The IMPRESSIONISTS IN CONTEXT

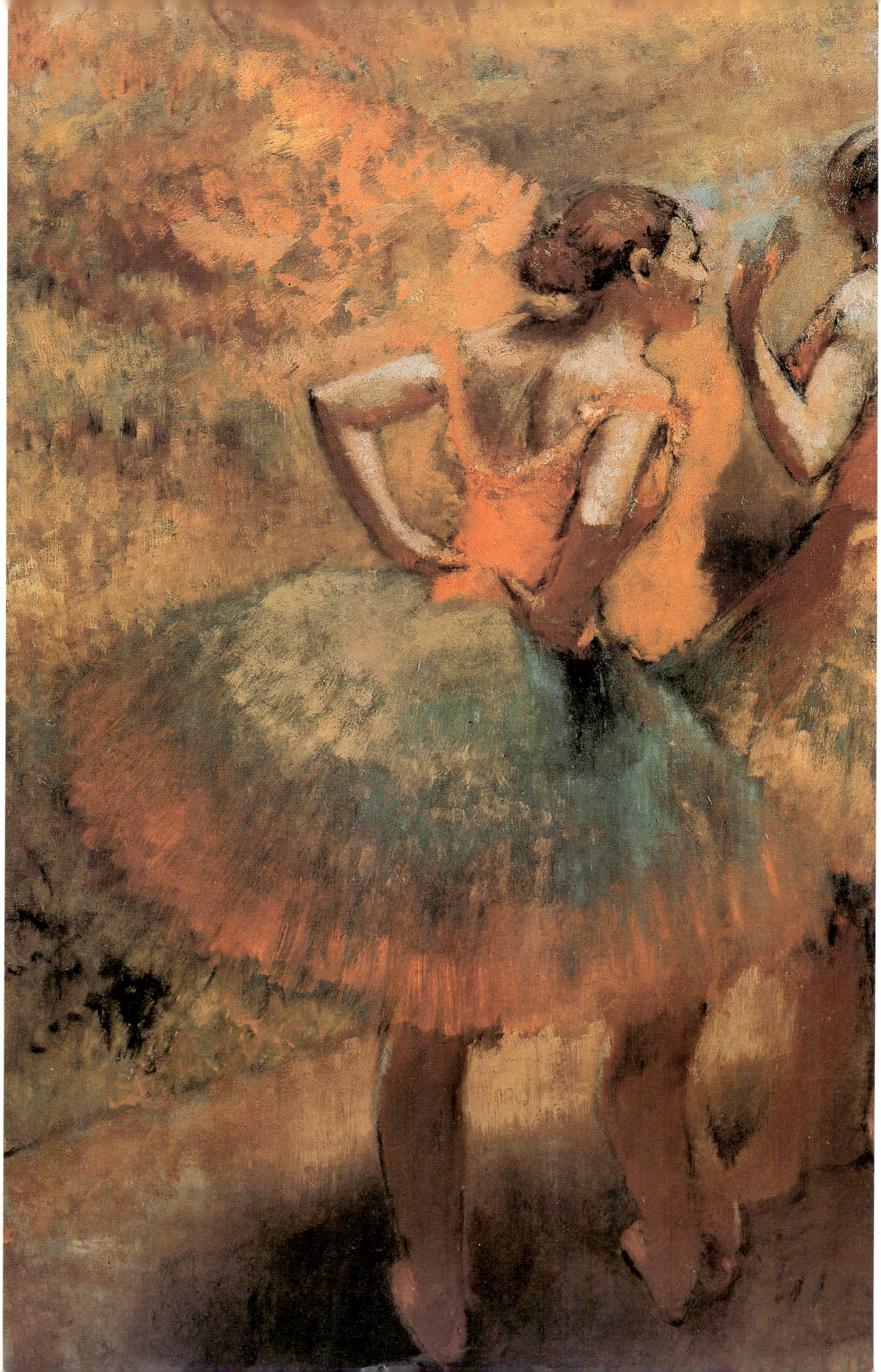

The IMPRESSIONISTS
IN CONTEXT

Robert Katz and Celestine Dars

Introduction by
Christopher Lloyd
Surveyor of The Queen's Pictures

ABBEYDALE PRESS

THE IMPRESSIONISTS IN CONTEXT

This paperback edition first published in 2003 by Abbeydale Press
an imprint of
Bookmart Limited
Registered Number 2372865
Trading as Bookmart Limited
Blaby Road, Wigston
Leicestershire, LE18 4SE
England

ISBN 1-86147-129-7

Printed in Singapore

CONTENTS

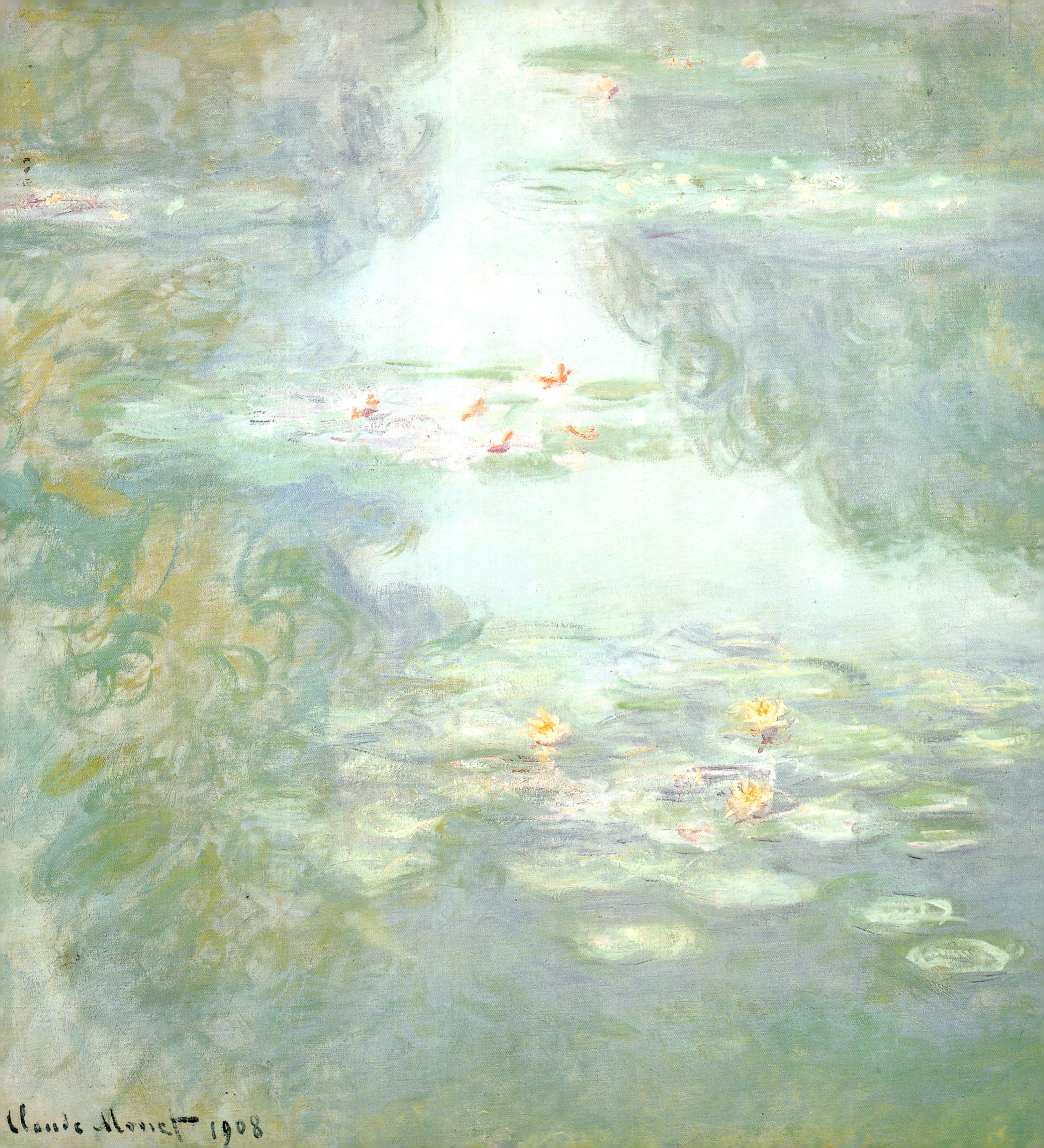
Claude Monet 1908

INTRODUCTION

The principal reason for the popularity of Impressionism today is, largely, because it is so accessible. Few people could fail to respond to a picture such as Renoir's *Luncheon of the Boating Party*; it positively breathes contentment. Such paintings depict an enviable lifestyle – the basic ingredients appear to include beautiful settings, sunlight, good food, plenty of drink, the easy companionship of elegant young people, clever conversation and high fashion. It seems as if everyone in France during the Third Republic was enjoying the pleasurable existence – *la jeunesse dorée* – mirrored by the Impressionists.

As a result there has been a tendency to reduce the radical nature of Impressionism – contemporary subjects, depicted in a new style based upon a broad range of brushwork and bold use of colour – simply to an admiration for middle-class values of hedonism. It is true that, to a limited extent, such an attitude is justified. The French nation had suffered not only a loss of prestige but also considerable hardship in the Franco-Prussian war of 1870 and the civil strife of the Commune that followed a year later. Impressionist painting, with its emphasis on the advantages of urban life, the pleasures of recreation and the sheer beauty of the countryside, can be interpreted as a resurgence of confidence and the rekindling of national pride.

There has, however, recently been a shift in the appreciation of Impressionist art away from the individual lives of the artists or formal analysis of their works. New research is directed more towards the context of Impressionist painting, in an attempt to discover more about the people in the pictures and the places they frequented. This contextual approach gives the

MONET
Nympheas
oil on canvas
1908. 91.5 × 81 cm

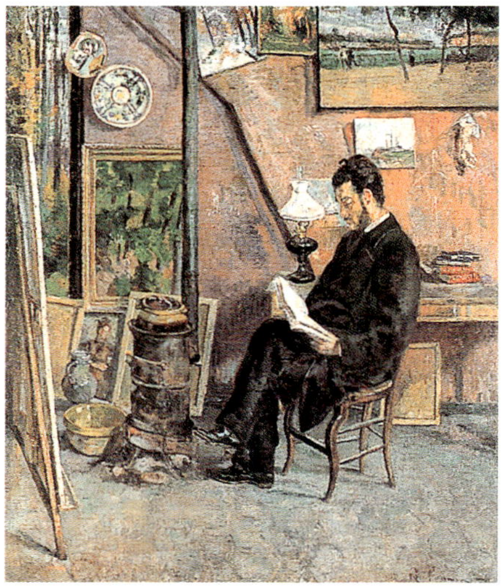

GUILLAUMIN
Doctor Martinez in the Studio
oil on canvas
1878. 89 × 74 cm

paintings a sharper resonance and brings them into clearer focus. What we find in Impressionist paintings are the political and social developments of late nineteenth-century France. As in the novels of Emile Zola, everyday life is portrayed in all its forms: the joyous festive occasions, both public and private; moments of intimacy; feelings of domesticity; the consequences of failure, corruption and ruin; the feeling of alienation produced by urban existence; the growth of decadence, the rise of political agitation and the advance of social idealism. This art is the product of Baudelaire's rallying call in the middle of the century for artists to reflect "the progress of fashionable life and thousands of floating existences – criminals and kept women – which drift about in the underworld of the great city . . . The life of our city is rich in poetic and marvellous subjects. We are enveloped and steeped as though in an atmosphere of the marvellous but we do not notice it."

For Baudelaire, the artist was an observer or spectator of the social scene: indeed he was part of the social scene. "To be away from home and yet to feel oneself everywhere at home: to be at the centre of the world and yet to remain hidden from the world." The hero of modern life was the dandy, the *flaneur*, the *boulevardier* or the *demi-mondaine*, because, simply, this was what life was about. The appeal to artists, then, was to extract the poetic and eternal qualities of their own highly transitional age. This was an important shift in artistic consciousness. Instead of the mythological and historical heroes that populated the canvases of successful painters, the Impressionists substituted the social and political tensions of the Third Republic. Such tensions spilled over into the country so that even the purest landscape painters, such as Sisley or Pissarro, were prey to them. Even when contemplating a landscape the Impressionist remained essentially an urban artist who had emerged from the city temporarily to sample the benefits of suburbia or immerse himself in country life. The recurring images of Impressionism involve the rebuilding of Paris, the development of the suburbs, the rise in popularity of the seaside resort, the technological advances in transport, notably the railway, the equation of city versus country, and increasing social mobility.

The world of Impressionist painters was one of constant flux, or what Baudelaire termed "the ephemeral, the fugitive, the contingent, the half of art whose other half is the eternal and the immutable." Trains, for example, hurtle through the countryside, while peasants move more sedately to market or work in the fields. Even where the artist chooses to depict the calmer, more reflective aspects of the countryside, in the broader context, the contrast between old and new, or past and present, is all the more marked. Because their subject matter was based on a fluctuating society, Impressionist artists were less limited in their selection or treatment of subjects than any previous group of painters. Their wide range of social types and variety of locations span the social spectrum. While it is true that Monet, Pissarro, and Sisley explored specific places (now well known as a result of their work), it is also true that the geography of Impressionism is fairly extensive.

Exploring the background to Impressionism involves a host of sources, often from related disciplines. Contemporary novels, guide books, newspapers, local histories, journals, maps, railway timetables, fashion magazines, the records and statistics produced for government departments – all provide the basis for the proper understanding of Impressionist art. It is important to know about the locations of *café-concerts*, the consumption of absinthe, the activities associated with *brasseries*, and the social standing of ballet dancers and shop-assistants. Such information forms the context of Impressionism.

If we fail to view Impressionist paintings against a clearly defined historical background, we are in danger of forgetting the radical nature of Impressionist art and its challenge to the establishment. These paintings are charged with subtle meanings. In 1869 both Renoir and Monet painted at a place called La Grenouillère, and it is in these pictures that we see the pure Impressionist style emerging. La Grenouillère was a fashionable open-air café and restaurant moored to the river bank. A contemporary description reads as follows: "La Grenouillère is Trouville on the banks of the Seine, a meeting place for the noisy, well dressed crowds that emigrate from Paris and set up camp in Croissy, Chatou or Bougival for the summer . . . Refreshments of all kinds are on sale in a large room . . . Most of the men and women who want to see the human race reduced to its most basic expression crowd on to this tiny islet. There is a small bathing area to the left of the islet; the river bed is of fine sand and the bathing area is roped off so that no one gets out of their depth . . . Boats are moored all around the island and the boaters, men and women alike, lie asleep in the shade of the great trees." In short, this is a bathing scene, but far removed from the famous and much vaunted scenes of established art. Furthermore, La Grenouillère was not such an innocent place as it may sound. Guy de Maupassant, in two of his novels, describes the crowds as "rowdy" and "screaming". He analyses the social breakdown of the scene as "a mixture of drapers' assistants, ham actors, hack journalists, gentlemen whose fortunes are still in trust, shady stockjobbers, degenerate revellers and corrupt old hedonists." For Maupassant, La Grenouillère reeked of "stupidity, vulgarity and cheap romance." Other Impressionists, likewise, were not attracted to the aspects of La Grenouillère that Monet and Renoir favoured. Pissarro, for instance, draws back from the scene and shows the general situation of the restaurant near a factory, which makes the whole site seem rather less attractive.

From one point of view Impressionist painting was concerned with coming to terms with modern life. Yet, from a technical aspect, it was also a question of redefining its relationship with the past. The standard theory of the birth of avant-garde art establishes a direct line of succession from Impressionism through to contemporary art. It views the progression through Post-Impressionism, Cubism, Dadaism, Surrealism, Futurism as a continuing reaction against the existing hierarchy. This view, however, ignores the background of activity against which the avant-garde was reacting and the considerable interplay between tradition and modern art. There is within the innovative qualities of Impressionism – colour, brushwork and composition – an inner tension. This stems from the dialogue that individual painters had with the art of the past.

Manet and Degas, and to a lesser extent, Cézanne, had an almost encyclopaedic knowledge of the old masters, revealed as much by the numerous copies they made, as by the visual quotations they incorporated in their work. For seventeenth- and eighteenth-century

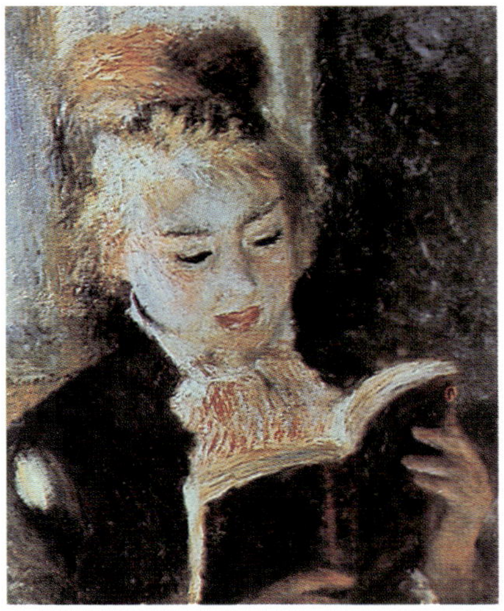

RENOIR
Woman Reading
1874. 46.5 × 38.5 cm

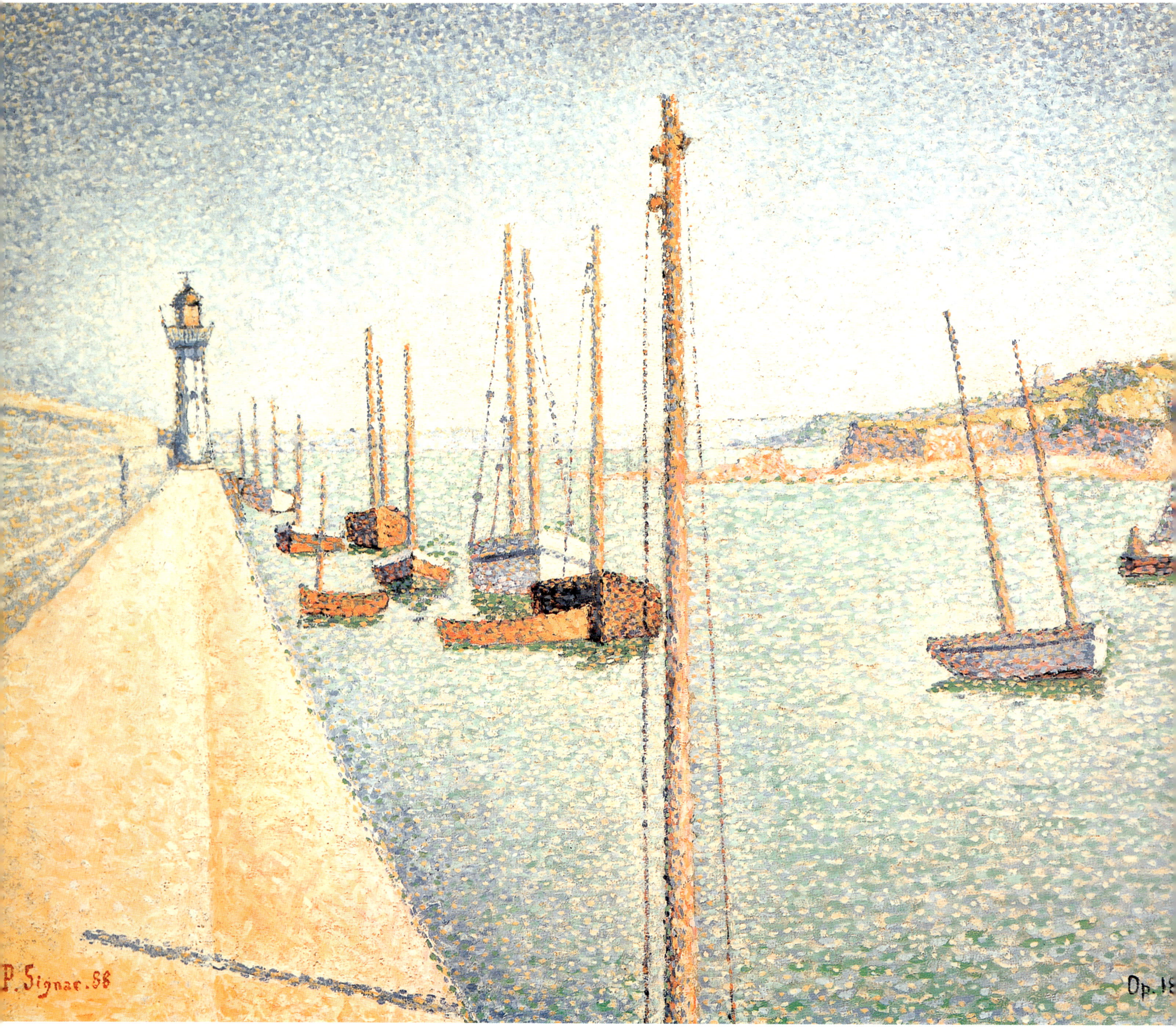
P. Signac. 88
Op. 18

artists such mimetic practices were regarded as respectable, but the Impressionists were brazen enough to flaunt their knowledge of the art of the past in order to give a greater potency to their representation of the present. In short, Manet, Degas, Pissarro and Cézanne used tradition as a weapon against itself. A famous and much discussed example is *Luncheon on the Grass*. Manet exhibited this picture in the Salon des Refusés in 1863, an officially sanctioned way of showing works by artists who had been refused by the main Salon. The reaction was one of outrage: one critic of the time described it thus: "A commonplace woman of the *demi-monde*, as naked as can be, shamelessly lolls between two dandies dressed to the teeth. These latter look like schoolboys on a holiday, involved in a prank in order to prove their manliness, and I search in vain for the meaning of this unbecoming puzzle-picture . . . This is a young man's practical joke, a shameful open sore, not worth exhibiting . . . The landscape is well handled . . . but these figures are slipshod." Even the more penetrating writers were bewildered. Théophile Thoré, a distinguished art historian who was sympathetic to Manet, wrote: "The nude hasn't a good figure, unfortunately, and one can't think of anything uglier than the man stretched out next to her who hasn't even thought of taking off, out of doors, his horrid padded cap. It is the contrast of a creature so inappropriate with this undraped bather that is shocking."

Why was the *Luncheon on the Grass* condemned when Cabanel's *Venus*, a smash-hit of the main Salon the same year, was decreed to be perfectly respectable? The answer is that Manet was breaking with convention. There was a well established tradition for female nudity in art. If Manet had it in mind to paint a picnic, there was a source of reference in pictures such as Watteau's *Embarkation for Cythère*. Manet's picture, however, depends on a dual ambiguity – one that introduces the peculiar arrangement of an undressed woman and two dressed men, and the other that flaunts historical tradition. The direct visual sources for the *Luncheon on the Grass* are Raphael and Giorgione. The grouping of the figures derives from details found in Marcantonio Raimondi's engraving after Raphael's *Judgement of Paris*, while the pastoral elements were clearly inspired by Giorgione's *Fête Champêtre*. Many artists paid lip service to their predecessors by quotation, but few were brazen enough to treat visual tradition in such a disrespectful way. Manet's purpose was to interpret modern life in terms of the great tradition of European art, transforming it through a respect for visual truth as complete and coherent as any shown by the masters of the past. The problem was that such a task was paradoxical: it seemed legitimate for the artist to look to the past for inspiration if the purpose was to uphold tradition; modernity, on the other hand, was incompatible with tradition.

Manet was also shattering the compositional conventions of the time. The public was educated to read mythological, historical or religious paintings according to certain well rehearsed principles, which did not extend to the gestures, direct confrontational stares and compositional gambits enlisted by Impressionist artists in order to depict modern life faithfully. In traditional works, invention was matched by execution. Primarily, there had to be a compositional unity with a dominant centre governed by the principal action; incidental matters were to be banished to the sides or placed in the background. The focus

SIGNAC
Portrieux, Brittany
oil on canvas
1888. 46 × 55 cm

RENOIR
Girl Wearing a Straw Hat
oil on canvas
1885. 42 × 31 cm

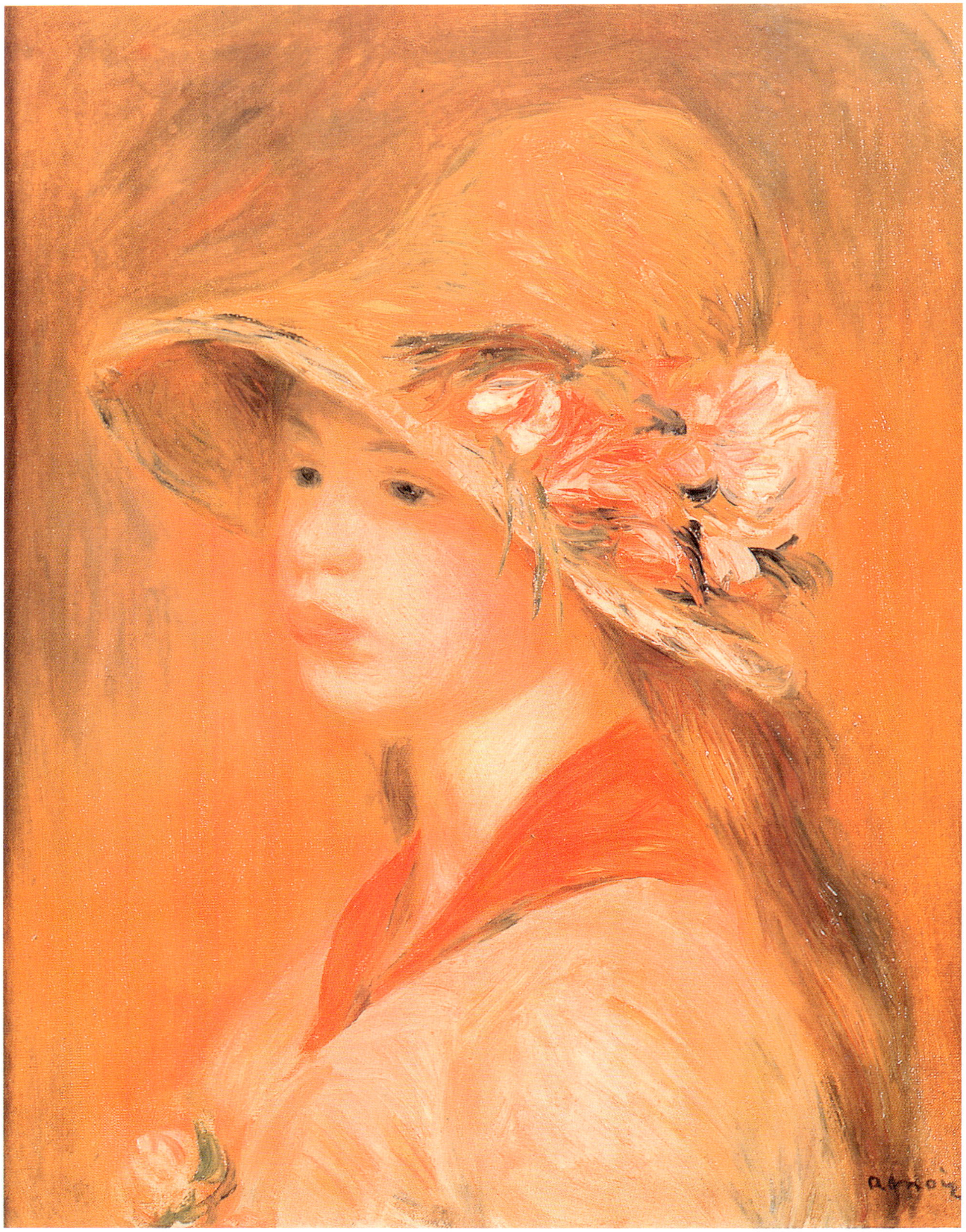

of action, or the narrative content, had to be clear so that the painting could be easily understood; lucidity was the chief component. The choice of subject was important, based preferably on a historical event, religious episode or mythological escapade, so that the content could be inspiring or ennobling. Everything in the painting had to relate to the central theme; the organization of the painting was all-important. The design, the figures, the treatment of light and handling of paint were subservient to the meaning, and the individuality of the artist was kept in check. Such pictures demanded a high finish built on accurate drawing, controlled brushwork, careful gradation of tones and the use of chiaroscuro, and a limited range of colours. There was also a hierarchy of subject, with narrative painting at the top and genre, landscape and still life being less significant.

Manet not only flaunted tradition in his subject matter, but also in his technique. The handling of his paint is vibrant to the extent that the flow of the brushstrokes evokes physical sensations. There is an immediate shift between light and dark with the elimination of the half-tones, a purity of colour and an exploitation of contrasts. This is a conscious attempt to paint a more truthful view of the world, as seen by the artist personally without resort to recorded precepts. This is the art of confrontation where in fact the present confronts the past.

The same tension between past and present exists in other artists, particularly Degas. His dilemma was to reconcile his deep respect for the artists of the past with an urgent sense of the modernity of his own culture – in the ballet, the horse-race and the brothel. Like Manet, Degas extracted from the past what he needed in order to forge a new style of painting, but unlike Manet, he was more subtle, more respectful, even though he was in the final analysis, more radical.

The essence of this vital relationship between Impressionism and the art of the past is further demonstrated in drawing. It is often assumed that Impressionists never drew because they were concerned with recording the sensations they experienced directly onto the canvas. Nonetheless, while not all the Impressionists relied on drawing to the same extent throughout their careers, there was an acknowledged dependency. Not all the Impressionists, however, put the same emphasis on drawing: the graphic *oeuvres* of Monet and Sisley, for example, are considerably smaller than those of Manet, Degas, Pissarro, Cézanne, Renoir, Caillebotte or Morisot. One of the principal results of this preoccupation with drawing is that the aesthetics of painting and drawing became interchangeable in Impressionism. The difference between them was really only a question of medium, not of style, finish or scale. This shift in the status of drawing amply demonstrates the nature of the dialogue between the past and the present that is omnipresent in Impressionist art. The pastels and drawings in mixed media by Manet, Degas, and Toulouse-Lautrec, or the watercolours by Cézanne, achieve equal status with the paintings in the search for contemporaneity. As Cézanne wrote, "To my mind, one does not put oneself in place of the past, one only adds a new link", or as he expressed it in another way, "The way to Nature lies through the Louvre, and the way to the Louvre lies through Nature."

CHRISTOPHER LLOYD
SURVEYOR OF THE QUEEN'S PICTURES

VAN GOGH
Sunflowers
oil on canvas
1888. 92 × 73 cm
It is ironical that this painting, popularly recognized as one of the great icons of Impressionism, was in fact created by a man whose serious artistic career began twenty years after the Salon des Refusés, and over ten years after the first Impressionist exhibition.

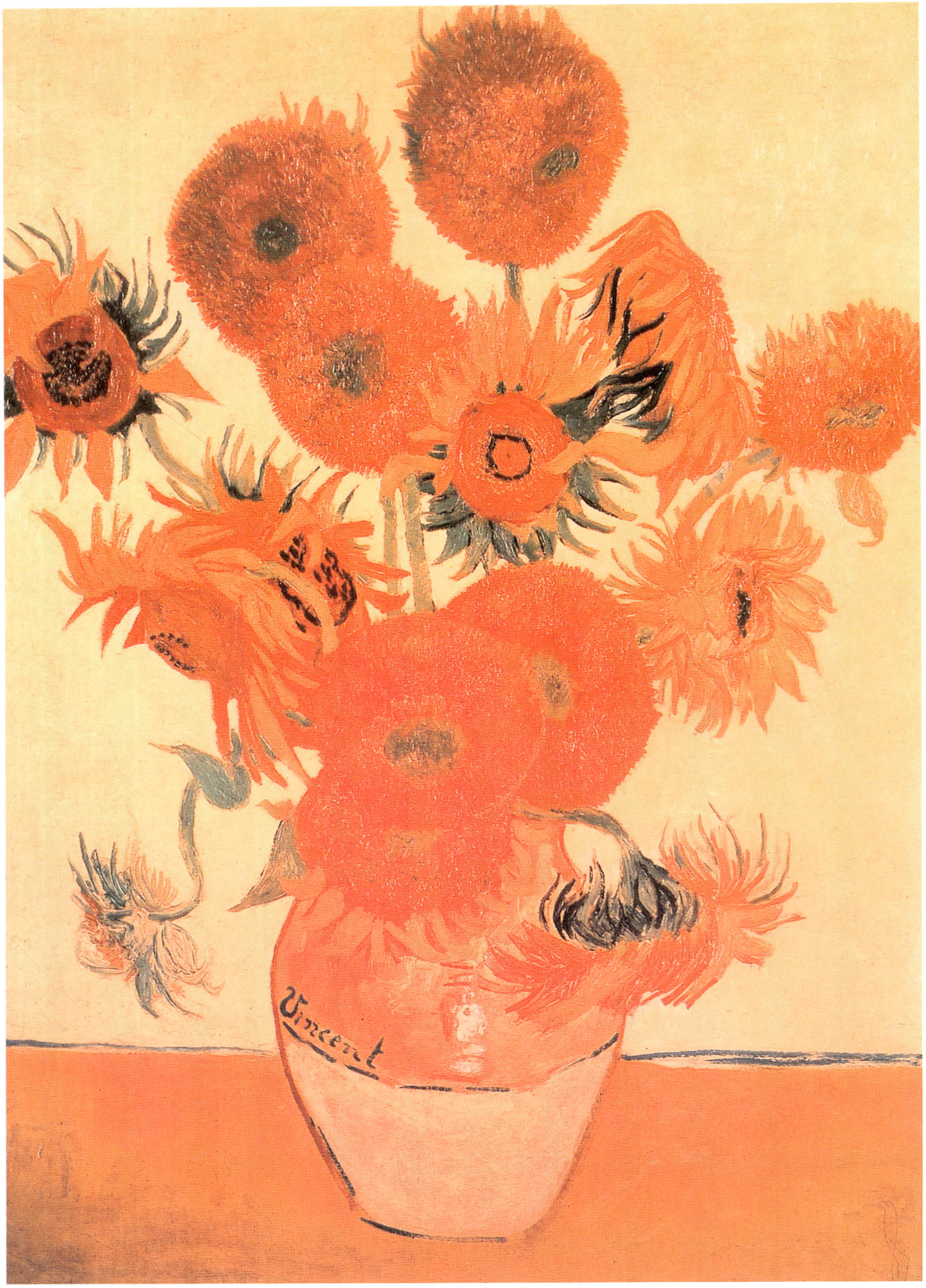

AUTHORS' NOTE

This is a book about the Impressionists in their historical, social, and artistic context. The term Impressionism is in itself an ambiguous and problematical one; it was originally coined in reference to a rapidly sketched painting by Claude Monet first exhibited in 1874 which bore the title *Impression, Sunrise.* This title was taken very much in vain by a contemporary critic and extended to characterize a quite heterogeneous group of artists, some of whom were developing a technique which used vibrant patches or strokes of colour to convey the unmediated visual impression of the scene before them.

Yet, the term Impressionism stuck, and has served its purpose well enough over the years: despite the fact that it embraces artists such as Edgar Degas and Camille Pissarro, who have little stylistically in common, it is a convenient way of describing an informal movement which radically changed the course of art. The main link between the principal artists discussed is that they took part in a series of exhibitions in Paris between 1874 and 1886 which came to be known as the Impressionist Exhibitions.

There are several ways of approaching the history and context of Impressionism. In a manner of speaking, this book begins before the beginning and ends after the end of the core period of French Impressionism. This was a brief but exciting decade or so which saw the launch into the world of the "New Painting", as one critic of the time called it, followed by its immediate rejection by the establishment and then its gradual acceptance, culminating in its rejection anew by a generation of artists who had grown up in its wake. A HISTORY OF IMPRESSIONISM follows the sequence of artistic trends which led to Monet's *Impression, Sunrise*, beginning with a discussion of outdoor or *plein-air* painting and the French landscape tradition, as well as the Realist art of Courbet and the explosion of Manet onto the scene in 1863, an event which shook the art establishment to its foundations. At the same time this section deals with the social, political, and literary background of France in general and Paris in particular; the conditions in which Impressionism was able to gain a foothold and eventually flourish. Impressionism was an art inextricable from its time and place.

THE LIFE AND WORKS considers the most important individuals who feature in the history of Impressionism, drawing out the biographical details that linked the Impressionists together as a functioning group and ultimately pulled them apart. Some of their stories, those of Sisley and Pissarro, for example, underline how they struggled to achieve recognition in an environment hostile to their work. The sections on the two women involved with the group, Berthe Morisot and Mary Cassatt, indicate in particular the special problems faced by women who would be artists in a man's world.

Finally, in THE LEGACY OF IMPRESSIONISM, we see how the world and the art of the Impressionists had changed in the decade and a half since the first exhibition in the boulevard des Capucines in Paris. In a relatively short period of time a reaction had set in which spelled the demise of Impressionism in France as a radical force in French art; yet the profound influence of Impressionism abroad – in Britain and America especially – ensured its survival for many years to come, while the impact it had made in France guaranteed it a critical shaping role in the stylistic development of a new generation of great artists, including Gauguin and van Gogh.

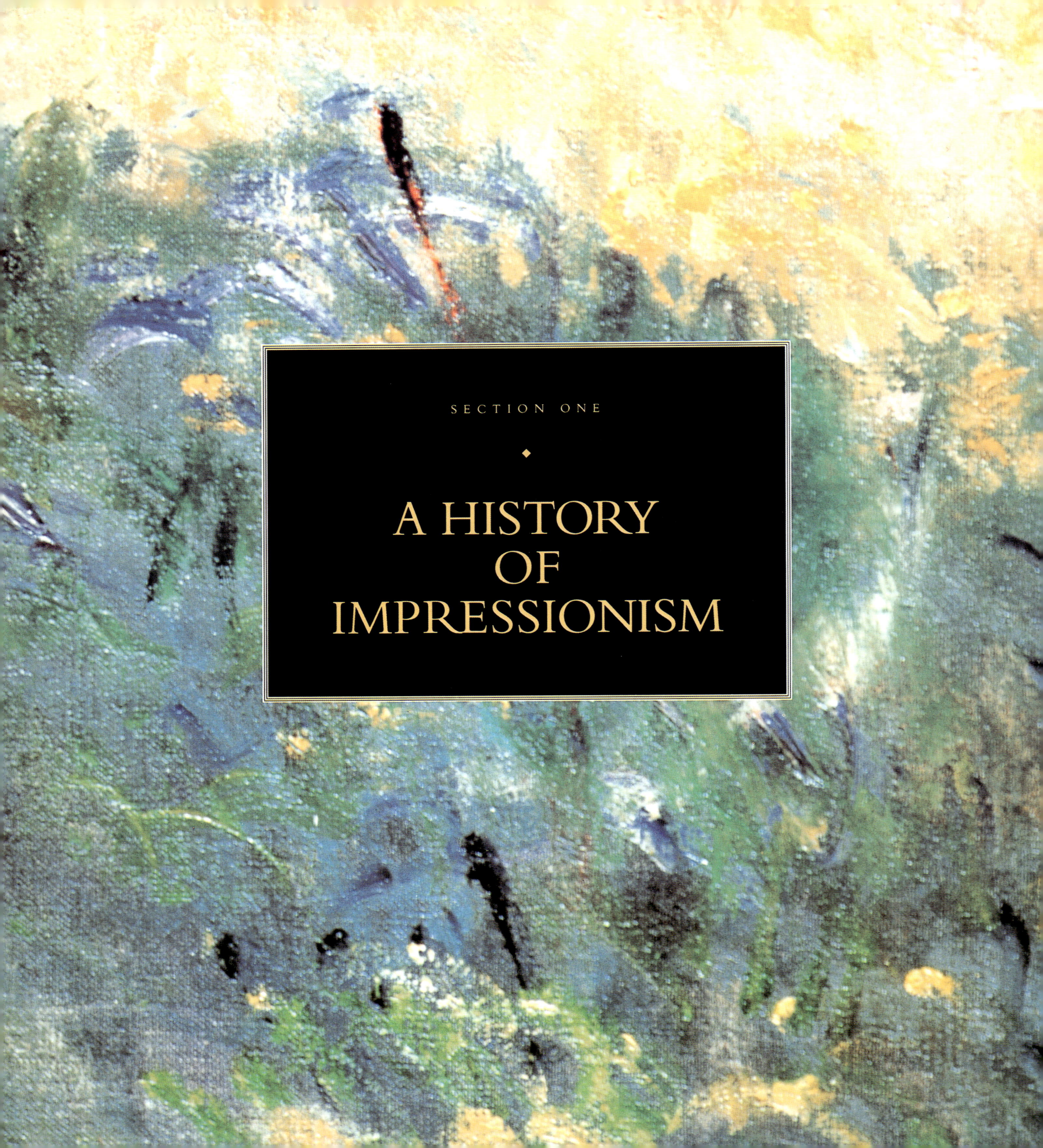

SECTION ONE

A HISTORY OF IMPRESSIONISM

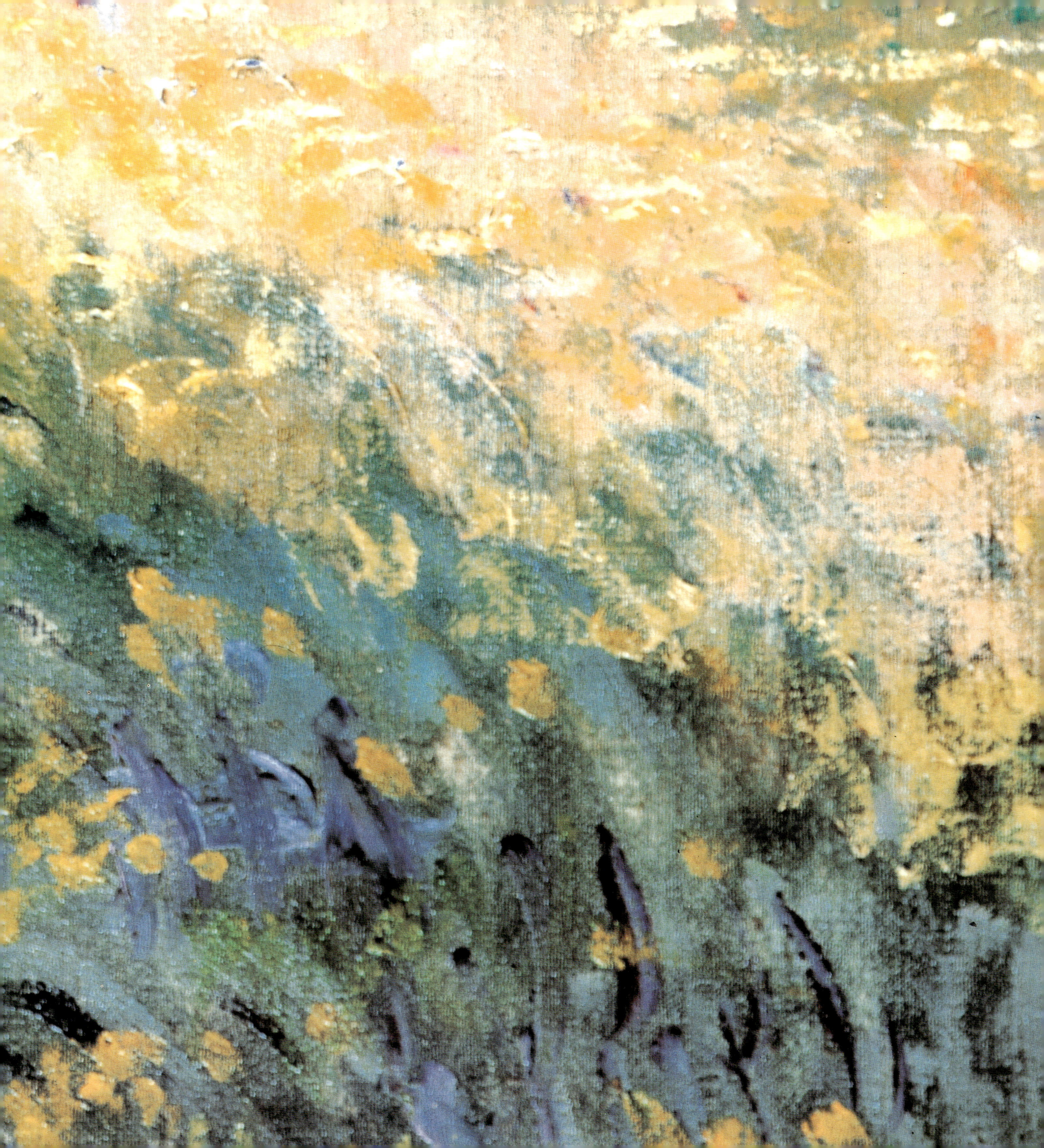

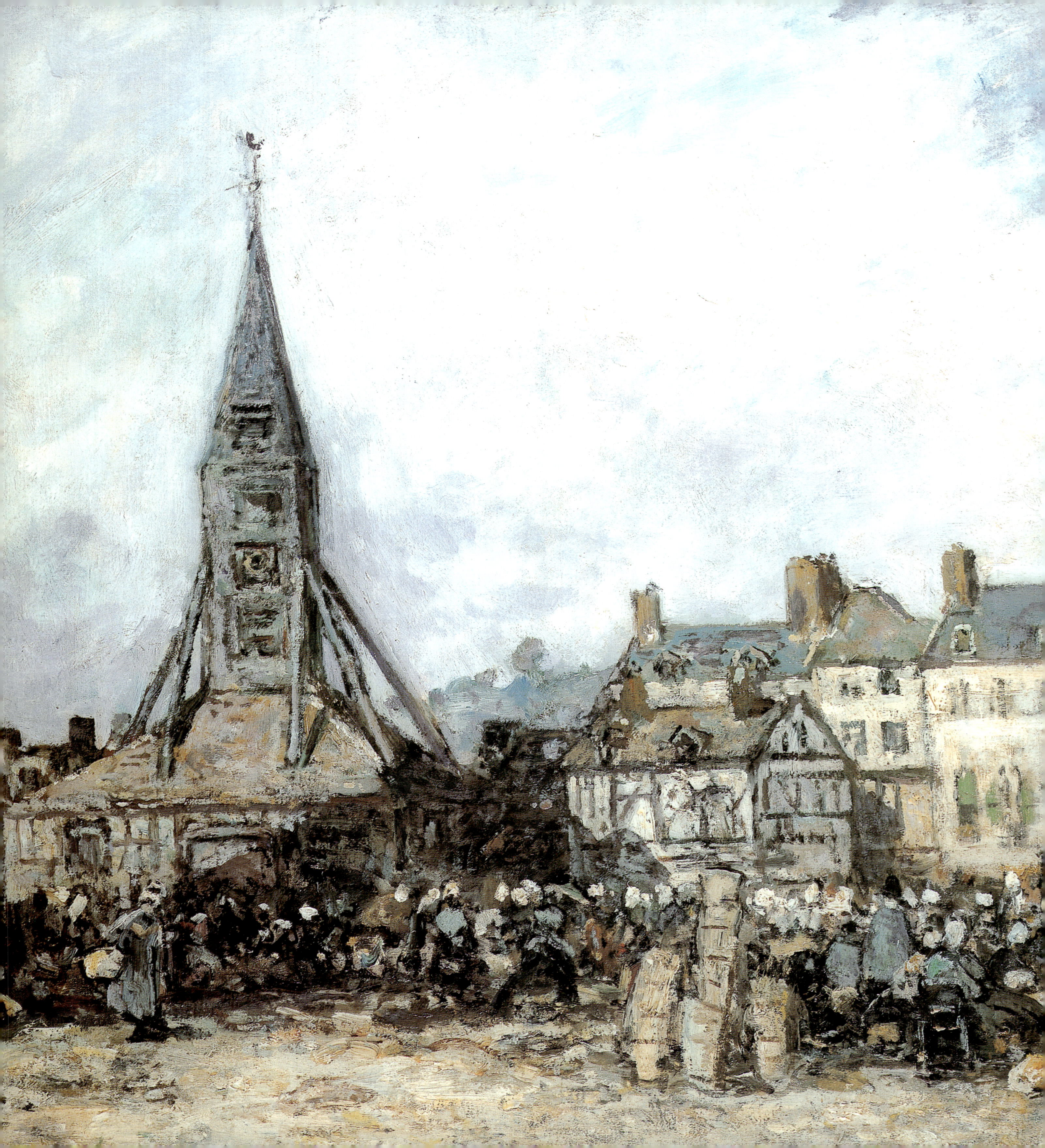

FRANCE AND IMPRESSIONISM

THE IMPRESSIONISTS DID NOT choose their name – it was foisted upon them in 1874 by a critic hostile to their work. However the name soon stuck and was used to describe a group of artists who never intended to be a unified radical movement, who never set out to shock or be revolutionaries. What they had in common was that they were all in Paris in the early 1860s and quickly got to know each other – some in art schools which they abandoned early on, some in the cafés where they would meet – and realized that they shared a desire to paint the landscape, cityscape, and modern life in new ways. The first Impressionist exhibition took place because none of these artists had achieved any regular success at the official Salon, the major venue for the Paris art market, whose juries were notoriously inconsistent and reactionary.

The first exhibition by this group did little to challenge the all-powerful Salon, but it crystallized critical opinion and pushed the so-called Impressionists into the limelight. They were pilloried by hostile critics and supported by writers such as Baudelaire and Zola who saw in their work an important advancement of art into the modern era. But the Impressionists did not seek to criticize their society; they were largely middle class and politically conservative in an age permanently on the brink of upheaval. They remained true to aesthetic ideas which, with few exceptions, kept them from depicting the grinding poverty caused by rapid industrial expansion, and the sporadic outbursts of war and violence that punctuated the history of their times.

JONGKIND
The Sainte Catherine's Market at Honfleur
oil on canvas
1865. 42 × 66 cm
(DETAIL)

April 1874: Shock of the New

The Impressionist eye is, in short, the most advanced eye in human evolution . . .

Jules Laforgue, 1883

For one month from 15th April 1874 a new exhibition was to be seen at 35 boulevard des Capucines in Paris. Félix Nadar, a well-known photographer, had lent his studio free of charge to a group of artists who had come together as the *Société anonyme des artistes peintres, sculpteurs, graveurs, etc.* (a joint stock company of artists, painters, etc.). The show was open from ten to six during the day and eight to ten at night for an admission price of one franc. Among the twenty-nine artists showing their work were Paul Cézanne, Edgar Degas, Armand Guillaumin, Claude Monet, Berthe Morisot, Camille Pissarro, Pierre-Auguste Renoir, and Alfred Sisley.

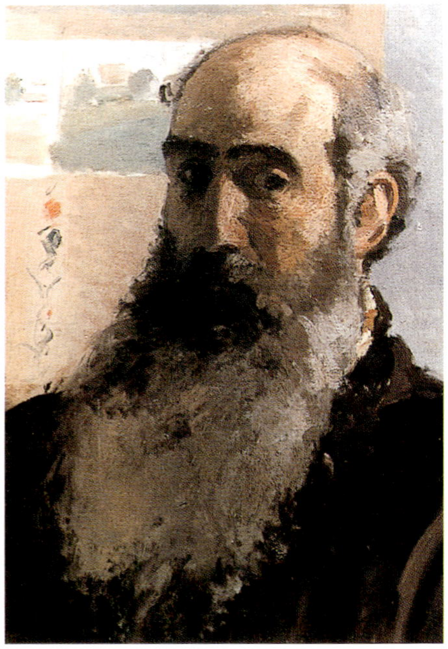

CAMILLE PISSARRO
Self-portrait
1873

The show was rapidly becoming a disaster. The members of the *Société anonyme* who had banded together to stage the show had of course aimed to generate sales as well as a greater awareness of their work with the public. Around 3,500 people visited the exhibition before it closed on 15th May but very few pictures were bought – the work of Degas and Morisot remained unsold, whilst Renoir had to knock down the price of his painting *La Loge* from 500 to 425 francs before he could sell it. In general the public came for the novelty value, to see a *cause célèbre* in the making. Only the critics were triumphant. Writing in the satirical journal *Charivari* on 25th April 1874, Louis Leroy, a minor critic and playwright, composed an acerbic satirical review of the exhibition in the form of a tour around it in the company of an imaginary landscape painter called Joseph Vincent. Having relentlessly debunked most of the other artists on show, Leroy devoted part of the climax of his satire to a picture by Claude Monet:

> A catastrophe seemed to be imminent, and it was reserved for M. Monet to contribute the last straw.
>
> "Ah, there he is!" he cried, in front of No.98. "I recognize him, *papa* Vincent's favourite! What does that canvas depict? Look at the catalogue."
>
> "*Impression, Sunrise.*"
>
> "*Impression* – I was sure of it. I was just telling myself that, since I was impressed, there had to be some impression in it . . . and what freedom, what ease of workmanship! Wallpaper in its embryonic state is more finished than this seascape."

Monet had chosen the title of this picture in some haste for the exhibition catalogue, not wanting to call it a simple "seascape", and in doing so he had unwittingly provided Leroy with the hook-line for his piece. The review appeared under the headline *Exhibition of the Impressionists.* Leroy had coined a name which would be certain to outlive his own.

What were these so-called Impressionists doing that was so unacceptable? Leroy had put his finger on the obvious qualities of one aspect of their work, what henceforth would be called the "Impressionist" use of paint – a method that was as shocking as it was new to its public. Standing in front of Monet's *Boulevard des Capucines*, Leroy's imaginary companion declares:

> "Is that brilliant enough for you now? There's an *impression*, or I don't know what it means. Only be so good as to tell me what those innumerable black tongue-lickings in the lower part of the picture represent?"
>
> "Why, those are people walking along," I replied.

Leroy, of course, could read the painting and see the effect that Monet's brushwork intended to convey, but a tradition of officially-sanctioned, respected and respectable Salon painting – which stressed the suitability of subject, quality and finesse of finish – inevitably meant that the public were looking at Monet's *Boulevard des Capucines* and *Impression, Sunrise*, or Degas' ballerinas, with a conservative, unprepared eye. To many, all that really could be seen from a couple of feet were blotches, strokes and scrapes of compacted pigment, which viewed from a "safe" distance would then coalesce into meaningful shapes. The "Impressionist technique" (in reality each artist was developing his own), allied with a new approach to colour and a new range of subject matter, made the *Société anonyme*'s first exhibition the laughing-stock of Paris. Yet it represented to the world at large a revolution in art that had been gathering since the early 1860s, when Edouard Manet caused a scandal with his *Luncheon on the Grass* (*Déjeuner sur l'herbe*).

In the early 1860s Frédéric Bazille, Monet, Renoir, and Sisley had met in Paris to study at the atelier of the Swiss painter Charles Gleyre, whilst Pissarro had come to know Monet and Paul Cézanne. The high period of Impressionism was brief; merely a decade later a somewhat diluted form of Impressionism had already been adopted by numerous conventional artists. Its influence, however, has lasted to this day.

The idea of an independent show outside the auspices of the Salon – the annual exhibition of the Académie des Beaux-Arts held in the Louvre's Salon d'Apollon and later in the enormous Palais d'Industrie – was increasingly discussed. Hitherto, the Académie des Beaux-Arts determined almost exclusively the showing of art. Without the sanction of the Salon an artist's work was practically unseen by the bourgeoisie which constituted his (and increasingly her) public. Furthermore, the atelier system of apprenticeship to a teacher who would prepare his students for the Ecole des Beaux-Arts, the teaching arm of the Académie, followed by the winning of one of the school's competitions, was the only way an artist could expect to learn and then progress in a career which depended on the patronage of conservative institutions and patrons. For good or ill, Leroy's insistence on the word "impression" tied together for posterity a group of artists whose aims were frequently at loggerheads, yet who had set out together, rejecting the Salon which had so often rejected them.

What the unimaginative public and critics like Leroy found gross and unpolished, slapdash and meaningless in the work of the Impressionists shown at Nadar's studio was exactly what later generations came to value most in it. Writing in 1883 to introduce a small show by Pissarro, Degas, and Renoir in Berlin, the poet Jules Laforgue (who died three years later at the age of twenty-seven) considered the Impressionists' work in a

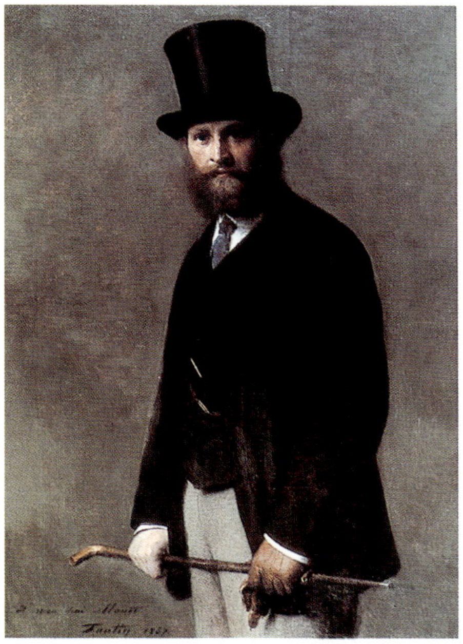

EDOUARD MANET
By Fantin-Latour
1867

remarkable essay. What he had to say then evokes the qualities that were to make Impressionism a lasting and vital phenomenon. He pays particular attention to the Impressionists' capturing of the conditions of light, colour, and form as they are transmitted unmediated to the artist's eye at a particular moment in time:

> In a landscape bathed with light, in which entities are modelled as if in coloured *grisaille* [i.e. monochrome painting in greyish colour], the academic painter sees nothing but white light spreading everywhere, whilst the Impressionist sees it bathing everything, not in dead whiteness, but in a thousand conflicting vibrations, in rich prismatic decompositions of colour. Where the academic sees only lines at the edge of things . . . the Impressionist sees real living lines, without geometrical form, built from thousands of irregular touches which, at a distance, give the thing life. Where the academic sees only things set down in regular, separate positions . . . the Impressionist sees perspective established by thousands of imperceptible tones and touches, by the variety of atmospheric states, with each plane not immobile, but shifting . . . The Impressionist sees and renders nature as she is, which is to say solely by means of coloured vibrations. Neither drawing, nor light, nor modelling, nor perspective, nor chiaroscuro: these infantile classifications all resolve in reality into coloured vibrations, and must be obtained on the canvas solely by coloured vibrations.

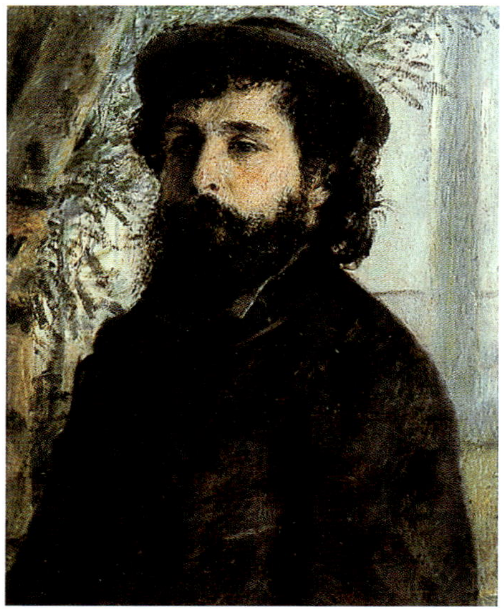

CLAUDE MONET
By Renoir
1875

Art in the Second Empire

Stop, monsieur le Président, here is France's shame.
Jean-Léon Gérôme to Président Loubet, 1900

Pissarro, Manet, Degas, Sisley, Monet, Bazille, and Morisot were all born between 1830 and 1841 into a France whose recent history had been as dramatic and changeable as the era the painters were to live through. France had not had a history of durable regimes; by the end of 1830 the King, Charles X, had abdicated after the July revolution in Paris, to be replaced by the Duke of Orleans, Louis Philippe, who assumed the lieutenant-generalship of France. Louis Philippe devoted himself to the bourgeoisie and the *juste milieu*, but ironically ruled amidst periodic riot and revolt until 1848 when Paris once again erupted in revolution, causing the abdication of Louis Philippe and the birth of the Second Republic. Two of the new republic's first acts were the Proclamation of Universal Suffrage and the Abolition of Slavery. In December 1848 Louis Napoleon, nephew of Napoleon I, was elected President of the Republic. Three years later, after the *coup d'étât* of 1851, Louis Napoleon became Emperor Napoleon III. Napoleon III marked the start of his rule with a crack-down on political dissent and a suppression of the press while at the same time regulating the price of bread and encouraging growth in industry and commerce. France had languished behind the rest of Europe as the Industrial Revolution gained momentum, but Napoleon III's reign saw the development of banking institutions – the Crédits Mobilier, Lyonnais, and Agricole – as well as railways and factories. As a patron of the arts, and of painting in particular, Napoleon III and his Arts Minister, Comte de Niewerkerke, were generous in reforming and developing a useful system of patronage, education and officially-commissioned works of art for public buildings.

In 1863 the Salon des Refusés, a massive exhibition of paintings which had been rejected by the Salon and for which Napoleon III bore great responsibility in many ways, marked the beginning of a new era of artistic freedom, even though it was a subtle attempt by the authorities to discredit critics of the official Salon. Not surprisingly, the Emperor's personal taste in painting favoured the academic style with its high finish and erudite classical and biblical subjects, although Romantics like Delacroix had little trouble making very successful careers for themselves under the Second Empire. However, a group of Realists who were more concerned with "common subjects", which had emerged under the vociferous leadership of Gustave Courbet, was anathema to Napoleon III's imperial sensibilities (as indeed were Courbet's socialist politics).

The new art, shortly to be named Impressionism, which succeeded Courbet, took as its subject matter not only nature, but also the prosperous middle class which had begun to make itself felt in the Second Empire. Edouard Manet's *Music in the Tuileries Gardens* (*Musique dans le Jardin des Tuileries*) of 1862 is regarded as one of the first great paintings of modern urban life, and what it shows is a bustling middle-class crowd of professionals and artists at their leisure. It is representative of a nation, transformed in part by the policies of Napoleon III into an economically competitive state ready to enjoy its new found success and confidence.

To advance his nation further, Napoleon III had embarked on a series of successful wars against Austria, Russia, and China. In 1855 and 1867 the spectacular Expositions Universelles in Paris, rivalling the British Great Exhibition of 1851, announced to the nation and the world that France had arrived. Alas, the vagaries of French history caught up with Napoleon III. In 1870, just as he was attempting a measure of political liberalization, he seriously misjudged the nation's readiness for conflict and engaged in war against Prussia on a point of diplomatic etiquette. (The French were so convinced they could win this war they issued their officers with maps of Germany only!) Hopelessly out-organized, outmanouevred and out-gunned by the very artillery pieces which Krupps had exhibited to great acclaim in the 1867 Paris Exposition, the French armies disintegrated, with the loss of the important eastern province of Alsace-Lorraine. The Prussians invaded Paris in September 1870, and the Second Empire fell soon after.

After the Prussians had paraded through Paris and the new, broadly-republican government had attempted to disarm the National Guard there, the city erupted into revolution resulting in the Commune of 1871. Victor Hugo called it *l'année terrible*, a brief violent revolution which rose against the

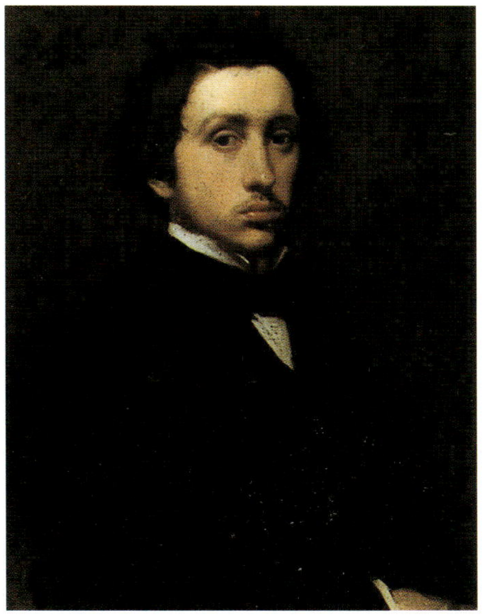

EDGAR DEGAS
Self-portrait
c.1855

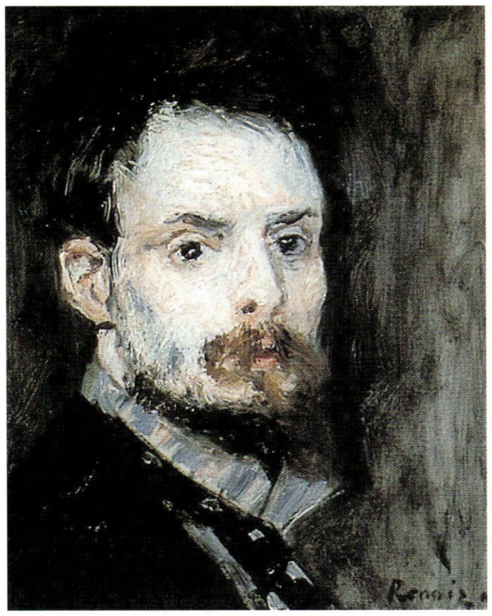

PIERRE-AUGUSTE RENOIR
Self-portrait
c.1875

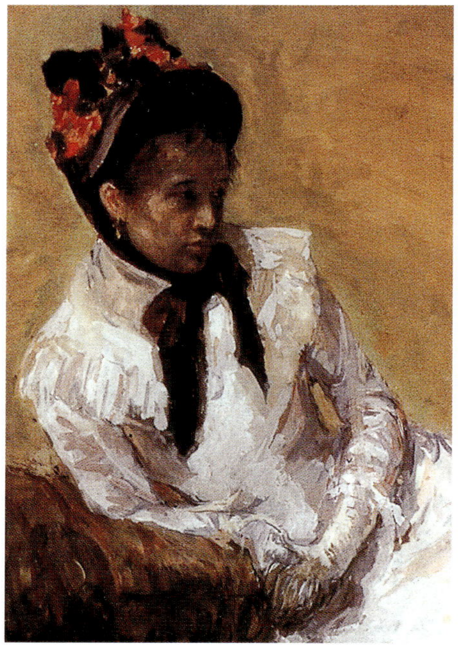

MARY CASSATT
Self-portrait
c.1895

government and ended in massacre. In one week 20,000 Parisians were killed as civil war erupted in the streets of what had recently been *la ville lumière*, the dazzling capital of Europe. Scarcely two years before Monet's *Boulevard des Capucines* went on show in 1873, the boulevards of Paris had been stripped of trees cut down for firewood; the animals in the zoos, including the elephants (but not the hippo, which no butcher could afford to buy), as well as the city's racehorses, had been slaughtered for food in the beseiged and starving city. Yet these momentous events touched the work of the Impressionists very little. There is no trace of upheaval in any of the Impressionists' paintings; most fled to avoid the war and only Manet and Degas remained in Paris. The former, who had been an anti-imperialist since the age of sixteen, was the only one amongst the group to record the bloody events of the Commune. But we shall see, the relationship of Manet and Degas with the other Impressionists is a special case in itself.

The Franco-Prussian war and the brief and bloody rise and fall of the Paris Commune formed the conclusion to the Second Empire. During the childhood and adolescence of the Impressionists many changes had swept over France, such as the massive construction of railways throughout the country to rival the systems of both Britain and the German states. Between 1851 and 1859 the French railways had trebled in length, facilitating the further expansion of industry and communications. Importantly for the Impressionists and their precursors who painted in the open air, the growth of the railways made the countryside available to the city-dweller in a way that was to have great consequences. During the Second Empire and well into the Third Republic, the cities, and Paris in particular, were undergoing fundamental change whilst in rural France the way of life was altered very little – only the occasional industrial chimney is to be seen poking up in the background of the Impressionists' landscapes.

In 1853 Napoleon III had appointed Baron Georges-Eugène Haussmann, Prefect of the Seine, to set about the reconstruction of Paris. This he began with grandiloquent gusto, aiming to transform a city of narrow streets and congested, practically medieval areas – a city with a hopelessly inefficient transport and sanitation infrastructure, a city where the bourgeoisie lived cheek by jowl with the very poorest underclass – into a modern European capital. Haussmann built great sewers after the example of London, but for the removal of rainwater, not, unfortunately, for sewage, and gutted huge sections in the centre of the city to make way for broad boulevards with pavements, avenues of trees and clear sight-lines for the military – popular uprisings would thus be easier to control. Haussmann built eighty-five miles of new roads that included the rue de Rivoli and the boulevard Saint-Michel. Along these new roads, modern buildings quickly sprang up, their height and style controlled by the authorities. For more than a decade Paris was a wonderland of new buildings, roads, squares, and other construction projects.

The Impressionists found the transformed city and its *banlieues* (suburbs) an ideal place for a new and modern kind of art, a place which, according to writer Edmond de Goncourt, made one a "stranger . . . to these new boulevards with no turnings, no chance perspectives, implacably straight, which are no longer of Balzac's world, but which make one think of some American Babylon of the future." The Impressionists, in contrast, were not so much afraid as fascinated by the new lines of Paris. The mile-long perspectives offered by the new boulevards, the St Lazare station in the centre and the railway bridges on the outskirts became the subjects, for example, of Monet's urban paintings.

What "Haussmannization" meant, above all, was the gentrification of Paris, making its centre the exclusive habitat of the bourgeoisie. However, behind these new streets the slums that had been cleared reappeared, only more cramped and squalid. Meanwhile hundreds of thousands of workers had been moved out to new industrial suburbs and slum areas, like Belleville and Menilmontant, where they subsisted much as they had done before, but this time dispossessed of their ancient city.

When the rubble of 1870–71, caused by heavy Prussian bombardment and violent civil war, was cleared away, Paris quickly became *la ville lumière* it had been during the Second Empire. By 1874 it was hard to imagine that dogs and rats had once been on the menu. Although memories of the civil war remained, the economic growth of the Second Empire resumed under a republican guise. Paris reclaimed its place as the centre of European art.

The Impressionists lived in an age of struggle between modernity and a traditional order. We see in their paintings a radical, and, for their time, shocking break with traditional notions of art, the culmination, but not the end, of a series of new ways of seeing. The Abstract movement of the twentieth century stemmed from experiments with existing art just as the Impressionists' innovations grew out of the paintings of Courbet, Corot, Delacroix, Constable, and the old masters who had gone before in the world of art.

We are surrounded by the art of the Impressionists – the legacy of a relatively brief period in the history of art which has endured in the most diverse of ways. There is scarcely a wall, a mug, a postcard, a jigsaw puzzle or indeed a box of chocolates which has not borne a reproduction of Degas' prima ballerinas, Manet's barmaid, Renoir's girl on a swing or one of Monet's haystacks. These images are perennial because they are windows on a bygone age of leisurely Parisian summers and intensely perceived light which appeal to us in this beleaguered post-modern century. They are also the masterpieces of a crucial period of change and works of art from an optimistic time of endless possibilities. The Impressionists' sense of wonderment at their world has, ironically, become for us a comforting reflection of times passed. Although it would be convenient to think that before Monet, Renoir, Sisley, and Pissarro light could never have been seen and set down in a series of broken, prismatic colours, that shadows were never blue or red, yet in fact these approaches were already becoming possible in the early nineteenth century. It is certainly true, nevertheless, that a short time after these artists had come together, blue shadows and green skies were, and have remained, commonplaces in the vocabulary of art.

The Impressionists were named in jest by a hostile critic; collectively they never published a manifesto – their name is a catch-all for a fragile movement of men and women briefly united in their belief that the time had come for a new art to be seen and appreciated. They came from different social backgrounds, from the patricians Manet and Degas to the working-class Renoir, and in the

BERTHE MORISOT
By Manet
c.1869

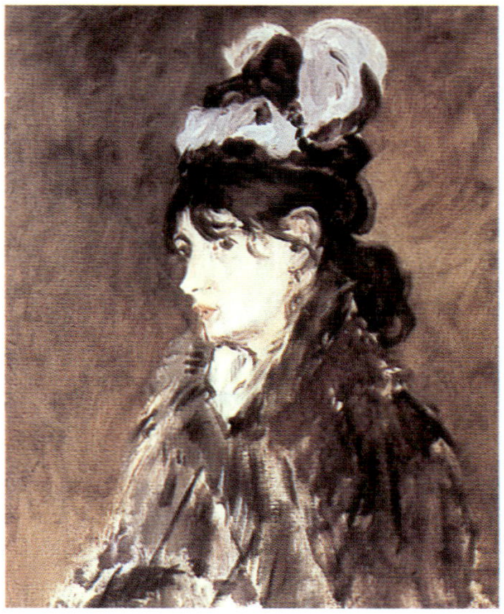

end their friendships broke up and they scattered across France. All of them, however, were in Paris during a critical period in French history; they knew and worked with each other and often lived in each other's pockets. Some – Monet, Sisley, and Pissarro, for example – were overwhelmingly attracted by the landscape and were driven to depict it. Others – Degas, Manet, and Renoir – were more concerned with the human figure and the life of the city and its suburbs. In their time they were all accused of being revolutionary; their supporters held them up as the iconographers of a new, modern age; their critics claimed they were subverting a set of artistic ideals and methods which had obtained for centuries.

In some ways the Impressionists were revolutionaries – in their use of colour, for example, or choice of subject and methods of exhibition, and in their assertion of the right to recreate the world as they saw it. The history of the Impressionists is full of contradictions. Edouard Manet (who together with Degas we should be wary of calling an Impressionist in any case), a generous and devoted supporter of the younger artists such as Monet, Renoir, and Sisley, never exhibited in the series of Impressionist exhibitions which shook the Parisian art world. However, he had caused a sensation a decade before with *Luncheon on the Grass* (*Déjeuner sur l'herbe*), and though he was considered to be their leader, he sought distinction through the Salon – a reluctant revolutionary. Degas, of the same generation as Manet, exhibited in all eight of the Impressionists' shows from 1874 to 1886. Monet, Renoir, and Sisley all dropped out of the group's exhibitions in the late 1870s, whilst the most politically revolutionary of them all, Pissarro, would not abandon Degas (politically an arch-Conservative and anti-Semite) or the Impressionist exhibitions even when the others begged him to. Despite all of these contradictions there existed for a short period in late nineteenth-century France a movement, a loose and informal "academy" whose members learnt from one another and changed the course of art.

When Claude Monet died in 1926, Impressionism was firmly enshrined in the past – new forces had been at work since the 1880s. In the lifetime of Monet and most of the Impressionists France had seen two revolutions, the rise and fall of the Second Empire and the establishment of the Third Republic. An industrial revolution had taken place and Paris had been rebuilt almost from scratch. The Impressionists' own revolution was intimately tied up with that of the world they inhabited. Innovations as seemingly mundane as the mass manufacture of oil paint in tin tubes and the portable easel had freed the artist from his or her studio. Monet's *Boulevard des Capucines* was painted from the window of Nadar's studio high up in the same boulevard, introducing literally a new angle on traditional views of Paris.

By the last years of the nineteenth century the Impressionist style had spread and prospered, evolving into Neo- and Post-Impressionism. But the shock waves of Impressionism continued to reverberate. In 1900, over a quarter of a century after the first Impressionist exhibition, the academician Gérôme, one of the most successful artists of his century, was guiding Président Loubet of France around the Exposition Universelle when he stopped him at the entrance to the Impressionist Room with these words: "*Arrêtez, monsieur le Président, c'est ici le déshonneur de la France!*"

MONET
The Artist's Garden at Argenteuil
oil on canvas
1872. 61 × 74 cm

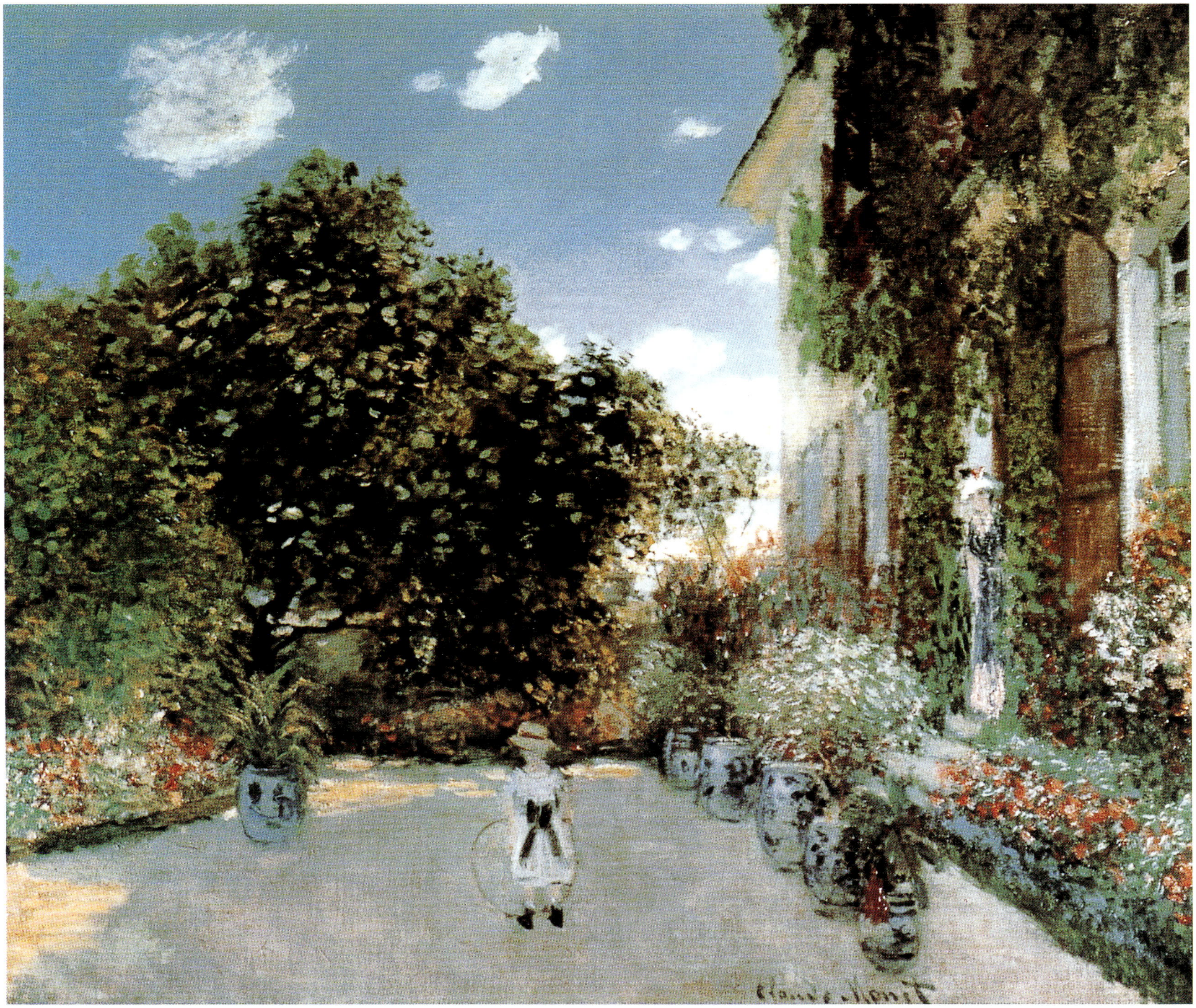

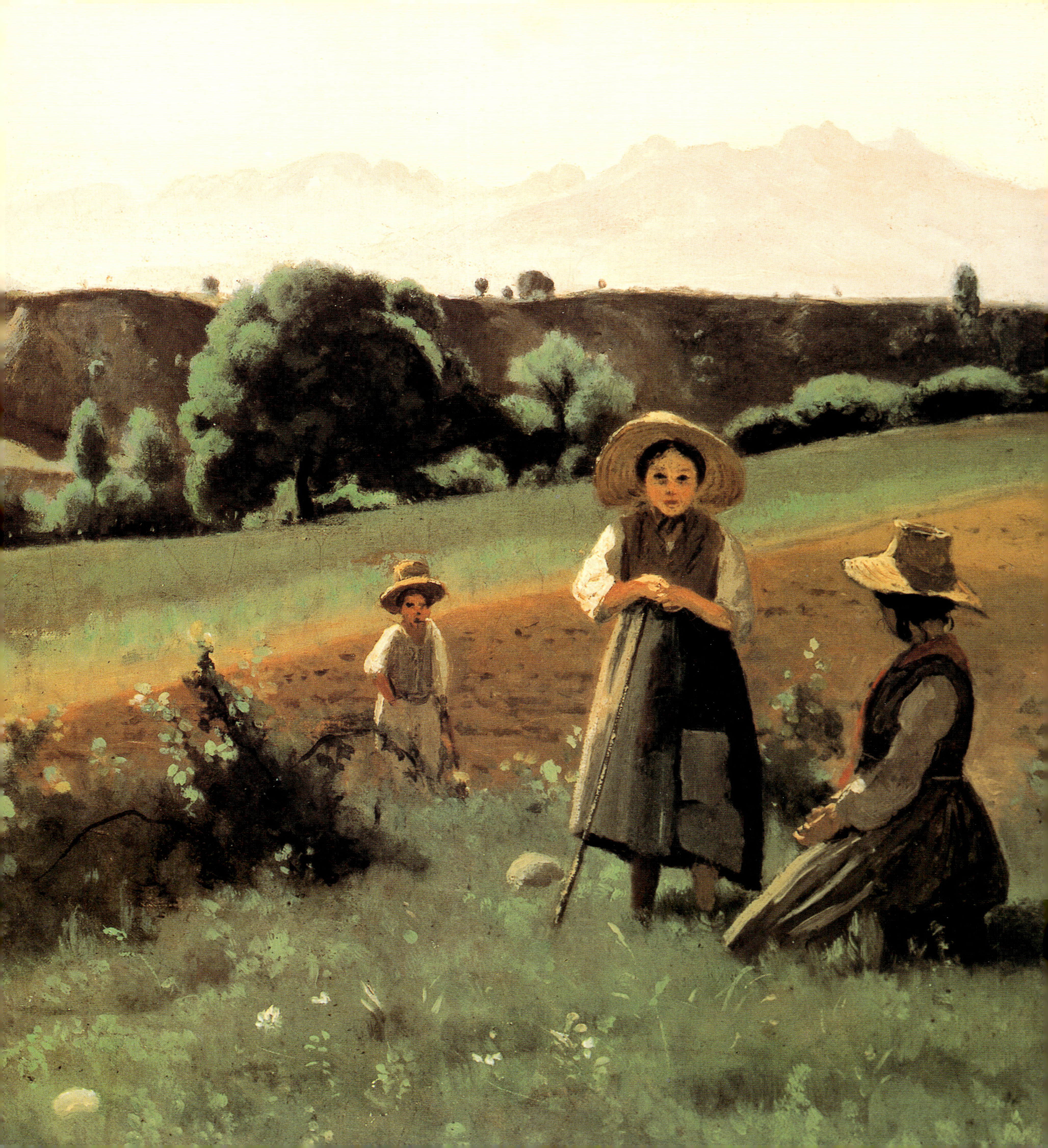

THE BIRTH OF IMPRESSIONISM

SEVERAL INFLUENCES IN THE earlier part of the nineteenth century are crucial to the development of Impressionism. In the first three decades of the century the inspiration of Dutch and English landscapists began to have an important effect on French landscape painting and art in general. Eugène Delacroix – who was to influence many of the Impressionists, especially Renoir – had brought a new brilliance of colour and virtuosity of brushwork to his paintings of exotic subjects and was a keen admirer of Constable, as were the Barbizon School of *plein-air*, or open air painters attempting a new naturalism in and around the Fontainebleau Forest. The latter were the precursors of Monet and Pissarro, who were also deeply influenced by the landscapists Eugène Boudin and Johan Jongkind working on the Normandy coast. By mid-century the Realists had come to prominence headed by Gustave Courbet, who had rejected the fanciful nature of Delacroix's Romanticism and was painting down-to-earth contemporary and allegorical subjects. All of these trends were significant in creating a world of art where Impressionism could flourish.

In 1863 the Salon was so oversubscribed that an exhibition of the thousands of rejected works was mounted after a popular outcry. Edouard Manet caused a scandal with his *Luncheon on the Grass* which portrayed its classical subject in a modern idiom to shocking effect and he became the reluctant leader of the younger generation of Monet, Renoir, Sisley, and Bazille who had come together the year before at the atelier of Charles Gleyre and formed the nucleus of the Impressionists.

COROT
Landscape at Mornex, Savoy
oil on canvas
undated. 40 × 61.5 cm
(DETAIL)

1820–1863: From the English Landscape to the Salon des Refusés

. . . I did not really see a less negative colour, but I felt as if it were an effort towards a less negative colour, the pulsation of a hesitant ray struggling to discharge its light.

Marcel Proust, *Swann's Way*

The Impressionists *par excellence*, Monet, Pissarro, Sisley, and Renoir, met in Paris in the early 1860s and were bound together in their admiration for the work of an older generation of landscape painters who had left their studios to paint in the open air in the countryside near Paris. Tracing the immediate origins of Impressionism, a phenomenon which began in the French countryside, takes us back to the English landscape and the excitement felt by early nineteenth-century French Romantic painters, such as Eugène Delacroix and Théodore Géricault, on encountering the experiments and achievements in oil and watercolour of the English landscape painters John Constable, J.M.W. Turner, and Richard Bonington.

In 1820 the French writer Charles Nodier, whose drawing room in Paris was an important place for the dissemination of news and ideas in the arts, was in London at the Royal Academy summer exhibition. In Nodier's journal, entitled *From Dieppe to the Mountains of Scotland*, he offered the following opinion of the summer exhibition:

> In painting, landscapes and sea views are the pieces in which the English have the fewest rivals in Europe . . . the palm of the exhibition belongs to a large landscape by Constable to which the ancient or modern masters have very few masterpieces that could be put in opposition. Near, it is only broad daubings of ill-laid colour which offend the touch as well as the sight, they are so coarse and uneven. At the distance of a few steps it is picturesque country, rustic dwellings, a low river where little waves foam over the pebbles, a cart crossing a pond. It is water, air and sky . . .

When Eugène Delacroix saw *The Hay Wain* at the Paris Salon of 1824 he was so impressed by the natural transparency and brilliance of colour in Constable's sky, trees, earth, and water that he immediately set about reworking his own *Massacre at Chois* (*Massacre à Scio*), a painting which he had almost finished, adding glaze and thick patches of pure pigment in various colours in an attempt to emulate the effect of the Englishman's work. Delacroix's radical use of colour and his technique of *flochetage*, using large flakes (*floches*) of colour to heighten his forms, was later to be developed further by the Impressionists.

Théodore Géricault, a fellow Romantic of Delacroix's, had seen *The Hay Wain* in London, two years before Delacroix's encounter with it at the 1824 Salon, and had expressed his astonishment to Delacroix and others on his return to Paris. With the enthusiasm of Nodier, the shock experienced by the critic Délécluze, who admitted that in comparison to *The Hay Wain* French landscape painting of the 1820s was "heavy, insensitive, and false", and the practical interest of Delacroix and Géricault in the English landscapists' work, an important step had been taken along the road which was eventually to lead to Monet and Pissarro.

During the 1820s and 1830s the sketches of Constable, Turner, and Bonington were of particular interest to Delacroix and his contemporaries. In order to capture "with a pure apprehension of natural effect," the incessantly changing qualities of light and colour, Delacroix observed that in the natural world "light and shadow never stand still." Consequently, the French Romantic painters developed the habit of making quick, but by no means cursory, sketches of a particular scene in oil and watercolour. These sketches, although they were not considered to be "finished" by the authorities and Salons of the time, are of importance in the development both of the artist's way of seeing the world and the technique of depicting it. They display to a remarkable degree the totality of the artist's vision and observation, and are nowadays often more highly prized than the "finished" work they frequently preceded. In fact, Delacroix and many others of his generation agreed that the vitality of outdoor sketches suffered from being transferred and reworked into studio compositions.

Until Constable and his fellow English landscapists had made their dazzling impact on the French art establishment in the 1820s, French landscape painting had enjoyed an honourable, if dull history. It is often, though quite wrongly, assumed that the Académie in

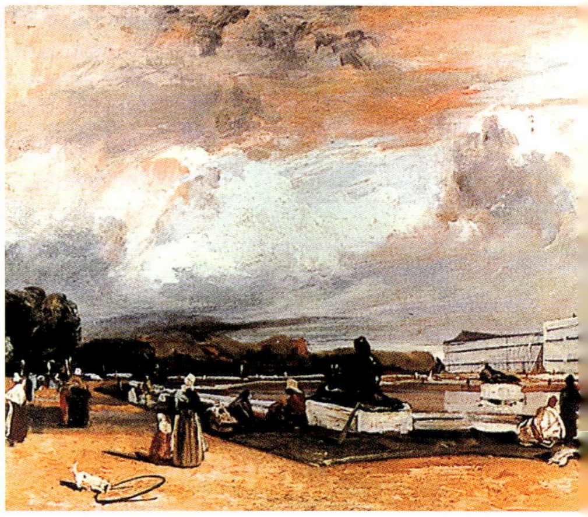

BONINGTON
The Large Pond, Palace of Versailles
oil on canvas
c.1820. 43.5 × 54.5 cm
Above Avoiding the popular aspects of Versailles, Bonington indicates the obvious touristic elements of the scene as sketchy masses in the background. Everything here is subordinated to the depiction of space and volume.

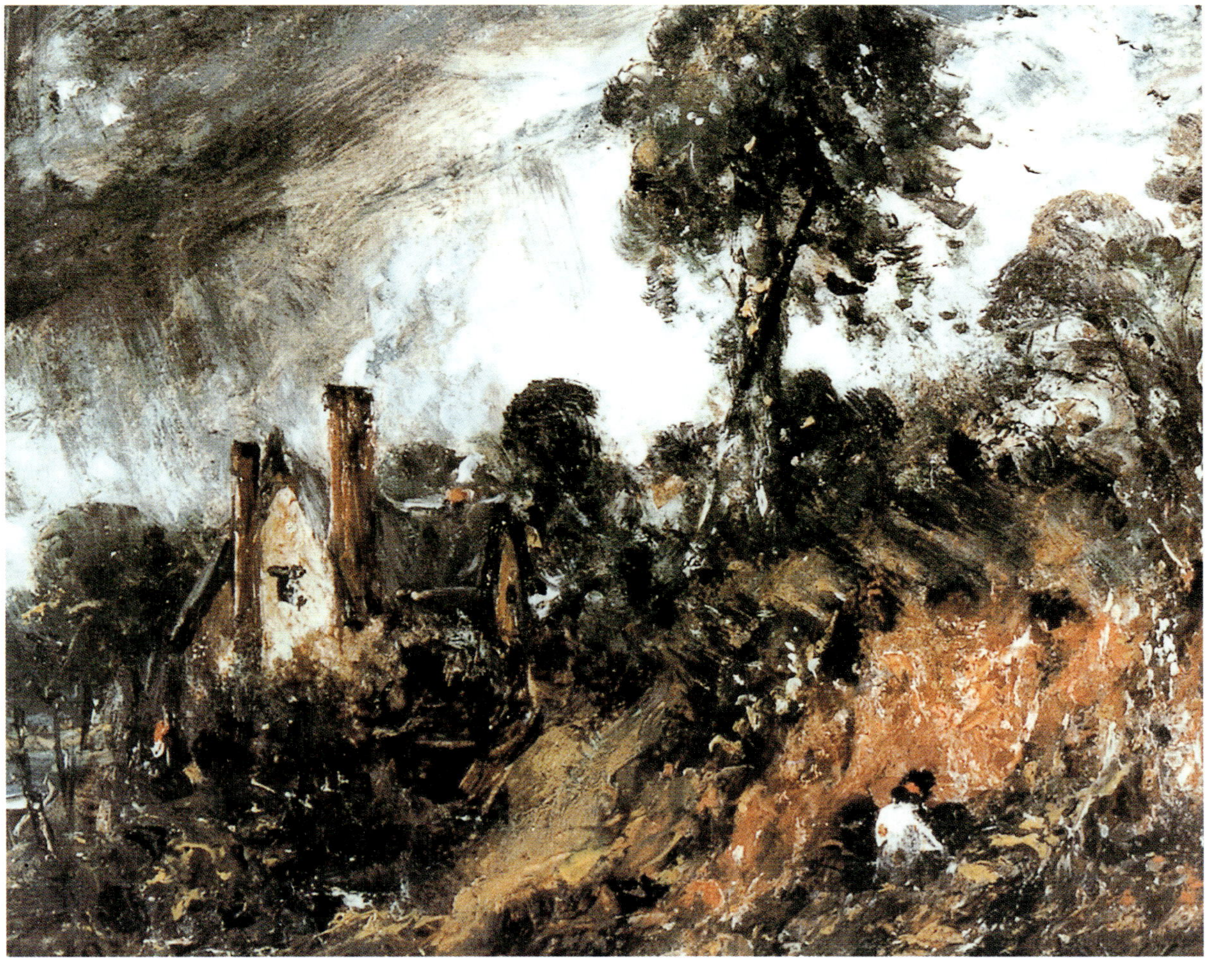

CONSTABLE
A Cottage among Trees with a Sand Bank
oil on paper on canvas
c.1830
Left An example of Constable's direct approach to landscape. The sketchy nature of works such as this was particularly influential in France.

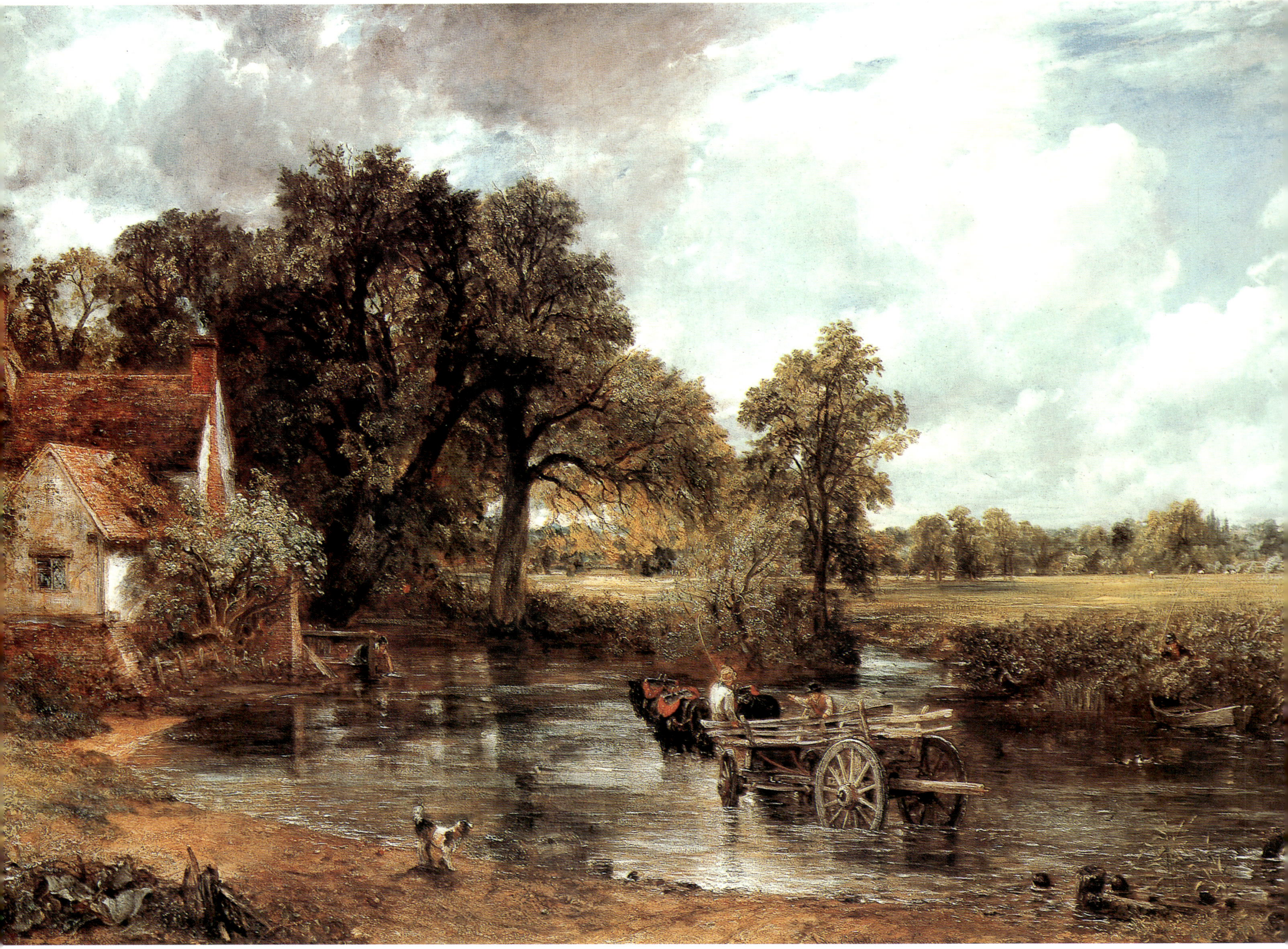

Paris at this time had no interest in the promotion of landscape painting. A major quadrennial competition in historical landscape painting, the Prix de Paysage Historique, had been instigated at the Ecole des Beaux-Arts in 1817 after many years of agitation by landscapists for the genre to be recognized within the school's establishment. Although the competition for the Prix de Paysage Historique was abolished in 1863 – a date central to the history of Impressionism as it marked the first Salon des Refusés – the teaching of landscape painting at the Ecole was at a significant level of development by the time Constable showed *The Hay Wain* at the 1824 Salon in Paris.

It is important to note that the Prix de Paysage Historique was precisely that – a competition for historical landscape, not landscape after nature or *paysage champêtre*. To compete, students had to choose a classical or biblical theme "of the noble and historical type" for their subject, and figures to be set in the landscape were not to exceed a prescribed height and disturb the proportions of a picture which was, after all, to be devoted to landscape. Despite this, the teaching of landscape after nature at the Ecole was surprisingly advanced, echoing some of the dicta of Constable and vaguely foreshadowing the loose theories of the Impressionists. J.B. Deperthes, who published his *Théorie de paysage* (*Landscape Theory*) in 1818, advised students of landscape painting that their aim in depicting nature was to paint it "in the light that falls on it at the exact moment when the painter sets out to capture the scene." According to the landscapist Pierre-Henri Valenciennes (who was partly responsible for the Prix de Paysage Historique), under whom Deperthes had studied, a study (*étude*) for a landscape painting made "from Nature should be done within two hours at the outside, and if your effect is a sunrise or a sunset, you should not take more than half an hour." Neither of these two instructions would have been out of place in a hypothetical manual of the art of Impressionism. Yet landscape painters such as Constable, Bonington, Valenciennes, and Deperthes were confined by tradition to their studios for the completion of their works of art. Painting outdoors did not lead to acceptably "finished" pieces of art. Indeed, Constable, as he was working in his London studio on *The Hay Wain*, was forced to dispatch an underling to the depths of East Anglia to make drawings of the eponymous cart. After the apprentice returned with the drawing Constable then completed the composition of the picture. This was the most practical approach.

CONSTABLE
The Hay Wain
oil on canvas
1821. 130 × 185.5 cm
OPPOSITE The quintessential English landscape, admired by Delacroix and Géricault for its dramatic naturalism. Delacroix reworked his own painting The Massacre at Chios *after he had seen Constable's great landscape at the Salon of 1824. This and other works by the English landscapists were a source of inspiration to the Barbizon School and their successors, the Impressionists.*

(GELÉE) LORRAIN
Landscape with Ascanius Shooting the Stag of Sylvia
oil on canvas
1682. 120 × 150 cm
BELOW Claude Lorrain was the great master of the "obedient" landscape, which aimed for a perfectly harmonious rendering of nature.

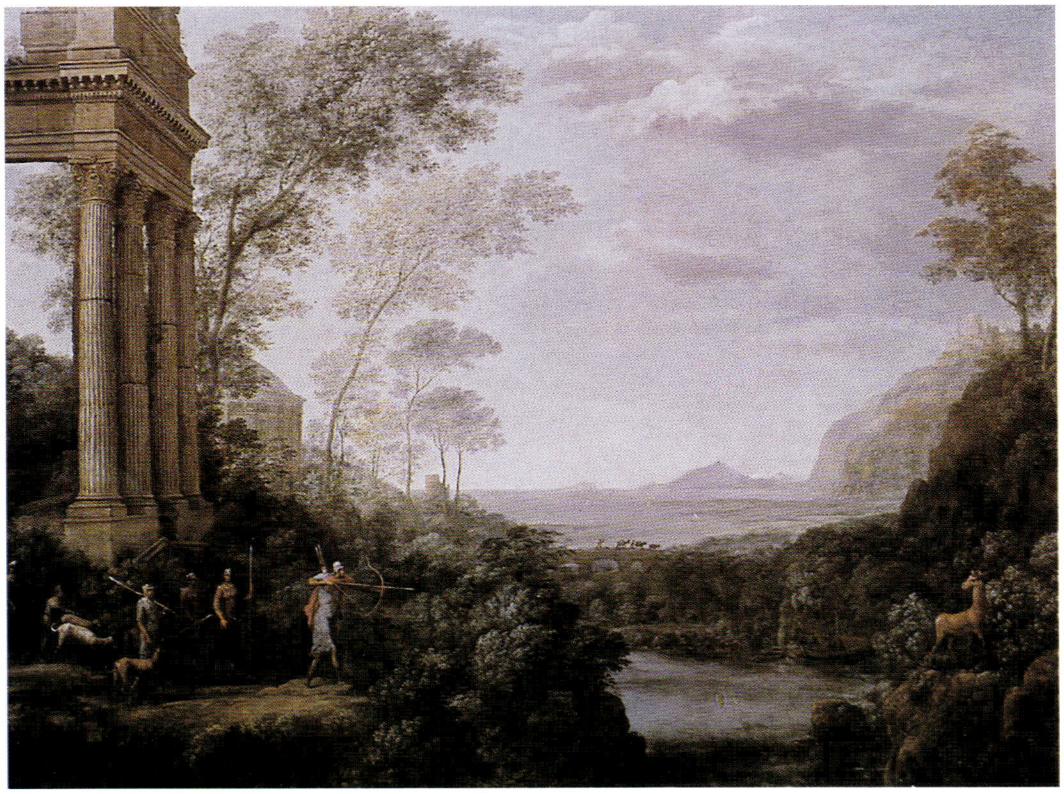

COURBET
Entrance to the Straits of Gibraltar
oil on canvas
1848. 18 × 26 cm
Below Small, hastily executed sketches were not made for public consumption, but the aesthetic of the sketch or study was gaining ground amongst French landscapists in the mid-nineteenth century.

COROT
The Roman Campagna with the Claudian Aquaduct
oil on canvas
c.1826–28. 21.5 × 33 cm
Right The Roman countryside was the classical landscape taught in the Ecole des Beaux-Arts. In an idealized form it provides the background for countless academic paintings of the time.

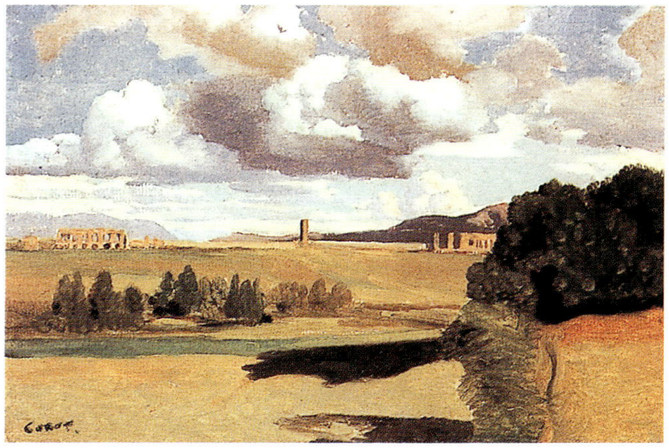

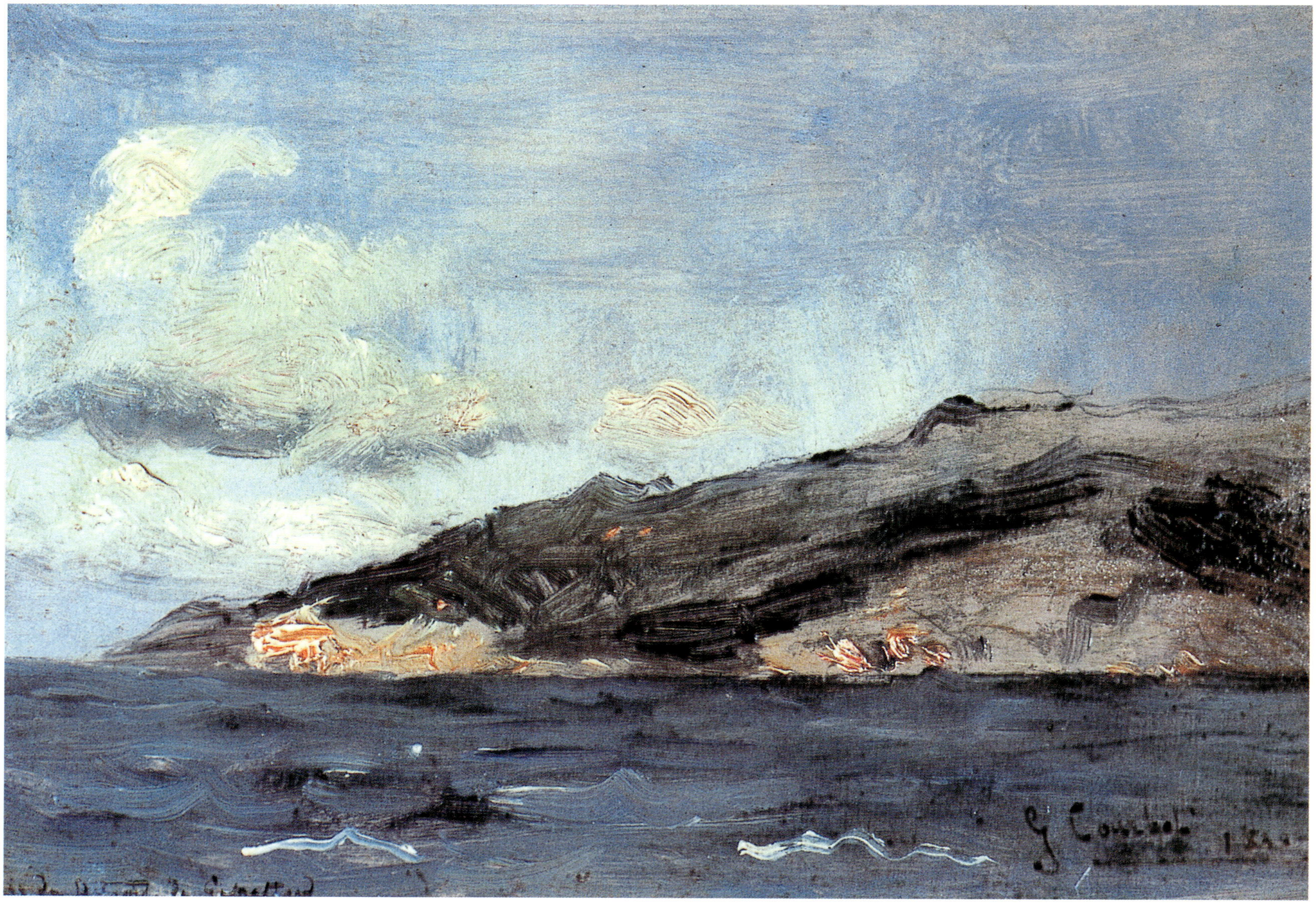

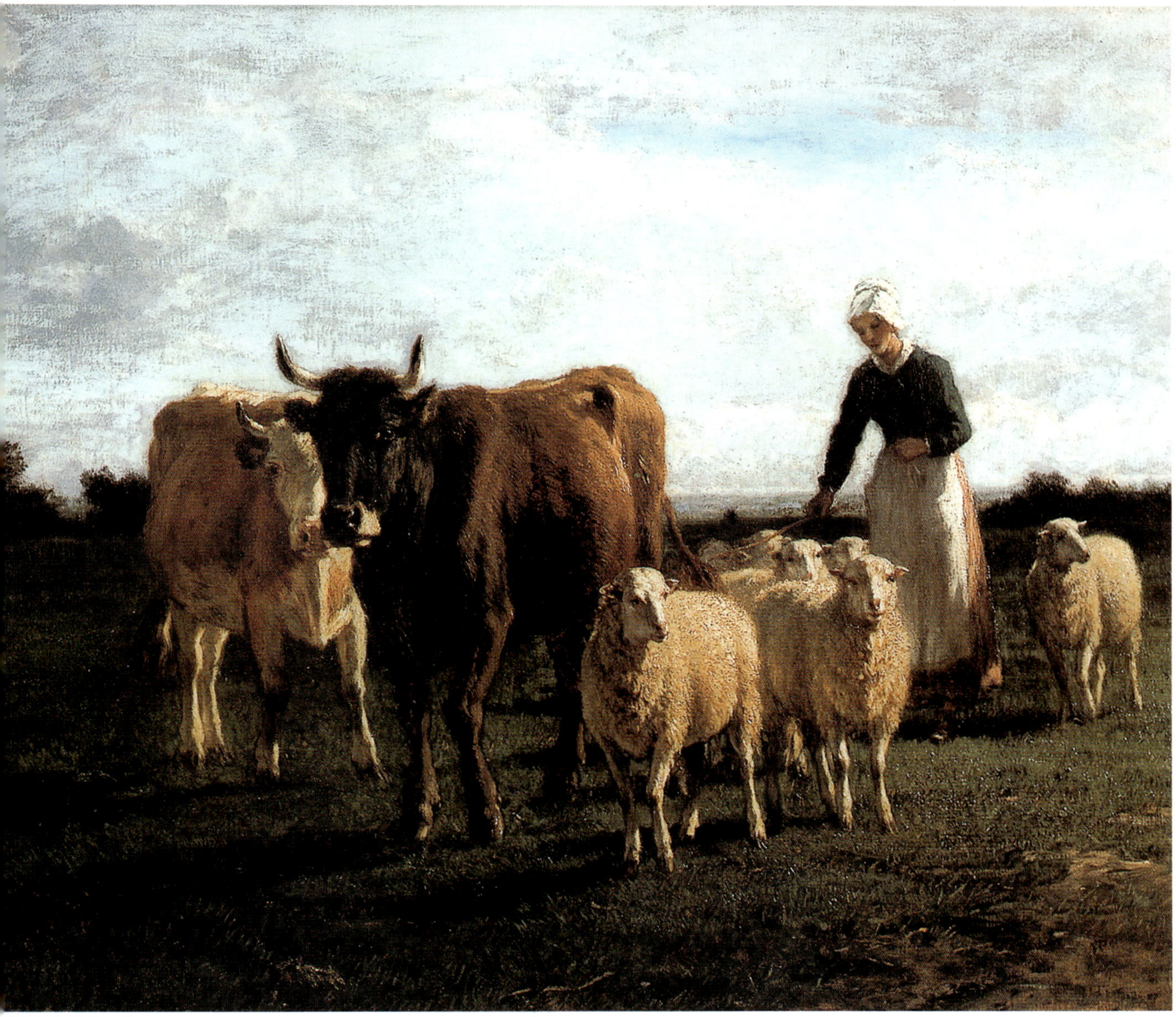

TROYON
Evening near Barbizon
oil on canvas
1859. 66 × 88 cm
The young Monet was particularly interested in the effects of light depicted in works such as this. On one of his first visits to the Salon Monet wrote to his friend and teacher Eugène Boudin that Troyon's landscapes had delighted him especially. Troyon was a friend of Boudin and he advised Monet to enrol in Thomas Couture's atelier, advice which Monet summarily rejected.

The move into the country and the development of the idea that a sketch made outdoors, *en plein-air*, was a legitimate end in itself came with a group of painters known as the Barbizon School. Barbizon is a village in the Fontainebleau Forest to the southeast of Paris. The Fontainebleau Forest and the nearby plain of Chailly had been locations for painters since the mid-eighteenth century, and had been suggested by Valenciennes as useful substitutes for the Roman Campagna, a landscape held in great esteem for its classical associations. Between 1830 and 1850 a group of landscape painters, which included Constant Troyon, Théodore Rousseau, Virgile Diaz de la Peña, François Daubigny, François Millet, and Jean-Baptiste Corot, made use of the area around Barbizon and often settled there for long periods. Daubigny was a devoted *plein-air* painter who built a studio boat in order to paint *in situ* on the river Oise (an example later followed by

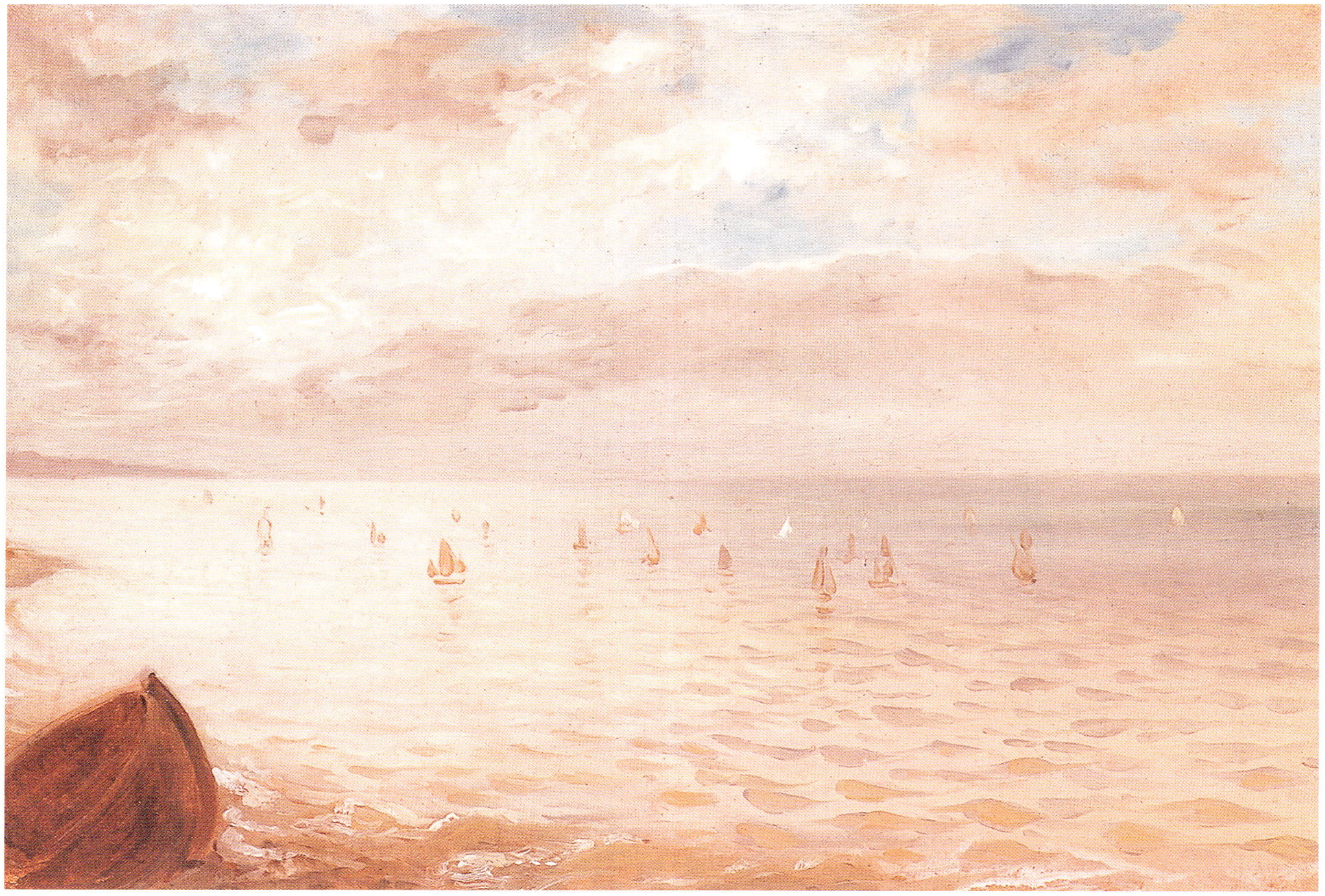

DELACROIX
The Sea from the Cliff-tops at Dieppe
oil on canvas
This is the landscape of the Normandy coast that Monet was to make his own. It is interesting to see that Delacroix was not only interested in exotic and Romantic figures.

Monet). In 1891 Frédéric Henriet, in his biography *The Campaigns of a Landscape Painter* (*Les Campagnes d'un paysagiste*), describes Daubigny's struggle with the elements:

> Daubigny attached his canvas to some posts solidly planted in the ground. And there it stayed, continually exposed to the horns of cattle and the pranks of naughty children until it was completely finished. The painter had specifically chosen a turbulent sky filled with large clouds chased by the angry wind. He was constantly on the alert for the right moment and ran to take up his work as soon as the weather corresponded to that of his painting.

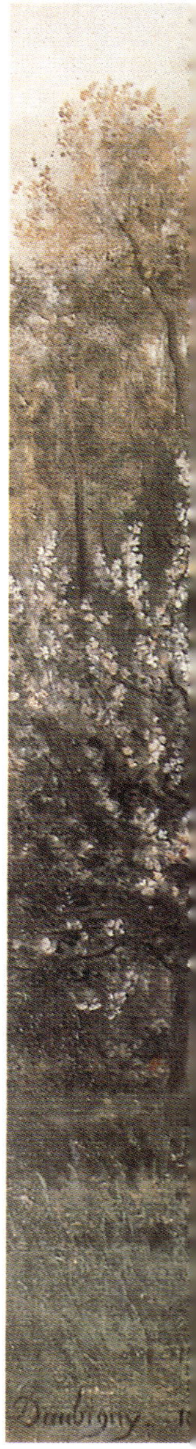

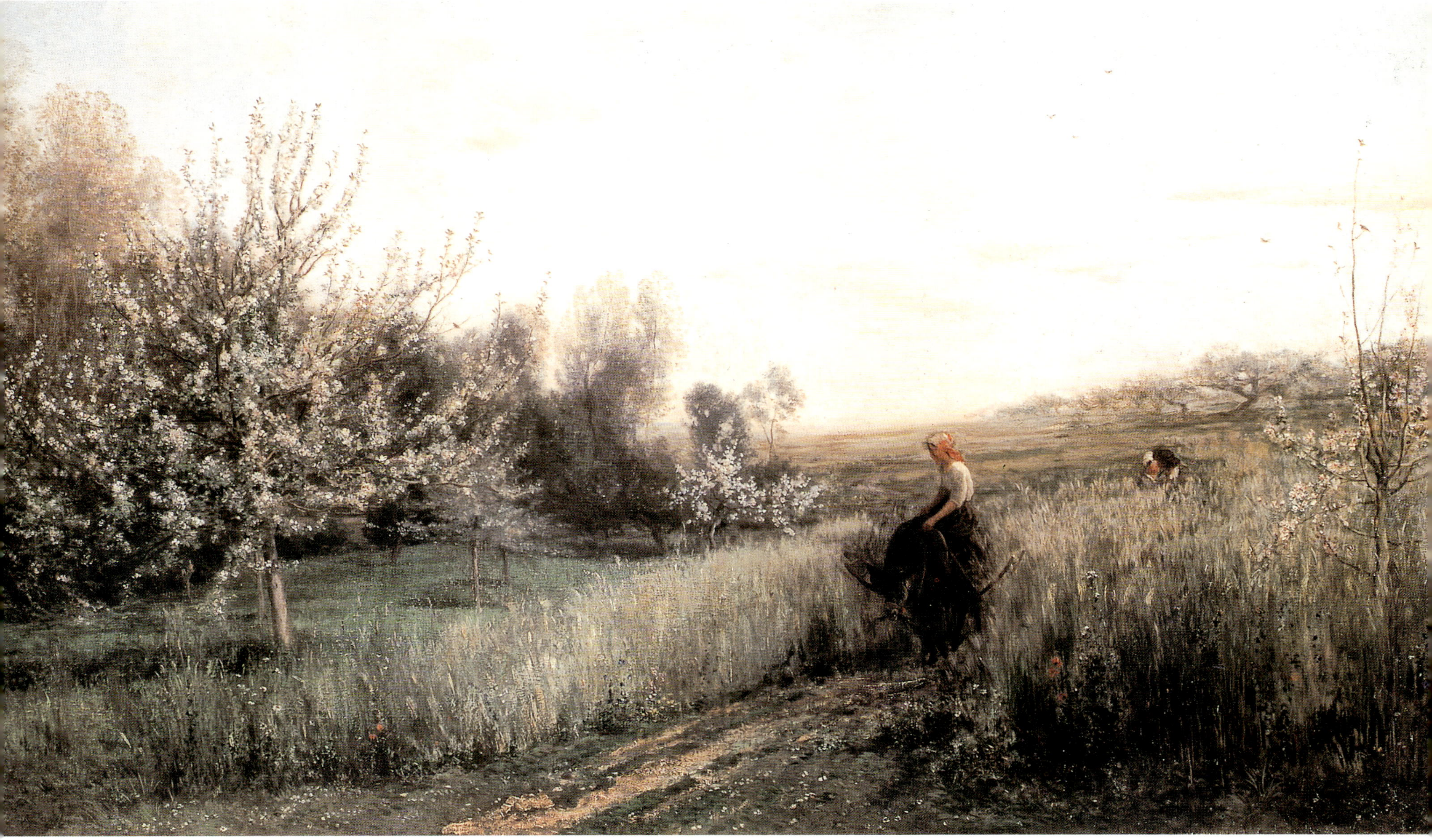

DAUBIGNY
Spring
oil on canvas
1857. 96 × 193 cm
A perfect example of the Barbizon landscape, Daubigny's painting was exhibited at the Salon of 1857 which was transferred that year from the Salon D'Apollon in the Louvre to the larger Palais de l'Industrie.

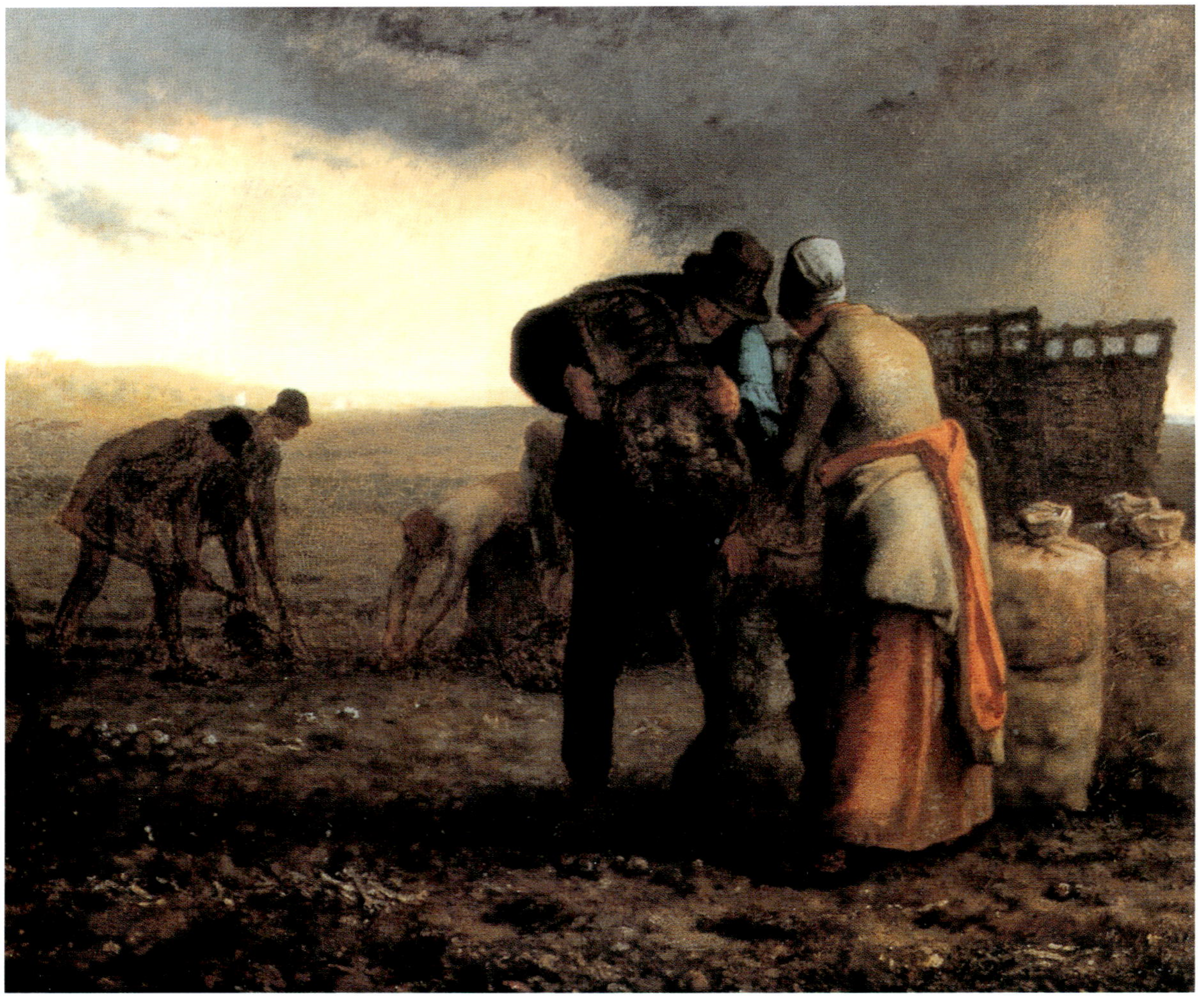

MILLET
The Potato Harvest
oil on canvas
1858. 54 × 65 cm
RIGHT The dignity of peasant labour was Millet's great, if somewhat sentimental theme. Pissarro, and later van Gogh, were influenced by Millet's depictions of the arduous life of the peasant. Millet's work did not find favour with the establishment which preferred idealized landscapes and peasants.

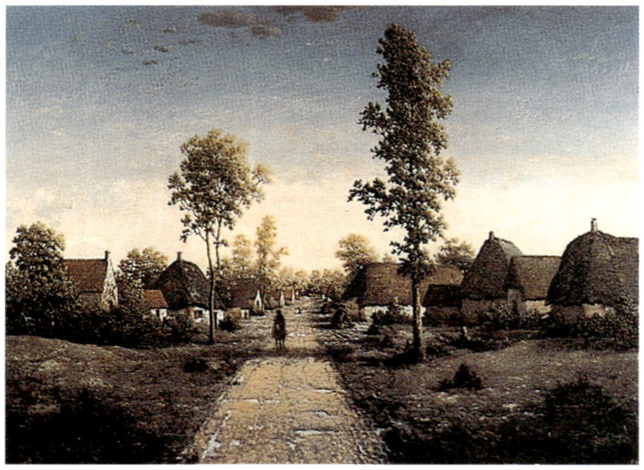

ROUSSEAU
The Village of Becquigny
oil on canvas
1857. 63.5 × 100 cm
RIGHT The composition may be a coincidence, but artists were assiduous museum-goers and learnt much from their predecessors. Baudelaire, however, was critical of Rousseau's lack of a personal vision: "He wants", he said "to be precise and to make something striking. A highly coloured photograph must be his ideal."

The Barbizon School was as indebted to the English landscapists as Delacroix although in historical terms the art being created around Barbizon quickly came to represent a strong reaction against the Romanticism of Delacroix and Géricault, who were not particularly interested in landscape or *plein-airisme* as a genre or method of painting. Just as the Romantics had rebelled against the ingrained Neo-Classicism of the Académie, as exemplified by David and Ingres and taught in the Ecole des Beaux-Arts, so the painting of nature for its own sake amounted to a rejection of both the erudite Neo-Classical and the flamboyant Romantic subject matter. The Barbizon painters, as well as admiring the English landscapists of their own era, were much taken with the eminent seventeenth-century Dutch School of landscape painting,

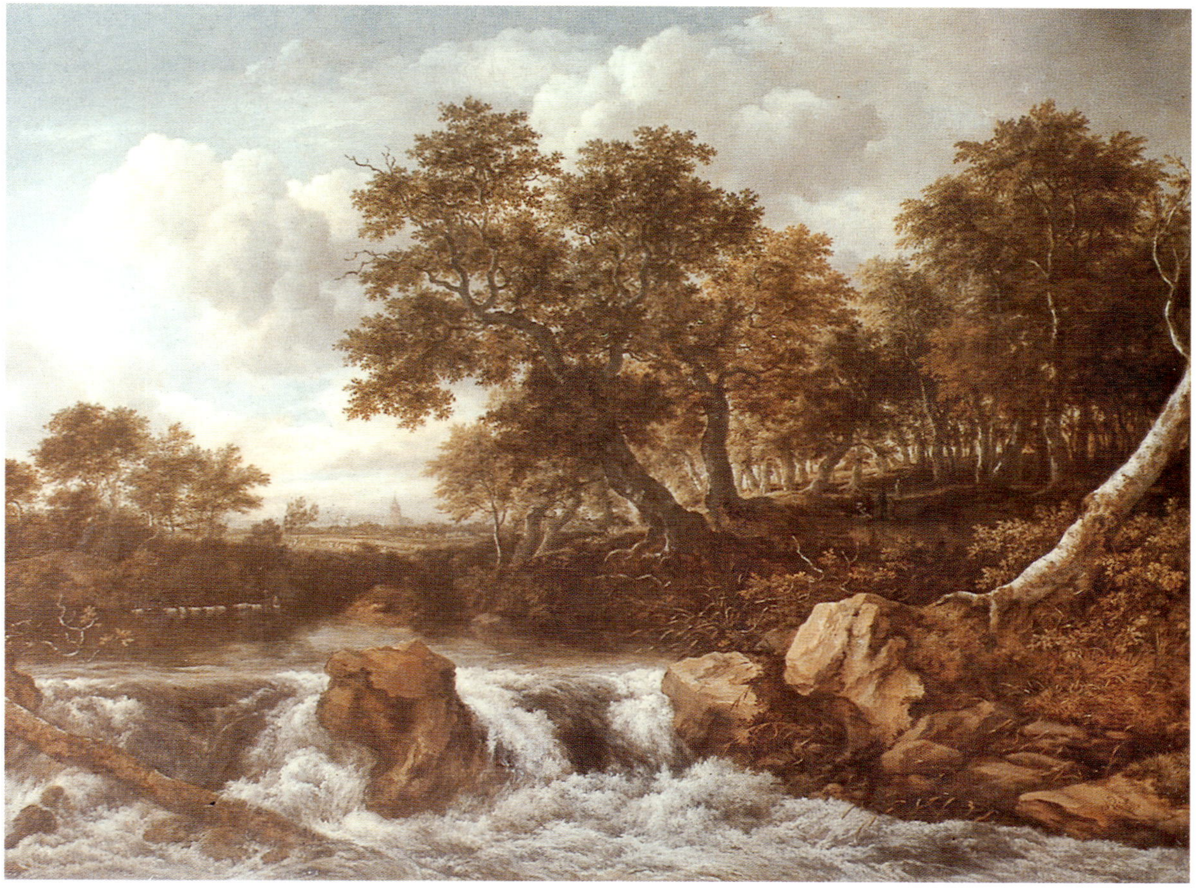

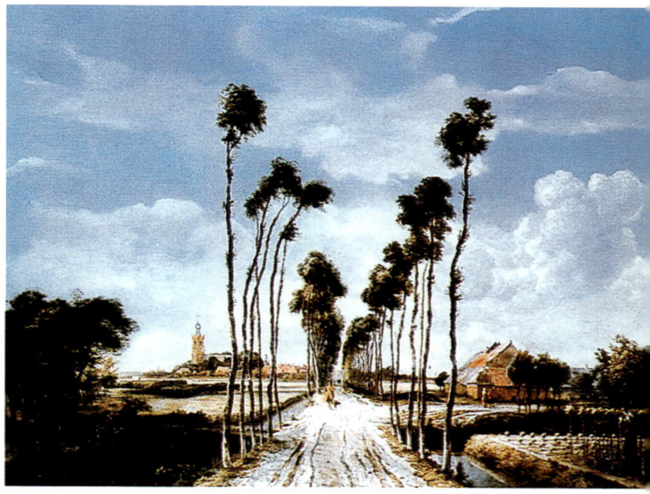

HOBBEMA
The Avenue, Middelharnis
oil on canvas
1689. 103.5 × 141 cm
ABOVE This was of course painted in the studio, but seventeenth-century Dutch artists were also concerned with studying their surroundings at first hand. Ruysdael warned his students that light and shadow never stand still; a sentiment close to Monet's heart in his later career.

RUYSDAEL
The Waterfall
oil on canvas
17th century
LEFT ABOVE The seventeenth century Dutch landscapists were the first great exponents of the genre. This scene is typical of their approach. Although it is highly formalised, great attention is paid to the details of movement in the torrent of water.

particularly the works of Ruysdael and Hobbema. In this the Barbizon School was supported by the Director of the Académie, Théophile Thoré, who had commissioned Rousseau and made an extensive study of Dutch art. On the other hand the Comte de Nieuwerkerke, the Director-General of National Museums after 1849, spoke for many when he described the Barbizon School in the following incandescent and patronizing terms: "This is the painting of democrats, of those who don't change their linen and who want to put themselves above men of the world. This art displeases and disquiets me."

Thankfully the Comte de Nieuwerkerke and the French authorities were increasingly disquietened to find their stranglehold on matters of taste weakening. The clear line of development from the Dutch to the English artists, and thence the French landscape painters and their attempt to capture "the exact moment", was leading to the art of Monet and his fellow Impressionists.

Capturing the landscape meant being in it, with all the attendant dangers and inconvenience of being away from the controlled environment of the studio. In 1841 John Goffe Rand, an American portraitist living in London, had invented the first collapsible paint tube, an idea quickly taken up by the colour merchants Winsor and Newton. As Pierre-Auguste Renoir is reported by his son, Jean, to have said, "Without paints in tubes there would have been no Cézanne, no Monet, no Sisley or Pissarro, nothing of what the journalists were later to call Impressionism."

Before the arrival of these new tubes, made of inert tin so as not to react with the various chemicals in the pigment, the ground pigment was supplied by the colour merchant, mixed with oil by the painter and kept in a small pouch of pig's bladder. To use the paint, the artist had to make a small hole in the wall of the bladder and squeeze it out. For centuries these bladders had been the only way of dispensing a ready mixed combination of pigment and oil, but paint could not be kept for long in them before the oil began to oxidize. Once opened, the life of the paint – made up of expensive pigments – was considerably shortened. The tin tube was a revolutionary device by comparison, both for the colour merchant, who had a new product with which to service an increasing clientèle of amateur or "Sunday" painters littering the banks of the Seine on summer days, and the serious artist, who could now venture outdoors confident that the paint was in a stable condition and swiftly to hand. The tube paint had the consistency of fresh butter, which made it ideal for application to the canvas in thick impasto brushstrokes, or even with the palette knife – both methods used by the Impressionists and after them to particularly remarkable effect by Vincent van Gogh. The paint could still of course be further tempered with linseed, walnut, or poppy oil, or diluted with turpentine.

To fill the new tubes a whole new range of bright, stable colours with well-understood drying properties began to appear on the market. The advancement of mineral and organic chemistry in the early part of the century had heralded new colours such as cobalt blue, artificial ultramarine (previously made of lapis lazuli, very expensive and available only in small quantities), chromium yellow with its shades of orange, red and green, emerald green, zinc white and a stable lead white. By the 1850s the artist had at his or her disposal a palette more brilliant, stable and convenient than ever before.

In 1839 the French chemist Eugène Chevreul, director of dyeing at the Gobelins tapestry workshop, who had begun an investigation into why some dyed colours seemed less brilliant than others, published his study *On the Law of Simultaneous Colour Contrast and the Arrangement of Coloured Objects* (better known as *The Principles of Harmony and Contrast of Colours*), which explained the phenomenon that when two colours are placed touching one another the differences between them are perceived to be at their greatest. From this he codified a theory of colours

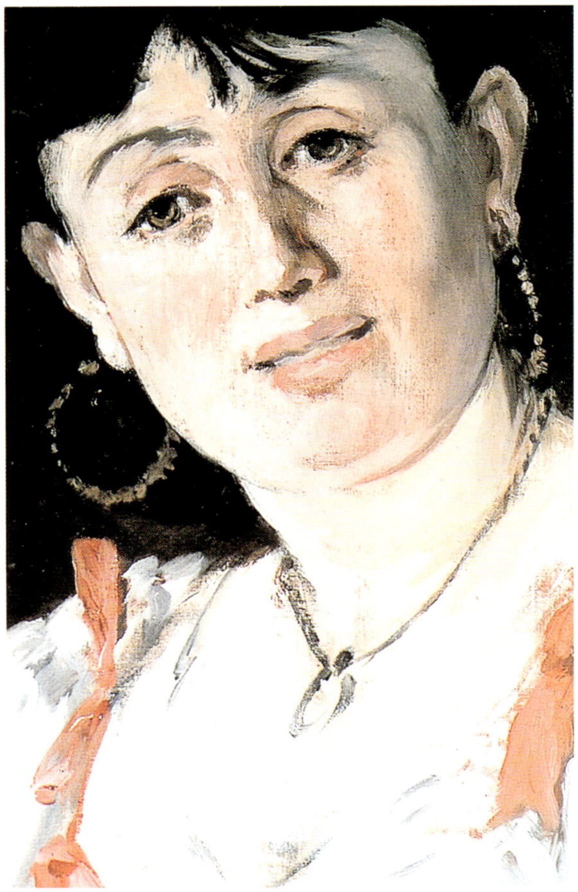

The four pictures here have been enlarged to show the details of the brushwork of the four master Impressionists – Manet, Pissarro, Monet, and Renoir. The essential similarity between them, and the obvious comparison to be made with the refined, concentrated brushwork of the classical schools and the conventional artists of the time, is the looseness and immediacy of the strokes.

MANET
An Italian Woman
oil on canvas
Private collection

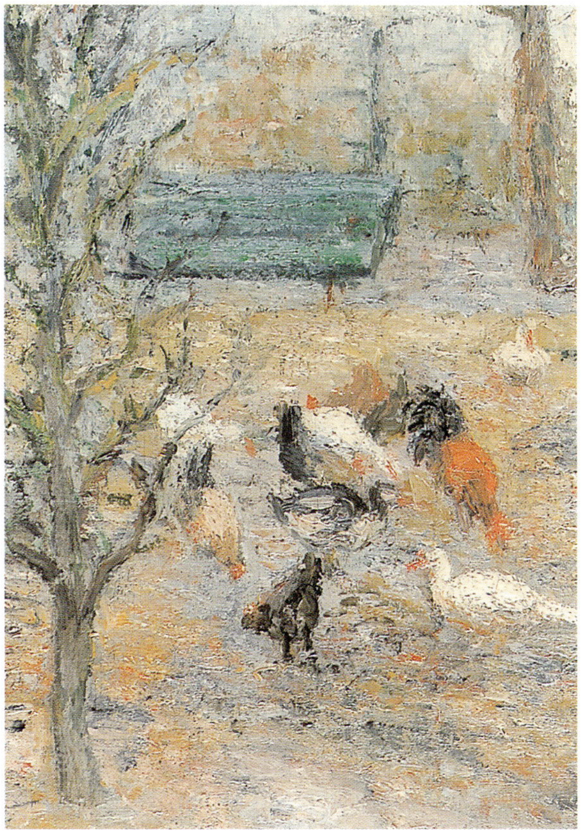

which says that certain pairs of colours, such as green and red, or violet and yellow, complement each other. This gives rise to the phenomenon of "negative or complementary after-image" where the complementary colour of a red, i.e. green, can be seen as an aura around the colour when staring at the red for a moment and then looking away. As the German poet and scientist Johan Wolfgang von Goethe had already observed in his *Theory of Colours* written in 1810, a deep red sunset produced the complementary colour of green in the shadows cast by the sunlight; likewise, the yellowish tinge of snow produced shadows of a violet hue. Delacroix had used coloured shadow in his work, and the Impressionists were to exploit their own perception and Chevreul's theory further with the bright new colours available to them, whilst the Neo-Impressionists were to take this phenomenon to its logical extreme.

PISSARRO
The Farmyard
oil on canvas
1877. 55 × 65 cm
Left

RENOIR
The White Hat
oil on canvas
1890. 55.5 × 46 cm
Below

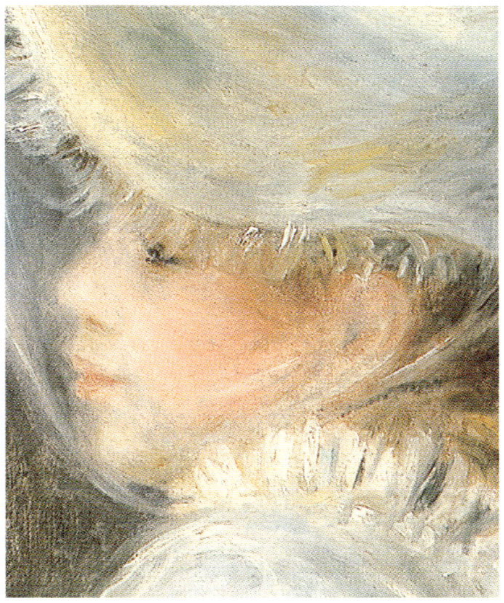

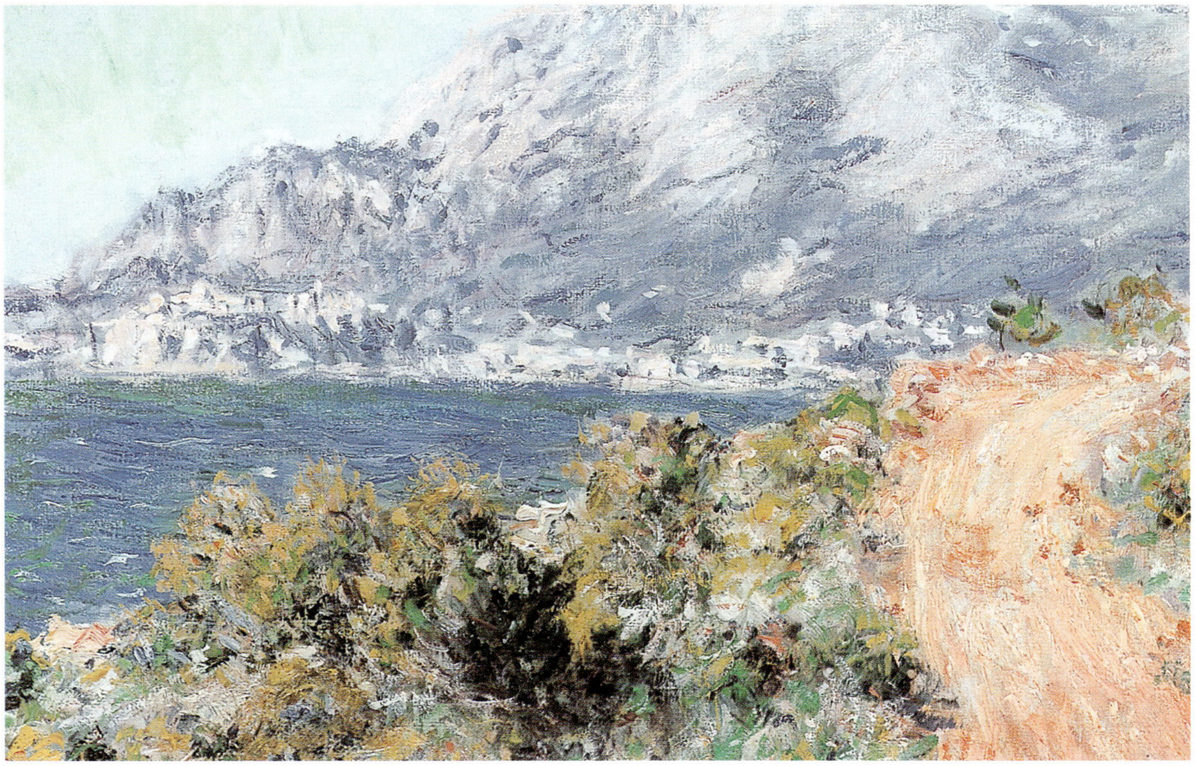

MONET
The Red Road
oil on canvas
1884. 65 × 81 cm
Left

MILLET
Bringing Home the New-born Calf
oil on canvas
1857–61. 81 × 99 cm
RIGHT Like The Potato Harvest, *this painting was ridiculed by some contemporary critics, who considered Millet's subjects to be vulgar and unworthy of fine art.*

COURBET
Joseph Proudhon and His Children
oil on canvas
1853. 147 × 198 cm
RIGHT BELOW This composition seems perfectly natural to us, but it was far too informal for the taste of the time.

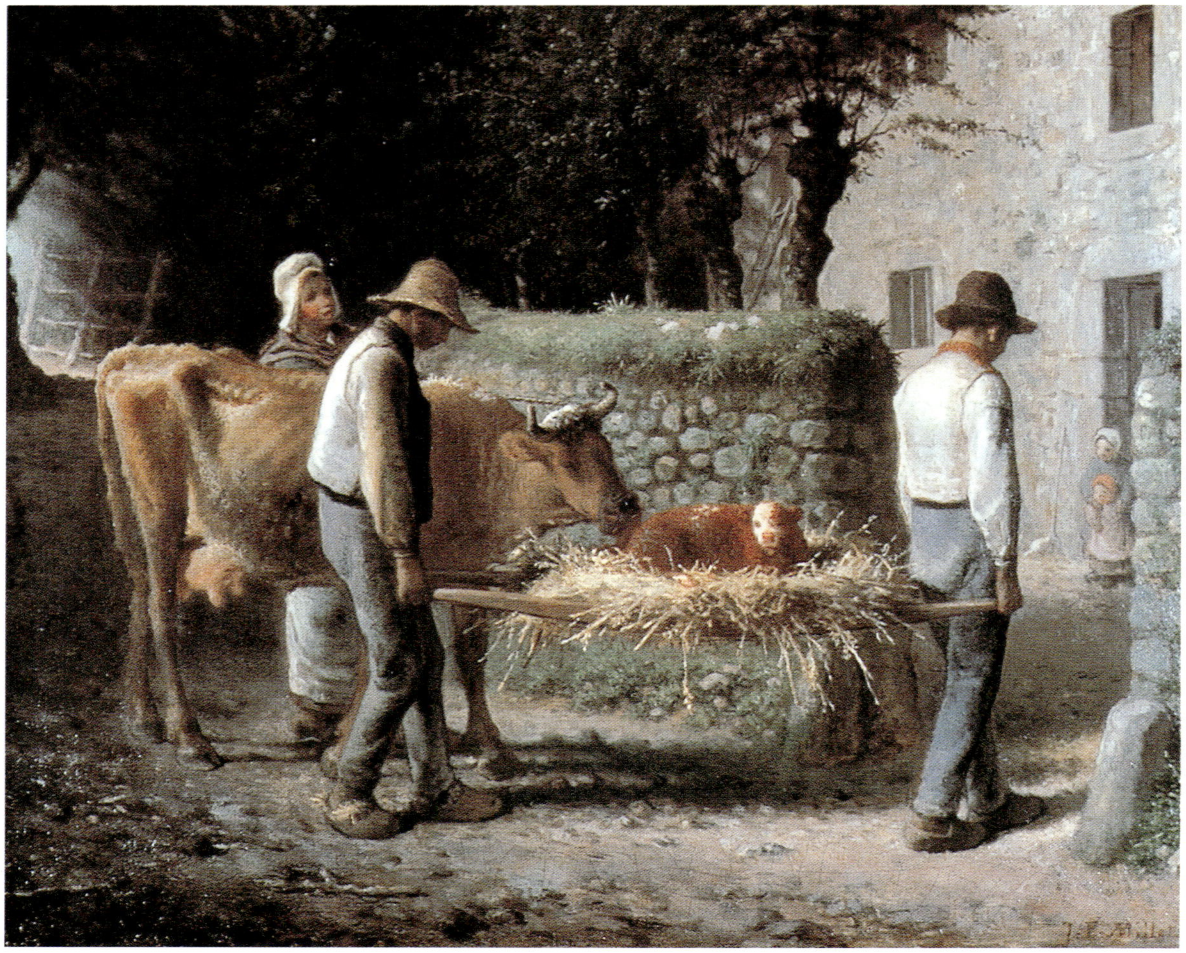

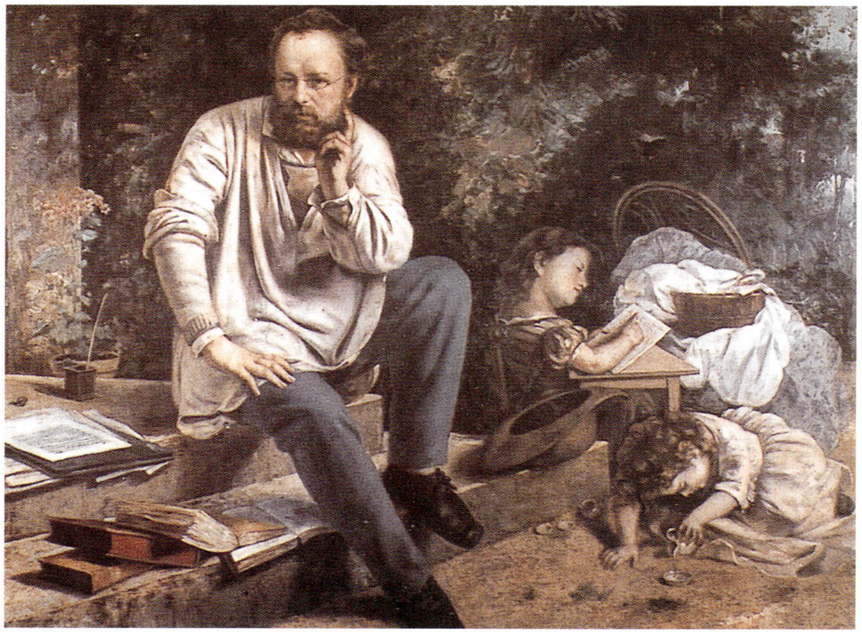

Meanwhile, the Realism developed by François Millet and Gustave Courbet, which was a complete rejection of Neo-Classical and Romantic styles, began, in the late 1850s and early 1860s, to have a strong influence on young painters like Monet. Millet's great achievement was to paint the peasantry as he found and remembered it, being himself the son of a Normandy peasant farmer. Although paintings such as *The Gleaners* (*Les Glaneurs*) and *Angèlus* show the peasantry at back-breaking work and pious rest, and do not appear today to be particularly realistic, their very subject matter was a cause for fierce controversy at the time among those traditionalists who thought agricultural labour a subject unfit for "proper" representation, and those at the other extreme who believed Millet's work to be the embodiment of socialist values. Despite the claims of the right and the left, Millet remained resolutely apolitical.

Not so Gustave Courbet, the son of a wealthy wine grower from Ornans near Switzerland. Courbet's art, like his politics, was uncompromising. His choice of subjects eschewed everything that had previously been thought suitable for fine art. They were, as Bernard Denvir observes, "unheroic, unhistorical, and entirely unconcerned either with religious symbolism or patriotic propaganda." Courbet was a friend and *comrade* of the printer Pierre Joseph Proudhon, the title of whose work of 1850 *What is Property?* (*Qu'est-ce que la proprieté?*) was answered with the immortal words: "It is theft" (*"C'est le vol"*). Courbet's staunch socialism ensured him a spectacular career in politics, eventually landing him in jail for taking part in the destruction of the Vendôme Column, a huge victory memorial in the heart of Paris. But in spite of his radicalism in painting and politics

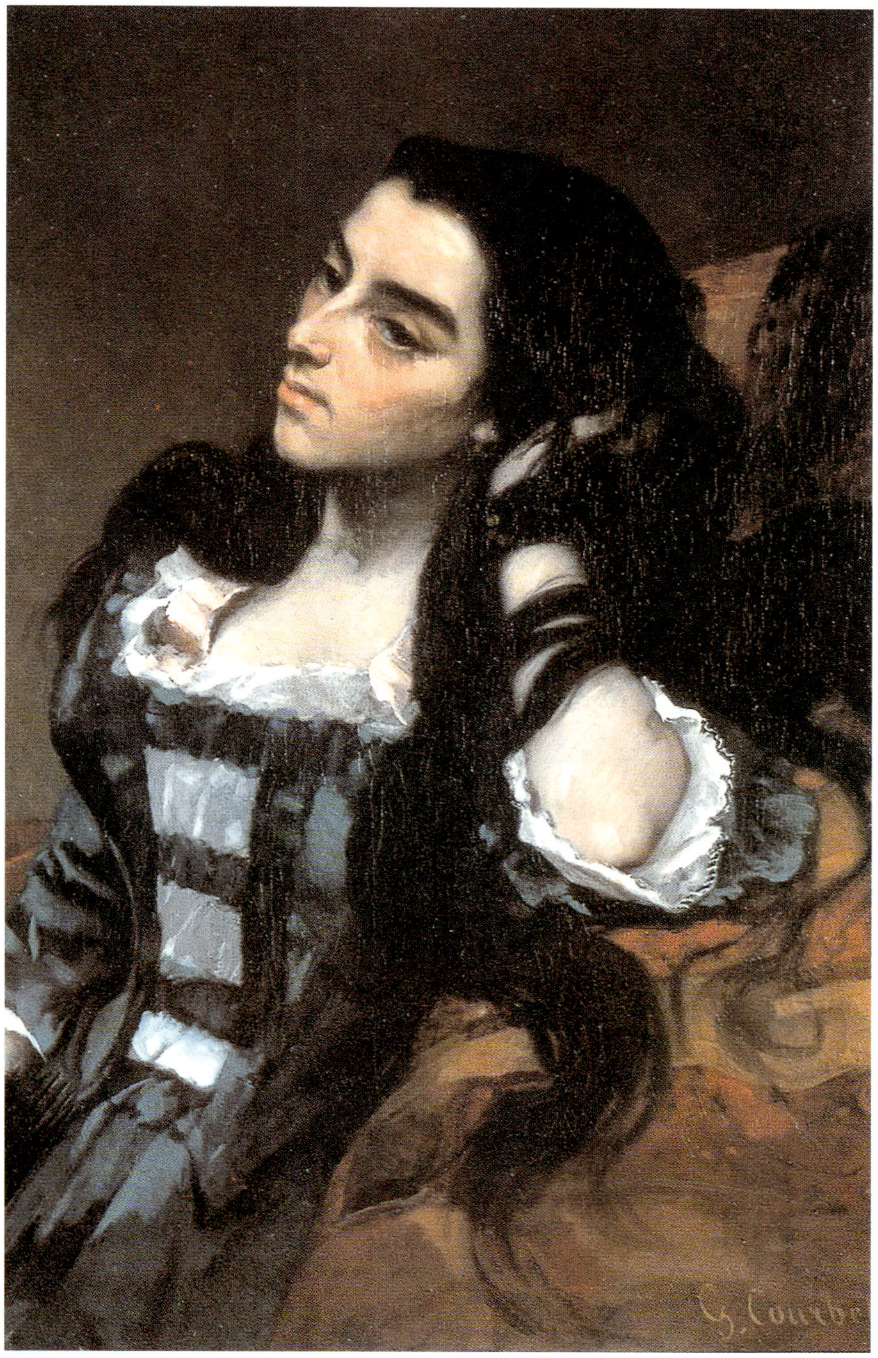

COURBET
A Spanish Woman
oil on canvas
1855. 81 × 65 cm
As usual, Courbet does not try to prettify his sitters.

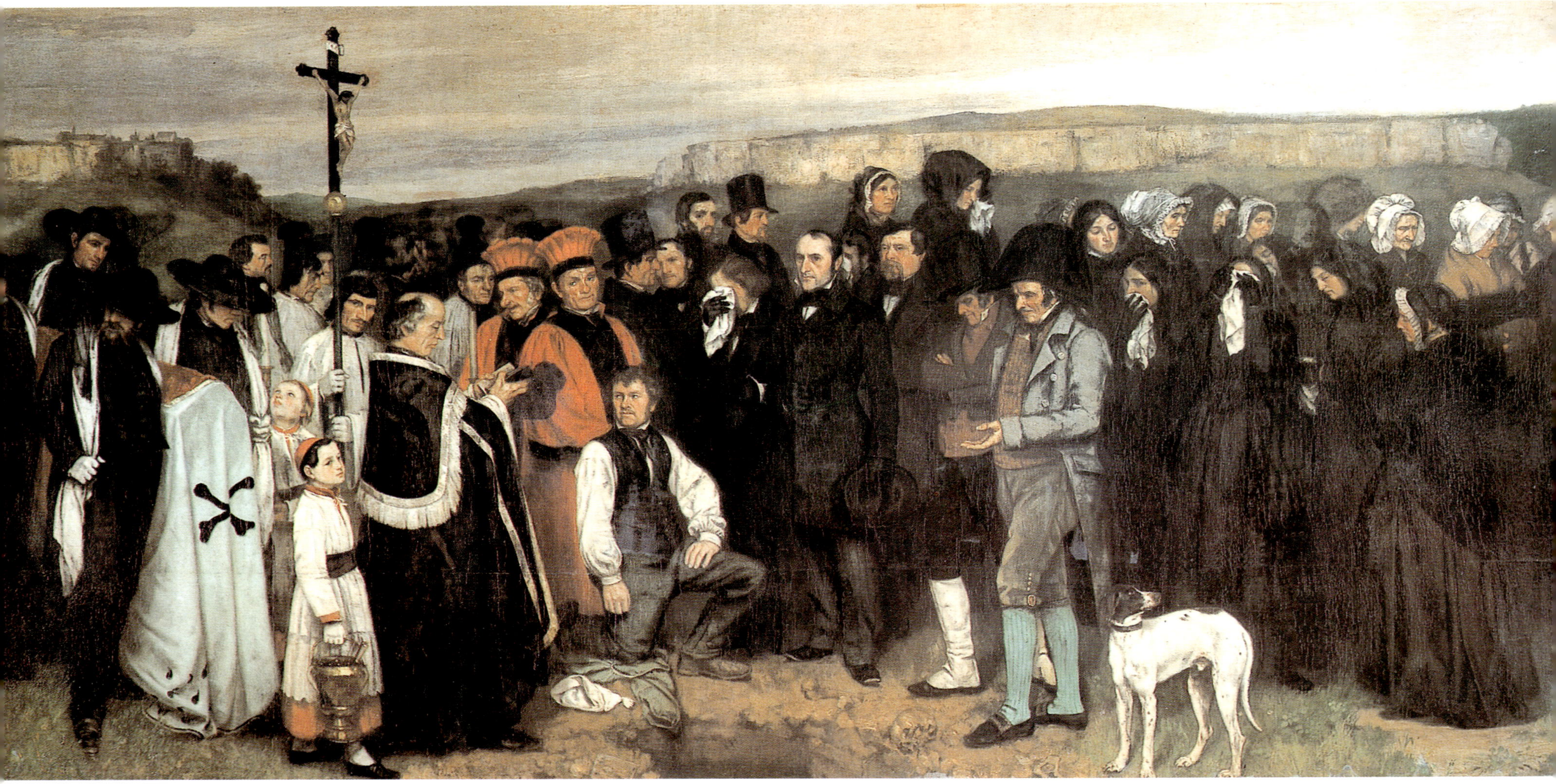

COURBET
The Burial at Ornans
oil on canvas
1849–50. 315 × 668 cm
ABOVE Courbet received a medal at the Salon in 1850, but not for this painting. The massive, dark, unconventional composition showing the lower echelons of society provoked outraged criticism. Courbet's Realism was deeply influenced by the political ideas of Pierre Joseph Proudhon, of whom he was a supporter. Courbet's rejection of historical and religious subjects made him a champion of the new generation of the "painters of modern life".

COURBET
The Artist's Studio
oil on canvas
1855. 360 × 600 cm
RIGHT This painting is subtitled an "Allegory of Realism", and the artist has indeed filled his picture with symbols and contemporary figures. Right, seated on the table: the poet Baudelaire. Right, centre: Champfleury. Right, third from left: another friend of Courbet's, the socialist writer Proudhon. In the shadow to the left, seated in profile: the barely disguised figure of Napoleon III, much disliked by Courbet and his radical friends. Left, seated, wearing a top hat: a right-wing journalist. Standing, left: a figure identified as the banker Fould. The woman nursing a child is Irish; she represents poverty and destitution. The dummy behind the easel has been symbolically discarded in favour of a real woman.

he exhibited two works, *The Stone Breakers* (*Les Casseurs de pierre*) and *The Burial at Ornans*, at the Salon of 1850. "I hold", Courbet wrote in 1861, "that painting is essentially a concrete art and does not consist of anything but the representation of real and concrete things". Five years later, at the Exposition Universelle in Paris, Courbet erected his own Realist Pavilion (Pavillion du Réalisme) where he rivalled the official Salon by showing forty pictures including the massive *The Artist's Studio* (*L'Atelier du peintre*), which depicts in "an Allegory of Realism" the artist and the influences at work on him.

In the decade after 1850 French painting underwent an unparalleled fragmentation of styles, partly tolerated but never promoted by the authorities. The experiments of the Barbizon School and the Realists were encouraging the young painters who had been born in the 1830s and 1840s along a path which was artistically a logical progression but which was to appear to the public and the arbiters of the Salon shockingly revolutionary. By the time the Impressionists began to show in the mid-1870s, the Barbizon artists were readily accepted by the Salon and their work was beginning to fetch high prices.

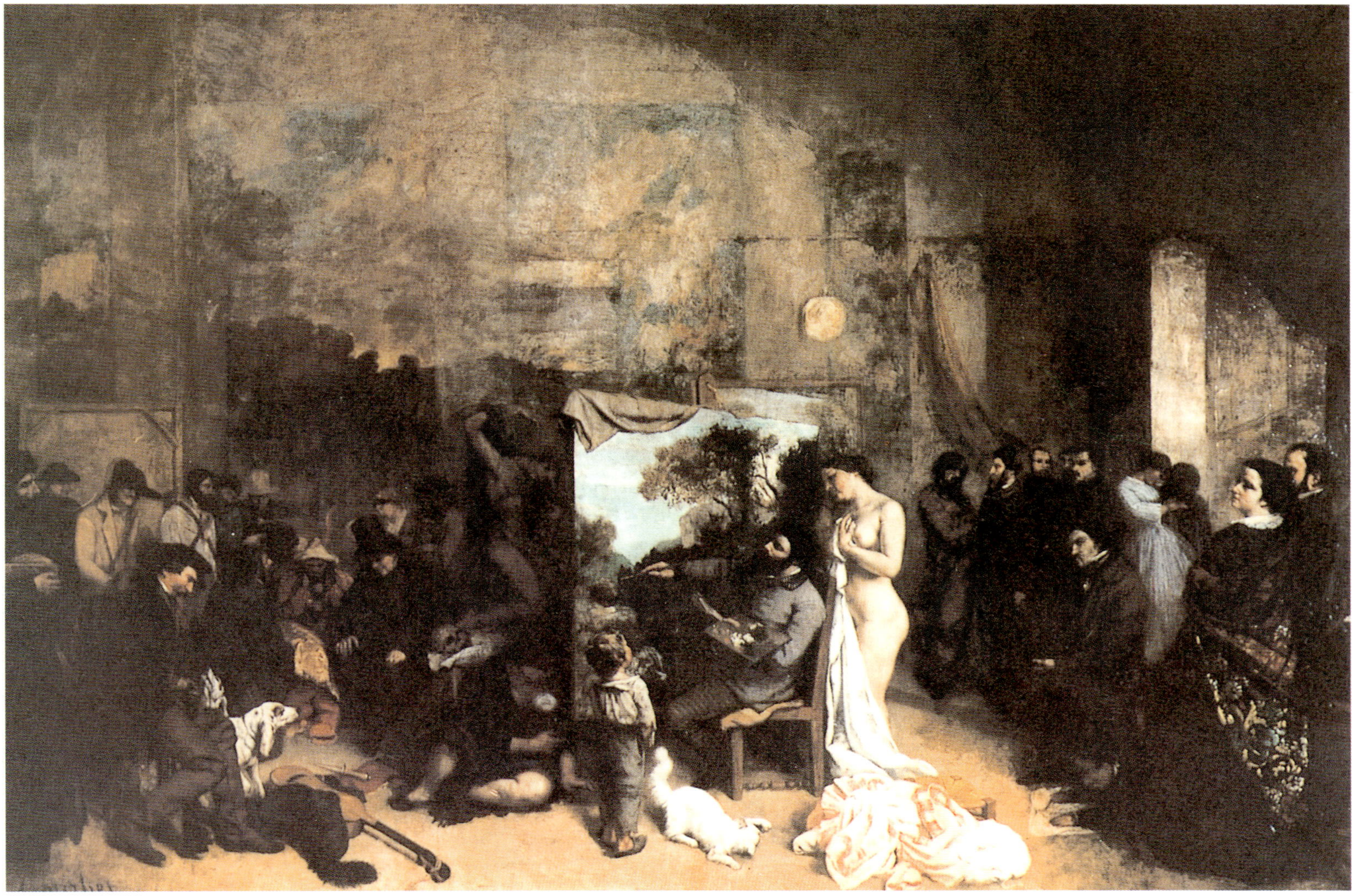

COROT
The Forest of Fontainebleau
oil on canvas
c.1855. 39 × 54.5 cm
The archetypal Barbizon landscape.

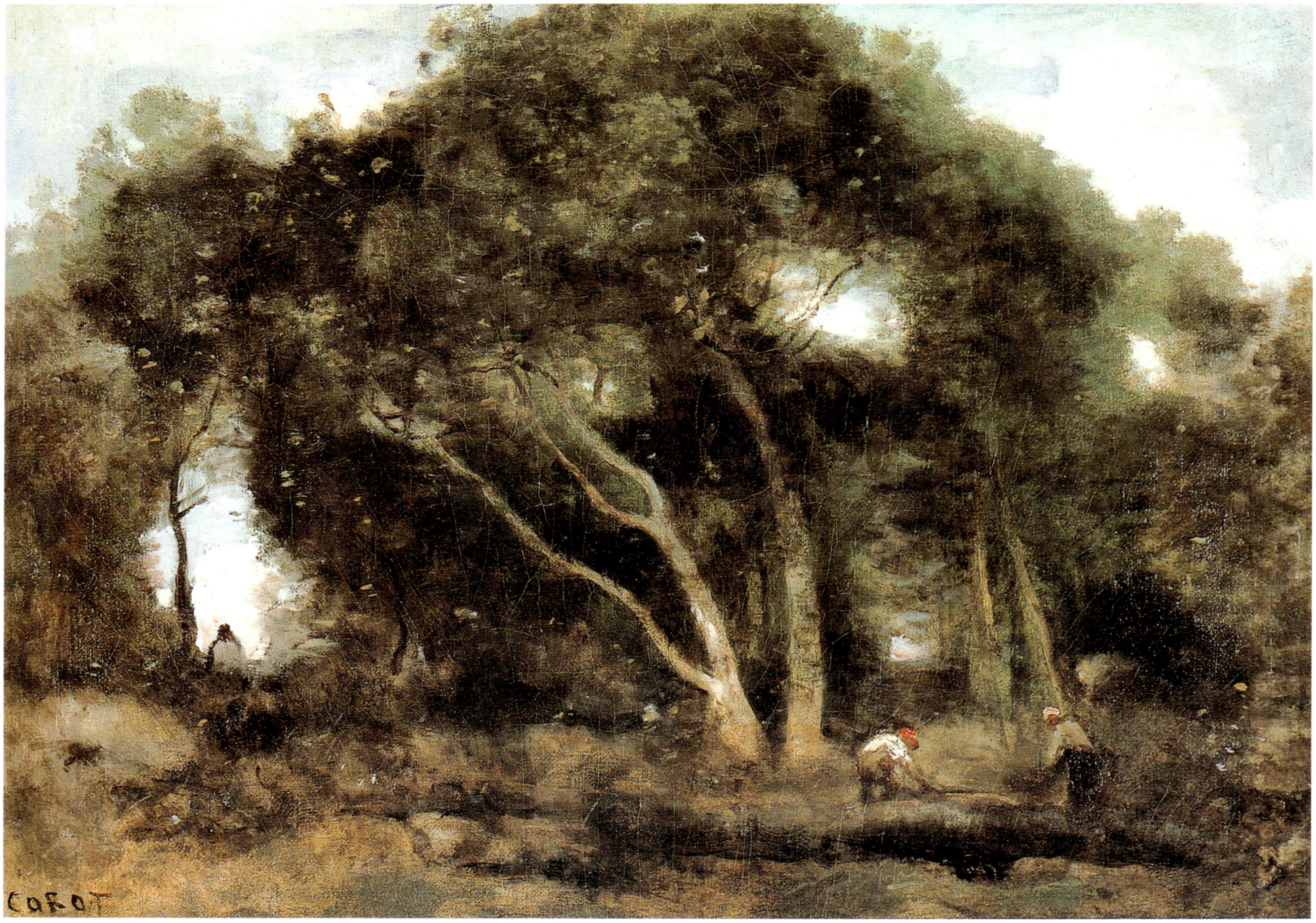

PISSARRO, MANET, AND DEGAS

Camille Pissarro, Edouard Manet, and Edgar Degas, born in 1830, 1832, and 1834 respectively, were in their twenties when the 1855 Exposition Universelle was proving to be the delight of Paris. The work of Delacroix, who was now fifty-seven and achieving great popular acclaim, was the main attraction, having been eloquently lauded by the poet and art critic Charles Baudelaire (who was later to befriend Manet). Work by Daubigny, Corot, and Millet was also to be seen hidden amongst the thousands of paintings on show, but it would have been difficult to miss Courbet's spectacular sideshow.

Pissarro, the third son of Franco-Jewish parents, had arrived in Paris from St Thomas, a Danish colony in the Virgin Islands where his father was a merchant. Camille had been to school in France, but after returning to St Thomas to work in his father's store, he had gone to Venezuela in 1853 to work with the Danish artist Fritz Melbye. Eventually his parents decided to send him to Paris to study art. He arrived in 1855, as the Exposition was in progress, to attend the Ecole des Beaux-Arts. He soon left the Ecole for the Académie Suisse, a studio in the quai des Orfèvres, run by an ex-model, which charged small fees, offered no teaching, but had models and equipment for young artists to study life drawing and painting as they wished. At the Exposition Universelle, Pissarro was particularly impressed by the six Corots on show – the young Pissarro had become a landscapist under the influence of his friend Melbye and later went to visit Corot in search of guidance. A couple of years later he was found by Claude Monet to be "peacefully working away in Corot's style"; ten years after the Exposition Universelle, Pissarro was officially exhibiting at the Salon as Corot's pupil. At that time it would be hard to imagine that he would become, with the exception of Claude Monet, perhaps the most influential of the landscape Impressionists.

In contrast to Camille Pissarro, Edouard Manet, twenty-three at the time of the Exposition, was the son of a Parisian magistrate, a member of the *haute bourgeoisie* and blessed, as was his slightly younger contemporary Edgar Degas, with the security of independent means. He had enrolled in the school of Thomas Couture in 1850, where he studied painting for six years. Couture had been a pupil of Paul Delaroche, whose *The Execution of Lady Jane Grey* exemplified the conservative but popular qualities of the Davidian academic style. The painting had delighted the Salon of 1834 where visitors are reported to have wept. They were no doubt moved by the sight of the young English noblewoman with her head on the block, a fate close to the hearts of all French citizens not so long after the mass executions that followed the 1789 Revolution.

COROT
Dardagny, near Geneva, Morning
oil on canvas
1853. 826 × 47 cm
A plain and simple landscape before photography influenced Corot's style. It is worked in large planes of colour with little or no detail to distract from the broad composition.

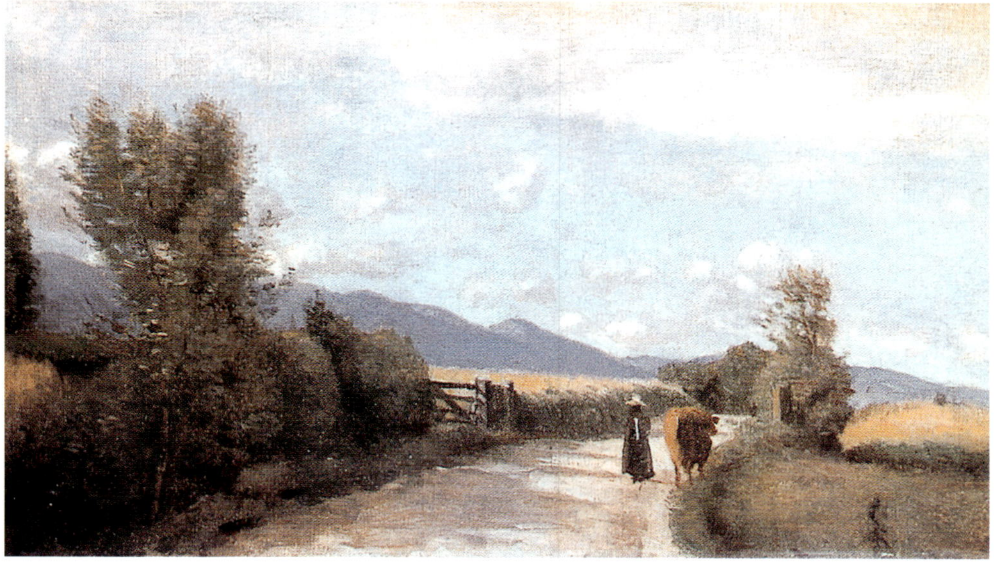

GÉRÔME
In the Harem
oil on canvas
1848. 150 × 200 cm
This is a good academic piece, with smoothly modelled bodies "à la Ingres" and a subject which lent itself to an acceptable form of voluptuousness.

Couture had caused controversy and ensured himself his own place in the popular imagination of the French public and critics with his huge painting *The Romans of the Decadence* (*Les Romains de la décadence*), a sprawling depiction of a Roman orgy which shocked and titillated Parisian society when it was shown at the Salon of 1847. In the same year, doubtless to make the most of his new-found notoriety, Couture had opened his own private art school in Paris, advertising it as offering "teaching based above all on the great art of ancient Greece, the Renaissance masters and the admirable Flemish school." Couture, in order to clarify his view further, declared himself against the "spurious classical school which reproduces the works of the past in a banal and imperfect fashion," and "hostile to that abominable school, known [as] Romantic."

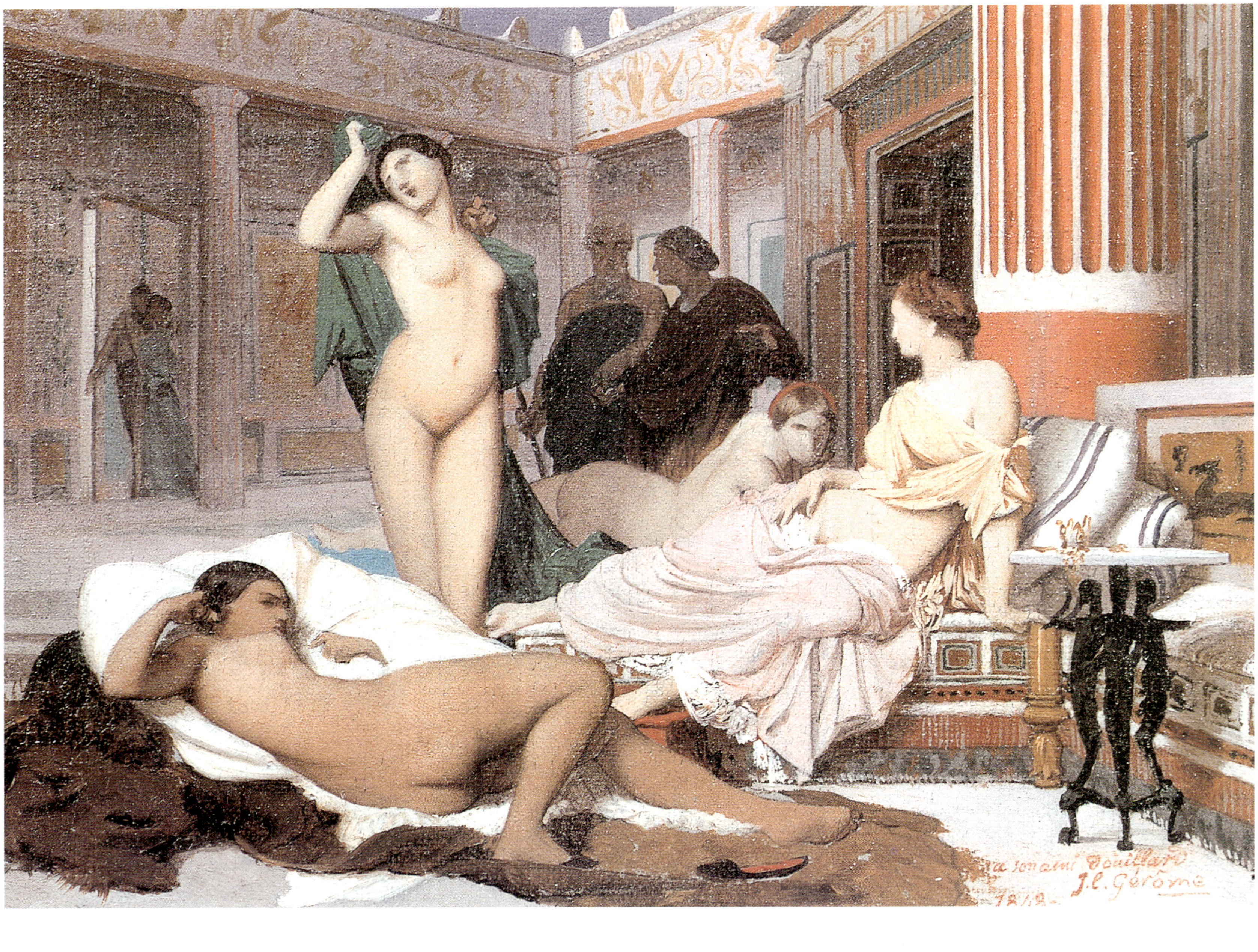

COUTURE
The Romans of the Decadence
oil on canvas
1847. 466 × 775 cm
Couture, the teacher of Manet, scored an immense success with this work at the Salon of 1847.

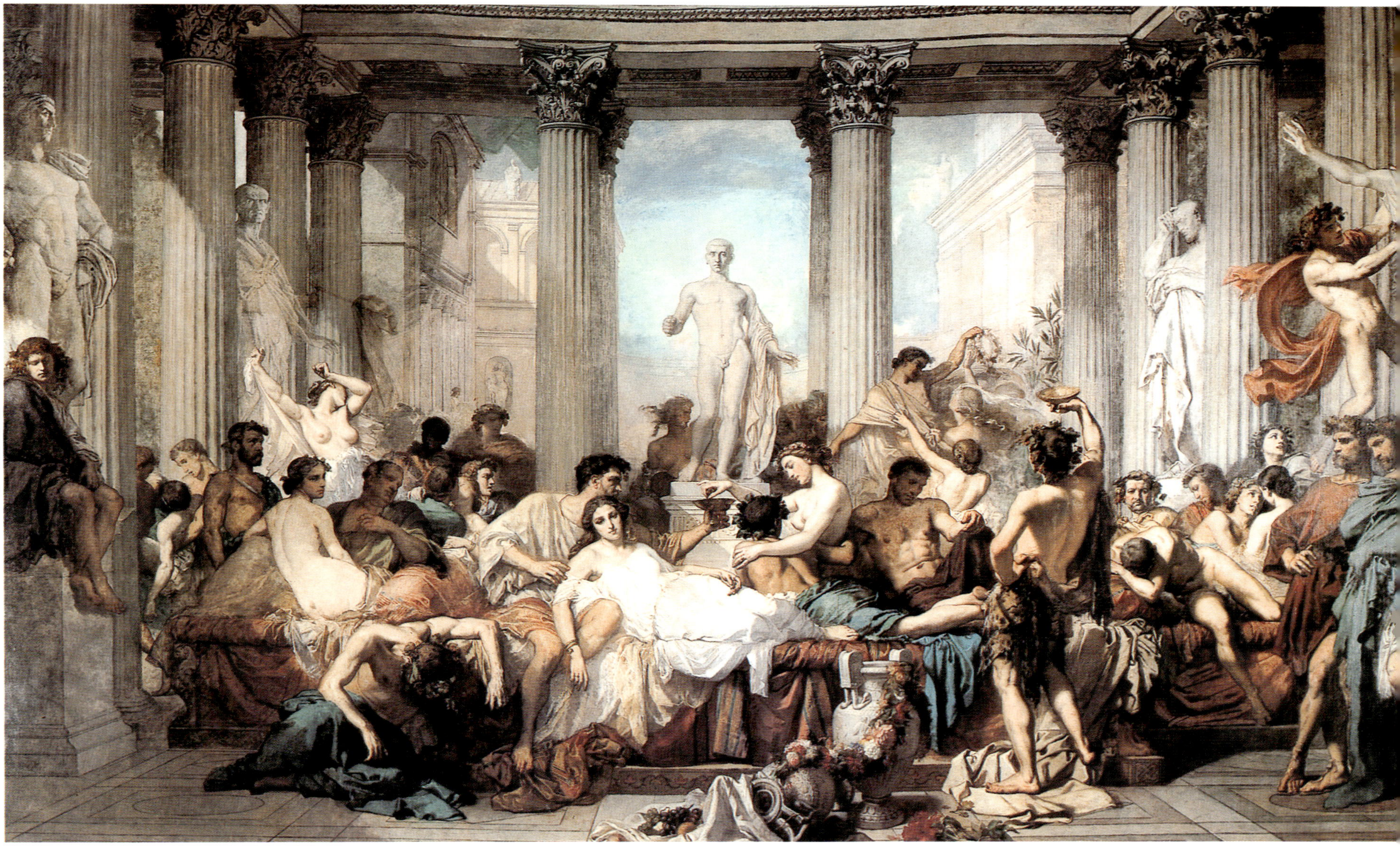

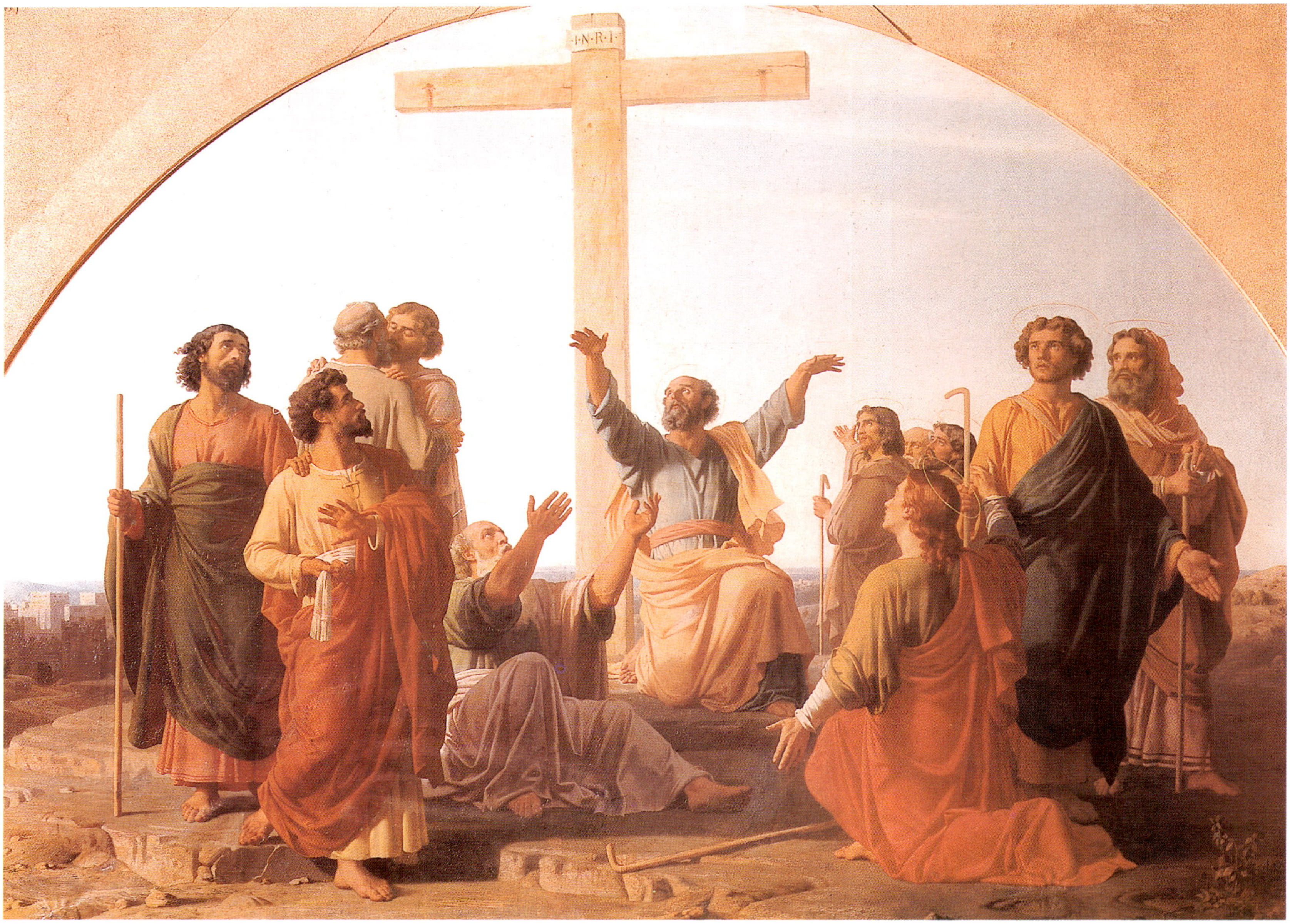

GLEYRE
The Apostles about to Embark on Their Evangelical Mission
oil on canvas
c.1844–45. 197 × 294 cm
The style of Gleyre's painting is derived directly from Raphael and Titian, but this sort of attempt to emulate past masters was exactly what the Impressionists rejected.

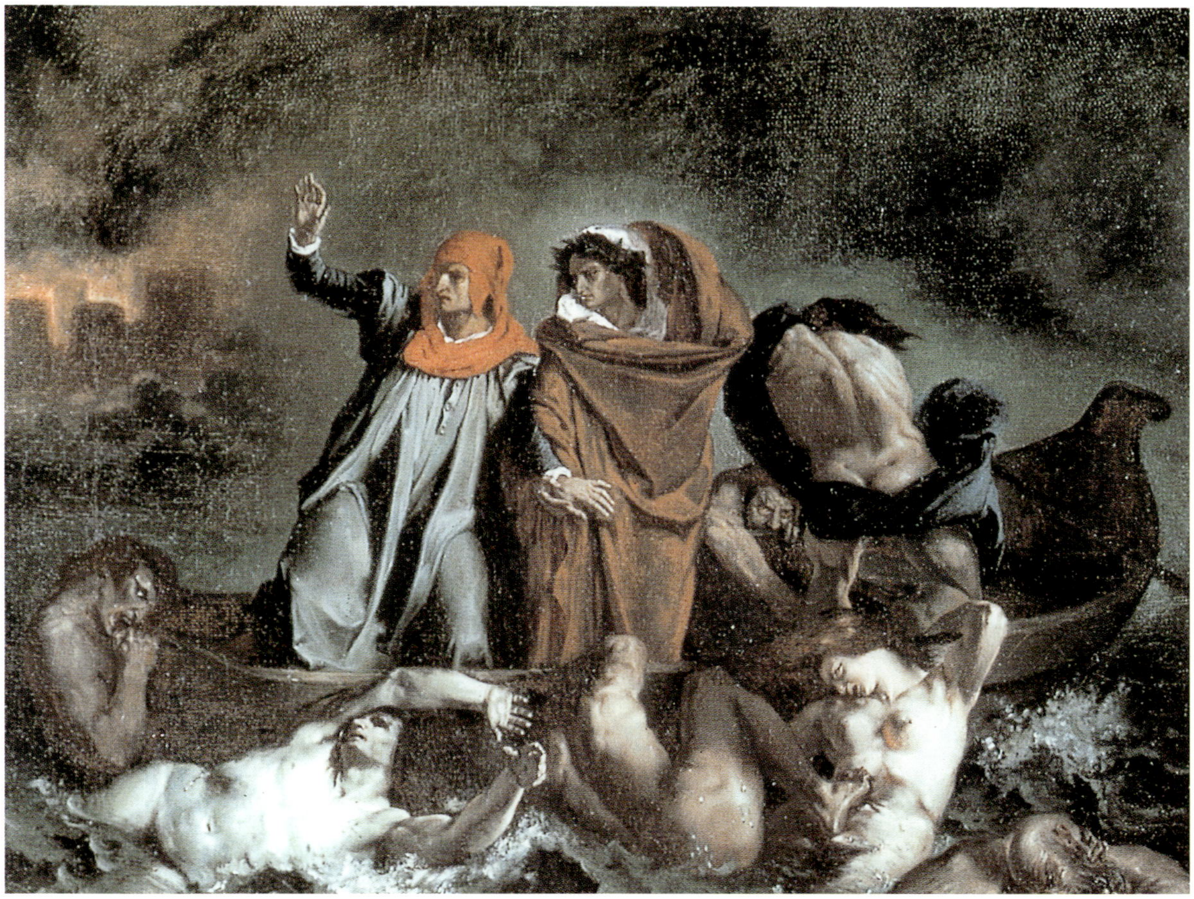

MANET
Copy after Delacroix's Dante
oil on canvas
1855. 33 × 41 cm
LEFT Manet went to see the deeply respected Delacroix with his friend Antonin Proust, and asked permission to copy his work.

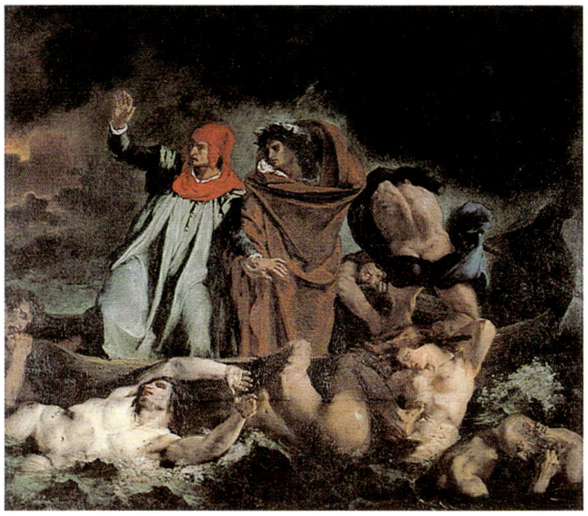

DELACROIX
Dante and Virgil in Hell
oil on canvas
1822. 189 × 246 cm
LEFT Manet and the Impressionists were profound admirers of Delacroix's individualistic style. This spectacular work is also commonly known as the Barque of Dante.

All this was true to the spirit of Louis Philippe's *juste milieu*, and linked Couture to his contemporaries such as Charles Gleyre and Alexander Cabanel, who were in fact content to use those elements of Classicism, Romanticism and even Realism which would make up an acceptable picture. As an allegory of contemporary hedonism veiled in the skimpy tunic of Classicism, *The Romans of the Decadence* stands in ironic contrast to the *juste milieu* professed by all and which was to continue after the fall of Louis Philippe and well into the Third Republic. The burgeoning French middle classes of the 1850s would have been outraged if Couture had depicted the contemporary French male bourgeoisie at one of its favourite leisure activities, the brothel. Yet, this is exactly what Couture's pupil Edouard Manet set out to do eight years later at the Salon des Refusés of 1863 with his *Luncheon on the Grass* (*Déjeuner sur l'herbe*). That painting scandalized Paris and pushed

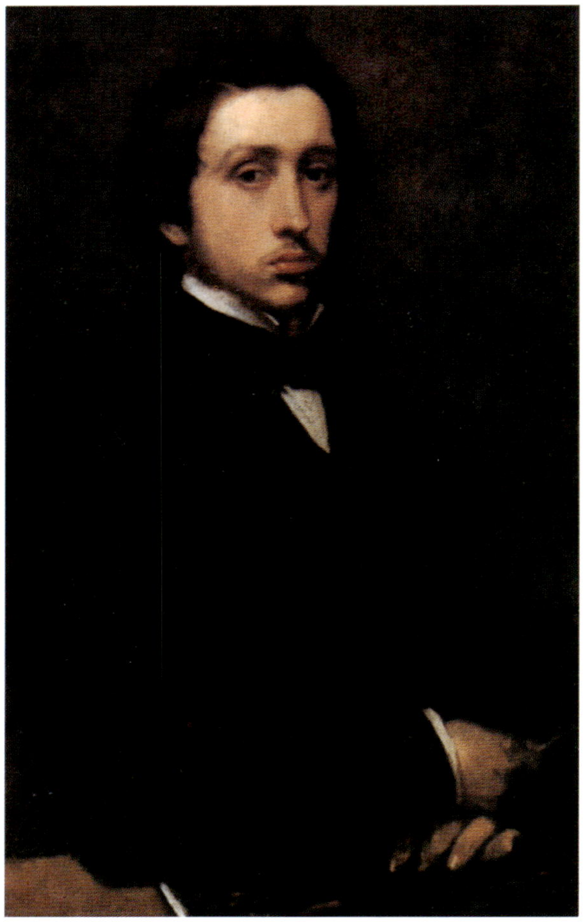

DEGAS
Self-portrait
oil on canvas
1854–55. 81 × 64.5 cm
One of many self-portraits the artist painted in his youth.

Manet reluctantly into the forefront of what became the Impressionist movement.

During his time as a young "apprentice" at Couture's atelier Manet was less concerned with shocking Paris than studying his master's teaching and pondering how literally to reverse the academic technique to his own ends. He also spent many hours in the Louvre studying and copying the techniques of the old masters. The Spanish artists Velazquez, Murillo, and Ribera particularly interested him; an influence which can be seen in his later paintings. During his time spent copying in the Louvre he also absorbed elements of a number of other masters including the French Le Nain brothers. Manet was in effect a pivotal force in the long tradition of European art. His wish was to evolve from the old masters, not reject what he had learnt from them. He was also significantly in awe of Delacroix, so much so that in 1855 he wrote to him asking permission to copy his *Barque of Dante* (*La Barque de Dante*).

Edgar Degas was the youngest of his generation of artists to study in Paris in the mid-1850s. He spent only one semester at the Ecole des Beaux-Arts, however, before an extended tour of Italy where part of his family lived. Degas was the son of Franco-Italian parents who had made their fortune in banking. He registered with the painting and sculpture section of the Ecole des Beaux-Arts on 6th April 1855 after passing an entrance competition at which the painter Henri Fantin-Latour was also successful. (Fantin-Latour, however, was found wanting and left three months later.) Degas' teacher during his brief studies at the Ecole was Louis Lamothe, who inspired him with his own deeply held respect for Ingres, whose pictures in any case Degas had been copying in the Louvre and at the homes of wealthy family friends for some time. In 1856 Degas was in Naples visiting his relatives, painting their portraits and touring the great museums of other Italian cities, absorbing all the Renaissance masters he could feast his eyes on. Although he was to be a prime mover in the *Société anonyme* just under a decade later, the relationship of Degas' work to the other Impressionists was to be marked both by his experiences in Italy and by his abiding interest in the human form as opposed to the landscape.

THE NURSERY OF IMPRESSIONISM

In 1862 France annexed Cambodia, Victor Hugo published *Les Misérables*, Edouard Manet painted *Music in the Tuileries Gardens*

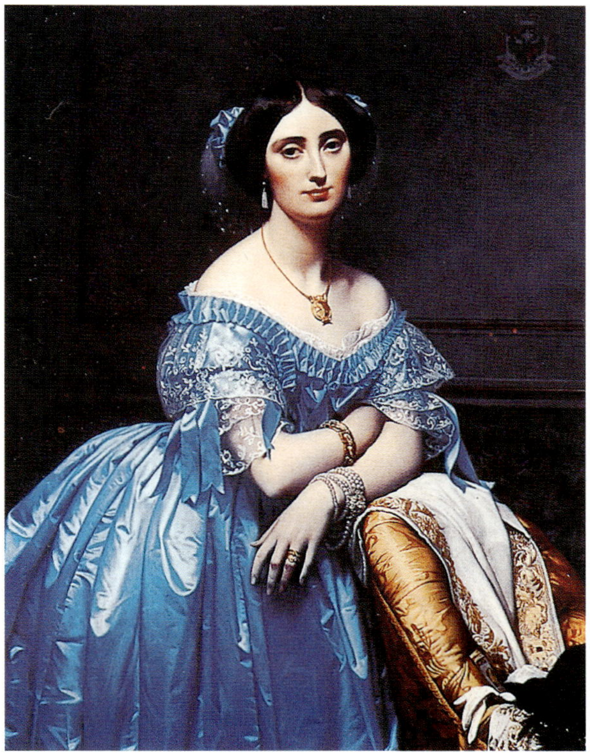

INGRES
The Princess of Broglie
oil on canvas
1853. 114.5 × 86 cm
LEFT Degas was a thorough draftsman and Ingres' perfection was an abiding model for him.

and four unknown young artists met in the Paris atelier of Charles Gleyre, a fifty-four-year-old Swiss artist who had been an instructor at the Ecole des Beaux-Arts. Claude Monet, the eldest son of a grain merchant in the northwestern port of Le Hâvre, Frédéric Bazille, whose family were affluent wine producers in the southern Hérault, Auguste Renoir, previously a porcelain-painter, and Alfred Sisley, at twenty-three the oldest in the group by two years and the son of an English businessman, had little in common except art. Gleyre's atelier had a reputation for being cheap and Gleyre himself was known to be fairly tolerant and kind to his *élèves* (pupils). Although he was neither famous nor a member of the Académie, one painting by him, *Lost Illusions* of 1843, had enjoyed great success at the Salon. The painting won him a medal and substantial respect from the critics of the day.

The teachers of the Impressionists were men raised in an academic ethos of painting which stretched back to principles laid down in the seventeenth century. To prepare for entry into the Ecole, aspiring artists in the mid-nineteenth century entrusted themselves (and their purses) to men such as Charles Gleyre and Thomas Couture who ran private independent ateliers where they could receive formal instruction (a system which persists to this day in France). Life at the atelier for a young *rapin*, or new boy, was often fraught with dangers. According to Albert Boime, the eminent historian of the Académie in the nineteenth century, the *rapin* would be first to arrive at the atelier in the morning and busied himself with menial tasks such as arranging the stools, sweeping the floor, washing the brushes, running errands and suffering occasional persecution by the older students.

DEGAS
The Bellelli Family
oil on canvas
1858–60. 200 × 250 cm
BELOW Degas started a series of portraits while visiting his relatives in Italy.

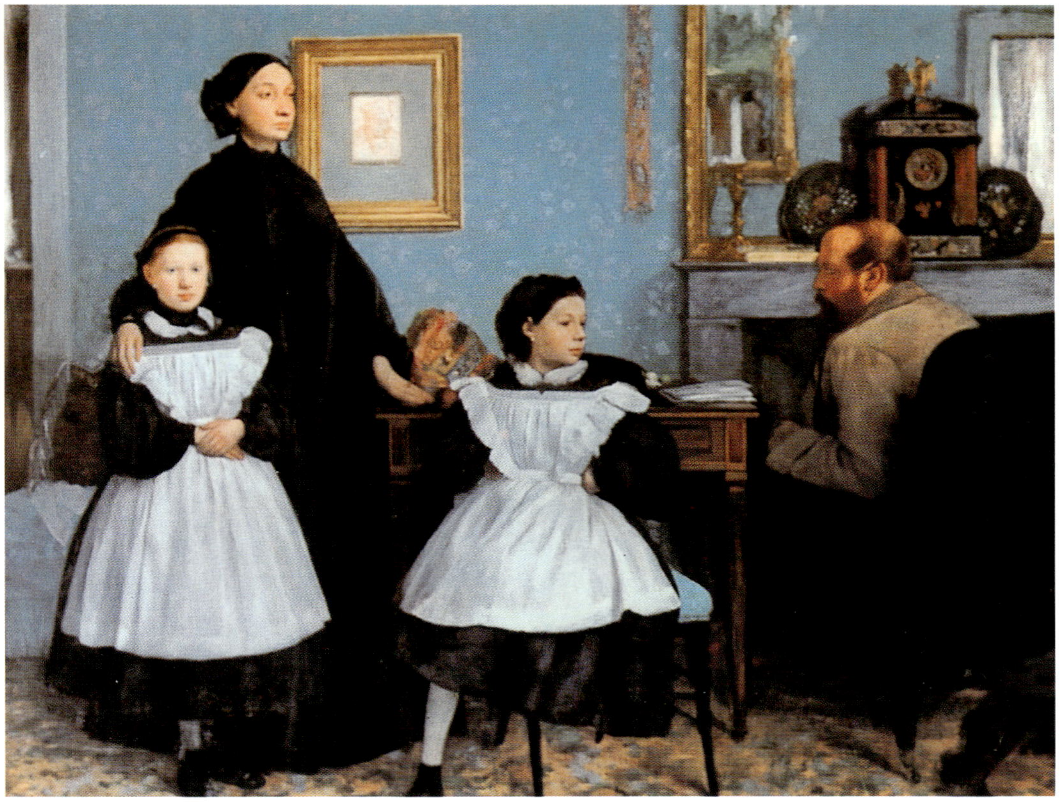

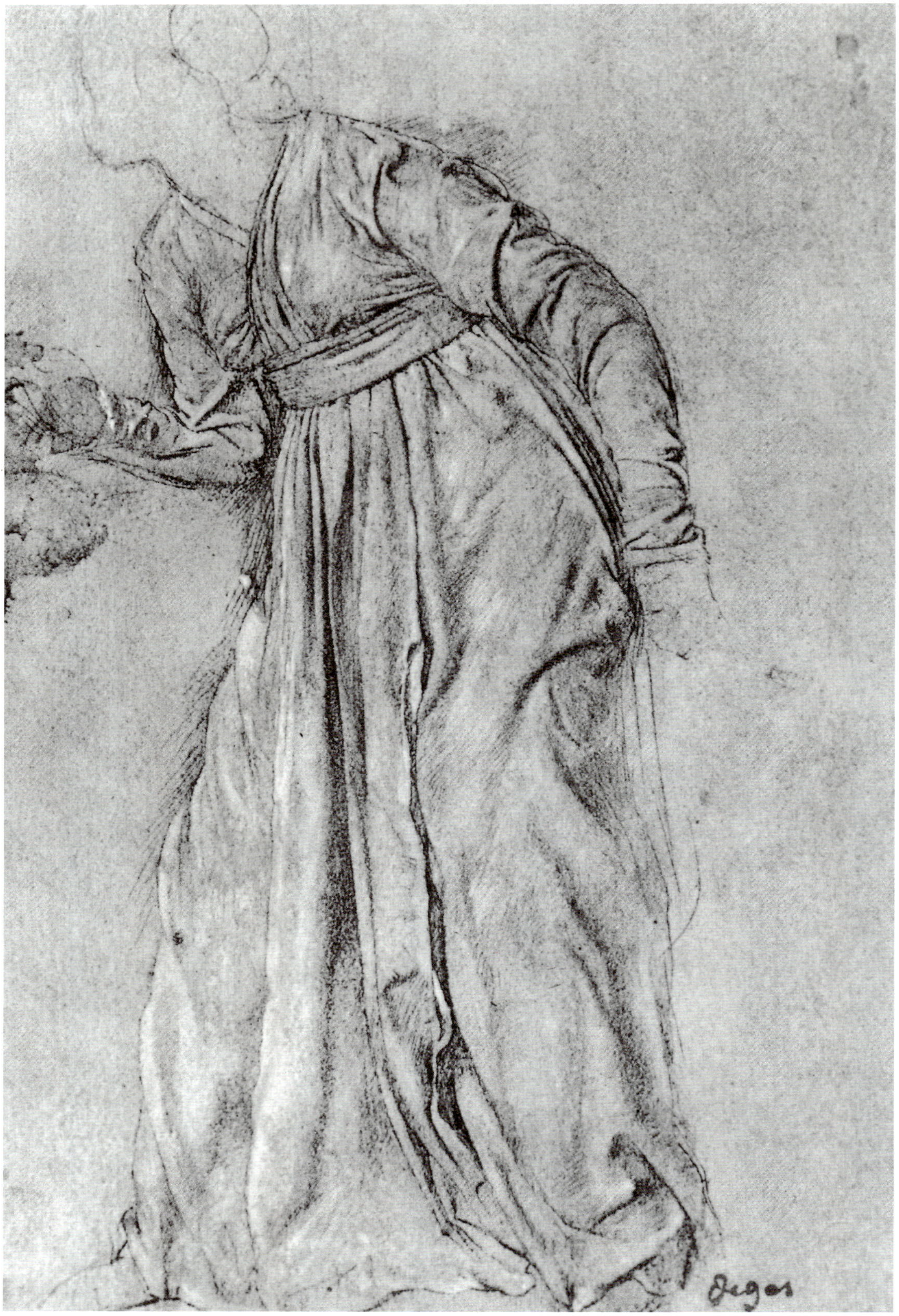

DEGAS
Study for Semiramis Building Babylon
pencil and gouache on grey paper
1861. 30.5 × 21 cm
Right

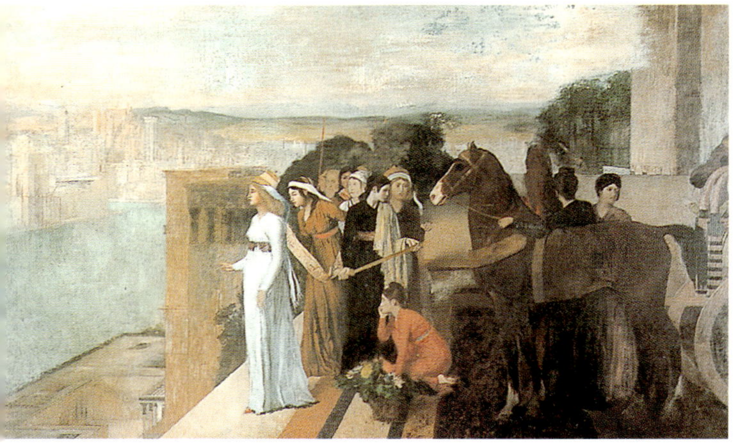

DEGAS
Semiramis Building Babylon
oil on canvas
1860–62. 151 × 258 cm
Above Semiramis *was Degas' first attempt at a large-scale history painting, and as this study and the final version show, the artist was clearly working within the academic tradition, making detailed plans for the work. Despite the conventional process followed by Degas here and to which he adhered for the rest of his career, there is nothing stilted and academic about the bright, realistic vision of the work, which manages to blend all that the young artist had seen in the museums of Europe with his own ideas.*

There were frequently initiation ceremonies, or *blagues*, for the hapless *rapins* to endure before they progressed in the social hierarchy of the atelier.

The course of studies pursued at the ateliers relied on a long tradition of ensuring that the student could draw proficiently before he could be allowed to touch a paintbrush. Drawing exercises which started with copying from engravings, then plaster casts of antique sculpture and finally the live models were rigorous and frequently mind-numbing. Only when the student had mastered drawing technique to a high degree would he be allowed to paint copies of the teacher's work or old masters in the Louvre, as did Manet, Degas and a reluctant Monet.

An equally rigorous system of painting was taught in the ateliers and the Ecole with varying nuances of emphasis according to the predilection of the master. The practical work of painting onto the canvas was as strictly taught as drawing. The student was guided towards producing a painting of a nude or model's head known as an *académie*, which displayed the classical technique of applying the oil paint to the canvas in layers of tones from dark to light. These *académies* were often undertaken in shades of grey or with a very limited palette to produce flesh-tones, for colour was considered a distraction, the sort of thing Delacroix was considered too free with by teachers, yet whose pupils revelled in it. The smoothness in texture and gradation of tone in the finished *académie* was of prime importance. Yet however stifling this kind of training might have been, it had served Degas and Manet well.

So in 1862, the young Monet and his friends found themselves sitting on their stools in Gleyre's atelier, perhaps sketching a

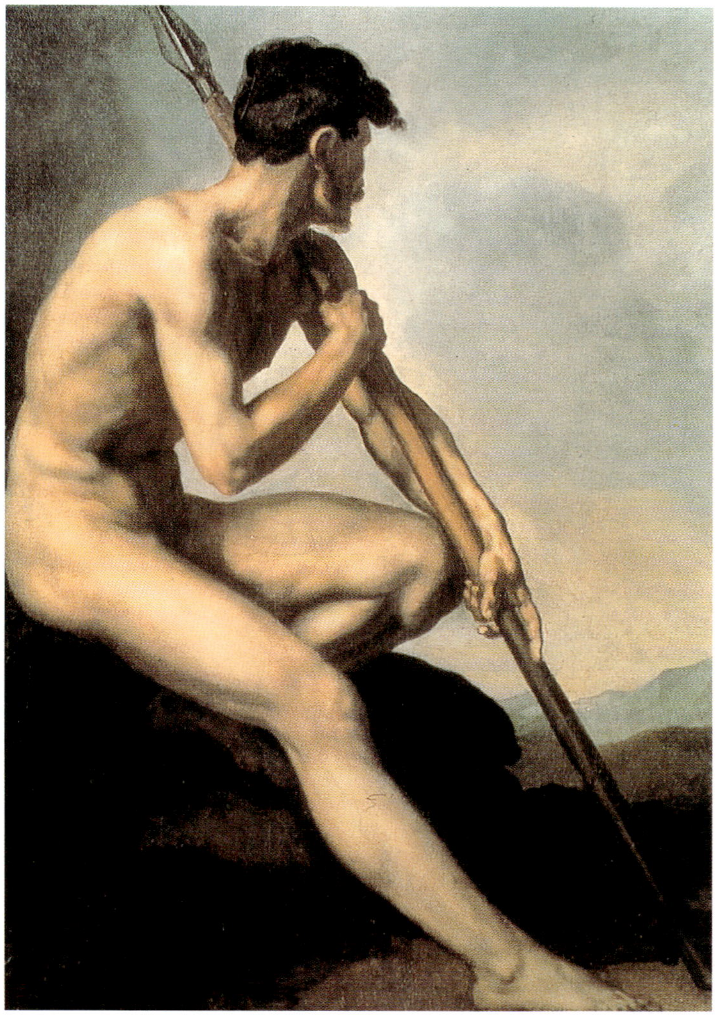

GÉRICAULT
Nude Warrior with a Spear
oil on canvas
1810. 93.5 × 75.5 cm
Though it was painted half a century earlier, this type of academic nude was still taught with the same rigor at the Ecole des Beaux-Arts and the independent ateliers such as those of Gleyre and Couture.

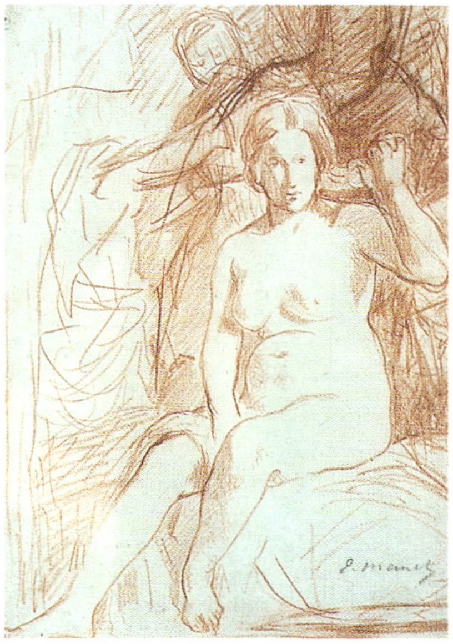

MANET
Study for La Toilette
red chalk on paper
1862. 28 × 20 cm
LEFT There is nothing remarkable about this study, which appears quite average in comparison to Degas' finely detailed sketches.

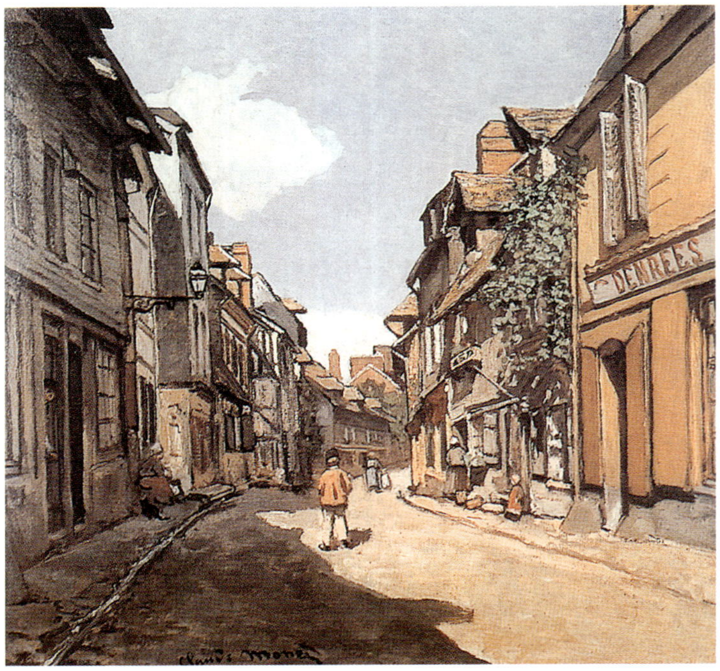

MONET
Honfleur, rue de la Bavolle
oil on canvas
1864. 56 × 61 cm
Right The free rendering is reminiscent of Corot's studies.

BOUDIN
Low Tide near Honfleur
oil on wood
1854–57. 26.7 × 36.5 cm
Below This small-scale work is reminiscent of earlier British studies.

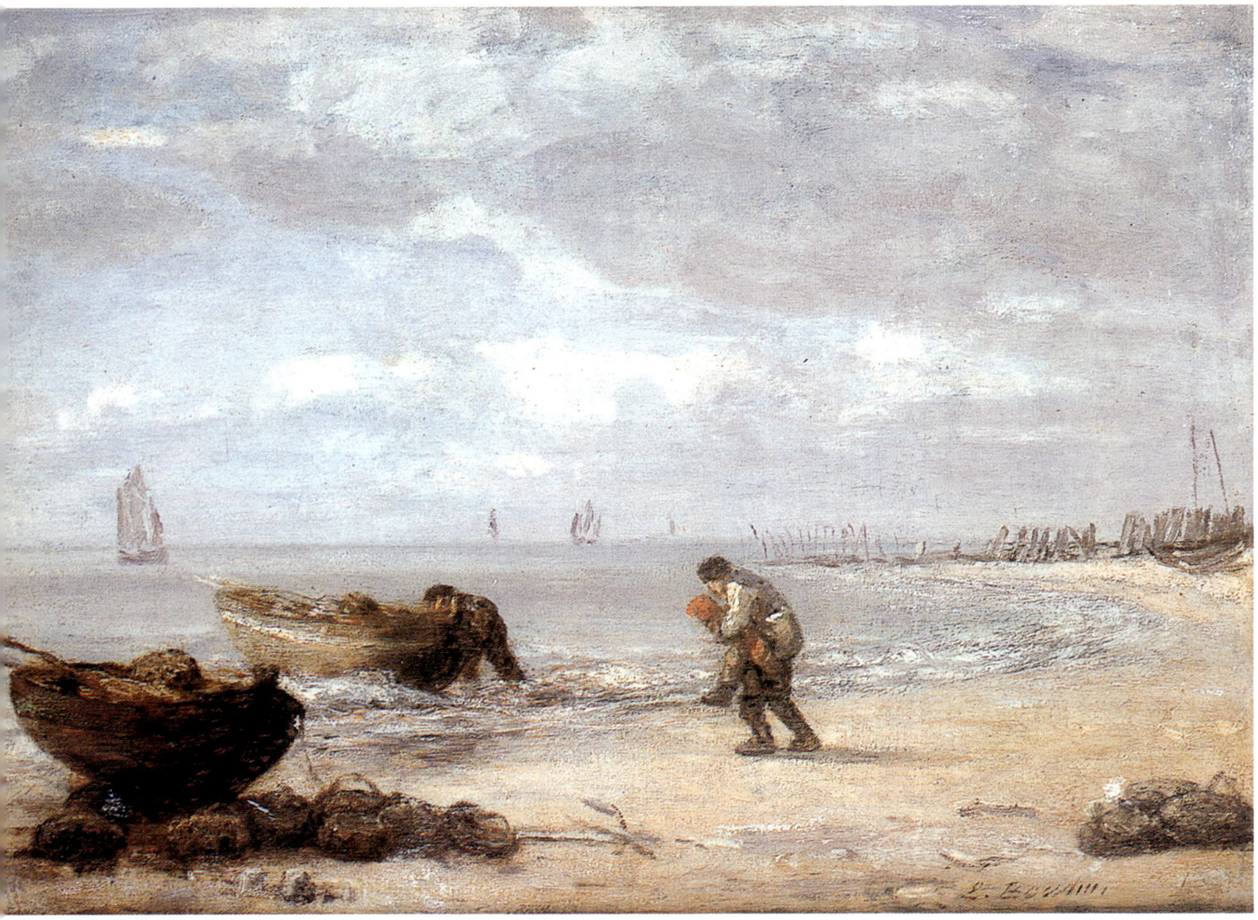

plaster copy of an antique statue as countless young art students had done before them. For Monet, the atelier must have been stuffy indeed. He stayed there for only eighteen months until Gleyre was forced to close, and afterwards attended the Académie Suisse. Monet was the son of a small businessman who had moved his family from Paris to Le Hâvre on the Normandy coast. The sea and the countryside of his youth were to become Claude Monet's natural habitat, not the Louvre or a Parisian atelier, and later years would find him braving the most appalling weather and terrain to capture a scene. He had returned to Paris on the sufferance of his father to study in the traditional way. Monet's artistic talents had already made an impact in Le Hâvre where he had been earning a reasonable living from selling caricatures. There he had met Eugène Boudin, a self-taught local landscapist, who persuaded him (initially reluctant, according to Monet) to take up painting in the open air. Of the four *rapins*, Monet was the most experienced in painting and with the new Realist philosophies – as exemplified in Courbet's paintings of "common" life – being thrown up around it. By the time he had gone to study with Gleyre he had already spent some time in Paris, done his military service in the French colony of Algeria and had been a habitué of the Brasserie des Martyrs at 75 rue des Martyrs, where Courbet, the art critic Jules Castagnary (who was to be a powerful spokesman for Impressionism), Baudelaire, and François Bonvin (a conventional painter with advanced views) would meet, talk, and drink. Edouard Manet's work was much discussed there even though he himself was an infrequent visitor, preferring to hold court in other cafés.

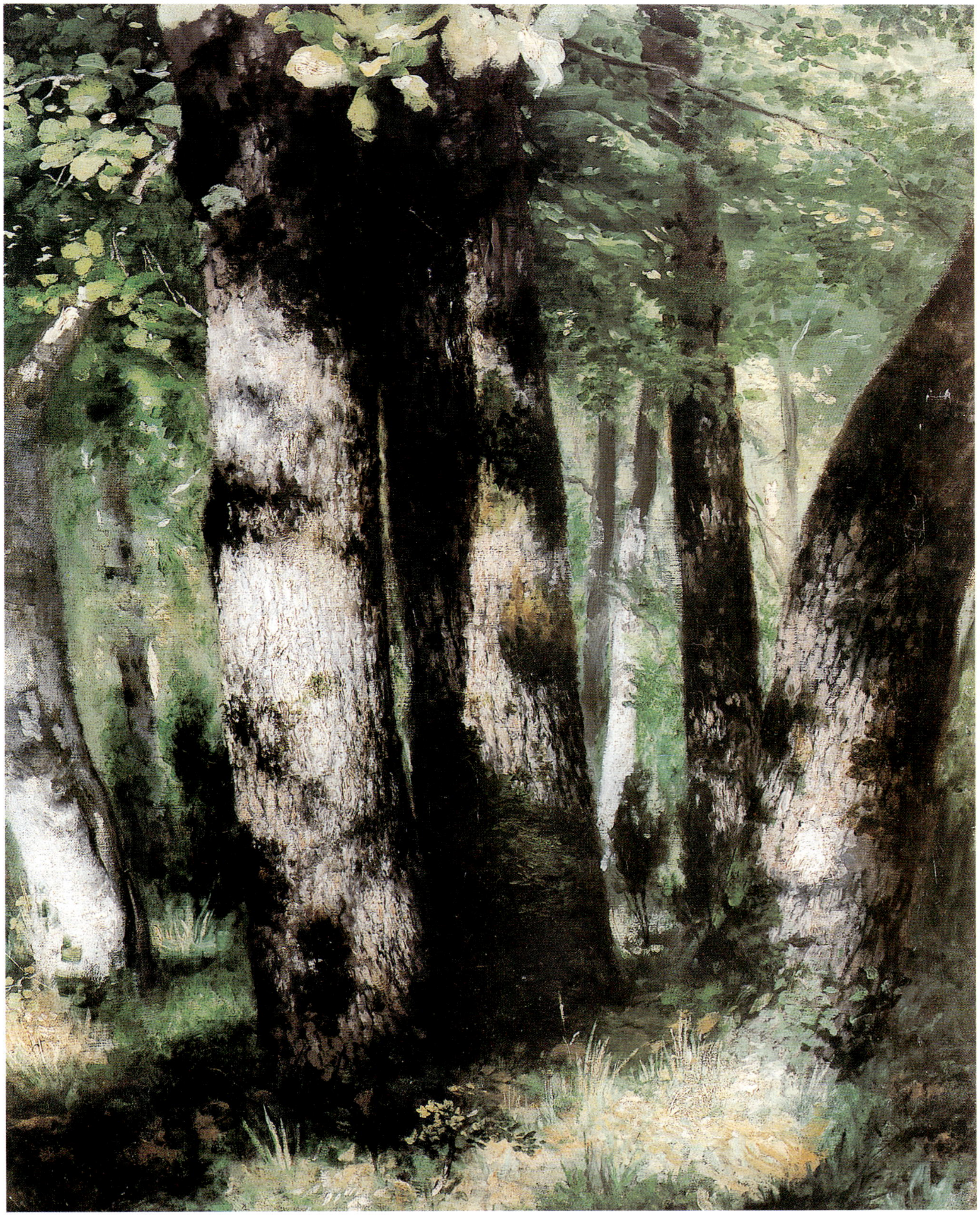

RENOIR
Trees in the Forest of Fontainebleau
oil on canvas
c.1860.
It would be difficult to guess that this robust and literal view is by Renoir, but his interest in the effects of light, even at this early stage, is quite evident.

Auguste Renoir's family were provincial tailors from Limoges who had moved to Paris shortly after he was born. He was apprenticed to a porcelain-painter (who went out of business in 1858) and then, for a living, Renoir painted fans, copying scenes from artists such as Fragonard, Watteau, and Boucher as well as painting blinds and other odd jobs before enrolling in Gleyre's atelier in 1861. Having been trained as an artistic craftsman, his whole philosophy in art was geared to the acquisition of technique. Like Manet and Degas, Renoir had studied the old masters in the Louvre, something Monet was reluctant to do. As the art historian John House has observed, by deciding to become a painter Renoir was moving from a trade to a profession, from the skilled working class into the middle class, yet from the very beginning he seems consistently to have thought of himself as a workman in paint, an "*ouvrier de la peinture*". Unlike Renoir, who in the mid–1850s had been painting to live, Alfred Sisley and Frédéric Bazille had been living to paint. Sisley had narrowly avoided a business career in London and Bazille had given up a career in medicine when they met Monet and Renoir at Gleyre's atelier.

Often spoken of as "the nursery of Impressionism," Gleyre's atelier became the meeting-place for four of the most important figures in the movement. There is little evidence that the four young painters immediately sympathized with each other in the cosmopolitan atmosphere of Gleyre's school, but they soon realized they had several interests in common one of which was landscape painting and often went on *plein-air*

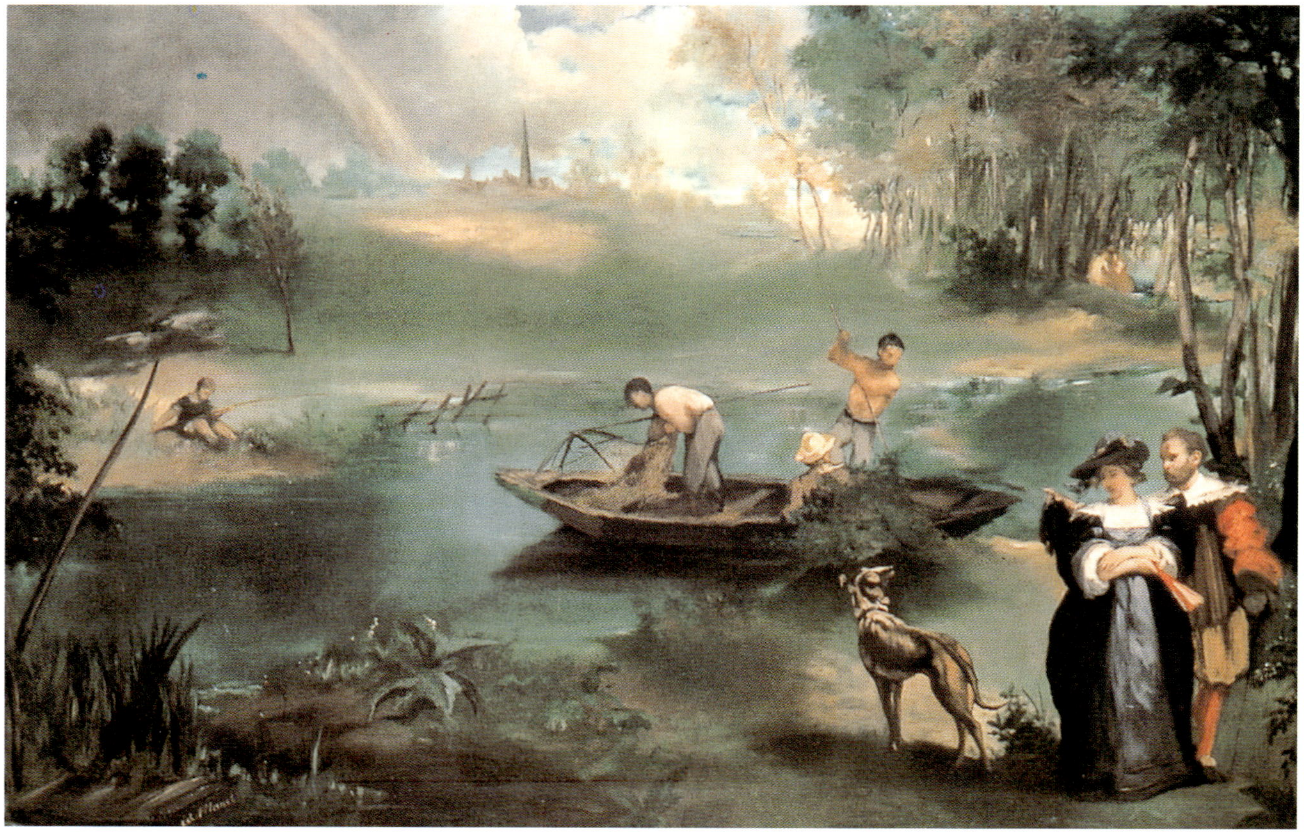

MANET
Fishing at St Ouen
oil on canvas
1860–61. 77 × 123 cm
This is an unusual and transitional work showing the influence of past masters.

expeditions into the countryside around Paris. In 1921, five years before his death, Claude Monet recalled the early days:

> At Gleyre's atelier I found Renoir, Sisley, and Bazille. As we were drawing from a model . . . Gleyre criticized my work. "It's not bad," he said, "but the breast is too heavy, the shoulder too powerful, the foot too large." "I can only draw what I see," I replied timidly . . . "Praxiteles borrowed the best elements from a hundred imperfect models to create a masterpiece," retorted Gleyre drily. "One must always think of classical antiquity."

It is tempting to think that the eighty-one year old Monet's memory had perhaps grown somewhat dim (if not bitter) on the subject of Gleyre, a teacher held in the highest respect by Renoir and many other *élèves*. Nevertheless, one evening during his time at Gleyre's Monet gathered together Sisley, Renoir, and Bazille and said "*Filons d'ici!*" ("lets get out of here!") "We left," Monet said in 1921 "after two weeks . . . We were well rid of the place, because I don't think any of the most promising students in the atelier ever made good." He was wrong on both counts: his memory must indeed have been failing him, for they remained with Gleyre until he closed down in 1864; and he and his friends were the most promising students in the place!

In addition to Monet, Renoir, Bazille, and Sisley, two more young artists who were to be involved in the Impressionist movement, Paul Cézanne and Armand Guillaumin, born in 1839 and 1841 respectively, had also gravitated to Paris by 1862. Twentieth-century art historians revere the former as the creative talent who was eventually to go beyond Impressionism, while posterity has largely forgotten the latter precisely because he became one of the most faithful exponents of the new genre.

Cézanne had come to Paris in 1861 on the urging of the novelist Emile Zola, a childhood friend from Aix-en-Provence where Cézanne's father was a banker. Cézanne had been studying law but had abandoned this to become a painter, working at the Académie Suisse. It was here that he met Armand

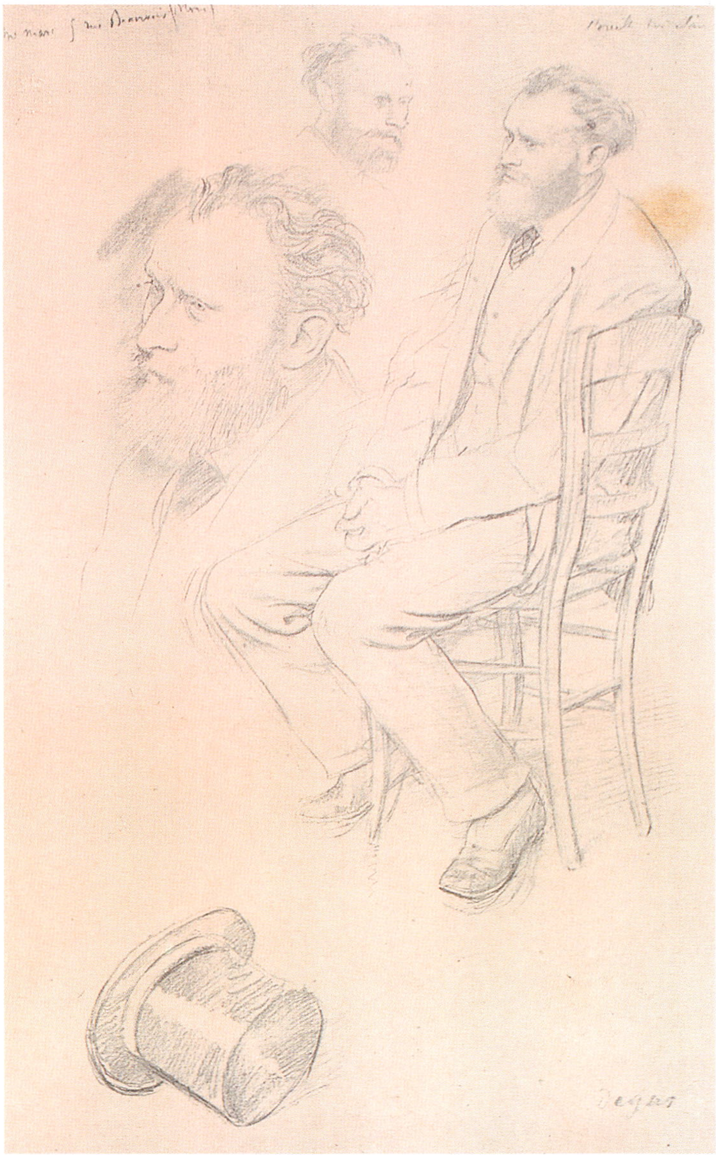

DEGAS
Study for a Portrait of Manet
pencil on paper
c.1864. 41.5 × 28 cm
Degas and Manet had met in the Louvre in 1862. Degas was copying onto a copper plate when Manet interrupted him with the suggestion that what he was doing was impossible.

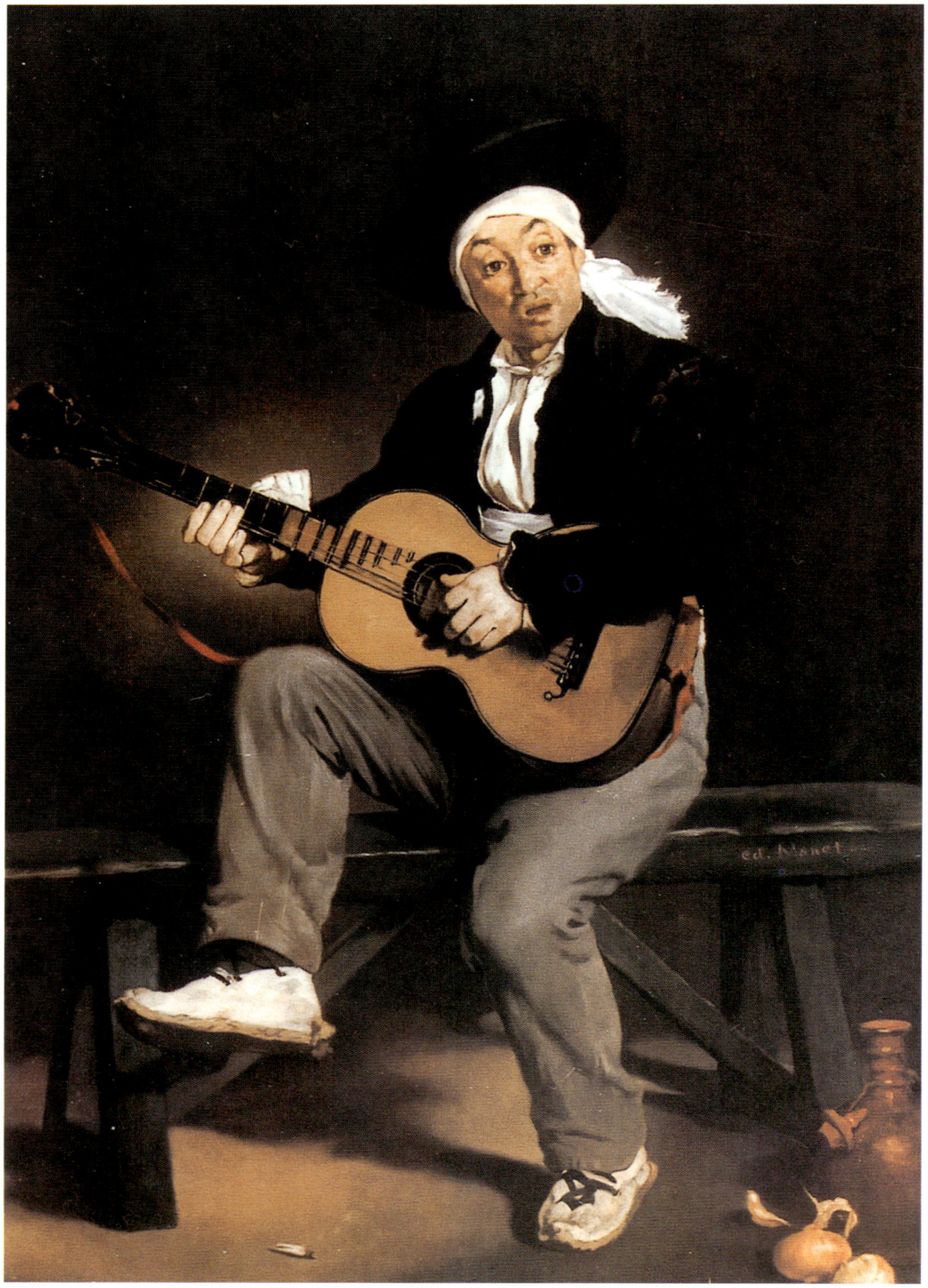

Guillaumin, who was painting during the time off from his job for the Paris-Orléans railway, and Camille Pissarro, who introduced them both to Monet and his friends from Gleyre's atelier.

DEPICTING MODERN LIFE

1862 was certainly a year of coincidental meetings which would have great consequences for art. That year, whilst he was copying Velazquez's *Infanta Margarita* onto a copper plate at the Louvre, Edgar Degas was interrupted in his work by Edouard Manet, signalling the beginning of an extraordinary relationship between the two men. They had much in common; both were of patrician Parisian families, and neither had been greatly influenced by the *plein-air* movement. Degas and Manet were also consciously resisting Courbet's call for a "social realist" art. Despite the fact that circumstances link them very closely with the "true" Impressionists such as Monet and Pissarro, their own artistic concerns in painting *la vie Parisienne* were largely to hold them together and apart from the others.

Manet and Degas were great admirers of one another's work (albeit on occasion very grudgingly), but they differed greatly in matters of politics and philosophy. On the one hand, Manet was staunchly republican in his politics and a considerable intellectual who craved and enjoyed the society of writers and critics involved with the new art such as Champfleury, Duranty, Baudelaire and later Mallarmé. Degas, on the other hand, was an arch-conservative and frequently a peevish anti-intellectual.

At the Salon of 1861 Manet exhibited his *Spanish Singer* (*Le Chanteur Espagnol*) to considerable acclaim. Reminiscent of Velazquez

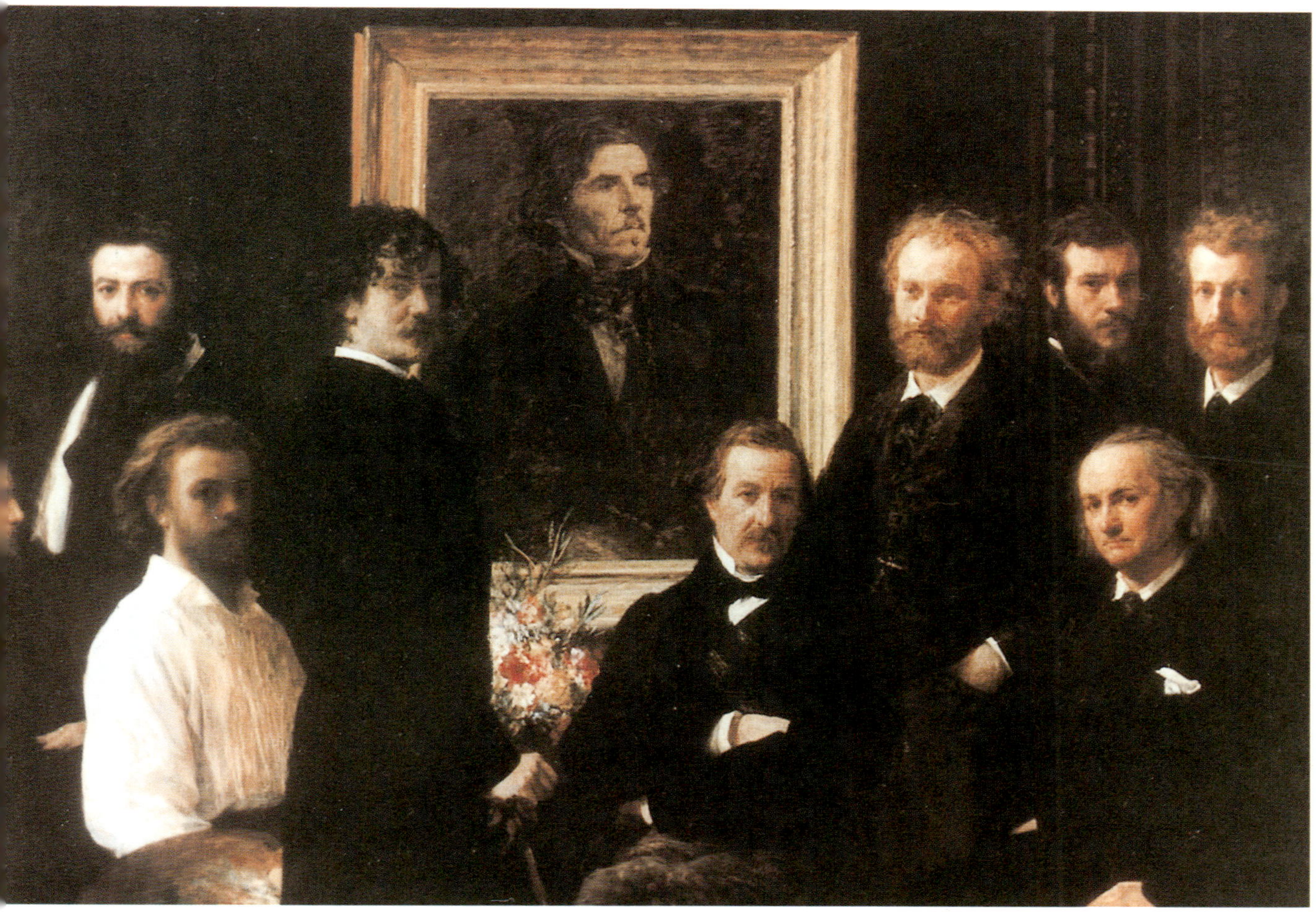

MANET
The Spanish Singer
oil on canvas
1860. 147.5 × 114.5 cm
OPPOSITE This painting and The Artist's Parents *were accepted at the Salon of 1861 and received an honourable mention, a welcome distinction after the rejection of* The Absinthe Drinker *in 1859.*

FANTIN-LATOUR
Homage to Delacroix
oil on canvas
1864. 160 × 250 cm
LEFT Inspired by a Dutch group portrait by Frans Hals, the group includes Whistler standing along the frame, Fantin-Latour, seated, wearing a white shirt, Duranty, Legros, the painter Cordier, the writers Champfleury and Baudelaire seated to the right, Manet standing right of the frame, Bracquemond and Albert Balleroy. This is the first of five group portraits, but Fantin-Latour destroyed one, keeping only three of the heads.

and Goya in style and of popular interest in its Spanish subject matter, the painting nevertheless displays the beginnings of the broad brushwork and rich colouration which were to be a feature of Manet's later work. Moreover the *Spanish Singer* disdained the fine finish of the Académic style and showed a sense of Realism which challenged Courbet at his own game attracting a cabal of critics, writers, and painters – Champfleury, Baudelaire, and Henri Fantin-Latour especially – to Manet's door where he welcomed their attentions and the beginnings of fame. Much later Matisse called Manet "the first great modern artist because his free and spontaneous brushwork liberated the artist's instincts."

In retrospect it is tempting to imagine at this time a republican-leaning, critical, artistic avant-garde armed with the desire for the untrammelled, the vigorous, the "real" in art, simply lying in wait for someone like Manet, a skillful, fresh, uncompromising and above all modern artist with metropolitan and cosmopolitan interests to come along and bear the standard of a new art. In many respects this was the case. Baudelaire, who in fact was twenty years Manet's senior, was respected as a rigorous art critic, he was a friend of Delacroix, an admirer of Courbet and lately a close friend of Manet. In 1862 Baudelaire was working on his *The Painter of Modern Life* (*Le Peintre de la vie moderne*) a critique which, as the title suggests, discusses in which direction art should go in the modern

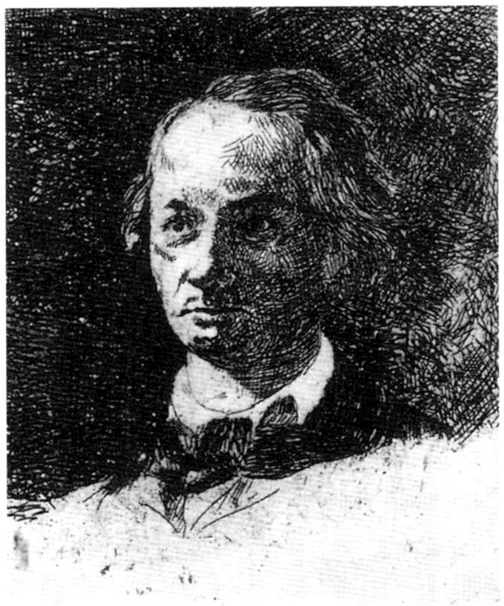

MANET
Baudelaire
etching
c.1869.
Baudelaire and Manet had met in 1858 and they were in frequent and close contact by 1860. The friendship lasted until the death of the poet in 1867. Baudelaire's views on the role of the artist in the modern world, published in 1863 as "Le Peintre de la vie moderne", were an important influence on Manet and his contemporaries.

world of the big city. The subject of *The Painter of Modern Life* is not Edouard Manet, however, who was as yet relatively unknown, but Constantin Guys, an illustrator and watercolourist who had covered the Crimean War for the *Illustrated London News* and whose pictures of Parisian life brought much admiration from artists and critics alike. Baudelaire's critique concerned itself with his own time and demanded an art which could deliver it up in all its present reality, not in anachronistic Neo-Classical allegories:

> The past is interesting not only because of the beauty which the artists of the past – whose present it was – have extracted from it, but because of its historical value. The same applies to the present. The pleasure which we derive from the presentation of the present derives from the beauty which it may possess, as well as from its essential quality as the present. Modernity is the transitory, the fugitive, the contingent, which make up one half of art, the other being the eternal and the immutable. This transitory fugitive element, which is constantly changing, must not be despised or neglected. If you do so you tumble into the emptiness of an abstract and undefinable beauty.

Manet was shortly to prove himself to be the painter of this modern life. He was already evolving compositions with subjects such as *The Old Musician* (*Le Vieux musicien*), *The Spanish Dancers* (*Le Ballet Espagnol*) and *Lola de Valence* which, although they were not the *actualités* of Guys, represented real people. Baudelaire considered Manet to "combine a vigorous taste for reality, modern reality – already a good sign – with an imagination which is both abundant and lively . . . "

In 1859 the Salon had rejected Manet's *The Absinthe Drinker*, a painting of modern Paris in its cups, but had accepted the more innocuous *Spanish Singer* two years later. In 1862 he finished *Music in the Tuileries Gardens*, perhaps the first great painting of "modern life"; its subject matter was on one level completely up to date; the Parisian élite had recently abandoned the Palais-Royale Gardens for the Tuileries, which was larger and closer to their residences. Whether consciously or not, Manet was answering Baudelaire's call; and whilst he was working on the subject of modern life, Degas, Monet, Sisley, Renoir, Bazille, Pissarro, Guillaumin, Cézanne, and Berthe Morisot (who later married Manet's brother, Eugène, and was a very close friend of Manet himself) were also becoming painters of the modern world. Reluctantly Manet was becoming, if not the leader of this wave of artists, then the whipping boy for the sins they were poised to commit in the art world.

Music in the Tuileries Gardens is a painting central to the development of Impressionism in that it seems to embody almost by design the transitory, the fugitive, the constantly changing. It has little in practical terms to do with the increasing desire of Monet, Pissarro, Renoir, and Sisley to find a way of capturing, in Jules Laforgue's elegant words, "nature as she is, which is to say solely by means of coloured vibrations," but it opens up a whole new realm of the possible. It is the view of a fashionable *flâneur*, a stroller in the park taking in the scene, a montage of frozen moments of Parisians at their leisure. We are in the age of photography after all and Manet studied photographs for some of the heads. The painting conveys movement and colour with virtuosic brushstrokes, yet the lighting

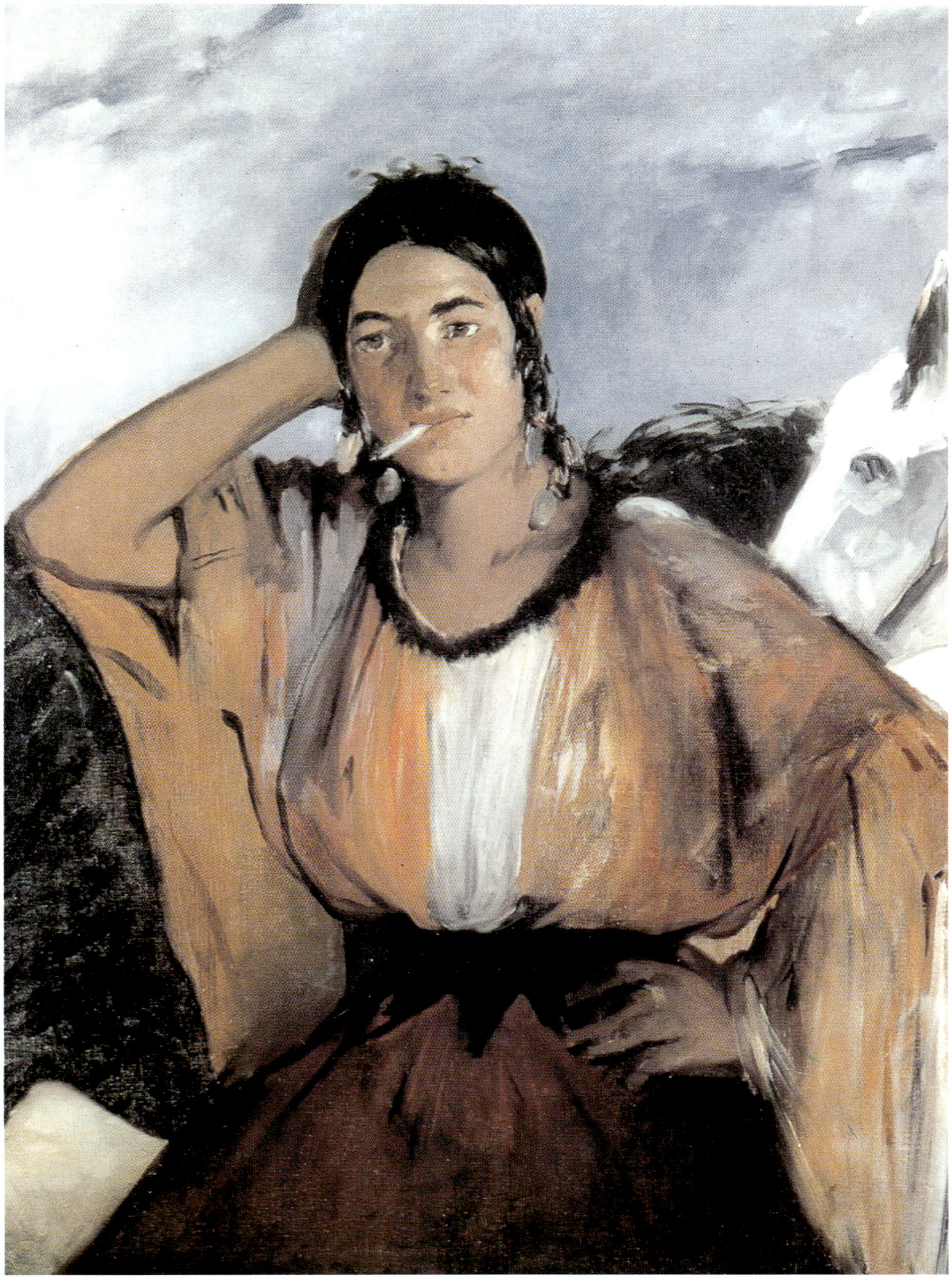

MANET
Gypsy Woman Smoking a Cigarette
oil on canvas
c.1862. 91 × 73 cm
This is probably what the Carmen in Prosper Merrimé's original story would have looked like. However, Bizet's opera was not performed before 1875.

is flat, the background has been scraped and smeared with the palette knife to give the impression, and not much more, of foliage; the figures at the extreme edges are real people. Baudelaire himself is there as well as the poet Théophile Gautier, Fantin-Latour, the Inspector of Museums Baron Taylor, the sculptor and poet Zacharie Astruc, Eugène Manet and Offenbach. These people are easily discernable but the woman seated in the centre of the picture exists in a confusion of yellow and violet next to an enigmatic, two-dimensional tree.

Two paintings by Edgar Degas from this period, the *Young Spartans* and *The Gentlemen's Race: Before the Start*, both painted between 1860–1862 (and reworked in the 1880s) continued to answer the broad demands of Baudelaire, and of Edmond and Jules de Goncourt who sought "a line which would precisely render life, embrace from close at hand the individual, the particular, a living human, inward line . . . "

The Young Spartans (*Les Jeunes Spartiates*), despite its classical theme, avoids the stock classical motifs; there are no temples or plane tree groves, the sky is not an attic blue; most importantly the figures are not characterized as Greek, but are modelled on contemporary Parisian boys and girls. The achievement is that of a thoroughly modern history painting. *The Gentlemen's Race* – together with two others, *At the Races* (*Aux Courses*) and *At the Races: The Start* (*Aux Courses: Le Départ*) – reflect the Parisian passion for the new racecourse which had opened at Longchamp in the Bois de Boulogne in 1857. The new track was a direct result of the rebuilding of Paris and presented a new venue for the *beau monde* to entertain itself; indeed some of Manet's and Degas' patrons were members of the Jockey Club which organized the races.

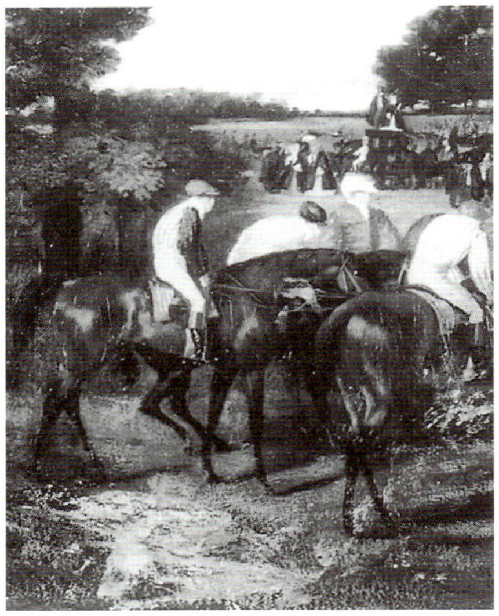

DEGAS
Derby Day
oil on canvas
c.1860–62. 26.5 × 21.5 cm
ABOVE This small picture is reminiscent of English sporting prints of the day.

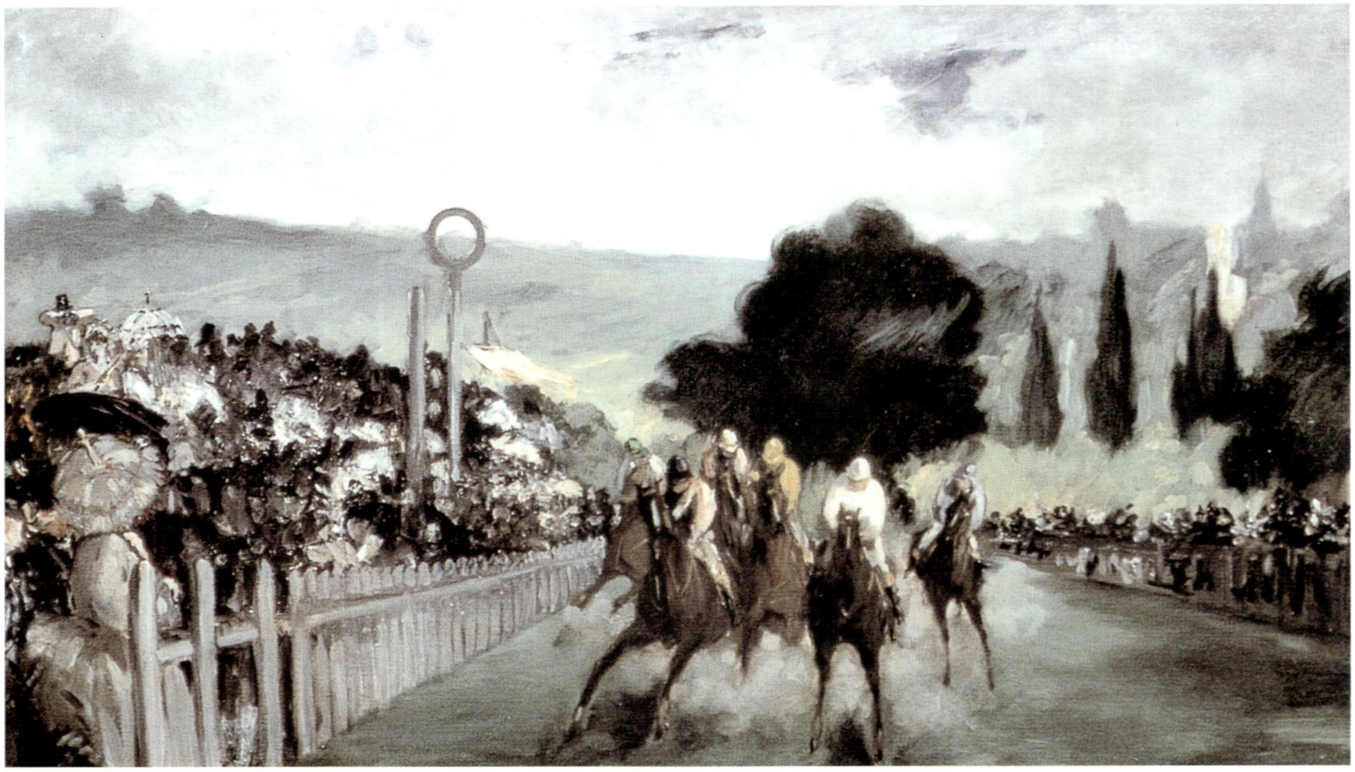

MANET
Races at Longchamp
oil on canvas
1864. 44 × 85 cm
RIGHT Longchamp was rapidly becoming an important social attraction for the wealthy bourgeois of Paris. Manet and Degas were frequent visitors.

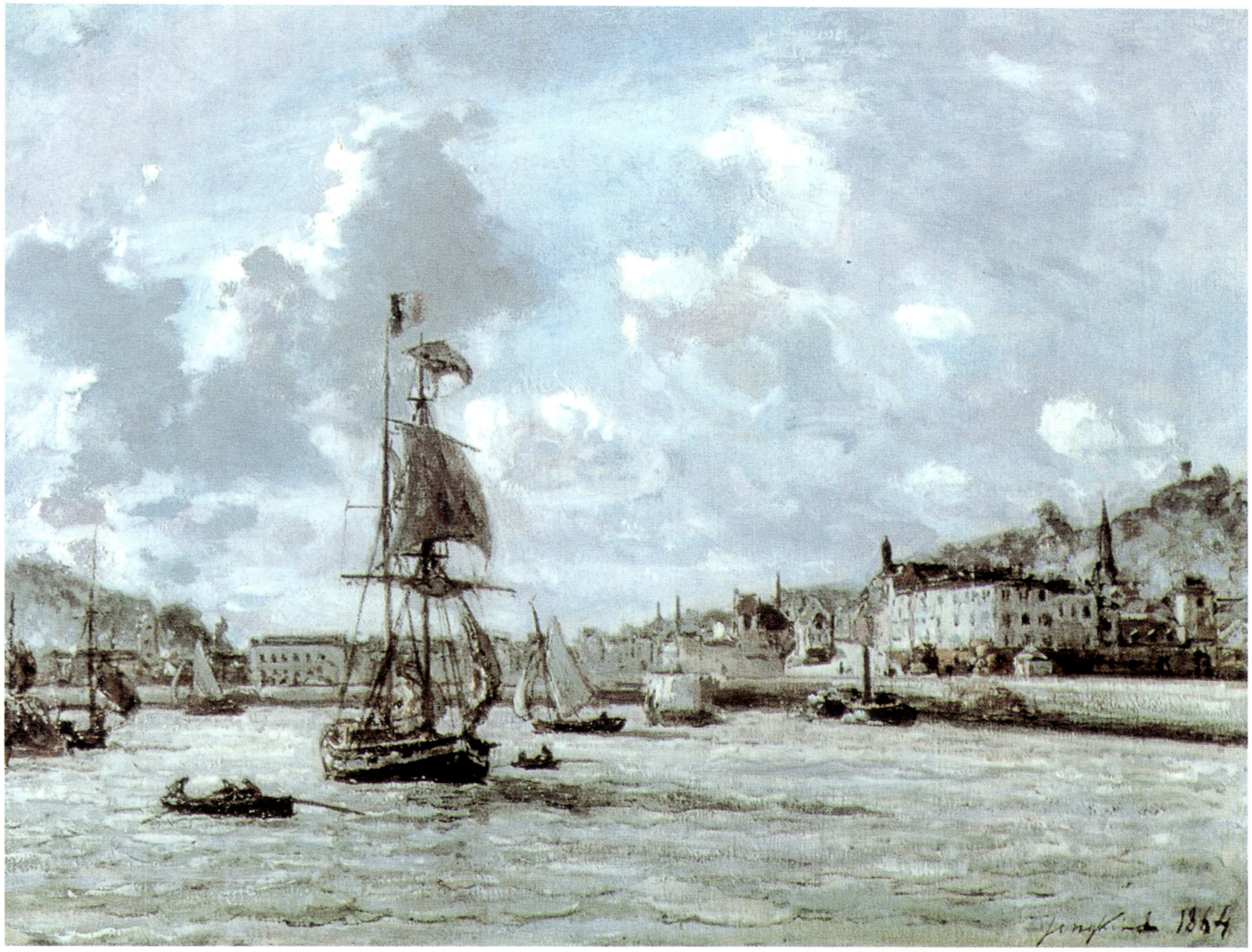

JONGKIND
Entrance to the Port of Honfleur
oil on canvas
1864. 42 × 56 cm
Like Boudin, and later Monet, on whom he was to have a great influence, Jongkind was primarily a self-taught painter of sea and rivers based in Normandy.

The new Paris being summoned into existence by Napoleon III and Haussmann was admirably suited to the realization of Baudelaire's project. The increasing wealth and number of people who made up the middle classes, the proliferation of entertainments, the sheer novelty of the new streets and squares with their airy prospects, were the new reality which a painter of modern life had to subsume in his or her work. In retrospect, we can see that the work of Manet and Degas outdoors in the city, and that of the Gleyre students led by Monet, who were escaping Paris to paint in the nearby countryside, would eventually coincide. In his eloquent essay of 1883 Jules Laforgue formulates a definition of *plein-air* painting which declares that "the open air concept governs the entire work of Impressionist painters, and means the painting of beings and things in their appropriate atmosphere . . . " This is what, in a sense, Manet and Degas were already about as early as 1862, strolling through Paris and its environs, sketch-book in hand. In fact Degas' range of vision was much wider than that of Manet, his notebook revealing subjects which included mourners and the local undertakers.

PISSARRO
A Clearing in the Woods
oil on canvas
c.1864. 26.5 × 21 cm
Although this is only a small study, it is quite clear that the artist had not yet found his own style.

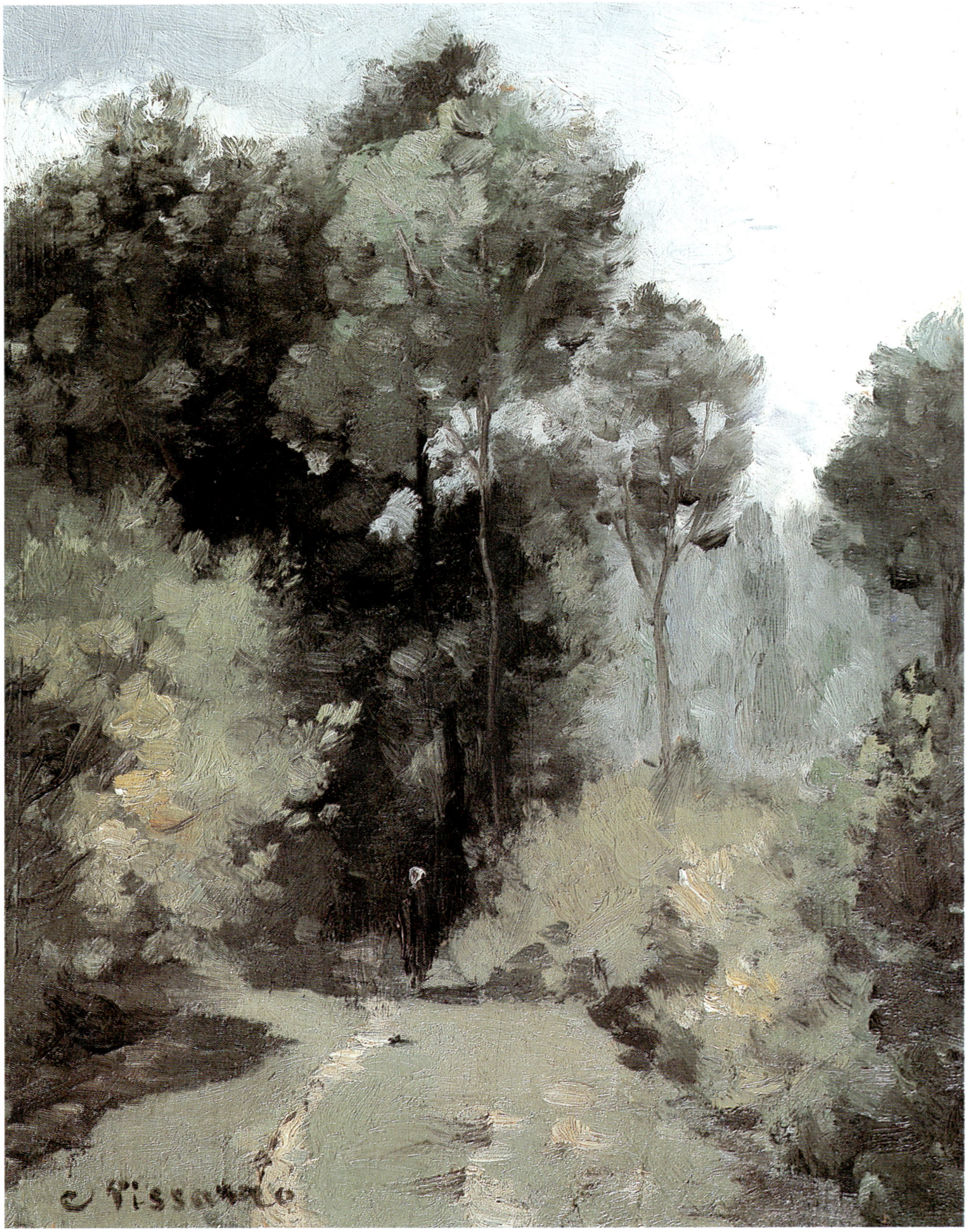

At this early stage in the story of Impressionism, in a year when Monet, Renoir, Sisley, Cézanne, Guillaumin, Morisot, and Bazille were still in their early twenties and searching for something new, the influence on them of the *plein-airistes* and the Barbizon School was still to bear substantial fruit. Monet's links to an older generation of landscape painters increased when he met and became a lasting friend of Johan Jongkind, a Dutch artist whose work is linked to that of Corot, Courbet, and Monet's first real teacher, Boudin. Meanwhile Berthe Morisot, born the same year as Renoir and Bazille, and daughter of the Secretary-General of the Crédit Financier, was working under the encouragement of Corot. He was teaching her landscape painting in Fontainebleau and Auvers where she was in frequent contact with Daubigny whose absolute devotion to *plein-airisme* was uncompromising.

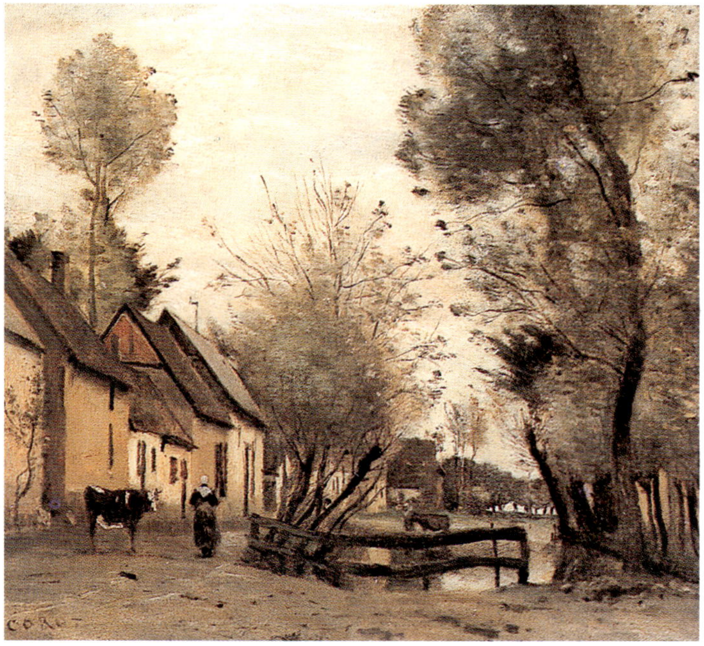

COROT
The Hamlet of Flesselles
oil on canvas
c.1862–65. 33 × 37.5 cm
Camille Corot was perhaps the most influential of the Barbizon painters on the younger landscapists, notably Pissarro, Morisot, Monet, and Renoir. His concern for rendering light and its effects in the landscape is of great importance in the prehistory of Impressionism.

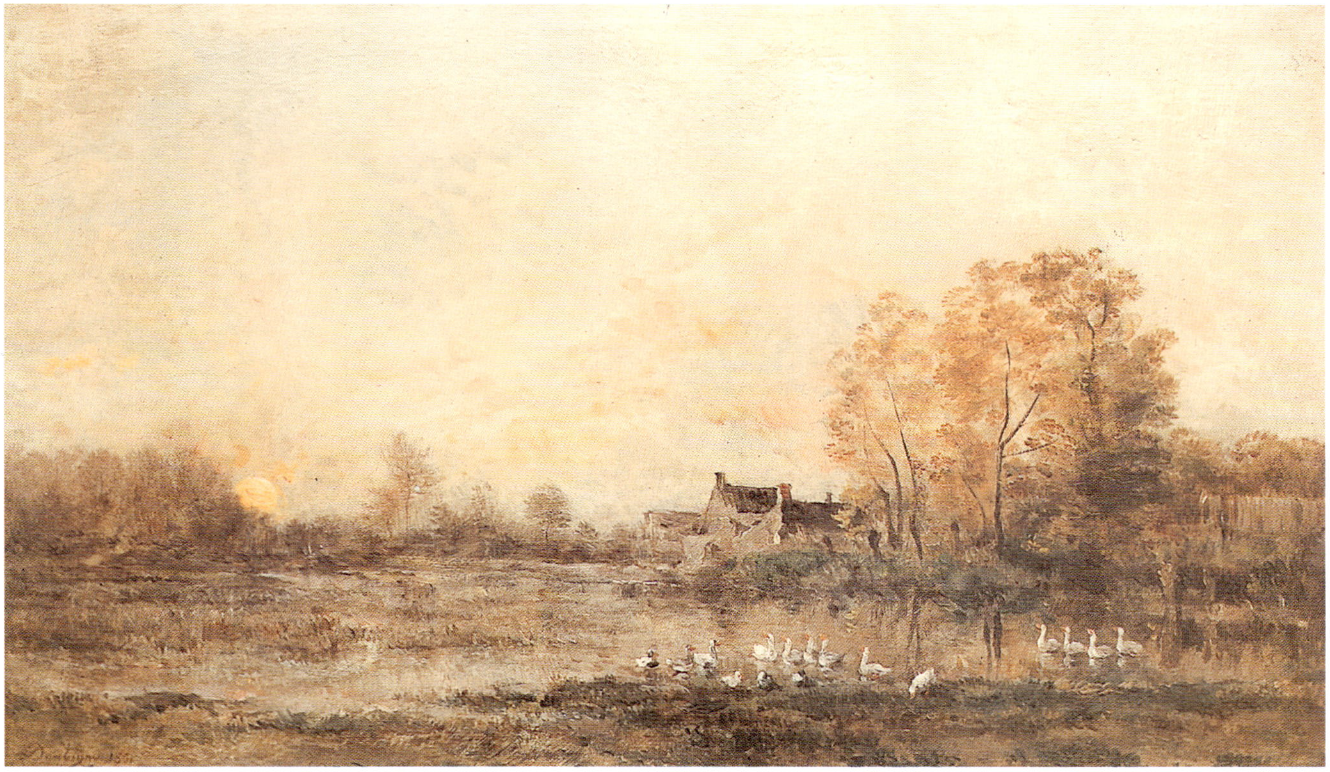

DAUBIGNY
The Marsh at Sunset
oil on canvas
1861. 33 × 57 cm
Daubigny, a devout plein-airiste, *had built a studio-boat to be able to paint from the river, an example later followed by Monet. Some critics said that he produced nothing but sketches and that he was satisfied with a first impression. Others praised his "delicious naivety, simple as a child, adding nothing and removing nothing".*

1863: The Salon des Refusés

. . . it is either a young man's idea of a joke, or it is a festering sore, unworthy of comment.

Louis Etienne, 1863

In 1863 the new railway line from Paris to Deauville was opened by the Duc de Morny, the internal combustion engine was invented, and in August, Eugène Delacroix, the source of so much colourful inspiration for the new artists, died. The 15th January was an ominous day for it marked the announcement by the Comte de Nieuwerkerke, the Director-General of National Museums, that the Salon (which had been held in the vast Palais de l'Industrie since the Exposition Universelle of 1855) was to be reorganized. For established artists, who had won medals at previous Salons, entry was now automatic as they did not have to pass the jury, but they were limited to three works each. The new rules were to present a serious blow to relative newcomers like Manet and Pissarro, whose work the jury was to reject later in the year.

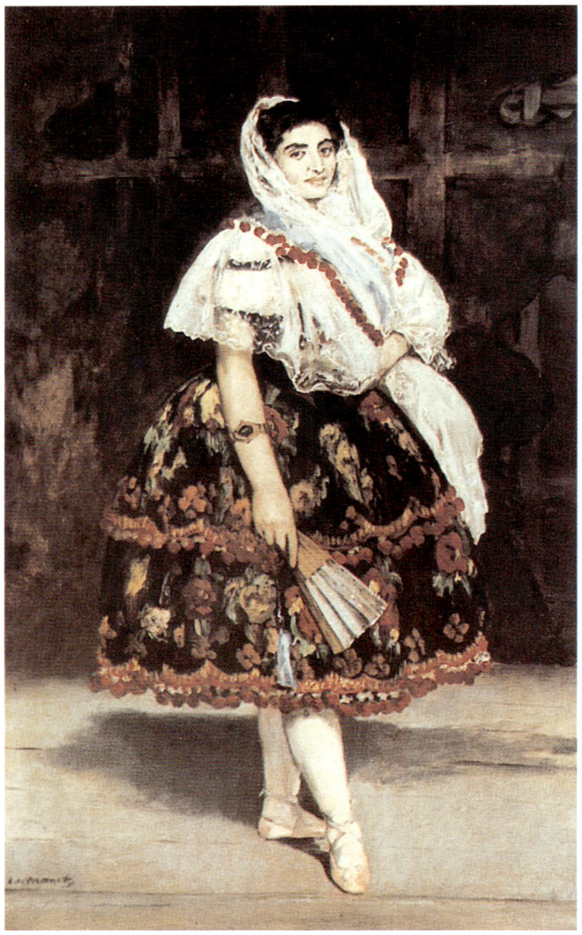

MANET
Lola de Valence
oil on canvas
1862. 123 × 92 cm
Manet produced a series of Spanish pictures as the ballet company was touring Paris. He had never been to Spain at the time, and did not go there until 1865.

Meanwhile Manet's first major exhibition went ahead at Louis Martinet's gallery in the boulevard des Italiens. It was here that *Music in the Tuileries Gardens* was first shown together with thirteen other paintings including *Lola de Valence* and *The Spanish Dancers*. The exhibition attracted the attention of Monet as well as Bazille who declared in a letter to his parents that one session spent looking at the Manets was worth a month of heavy work.

In April it was becoming clear that the Salon was making heavy work of its new rules. Of the 5,000 works which had been submitted, 2,783 had been rejected by the jury, led by a traditionalist of the history painting school, Emile Signol, who had once been furious with Renoir for using colour in the flamboyant style of Delacroix. In fact Delacroix and Ingres were members of the jury, but were not involved in the selection of works. All three of Manet's submissions, which included *Luncheon on the Grass* were refused entry to the exhibition.

The importance of being shown at the

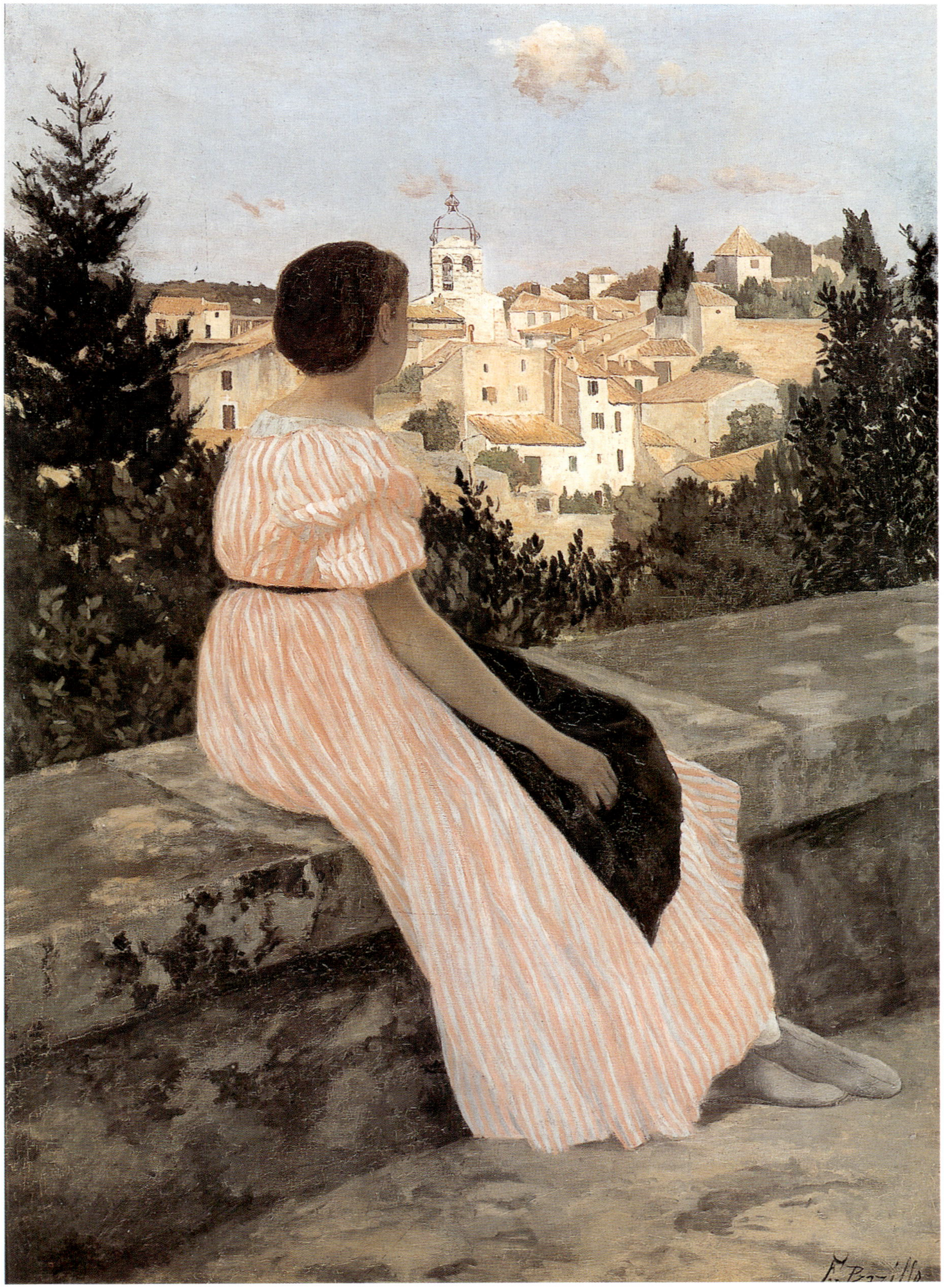

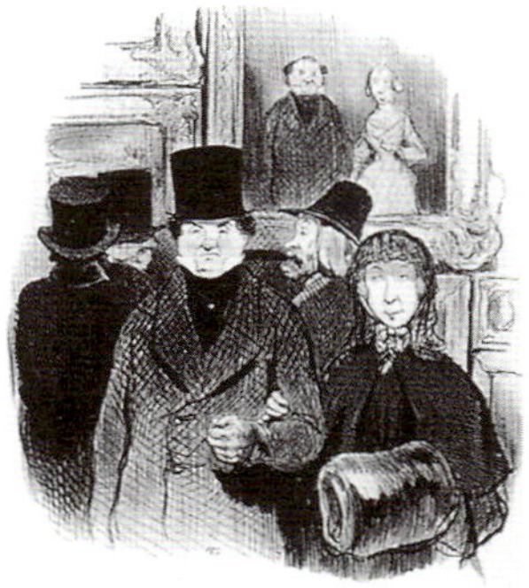

DAUMIER
The Pride of Having One's Portrait at the Salon
lithograph
1845. 26 × 17 cm
ABOVE Honoré Daumier is best known as a prolific and scathing caricaturist of political and artistic events in nineteenth-century Paris. His paintings of contemporary life form a less accomplished background to the work of Manet and Degas – Manet's teacher Thomas Couture had once warned his pupil that he would end up as a Daumier if he carried on in his usual irreverent fashion.

BAZILLE
The Pink Dress
oil on canvas
1864. 147 × 110 cm
LEFT This rich and finely-finished piece – also known as View of a Village *– shows just how much the twenty-three-year-old artist's technique and vision were beginning to mature.*

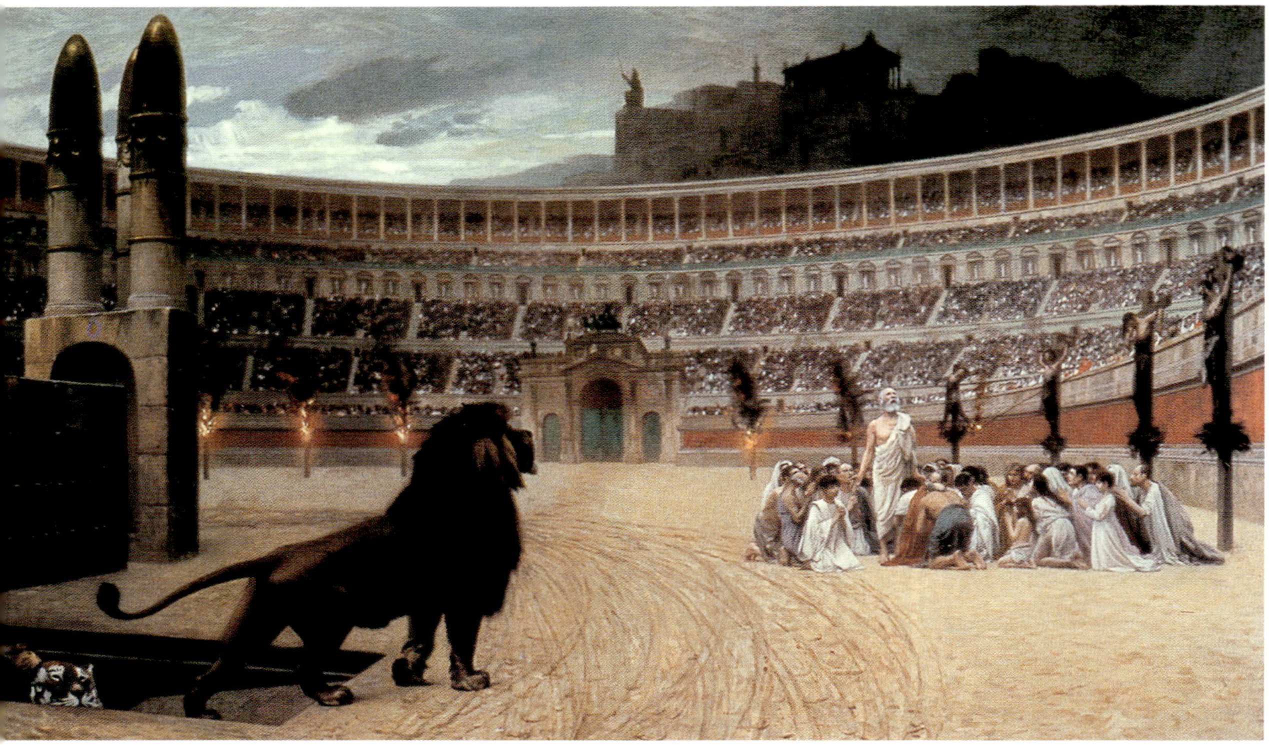

GÉRÔME
Christian Martyrs
oil on wood
1863–73. 88 × 150 cm
Gérôme was one of the most popular Salon artists of his day. His taste and technique in classical and biblical subjects was not shared by the Impressionists.

Salon for artists at this time cannot be underestimated. There were certainly well over a hundred independent galleries like Martinet's, but the Salon was the only marketplace with an assured audience of thousands; *le tout Paris* would be certain to be there, and failure to show at it meant another year without significant exposure to the public, the commissioning authorities, the dealers, and the critics. Although Manet had been rejected before, in 1857 and 1859, he was well aware of the benefits of appearing at the Salon and continued to strive to be accepted there as did the younger artists such as Monet and Renoir. To make things worse, several regular exhibitors had also fallen at the new hurdles, artists with official commissions already behind them who would in the normal course of events be expected to show at the Salon. One artist had even submitted works done for the Empress Eugènie – a more important patron, save the Emperor himself, could not be imagined – and had them rejected. The press seized upon the opportunity offered by the fiasco that the Salon was turning into, and the traditionalists as well as supporters of Manet and the younger artists demanded that something should be done. In the end the Emperor paid a visit to the Salon to judge for himself and, with his wife's rejected commission no doubt firmly in his mind, he too declared that something must be done. However, the jury refused to reconvene and the exhibition had in any case already been hung. On 24th April just three weeks before the opening of the Salon the following announcement appeared in the *Moniteur Universel*:

> Numerous complaints have reached the Emperor on the subject of works of art which have been refused by the jury of the Exhibition. His Majesty, wishing to allow the public to judge the legitimacy of these complaints, has decided that the rejected works shall be exhibited in another part of the Palais de l'Industrie. This exhibition will be voluntary, and artists who do not wish to participate need only to inform the administration of the exhibition, which will hasten to return their works to them.

In a sense Napoleon III had pulled off another coup; this time he had succeeded in showing himself as an enlightened liberal ruler concerned with art and ready to listen to public opinion. The press enjoyed a field day on this issue not least because there were few other causes for them to champion under the strict regime of censorship that had then been imposed by the Emperor.

The new exhibition came to be known as

MEISSONIER
French Campaign, Napoleon
oil on canvas
1864. 49 × 75 cm
BELOW Edifying subjects, whether religious or heroic or both, were the staple diet of the Salon during the second half of the century.

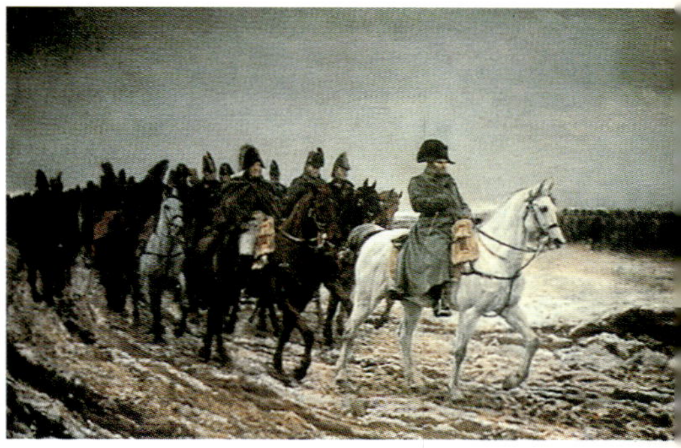

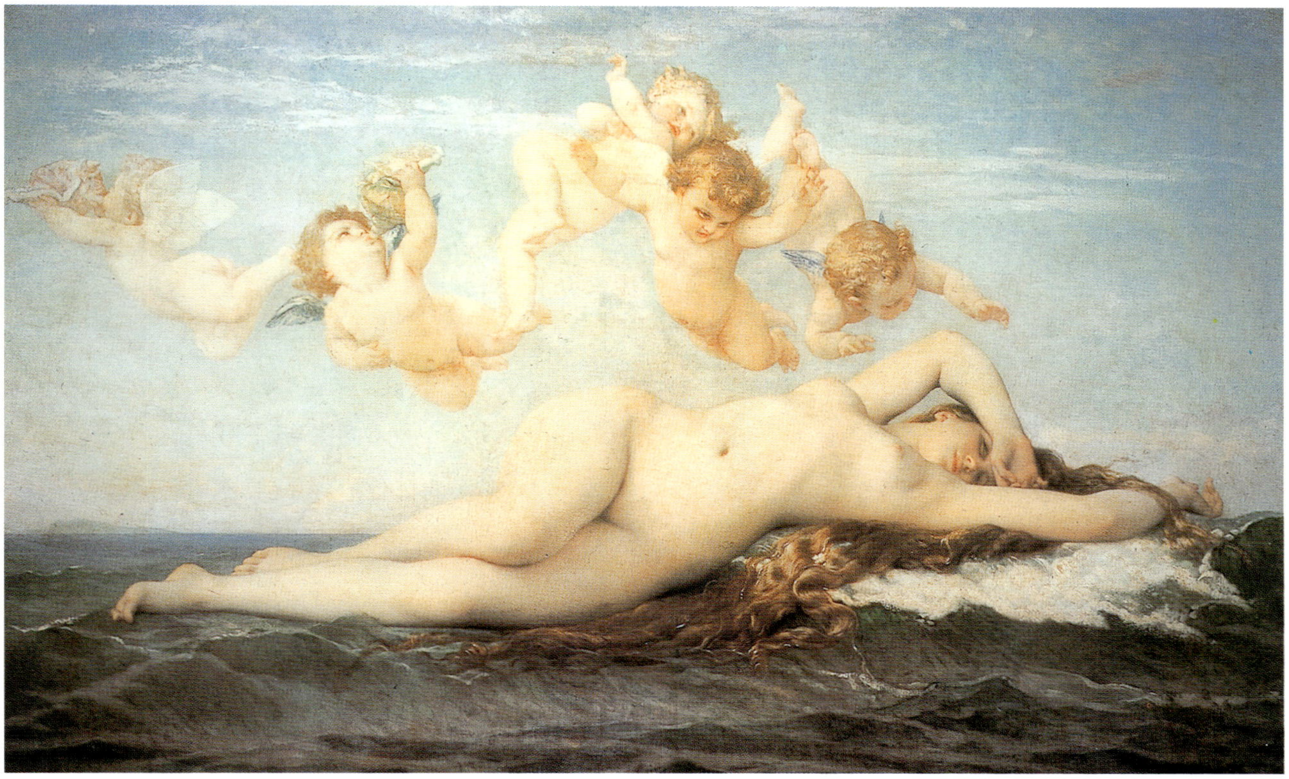

CABANEL
Birth of Venus
oil on canvas
1863. 130 × 225 cm
ABOVE LEFT The star of the official 1863 Salon, Cabanel's Venus *embodies perfectly all that Manet, Degas and the nascent Impressionists were trying to avoid. The highly finished, quintessentially classical composition with its hint of eroticism was bought by Napoleon III. On show next door in the Salon des Refusés Manet's frankly realist* Luncheon on the Grass *drew outrage and condemnation.*

the Salon des Refusés, and, when it opened its doors directly adjacent to the Salon proper on 17th May, over 10,000 people came to marvel at it. Amongst the jumble of paintings which had been hung with no particular order or care (of course many pictures which deserved to be rejected were on show) were two which caused an especially violent reaction, James McNeill Whistler's *White Girl* which had previously been rejected by the Royal Academy in London, and Manet's *Luncheon on the Grass*. Whistler's painting was ridiculed by many whilst "Manet in the furthest hall," as the *refusé* Jean-Charles Cazin observed, "went right through the wall with his *Luncheon on the Grass*." If *Music in the Tuileries Gardens* had caused a positive stir amongst his fellow artists and the Spanish paintings had delighted the public, *Luncheon on the Grass* was an instant *succès de scandale*.

Manet's technique aside, the general public was outraged at the depiction of a female nude together with two clothed young bourgeois, and Napoleon III pronounced it to be an offence against modesty. (The Emperor was not too modest however to purchase Alexandre Cabanel's studiously academic but erotic *Birth of Venus* (*La Naissance de Vénus*), which was on show in the official Salon next door to the *refusés*.) Zola defended the picture by drawing attention to the fact that there were several paintings in the Louvre with clothed and nude figures. Zacharie Astruc also leapt to Manet's defence, going so far as to publish a newspaper *Le Salon de 1863* which called Manet "one of the greatest artistic characters of the time," lauding his work for "brilliance, inspiration, power, flavour, surprise." Manet professed himself to be distressed by all this attention, complaining to his friend Baudelaire that abuse was raining down on him like hail.

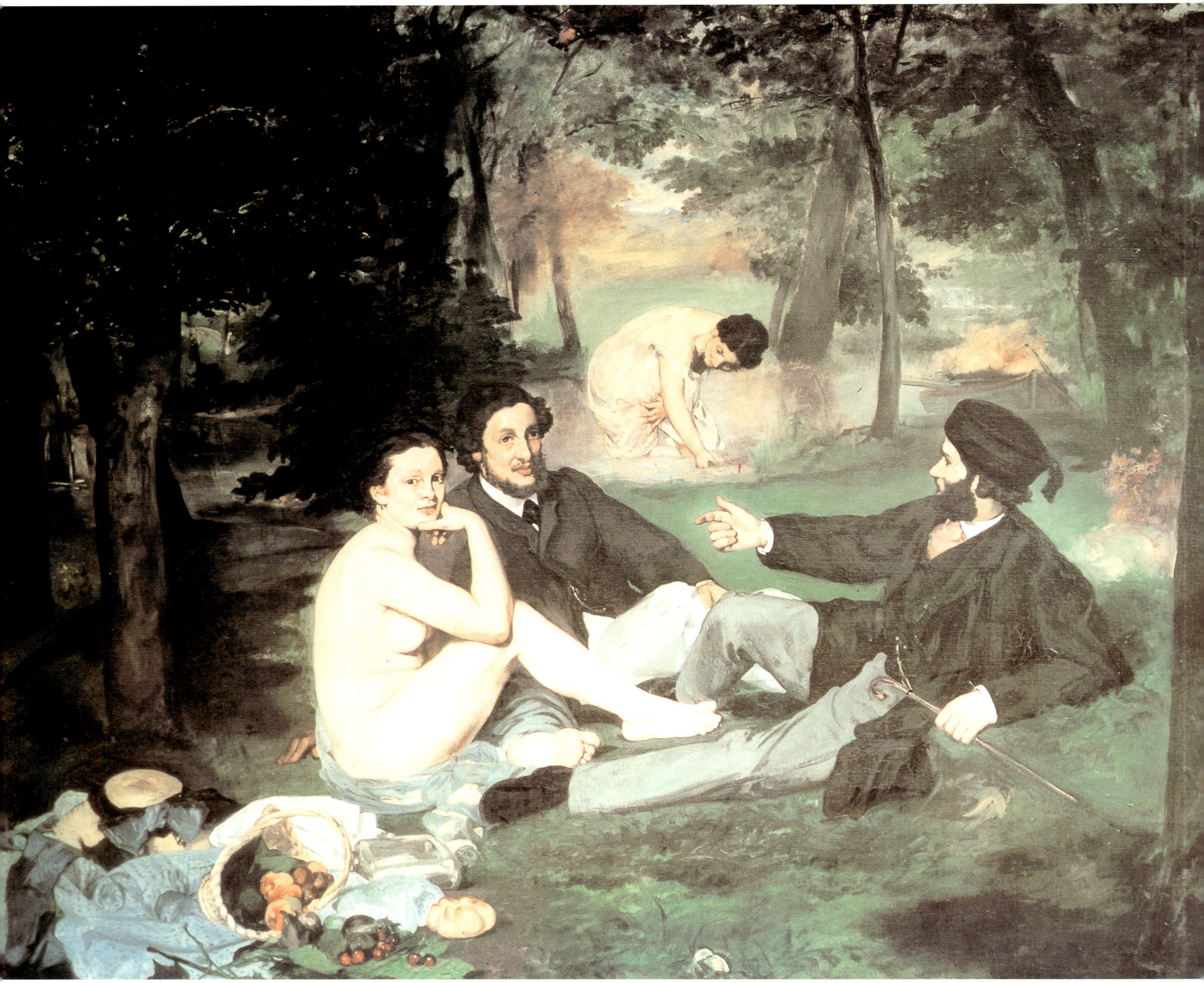

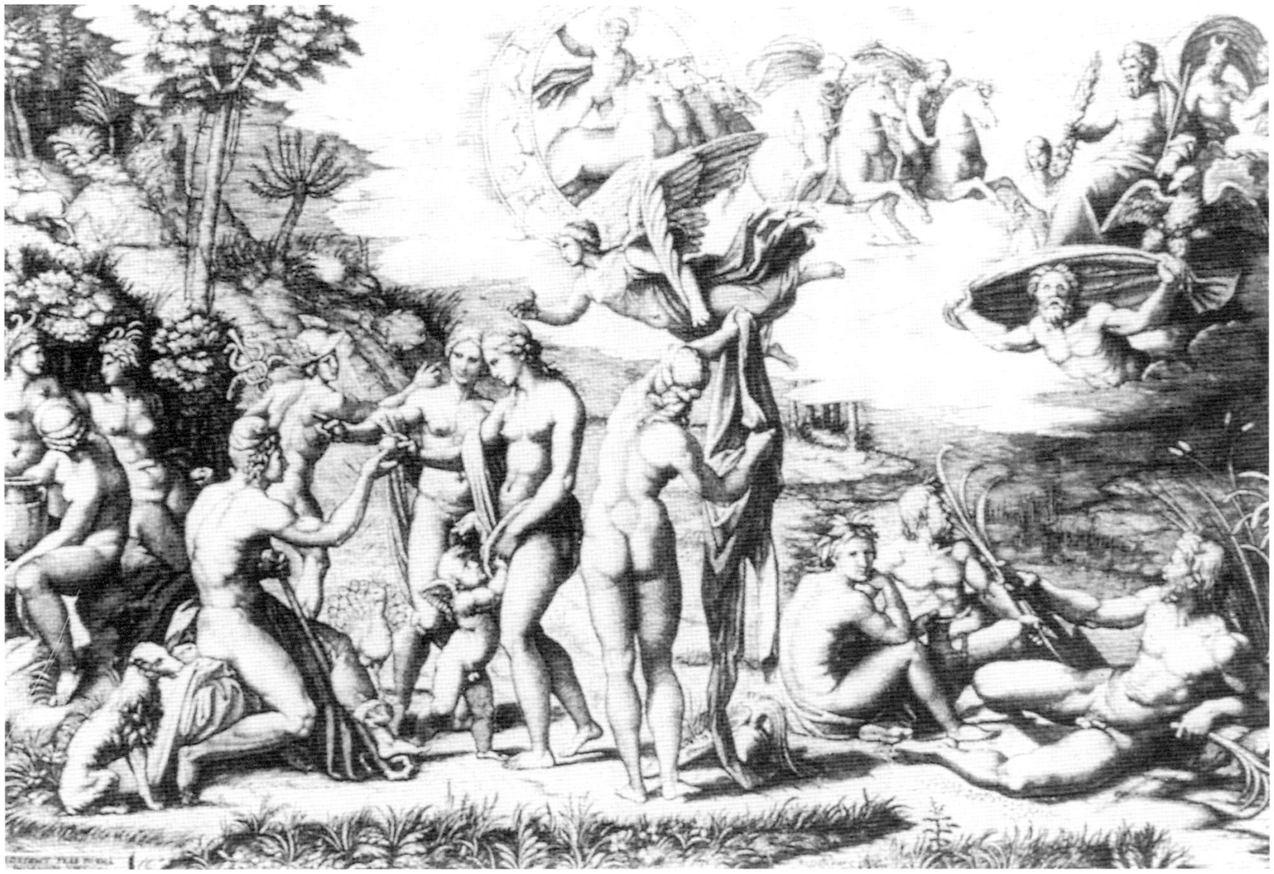

MANET
Luncheon on the Grass
oil on canvas
1863. 208 × 264.5 cm
OPPOSITE Neither the critics nor public could accept a classical scene in modern dress, and although there were several precedents for this subject in the Louvre, the shock of seeing a female nude in the company of two modern-day dandies was simply too much. The flat lighting and uncompromising realism in the depiction of the main figures also brought much criticism of Manet's technique.

RAIMONDI
The Judgement of Paris, after Raphael
engraving
c.1550.
LEFT One of the revered precedents for Manet's Déjeuner sur l'herbe.

Manet's painting had ultimately derived from a work of 1510–11 in the Louvre (by Titian, Giorgione, or both) known as *La Fête champêtre*; it also had a respectable precedent in an engraving by Marcantonio after Raphael. Yet the flat yellowish lighting on the central nude depicts her without a trace of the customary *pudeur* so obvious and conventionally appealing in Cabanel's pinkly suffused Venus, the star of the "official" Salon. One critic, Théophile Burger, a friend of Baudelaire's "[failed] to see what could have induced a distinguished and intelligent artist to adopt such an absurd composition." But he admitted that "there are qualities of colour and light in the landscape, and indeed some very fine passages of modelling in the torso." These fine passages were passed over in a pamphlet by Louis Etienne who pronounced what was on everyone's mind, describing the painting as:

> A nonchalant *bréda* [a prostitute] . . . completely naked, impudently lounges between two dandies dressed up to the nines. They give the impression of two students on holiday who are behaving outrageously, to try and give the impression of real men . . . It is either a young man's idea of a joke, or it is a festering sore, unworthy of comment.

The prostitute in Manet's painting is referred to by Etienne as a *bréda* after the rue Bréda in the Batignolles district of Paris where the women worked. At the time of the Salon des Refusés Manet lived and worked nearby. It

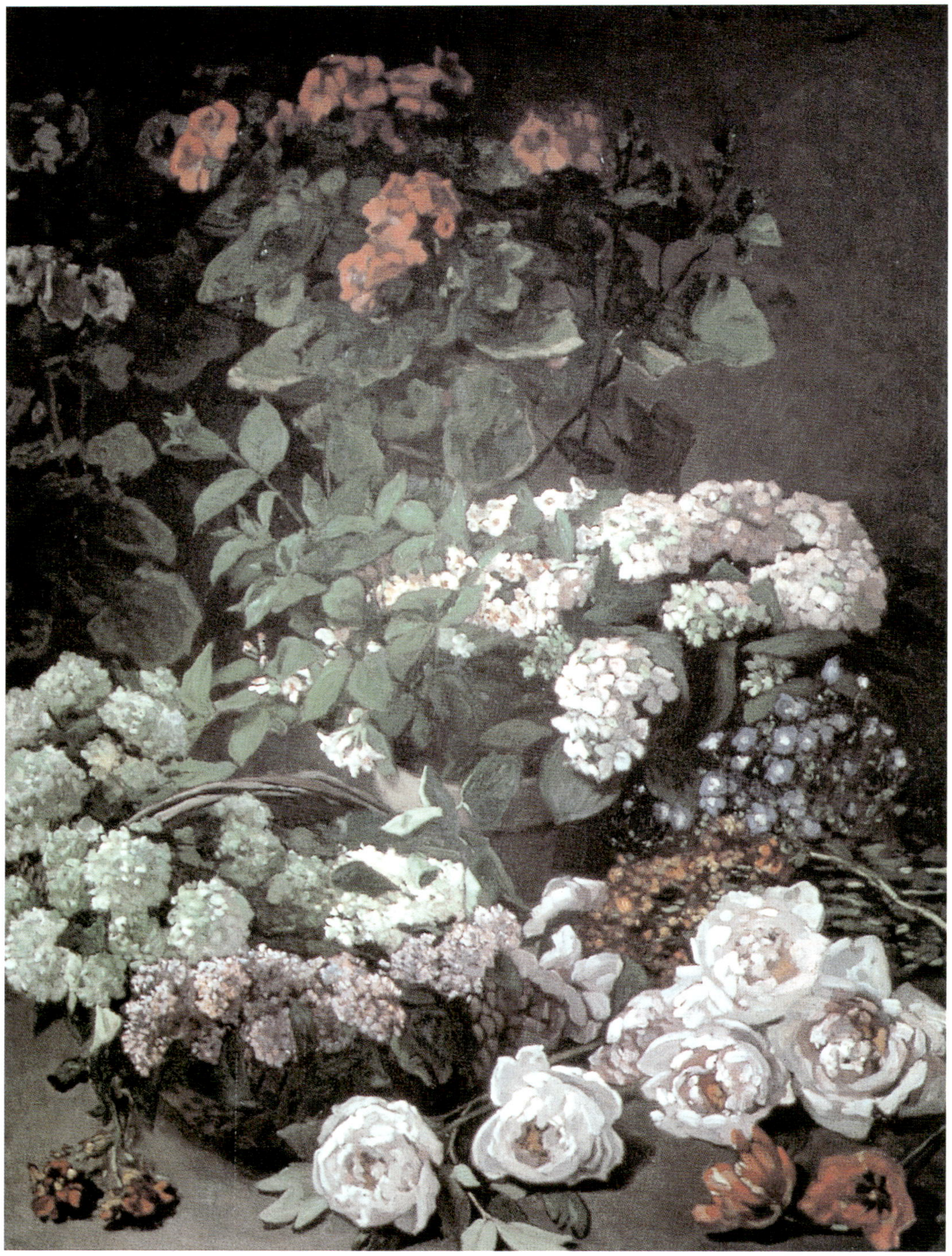

MONET
Spring Flowers
oil on canvas
1864. 117 × 89 cm
This early piece proves that Monet was able to produce commercially accessible work.

was in the Café Guerbois at 11 Grande rue des Batignolles that a group of like-minded artists and intellectuals, amongst them Manet, Monet, Pissarro, Bazille, Degas, Renoir, Zola, and Nadar would meet in the coming years to discuss their life and work. They became known as the Batignolles Group.

Zola's view, fortunately the one that has prevailed, was that:

> What you have to look for in the picture is not just the picnic on the grass, but the whole landscape with its bold and subtle passages, its broadly painted, solid foreground, its light and delicate background and that firm flesh modelled in broad areas of light, those supple and strong pigments, and, particularly, that delicate splash of white among the green leaves in the background; in fact to look at the whole of this vast, airy composition, at this attention to nature, rendered with such accurate simplicity.

Festering sore or airy composition, *Luncheon on the Grass* pushed modern life into the Salon and out into the world even though it was literally and figuratively one of the *peintures refusées*. Nowadays we find it extremely difficult to find anything scandalous in this picture, but at the time nudes were only acceptable in certain highly stylized and sanitized forms like Cabanel's. The "real thing" was wholly intolerable.

One more event was to cause uproar that year. In a decree dated 13th November the government announced sweeping reforms of the Ecole des Beaux-Arts, removing it from the control of the Académie des Beaux-Arts, installing a system of ateliers to teach painting within the Ecole which had previously only taught drawing, and abolishing several important competitions, one of which was the Prix de Paysage Historique. Many of the Barbizon landscapists had taken part in the competition; Rousseau and Daubigny had both attempted it and, as art historian Albert Boime points out, Corot and Gleyre had trained their students to compete for it whilst Monet and Sisley were both interested in it. The government had decreed the reforms partly under the pretext that they would foster more originality, but they were popular with neither the Académie nor the students, who feared they would no longer be able to choose which master they worked under in preparation for the Ecole. Sisley was one of those who signed a petition protesting against the changes, proving, according to Albert Boime, that the group of students of Gleyre's atelier had not yet relinquished hope of official recognition through the Ecole's competition structure and the official Salon to which they still aspired, despite the success of the Salon des Refusés.

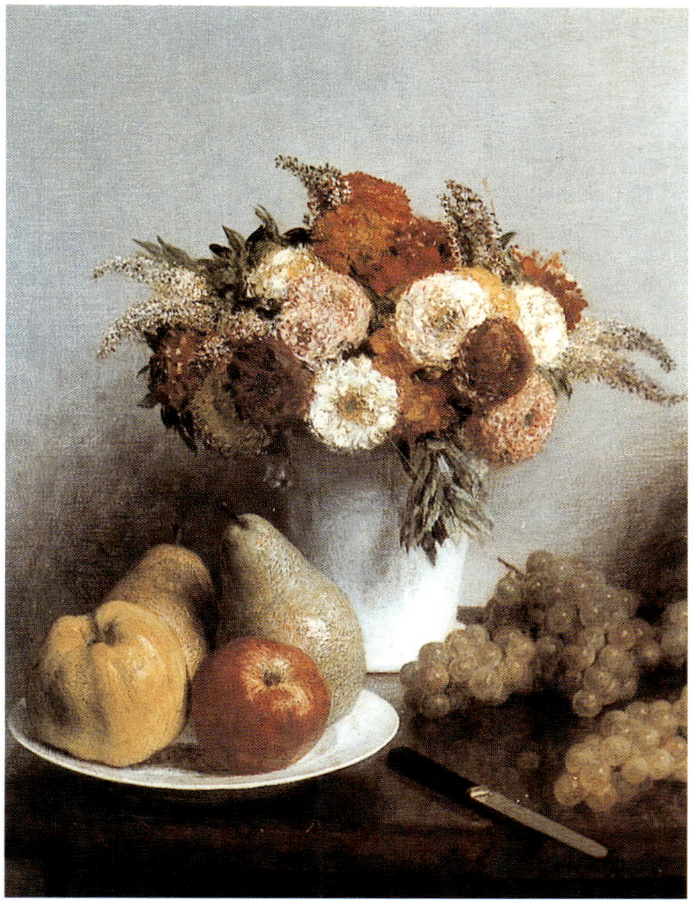

FANTIN-LATOUR
Flowers and Fruit
oil on canvas
1865. 64 × 57 cm
LEFT Fantin-Latour's paintings of flowers sold particularly well in London where he was seen as the highly desirable face of French art.

1864–1866: "OLYMPIA WAKES"

In 1864 the Duc de Morny, who organized the building of a coastal resort at Deauville and connected it to Paris with a railway line so that affluent Parisians could take advantage of it, inaugurated the new race track there. Nothing was unusual about this commonplace development in an era of rapid industrial and economic expansion in France. It is simply another example of the new middle-class prosperity and (expensive) free time which many could now spend in a variety of pursuits. That year the first international victory at Longchamp by a French racehorse was celebrated. Speed was of the moment; the railway had already revolutionized travel and was helping France on its way to becoming a major industrial power.

The Second Empire was attempting to extend its power base in other ways too; in Mexico Napoleon III installed Maximilian of Austria as the puppet ruler, but like so much of the Emperor's foreign policy, this was to prove a disastrous chimera. Meanwhile, Eugène Chevreul published his second work on colour, and Charles Gleyre was forced to close down his atelier due to failing health and lack of funds. In the summer Morisot, Renoir, and Pissarro had work accepted at the Salon which was now to be run annually. Manet, however, was rejected and out of the limelight for a year.

With the demise of Gleyre's atelier, Monet and his friends took off to the country to

MANET
Peonies
oil on canvas
1864. 38 × 46.5 cm
BELOW Manet produced still lifes throughout his career, but no painter could rival Fantin-Latour for the popularity of his flower pieces.

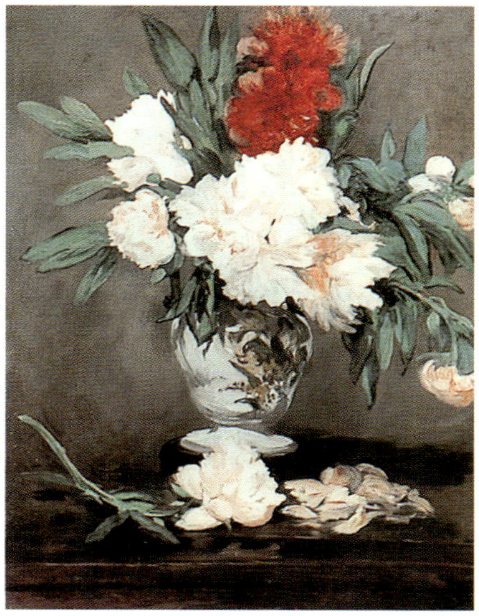

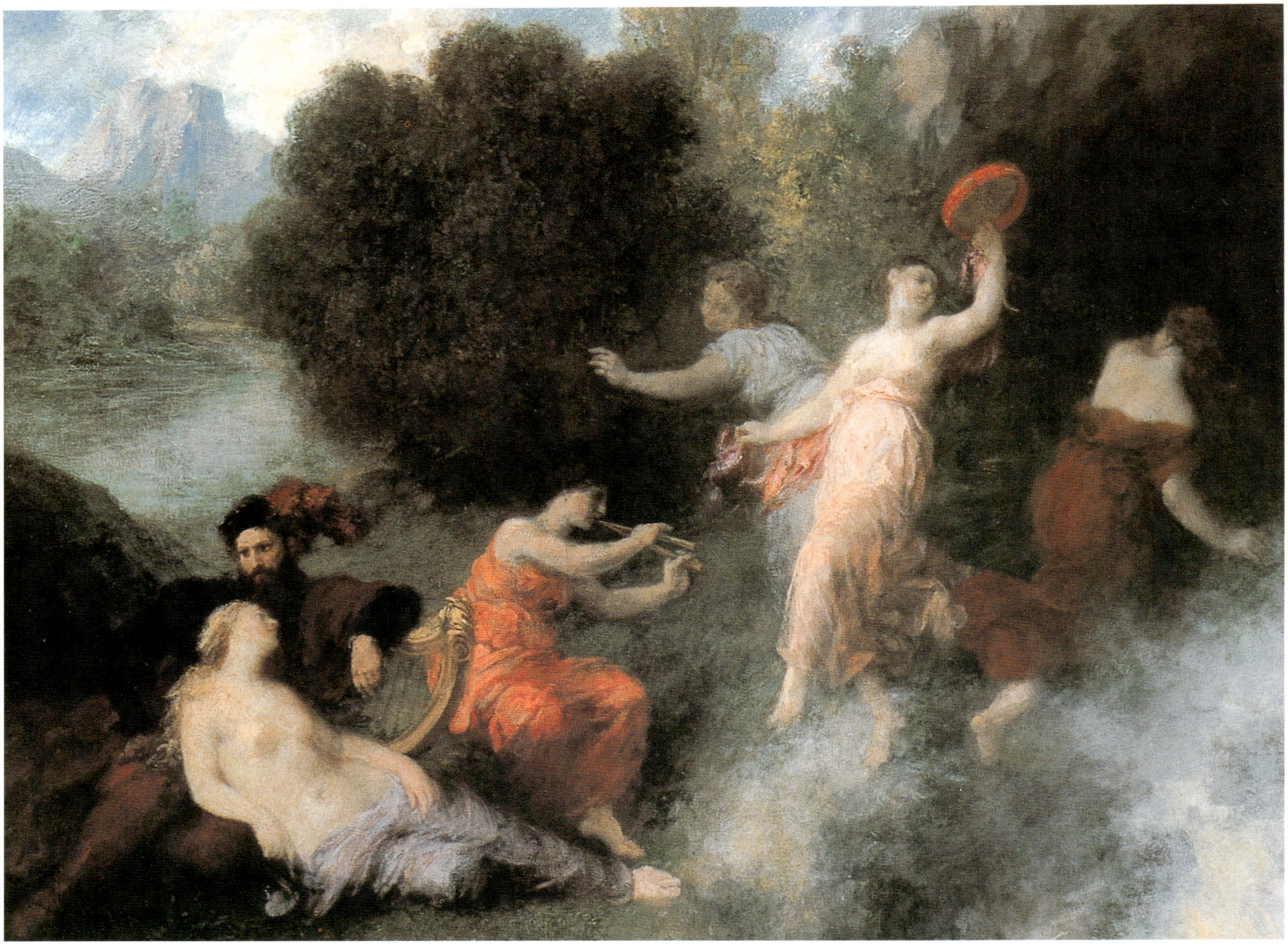

FANTIN-LATOUR
Tannhäuser on the Venusberg
oil on canvas
1864. 98 × 130 cm
Fantin-Latour had discovered Wagner the previous year. Tannhäuser failed in Paris but Fantin-Latour adored the music of Wagner and Berlioz, an enthusiasm shared by Bazille.

paint. In the early spring Monet had been working in and around Fontainebleau with Renoir and Sisley. That summer Monet returned to the Normandy coast at a farm near Honfleur, where Bazille, Boudin, and Jongkind later joined him. Bazille had returned to Paris when Monet wrote to him from Honfleur, entreating him to come back to the country and declaring that:

It really is appallingly difficult to do something which is complete in every way, and I think most people are content with mere approximations . . . I intend to battle on, scrape off, and start again . . . and when I look at nature I feel as if I'll be able to paint it all, note it all down . . . it's on the strength of observation and reflection that one finds a way. So we must dig and delve unceasingly.

The influence of Boudin and especially Jongkind is clearly evident in Monet's work from this early period. He even admitted to touches of Corot in some of the landscapes he was producing near Honfleur. But *Rue de la Barolle* and *Farmyard in Normandy* (*La Ferme Normande*), both painted at this time, display the beginnings of his rapidly developing technique. At this point he was producing work at a phenomenal rate and he continued to do so for the rest of his life; his head was, as he wrote to Bazille in July 1864, "bursting with the desire to paint." This was just as well, for he lived on the edge of destitution and often had to call on friends like Bazille to help him out of financial difficulties. His diligence paid off in the next year's Salon where two works were accepted, along with Degas' first successful submission and what proved to be his last history painting, *Scene of War in the Middle Ages* (*Scène de guerre au Moyen Age*).

Monet showed two seascapes at the Salon of 1865, *The Mouth of the Seine at Honfleur* (*L'Embouchure de la Seine à Honfleur*) and *Pointe de la Hève at Low Tide* (*Pointe de la Hève à marée basse*). In both the influence of Jongkind and Boudin is evident, but the critic Gallet was moved to describe Monet as "a young realist who promises much. His two seascapes . . . display the work of a powerful hand uninterested in prettiness and greatly preoccupied with accuracy of effect." Another critic, Victor Fournel, offered a withering dismissal: "What is there to say, for instance, about this *Mouth of the Seine at Honfleur*? The waves are represented by

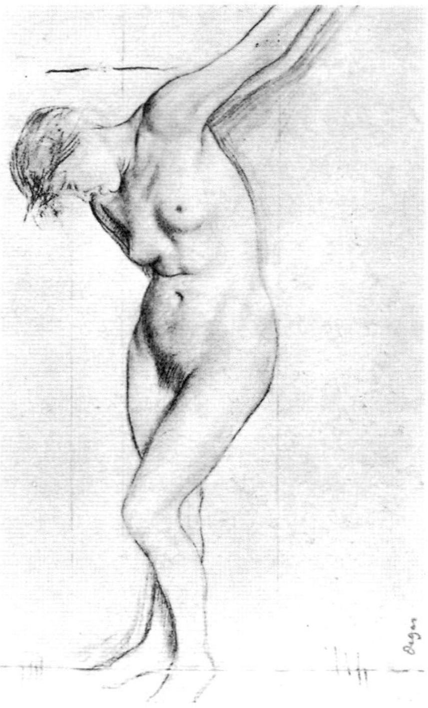

DEGAS
Study for A Scene of War in the Middle Ages
pencil on paper
1865. 35.5 × 22 cm
ABOVE Degas rigorously followed the tradition of drawing nude figures before painting them clothed in order to obtain accurate volumes.

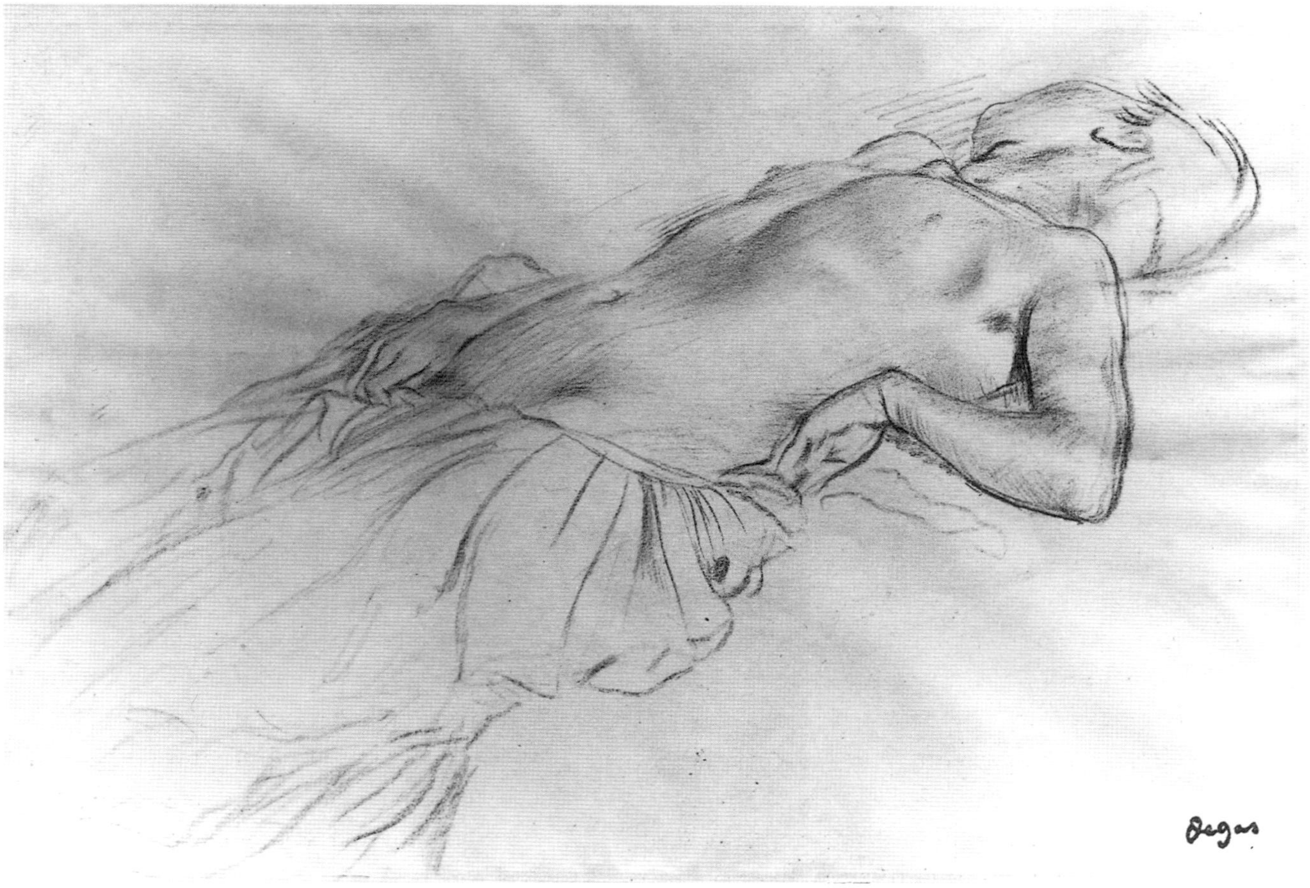

DEGAS
Study for A Scene of War in the Middle Ages
black chalk on paper
1865. 26.5 × 31.5 cm
LEFT Degas' studies were always carefully worked towards the finished painting; he left nothing to chance, a trait which kept him stylistically apart from the mainstream of Impressionism.

CARAVAGGIO
Ecce Homo
oil on canvas
1606. 128 × 103 cm
FAR RIGHT Caravaggio's naturalism was considered outrageous at a time when most subjects were idealized and sanitized; Manet suffered the same fate.

MANET
Christ Mocked by the Soldiers
oil on canvas
1865. 191.5 × 148.5 cm
RIGHT "You are the foremost in the decrepitude of your art", Baudelaire wrote in a vitriolic vein to an extremely unhappy Manet after the scandal of Olympia *and* Christ Mocked *had broken at the Salon. Both paintings were taken down from their prominent position and rehung in the darkest corner of Room M.*

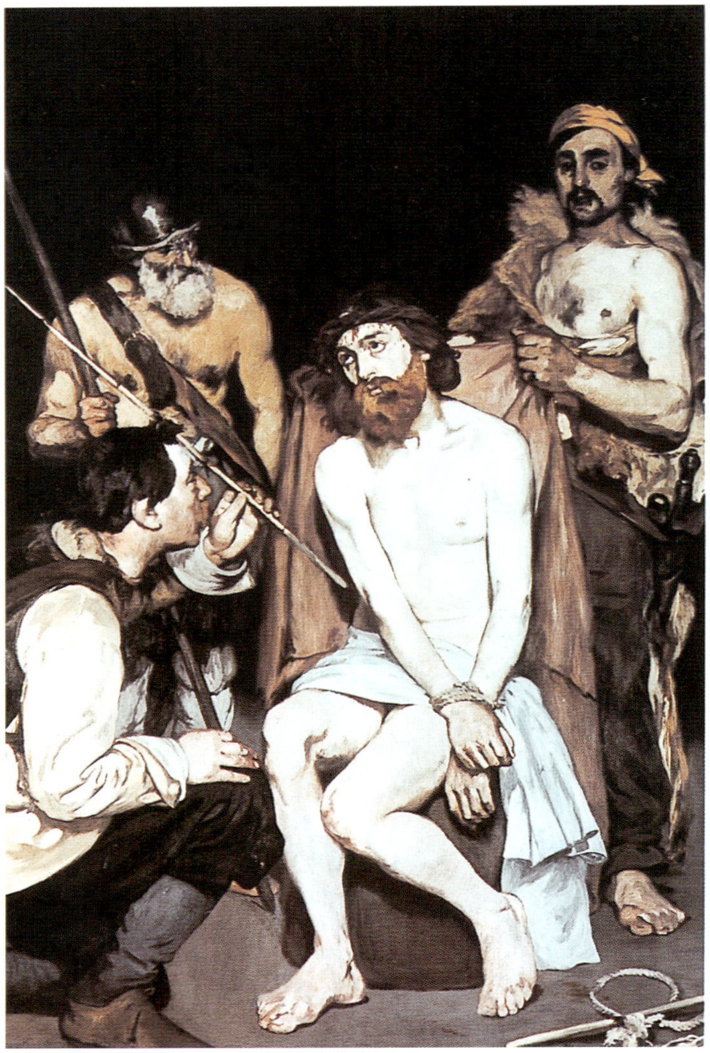

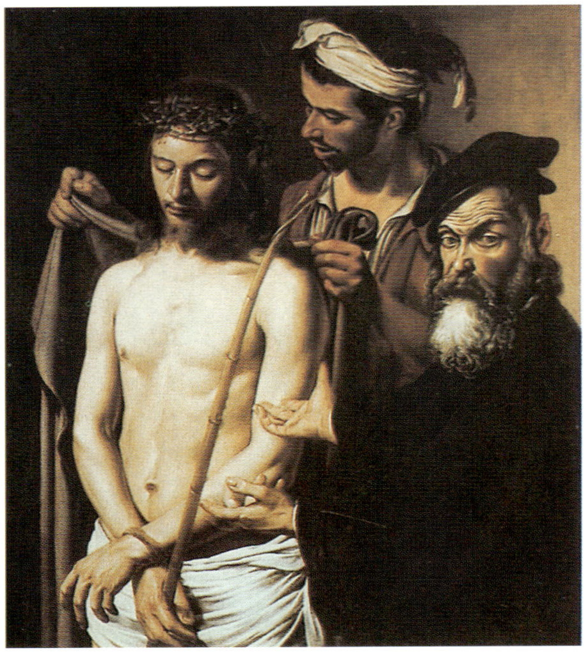

lumps of earth, the sails of the boats by triangles of black wood: one might well think it had been scrawled by a child of twelve on the cover of his Sunday school book." But both Monet and Degas, as well as Pissarro, who was again successful at the Salon, were to be overshadowed by Edouard Manet and his *Olympia*.

Earlier in 1865 Manet had again exhibited at the Galerie Martinet to some acclaim. In May the Salon opened to a hysterical onslaught. The objects of the critics' scorn and the public's distaste were Manet's two submissions, *Christ Mocked by the Soldiers* (*Jésus insulté par les soldats*) and *Olympia*. Hanging together, they attracted crowds of curious viewers. The critic Victor de Jankovitz waxed sardonic: "Thanks to his brushwork, *Christ Mocked* by M. Manet, is a picture beneath all criticism. It is Raphael as corrected by a third-rate Courbet." *Christ Mocked by the Soldiers* came away from its confrontation with the critics fairly unscathed in comparison with *Olympia*. Gentlewomen were said to have averted their eyes from the shameful sight. Nevertheless they and their gentlemen-folk crushed into Room M to assure themselves of the veracity of the shocking reports.

Olympia's notoriety quickly transcended that of *Luncheon on the Grass* which, it should be remembered, had been shown outside the official Salon as a work which had been rejected as being unworthy of recognition. The Salon catalogue entry for the painting carried the following verse by the painter's friend Zacharie Astruc:

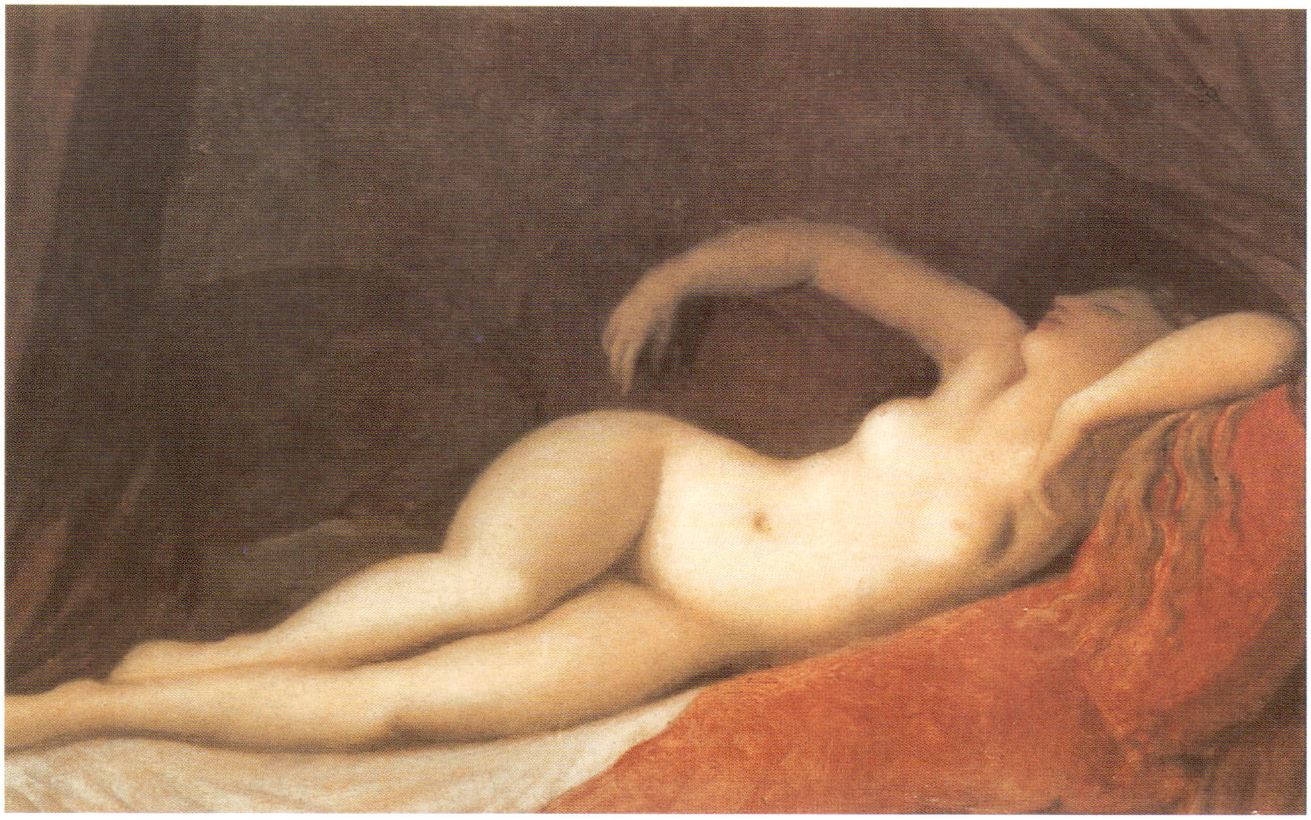

INGRES
Sleeping Odalisque
oil on canvas
1829. 30 × 47.5 cm
It might be that Ingres' nude is more provocative and erotic than Olympia, *but nevertheless she is devoid of the plain everyday look of Manet's model, too easily linked to prostitution by a hypocritical bourgeois society.*

When, weary of dreaming, Olympia wakes,
Springtime arrives in the arms of a gentle black envoy;
It is the slave, like unto a night of passion,
Who comes to make the day bloom, a delight to behold;
The august young girl in whom the flame burns.

Everything about the painting – the disposition of its subject, her dishevelled sheets and her scant accoutrements, the black maid, the little black cat, the flowers, the technique, with some passages finely modelled and some blocked in with broad sweeps of the brush – conspired to confuse and dismay its viewers. There was little doubt that this was another *bréda*, a prostitute, weary, not from dreaming, but from a night of work. Paris was awash with prostitutes; from the poorest streetwalker in the rue Bréda to the richest *courtesane*, lavishly entertaining in apartments along the *grands boulevards*. But painting them, other than in the enciphered form of a Venus or some demi-goddess, was unheard of until the first Salon des Refusés and now *Olympia*. Manet had liberated a new territory which others, Degas in particular, were later able to exploit with more or less impunity. Directly based on a pose much used by sixteenth-century Italian painters, the English painter Peter Lely, and eighteenth-century French artists such as François Boucher, *Olympia* did not try to charm the public. Here was a real woman, unashamed, addressing the viewer directly and without pretence or any attempt at seduction.

The Second Empire was all artifice. Away from the massive façades of the new Paris designed by Haussmann, half of the population, which Haussmann himself had described as "living in poverty bordering on destitution," was in the process of being relocated to featureless *faubourgs* (suburbs) or concentrated into areas like Belleville. It is significant that one critic openly described Olympia as *une petite faubourienne*, which is to say a common working-class girl, not as *une cocotte*, the euphemism most commonly used. The hypocrisy of the time may appear to be staggering, but it was a hypocrisy which tolerated its *courtesanes* as long as they hovered above the dirt and grime of reality. Manet broke the silence in this respect so thoroughly that, as T.J. Clark has penetratingly observed, it caused a crisis in the language of art criticism itself. Far from being lost for words, the arbiters of the nation's taste, from the meanest hack to the loftiest intellectual, were volubly falling over each other to avoid describing *Olympia* in traditional terms. Whilst they were busy likening Olympia's skin to India rubber, all but two of them could not or would not see the obvious reference to Titian's *Venus of Urbino* which Manet had once copied in oil at the Uffizi in Florence. The irony of calling a *faubourienne* "Olympia" was not however lost on them; any one of the several licensed brothels in Paris would have offered up a number of women working under the classical *noms de guerre* of Olympia, Lucretia, Calliope or the most popular, Virginia. The chief problem for the critics and public alike was that *Olympia* had appeared *dans le Salon-même*, and this had stretched their tolerance beyond reason and their reason beyond tolerance. The

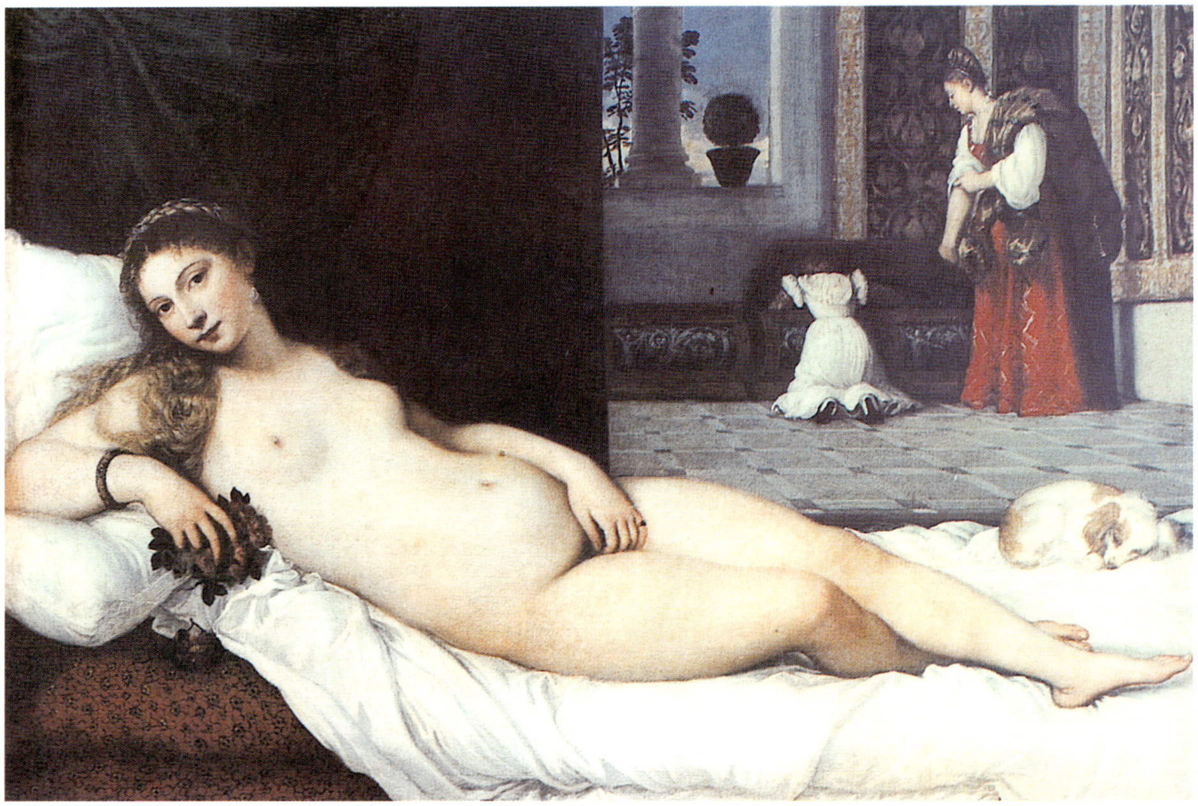

TITIAN
The Venus of Urbino
oil on canvas
c.1538. 120 × 165 cm
An archetype for Olympia. *The compositional similarities between this and Manet's painting are obvious.*

outcry against the painting and its companion *Christ Mocked* was so great that they were eventually both removed to the furthest, darkest corner of the huge Palais de l'Industrie. Manet's fame (or infamy) was assured for the rest of his life. His position as the reluctant champion of the new artists of modern life was affirmed once and for all.

In the world at large life and death went on: across the Atlantic Ocean in the United States President Abraham Lincoln was assassinated, in Paris the First Communist International was held and in England a young mathematics don at Christchurch College Oxford, published a story called *Alice in Wonderland*, under the pseudonym of Lewis Carroll.

Encouraged by his own reception at the Salon, albeit mixed, and the example of Manet, Claude Monet had embarked in 1865 on his own monumental *Luncheon on the Grass*, obviously intended to make a much bigger splash in the Paris art world. Sadly the painting was abandoned in March 1866, when the deadline for that year's Salon expired, and survives only in fragments and an oil sketch of what was once a vast picture almost fifteen feet high by twenty feet wide. Monet left the canvas in Bazille's studio for years as security against unpaid rent before he reclaimed it, by which time part of it had gone mouldy. Monet removed this portion and cut the remainder into two sections. The sketch for the painting indicates that Monet's conception was for a major *plein-air* work, using the relatively novel idea of figures sketched on the spot; these included Sisley, Bazille, and Monet's mistress, Camille Doncieux. By all accounts Monet was obsessed with the massive project and spent the whole of the summer of 1865, as the *Olympia* scandal raged

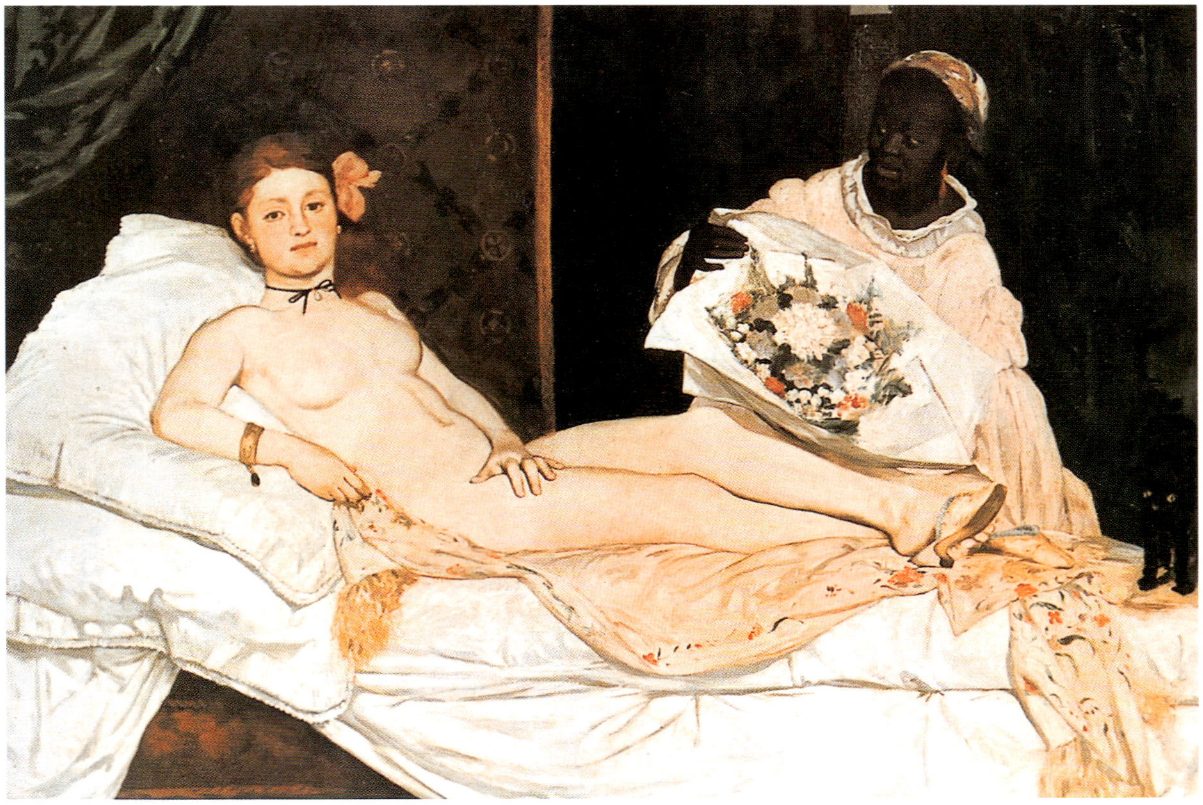

MANET
Olympia
oil on canvas
1863. 130.5 × 190 cm
This painting caused a storm verging on outrage at the Salon of 1865, and established Manet's reputation and fame, though not, perhaps, in the way he had immediately hoped. It has been referred to as a turning point in the history of modern art, combining with Luncheon on the Grass *to entirely subvert the traditional artistic view of the nude, as it was previously encapsulated in the Titian opposite.*

in Paris, devoted to it. He frequently begged Bazille by post to come down to the forest of Fontainebleau and sit for him. Throughout his work on the painting Monet was harrassed: firstly he was hampered by an injury to his leg in 1865 and then, having moved to Bazille's Paris studio in order to finish the picture for the 1866 Salon, he was forced to leave the studio and move across the river to another. Unable to complete the painting, Monet furiously produced (in four days) a full-length portrait of Camille known as *The Woman in the Green Dress* (*Femme en vert*), which in turn proved a success at the Salon.

Luncheon on the Grass was a prodigious undertaking in every respect; and as Andrew Forge has suggested, "It was something as different from Courbet's earthy social analysis as it was from Manet's sophisticated reflections on the erotic in modern life.

MONET
Luncheon on the Grass
oil on canvas
1865–66. 130 × 181 cm
A sketch of the unfinished work.

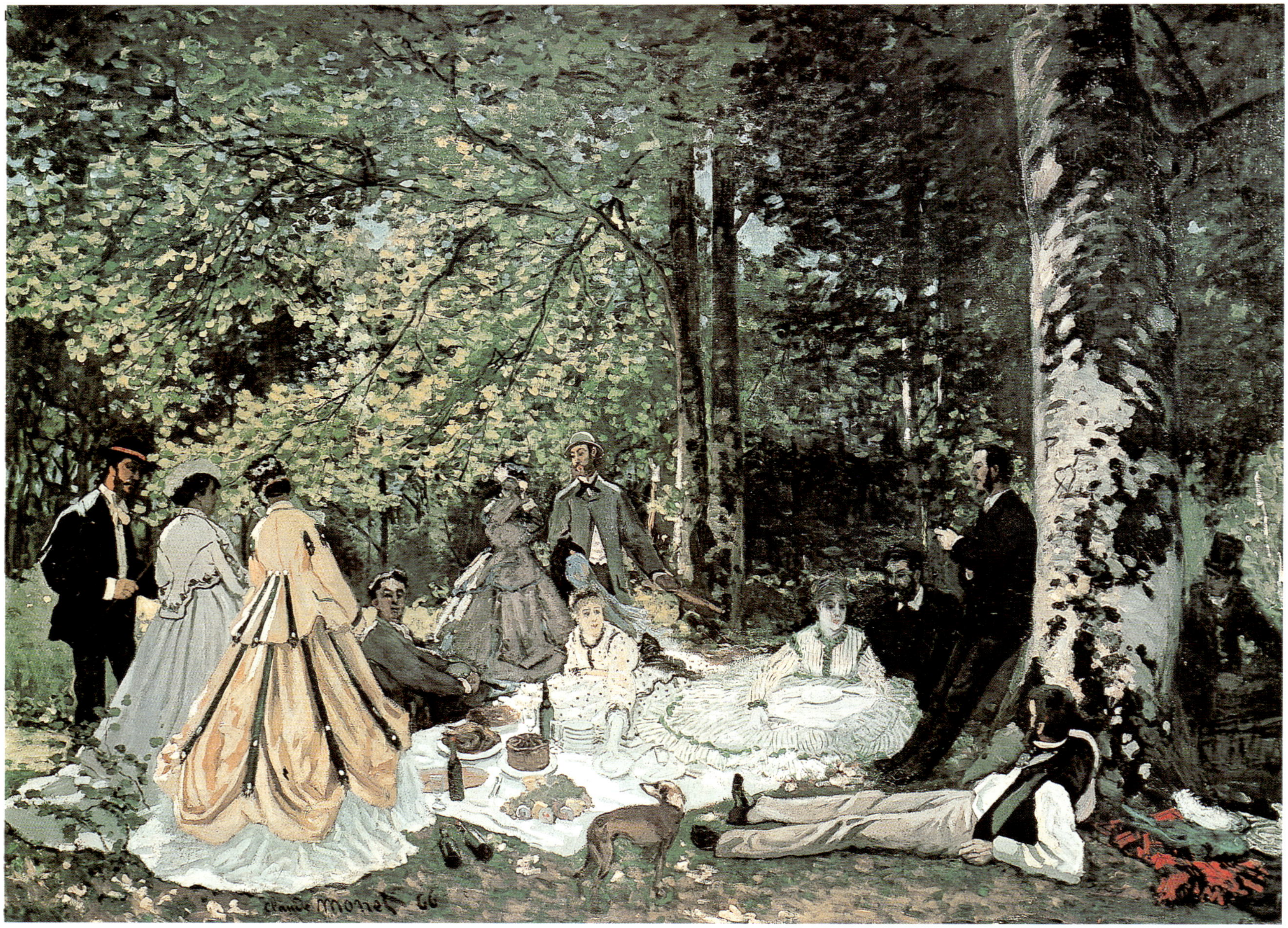

Monet was trying to present on an exhibition scale that particular area of painting that was specific to the direct study. He was trying to monumentalize the syntax of a sketch."

Undaunted by his failure to complete *Luncheon on the Grass*, in early 1866 Monet embarked on another large picture, nine feet by six feet in size, the *Women in the Garden* (*Femmes dans un jardin*). He had rented a house near Paris and dug a trench for the painting to be lowered into by pulleys so that he could work without moving his position relative to the subjects in front of him. The idea, ridiculed by Courbet, was to complete the whole picture *en plein-air*. The painting was finished but the Salon of 1867 rejected it, a bitter blow to Monet.

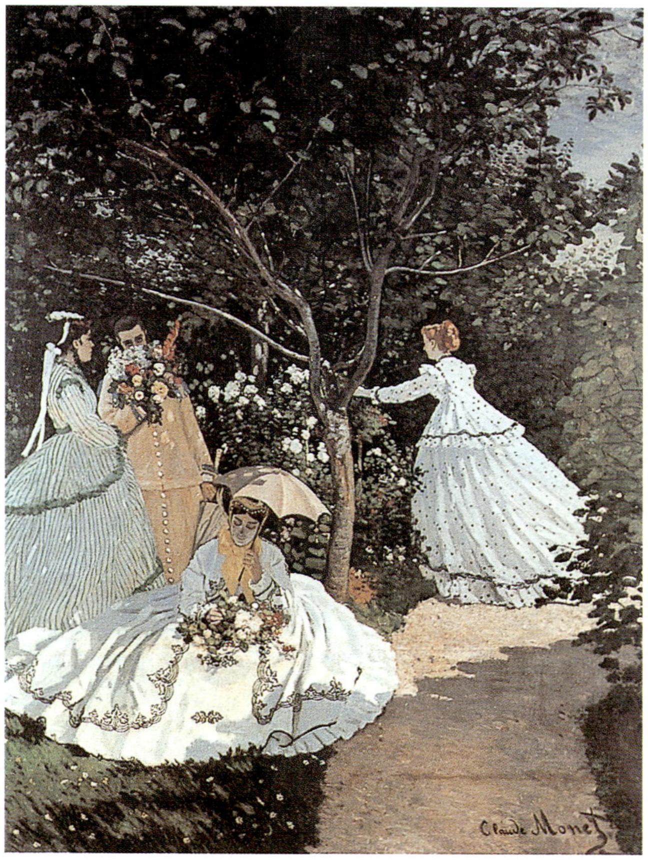

MONET
Women in the Garden
oil on canvas
1865–66. 418 × 150 cm
This is Monet's last attempt at a large-scale figure composition. Two possible sources for the picture's inspiration are thought to have been a photograph of his friend Bazille's sisters and a costume illustration from a fashion magazine. Camille posed for no less than three of the figures.

THE BATIGNOLLES GROUP

The year 1866 saw the invention of dynamite by Alfred Nobel. In France Napoleon III ordered the withdrawal of his forces from Mexico, a move that was to have disastrous consequences for the puppet Emperor Maximilian. In his own salvo of explosive prose, Zola published an article entitled "Mon Salon en L'Evènement" defending the work of Cézanne, Bazille, Monet, and Pissarro and supporting a letter Cézanne had written to the Comte de Nieuwerkerke demanding another Salon des Refusés. In it Cézanne had felt obliged to "content myself with pointing out to you again that I cannot accept the unlawful judgement of colleagues to whom I have not personally given the task of assessing me . . . I wish to make a direct appeal to the public and have my work exhibited without any restriction."

A complex network of relationships between Monet, Pissarro, Bazille, Cézanne, Guillaumin, Morisot, Renoir, Sisley, Manet, and Degas had already begun to form by this point. During the private view of the 1866 Salon Monet and Bazille had encountered Manet and his entourage leaving the exhibition. Monet's signature on his *Woman in the Green Dress* had been mistaken for Manet's, who had entered the Salon to a chorus of acclaim for his supposed work. Monet recounted the story in 1900 to *Le Temps*:

> . . . imagine his consternation when he discovered that the picture about which he was being congratulated was actually by me! The saddest part of all was that on leaving the Salon he came across a group which included Bazille and me. "How goes it?" one of them asked. "Awful," replied Manet, "I am digusted. I have been complimented on a painting which is not mine."

MONET
Quays of Paris
oil on canvas
1866–67. 66 × 94 cm
Right The Impressionists took quickly to painting cityscapes from windows high above the streets. Apart from the interesting perspective such a position offered, it was certainly much more comfortable than painting outdoors and they were not disturbed by passers-by.

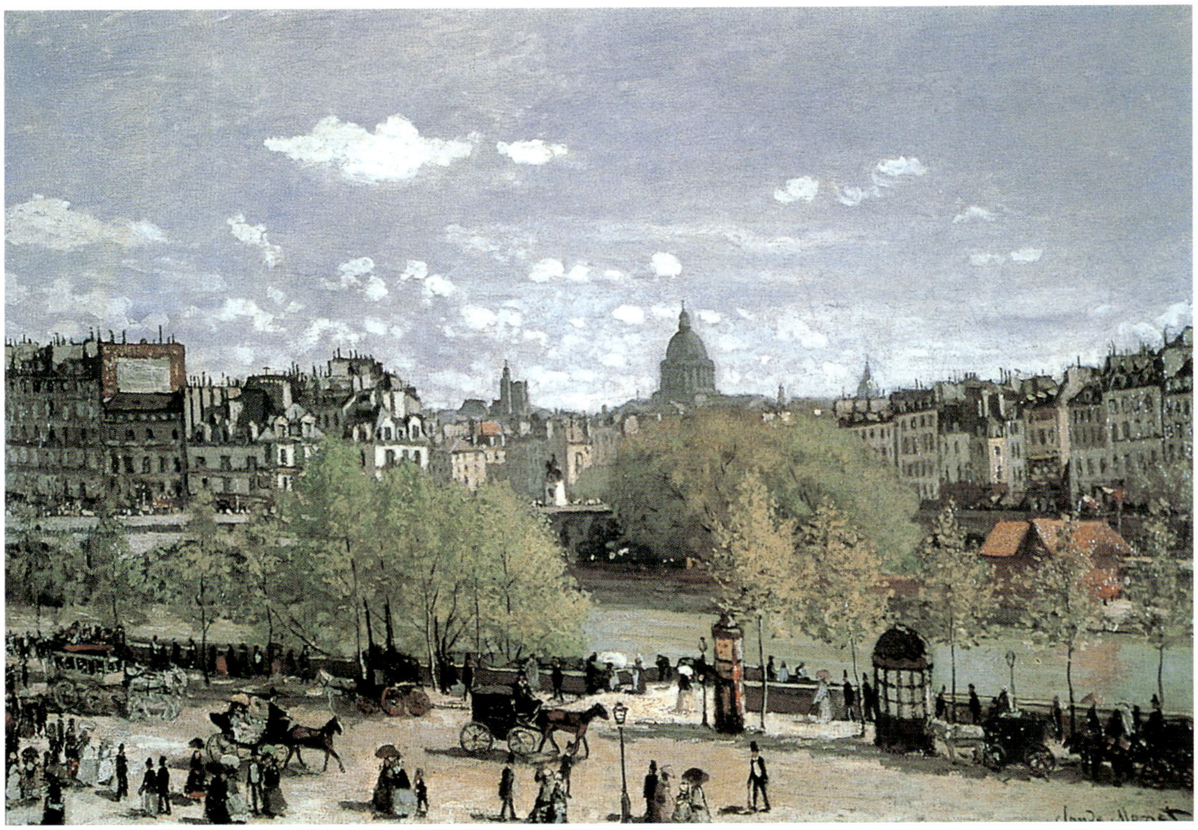

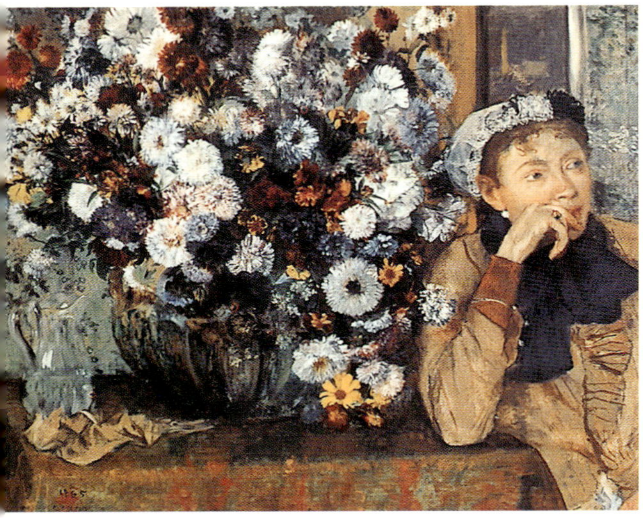

DEGAS
Woman with Chrysanthemums
oil on canvas
1865. 71 × 92 cm
Above Although he used a photograph to make this picture, Degas also made exhaustive preliminary studies from life.

The next day Manet is supposed to have refused to be introduced to Monet because he was still bitter about Monet's purely unintentional slight on the young master. But as Monet recalled:

> It was only in 1869 that I saw him again, and then we at once became firm friends. At our first meeting he invited me to join him every evening at a café in the Batignolles district where he and his friends gathered at the end of the day to talk. There I met Fantin-Latour, Cézanne, Degas . . . the art critic Duranty, Emile Zola and many others. For my part I used to take Sisley, Bazille, and Renoir there. Nothing could have been more interesting than the discussions we had, with their perpetual clash of opinions. They kept our wits sharpened, encouraged us to press ahead with our own experiments, and provided us with the enthusiasm to keep on painting for weeks on end until our ideas became clear and coherent . . . we emerged more finely tempered, our resolve firmer, our thoughts clearer and less confused.

1866 marks the beginnings of what came to be known as the Batignolles Group. Whilst Monet, Bazille, Renoir, Sisley, and Pissarro were working in the country, the Batignolles area of Paris was becoming a focus of artistic attention. During Haussmannization this area of Paris had expanded greatly, along with the large new boulevard des Batignolles. Between 1842 and 1866 the population of the district had increased from 15,000 to 200,000. Its position away from the centre of the city but close to the Gare St Lazare made it

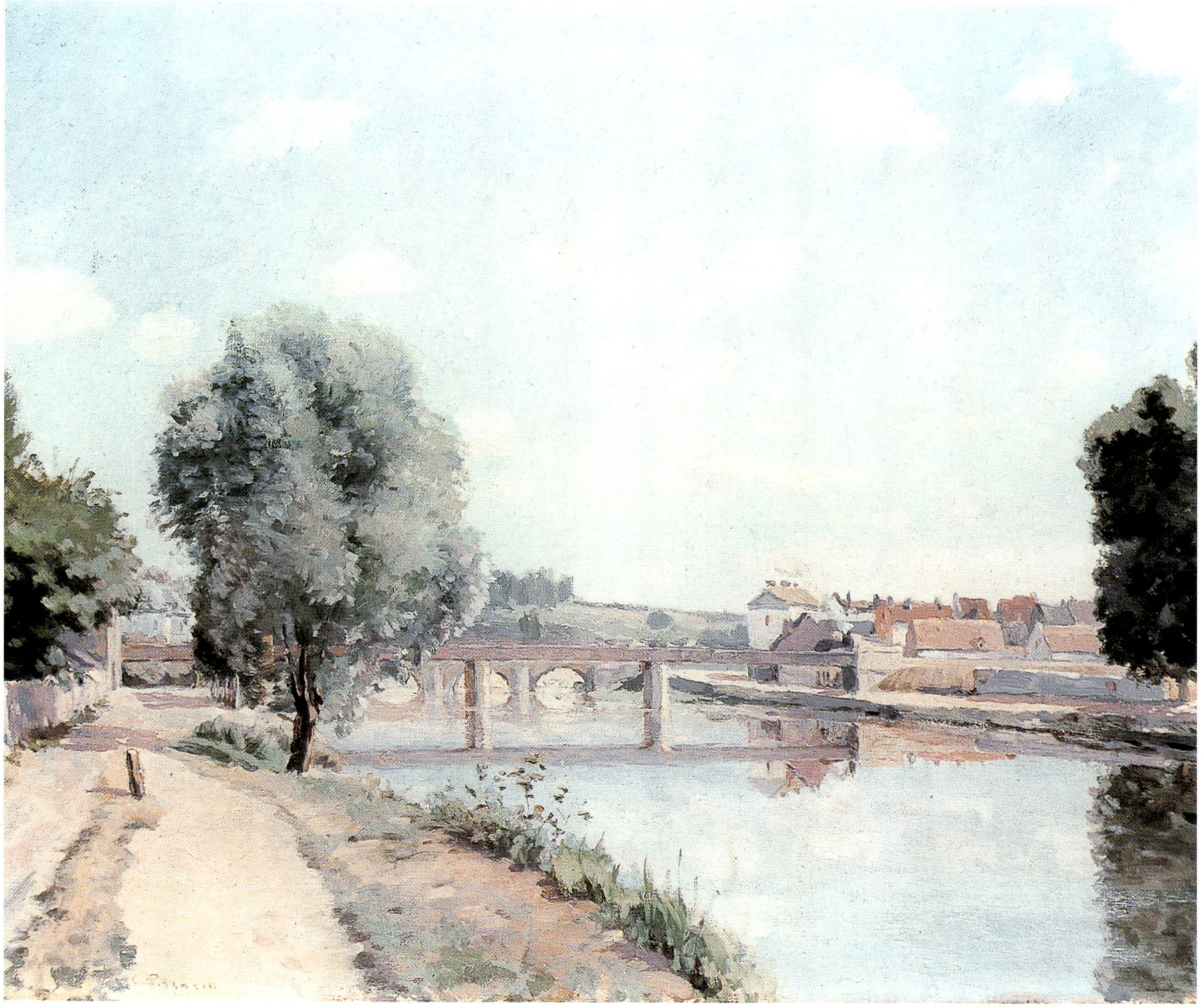

popular. The buildings were modern, comfortably bourgeois and the area had become residential but still affordable. A letter of Renoir's to his parents a couple of years later when he and Bazille lived in the rue de la Paix confirms this, "Tell Mama not to worry, the Batignolles is a quiet area and cheaper than the rest of Paris."

Parts of the old village of Batignolles remained, populated by poor immigrants, rag-pickers, and prostitutes, amongst whom Manet found some of his subjects and models. Manet had lived there for some time at various addresses and had recently begun to haunt the Café Guerbois at 11 rue des Batignolles. During the next three years practically everyone of importance to Impressionism began to gather there in the evenings – Thursday nights were the favourite – to talk about art and literature. If Gleyre's atelier had been the nursery of the *plein-air* Impressionists, the Café Guerbois was undoubtedly its common

PISSARRO
The Railway Bridge at Pontoise
oil on canvas
c.1865. 50 × 65 cm
Pissarro and his family moved to live in Pontoise, a village on the river Oise (seen here) near Auvers, in 1867, about two years after this picture was painted.

room. Anyone looking for the artistic avant-garde in Paris would need go no further than the Café Guerbois, one of many cafés that had sprung up in the new Paris of wide pavements and rolling boulevards. Manet was certainly the first amongst his peers and held court with aplomb. The writer and critic of Impressionism Armand Silvestre described Manet as a revolutionary with the manners of a perfect gentleman: "he had in the extraordinary vivacity of his gaze and the mocking expression on his lips a very strong dose of the Parisian street urchin. He had a marvellous command of the annihilating and devastating phrase." Yet he still yearned for official recognition.

1867–1868: LA VILLE LUMIÈRE

The year 1867 brought with it crisis for the Second Empire. Since the proclamation of Napoleon III as Emperor in 1852 France had spent itself into a prosperity that was in essence conservative and favoured the middle and upper classes. The new boulevards and buildings of Paris were symbolic of this prosperity, as were the resorts springing up on the Normandy coast. But they had all been constructed on credit and the equivalent of

BELOW Birds-eye view of the World Exhibition of 1867.

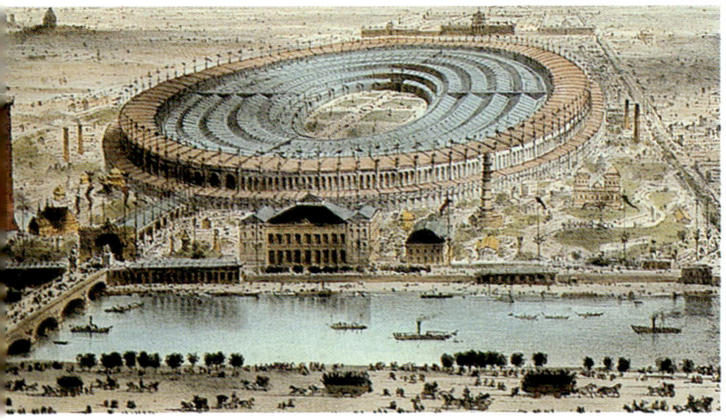

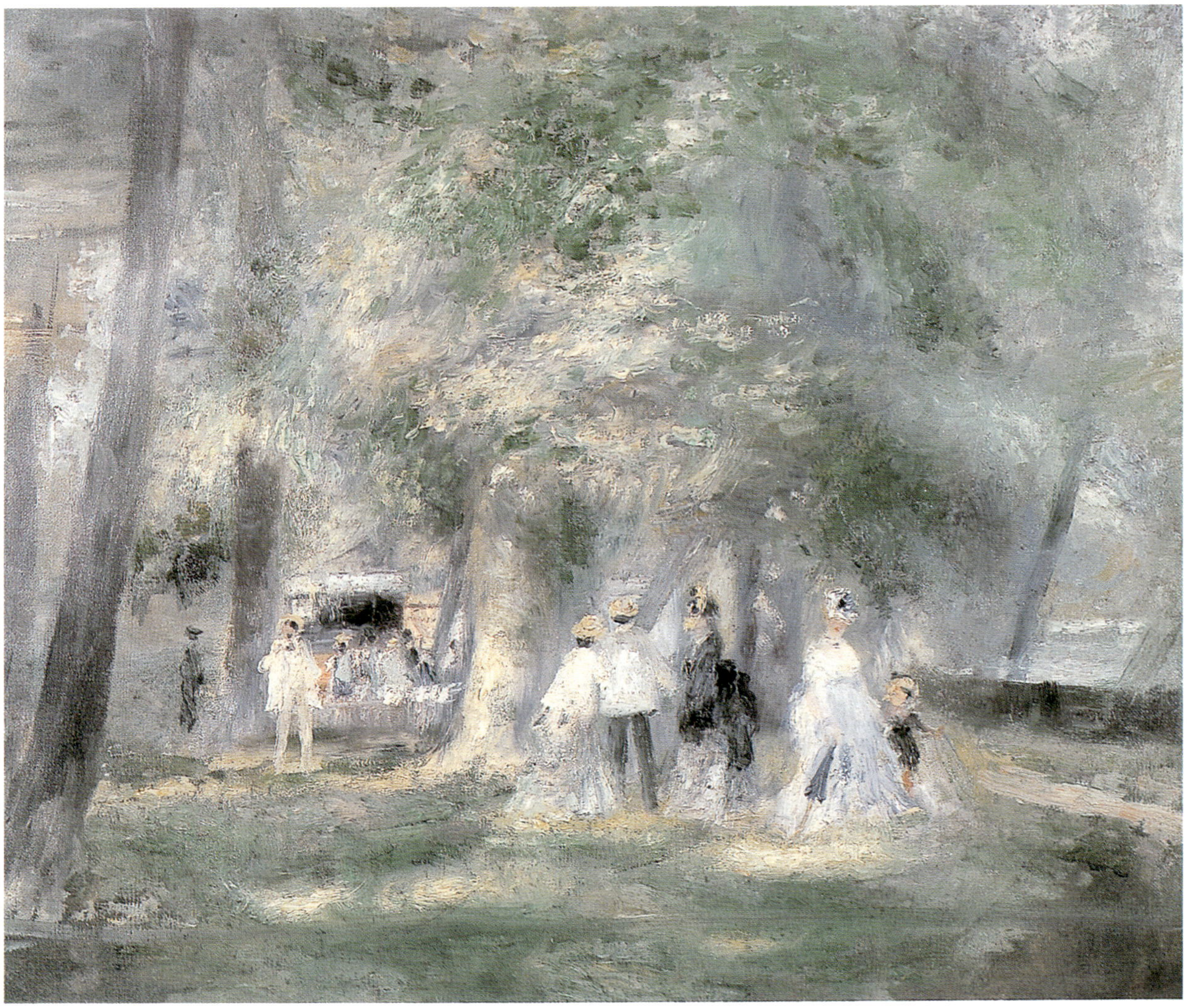

RENOIR
The Park of St Cloud
oil on canvas
1866. 50 × 61 cm
RIGHT An early, surprisingly impressionistic painting by Renoir painted three years before the work with Monet at La Grenouillère.

the modern junk bond. In 1866 the Crédit Mobilier, which had financed a great part of the new Empire, found itself with a monumental liquidity problem. Its shares fell the next year from 1,982 francs to just 140 francs. The Mexican fiasco ended with the death of Maximilian who was abandoned by the French and executed by rebels. Manet, who rightly saw this crisis as a failure of imperial politics, began a painting of the execution, making use of photographs, but also basing part of its composition on Goya's *The Third of May* which he had seen in Madrid in 1865. He was given to understand by the Salon that it would not be admitted on the grounds of its political sensitivity. A lithograph of the picture was officially banned by the censors.

Elsewhere in the world tensions ran high. In an attempt to help the Papal States French battalions were dispatched to Rome to defend them against the revolutionary Garibaldi. As usual relations with Prussia were tense. In January Napoleon III had announced constitutional changes with a move towards representative government for the Empire, but it was to be of no avail. The American Civil War had disrupted cotton trade, and the vineyards were suffering from the phylloxera disease which had appeared in 1863 and taken hold, steadily reducing the crop. The outward success of the Second Empire had, as Alastair Horne claims, "blinded French eyes to the realities beneath the surface. Syphilis was rampant and many of the great Frenchmen of the age were to die of it; Maupassant, Jules Goncourt, Dumas *fils*, Baudelaire [in 1867], and Manet. The dread disease was symptomatic of the Second Empire itself; on the surface, all gaiety and light; below, sombre purulence, decay, and ultimately death."

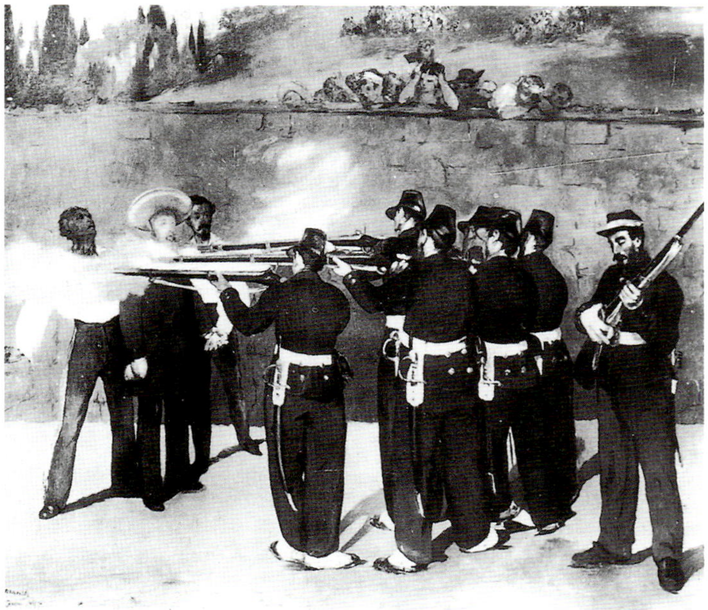

MANET
The Execution of the Emperor Maximilian
Left Manet was making a habit at this time of challenging the sensibilities of the Salon, which took the precaution of telling him well in advance that this painting would not even be considered due to its political content. Manet drew inspiration for the work from Goya's The Third of May, *which he had seen in Madrid.*

GOYA
The Third of May
oil on canvas
1814. 266 × 345 cm
Below

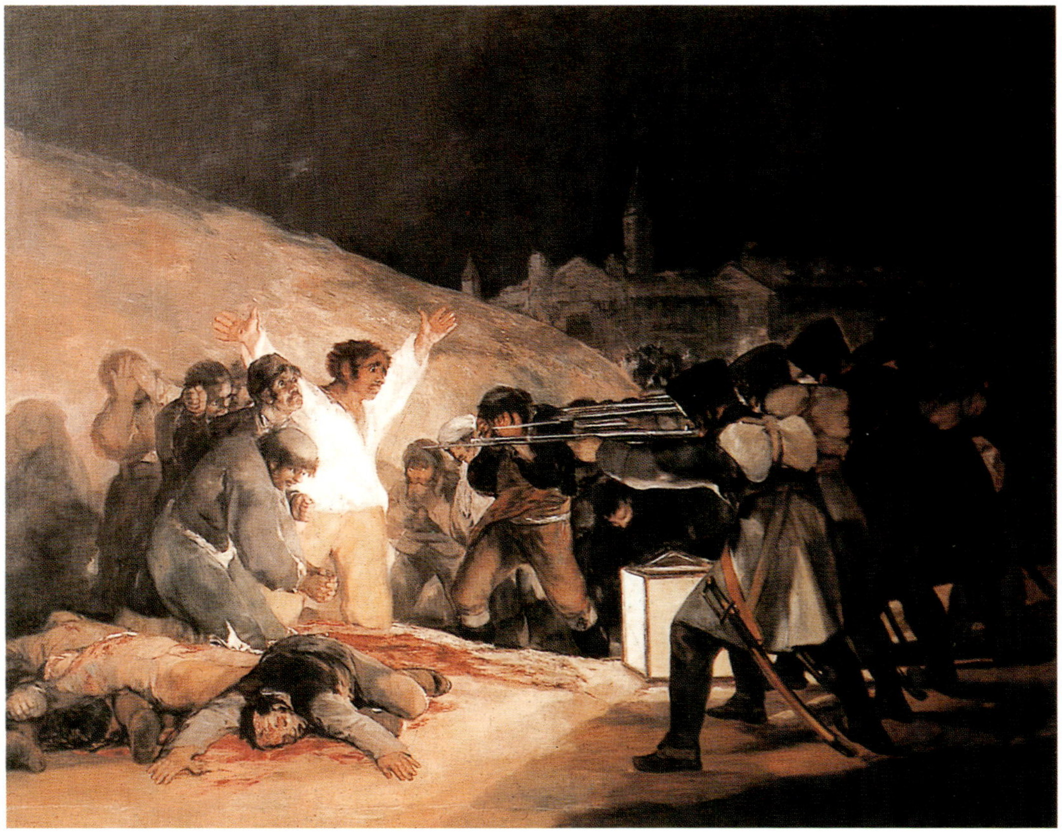

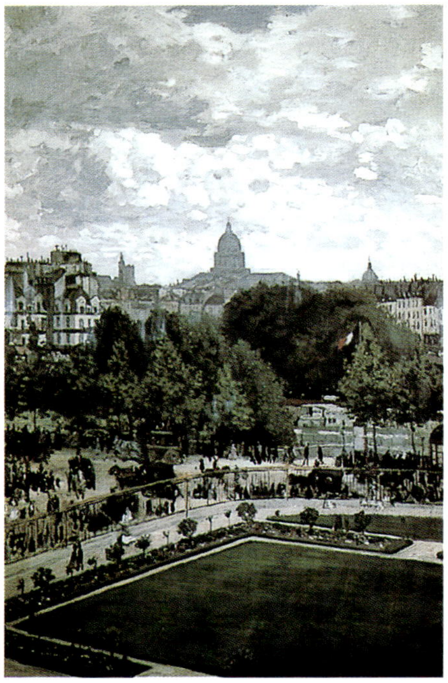

MONET
The Garden of the Princess
oil on canvas
1867. 92 × 62 cm
ABOVE This was one of three works that the Louvre allowed Monet to paint on its balcony. It shows the influence of photography in the angle of the view and the seemingly arbitrary points at which the subject is cut off by its framing.

A visitor to Paris in the summer of 1867, and there were thousands, would have been hard pressed to believe all this doom, for the second Exposition Universelle had taken over a city which was already crammed with hundreds of theatres and cafés, all full of Parisians enjoying themselves. Visitors to the Prussian display of armaments marvelled at the Krupp artillery pieces. The implements of modern warfare certainly looked impressive and if the French had taken more stock of them they might have thought twice about engaging the Prussians in battle a couple of years later. A picture by Manet painted at the time, *View of the Paris World's Fair* (*Vue de Paris pendant l'Exposition Universelle*) shows the French and English lighthouses erected for the Fair and the photographer Nadar's balloon, known as "The Giant", hovering over the city. Renoir's *Champs-Elysées during the Paris Fair of 1867* (*Les Champs-Elysées pendant l'Exposition Universelle de 1867*) depicts leisurely strollers; the women wear summer dresses, the sky is temptingly blue with fluffy clouds. In the background a *tricouleur* flies over the Palais de l'Industrie which had been built for the previous Exposition Universelle when Pissarro had marvelled at the Corots and when Courbet's Realist Pavilion had challenged the establishment.

The same was to occur in 1867. Again Courbet erected a pavilion to rival the official Salon, and Manet, who had boycotted the Salon in disgust at having been rejected again, did the same. Pressure for another Salon des Refusés was strong: Monet, Renoir, Pissarro, Sisley, Jongkind, Manet, and Daubigny had all signed a petition to the authorities requesting one, but the *refusés* request was rejected. Unfortunately, Manet's pavilion did scant business. Times were getting harder for the avant-garde painters. The arbitrariness of the Salon juries who changed their views on what was acceptable from year to year was a cause of intense frustration. In May Bazille had written to his parents outlining a plan which

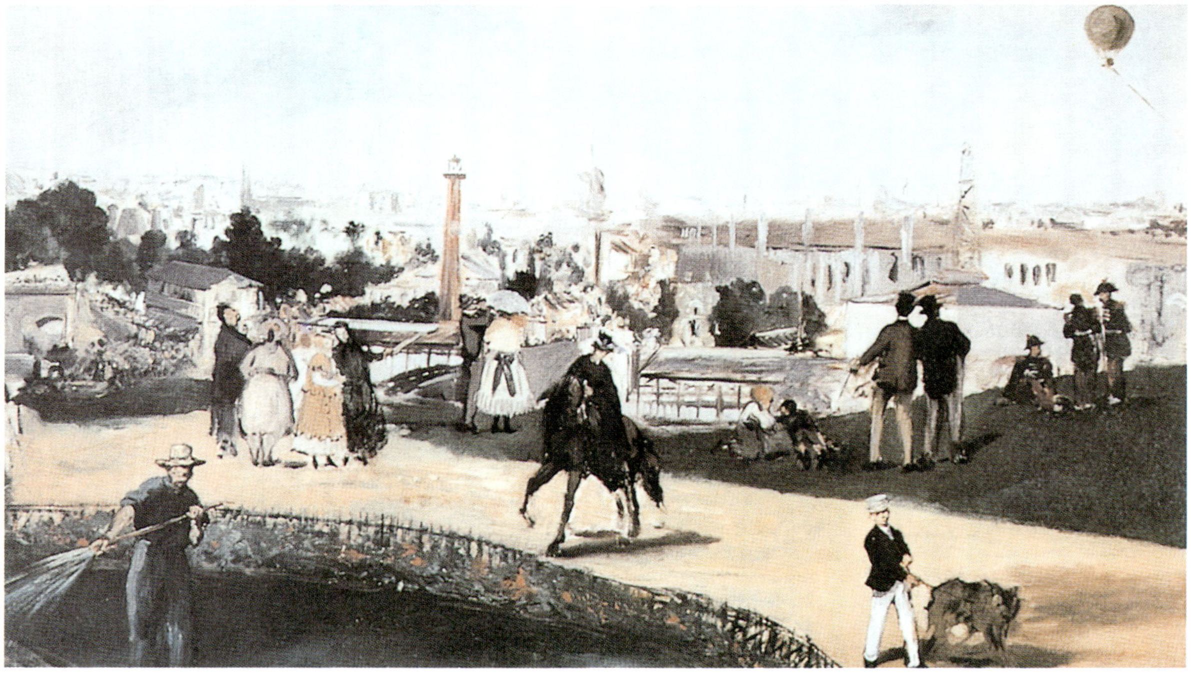

MANET
The World's Fair in Paris
oil on canvas
1867. 108 × 196 cm
RIGHT Manet's picture shows a cross-section of Parisian society, from the gentlewoman on her morning ride, to the lower-class figures on the grass. Nadar's famous balloon hovers above the scene.

had emerged among the group to:

> . . . rent a big studio every year where we will be able to show as many of our paintings as we want. We will invite the painters we like to send paintings. Courbet, Corot, Diaz, Daubigny and many others with whom you may not be familiar have promised to send their work and strongly approve of the idea. With the latter, and Monet who is better than all of us, we are sure to succeed.

The plan came to nothing; the funds to mount the exhibition could not be found amongst the contributors, but this was essentially the first attempt to launch the *Société anonyme des artistes peintres, sculpteurs, graveurs, etc*, which upstaged the Salon of 1874.

In the meantime Claude Monet had gained permission from the Louvre to paint from one of its second floor balconies. One of the three pictures that resulted is the *Garden of the Princess* (*Le Jardin de la princesse*). This, and the views of the *Quai du Louvre*, and *Saint-Germain l'Auxerrois* mark what Forge has called "crucial experiments in which [Monet] seems to be pushing the principles of Realism to their furthest limits." The *Garden of the Princess* indicates a new vision of the city using the technique Monet had been developing in his landscapes and the two large-scale figure paintings. The angle of the view shows the influence of the framing and distortive effects of photography which tend to "wrap" the field of vision at the edges and cut off the composition at arbitrary points producing a vertiginous sense of height, distance, and space. Monet's landscapist's eye, however, shows the crowds down below as a mobile element of the cityscape rendered with the swift brushstrokes later to be denounced as "tongue-lickings". The much altered topography of Paris attracted many of Monet's friends. They could also hope to sell paintings of the new Haussmann boulevards which were not controversial subjects.

Visitors to the Exposition Universelle were seduced and intrigued that year by the exhibition of Japanese prints and artefacts which soon launched an enduring fashion for all things Japanese. Many artists were influenced by the composition of these prints, especially Degas, like Whistler before him. Japanese prints had trickled in to Europe from the 1850s, mainly used to wrap artefacts.

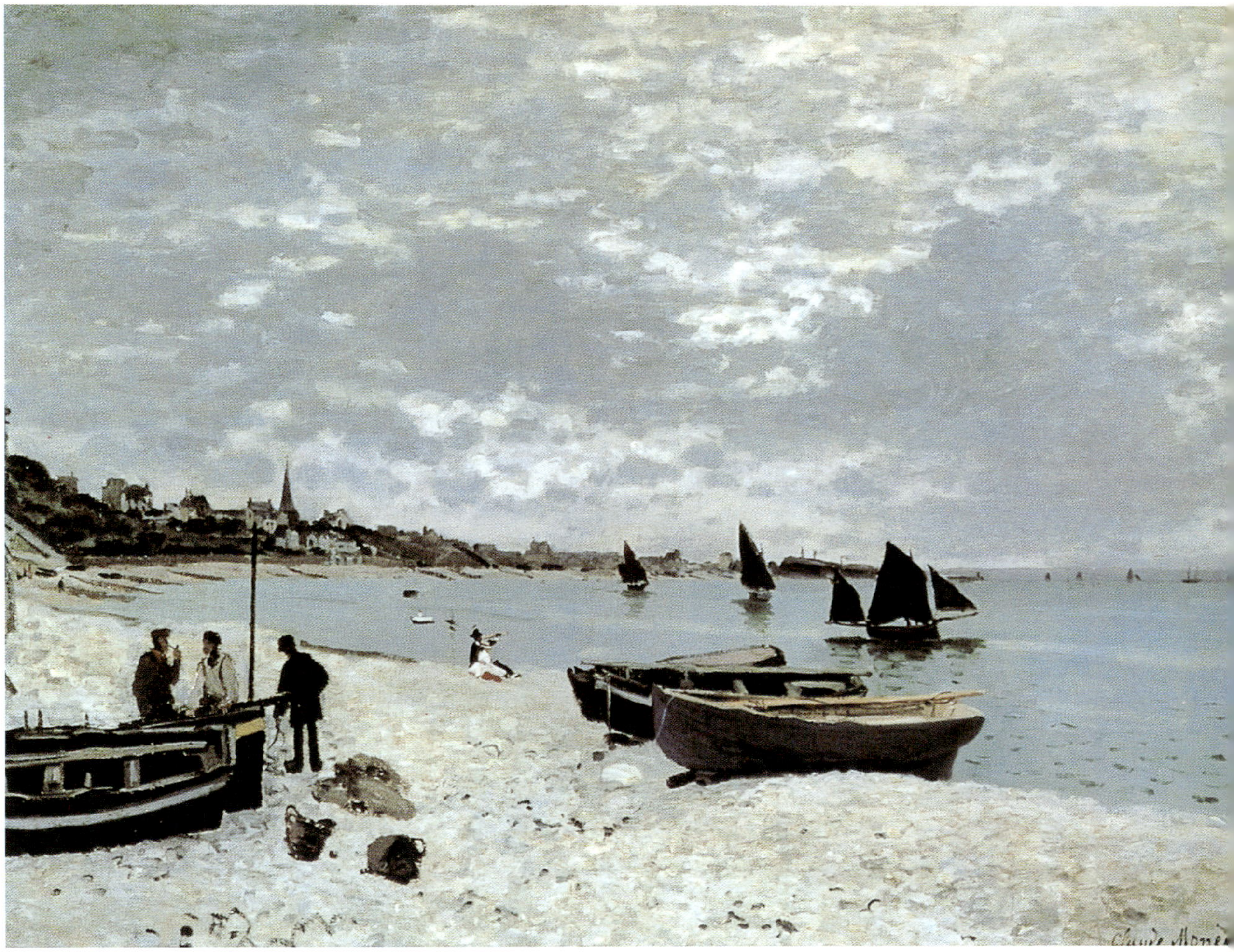

MONET
Beach at Sainte-Adresse
oil on canvas
c.1867. 75 × 101 cm
Monet never tired of painting the coast of Normandy in his youth and he worked along this stretch of coastline nearly all his life.

RENOIR
Rose Field
oil on canvas
Undated. 33 × 46.5 cm
Right Renoir's loose style was at the vanguard of Impressionism, but the artist later found that it was too limiting.

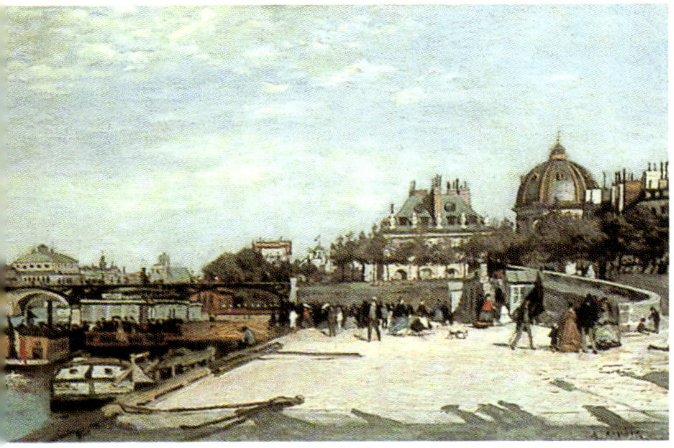

RENOIR
Le Pont des Arts, Paris
oil on canvas
1867. 62 × 100 cm
Above This was the new Paris with the recently cleared embankments where houses had stood before.

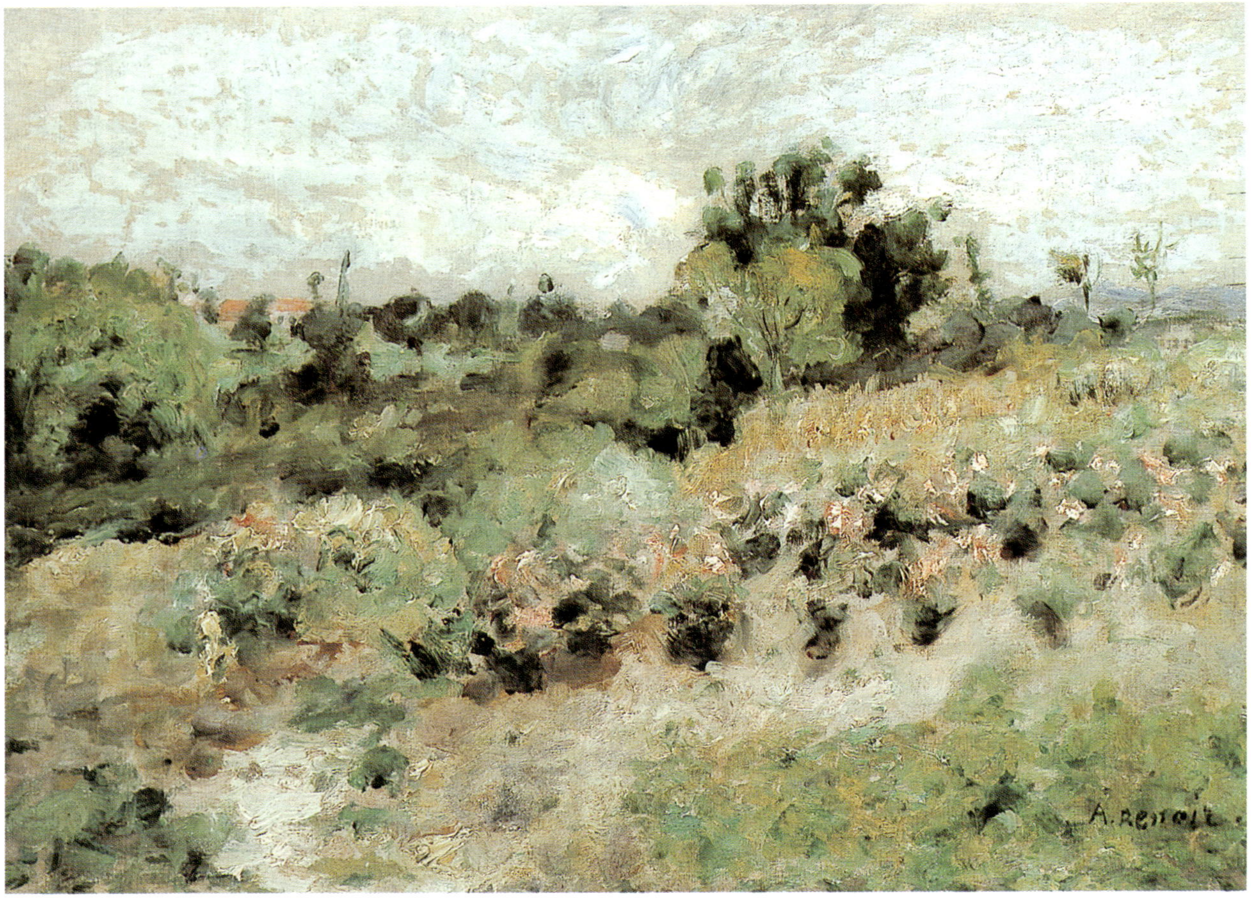

Following several centuries of seclusion, at last Japan opened its doors to the West in 1867, and two shops in Paris were selling this new exotica. The studios of Whistler, Manet, Degas, and Monet were graced with Japanese china, fans, and prints, and these feature in several later paintings. Castagnary even called the Batignolles Group "the Japanese of painting". Monet said, that "[the Japanese] refinement of taste has always pleased me, and I approve of their aesthetic doctrine which evokes the presence of something by a shadow; and the whole by means of a fragment." Degas' work was increasingly reinforced by the Japanese print masters' sense of space and (to Western eyes) unusual perspectives and framings, as well as their subject matter which was often urban and refined. This new view was much in keeping with Degas' artistic interests.

Napoleon III's last years in power were marked by an increasing desire on his part to free up the country's moribund political and social system. Accordingly, in 1868 new laws allowed limited freedom of the press and the right to assembly for the first time since the First Republic. In a move symptomatic of the decline of the Second Empire, Baron Haussmann was forced to approach the ruling Legislative Body and request a loan to pay for the rebuilding of Paris which amounted to a quarter of the whole French budget. Haussmann was almost finished, but so was Paris.

Manet, Degas, Morisot, Pissarro, Monet, Sisley, and Bazille all made it into the Salon of 1868 after the dismal failure of the previous year and they had François Daubigny to thank because he had been invited to sit on the jury. Daubigny's inclusion was a sign that *plein-airisme* had finally been accepted by the Salon as a legitimate method of painting, although this did not make it any easier for the avant-garde. To artists like Manet, Bazille, and Degas, who were reasonably wealthy, not selling their work did not ultimately mean starvation.

Monet himself had none of the luxuries of a Manet or a Bazille; he was forced to sell or starve, and since he had few buyers in the late 1860s the latter fate stared him and his wife relentlessly in the face. In 1867 he had been forced by his family (on whom he relied for an allowance) to abandon Camille, then pregnant with a son, Jean. In June 1868 Monet had to ask Bazille (once again) to help him out by sending Camille some money to support herself and the child. In his begging letter he signs himself, "Your loyal and tormented friend," and adds curtly and ominously, "I was so upset yesterday that I was foolish enough to throw myself into the water. Fortunately no harm was done." It seems that Monet was too much in love with painting and life to make a serious attempt at suicide even though his despair was deep.

Despite the collapse of the Crédit Foncier and Haussmann's exorbitant claims on the national budget, *la ville lumière* thrived. Paris in the early part of 1868 was depicted with increasing acuity and originality by artists. Degas, the most consistent of the "slice of life" painters, spent all of his time in the streets, cafés, theatres, and concert halls of the city; noting, sketching, and observing with a sharp eye the effervescent activity around him. Not a *plein-airiste* by any stretch of the imagination, he composed his pictures very carefully *post hoc* in the studio. His *Orchestra of the Paris Opera* (*L'Orchestre de l'Opéra de Paris*) of 1868–69 is an excellent example of both his devotion to Ingres, his finely detailed technique and a thoroughly modern sense of composition: again the influence of photography is evident, with the figures cropped by the edges of the painting and the double-bassist turning his back to us looking at a conductor "out of shot". One of the second violinists is even captured gazing up at the incandescent tutus of the ballerinas, obviously bored with his part.

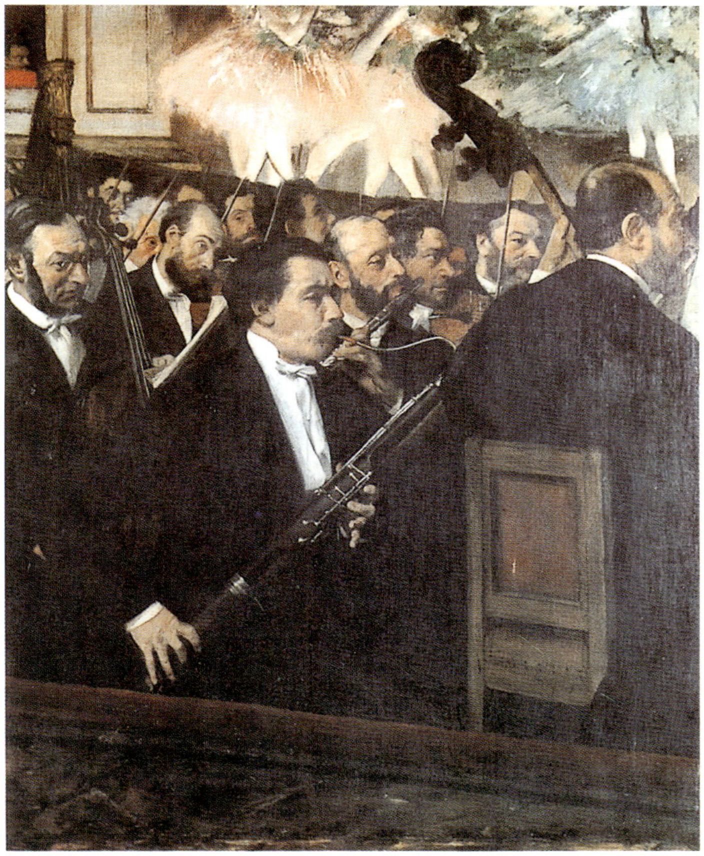

DEGAS
Orchestra of the Paris Opera
oil on canvas
1868–69. 56.5 × 46 cm
A fine example of the new theory of composition that the Impressionists were beginning to shape. The figures are caught as though in a photograph – cut off at seemingly random points, and standing at odd angles to the artist. This is very different from the highly stylized, carefully posed, and fully framed tableaux of the classical schools, and represented a radical departure.

Away from the bustle of the city, Bazille was succeeding to a great extent in meshing the forms of landscape and figure painting which had been started and abandoned by Monet. *View of the Village* (*Paysage avec un village*) and *The Family Reunion* (*La Réunion de*

Famille) show the influence of Manet and Monet, but taking a firm grip on the elements of the pictures. Bazille is especially fearless in the use of bright colours applied in flat areas. Berthe Morisot said of the *View*, "He is seeking what we have all so often sought: how to place a figure in outdoor surroundings. This time I think he has succeeded."

Whilst Monet, Renoir, Bazille, and Sisley had been working in and around Paris and on the coast, Camille Pissarro, (older than them by ten years and yet stylistically much more a part of their generation than Manet or Degas), had been living in Pontoise, a town to the northwest of Paris where in 1866 he had settled with his mistress, Julie Vellay. His frequent visits to Paris included the Café Guerbois where he expressed himself openly and eloquently in matters of art and politics: he was a radical republican, an anarchist in fact. Thanks to Daubigny two of Pissarro's views of the *Hermitage at Pontoise* (*L'Ermitage à Pontoise*) were shown at the Salons of 1868 and 1869. They were attacked as being vulgar, coarse, primitive daubings. The paint is certainly applied with vigour and Pissarro's denial of detail and his concentration on structure using planes of colour prefigures the later work of Cézanne. But Zola considered that "the originality here is deeply human, not derived from a mere facility of hand or a falsification of nature: it stems from the temperament of the painter himself and comprises a feeling for truth resulting from an inner conviction."

MANET
Study for The Balcony
pencil and wash on paper
1868.
BELOW Manet was a diligent technician, and spent endless days in the Louvre copying the works of the great masters when he was a student at Couture's atelier. His wish to evolve from the masters, rather than to reject them, is reflected here in his use of the classical methodology of producing a careful study for a larger work.

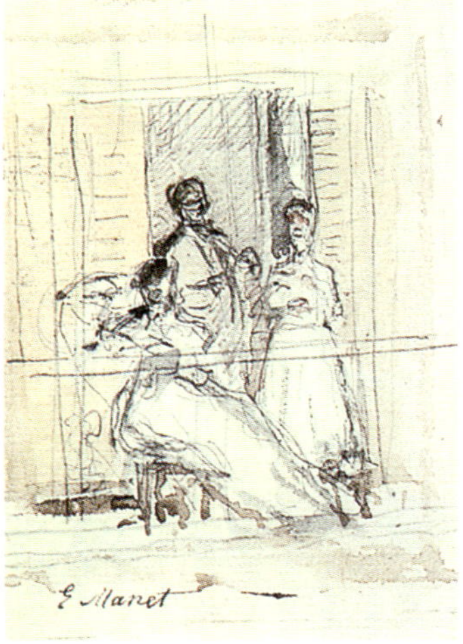

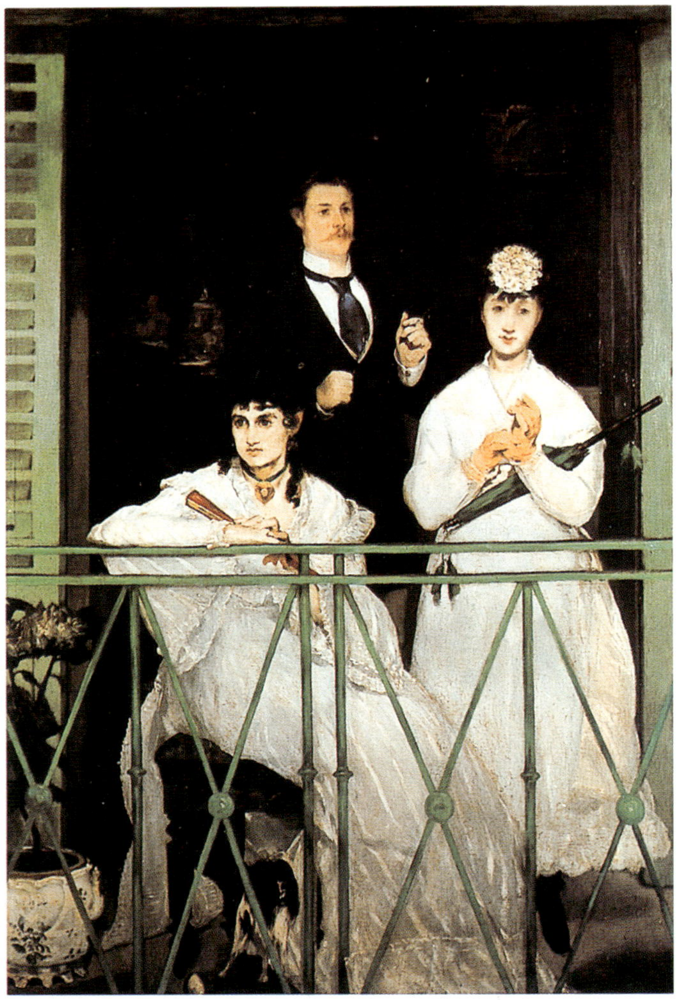

MANET
The Balcony
oil on canvas
1868–69. 170 × 124 cm
RIGHT Berthe Morisot had met Manet two months before she posed for this painting. Their friendship lasted till his death in 1883.

1869: "ROTTEN SKETCHES"

The French elections of May 1869 produced a massive upsurge of support for the opposition parties – mostly varying shades of republicanism. Government control of the Legislative Body was sharply reduced and the Prime Minister was forced to resign. Haussmann's fortunes continued to wane as his opponents questioned the exorbitantly high cost of his rebuilding of Paris. Napoleon III's "Liberal Empire" was in its last days. A left-wing slogan frequently heard on the streets of the big cities was "Moderation is Death".

The convulsive politics of the Empire must have been on the agenda at the Café Guerbois, but of more prurient interest may well have been the erroneous gossip amorously linking Manet and Berthe Morisot who had been introduced to the clique via Fantin-Latour. At this stage gentlewomen were not in the habit

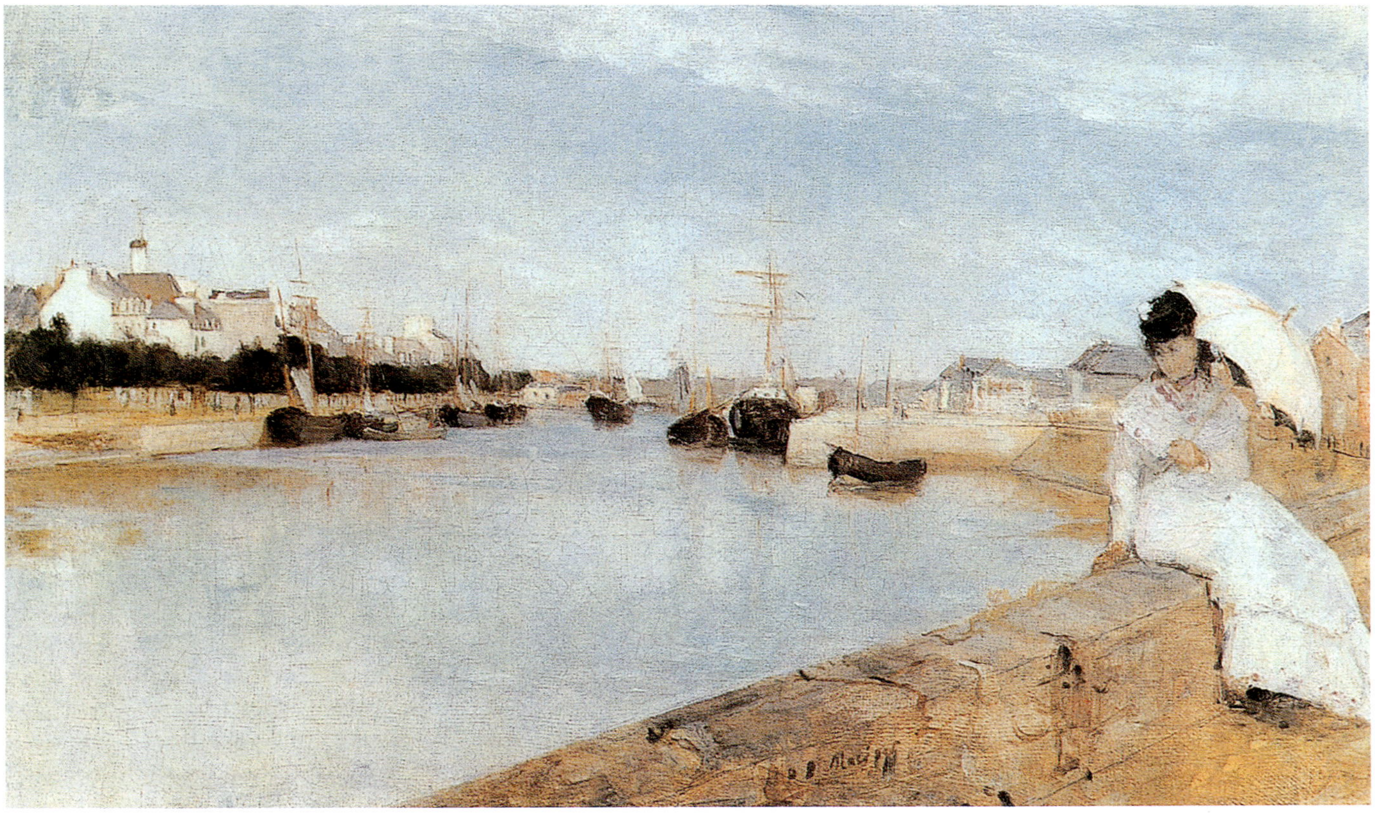

MORISOT
The Harbour of Lorient, Brittany
oil on canvas
1869. 43.5 × 73 cm
Morisot was visiting her sister, who posed for her here.

of frequenting gentlemen's café societies, so Morisot's acquaintance with Manet would have been consolidated outside the auspices of the Café Guerbois, and thus she would have been denied what Monet had called the "constant clash of opinions" and the lapidary wit-sharpening of Thursday nights.

Nevertheless Manet and Morisot had become very close – Manet's main exhibit at the 1869 Salon shows a moody Berthe on *The Balcony* (*Le Balcon*), for which she had posed a few months after they had met at the Louvre, where she was also a copyist. Manet's ponderous influence on Berthe can be seen in a portrait of her sister, Edma, and her mother which Manet had retouched into what Berthe called "the prettiest little caricature". For her part Berthe, who had been brought up by Corot and Daubigny as a *plein-airiste*, encouraged Manet to take to the outdoors and lighten his otherwise sombre palette. At this time another woman painter, Eva Gonzalès, the daughter of a novelist, appeared on Manet's horizon and much to Berthe Morisot's dismay he agreed to take Eva as his pupil – the first and last time he chose to teach.

In the spring of 1869 Monet had installed himself in the village of Saint-Michel near Bougival. This was an increasingly popular resort on the Seine linked to Paris by the Paris–Saint-Germain railway and the stop at Chatou. This area had long been a retreat for landscapists such as Corot. Pissarro had meanwhile moved from Pontoise to nearby Louveciennes, where Renoir was staying with him. At a branch of the Seine near Croissy there was a popular floating restaurant and bathing establishment called La Grenouillère (literally "The Froggery") where jaded Parisians would retire on day trips

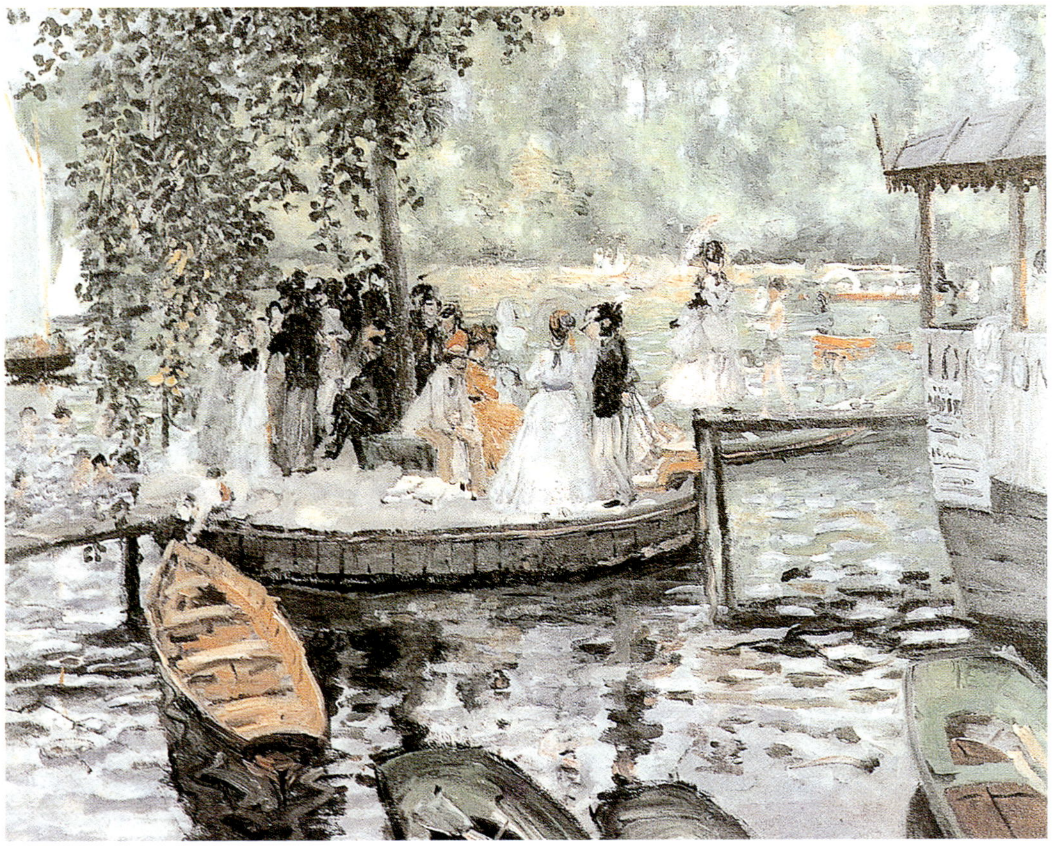

RENOIR
La Grenouillère
oil on canvas
1869. 66 × 86 cm
Above Renoir and Monet painted a series of pictures from the same viewpoints. The influence of Monet on Renoir's work is evident.

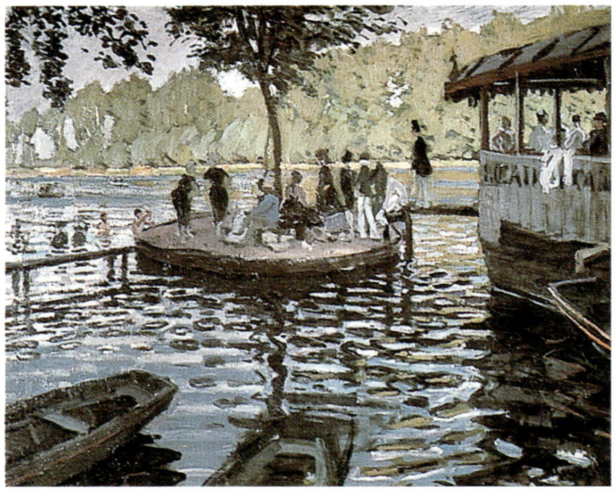

MONET
La Grenouillère
oil on canvas
1869. 79 × 60 cm
Right

during the summer months to eat, drink, and swim. It was so popular that it was often illustrated in gazettes; the Imperial couple had once stopped there in their boat, adding to its fame. It was here that Renoir and Monet spent much of the summer of 1869.

In yet another begging letter to Bazille from this period Monet also mentions that "I had indeed a dream, a *tableau*, the bathing place at La Grenouillère, for which I have made some rotten sketches . . . " The "rotten sketches" that he and Renoir had been working on that summer were a turning point, they mark the first major examples of the Impressionism to come in the next decade. The conditions were right: the two artists, each working with an eye on the other's canvas, were using paint with an unheard of directness and speed to capture all the elements in view in as unmediated a way as possible. We begin to see in his *Bathers at La Grenouillère* (*Baigneurs à la Grenouillère*) the genesis of Monet's famous advice:

> When you go out to paint, try to forget what objects you have before you; a tree, a house, a field or whatever. Merely think here is a little square of blue, here an oblong of pink, here a streak of yellow, and paint it just as it looks to you, the exact colour and shape, until it gives you your own naïve impression of the scene before you.

Despite the insistence of Monet and Renoir that the Grenouillère paintings were merely *pochades*, or sketches, the distinction between sketch and finished painting was by now becoming blurred. A painting done at La Grenouillère and submitted to the Salon of 1870 (it was rejected and is now lost) appears hardly more "finished" than the *pochades*.

1870–1871: WAR AND THE COMMUNE

In May 1870 the new decade seemed to promise a bright future for the Second Empire. A plebiscite on constitutional changes to establish a cabinet government responsible to parliament was approved by an overwhelming majority of six million. As Cobban describes it, "In the early summer of 1870, though the Empire was in a process of evolution, there seemed not the slightest danger of revolution." By 2nd July the Second Empire was in peril. Following a byzantine and mischievous piece of statecraft on the part of the Prussians, Prince Leopold of Hohenzollern was offered as a candidate for the vacant throne in Spain. France could not tolerate the idea of Prussian involvement within its southern neighbour. The scheme brought back old memories of continual war between the Hapsburg Empire and France. The Prussians withdrew the offer to Spain ten days later, but this was not satisfactory to Napoleon III and the belligerent Empress Eugénie, a Spaniard, who took it upon herself to demand through the government an assurance from Wilhelm I of Prussia that no more claims would be made to the Spanish throne. The French were looking for the diplomatic victory over Bismarck such an assurance would provide, but they were outmanouevred when on 14th July a provocative telegram arrived from Ems which had been written by Bismarck and calculated to infuriate the French. When the telegram was published in the press, France exploded in patriotic fervour and demanded war with the Prussians. Napoleon III was too ill at the time to resist this tide of emotion and five days later, on 19th July, he was forced to declare war on the Prussians.

By August the French armies had suffered heavy defeats on all fronts. The Prussians' Krupps guns, so admired at the 1867 Exposition Universelle, had been used to devastating effect; the French army was ill equipped, badly led and swiftly demoralized. Napoleon III himself was barely able to sit astride his horse through illness. The Prussians, on the other hand, had built up a formidable war machine under Bismarck, who made use of the railways to transport men and artillery to the fronts; they took Alsace and Lorraine in the first week of fighting. A series of humiliating defeats followed for the French. On 1st September Napoleon III surrendered his army at Sedan and was taken prisoner of war. Paris erupted in pent-up revolutionary fervour; the Empress Eugénie and the Prince Imperial escaped out of the back door of the Palais de Versailles to England. The chronicler of Parisian life Edmond de Goncourt attempted to describe the chaotic scene as the bad news hit Paris:

PISSARRO
The Orchard
oil on canvas
1870. 56.5 × 84 cm
This painting was created shortly after Pissarro's move to Louveciennes. He worked consistently outdoors during the period, but also kept a studio in Paris. He did not neglect his association with the rest of the Impressionists, attending regularly the meetings at the Café Guerbois.

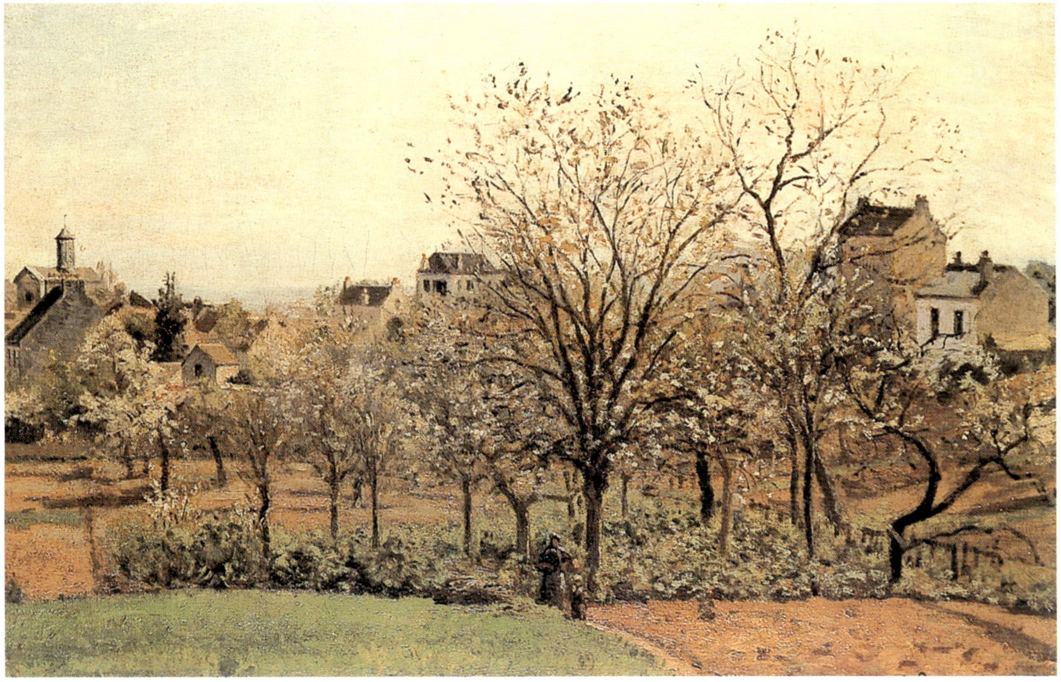

MONET
L'Hôtel des Roches Noires, Trouville
oil on canvas
1870. 81 × 58.5 cm
The Monets were not staying at the luxurious 150-room hotel but in a modest establishment which they left without paying. The bill was settled much later.

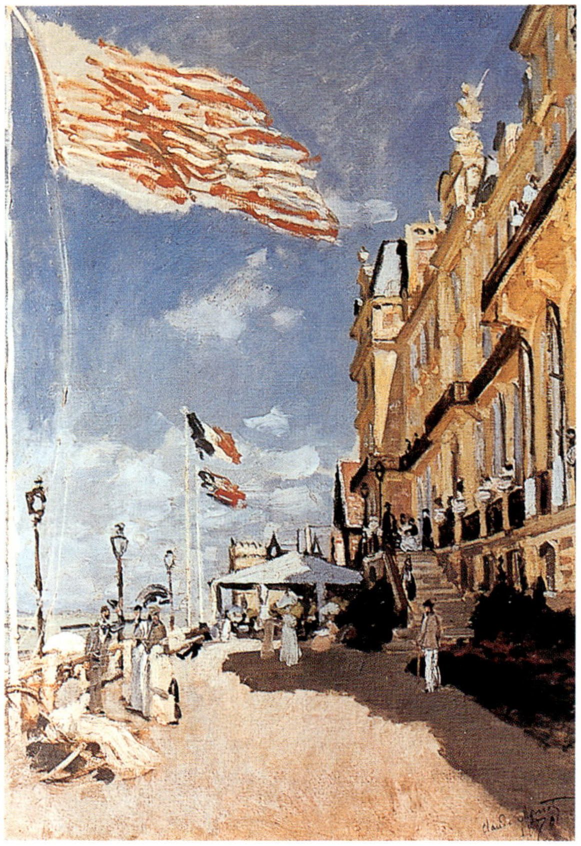

> Who can describe the consternation written on every face, the crowds collecting at street corners and outside town halls, the siege of the newspaper kiosks, the triple rows of readers gathering around every gas lamp? Then there is the menacing roar of the crowd in which stupefaction has begun to give way to anger. Next there are crowds moving down the boulevards shouting "*A bas l'Empire!*" ["Down with the Empire!"] . . . And finally there is the wild, tumultuous spectacle of a nation determined to perish or save itself by an enormous effort, by one of those impossible feats of revolutionary times.

A republican government of National Defence was proclaimed by the moderates in the Legislative Assembly. Within three months the Second Empire no longer existed.

On 28th November, a year short of his thirtieth birthday, Frédéric Bazille was killed in battle at Beaunes-la-Rolande near Orléans. One of his last paintings, *Studio in the rue de la Condamine*, depicts some habitués of the Café Guerbois, Monet, Manet, Renoir, Zola, the musician Maître and the artist himself (painted in by Manet) in happier, more peaceful times.

Manet had remained in Paris, a lieutenant in the National Guard under the painter Meissonier. Renoir was sent to Bordeaux, in the southwest and thus saw no action. In Paris Manet was to be seen swanning around in his officer's uniform, although neither he, Renoir, nor Degas were involved in any action. Cézanne had fled back to Aix-en-Provence in the south to avoid being conscripted into a war which was largely being fought in the northeast. Pissarro had painted on in Louveciennes until the Prussians advanced towards it. Over 1,100 of his paintings (which shows how prodigious his output was) were badly damaged or destroyed when his house was commandeered by several enemy troops.

As the war raged in the east Monet was at Trouville painting a number of pictures of the beach and seafront, notably the two *Beach at Trouville* (*La Plage à Trouville*) paintings and *L'Hôtel des Roches Noires, Trouville* which confirm his increasingly impressionistic style. In the autumn, with the Prussians advancing westward to encircle Paris, Monet and Pissarro fled separately to London.

If the war had proved fatal for Bazille, Monet's closest friend and as promising an artist as any of the group, it provided Pissarro and Monet with the opportunity to meet Paul Durand-Ruel, an important dealer who had opened a gallery in London and was later to

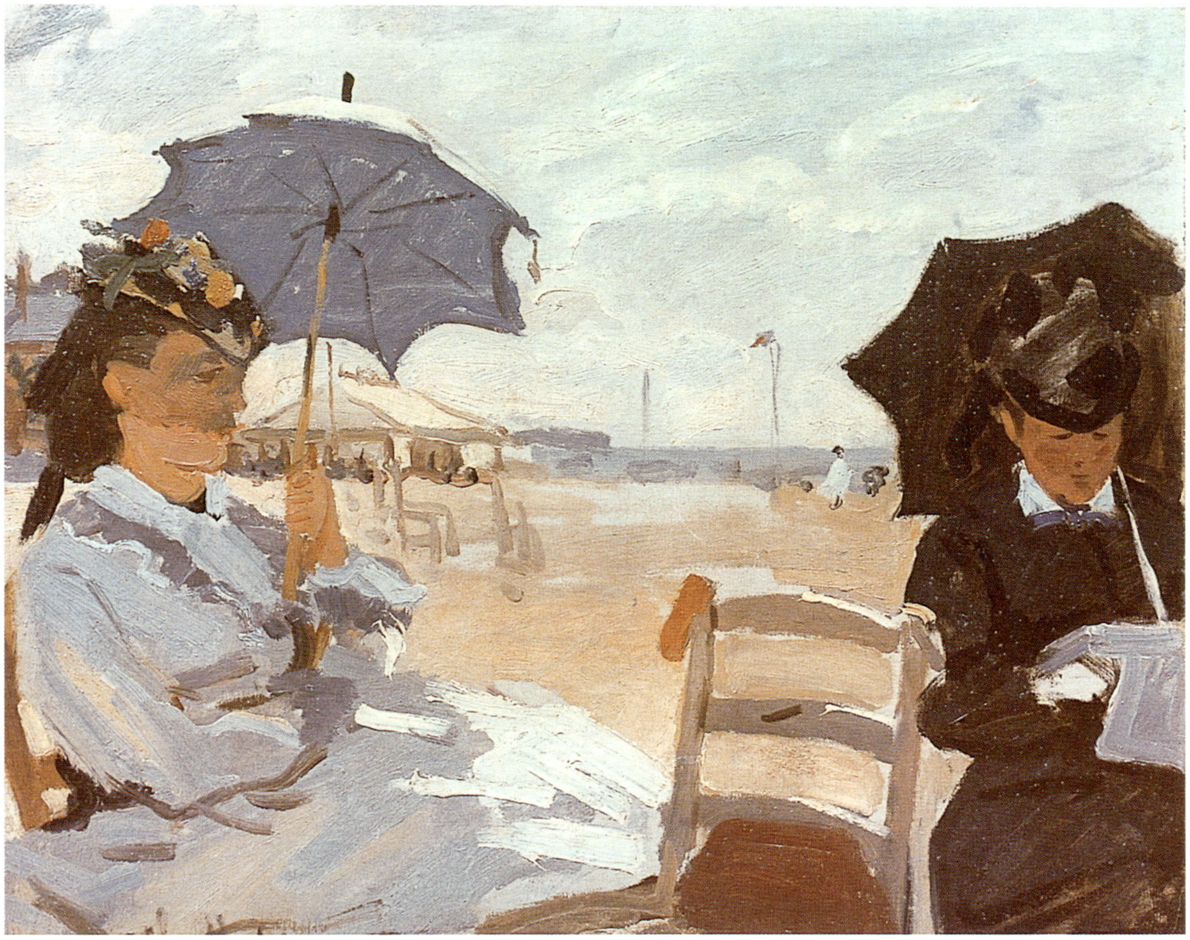

MONET
Beach at Trouville
oil on canvas
1870. 37.5 × 45.5 cm
This sketchy picture, an important step on the road to Impressionism, can be compared to an enlarged detail of Boudin's painting of the same subject. The painters were working together that summer, and Mme Boudin is perhaps the other woman in the picture.

faithfully champion their work and stage exhibitions of the Impressionists in New York. "A true picture dealer," said Durand-Ruel, "should also be an enlightened patron; he should, if necessary, sacrifice his immediate interest to his artistic convictions and oppose rather than support the interest of speculators." Living in the West End of London, Monet had been introduced to Durand-Ruel by Charles Daubigny, who was making a good living painting scenes of the Thames. Durand-Ruel in turn put Monet in touch with Pissarro who was staying with his mother in South Norwood, a quiet, picturesque village to the southeast of London.

By 20th September 1870 the Prussians had completely surrounded Paris, cutting it off from the rest of France. An attack by the crack Zouaves Regiment had been routed the day before. Edmond de Goncourt heard a terrified national guardsman on the street "relating that the Prussians numbered a hundred thousand in the Bois de Meudon . . . One senses in these accounts the madness of fear, the hallucinations of panic . . . " The Bois de Boulogne had been turned into a farmyard, siege fortifications had been built in and around the city which thronged with soldiers from the National Guard. Throughout the autumn and winter and on into 1871 the war continued, with food supplies running short and starvation becoming rampant.

One of the few links to the outside world was via hot air balloons. On 8th October,

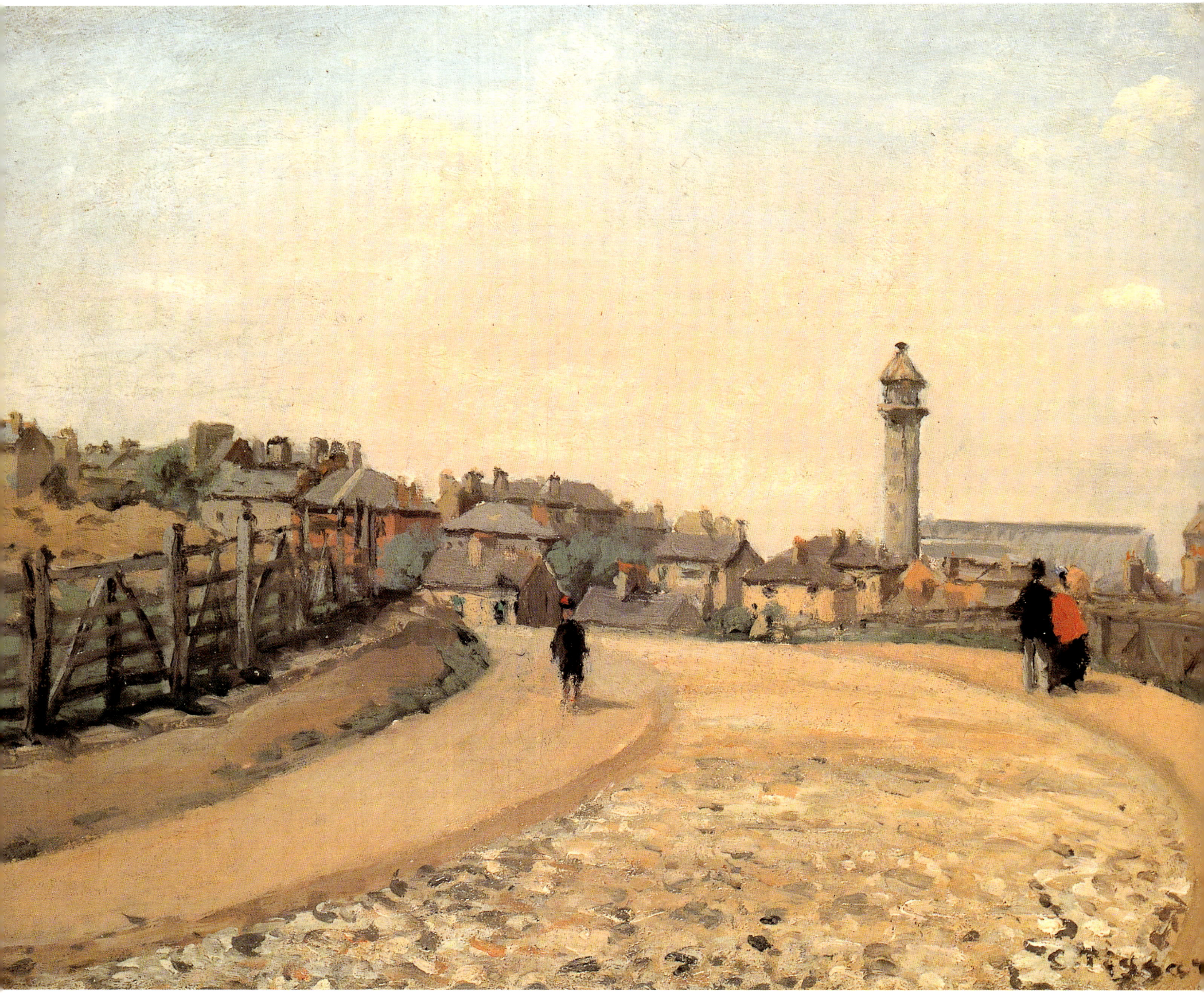

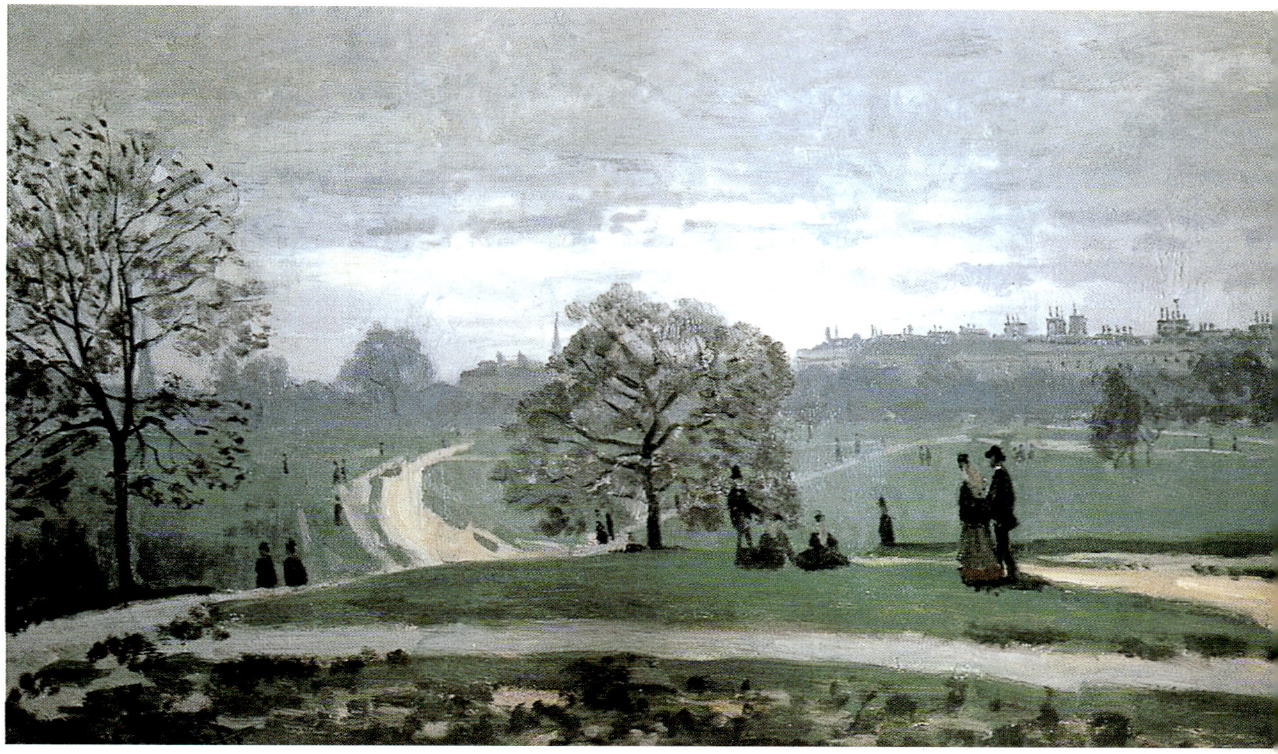

Léon Gambetta, a fiery and popular orator and Minister of the Interior, had made an heroic escape to Tours in a balloon launched from the heights of Montmartre. Taking advantage of this, Nadar organized letters to be sent by balloon post. One letter from Berthe Morisot to her sister, Edma, describes the noise of the Prussian bombardments which began in November, the corpses lying in the streets and grim warnings from Edouard and Eugène Manet that Berthe would be better off if she lost her hand or became disfigured. On 19th January the Paris garrison attempted to break out of the city and through the Prussian lines, but failed. This attempted *sortie en masse* was the last significant action of the war. Nine days later Paris surrendered to the Prussian army.

In February a republican National Assembly was elected to make peace with Prussia and approve massive reparations. But the National Guard was still armed in Paris and when on 18th March troops loyal to the new republican government attempted and failed to seize the cannon in Montmartre, Paris – led by a coalition of revolutionaries – was at war with the Republic. On 28th March the Paris Commune was elected amid scenes of jubilation that harked back to the days of the Revolution in 1789 and the first Commune. On 2nd April the second siege of Paris began; the Commune held out until the "Bloody Week" which began on 21st May when more than 20,000 Parisians were killed in indiscriminate reprisals as government forces overran the city.

Gustave Courbet, who had been elected chairman of the Arts Commission after the fall of the Empire, was a prominent member of the Commune and became implicated in the destruction of the Vendôme Column, which stood as a bitter reminder of Napoleonic power to the Communards. When the government "liberated" Paris he was imprisoned and later exiled to Switzerland where he died in 1877.

Amidst the dramatic events of this period Degas' eyesight had begun to deteriorate, Renoir had obtained a pass during the Commune and left to continue his landscape studies and most of the others of the Batignolles Group had fled to safety.

Manet was the only member of the group concerned with depicting the war in Paris and its effects. Standing on the corner of the boulevard Malesherbes, he sketched the dead bodies lying there. The lithograph *The Civil War* (*La Guerre civile*) shows how readily his *Execution of Maximilian* must have come to his mind as he observed the horror in the streets of Paris at that perilous time: the starvation, sheer anarchy, and devastation.

MONET
Green Park, London
oil on canvas
1871. 40 × 73 cm
Above

PISSARRO
Upper Norwood, Crystal Palace
oil on canvas
1871. 40 × 51 cm
Opposite This work by Pissarro and the painting above by Monet were each the product of the artists' voluntary exile in England during the Franco-Prussian war. It was an important time, as it brought the two men together, but was commercially unsuccessful, as the English public was not yet ready for the Impressionists, and the Royal Academy – equivalent to the French Salon – rejected their work.

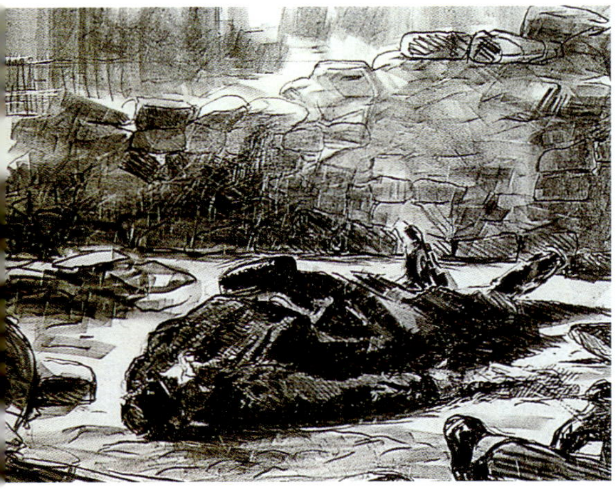

MANET
Civil War
Lithograph
1871. 40 × 51 cm
Above The artist had seen corpses lying in the streets near his home.

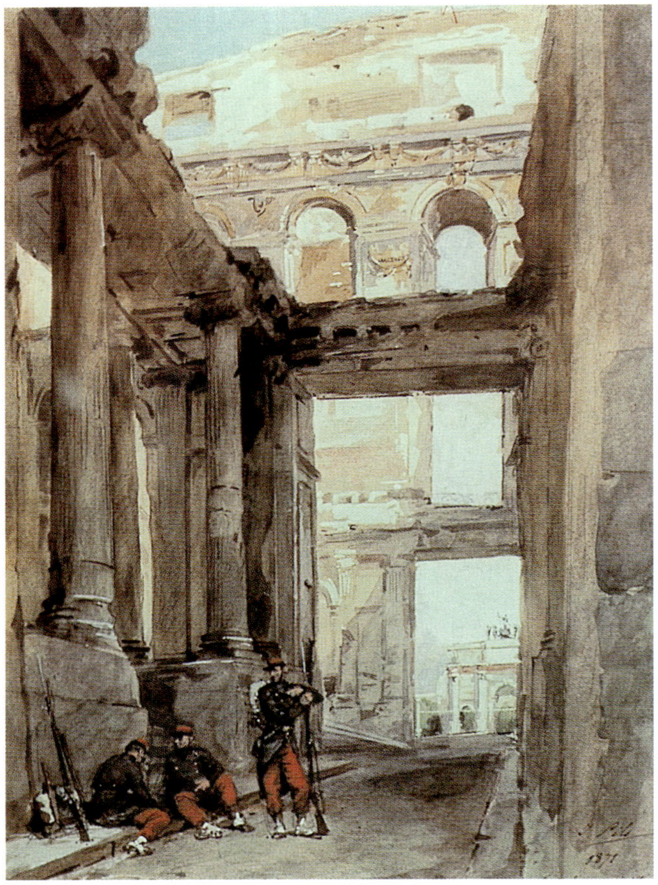

PILS
The Ruins of the Tuileries Palace
watercolour on paper
1871. 38 × 51 cm
Right We have to turn to topographical artists, or to Meissonier, to find pictures of the devastation of war. Most of the Impressionists were out of Paris at the time and in any case had no desire to paint such scenes.

DEGAS IN NEW ORLEANS

For illustrations of the Commune we have to turn to photography and the topographic artists who remained in Paris to record the suffering and destruction. None of the Impressionists was interested in the ruins of the Tuileries Palace, which had stood in the heart of the city, an area they had often depicted before the war.

In the end, the war against Prussia and the Commune had little effect on the French economy. France was now a *de facto* republic for the third time in her history. In the climate of expansion which immediately followed the end of the troubles Durand-Ruel began to invest heavily in the Batignolles artists. He bought 30 Monets and paid Manet 51,000 francs for 29 of his paintings, a fantastic sum considering Claude Monet's income the next year was 25,000 francs. For Monet in particular things were looking up at last. From England he had gone to Holland and then to Argenteuil on the Seine near Paris where Renoir frequently joined him as before. Pissarro had returned to Louveciennes and then decamped to Pontoise where Cézanne visited him. The Café Guerbois evenings continued for another year. In November Degas and his brother René arrived in New Orleans to stay with their mother. In a letter to his friend Lorentz Fröhlich, Degas described the effect the new world was having on him:

> Everything attracts me here, I look at everything . . . I accumulate plans that would take a lifetime to complete. I will abandon them in six weeks to return and never again leave my home . . . My eyes are much better.

Ten days later he wrote to Henri Rouart:

> The light is so strong that I have not yet been able to do anything on the river. My eyes are so greatly in need of care that I scarcely take any risk with them at all . . . Manet would see lovely things here, even more than I do . . .

Indicative of his friendly rivalry with Manet he went on:

> . . . but not many more of them. One loves and gives art only to the things to which one is accustomed.

Among the results of Degas' period in New Orleans, chiefly devoted to painting portraits of his family, are two remarkable pictures,

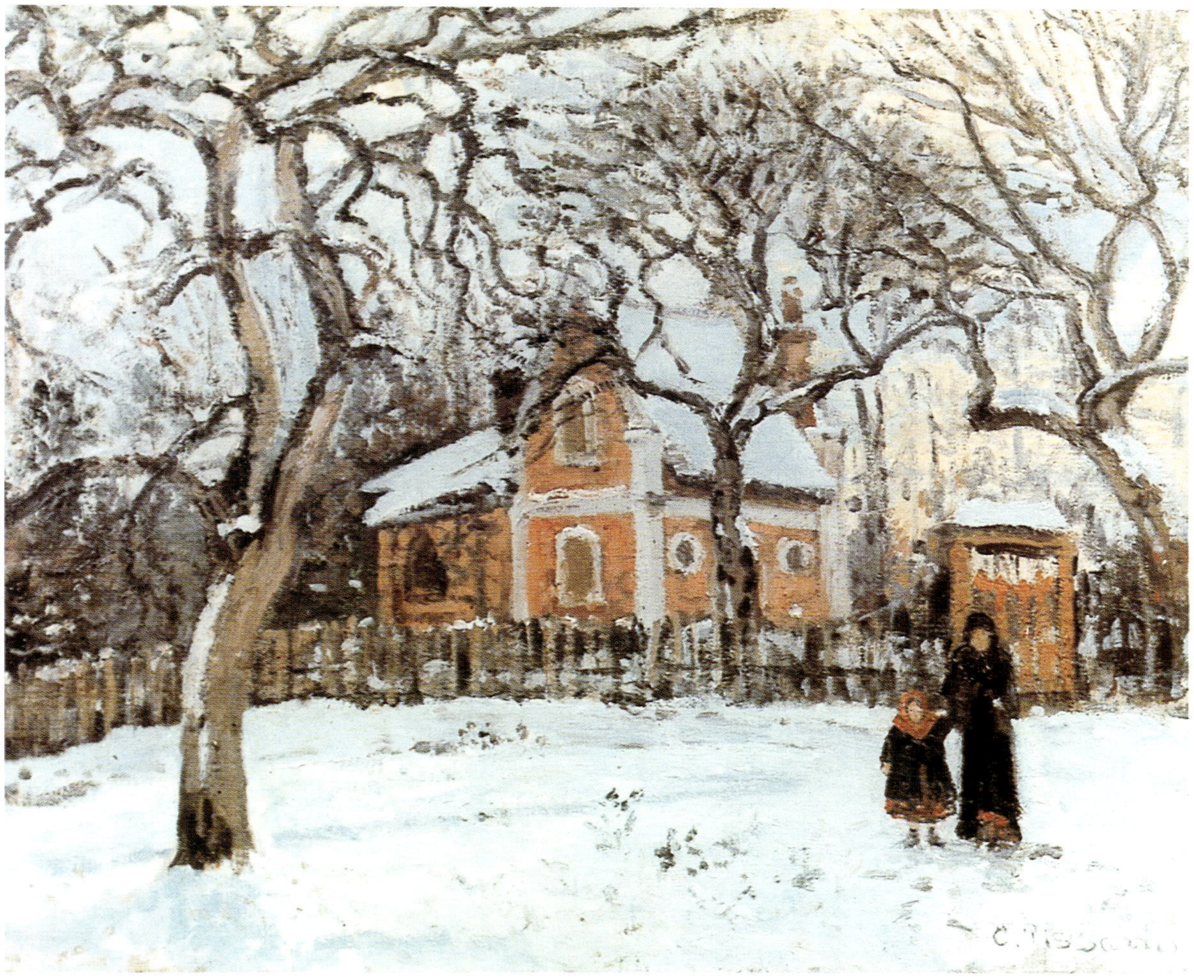

PISSARRO
Horsechestnut Trees at Louveciennes
oil on canvas
c.1872. 41 × 54 cm
This evocative snow-scene was painted close to the artist's home at Louveciennes, where he had moved with his family three years before.

The Invalid (*L'Invalide*) and *Portraits in an Office – New Orleans* (*Portraits dans un bureau à Nouvelle-Orléans*) better known as *The Cotton Market* (*Le Bureau de Coton*). The former is one of Degas' most atmospheric works, conveying what Henri Loyrette calls "the stifling sense of the sickroom" in broad, swift brushstrokes; the latter, making the modern business world a legitimate subject for art, was described by Armand Silvestre as "an exceedingly witty painting that one could spend days contemplating." This painting is perhaps as epochal as Manet's *Music in the Tuileries Garden* had been a decade earlier. After this Degas' failing eyes allowed him to paint few pictures of such acute detail.

1873: SOCIÉTÉ ANONYME

The post-war boom soon gave way to a period of economic recession which lasted for five years and affected the Impressionists, their patrons, and especially Durand-Ruel, forcing him to close his London gallery in 1874. As in 1863 the Salon was hugely oversubscribed but this time the *refusés* succeeded in pressurizing the government to mount another Salon des Refusés. A huge Renoir painting, almost eight and a half by seven and a half feet, the *Morning Ride in the Bois de Boulogne* (*Allée cavalière au Bois de Boulogne*) had been rejected by the Salon but was shown to great acclaim at the alternative exhibition.

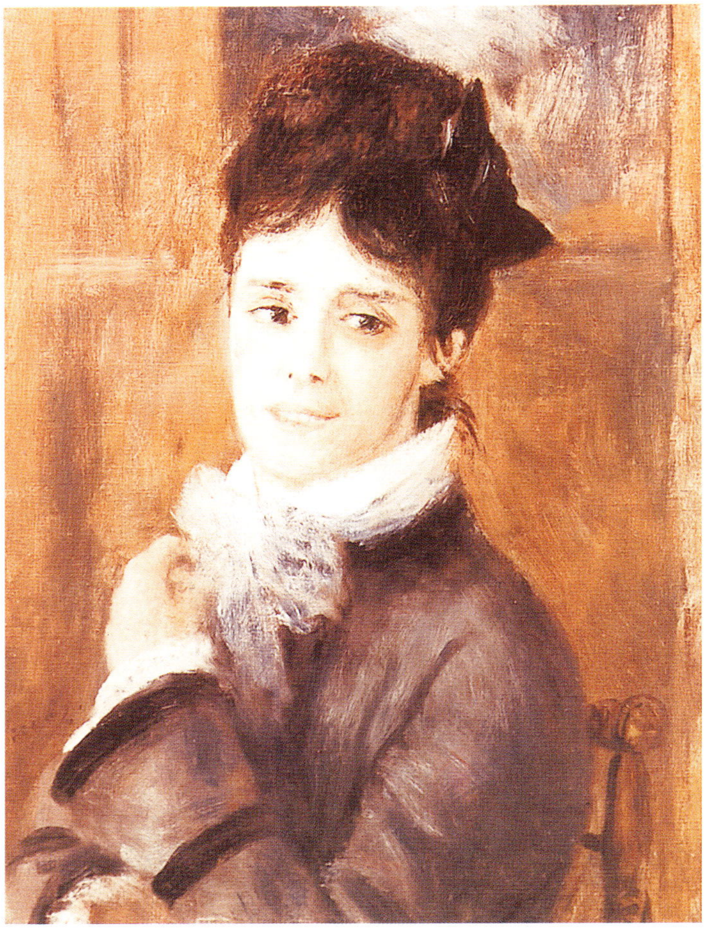

RENOIR
Madame Camille Monet
oil on canvas
1872. 61 × 50 cm
There are hundreds of instances of the Impressionists painting the other members of the group and their families – this is perhaps one of the finest. It was painted shortly after the Franco-Prussian war, when Renoir and Monet developed the habit of painting together on trips along the banks of the Seine.

Monet's influence on Renoir, after long months working with him before and after the war, had led to a brightening of his palette and more delicate brushwork. Renoir's *Pont Neuf* of the previous year was one of his most impressionistic pictures to date; the briefly sketched-in figures highlighted with dabs of pure pigment betray the influence of Monet, as do the complementary colours blue-violet and yellow in the overall composition, and the bluish shadows, which create the effect of colour contrast in brilliant sunlight.

Unlike the events a decade earlier, the Salon des Refusés of 1873 was remarkably devoid of scandal. The painter most likely to cause an uproar, Edouard Manet, was showing two works at the official Salon, a portrait of Berthe Morisot and *Le Bon Bock* – a portrait of the engraver Bellot at a table in the Café Guerbois. The latter proved a welcome success for Manet, sensitive as ever to the barbs of the critics. The influence of Frans Hals, whom Manet had been studying during a tour of Holland the year before, as well as the deliberate lack of a scandalous subject gently reassured the Salon-going public of Manet's talent.

The Salon des Refusés did little to placate the rest of the Batignolles Group who were still desperately looking for outlets for their work. Ironically, the war had promoted a deeply conservative streak in the Salon jury which made Nieuwerkerke's *ancien régime* appear liberal by comparison. This conspired against an avant-garde whose influence was by now becoming widespread. With Durand-Ruel's business suffering in the recession and unable to support them they were forced to look elsewhere. The idea first mentioned by Bazille in 1867 of forming an independent organization to stage an exhibition was rekindled. A much heated discussion between Pissarro, who was for a highly complex association based on a social and political union, and the others in the group, including Renoir and Monet, who demanded a simpler, looser collective, resulted in a document signed on 27th December founding the *Société anonyme des artistes peintres, sculpteurs, graveurs, etc.* Only Manet refused to join the new body, arguing in common with Cézanne, that still "the Salon is the true battlefield." Degas was in favour, writing to Tissot that "the realist movement no longer needs to fight with the others. It is. It exists, it must show itself as something distinct . . . So forget the money side for a moment. Exhibit. Be of your country and your friends."

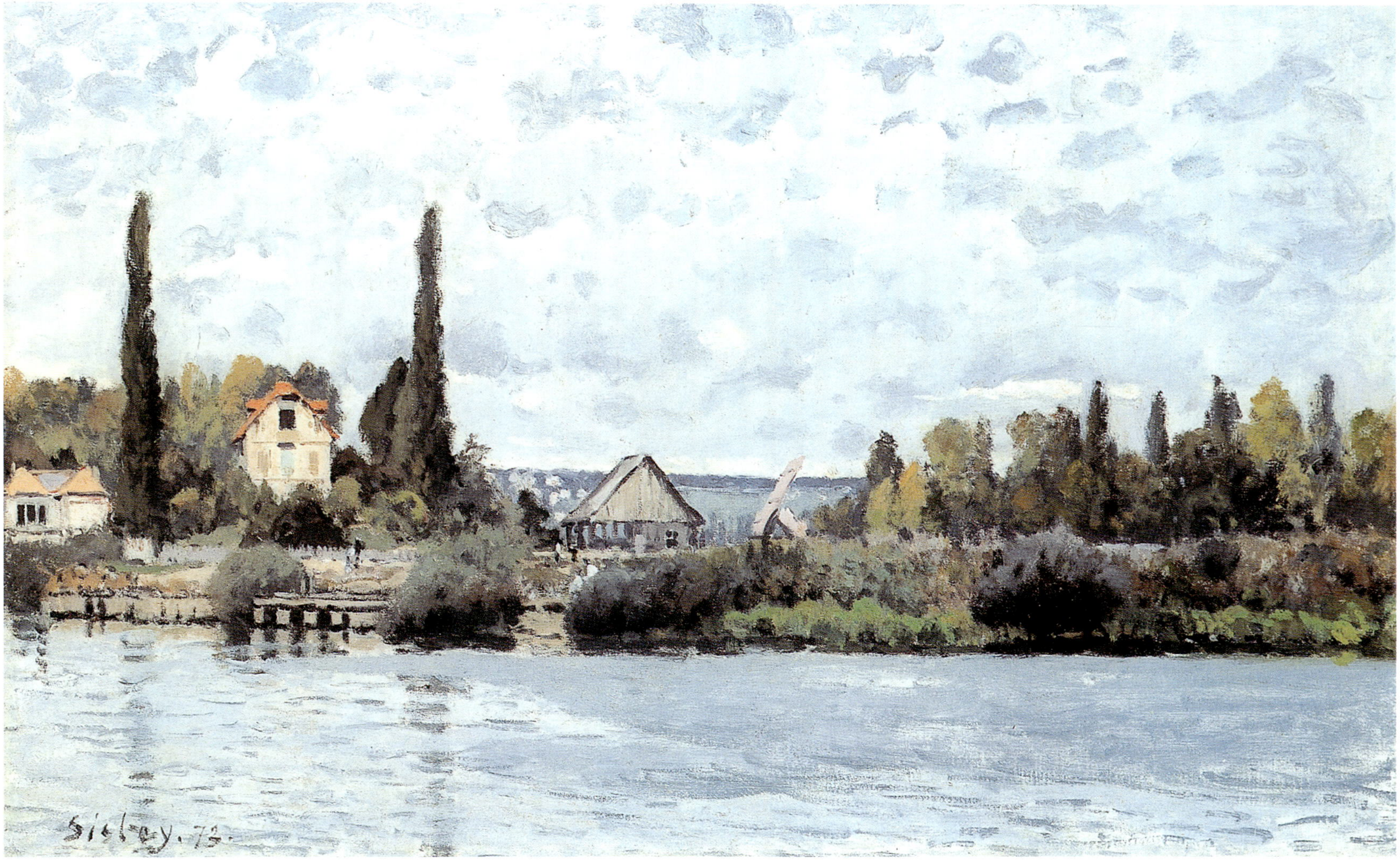

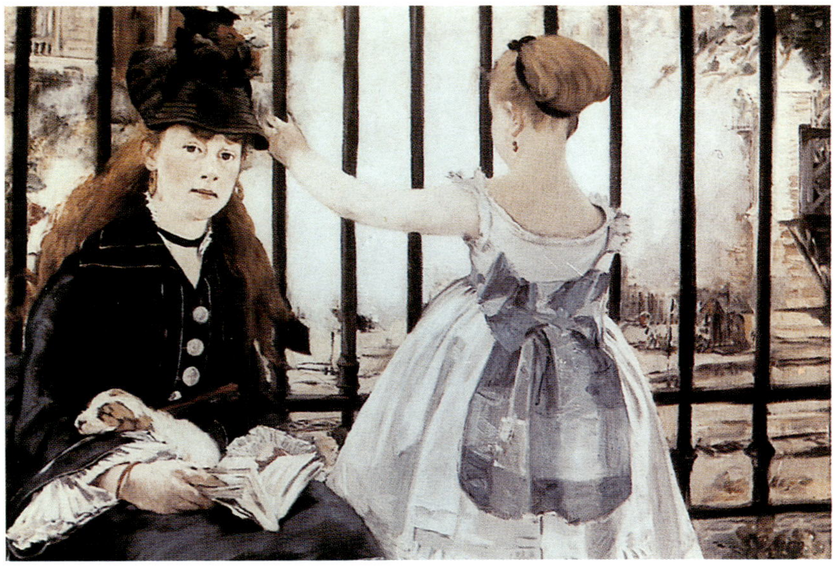

MANET
The Railway
1872–73. 93.5 × 114.5 cm
LEFT Also called The Gare St Lazare, *we can hardly guess that there is a railway station behind the cloud of smoke. Most Impressionists painted scenes with trains at this time.*

SISLEY
The Seine at Bougival
oil on canvas
1872–77. 38.5 × 62 cm
ABOVE Sisley was interested at this time in the problems of depicting water and sky. His palette was somewhat dark and sombre compared to most of the other Impressionists.

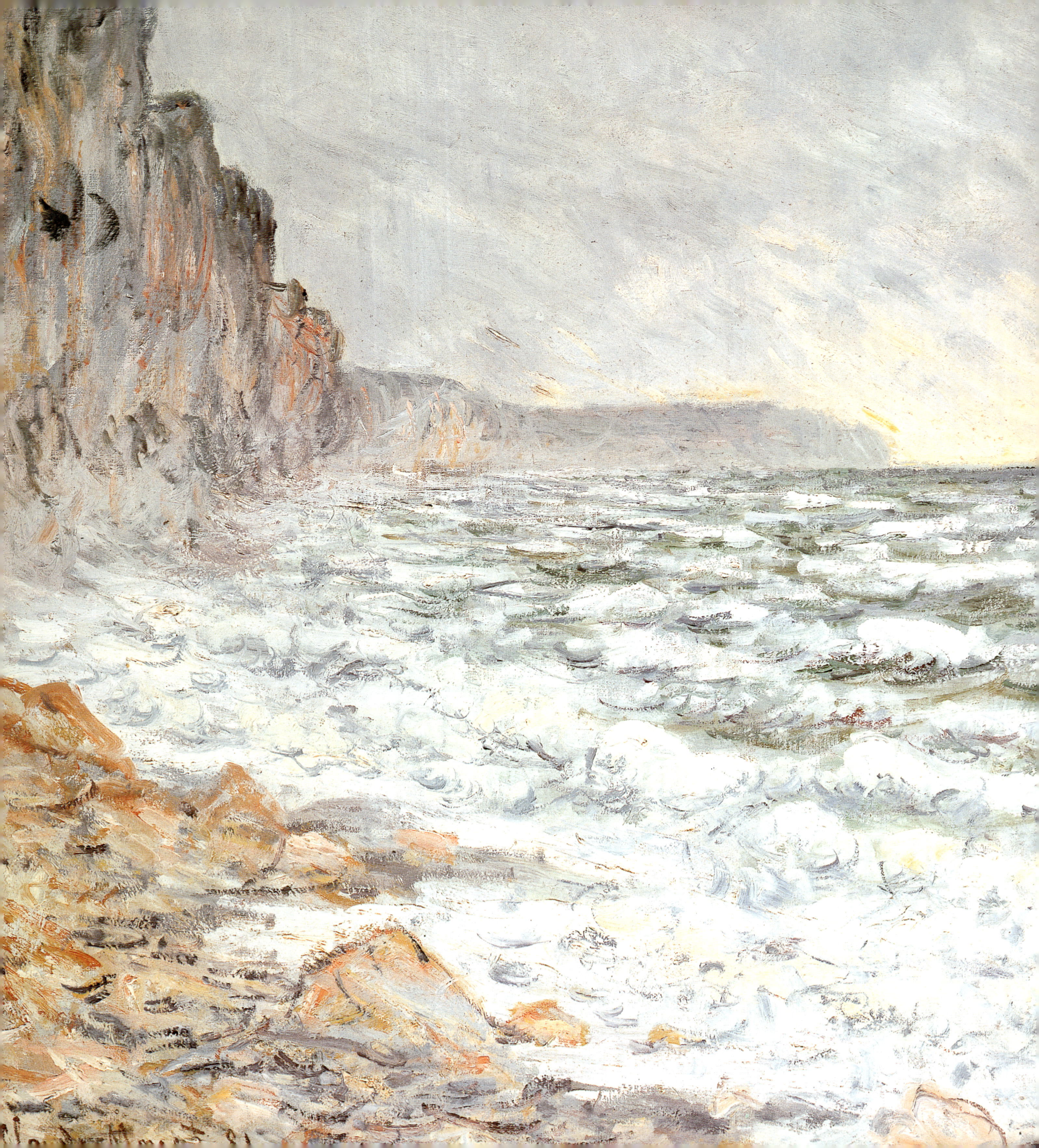

THE AGE OF IMPRESSIONISM

The works of Monet, Renoir, Manet, Morisot, Pissarro, and Sisley, which characterized the Impressionist idiom in its most popularly recognizable form, were painted in the 1870s. Degas, who played an important role in organizing the series of Impressionist exhibitions which marked the 1870s and 1880s, remained resolutely opposed to *plein-air* painting. He nevertheless produced the most striking images of modern Parisian life, taking inspiration from Japanese prints and photography, and, like Manet, basing his technique on a thorough appreciation of the old masters. Towards the end of the 1870s serious rifts began to appear in the group and Monet, Renoir, and Sisley dropped out as Degas and Pissarro exerted more and more control over the exhibitions, replenishing the group with new artists. For most of the Impressionists this was a time of personal consolidation, with patrons and dealers securing them a regular income despite periodic economic recessions. The penultimate Impressionist exhibition – minus Degas – took place in 1882 and essentially represented the fragile group's last stand. The next year Manet died having completed his masterpiece *Bar at the Folies-Bergère*. He had remained highly supportive of the group but never exhibited with them.

By 1886 the final Impressionist exhibition featured the work of Degas, Pissarro, and a new generation including Georges Seurat, Paul Signac, and Paul Gauguin.

MONET
The Sea at Fécamp
oil on canvas
1881. 65 × 80 cm
(Detail)

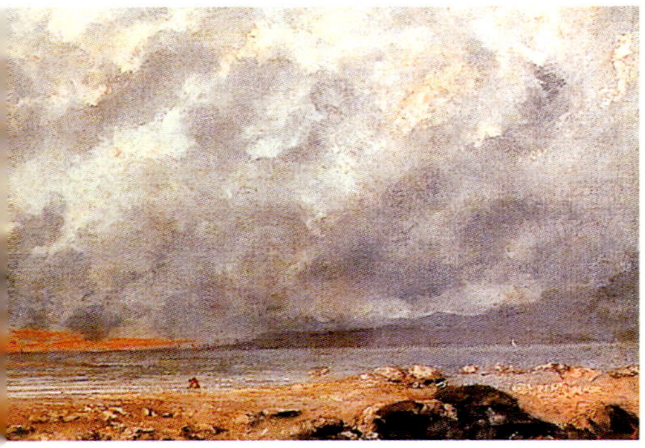

COURBET
Beach Scene
oil on canvas
1874. 37.5 × 54.5 cm
ABOVE Courbet's choice of subjects from ordinary life and his very simple artistic philosophy ("Painting is an art of sight and should therefore concern itself with things seen") made him a natural precursor of the Impressionist movement.

1874: THE FIRST IMPRESSIONIST EXHIBITION

We were all one group when we first started out. We stood shoulder to shoulder and encouraged each other . . .

The quotation above was given by Renoir, twenty years after the inaugural collective Impressionist show: the *Société anonyme*'s first (and last) exhibition opened in mid-April, deliberately timed to upstage the official Salon. Situated in Nadar's old studio, it was close to the premises of several dealers and photographers, including Durand-Ruel's gallery. The choice of a *grand boulevard* was in itself a fitting one for the generation of artists who had grown up in Haussmann's Paris painting Baudelaire's *vie moderne*.

The exhibition was immediately a critical *cause célèbre*; not only did it provoke the aspersions of critics such as Leroy, it also rallied the influential theorist Edmond Duranty (with whom Manet had once fought a duel!) to the Impressionists' defence. At the time, Jules Castagnary also showed particular insight in putting his finger on the fact that Monet, Pissarro, Sisley, Morisot, and Renoir were "Impressionists in the sense that they render not the landscape, but the sensation produced by the landscape."

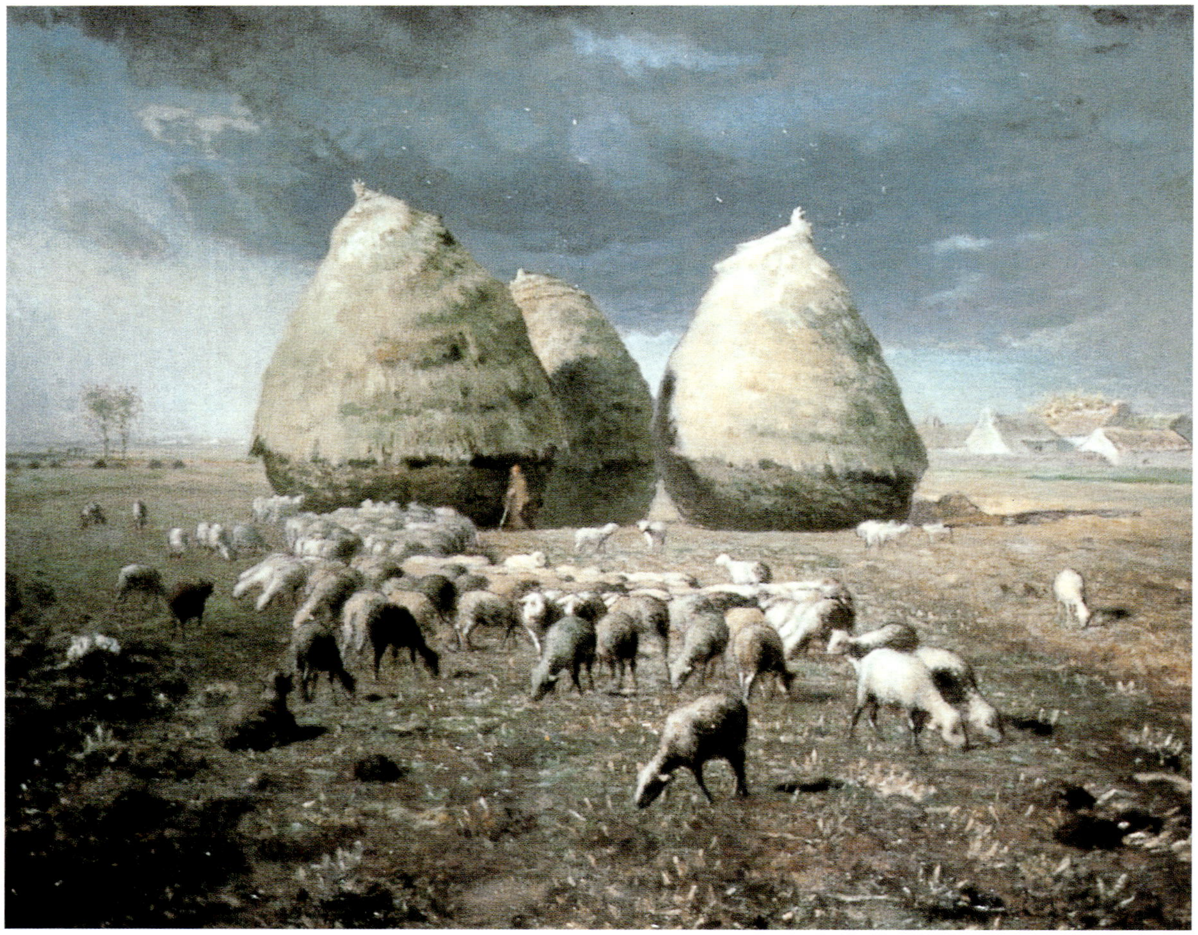

MILLET
Haystacks in Autumn
oil on canvas
1873–74. 85 × 110 cm
RIGHT Though charmingly done in their own right, Millet's haystacks are perhaps of more interest through their very obvious foreshadowing of the magnificent series by Monet.

However, the exhibition was such a financial disaster that the *Société* was later forced to meet in December to wind up its affairs. Thanks to Louis Leroy's scurrilous satire in *Charivari*, the group, which had laboured under several titles, none of them really appropriate – *la bande à Manet*, the Batignolles Group, the Realists – was now known as "the Impressionists". There were seven more Impressionist exhibitions, the last in 1886, although none of them bore the title "Impressionist", their participants typically preferring the name *Expositions de Peinture*, or on one occasion, an *Exposition des Independants*.

All but forgotten in a new world of painting, Charles Gleyre died that same year. Renoir, for one, maintained to the very end that Gleyre had taught him his *métier*. He recalled a scene at Gleyre's a decade before:

> Whilst the other students yelled and broke the windows, tormented the model and distracted the teacher I would quietly sit in the corner, observant and prepared, studying the model and listening to the master. And they accused me of being a revolutionary.

1875: CRITICS AND COLLECTORS

The Salon of 1875 was graced with the results of Edouard Manet's work at Argenteuil where he had spent the previous summer with Monet and Renoir. Manet had helped Monet's family to find new lodgings in this picturesque village on the banks of the Seine and proceeded under the latter's influence to create a series of highly impressionistic figures in landscapes. Liberated from the studio and surrounded by the most devoted of Impressionist *plein-airistes*, Manet's technique underwent a revolution. *Monet Painting in his Studio Boat* (*Monet dans son studio flotant*),

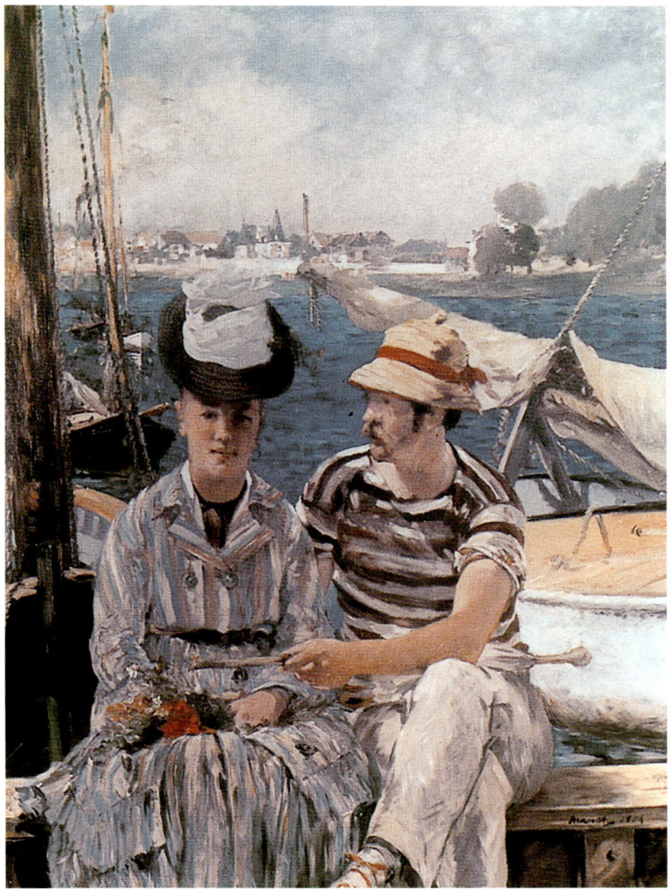

Banks of the Seine at Argenteuil (*Les Bords de la Seine à Argenteuil*) (the two figures are Camille Monet and Jean), and *The Monet Family in their Garden* (*La Famille Monet au jardin*) are remarkable for the breathtaking speed of their execution and the abandonment of Manet's otherwise sombre palette in favour of strokes of pure pigment. The contrast between Monet's insistence on landscape as his *motif* – his reluctance to attempt large figures after *Women in the Garden* some ten years earlier is palpable – and Manet's abiding concern with the human figure is still marked, even at the point where their styles most obviously converge.

The respite offered by Durand-Ruel to the poorest Impressionists, Monet, Renoir, Pissarro, and Sisley (whose father's business had

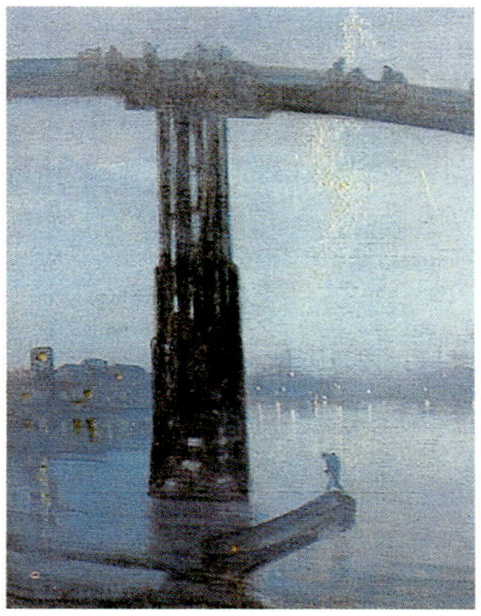

WHISTLER
The Old Battersea Bridge, Harmony in Blue and Gold
oil on canvas
c.1872–75. 68 × 51 cm
ABOVE The Japanese influence is obvious, but Whistler is not the only artist who succeeded in blending Impressionism with the Japanese style.

MANET
Banks of the Seine at Argenteuil
oil on canvas
1874. 148 × 115 cm
ABOVE LEFT Manet's technique shows the liberating influence of Monet and Renoir; his palette is brighter than ever and his style is at last truly impressionistic.

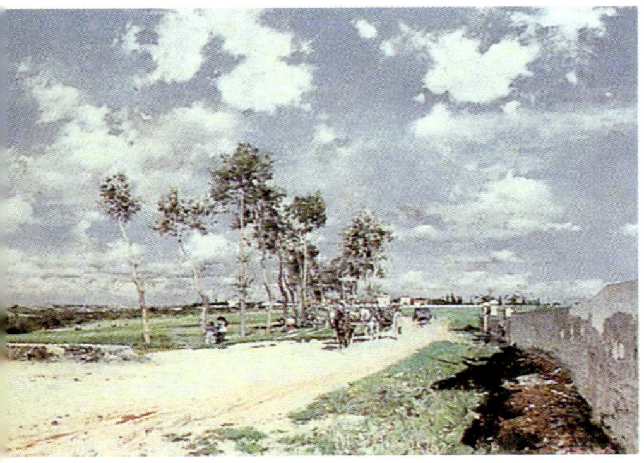

BOLDINI
Highway at Combes-la-Ville
oil on canvas
1873. 70 × 102 cm
ABOVE Boldini was one of several artists whose work was close to Impressionism for a while, although most of them did not persevere in this style.

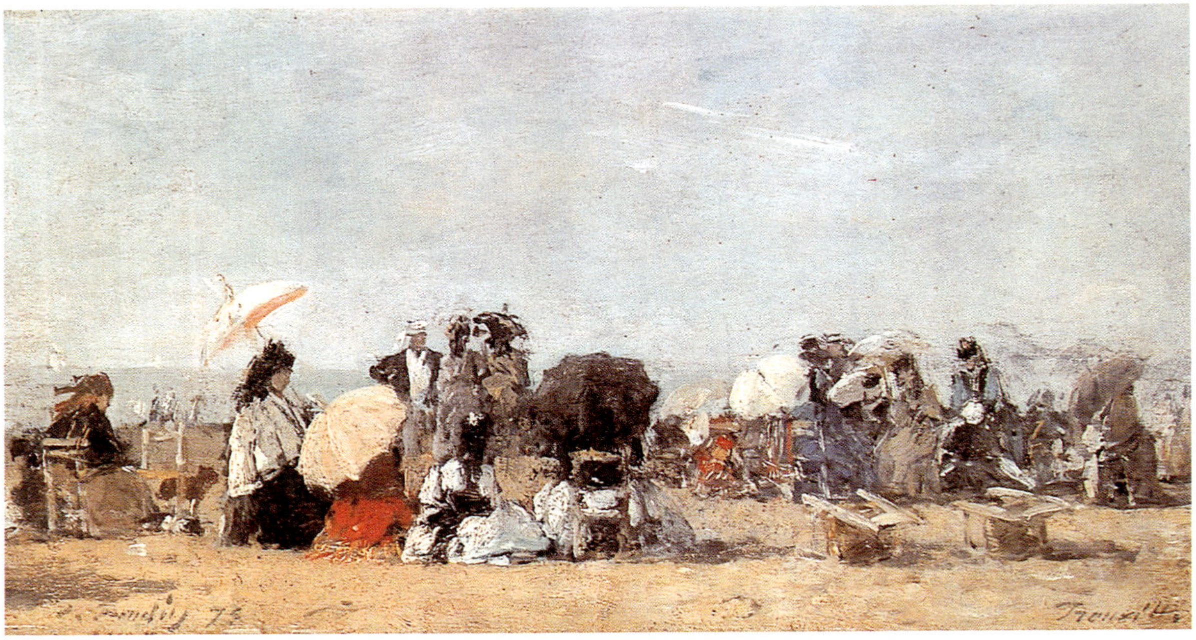

BOUDIN
Beach Scene, Trouville
oil on canvas
1873. 15 × 30 cm
RIGHT One of many scenes of this kind by Boudin. He deplored the invasion of tourists but could not avoid depicting them. Like Boldini (above), Boudin flirted with Impressionism, and indeed his work was included in the first Impressionist exhibition. Yet he was a free spirit, refusing to permanently ally himself to any specific grouping.

MANET
Nina de Callias
oil on canvas
1873–74. 113.5 × 166.5 cm
OPPOSITE She was Anne-Marie Gaillard, also known as Nina de Villard, wife of Hector de Callias, a musician. A warm woman, easy going but sometimes hysterical, she held a salon between 1868 and 1884. She became insane in 1881 and went to an asylum where she died in 1884. She asked to be buried in this outfit.

collapsed in the war) had temporarily evaporated; sales had plummeted in the recession. Even Degas was in trouble after the death of his father had entailed the Degas estate. An auction of Impressionist work arranged by Renoir and held at the Hôtel Drouot ended in farce and near riot. So derisory were the bids that the artists were forced to purchase many of their own works. Albert Wolff, the art critic of the important daily *Le Figaro*, had been asked by Manet to promote the sale. His answer was to write "the impression the Impressionists achieve [is] that of a cat walking on a piano keyboard or a monkey who might have got hold of a box of paints."

Gradually, however, patrons were beginning to come to the aid of some of the Impressionists. An eccentric customs official called Victor Chocquet, who had devoted his life to collecting the work of Delacroix and many other objets d'art, had become enamoured of Renoir's work at the Hotel Drouot and began to support the Impressionists. Renoir introduced him to Cézanne, also in need of more patronage and the result was a series of portraits of M. and Mme Chocquet by the two artists. A comparison of Renoir's and Cézanne's 1876 portraits of the collector shows the difference in the two artists' approach to their subject. Renoir's picture is executed with feathery brush strokes evoking a gentle, kindly, almost ethereal individual; Cézanne's portrait (like the later portrait of 1879–82) shows his increasing concern with structure and volume, and the paint is applied in thick patches and with the palette knife.

The second Impressionist exhibition planned for 1875 was unable to go ahead because there were no available funds to mount it. Although this decline of the *Société anonyme* was only a temporary setback, some serious rifts were already beginning to appear in the group. In August Pissarro and his friend Alfred Meyer set up *L'Union* to carry on the work of the defunct *Société anonyme*. Cézanne and Monet objected to this upstart organization, especially the involvement of Meyer who they believed was plotting against the

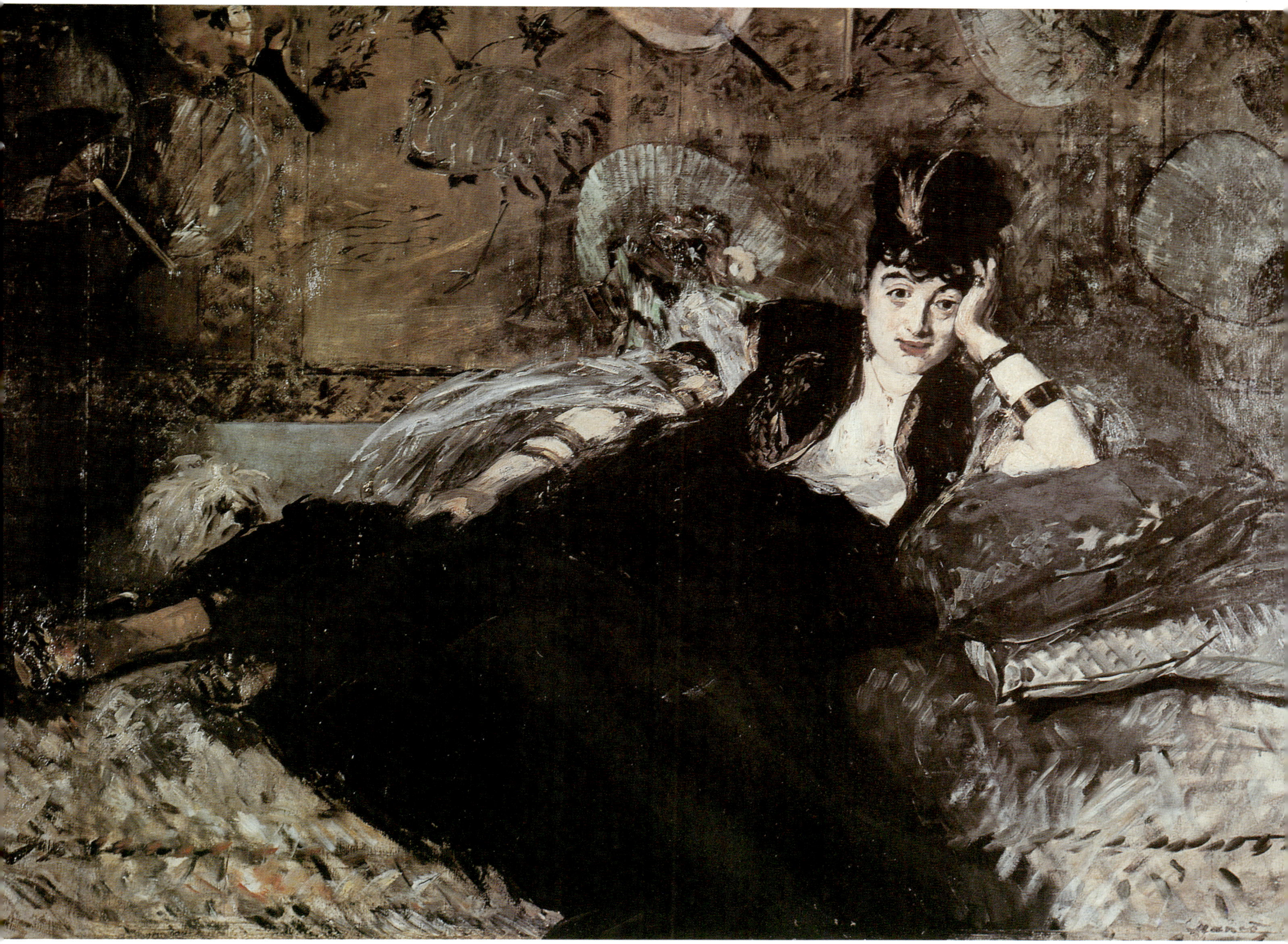

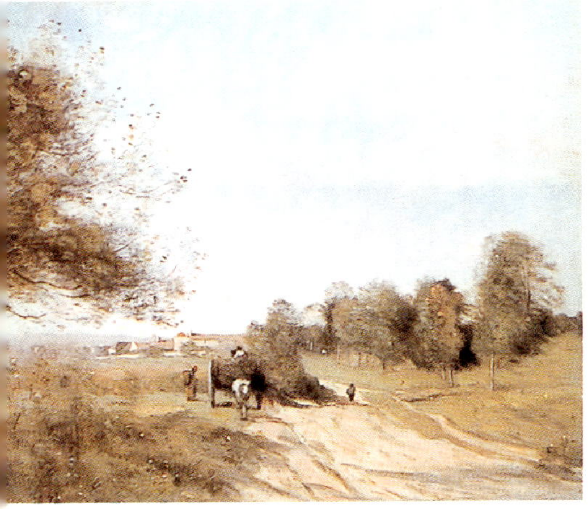

COROT
The Waggon, Souvenir of Saintry, near Corbeil
oil on canvas
1874. 47 × 57 cm
Above Amidst the excitements of 1874, with the first Impressionist exhibition, the old war-horse Corot continued on in his own inimitable fashion. The group, to whom he had been both an inspiration and a supporter, was greatly saddened by his death in the following year.

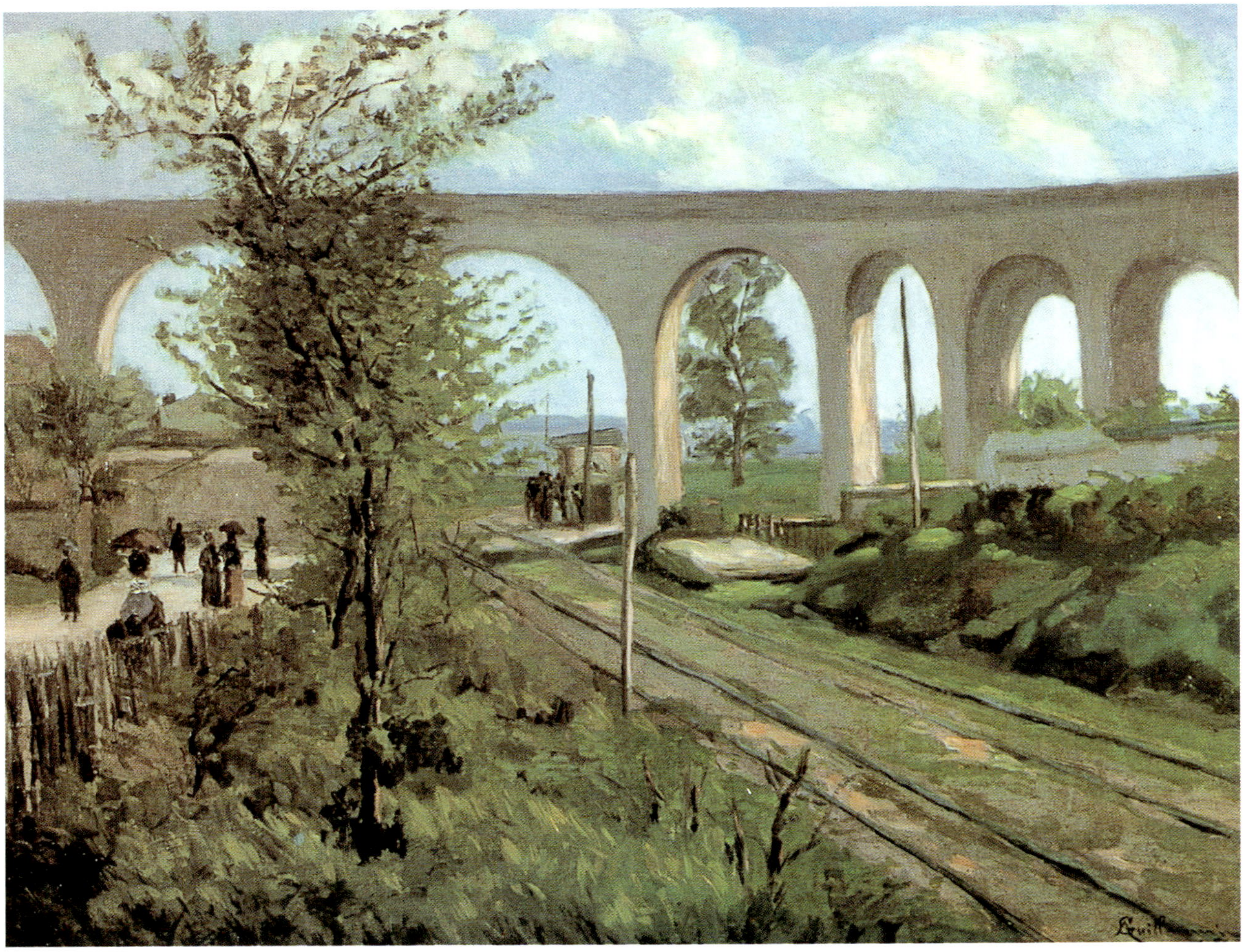

GUILLAUMIN
The Aquaduct at Arcueil
oil on canvas
1874. 51 × 65 cm
Right Among the Impressionists Guillaumin was one of the few to depict the grim aspects of the urban industrial landscape.

artistic objectives of the Impressionists. Although *L'Union* had recruited several minor painters to its ranks, including Guillaumin, it attracted little attention from the critics and eventually faded into oblivion. However much this singular group of artists was identified by the critics, the public and other artists as a homogenous circle their talents and personalities were formidably individual. A mutual struggle against the inflexibility of the art world brought them "shoulder to shoulder", but that alone was not enough to keep the Impressionists together for very much longer.

The death of Camille Corot in 1875, the inspiration for so many of the Impressionists, was an occasion for much sadness in the group, especially for Berthe Morisot and Camille Pissarro who had been closest to him and learnt the most from his work and artistic guidance. "We don't see in the same way; you see green and I see grey and silver," Corot once said to Pissarro, " . . . but this is no reason at all for you not to work at [tonal] values, for this is the basis of everything, and in whatever way one may feel and express oneself, one cannot do good painting without it." Morisot had outgrown Corot's style by the time of the first Impressionist exhibition, as her painting *The Cradle* (*Berceau*) indicates, but Corot's influence on Pissarro persisted well into the 1870s.

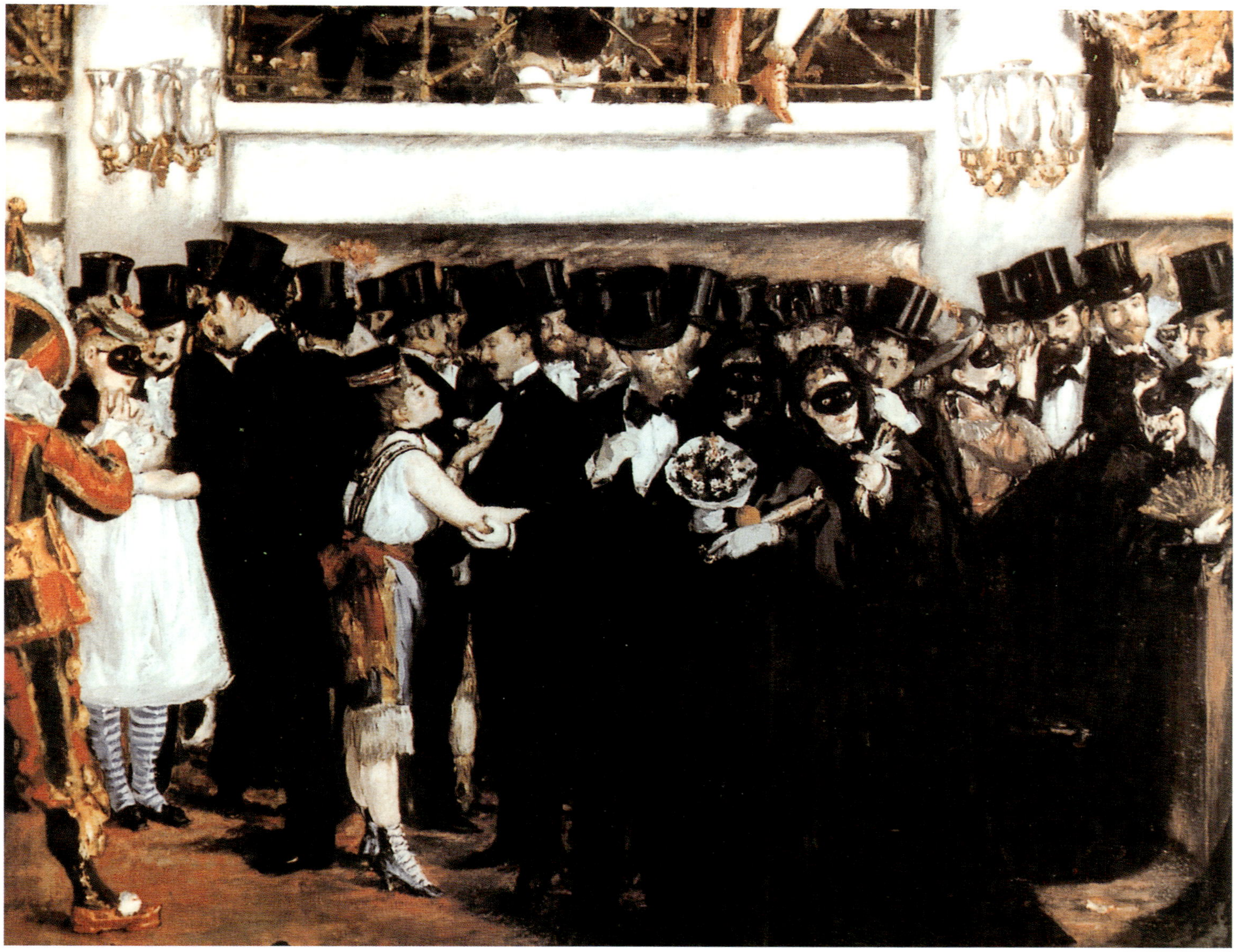

MANET
Masked Ball at the Opera
oil on canvas
1873–74. 60 × 73 cm
On the left, talking to a masked woman in white, is the composer Chabrier, a friend of several Impressionists. This kind of entertainment was not suitable for the respectable Mme Manet or Berthe Morisot.

PHOTOGRAPHY AND IMPRESSIONISM

Of great interest to art historians is the fact that over three hundred photographs were found in Corot's studio after his death. These photographs are now lost, but a contemporary source described two hundred of them as being "studies from nature".

The first reliable photographic process had been discovered by Louis Daguerre and announced to the French Académie des Sciences in 1839. (In 1822 Joseph-Nicéphore Niepce had succeeded in fixing a photographic image on glass, and William Henry Fox Talbot in England was developing a rival process which could reproduce from negatives.) The daguerreotype was capable of producing a positive image fixed on a highly polished metal plate and soon became widely available. The new invention had an immediate effect on artists, especially miniature portrait painters: it put many of them out of business. Nevertheless the practical applications of the new medium were apparent to

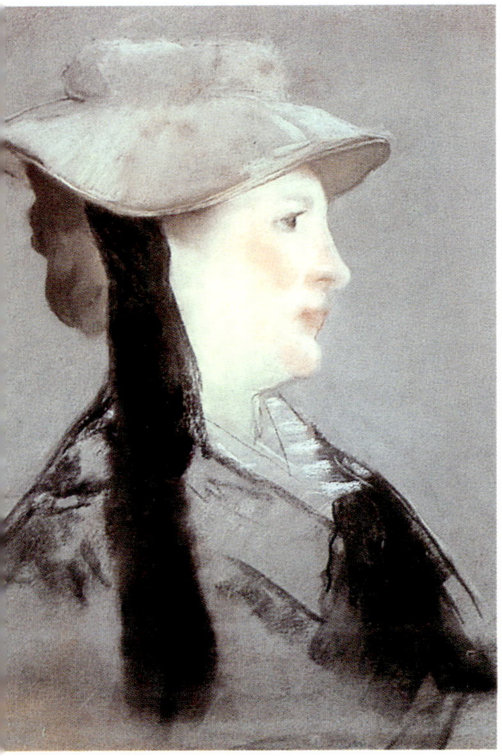

MANET
Madame Manet
pastel on paper
1873. 54 × 39 cm
ABOVE The use of pastel and other media apart from oil paint was revived by Manet and Degas in particular.

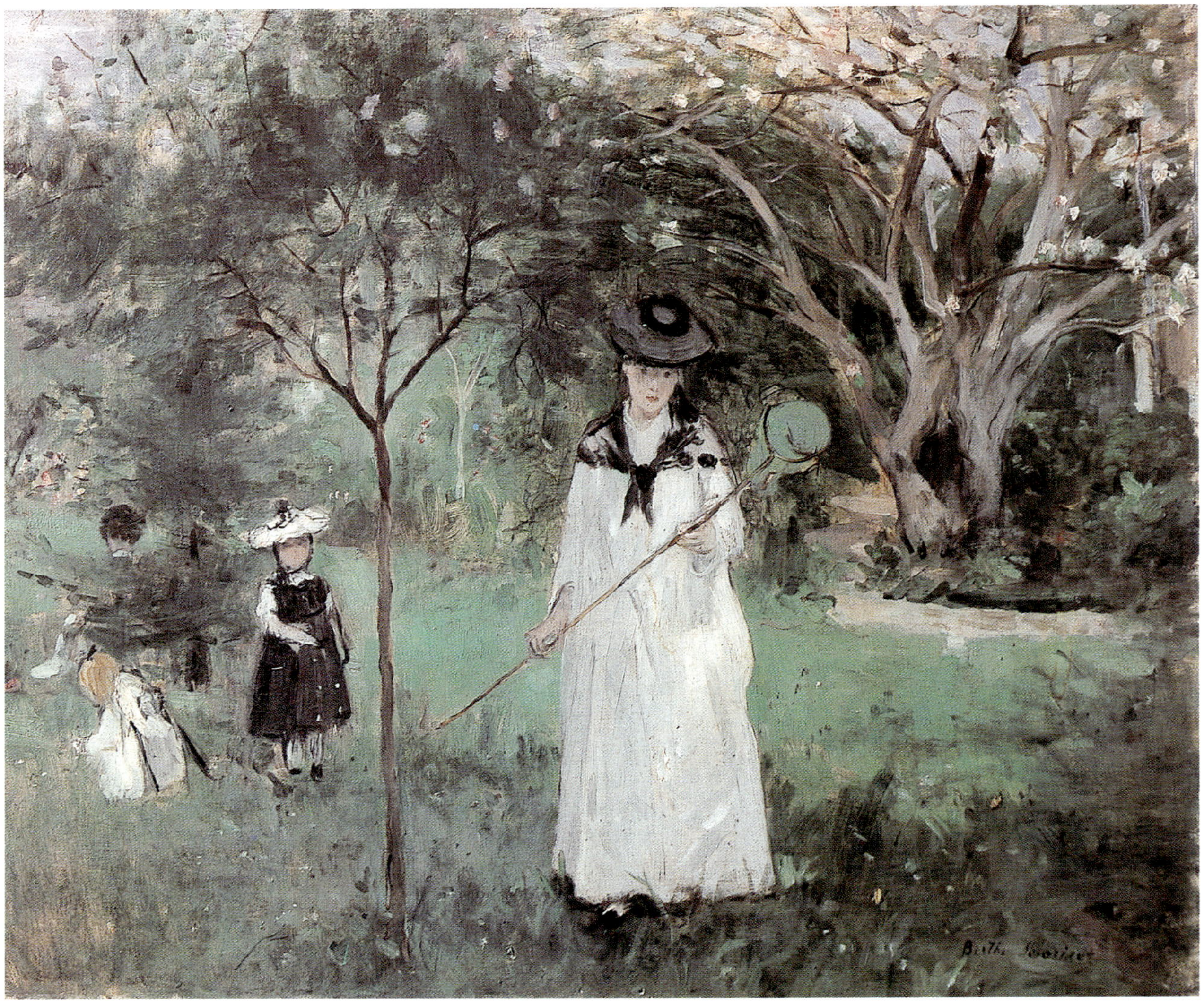

MORISOT
Chasing Butterflies
oil on canvas
1874. 47 × 56 cm
RIGHT Morisot had work accepted by the official Salon as early as 1864, when she was only twenty three: but it was not until 1879, five years after their inaugural exhibition, that she first showed with the Impressionists.

major artists such as Ingres and Delacroix. The latter made no secret of his admiration, a daguerreotype, he said:

> . . . is a mirror of the object, certain details, almost always neglected in drawings from nature . . . in the daguerreotype take on a great importance and bring the artist into a full understanding of the object's construction. There, passages of light and shade show their true qualities . . .

In fact the daguerreotype was often more prone to distorting reality. Very slow exposure speeds in the 1850s meant that gently moving objects like trees were recorded on the plate in a blurred image, the light from the sky eating into the moving edges of the foliage. Corot and the Barbizon School were closely acquainted with the landscape photographers of the time who, as the historian of photography Aaron Scharf suggests, must have been setting up their tripods right next to the painters' easels in the leafy recesses of the Fontainebleau Forest and in other landscape sites. After 1840 there is increasing and direct use of the "halated" or blurred effect in the outline of Corot's trees as well as the influence of photographic over- and under-exposure in his astute handling of light and dark areas.

By the 1860s "snapshots" with fast exposure times were possible and Talbot's system of producing copies on paper from a negative had made the photograph widely available. Manet's *The Execution of The Emperor Maximilian* (*L'Execution de l'empereur Maximilien*) is partly indebted to photographs taken in Mexico of the doomed Emperor and his aides. As a cultural expression of its time, *The Execution* stands poised between the instantaneous modernity of the photograph with its ability to capture current events, and the art of Goya who had painted his *Third of May* (1808) in the first Napoleonic era.

Describing Monet's painting in 1874 Ernest Chesneau perceptively wrote: "Never has the elusive, the fleeting, the instantaneous movement been caught in its incredible flux and fixed, as it is in this extraordinary *Boulevard des Capucines*." The previously unseen, blurred forms of moving people and objects which the camera could reveal had now become part of the vocabulary of the Impressionists, whether or not the influence was a conscious one.

In the year Corot died Degas painted the *Place de la Concorde* (now sadly lost). Of his contemporaries it was Degas who exploited the photograph to its fullest potential, later using it to help him with studies of dancers and horses. The view of the *Place de la Concorde* with the Vicomte Lepic and his daughters frozen in motion, sliced off by the bottom of the picture, and an onlooker on the left similarly clipped by the frame, is clearly reminiscent of a snapshot and influenced by the new ways of framing made possible by the camera.

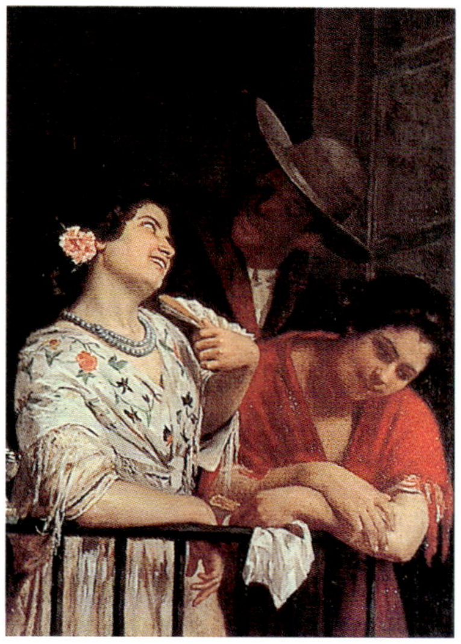

CASSATT
On the Balcony
oil on canvas
1873. 101 × 83 cm
LEFT An unusual Spanish-style picture for Mary Cassatt who, like Berthe Morisot, had to rely on sitters from among the members of her family.

MONET
Boulevard des Capucines
oil on canvas
1873–74. 79 × 59 cm
BELOW The picture was painted in the autumn from Nadar's old photographic studio on the second floor. The brand-new Grand Hotel is on the left.

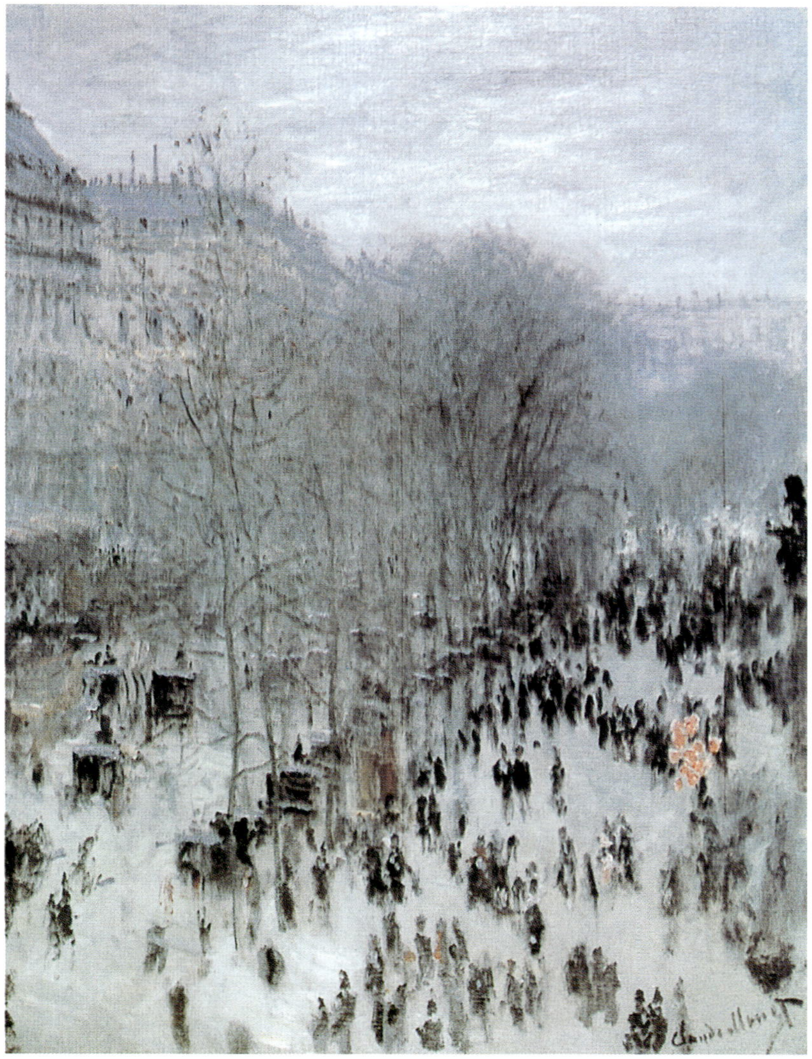

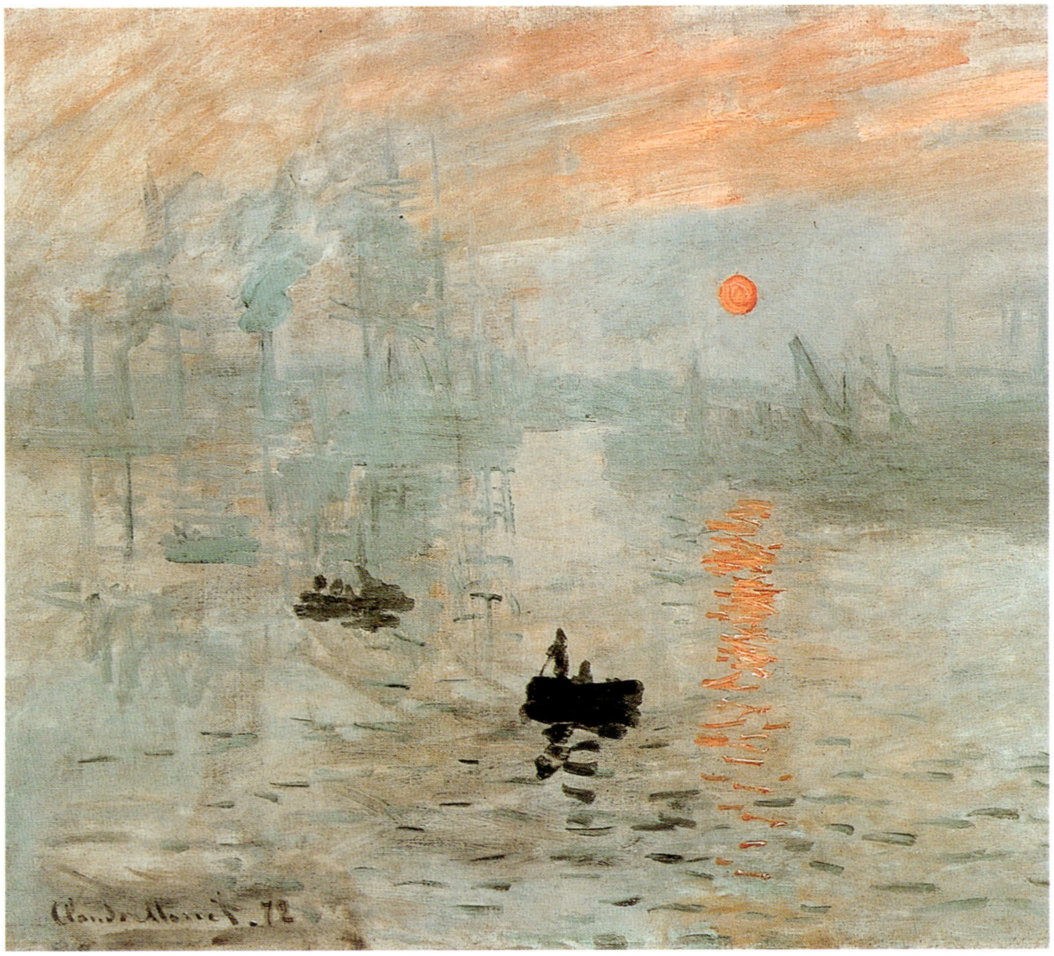

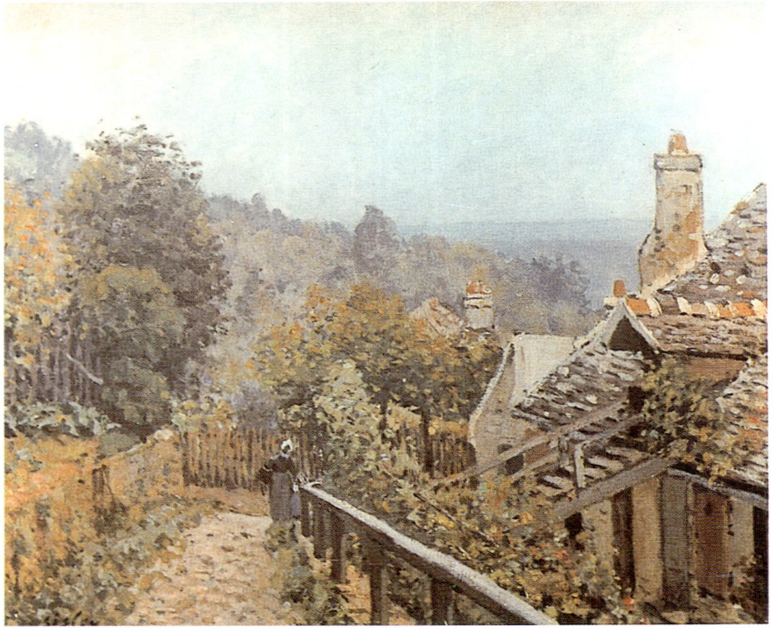

1876–1877: LA NOUVELLE PEINTURE

"None of its members show signs of possessing first-rate talent, and indeed the 'Impressionist' doctrines strike me as incompatible, in an artist's mind, with the existence of first-rate talent. To embrace them you must be provided with a plentiful absence of imagination."

HENRY JAMES, *THE NEW YORK TRIBUNE*
13TH MAY 1876.

The second Impressionist exhibition opened in mid-April 1876 at Durand-Ruel's gallery in the rue Le Pelletier. Some of the more extreme critics had seized the opportunity of likening the group to madmen and syphilitics, so Henry James's criticism seems mild by comparison. Yet it was typical of the prevailing school of thought which still could not accept Impressionism in any form. A critical defence was needed and several writers sympathetic to the Impressionists came to their aid. In his pamphlet *La Nouvelle Peinture*, Edmond Duranty analyzed the "new painting" in some depth. Monet, Renoir, and Pissarro were less than pleased with Duranty's tacit praise of Degas at their expense, but *La Nouvelle Peinture* offers some thoughtful insights into the Impressionists' work. This is what he had to say about the Impressionist use of colour:

> Their real discovery consists in the realization that a strong light *discolours* tones, that sunshine reflected off objects tends by virtue of its clarity to blend its seven prismatic rays into a single, uncoloured brilliance which is light. From one flash of intuition to another, they have succeeded in breaking up solar light into its rays, its elements, and to reconstruct

MONET
Impression, Sunrise
oil on canvas
1872. 48 × 63 cm
OPPOSITE ABOVE This is the painting which provoked Leroy into coining the name Impressionism at the group's first joint exhibition in 1874.

SISLEY
Louveciennes, Heights of Marly
oil on canvas
1873. 38 × 46 cm
OPPOSITE BELOW Sisley painted this scene in the region of Louveciennes, very much the home territory of Pissarro. In this period, shortly before the first Impressionist exhibition of 1874, Sisley was experiencing the life of the professional painter for the first time. Up until 1871, when his father's business collapsed, he had been very much the leisured, gentleman painter: now, he painted to eat.

PISSARRO
La Côte du Chou, Pontoise
oil on canvas
c.1875–76. 81.5 × 65 cm
RIGHT At this stage of his career Pissarro was increasingly being sought out by his younger Impressionist colleagues for help and advice. Cézanne, in particular, was a frequent visitor to Pontoise (where Pissarro and his family had returned in 1872), and once said that his friend was "a little like the good Lord."

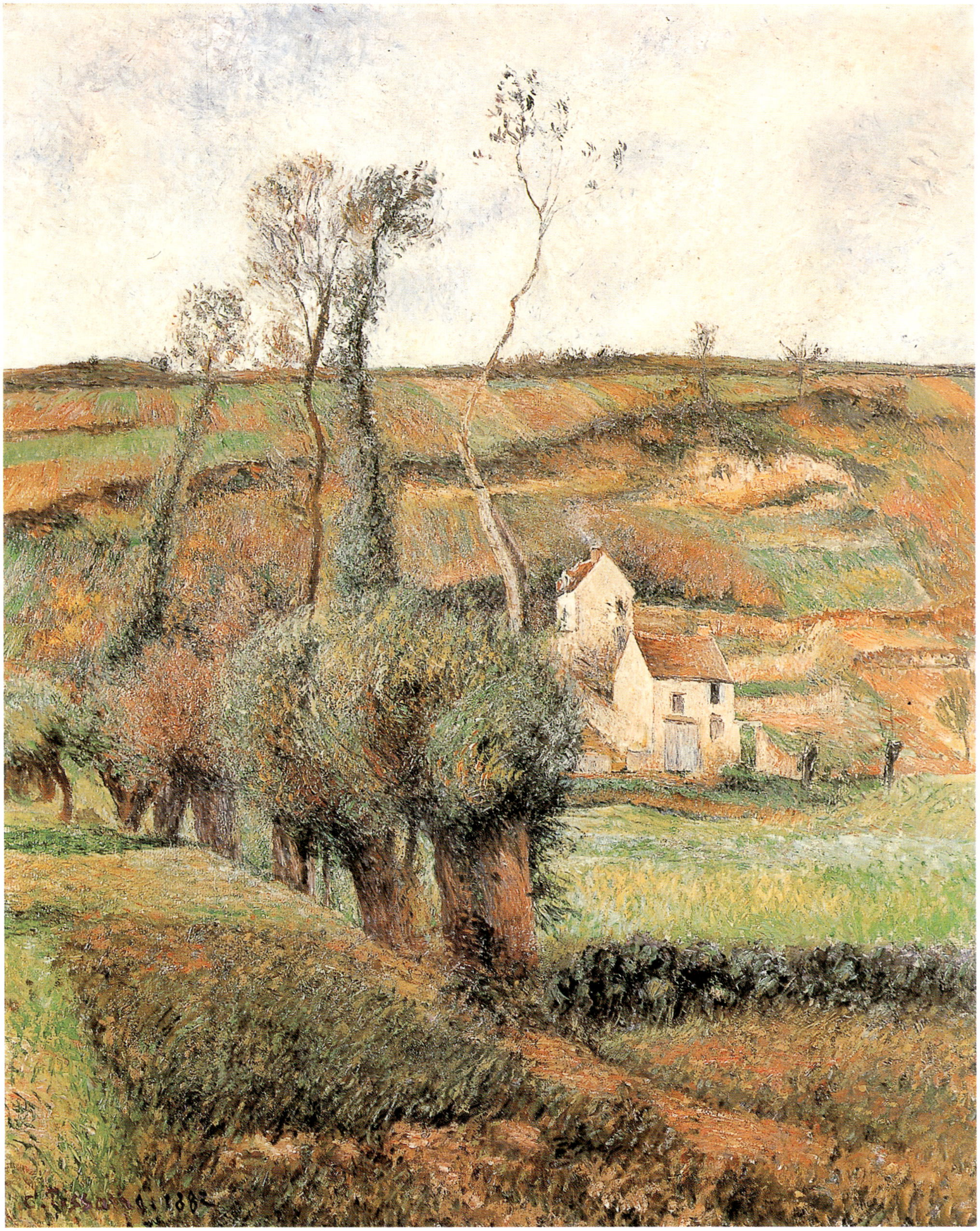

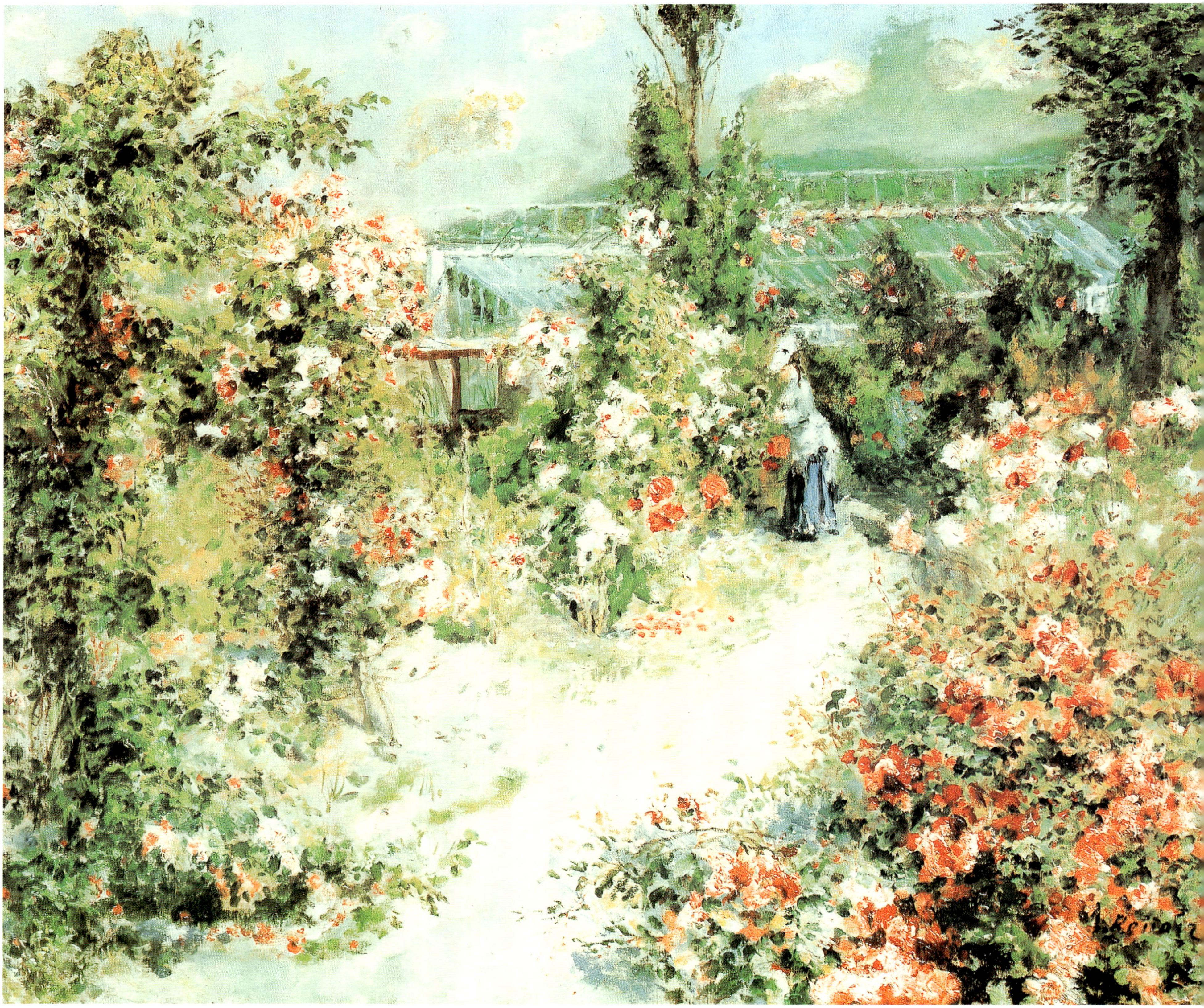

> it as a unity by the general harmony of the iridescence they spread on their canvases. From the viewpoint of the refinement of vision and the subtle penetration of colours, it has produced an extraordinary result. The most astute physicist could find no fault with their analysis of colour.

Other critics did not agree. One of the fifteen works by Renoir at the second exhibition (several were on loan from Victor Chocquet) was the *Étude*, better known as *Nude in Sunlight*. In his satire on the first exhibition Leroy had conceded that the painter "has a certain understanding of colour"; and Silvestre in *L'Opinion* thought *Nude in Sunlight* "the work of a true colourist." Wolff, however, in *Le Figaro* made a devastating attack focused on Renoir's palette:

> Would someone kindly explain to M. Renoir that a woman's torso is not a mass of decomposing flesh with the green and purplish blotches that indicate a state of complete putrefaction in a corpse . . .

Not to be outdone in similes of corrupt flesh, Louis Enault in *Le Constitutionnel* offered his readers this opinion:

> It is depressing to look at this large study of a nude woman; her purplish flesh is the colour of game that has been hung for too long, and someone really should have made her put on a dress.

Despite these attacks this was, as art historian Phoebe Pool says, Renoir's *annus mirabilis*. Not only do two of his finest paintings, *The Swing* (*La Balançoire*) and the *Ball at the Moulin de la Galette* (*Bal du Moulin de la Galette*), date

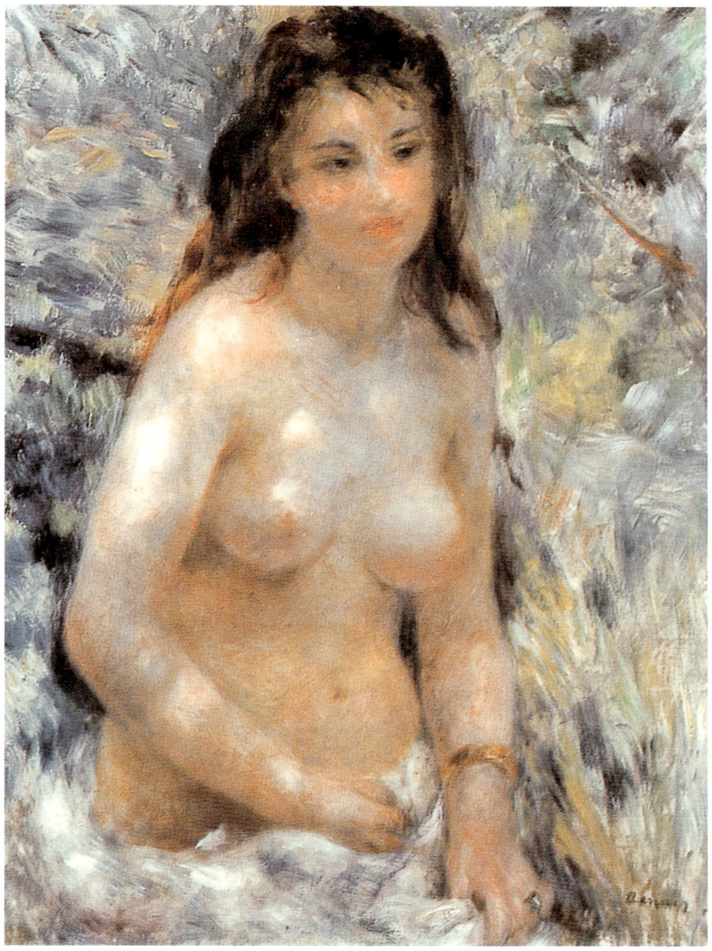

RENOIR
Nude in Sunlight
oil on canvas
1876. 81 × 65 cm
Left Where Monet concentrated on the overall lighting in a picture, Renoir preferred the contrast of light and shade. The picture was bitterly condemned by critics, one of whom, Albert Wolff, likened it to decomposing flesh. Georges Rivière, a friend of Renoir said of Wolff: "When I see Albert Wolff I can forgive him the harsh words he has written about my friends. Nature has treated him far worse."

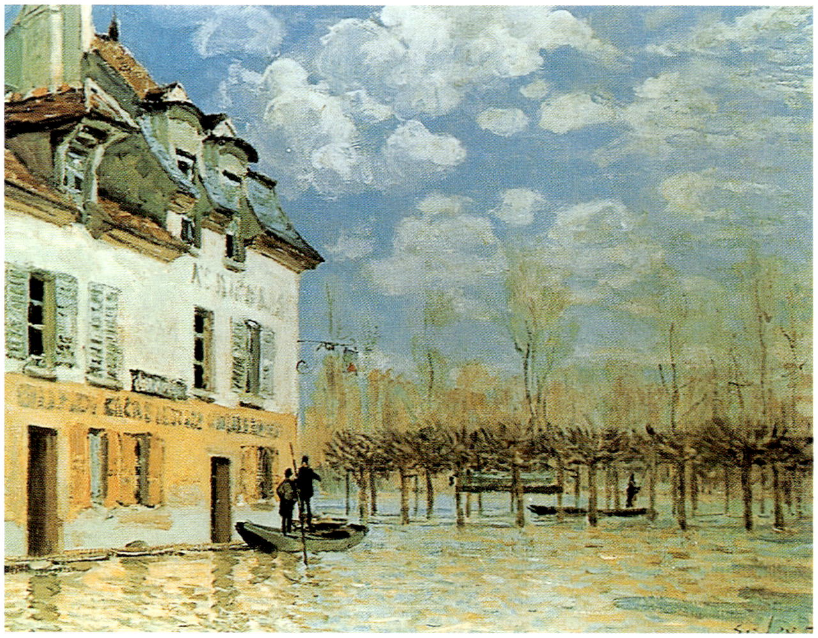

SISLEY
Flood at Port Marly
oil on canvas
1876. 50 × 61 cm
Below left

RENOIR
The Greenhouse
oil on canvas
Undated. 60 × 74 cm
Opposite

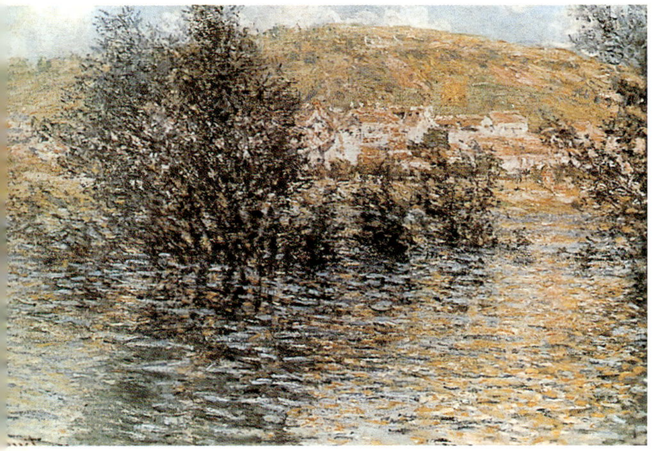

MONET
The Seine at Vétheuil
oil on canvas
1879. 60 × 81 cm
ABOVE This picture was painted during a period when Monet's fortunes were at a very low ebb: personal or financial difficulties never did effect his incredible work-rate.

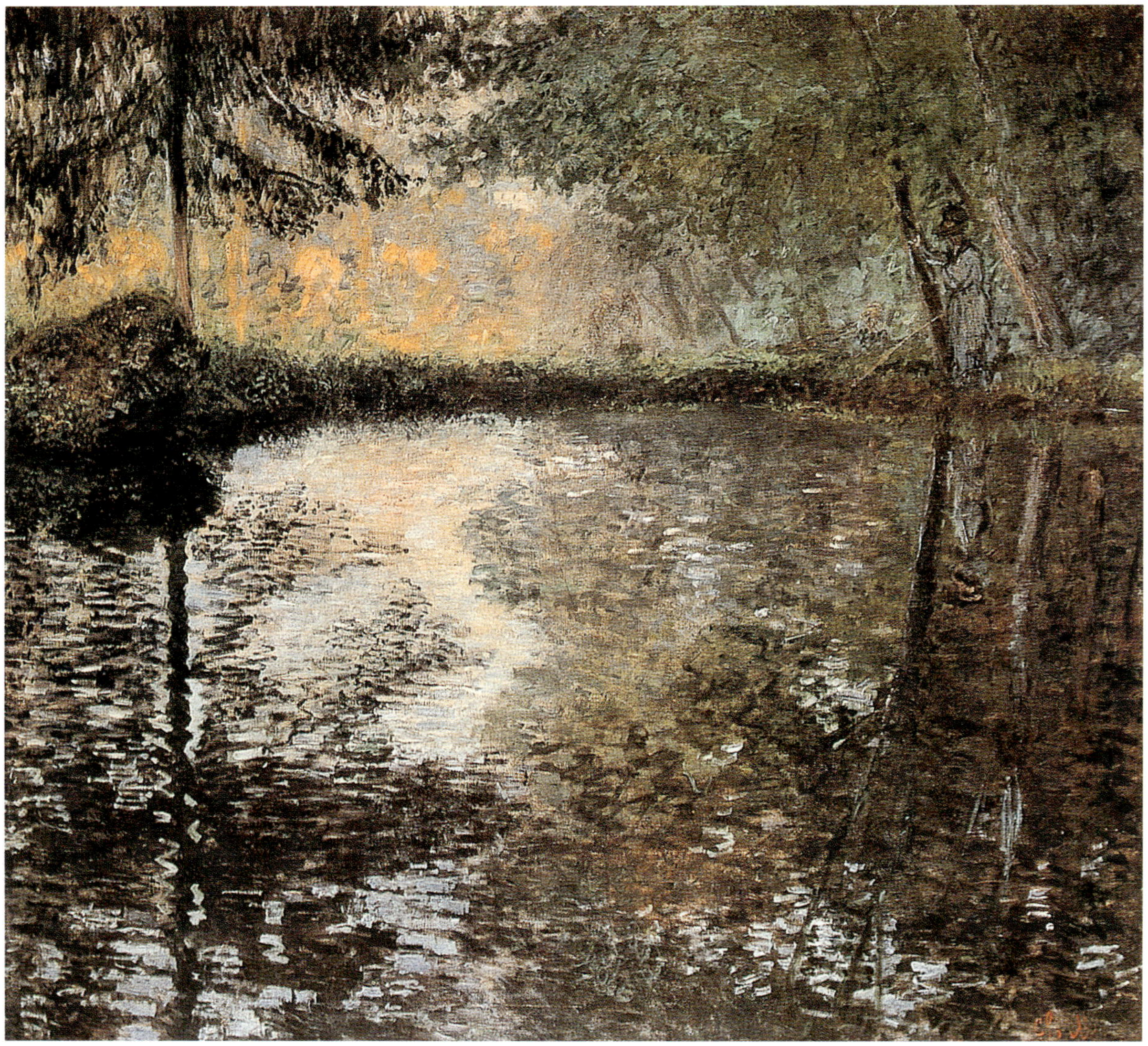

from this period, but he had the good fortune to meet Georges Charpentier, a wealthy young publisher who became an important patron. Mme Charpentier's salon was an important meeting place for the intellectual and social élite of the day. Renoir's later portrait of Mme Charpentier is described by Proust in *Time Regained* (*Le Temps retrouvé*) as being comparable to the best of Titian.

It was also around this time that a young painter of independent means, Gustave Caillebotte, became an important force amongst the Impressionists. His *Floor Scrapers* (*Les Raboteurs de parquets*) and *Le Pont de l'Europe* were shown at the second Impressionist exhibition. The influence of Degas and photography is discernible in the deep perspective, and whilst the style can hardly be called "impressionistic" in the sense of Monet, Sisley, or Renoir, these and several later paintings, notably the *Boulevard Seen from Above* (*Boulevard vu d'en haut*) have often been mentioned as some of the most memorable urban images of his century. Seven years younger than Renoir and Monet, Caillebotte was soon engaged in organizing the 1877 exhibition and funding the group through the extensive purchase of some of their most important works, with the intention of bequeathing them to the State. (There were sixty in all, including the two by Renoir mentioned above, now in the Musée d'Orsay, in Paris).

As Renoir's fortunes waxed for the time being, Monet's waned. During the years between 1876 and 1880 Monet was consistently forced to rely on the largesse of others. He described himself as being penniless and destitute, although he was still earning (and spending) six times more than the average workman whilst occasionally living in some style. Nevertheless the third Impressionist exhibition held at Durand-Ruel's and funded by Caillebotte, showed that penury could not stop Monet's outflow of work.

In January Caillebotte had rented a small apartment and studio for Monet close to the Gare St Lazare, the main station for points west of Paris, including the Normandy coast, Argenteuil, and Bougival (in 1877 it handled 13 million passengers). With the sort of bravado only a penniless artist like Monet could summon up, he went to call on the Superintendent of the railway who assumed him to be a famous artist and offered him the freedom of the station. A series of twelve paintings was the result, seven of which were shown at the third exhibition. Greeted with astonishment, they proved to be the last of his urban landscapes. Georges Rivière, an art critic of the time held the overall view that "these paintings are amazingly varied, despite the monotony and aridity of the subject. In them more than anywhere else can be seen that skill in arrangement, that organization of the canvas, that is one of the main qualities of Monet's work." Trains and the new railways

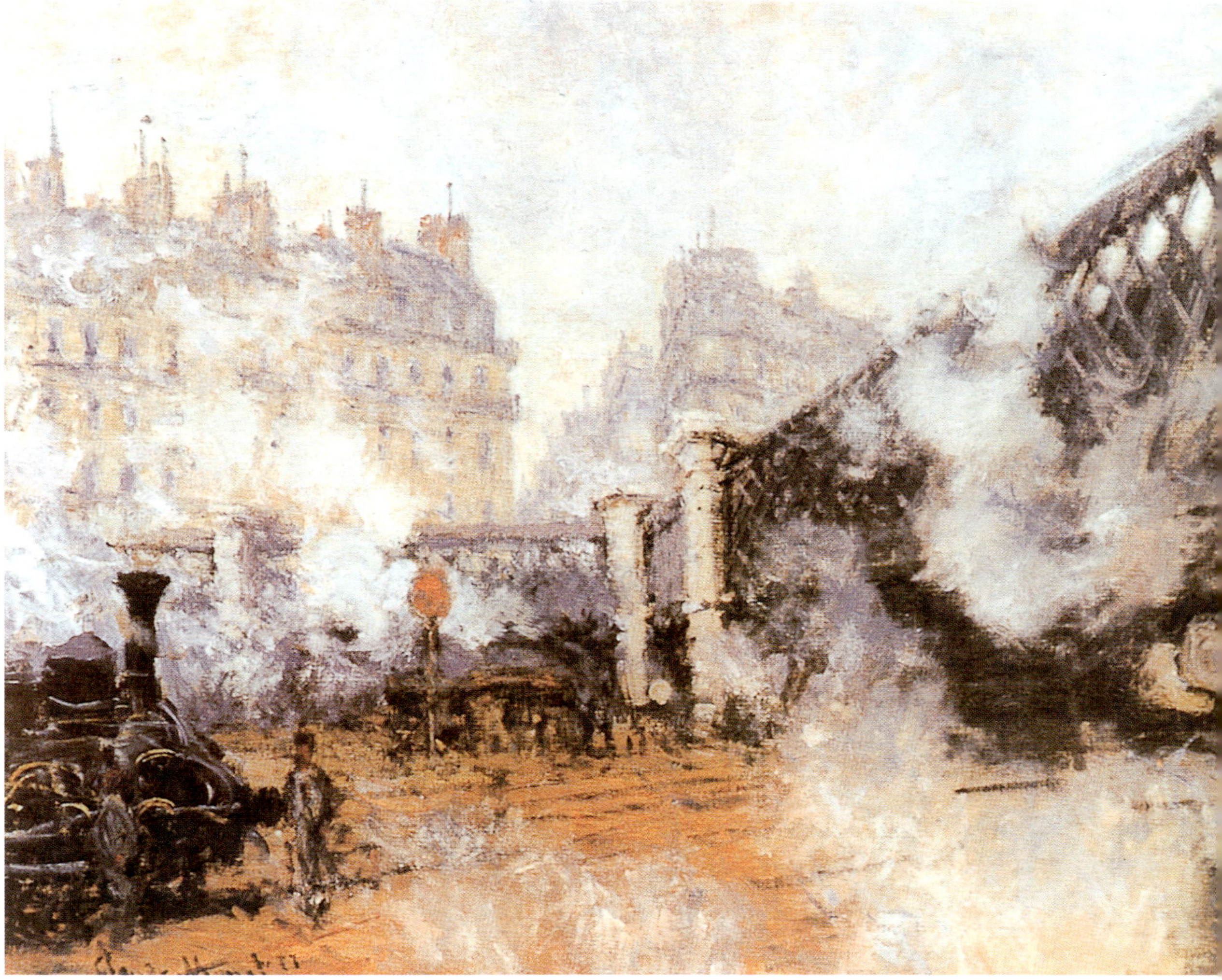

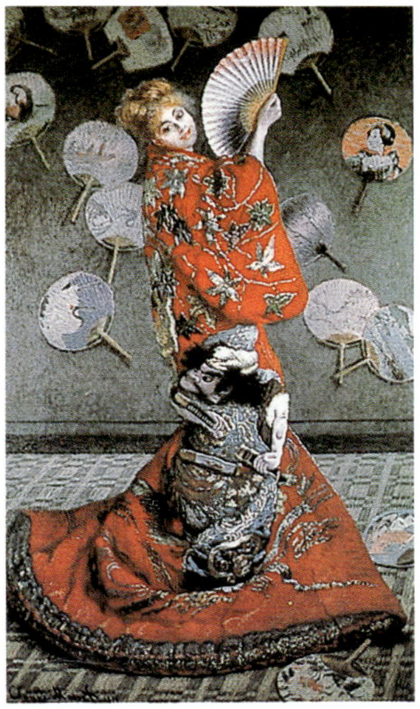

MONET
Gare St Lazare, Pont de l'Europe
oil on canvas
1877. 64 × 81 cm
Above The railway bridge seen at train level, a much more animated and interesting composition than Caillebotte's work.

MONET
The Japanese Kimono
oil on canvas
1876. 231 × 142 cm
Left The model is Monet's first wife, Camille.

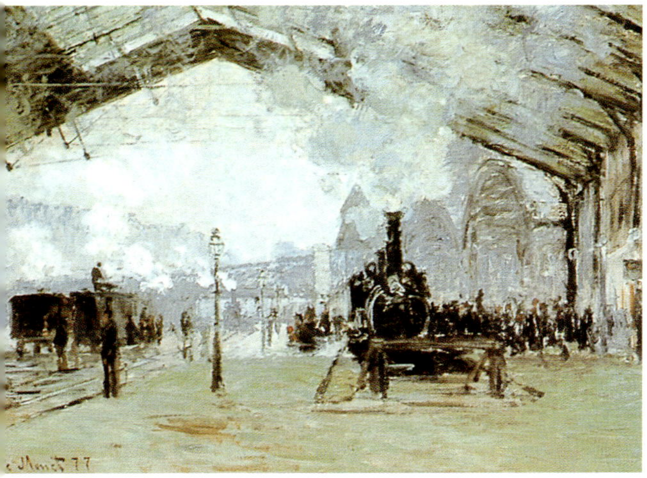

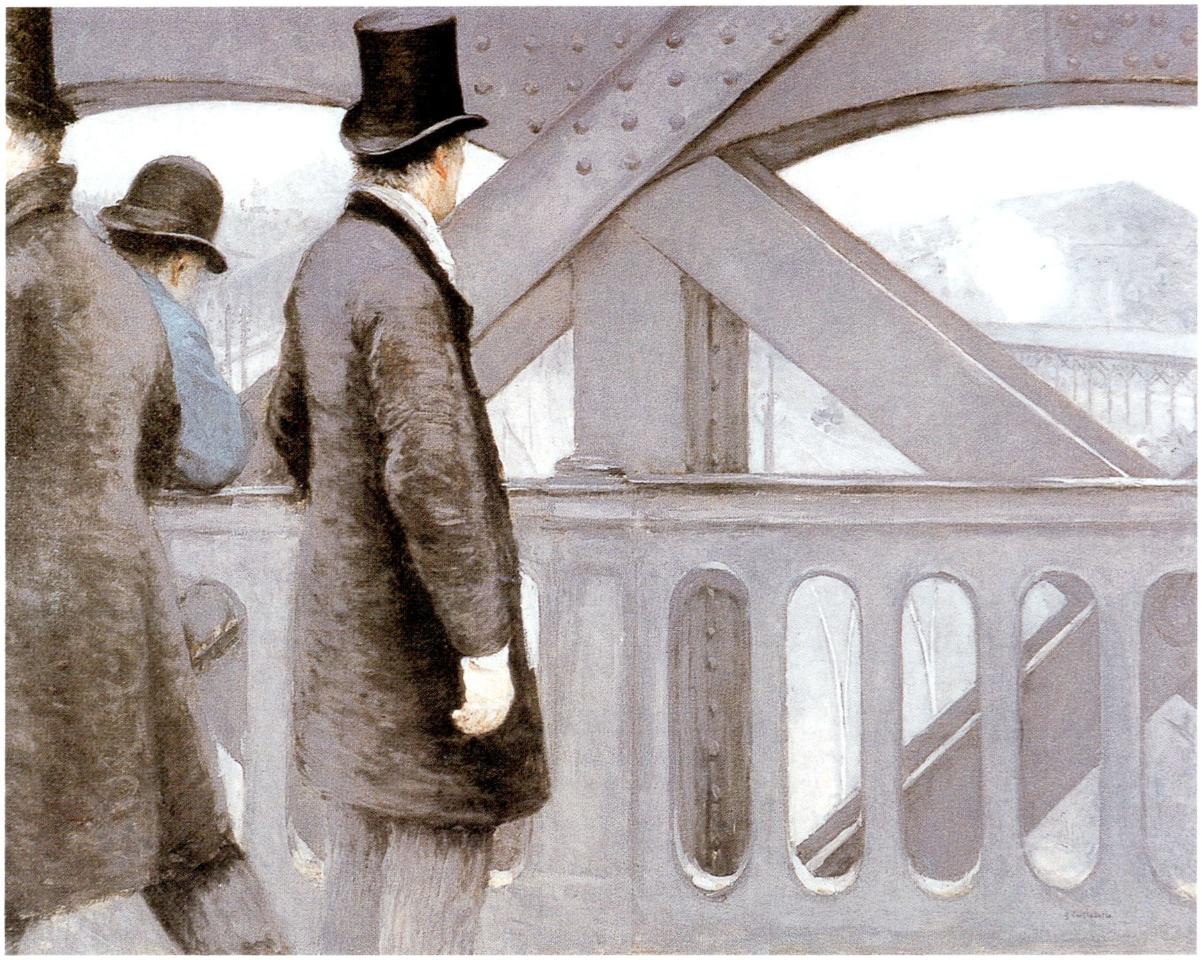

MONET
Gare St Lazare
oil on canvas
1877. 60 × 80 cm
ABOVE Monet put on his best suit, went to the director of railways and asked permission to paint inside the station. Mistaken for a famous artist, the station was cleared for him, the engines stacked to provide abundant smoke, and he was escorted by railway officials. He painted twelve views of the station and showed seven of them at the third Impressionist show of 1877.

CAILLEBOTTE
Pont de l'Europe
oil on canvas
1876–77. 105 × 130 cm
RIGHT Caillebotte lived in the area of the St Lazare railway station, like Manet.

were indeed an important feature in the work of the other artists, notably Pissarro, Sisley, and Manet. Manet's *The Railway* (*Le Chemin de fer*) of 1873 tells us a great deal about the difference between him and Monet. It is primarily a figure painting: the railway itself is beyond the picture and represented by a cloud of steam; the little girl stands (like Degas' double-bass) with her back to us. Manet, unlike Monet, is not primarily interested in the railway as such, but in the relationship between it and his figures. As an icon of its time it is a powerful image, portraying a sense of wonderment (the girl) and banality (the woman) in the modern world.

Looking at this modern world from an entirely different perspective, Degas' contribution to the exhibition included two celebrated images of Parisian vice; *In a Café* (also known as *The Absinthe Drinker*) and *Women on the Terrace of a Café in the Evening* (*Femmes à la terrasse d'un café soir*). Of the latter, the contemporary critic Alexandre Pothey confessed, "the terrifying realism of these painted, faded creatures, exuding vice, who cynically tell each other about their day's activities and accomplishments." The scandal caused by Manet's *Olympia* twelve years before in the long summer days of the Second Empire had been instrumental in clearing the way for Degas' explicit depiction of prostitution and alcoholism, now tacitly acceptable in polite

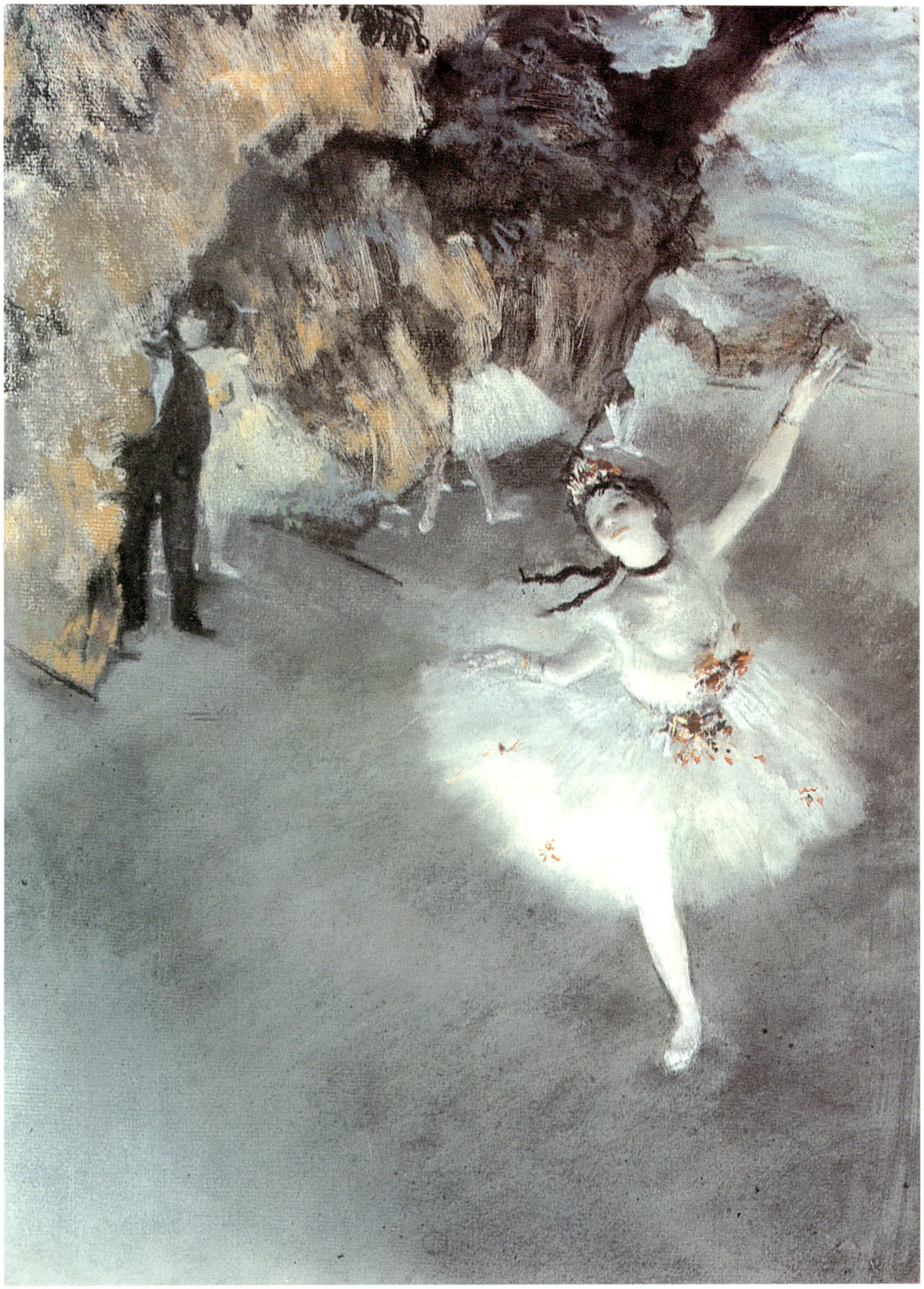

Third Republic society. If Baudelaire had survived he would have been delighted, for Degas was now the painter of modern life *par excellence*, making art of everything that went on in Paris, from the loneliest bar to the heaving café-concert. His interest in ballet had resulted in *The Star* (*L'Etoile*) and *Dancers at the Barre*, whilst the café-concert, a sort of vaudeville or music hall at the height of its popularity in the 1870s, was the trigger for several pictures on this subject, as indeed it was for Renoir and Manet.

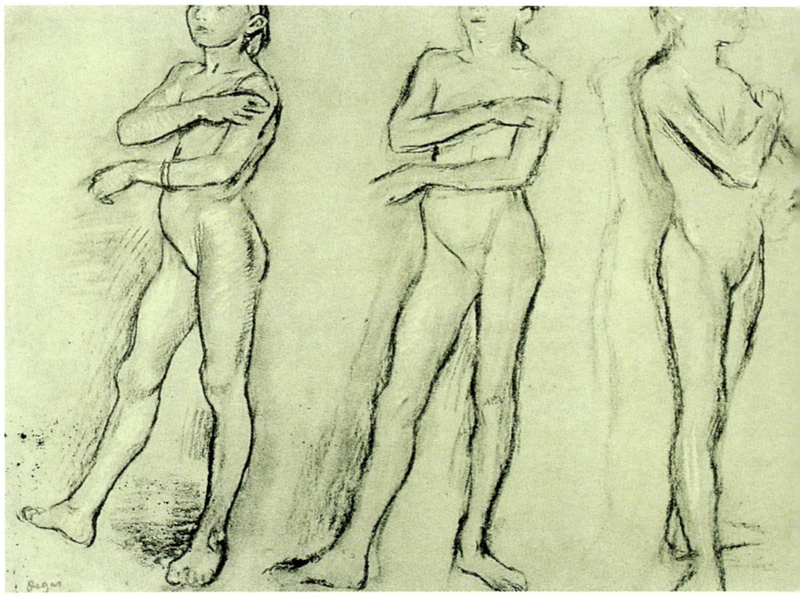

DEGAS
The Star
pastel/monotype
c.1878. 60 × 44 cm
LEFT Degas said, "People call me the painter of dancing girls. It has never occurred to them that my chief interest in dancers lies in rendering movement and in painting pretty clothes."

DEGAS
Three studies for a Fourteen-year-old Dancer
chalk and charcoal on green paper
c.1876–80. 48 × 63 cm
ABOVE The exhaustive studies for this sculpture demonstrate both Degas' determination to master his subject completely, and his cautious move into a new medium, that of sculpture, which became increasingly important in later years when his eyesight began to fail.

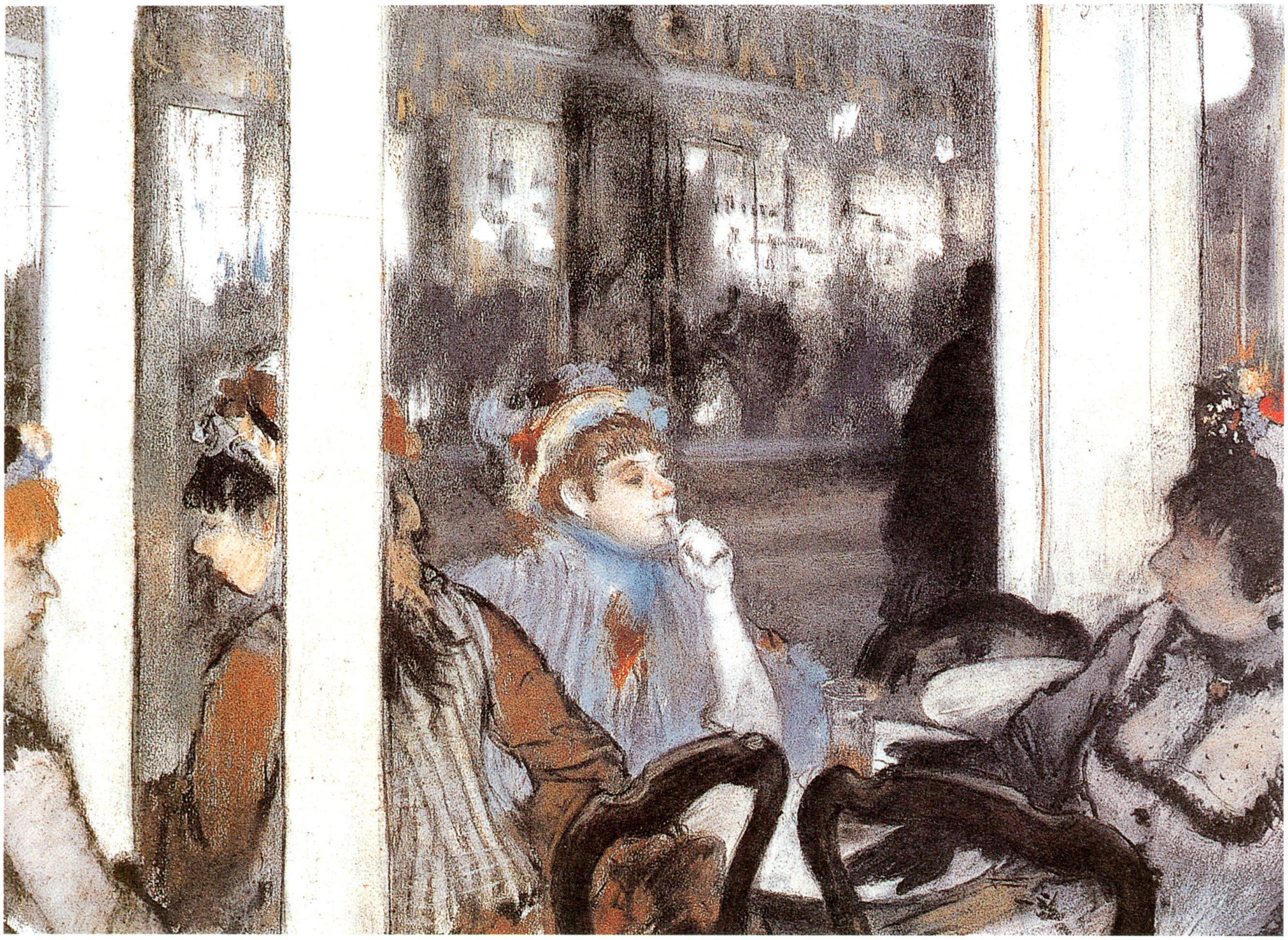

1878–1881: Beginning of the End

We are far from the moment when we are able to do without the prestige attached to the official exhibitions.

Alfred Sisley, 1878

In 1878 an important patron of the Impressionists, Ernest Hoschedé, the director of a Paris department store, was in serious financial difficulties which later forced him to sell a sizeable collection of works he had accumulated after the first Impressionist exhibition in 1874. Monet in particular was affected by the impending fall of Hoschedé; he had made extensive use of Hoschedé's country house at Montgeron near Paris and had produced some important work for the collector. The loss of a patron was bad enough; Monet and Camille now had a second child to support, they had recently been forced to leave their house in Argenteuil, relying on Edouard Manet to find them lodgings at Lavacourt near Vétheuil, a village over thirty miles from Paris. The Monets were already desperate, as Camille was ill with cancer of the uterus, and to make things worse, the Hoschedés were ruined, and they came, with their six children, to stay. To complicate matters Claude had been having a secret liaison with Hoschedé's wife, Alice, for some time. Thus began a strange *ménage à douze*. From around this time Monet began to be more and more isolated from the other Impressionists, rarely venturing into Paris.

One of the founding members of the *Société anonyme* who had already cut himself off from the group to a certain extent, pursuing his own aims and methods, was Alfred Sisley. He was becoming a recluse; some years later he crossed the street to avoid Renoir who had once been one of his closest friends. Eight years earlier Sisley's father's business had crashed during the Franco-Prussian War and from this time to his death in 1899 his life was a continual struggle to support his family. His finest work dates from the mid-1870s. Sisley had lived near Argenteuil in the earlier part of the decade and between 1875 and 1877 he had gone to Marly-le-Roi to continue his landscapes. In 1878 he got his work into the Salon along with Renoir; both artists had now officially left the Impressionists. Sisley told Duret that:

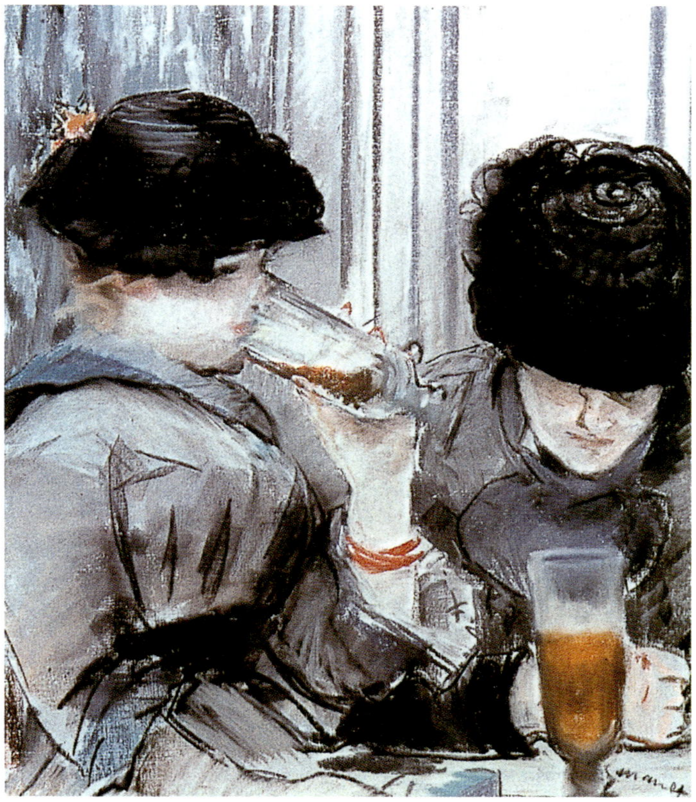

DEGAS
Women on the Terrace of a Café in the Evening
pastel/monotype
1877. 41 × 60 cm
Opposite

MANET
Women Drinking Beer
pastel on paper
1878. 61 × 51 cm
Left Manet and Degas were the resolutely urban painters of the group. Scenes of modern Parisian life were just the sort of thing that Baudelaire had in mind when he demanded a new art.

SISLEY
Snow at Louveciennes
oil on canvas
1878. 61 × 50.5 cm
RIGHT Like Monet and Pissarro, Sisley was concerned with capturing the blue winter light on the snow. Renoir hated it and painted only one snow scene.

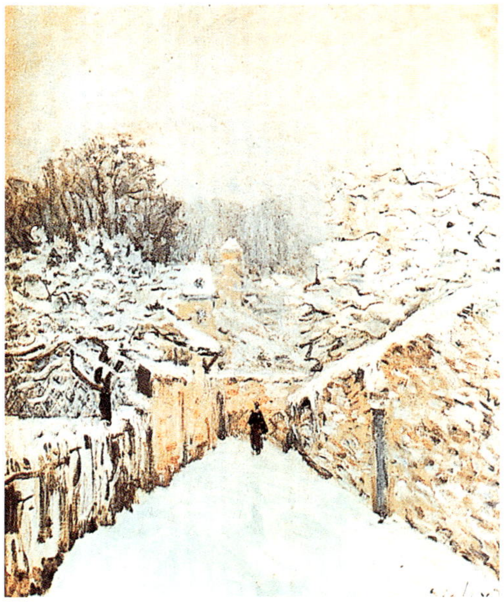

PISSARRO
The Kitchen Garden
oil on canvas
1879. 55 × 65 cm
BELOW Whereas Renoir had a longing to be accepted by high society, Pissarro remained staunchly loyal to his principles and continued to paint humble subjects.

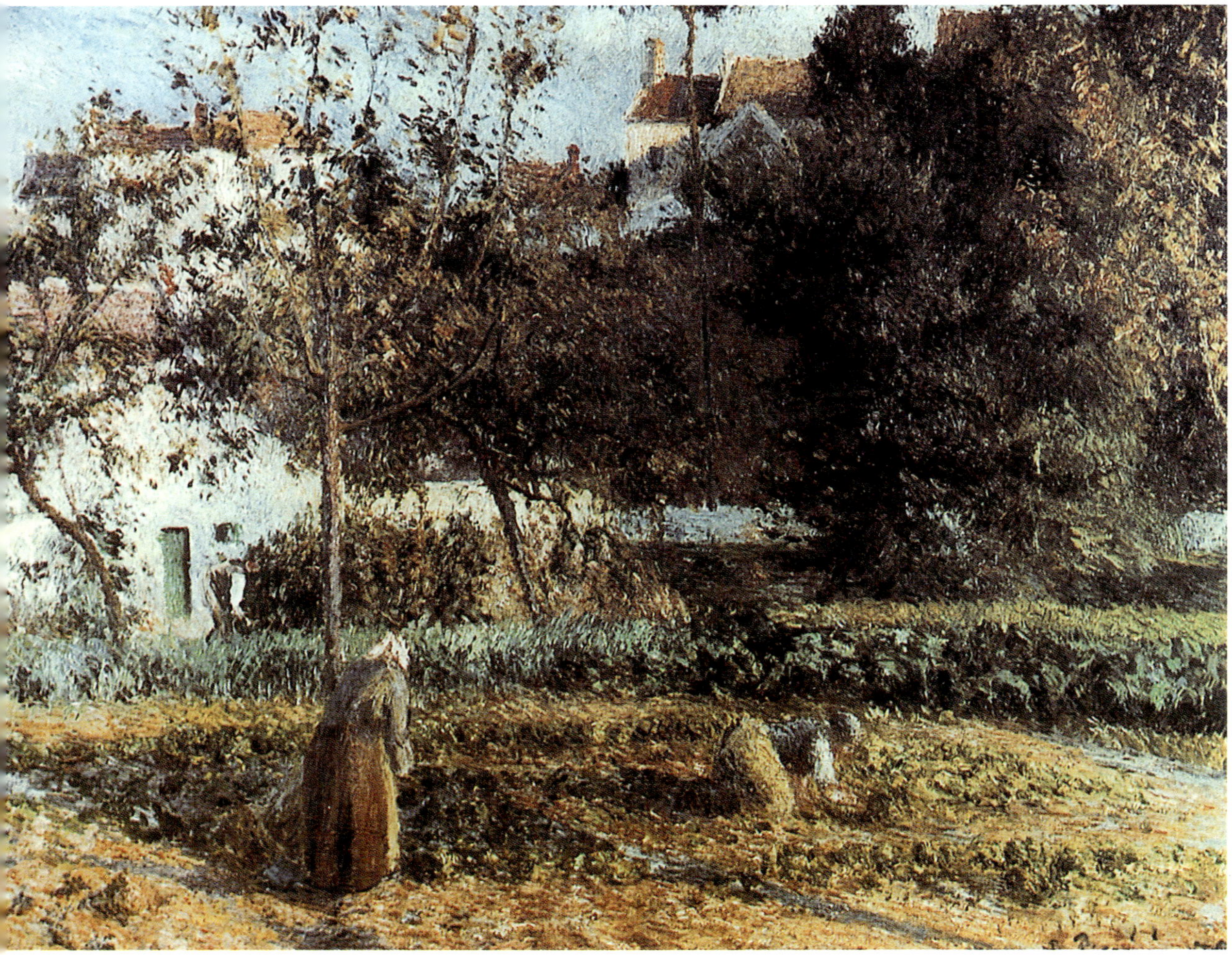

> It is true that our exhibitions have served to make us known and in this they have been very useful to me, but I believe we must not isolate ourselves for too long. We are far from the moment when we are able to do without the prestige attached to the official exhibitions. I am therefore determined to submit to the Salon.

Underlying this dissatisfaction was the increasing dominance that Degas (and Caillebotte) seemed to be exerting on the group. A benign example of Degas' influence can be seen in his patronage of a young American, Mary Cassatt, who had been living in France since 1866 and had shown twice at the Salon. But other, lesser artists were now to be drafted into the Impressionist exhibitions to make up for the loss of Renoir, Sisley, and later Monet himself. Clearly the Impressionist exhibitions had partially succeeded in promulgating the "movement" but the Impressionists themselves could not expect to live on the proceeds. Chocquet, Charpentier, and other patrons (Manet and Caillebotte also fulfilled this role) were still vital to their livelihood, and, as frustration with the relative failure of the independent shows grew, Renoir, Sisley, and Monet in particular looked once again to the Salon. The radical Pissarro would not countenance this and in 1878, a year when there was no Impressionist exhibition, he rented a room in the Montmartre quarter of Paris to exhibit his own pictures, which were ironically less radical than ever before, to potential clients. Pissarro, like Monet, had recently lost a friend and patron, Ludovic Piette, a landscapist of some talent who had exhibited with the Impressionists and had died in 1877, depriving Pissarro of an important source of income.

"A BANAL SCHOOL"

The fourth Impressionist exhibition opened on 10th April 1879 at 28 avenue de l'Opéra in Paris without Sisley, Renoir, Morisot (who was pregnant) and Cézanne, but it had works by Cassatt, Forain, Zandomeneghi (all protégés of Degas) and an as yet unknown painter by the name of Paul Gauguin, who had been befriended by Pissarro. For once it was a success and the irony was that as the crowds flocked to see the exhibition there were precious few of the major Impressionists on view. The Salon was now the place to see works like Renoir's *Portrait of Madame Charpentier and Her Children* (*Madame Charpentier et ses enfants*) and Manet's *Boating* (*En Bateau*), both of which received considerable acclaim. That April Georges Charpentier published the first edition of *La Vie Moderne*, a magazine of style, science, comment, and criticism aimed at the well-to-do Parisian. *La Vie Moderne* instituted a series of exhibitions at which Renoir in 1879, and Manet and Monet in 1880, were to have hugely successful one-man shows. As Monet's work finally began to receive the praise he had longed for he was at his most isolated, declaring, "I am still and always intend to be an Impressionist – but very rarely see the men and women who are

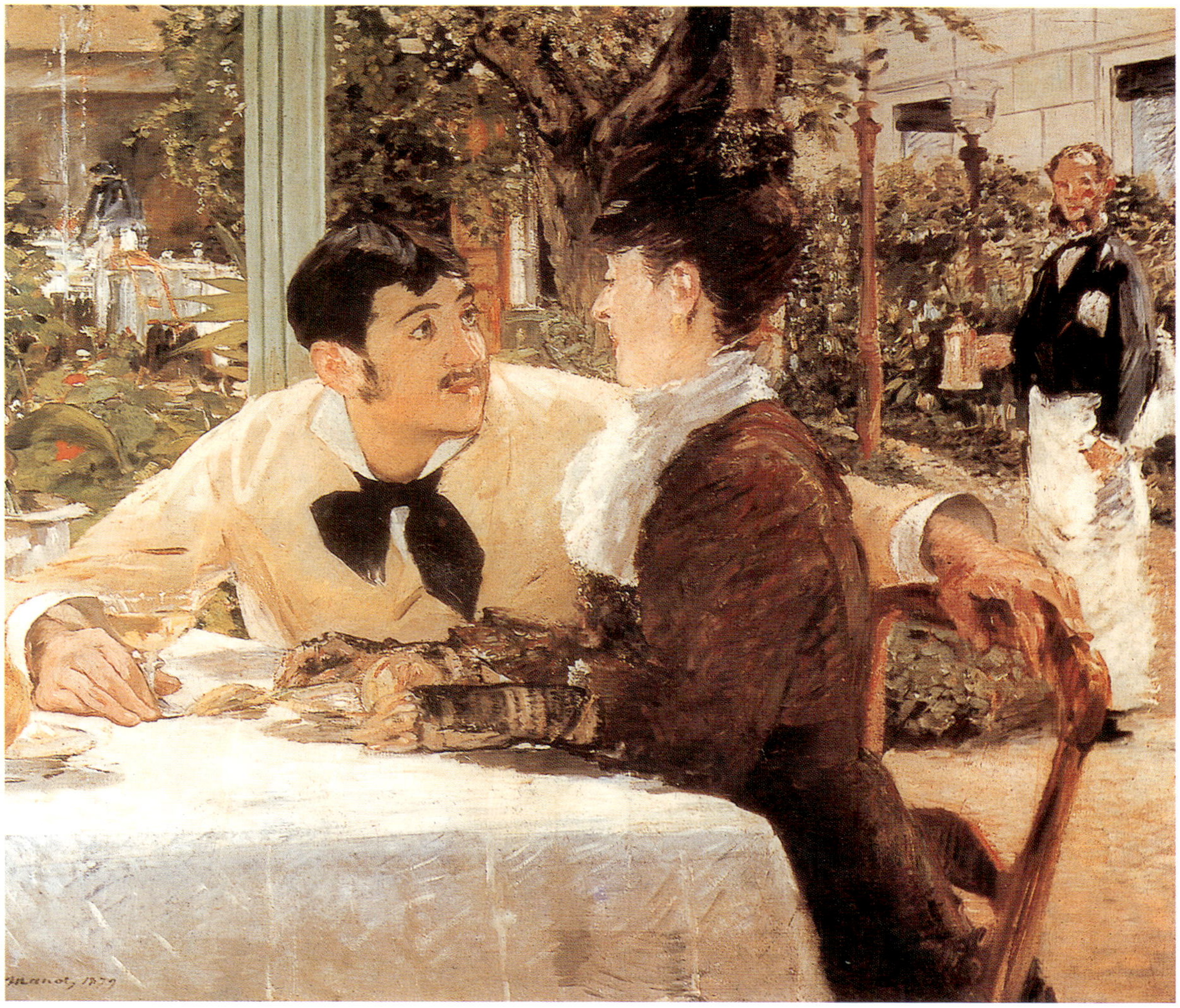

MANET
At the Père Lathuille
oil on canvas
1879. 93 × 112 cm
The Impressionists challenged not only the technique but also the subject matter of the academic style as taught in the Ecole. Manet, although not radically different in technique, turned his eye away from the traditional, classical content of painting by depicting the modern life of Paris. Here he has chosen a restaurant in the Batignolles area near where he lived as the setting for what could have been an ordinarily bourgeois scene.

CASSATT
Young Lady in a Park
oil on canvas
c.1880. 71 × 90 cm
RIGHT In his essay in Le Figaro *entitled "The Painter of Modern Life", a seminal influence on the Impressionists, Baudelaire set forth his views on the status of women in this new art. "Woman", he wrote, "is for the artist in general . . . she is divinity, a star . . . a glittering conglomeration of all the graces of nature, condensed into a single being . . . she is an idol, stupid perhaps, but dazzling and bewitching . . ." Clearly this attitude had little to do with the lives and work of Cassatt and Morisot, who could not walk the streets of Paris, or even copy in the Louvre, without being chaperoned.*

CASSATT
Mother and Child
pastel on paper
Undated. 55 × 45 cm
OPPOSITE Mary Cassatt, who had no children, nevertheless made motherhood and child-rearing her personal artistic domain. As this pastel shows, she was influenced by Degas, her initial mentor, and treats her subjects with the detailed observation not to be found amongst her truly impressionistic contemporaries.

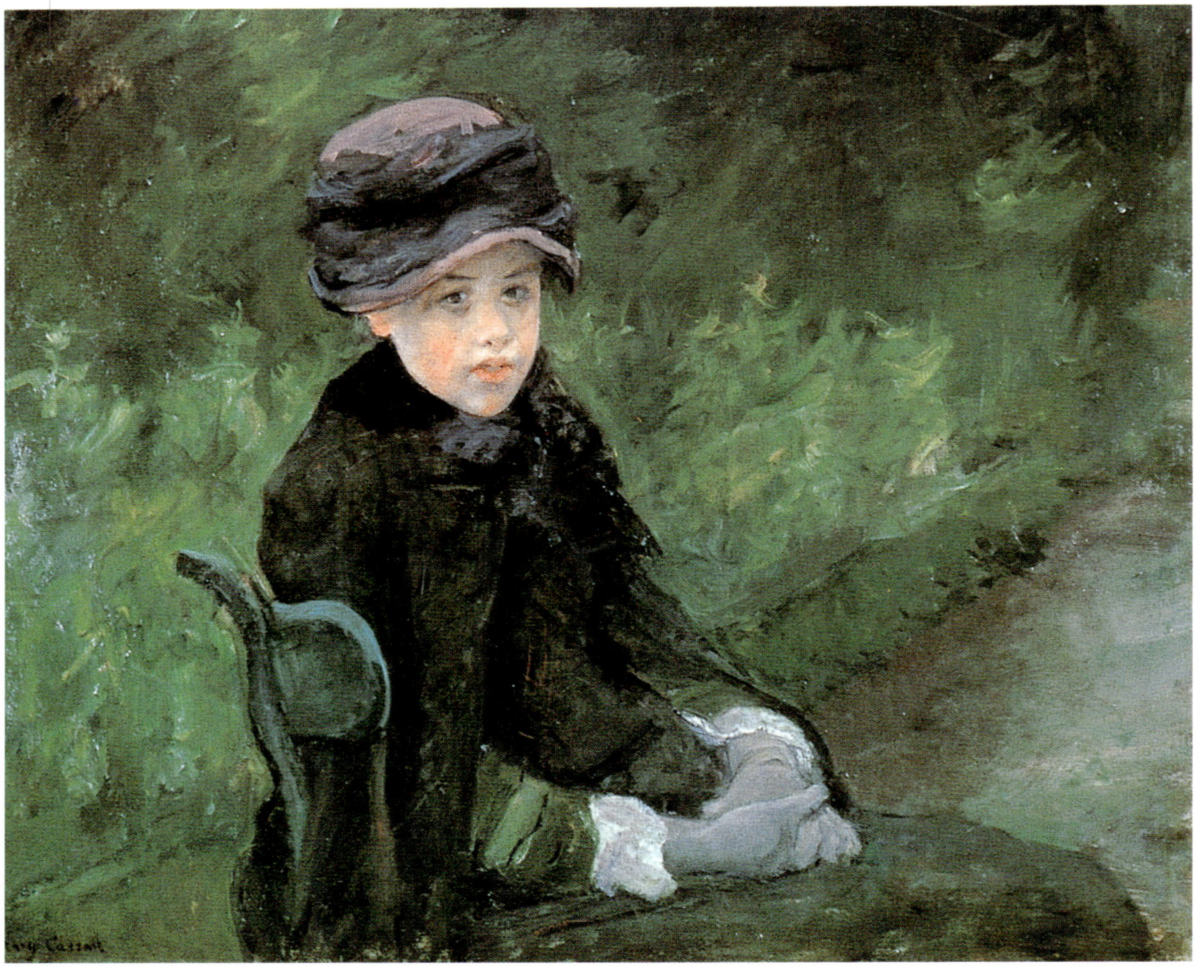

my colleagues. The little church has become a banal school which opens its doors to the first dauber that comes along."

Camille died in September 1879. As he watched her growing cold, Monet could not resist painting her portrait for the last time. 1880 marked the beginning of a new decade and the end of an era. Duranty, Flaubert, and Offenbach had died. Manet's illness was now seriously affecting him, making a trip to the Café de la Nouvelle-Athènes, which had replaced the Café Guerbois as Manet's haunt, a rare occurence. Of the original subscribers to the *Société anonyme* only Degas (who had appeared in every show so far), Pissarro, and Berthe Morisot were to exhibit in the Impressionist exhibitions of 1880 and 1881. Renoir was moving in a higher strata of society and was now financially secure although an artistic crisis was looming for him. Degas' increasing grip on the Impressionist exhibitions in which he included more and more of his followers drove Pissarro and Caillebotte to beg him to allow Monet, Renoir, and Sisley back into the fold. Caillebotte finally turned against Degas, bitterly attacking him in a letter to Pissarro:

> This man has gone sour. He doesn't hold the big place that he ought to according to his talent and although he will never admit it, he bears the whole world a grudge. One could

> put together a volume from what he has said against Manet, Monet, you . . .

Pissarro would not be swayed and remained faithful to Degas to the last. The 1881 exhibition opened at the boulevard des Capucines where seven years earlier Monet's *Impression, Sunrise* had given the history of art a new -*ism*. Caillebotte did not participate. A new generation of Impressionists joined Degas, Morisot, Guillaumin, and Pissarro; this was the third Impressionist show for Mary Cassatt, the second for Paul Gauguin; the others included Rouart, Vidal, Vignon, and Zandomeneghi.

Meanwhile the dying Manet had been awarded the *Légion d'Honneur* by a Third Republic which had finally come to terms with him. The pronouncement of Gambetta, the hero of the Siege of Paris in 1870, that "You are revolutionaries, that's the trouble . . . It is better for the Republic to live with bad painting than to die for the sake of great art . . . " had been overturned. The love-hate relationship between the Salon and Manet, the continual rejections and occasional triumphs, had at last resolved itself in favour of the artist. Manet had always tried to play both sides against the middle, encouraging and supporting the Impressionists in their darkest hours whilst resolutely maintaining that he was neither a revolutionary nor an Impressionist. Astruc had said of him in 1867, "M. Manet . . . has no intention to overthrow the old methods of painting or to create new ones. He has merely tried to be himself and no one else." Hearing that he had won the *Légion d'Honneur*, Manet complained with typical barbed wit, "It would have made my future once, but now it is too late to make up for twenty years of failure."

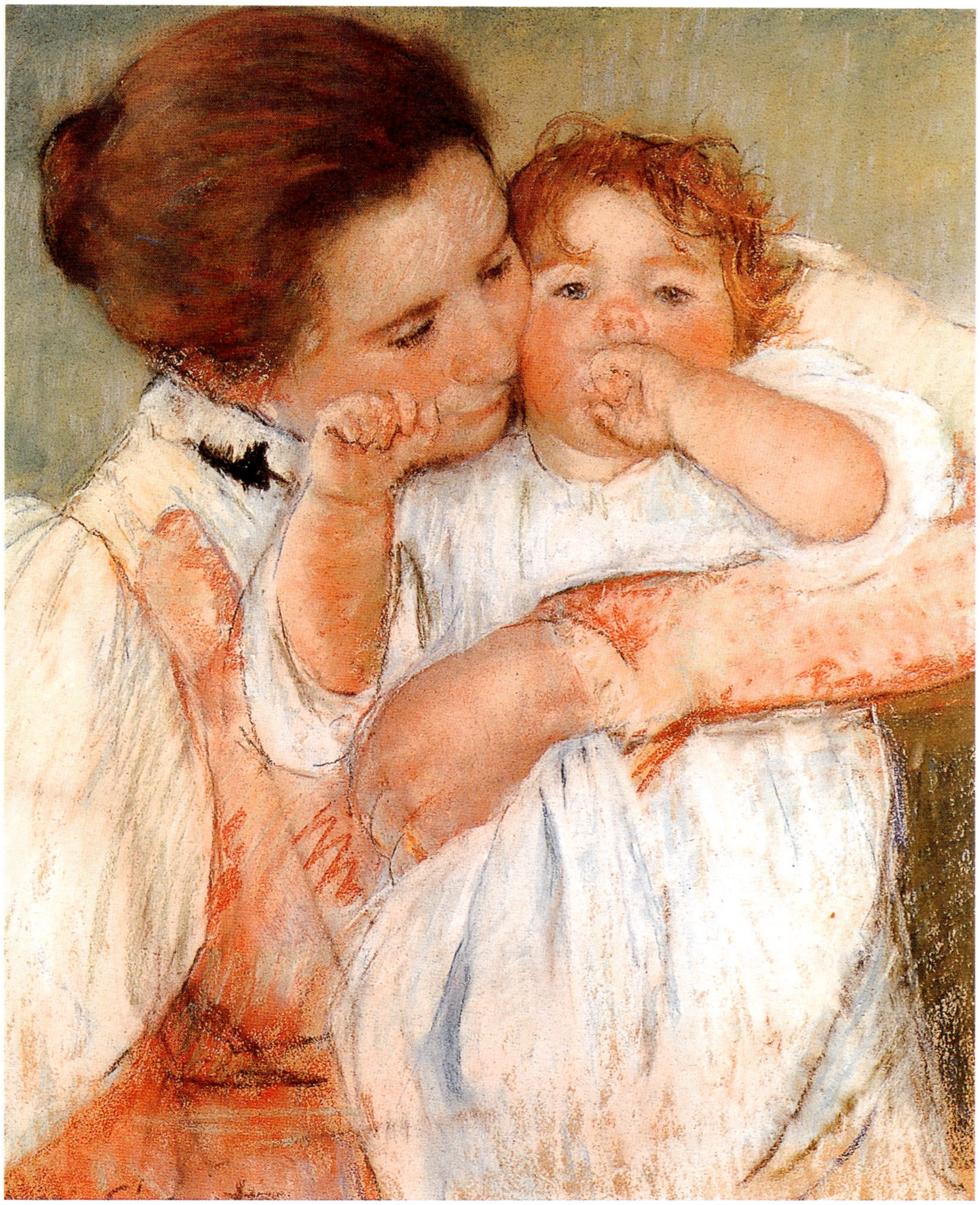

In 1882, with the notable absence of Degas and Cassatt, the Impressionists held their penultimate exhibition in the rue Saint-Honoré. Although there was to be another show in 1886, this was in reality their last stand. For a final time, and with great difficulty, Caillebotte and Pissarro (with the aid of

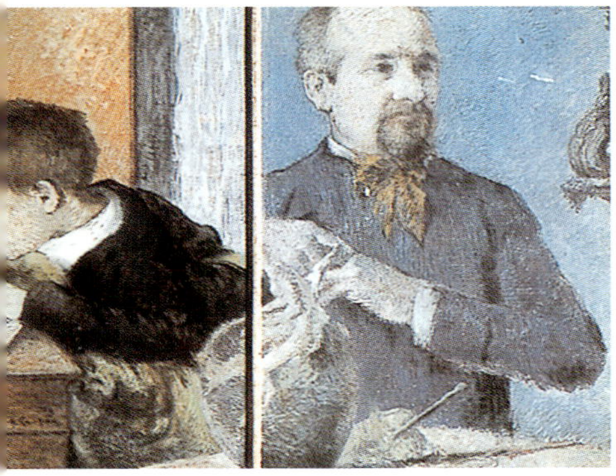

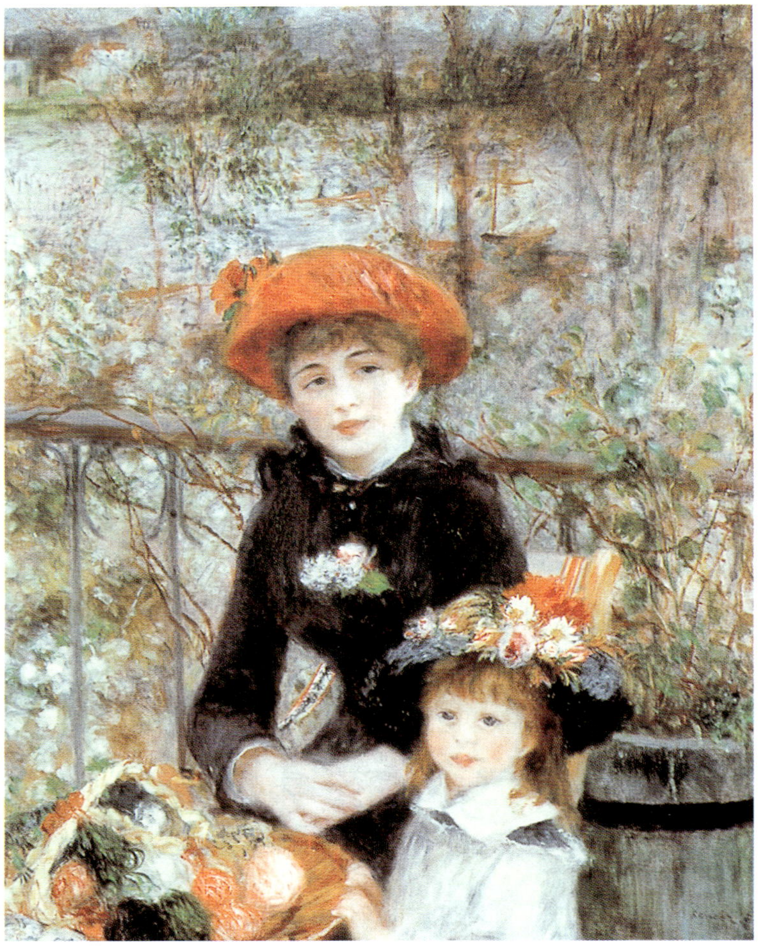

GAUGUIN
The Sculptor Abbi and His Son
oil on canvas
1882. 53 × 71 cm
ABOVE An almost conventional double portrait, with no overt symbolic content, although the composition is strangely disconnected by the vertical join in the centre of the picture.

RENOIR
The Terrace
oil on canvas
1881. 100 × 81 cm
RIGHT Renoir was still painting landscapes, but portraits were a favourite subject.

Durand-Ruel) had gathered together the work of Monet, Morisot, Renoir, and Sisley (with Gauguin, Guillaumin, and Vignon) under one roof. At the last moment Edouard Manet was struck with indecision about whether to join the group. At any rate he was now in the final stages of his illness, a form of locomotor ataxia it is believed, which was steadily paralyzing him. His appearance with the others would have been a fitting conclusion to a decade he had spent devoted to them. Nevertheless his last great masterpiece, *A Bar at the Folies-Bergère* (*Le Bar aux Folies-Bergère*) was shown at the Salon of 1882 as he received for the last time the official recognition he so desperately desired.

The painting can perhaps be seen as a summation of his adventure as a "painter of modern life". It shows a barmaid, blank-faced, before a mirror reflecting the incessant nightlife of Paris; there is an improbable reflection of her and her customer to the right which touches the borders of surrealism: we might be that customer. In the top left hand corner the legs of an acrobat are bizarrely severed by the frame. A moment of staggering insignificance captured in the very heart of the City of Light.

Manet died on 30th April 1883, at the age of fifty-one. A sale of his work in 1884 realized the modest sum of 116,637 francs for 167 paintings, an average of less than 700 francs per work, far below anything paid for an official Salon painting, or even the Barbizon School which had now become highly collectable.

1883–1886: THE LAST SHOW

Renoir was in the throes of a crisis: "I had come to the end of Impressionism. I was reaching the conclusion that I didn't know how either to paint or draw. In a word, I was at a dead end." In 1882 he had been travelling in Italy and Sicily where he had painted a portrait of Richard Wagner; from there he had joined Cézanne at l'Estaque on the Côte d'Azur and fell seriously ill with pneumonia. His journey to Italy was mainly a quest for classical art and technique. He studied the wall paintings of Pompeii and even more so the perfect smoothness of Raphael's works in Rome, which led him to work in a tighter, more refined and precise style for a while, before he returned to his instinctive, less disciplined brushwork. The conflict of his styles heightened a personal and artistic crisis which is eloquently demonstrated in his painting *The Umbrellas* (*Les Parapluies*),

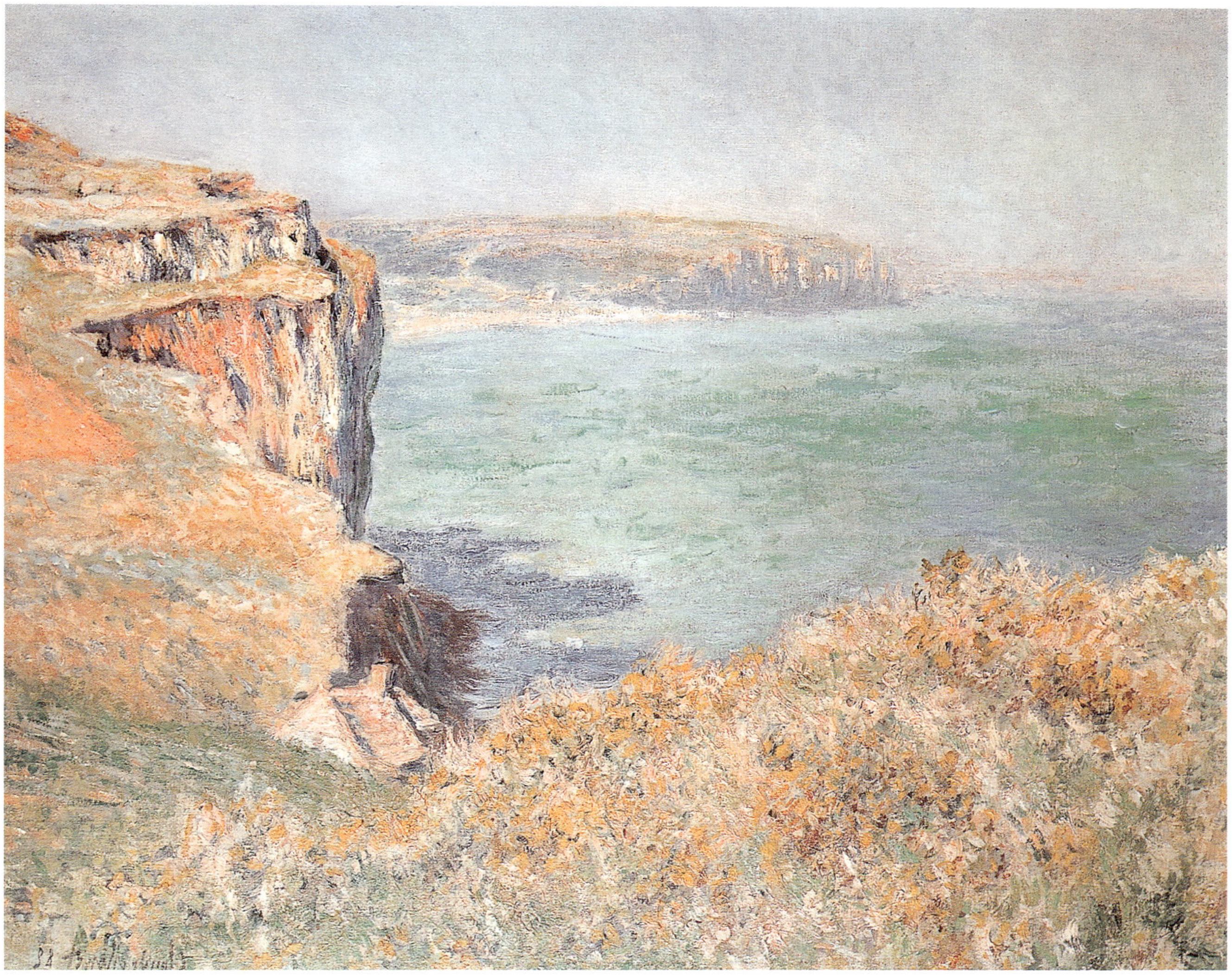

MONET
The Cliffs at Varengeville
oil on canvas
1882.
A favourite subject for Monet, the cliffs along the Normandy coast provided him with a spectacular mixture of land- and seascape.

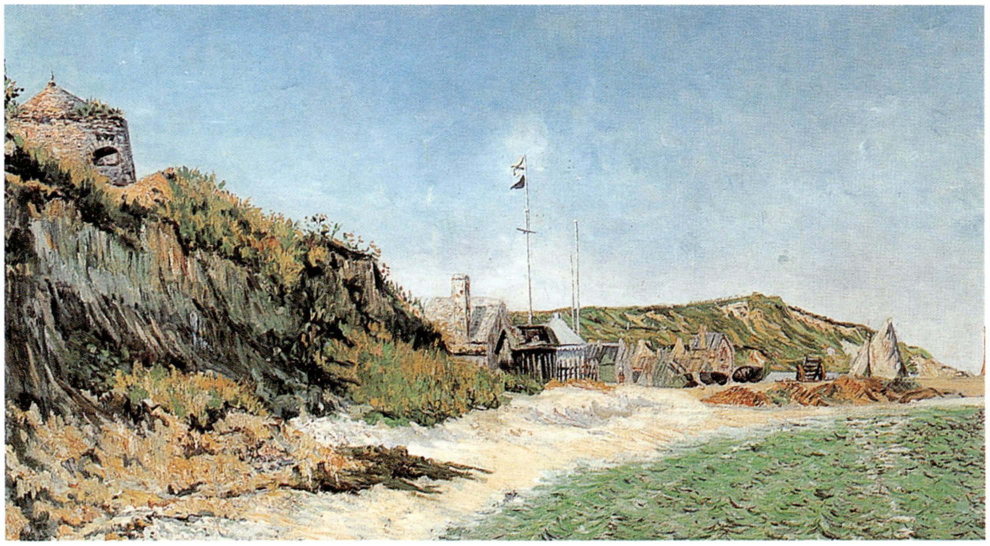

SIGNAC
Port-en-Bessin
oil on canvas
1884. 68 × 127.5 cm
Although Signac claimed some credit for the Pointillist technique that Seurat developed, it is clear in this work that he was not yet using it himself. He later codified the aims and methods of Pointillism, or Divisionism, in his book From Delacroix to Neo-Impressionism *(1899).*

reworked during the 1880s and left unfinished. Cézanne's powerful influence is evident in Renoir's solid handling of the umbrellas; the group on the right is painted in the delicate, feathery style associated with his high Impressionist period, whilst the girl on the left shows the beginnings of a brief flirtation with classical purity of form and line. A series of *Bathers* illustrates well the more restrained rendering which he tried to apply in later years to commissioned portraits.

In 1883 Monet, Alice Hoschedé and their respective children settled in Giverny, a small village near the Seine and close to Rouen. Ernest Hoschedé had gradually been estranged from his wife and had left the double household. After years of poverty, moving from house to house, relying on others to pay his way, Monet was now firmly established with a decent income; his pictures were fetching excellent prices, especially in America. He could now devote himself to exploring the *enveloppe* of light he perceived to hold the world together. For the next forty-three years he lived at Giverny, established and tended his celebrated garden, and painted more than ever before. Foreign artists, many of them American, settled nearby; others frequently visited him. The other Impressionists had spread out across France: Pissarro had moved north of Paris to Osny, Cézanne rarely left Provence, and Renoir had decamped to Essoyes in Burgundy with his mistress (later his wife) Aline Charigot.

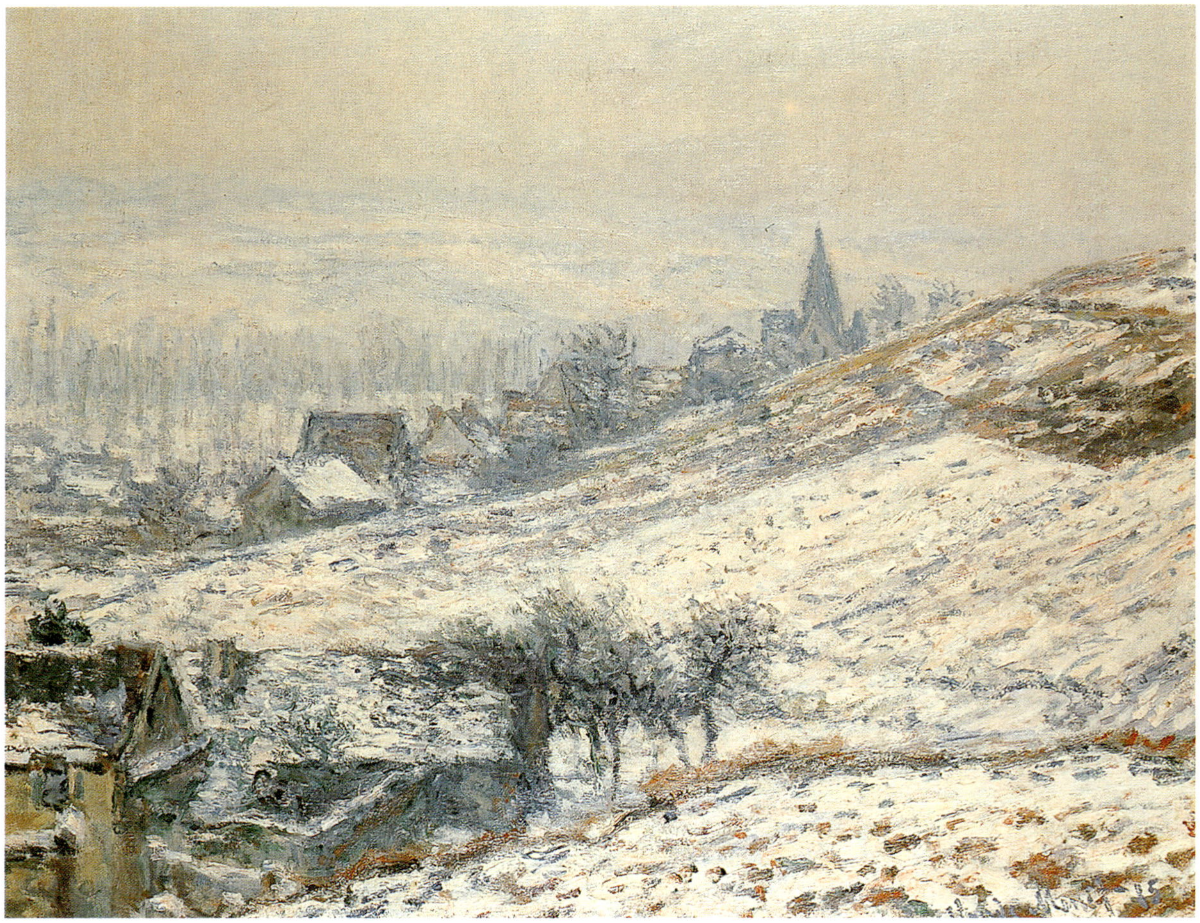

MONET
Giverny in Winter
oil on canvas
1885. 64.5 × 88.5 cm
At this time Monet was exploring the area where he was to live until his death in 1926. No weather was cold enough to discourage him.

The last Impressionist exhibition took place in 1886. Degas was back with his protégés, but their thunder was stolen by the Neo-Impressionists, or Divisionists, Seurat and Signac, who had already begun to influence Pissarro, after he, like Renoir, had reached a stylistic dead end. Seurat's huge painting *La Grande Jatte* caused a storm at the exhibition, and closed the decade of Impressionism with a new form of painting as controversial as that which had begun it.

The great age of Impressionism lasted barely more than a decade. By 1886 it had permeated the entire world of art, spawning Impressionist movements in the United States, Britain, Germany, and Scandinavia which were to continue for many years to come. Impressionism as an innovative force was still influential, but was also beginning to be challenged, especially by Gauguin, and in 1886 a thirty-three-year-old Dutchman, Vincent van Gogh, arrived in Paris to study at Félix Cormon's atelier . . .

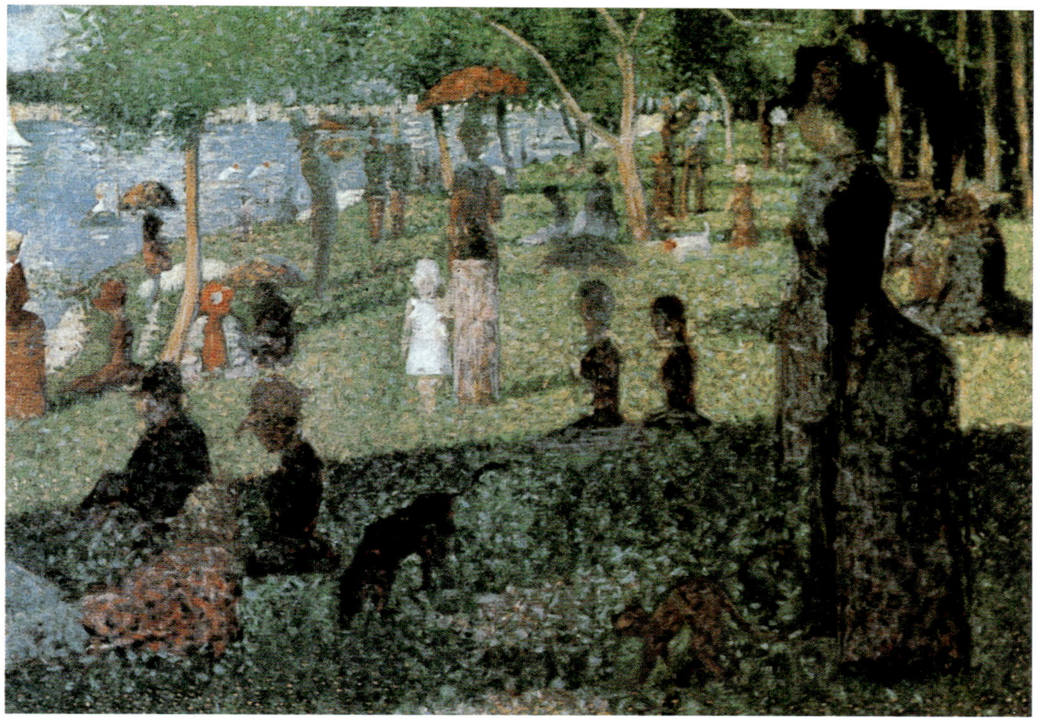

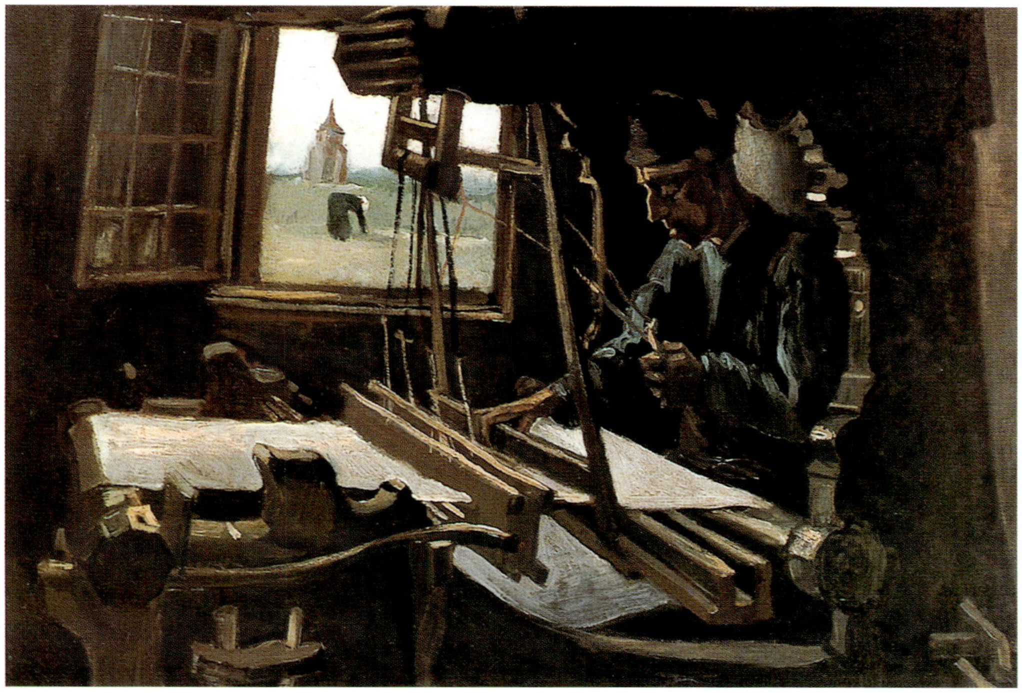

VAN GOGH
The Weaver
oil on canvas
1884. 67.5 × 93 cm
LEFT Despite the important influence of the Impressionist and Neo-Impressionist use of colour on van Gogh's palette, he was no more an Impressionist than the renegade Gauguin. Van Gogh arrived in Paris in 1886, just in time to catch up with the last days of the movement.

SEURAT
Study for La Grande Jatte
oil on canvas
1883. 71 × 104 cm
ABOVE This is one of several finely detailed studies for the finished painting which Seurat made. Pissarro said of him: "he has something new to contribute . . . I am totally convinced of the progressive nature of his art and certain that in time it will yield extraordinary results . . ." Seurat died at the age of thirty-two in 1891 before he could witness the profound influence his work was to have on the Post-Impressionists.

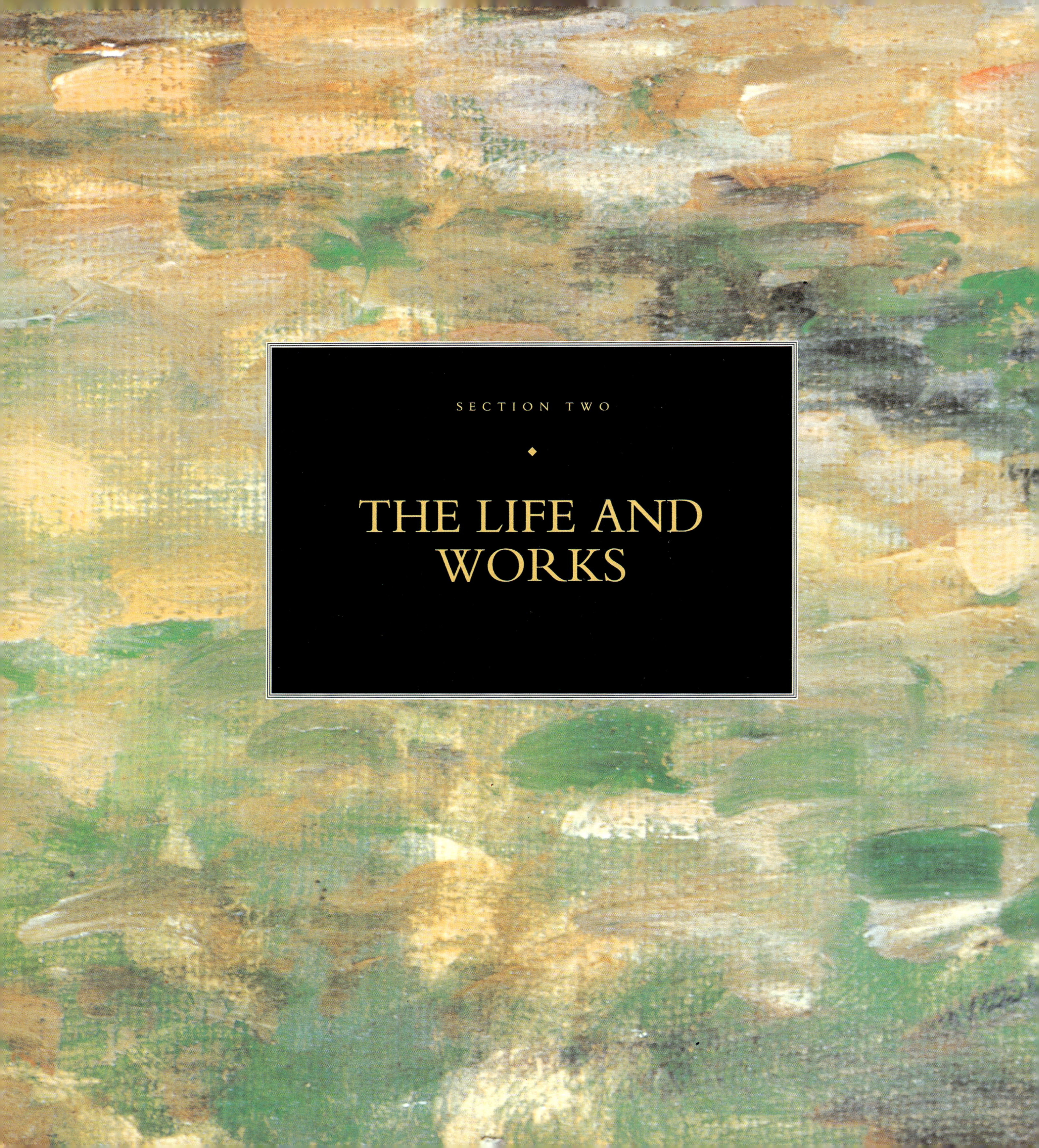

SECTION TWO

THE LIFE AND WORKS

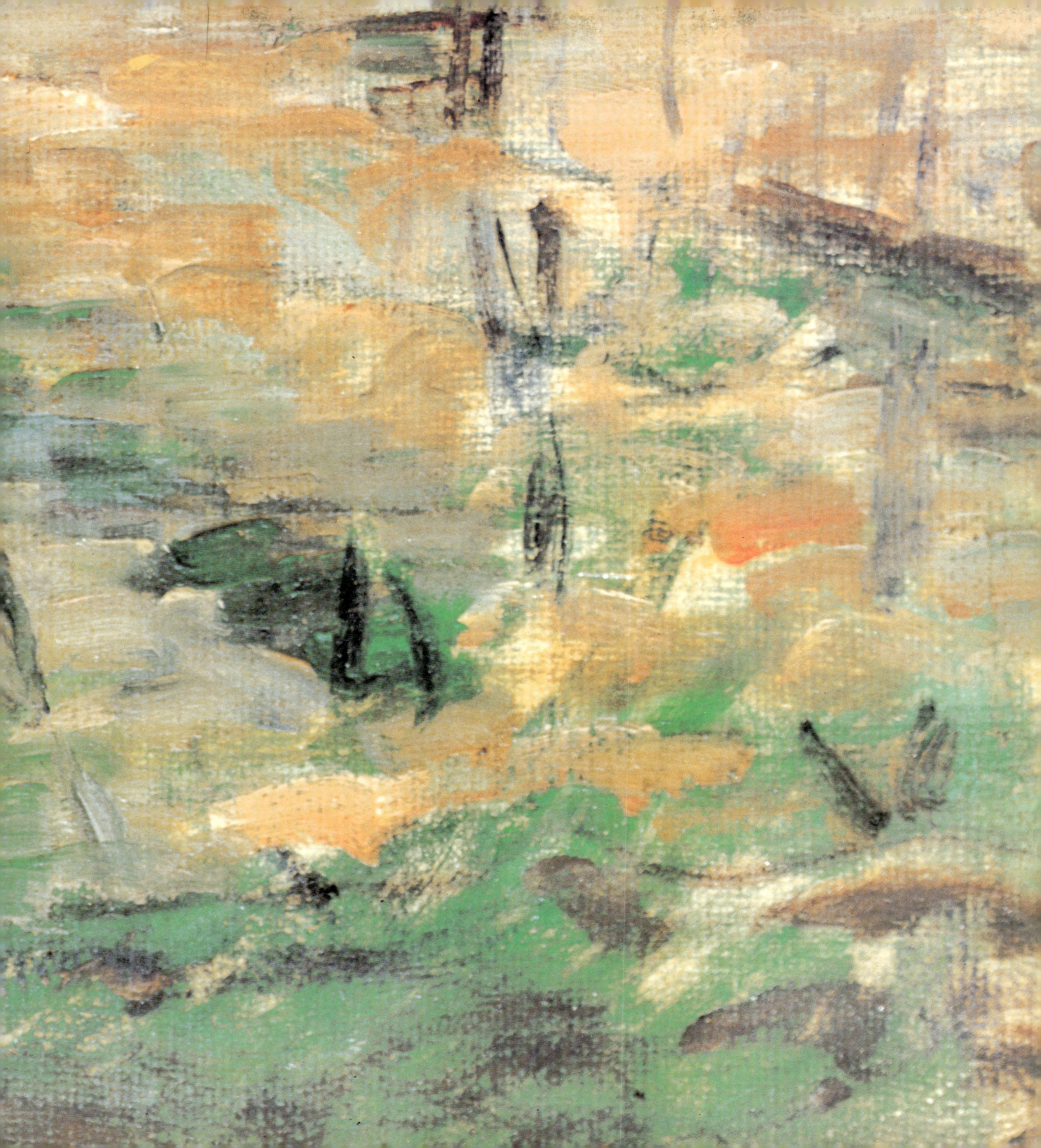

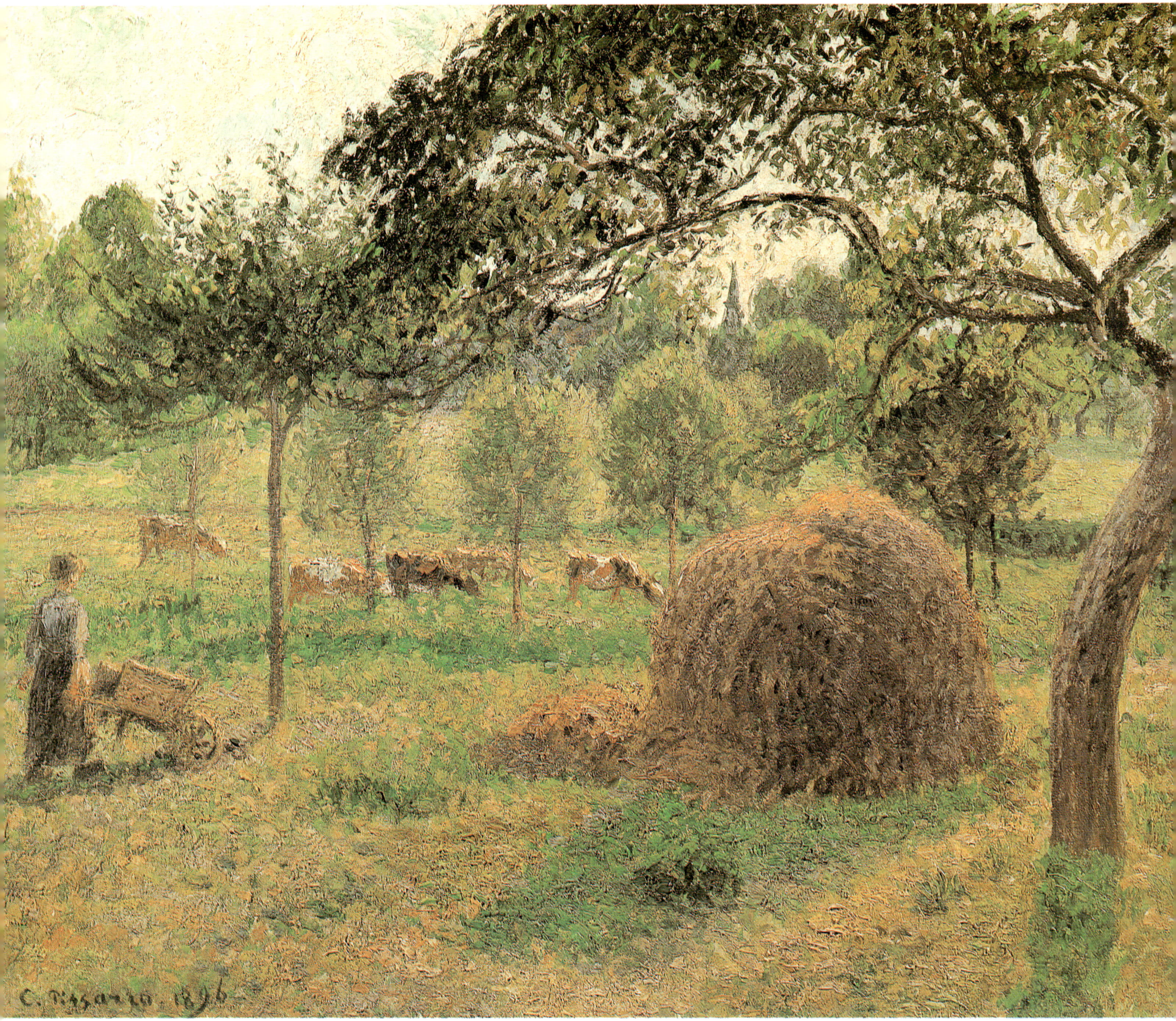
C. Pissarro. 1896

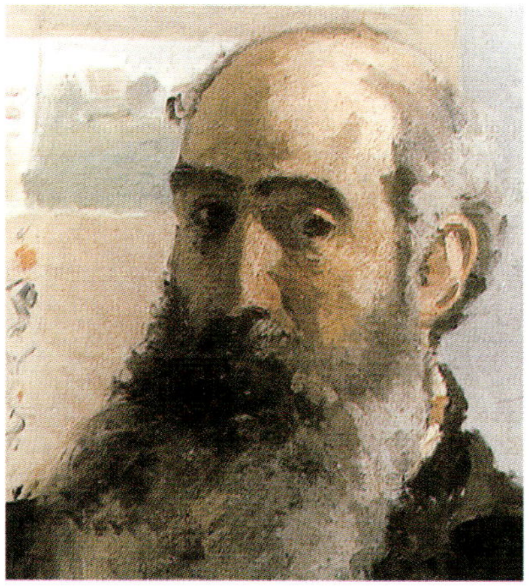

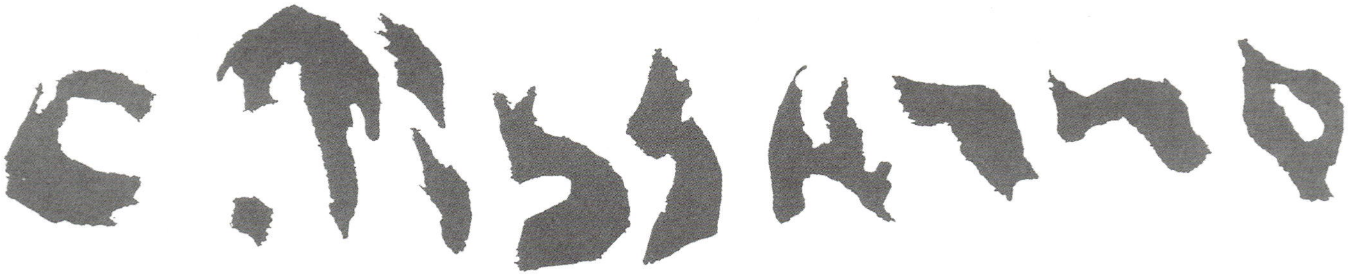

TALENTED ARTISTS as diverse as Gauguin, Cassatt, and Cézanne held Camille Pissarro in the utmost reverence as a teacher and a man of integrity. His selfless devotion to the cause of art and his fellow artists endeared him in a way that few, if any, of his contemporaries could claim. His openness enabled him to transcend his (at best theoretical) anarchist convictions and get on with the likes of the extremely reactionary Degas and the innately conservative Renoir, whilst he was a natural friend and ally to Monet and Sisley, who both struggled, as indeed Pissarro did, long and hard to secure their place in the art world.

Although Pissarro was able to instil confidence in others, he was himself deeply uneasy about his own ability and only settled into a mode of expression which began to satisfy him very late in his life, following a brief but productive flirtation with Neo-Impressionism.

CAMILLE PISSARRO
Self-portrait
1873
Above

PISSARRO
Sunset at Eragny
oil on canvas
1896. 54.5 × 65 cm
Opposite

Life and Works: Camille Pissarro (1830–1903)

Remember that I have the temperament of a peasant, I am melancholy, harsh and savage in my works. It is only in the long run that I can expect to please, and then only those who have a grain of indulgence.

Camille Pissarro

Camille Jacob Pissarro, "the First Impressionist" as Cézanne referred to him, was born on 10th July 1830 on the island of St Thomas in the Danish West Indies (now the U.S. Virgin Islands), the fourth son of Abraham Pissarro, a French Jew from Bordeaux, and Rachel Manzana-Pommié, a Creole from Dominica who had been widowed and was seven years older than her second husband. Abraham Pissarro ran a general store in Charlotte Amalie, the capital and port of St Thomas.

Though he and his family lived on a tiny island thousands of miles from France, Abraham Pissarro was keen to bring up his children in the French manner, so between the ages of twelve and seventeen Camille attended a boarding school, the Académie Savary in Passy, a suburb of Paris. M. Savary, the director of the Académie, is said to have encouraged the boy's artistic leanings by imploring him to draw coconut palms from nature when he returned to the West Indies. In 1847 Camille was back in St Thomas working in his father's store and he must have indeed followed M. Savary's advice in his spare time, for nine years later (in Paris again) he was painting tropical landscapes from memory.

Camille remained with his family in St Thomas until 1853 when, after five years of working as a clerk, its charms were no longer able to detain him. He decided he had to see more of the world and took off without parental consent to Venezuela with the Danish artist, Fritz Melbye. For the next two years they rented a studio in Caracas where Pissarro practised drawing and attempted his first watercolours under the thoughtful eye of Melbye who had studied at the Copenhagen Academy and was able to teach his friend the basics of the Academic Style. By the time he had obtained his father's blessing and sailed to Paris to study with Melbye's brother Anton, Pissarro was already an accomplished landscape painter.

The Exposition Universelle of 1855 was in its last few days when Pissarro arrived in Paris. Courbet's Realist Pavilion was creating a stir, but Pissarro was more interested in the few landscapes by Corot on show and later introduced himself to the master landscapist. During the next couple of years Pissarro worked as Anton Melbye's assistant, took some private lessons at the Ecole and studied at the free Académie Suisse where he met Claude Monet; he was also an occasional pupil of Corot, describing himself as such in his first submission to the Salon in 1859.

Pissarro passed the Salon hurdle at the first attempt. His parents had recently returned to France and settled in Paris, and were suitably impressed (and no doubt relieved) that their youngest son had begun to make his mark in the art world. The Salon was the summit of exhibitions and Pissarro's carefully worked landscape of Montmorency had enough of Corot in it to succeed in academic terms, but it also proved that Pissarro's talent was to be uncompromising. The move from the exotic Virgin Islands and South America to what the art historian Linda Nochlin calls "the infinitely civilized" French countryside had produced in Pissarro a lighter, more naturalistic vision than that of Corot. In the years to come he was frequently to be accused of painting vulgar and unaesthetic landscapes far from Corot's comparatively idealized works.

From his earliest drawings in St Thomas to his death in 1903, Pissarro's style and method were in a continual state of flux. As the art historian John House has said, "to chart Pissarro's stylistic evolution . . . we meet in turn Corot, Daubigny, Courbet, Jongkind, Monet, Cézanne, Renoir, Millet, Seurat, Turner, and Monet again." Although he was the oldest of the Impressionists, Pissarro never ceased assimilating the work of others in an artistic evolution which is unparalleled among his contemporaries. In the late 1850s and early 1860s the Salon and the French art world were in a deep debate about the acceptability of Daubigny's sketchy *plein-airisme* and the consequences of Courbet's realism. Having succeeded on the safer ground of Corot, Pissarro began to appreciate the attempts of Daubigny and Courbet to paint what they saw and wanted to see. At the age of twenty-nine Pissarro met Monet, ten years his junior, at the Académie Suisse and soon became part of a new generation of artists fired by the example of Courbet and Daubigny, impatient with the academic landscape.

COROT
Dardagny, Morning
oil on canvas
c.1853. 26 × 47 cm
Pissarro had seen the few Corots on show at the 1855 Exposition Universelle and a year later went to see the master landscapist. Corot's style was a profound influence on Pissarro for many years. This small, sketchy picture displays the freer side of Corot which suited Pissarro's early vision.

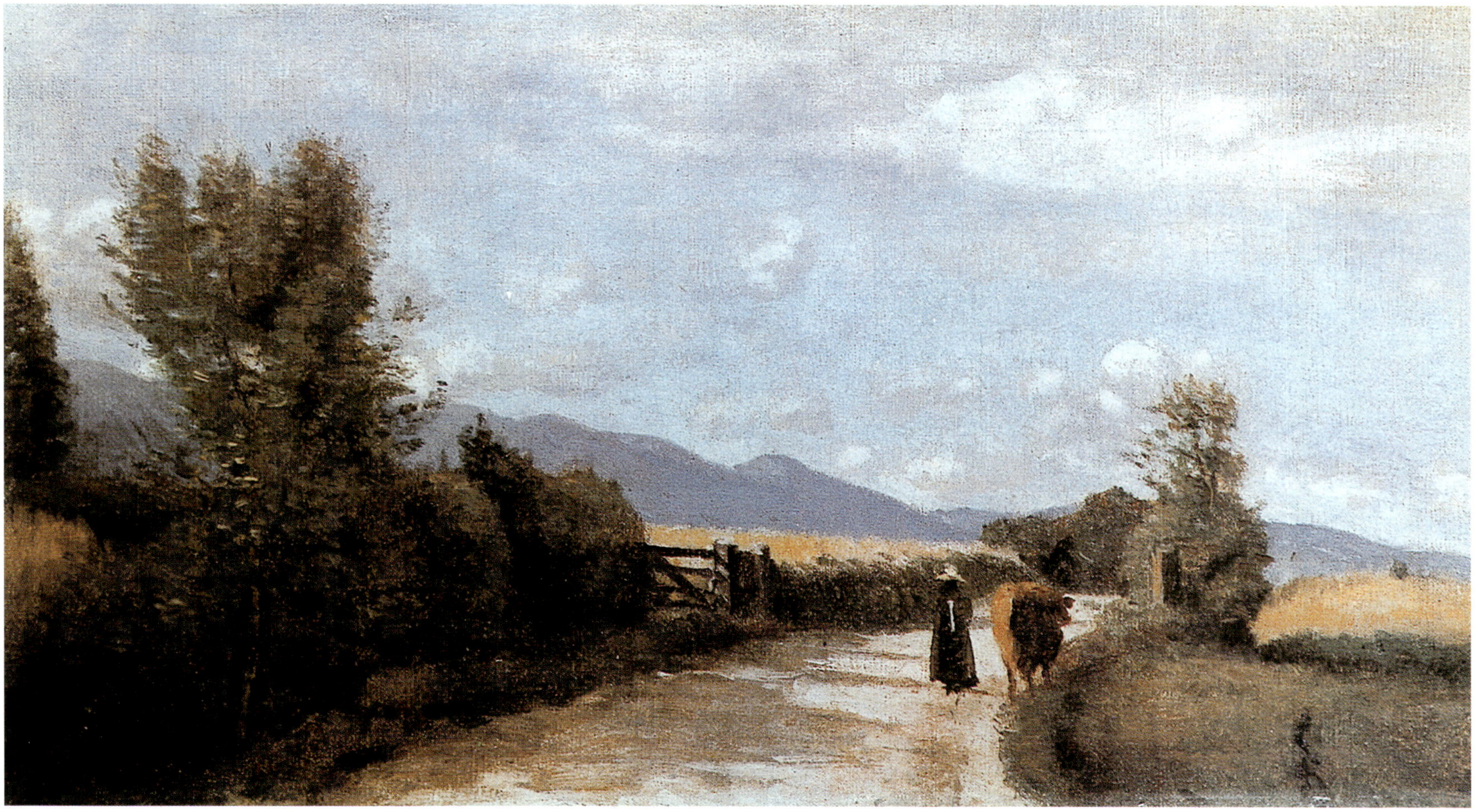

Unlike Monet, Renoir, Sisley, and the other budding Impressionists with whom he was soon to have a remarkable relationship, Pissarro's view of the world had already become deeply politicized. The glory of the Second Empire was skin deep as far as he could see and the dehumanizing effects of rapid industrialization hidden behind the glittering façade of the Empire were not lost on him. He grew increasingly attracted to the extreme radicalism of Proudhon and Prince Kropotkin. Proudhon had said that "art should show us exactly as we are, not in a mediated fantasy that no longer represents us." The artist he had in mind for his project was Courbet; Pissarro was already well acquainted with Courbet's work in the late 1850s and had read Proudhon's huge tract *On Justice in the Revolution and the Church*, published in 1858. Somewhat anarchic by nature, Pissarro began to espouse some of Proudhon's anarcho-federalist ideals and was to become more avowedly anarchist as the years went by. (Proudhon was, as the art historian Ralph Shikes points out, "a passionate advocate of Justice, Liberty, and Equality, yet his Equality did not embrace universal suffrage; blacks, whom he regarded as inferior; and women, equally inferior, whose place he felt was in the home.") The task of the artist, as Pissarro was to say many years later, echoing Proudhon, "is to seek with our own senses the elements of what surrounds us. This can only be achieved by observing

MILLET
The Gleaners
oil on canvas
1857. 83.5 × 111 cm
Millet was also an important early influence on Pissarro, who was attracted to subjects like this and continued to paint them throughout his career. Millet's plain and sentimental paeans to peasant life were criticized for the "vulgarity" of their subject matter, but formed an important model for artists such as Pissarro and later van Gogh.

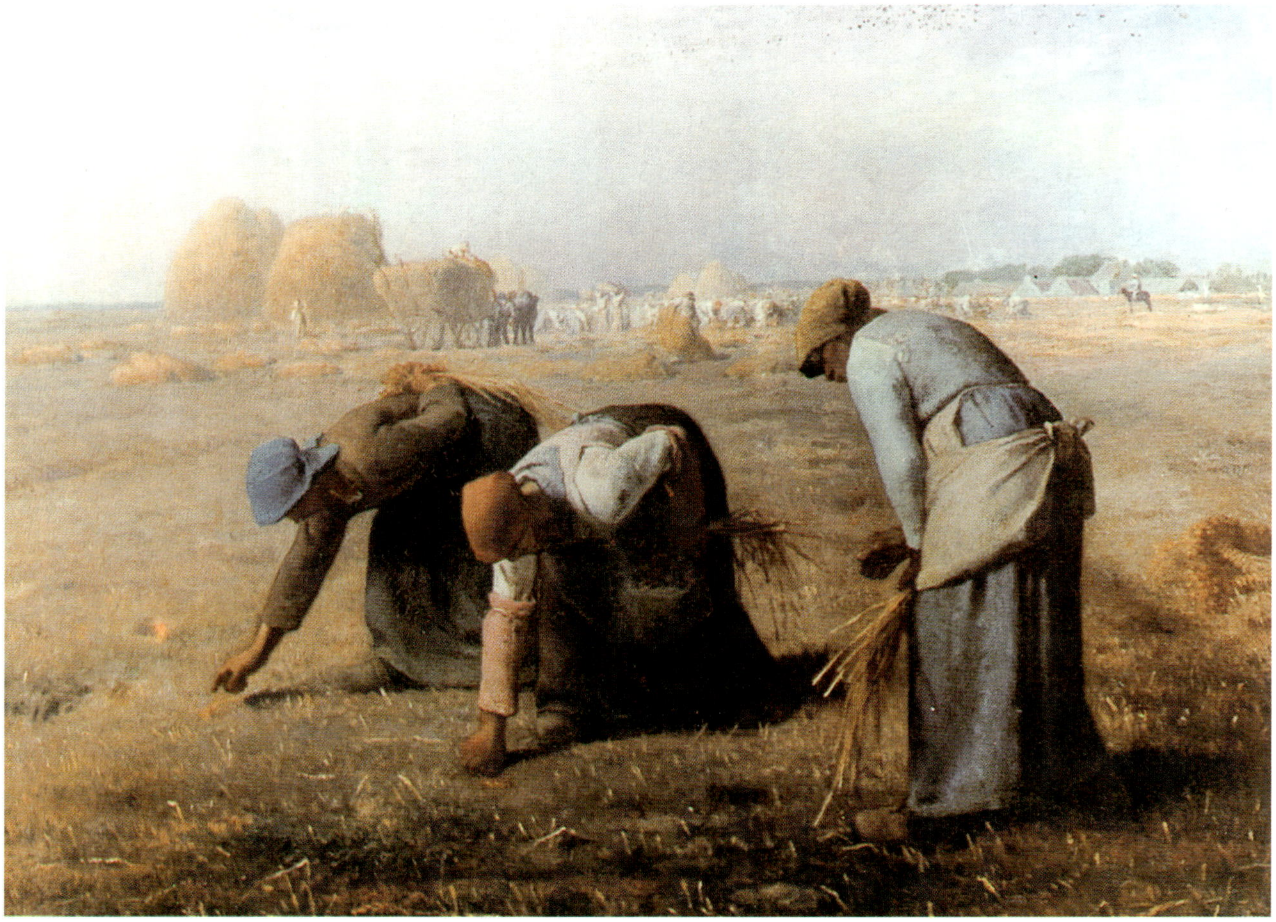

nature with our own contemporary sensibility. It is a serious mistake to believe that every form of art is not closely linked to its time."

In 1860 when it seemed little could shake the foundations of the Second Empire, Proudhon's views were considered dangerous but tolerated. Despite his growing convictions, Pissarro's talents clearly lay in the reality of nature and agriculture, in landscapes with figures – what one critic has called humanist landscape – not social realism, although the two could combine successfully to a certain extent in his *Railway Bridge at Pontoise* (*Le Pont de chemin de fer à Pontoise*) of 1860, and yet prove stilted and sentimental in *Donkey Ride at La Roche-Guyan* (*Promenade à l'âne à La Roche-Guyon*), what Shikes calls "the only canvas of his career with an overt social message."

Several important relationships developed for Pissarro in 1860. Working in the countryside around Paris one of his constant companions was Ludovic Piette, a landscape painter four years older than Pissarro who had studied at the famous atelier of Couture and then at the Académie Suisse. Pissarro struck up a life-long friendship with Piette, who was moderately well off and had a farm at Montfoucault in Brittany which in future years became indispensable to the penniless Pissarro. At about this time Pissarro became closely attached to Julie Vellay, the daughter of a viticulturist from Burgundy, who had found employment as his mother's maid. There had been no Salon in 1860, but after his initial success two years earlier the vagaries of the Salon were against Pissarro this time. The jury was severe and rejected his entry but accepted Manet's *Guitar Player* (*Le Joueur de guitare*) with an honourable mention. Pissarro continued to work in Paris, copying at the Louvre and working at the Académie Suisse where he met two important allies, Paul Cézanne, on whom he was to have a great influence, and Armand Guillaumin.

1863 was the year of the Salon des Refusés and the scandal of Manet's *Luncheon on the Grass* (*Déjeuner sur l'herbe*) which overshadowed the contributions of Pissarro, Cézanne, Jongkind, and Guillaumin and launched the reluctant Manet as a figurehead of the avant-garde. The year had begun auspiciously for Pissarro and Julie Vellay; in February the first of their seven children, Lucien,

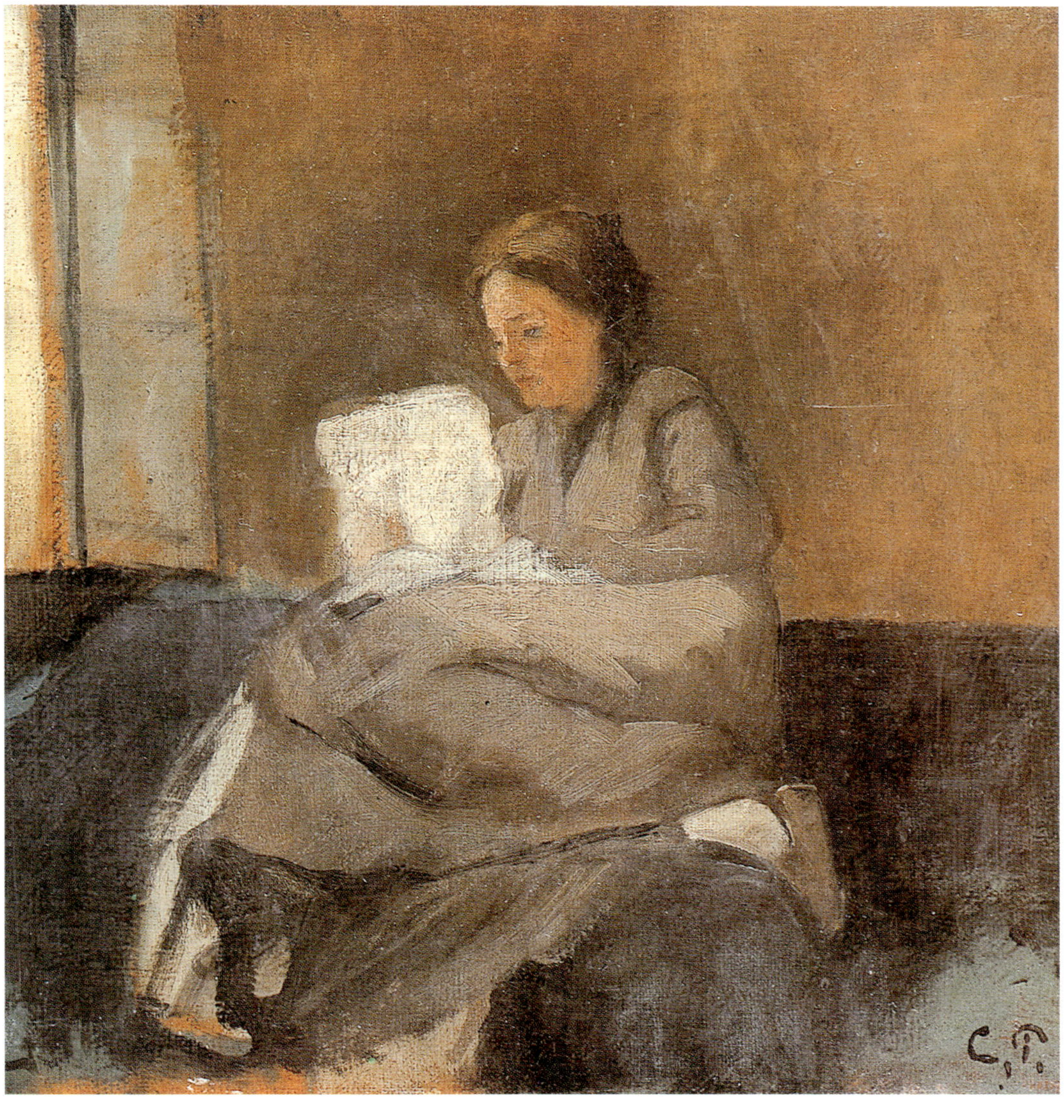

PISSARRO
Woman Reading
oil on canvas
1860. 26.5 × 29 cm
The sitter is Julie Vellay, the maid of Pissarro's mother, whom he met the same year, and who was quite a few years younger than him. They had seven children and married ten years later, in 1870, while they were in London.

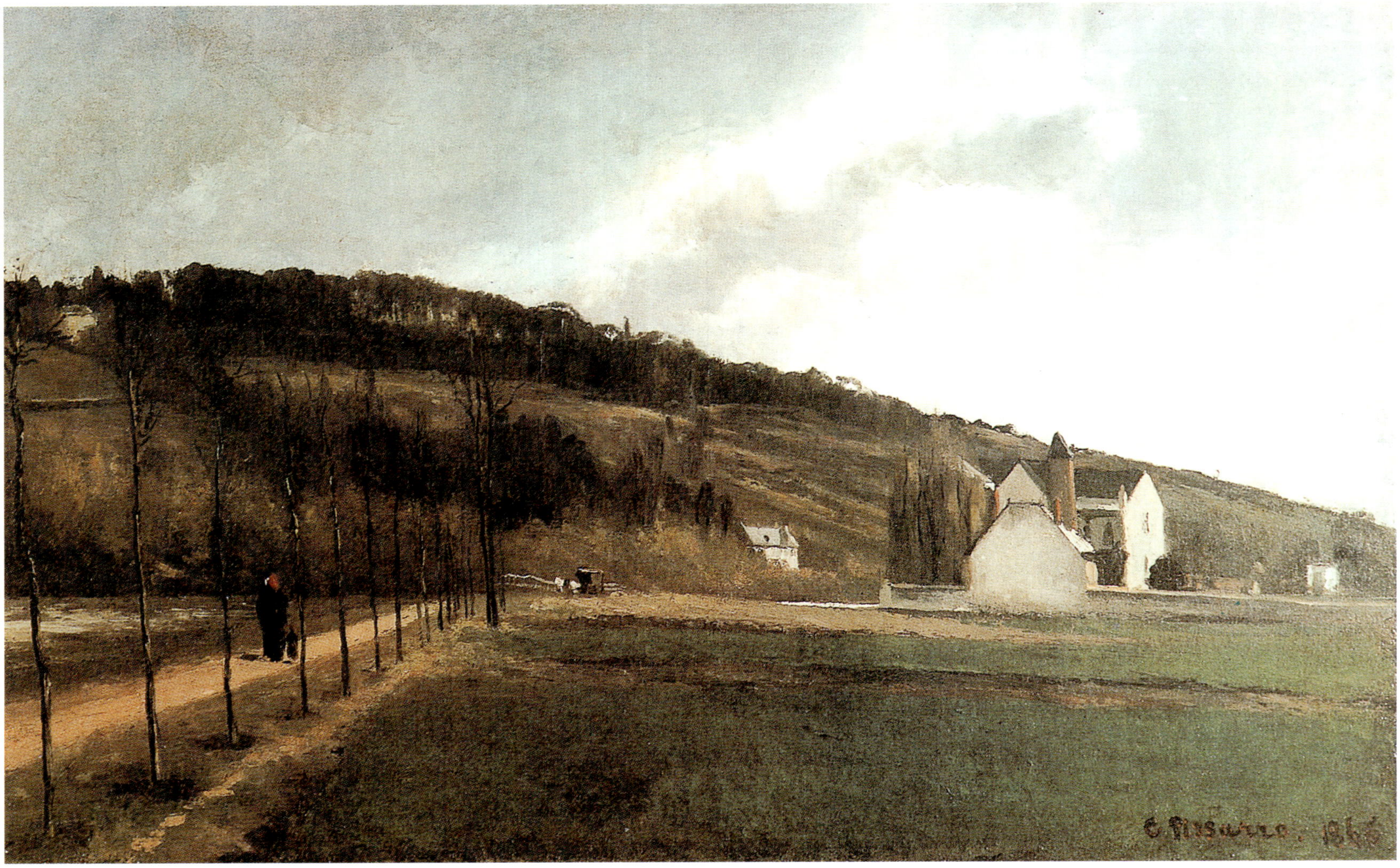

PISSARRO
Banks of the Marne in Winter
oil on canvas
1866. 92 × 150 cm
The influence of Corot is manifest in this bare work, which was shown at the Salon, where the subject was found vulgar and the painting ugly. It was indeed not decorative enough for its time, but Pissarro was never concerned by prettiness.

was born (Julie had in fact suffered a miscarriage the year before). Pissarro was a devoted father to his children; his extensive correspondence with Lucien, who moved to London in the 1890s to set up a book illustration press, forms a large part of our knowledge about Pissarro's later life.

Two years later Abraham Pissarro died, precipitating a financial crisis for Camille Pissarro and his growing family – they now had a daughter, Jeanne. The Salon of 1864 had accepted two landscapes from the artist, described in the catalogue as a pupil of Corot and (Anton) Melbye, and Pissarro appeared in the Salon until rejected along with Renoir, Sisley, and Monet in 1867.

Despite this relatively steady success rate at the most important of art markets, Pissarro's sales were few and far between; he was already beginning to call upon the largesse of friends such as Ludovic Piette whose farmhouse in Montfoucault he had visited in 1864. At this time he also began to fall out with Corot who did not approve of the increasing influence of Courbet in Pissarro's work and thereafter Pissarro stopped calling himself a pupil of Corot. The painting Pissarro showed at the 1866 Salon, *Banks of the Marne in Winter*

(*Les Rives de la Marne en hiver*) drew the praise of Zola for its modernity, whilst another critic said: "M. Pissarro is not commonplace for want of the ability to be picturesque, he has used his robust and exuberant talent to depict the vulgarity of the modern world." The influence of Corot and Daubigny in Pissarro's use of dark and subdued pigments, as well as Courbet's palette knife technique is evident here, but even at this early stage in his development Pissarro's choice and control of his admittedly banal subject stands out as an intensely personal vision of the countryside (near Pissarro's home at the time, La Varenne-Saint-Hilaire) that he painted.

By 1867 Pissarro and his family had moved to Pontoise, a village on the river Oise near Auvers, where they remained until 1869 and then settled in Louveciennes. Pissarro worked consistently outdoors at landscapes during these years but kept a studio in Paris and was close to the rapidly growing movement that met in the Café Guerbois. The 1867 Salon which coincided with the Exposition Universelle was particularly conservative in its selections and Pissarro, one of the many *refusés*, had joined Renoir, Sisley, Monet, Bazille, and Cézanne in signing a petition

PISSARRO
Springtime in Louveciennes
oil on canvas
c.1868–69. 53 × 82 cm
The Pissarros had recently moved to Pontoise, a small town on the banks of the Seine not far from Marly, where Sisley lived, and Bougival, where Monet worked. This landscape is still close in style to Corot, especially in the rendering of the trees on the right.

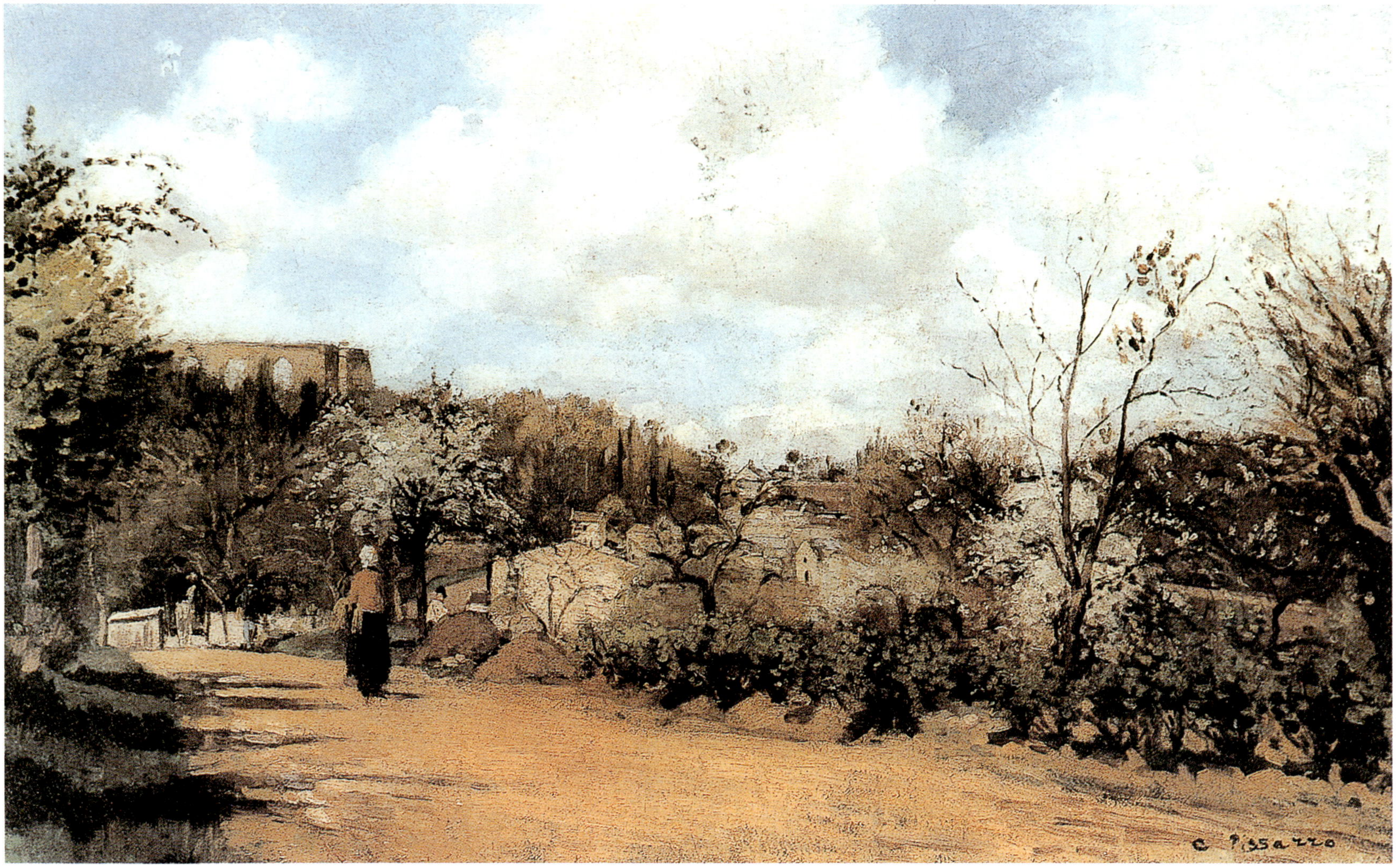

PISSARRO
The Diligence at Louveciennes
oil on canvas
1870. 25.5 × 35.7 cm
Pissarro has at last found his own style: the brushstrokes are less unified and he captures well the atmosphere of a rainy day. The diligence was the public coach transporting local passengers, here seen on its slow round.

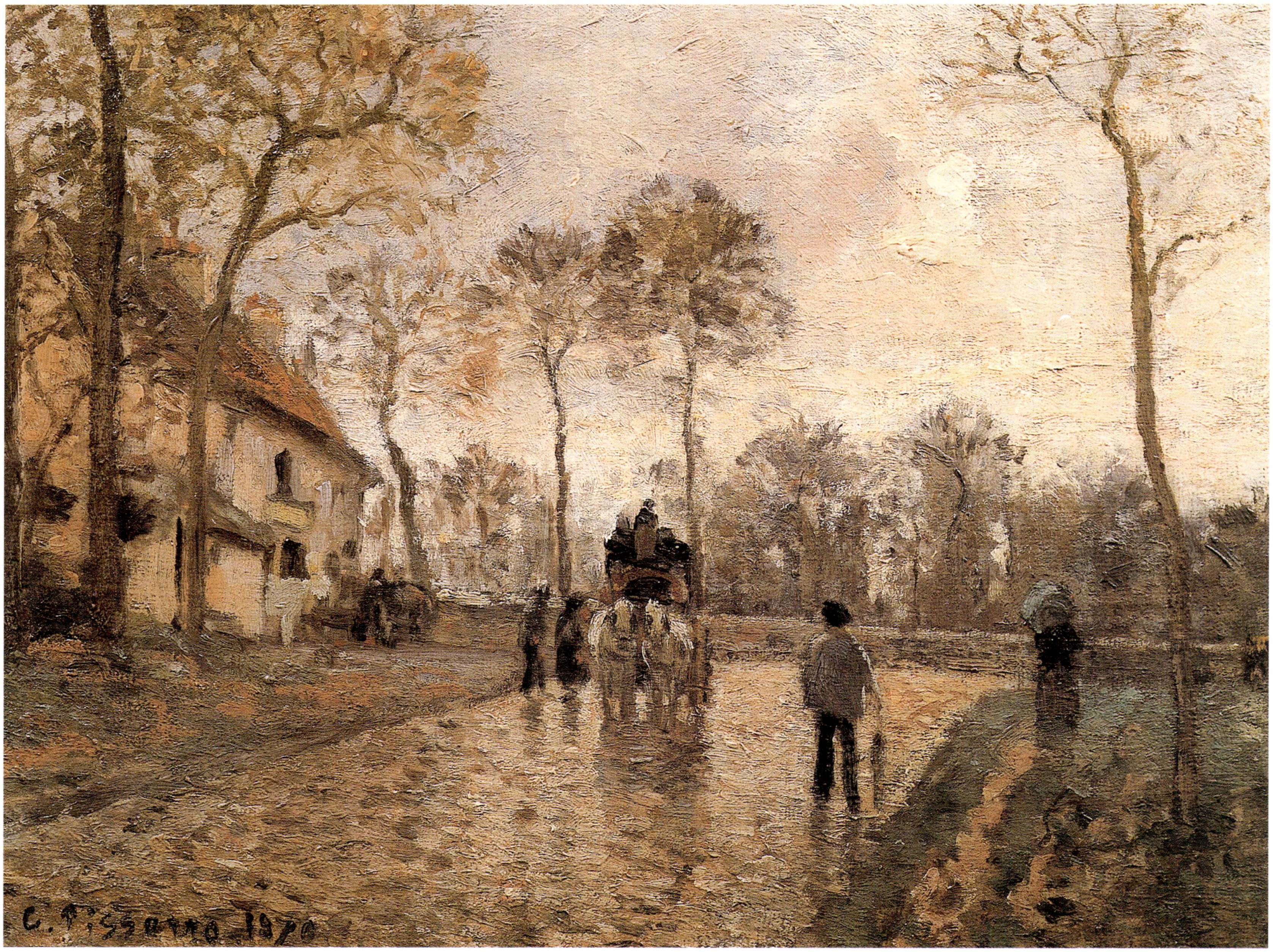

demanding another Salon des Refusés. There was now talk of an independent exhibition amongst the Gleyre students and Pissarro, Cézanne, and Degas. Pissarro was by now deeply involved in the emerging group and was to play an increasing role in its future development. Daubigny's inclusion on the Salon's jury the next year secured the exhibition of two of Pissarro's Pontoise landscapes, moving Zola to pronounce Pissarro "one of the three or four true painters of our day. I have rarely encountered a technique that is so sure . . . *C'est là la campagne moderne* [this is truly the modern countryside]." Sadly this praise was of little avail to the Pissarro family, now in financial straits. Their income was so erratic that Camille was occasionally forced to join with Armand Guillaumin decorating shop fronts and blinds.

A brief period of relative calm and consolidation ensued in Louveciennes, where Pissarro's researches into landscape continued. He was joined by Claude Monet, who had been working with Renoir at La Grenouillère (Pissarro had briefly worked there as well during the summer). In the winter of 1869–70 under varying weather conditions both artists painted similar views of the road to Versailles where Pissarro's house stood.

The outbreak of war on 19th July 1870 forced the Pissarro family to move to safety, first to Piette's farm in Brittany and then in December they crossed the English Channel to a suburb of London where Pissarro's mother was already living. There he finally married Julie Vellay, already pregnant with their third child.

Monet had fled to London as well, and through the auspices of the sympathetic dealer Durand-Ruel, also a refugee in London, Pissarro made contact with him: "Monet and I were very enthusiastic over the London landscapes," recalled Pissarro in a letter of 1902. "Monet worked in the parks whilst I, living in Lower Norwood, at that time a charming suburb, studied the effect of fog, snow, and springtime. We worked from nature . . . We also visited the museums. The watercolours and paintings of Constable and Turner and the canvases of Old Crome [i.e. John Crome, 1768–1821, leading artist of the Norwich School of landscapists] have certainly had an influence upon us. We admired Gainsborough, Lawrence, Reynolds, etc., but were struck chiefly by the landscape painters who shared more in our aim with regard to *plein-air*, light and fugitive effects." As the art historian Phoebe Pool notes, Pissarro's initial delight at the English landscapists was grudgingly tempered. In the last year of his life he

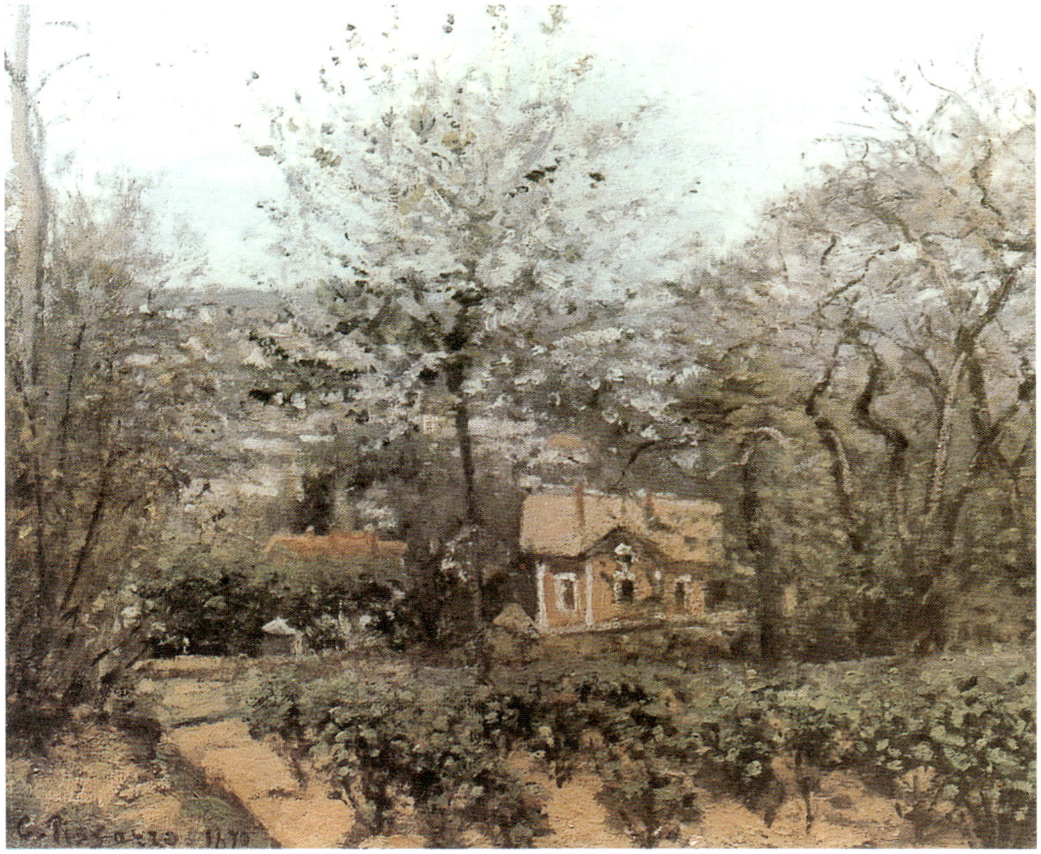

PISSARRO
The Pink House
oil on canvas
1870. 46 × 55 cm
Pissarro's subjects are always factual and completely unpretentious, true to his own temperament. Like most true Impressionist artists, he was satisfied to choose a spot and to paint it. Monet joined Pissarro at Louveciennes, where they painted the local streets side by side.

PISSARRO
Fox Hill, Upper Norwood
oil on canvas
1870. 35.5 × 45.5 cm
The war prompted Monet and Pissarro to leave for England, where Pissarro's mother was already living in Norwood and Pissarro painted a series of local landscapes, of which a dozen have survived.

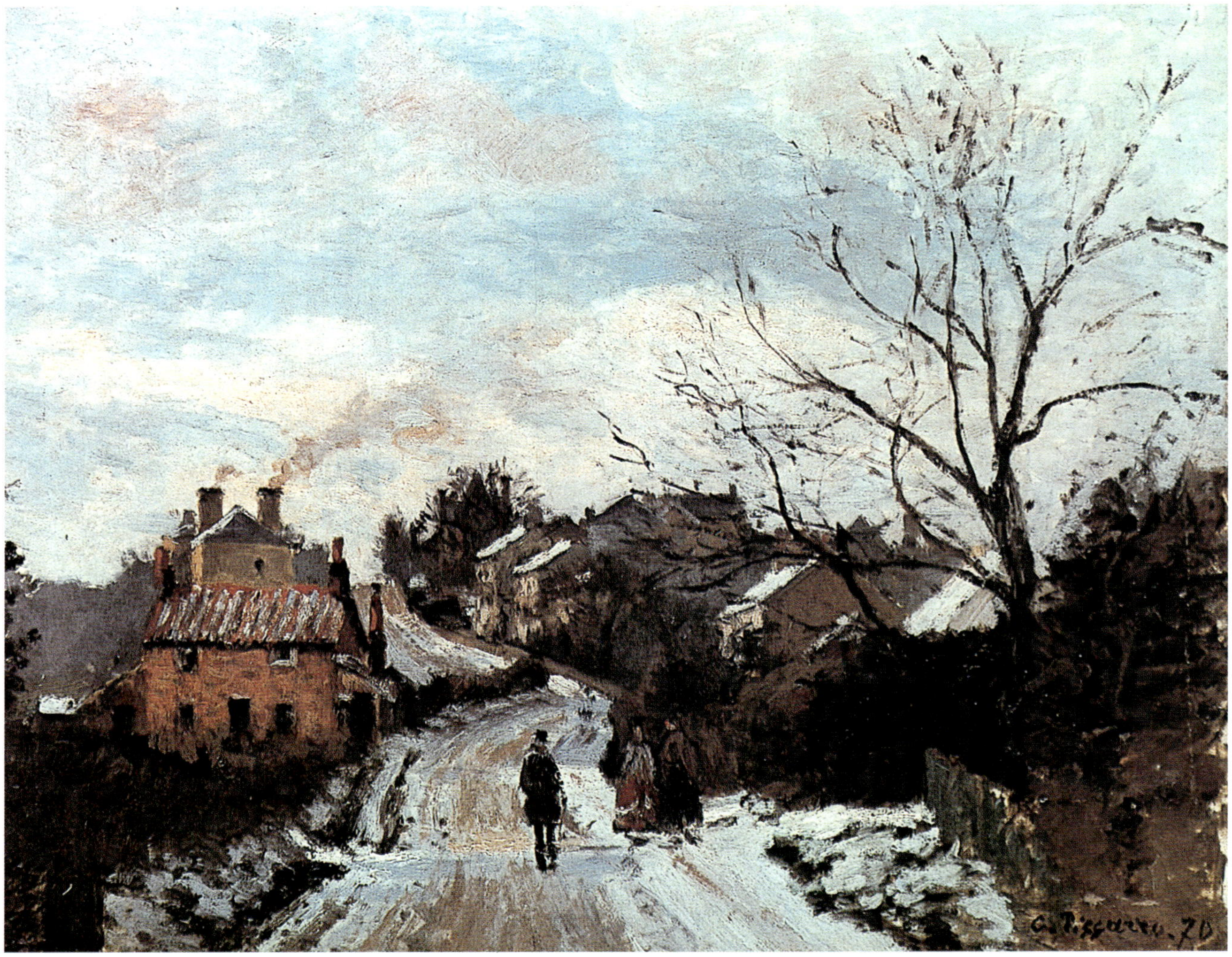

wrote to Lucien saying, "Turner and Constable . . . showed us in their work that they had no understanding of the analysis of shadow, which in Turner's painting is simply used as an effect, a mere absence of light. As far as tone division is concerned, Turner proved its value although he did not apply it correctly and naturally."

The important contact with Durand-Ruel aside, Pissarro's fortunes did not improve in London; the public were not keen to buy his paintings and the Royal Academy's annual exhibition refused both his and Monet's work. Twelve paintings and some studies survive from Pissarro's time in London, ranging from the highly impressionistic *Fox Hill, Upper Norwood* and *Dulwich College* to the more highly polished *The Avenue, Sydenham*, which Durand-Ruel eventually bought in 1871, but which Pissarro must have hoped to sell to the London market.

The net result in artistic terms of Pissarro's exile in London, his contact with Monet and the English landscape school, was a freer handling of brighter pigments, using the swiftly applied patches of colour which Monet had been developing since La Grenouillère and was now employing to great effect in his views of the Thames. Compared to Monet, now approaching Impressionism

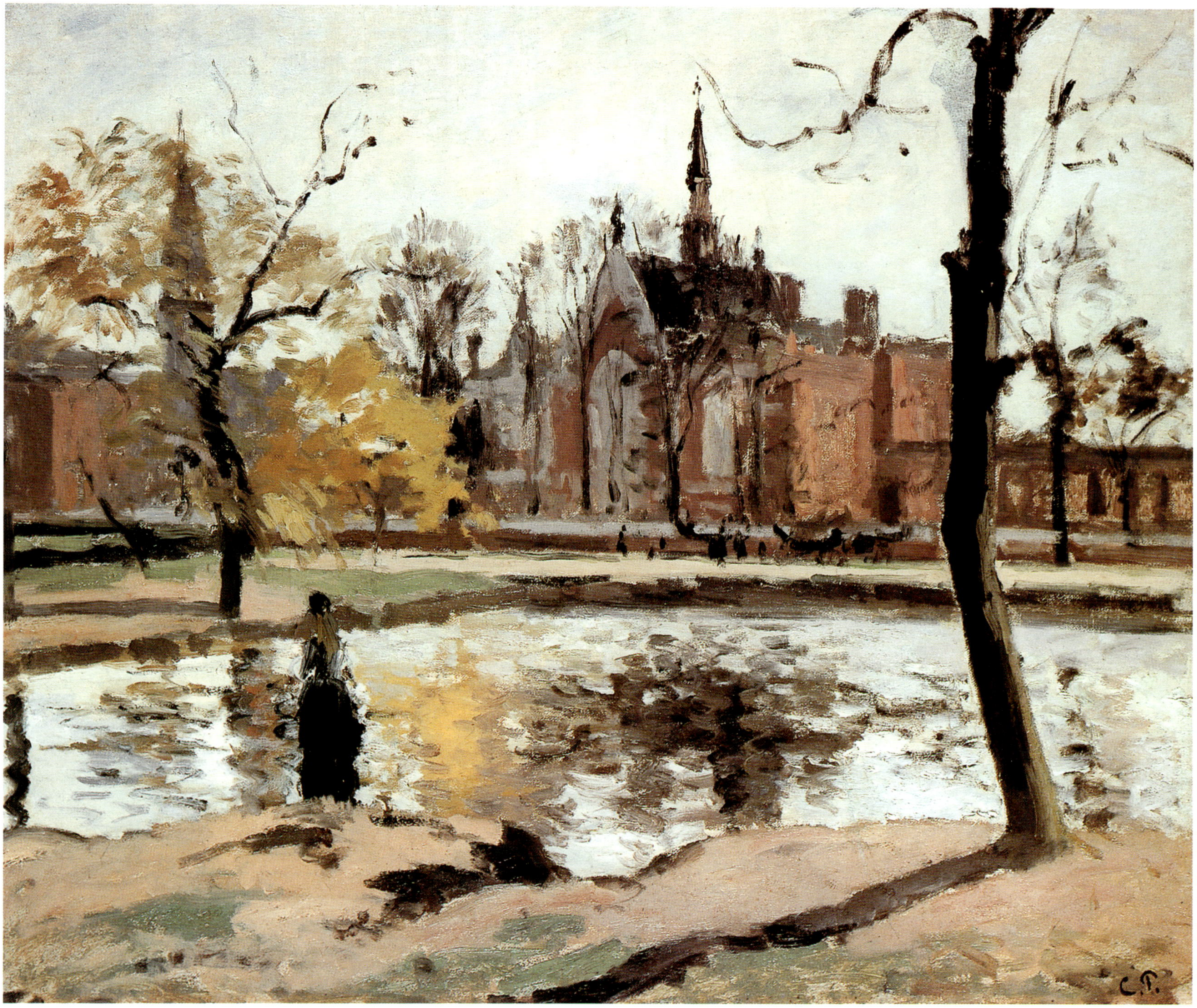

PISSARRO
Dulwich College
oil on canvas
c.1870. 50 × 61 cm
Save the rather systematic rendering of the branches, the careful if plain rendering of some of Corot's work has now disappeared from Pissarro's. Dulwich College was and remains one of the landmarks of the area.

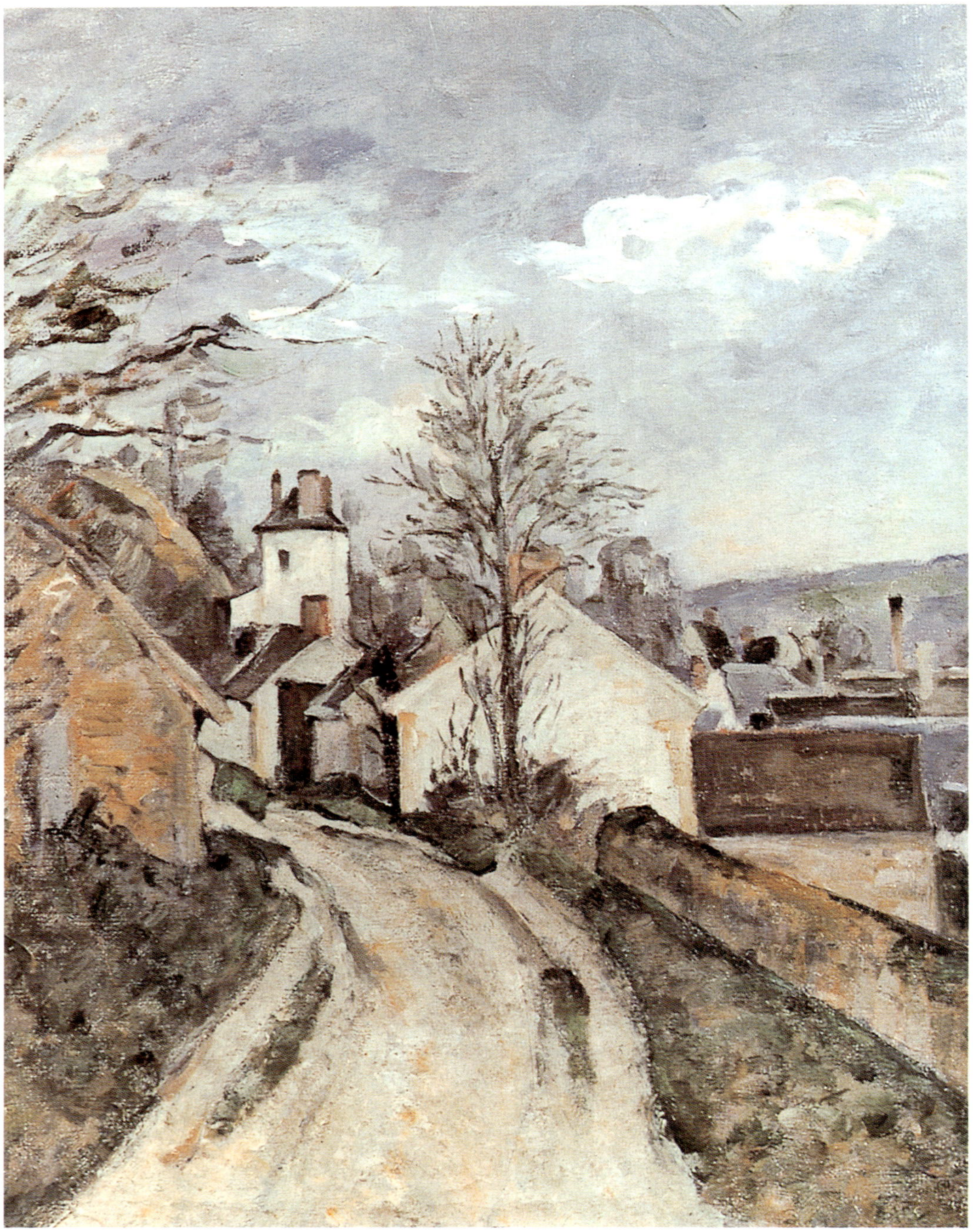

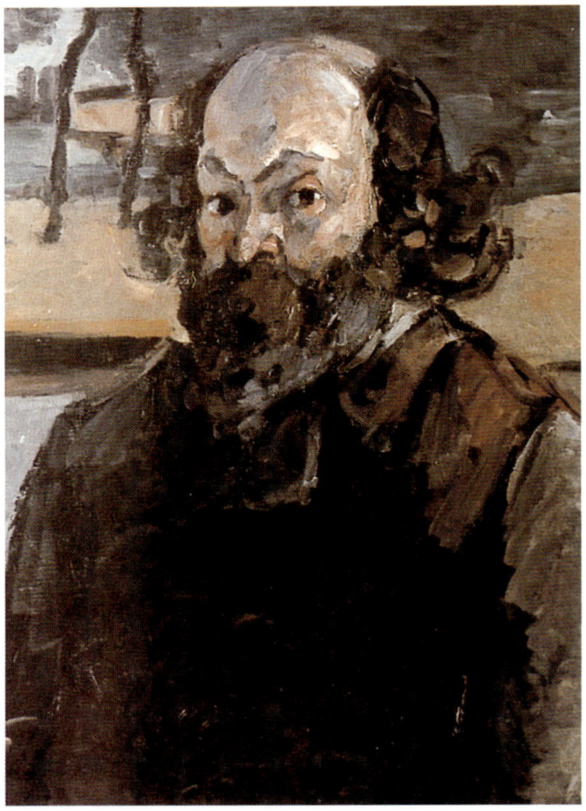

par excellence, Pissarro's ongoing debt to the first of his mentors, Corot, as well as to Daubigny and Courbet is still evident in *The Avenue, Sydenham*. Solidity and consonance of composition characterize his work in comparison to Monet's search for "fugitive effects" in light and water.

The fall of the Paris Commune and the end of war in 1871 allowed Pissarro and his family to return to Louveciennes. What they saw when they got there horrified them. The Prussians had commandeered their house and used it as a butchery. Of the 1,500 paintings the artist had stored there, only about forty remained; the rest had been ripped from their stretchers and placed on the ground for the soldiers to walk on. Pissarro found the abused canvases discarded on the compost heap. Undeterred, Pissarro carried on painting as prodigiously as before. In November their second son, Georges, was born. In 1872 they moved back to Pontoise where they remained until 1882. Cézanne, invited by Pissarro to continue his landscape studies in Pontoise, arrived in the winter of 1872 with his companion Hortense Fiquet and their son Paul. They took up residence in a local hotel, later

CEZANNE
Dr Gachet's House at Auvers
oil on canvas
1873. 46 × 38 cm
FAR LEFT Cézanne worked with Pissarro between 1872 and 1874, and his technique improved considerably under Pissarro's tuition. Here we can see how Cézanne emulates Pissarro's style, abandoning a thick impasto worked with a palette knife for a lighter and more sober rendering.

CEZANNE
Self-portrait
oil on canvas
1873–76. 64 × 53 cm
LEFT He has depicted himself tormented and scruffy, seeking himself and not often pleased with the result of his efforts.

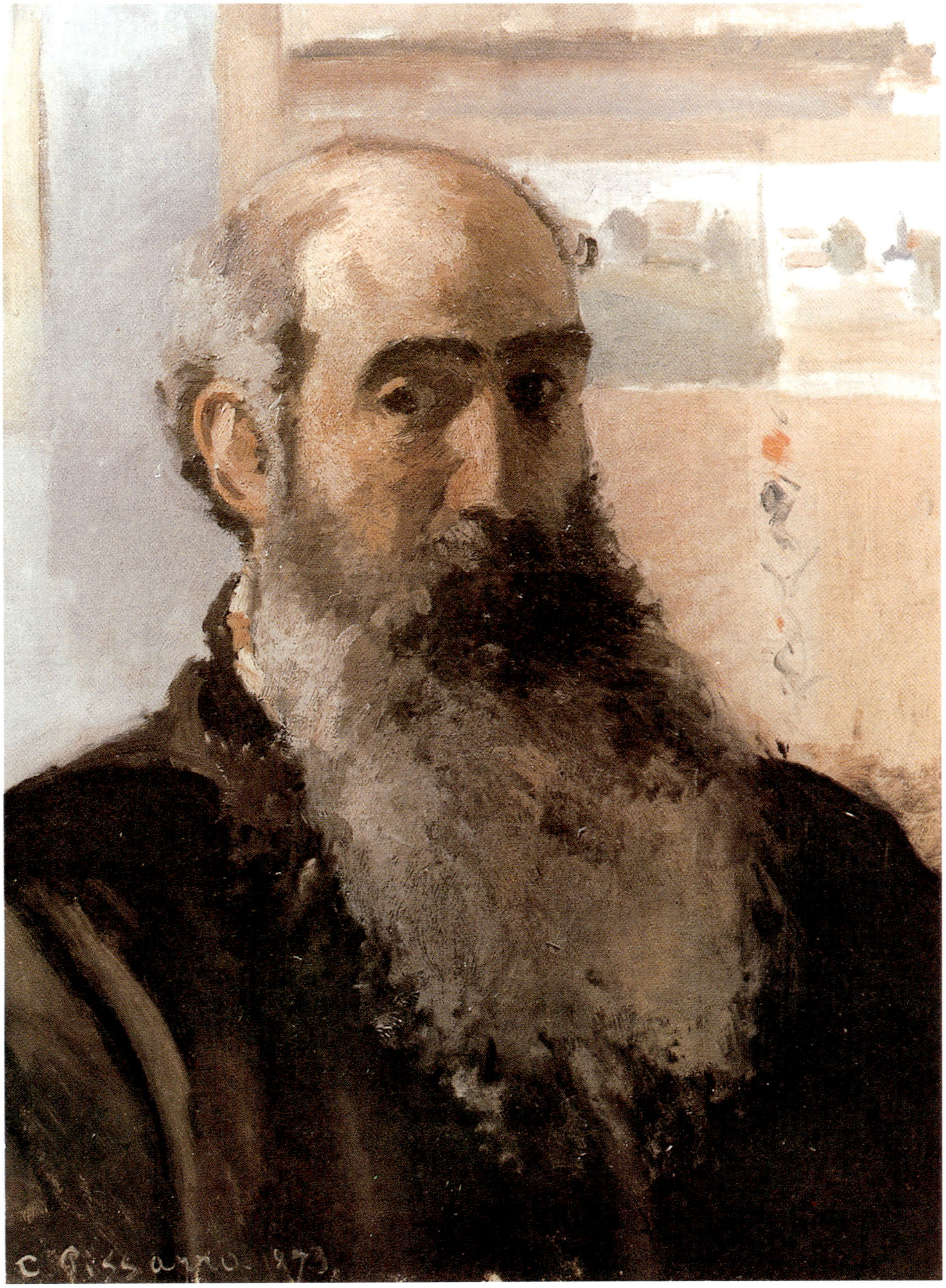

PISSARRO
Self-portrait
oil on canvas
1873. 56 × 46.5 cm
RIGHT Pissarro was only forty-three when this portrait was made, but he looks much older by our standards. Renoir complained of being old at the same age.

PISSARRO
Early Frost
oil on canvas
1873. 65 × 93 cm
RIGHT Pissarro was the only Impressionist to share with the previous generation a taste for pastorals, peasants and villages, and he preferred orchards and kitchen gardens to the cultivated gardens dear to Monet. This composition is sophisticated in its simplicity and it is remarkably well balanced and delicate.

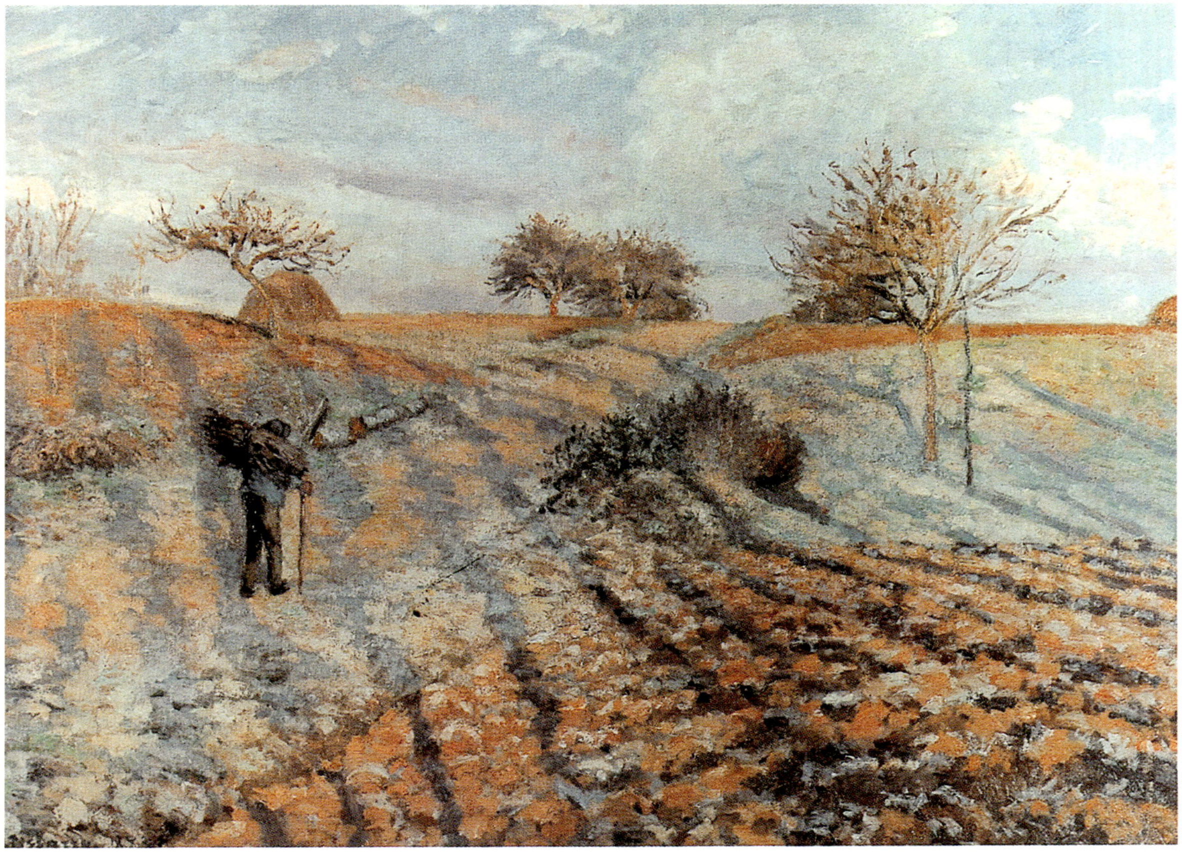

PISSARRO
Red Roofs
oil on canvas
1877. 54.5 × 65.5 cm
BELOW Pissarro painted Red Roofs *during the winter of 1876–77. It was a cluster of houses at the bottom of the Côtes des Boeufs, very near Pissarro's house.*

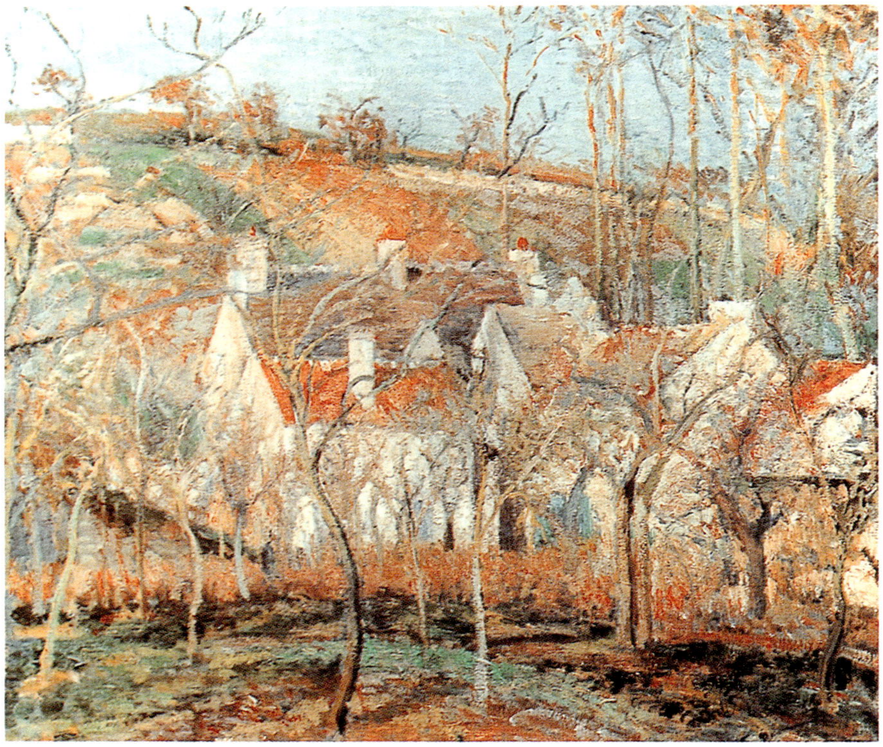

moving to nearby Auvers-sur-Oise. Cézanne's *House of the Hanged Man at Auvers* (*La Maison du pendu à Auvers*) from this period is greatly influenced by Pissarro's increasingly impressionistic style.

Pissarro's fortunes were temporarily looking up. Auctions in Paris were fetching high prices, whilst the influential, sympathetic and extremely wealthy journalist and art critic Théodore Duret, the Comte de Brie, was beginning to champion the work of Pissarro and others in the group. The soon-to-be-named Impressionists, including Pissarro, were thrashing out the details of the new *Société anonyme* that they were about to form in order to launch their first exhibition. Pissarro was deeply involved in organizing the new venture, foreseeing a sort of co-operative or collective bizarrely based on the

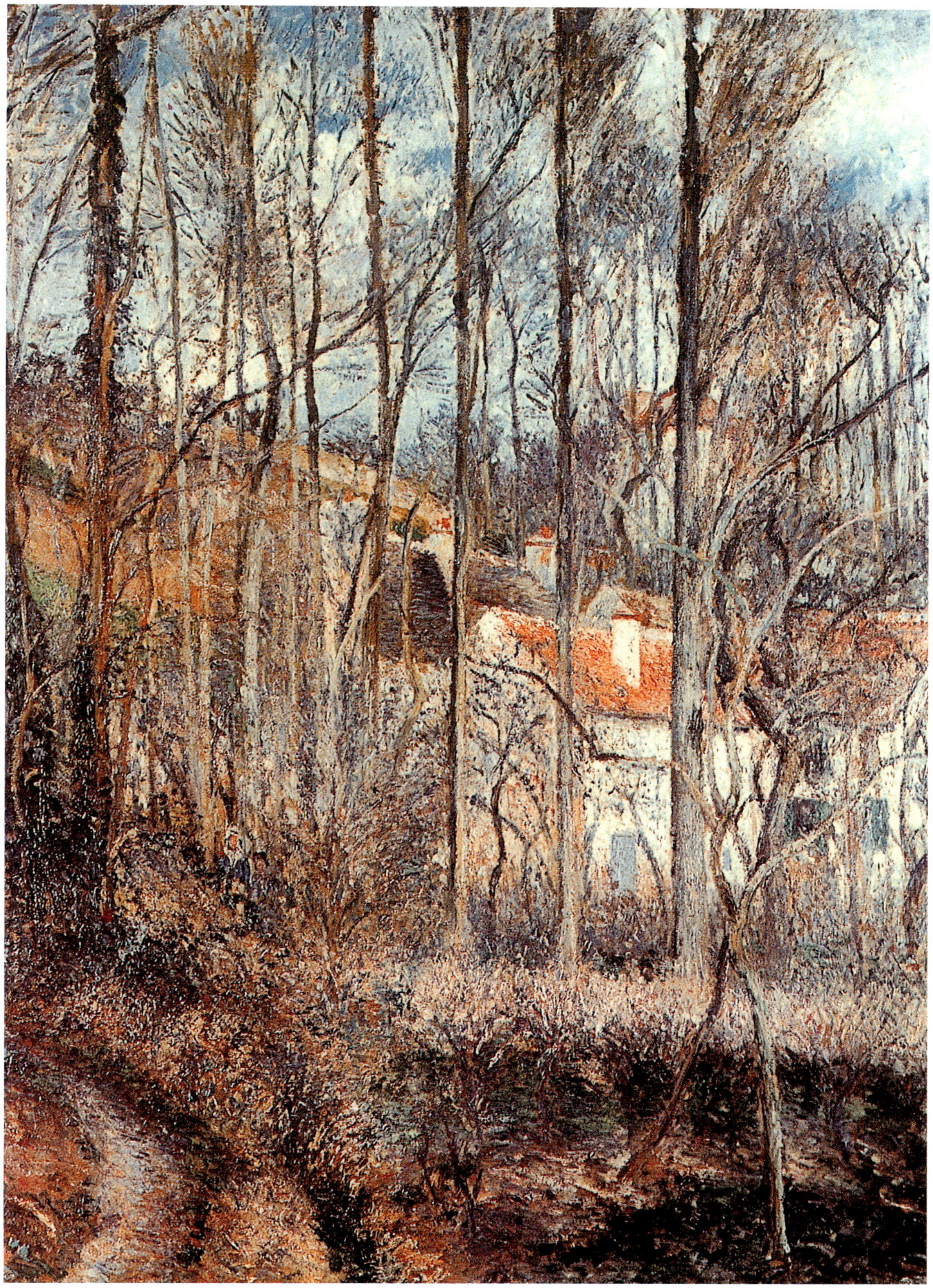

PISSARRO
La Côte des Boeufs at the Hermitage, near Pontoise
oil on canvas
1877. 115 × 87.5 cm
This year Cézanne had returned from the south of France to work with Pissarro. Here we find a similar view of cottages seen through trees, and a hill blocking part of the background. Pissarro was beginning to apply thicker coats of paint, giving more texture to his canvases.

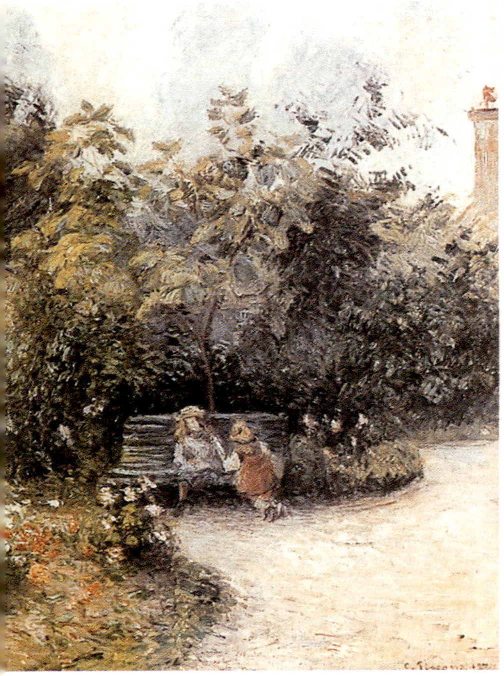

PISSARRO
The Garden at the Hermitage
oil on canvas
1877. 55 × 46 cm
ABOVE Abandoning for once the open country, Pissarro depicts two of his children in the family garden, which does not look as well cared for as Monet's.

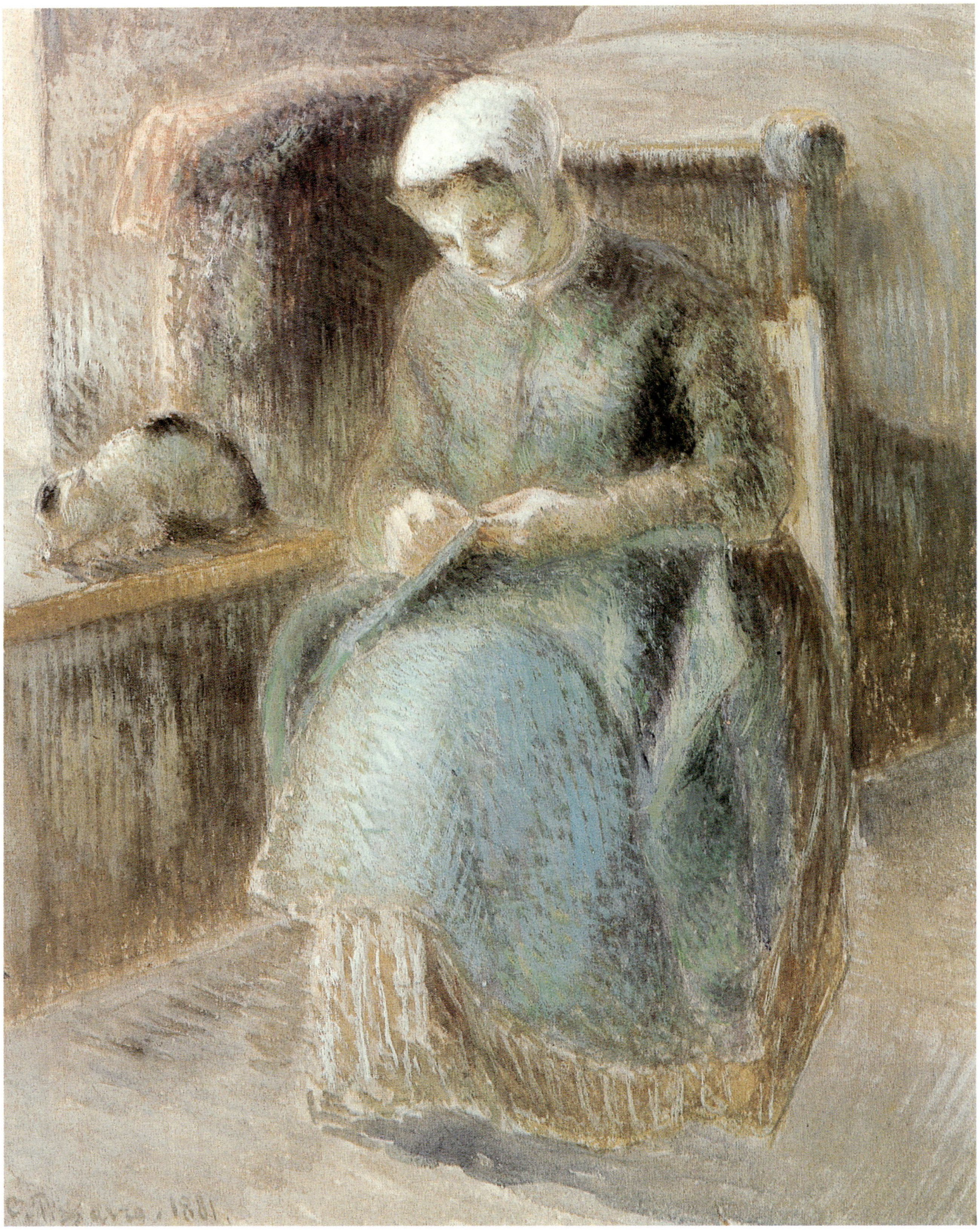

PISSARRO
The Seamstress
pastel on canvas
1881. 25 × 20 cm
RIGHT In this small study, Pissarro depicts the humble life of a peasant woman in the peace of her home.

principles of the Pontoise bakers' union and the *Association des artistes, peintres d'histoire et de genre, etc* which he had joined thirteen years before. Renoir, Monet and the rest of the group found the complexities of Pissarro's plan too much and eventually a joint stock company was founded with the fifteen artists as equal shareholders. Further tension was created by Pissarro insisting on Cézanne and Guillaumin joining the *Société*'s exhibition but Pissarro had his way. Duret was against the whole idea of an independent exhibition and urged Pissarro to follow Manet's example and stick to the Salon. This Pissarro ignored and thus remained faithful to the concept of the Impressionist exhibitions; he went on to contribute to all eight.

April 1874 was an eventful, albeit traumatic

PISSARRO and GAUGUIN
Respective portraits
c.1879–80.
Gauguin, self-centred and opinionated, was one of the young artists who profited from Pissarro's benevolent tuition. Gauguin was to find Pissarro's world all too simplistic and pursued his own very different quest. He turned against his mentor but later acknowledged how much he owed him.

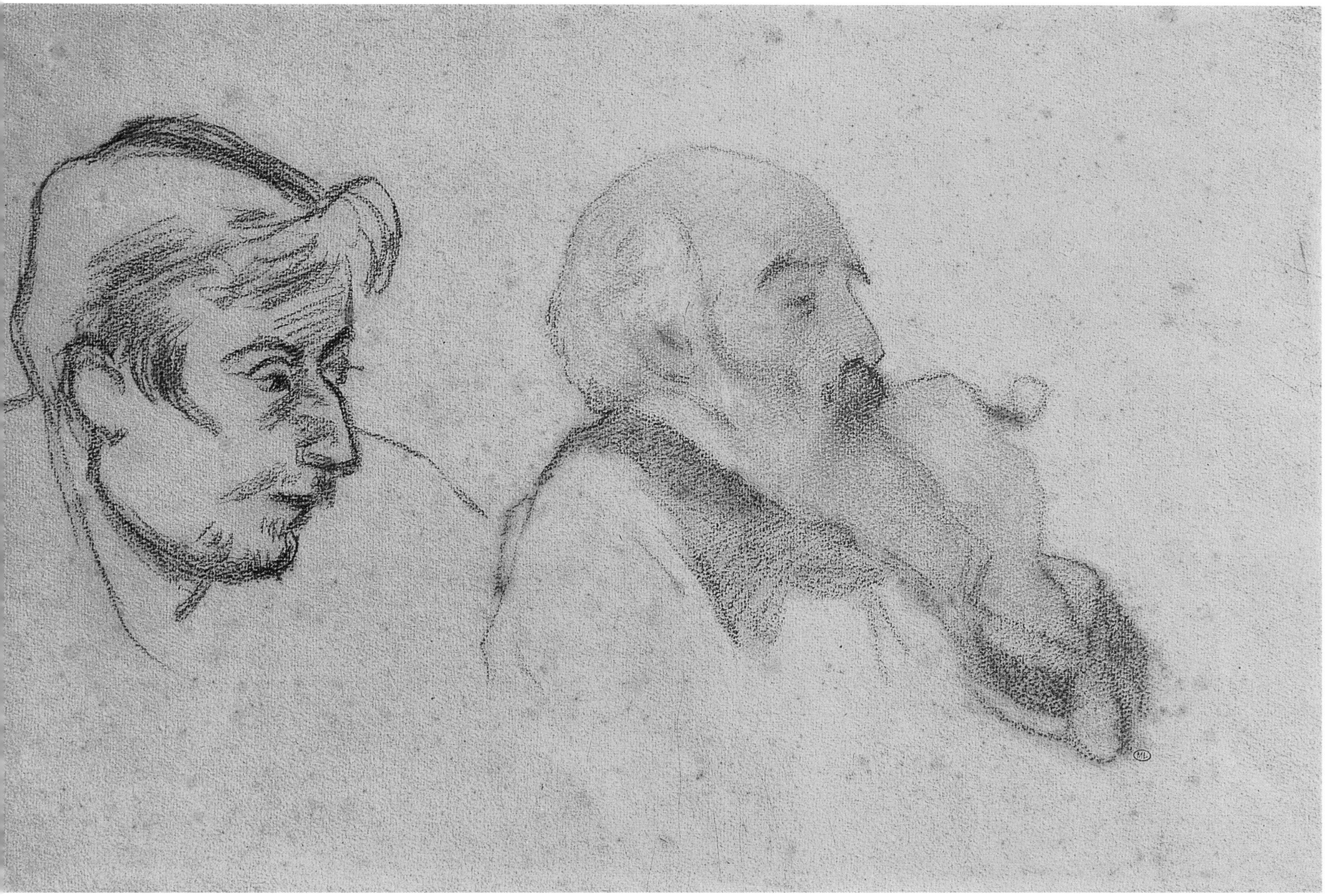

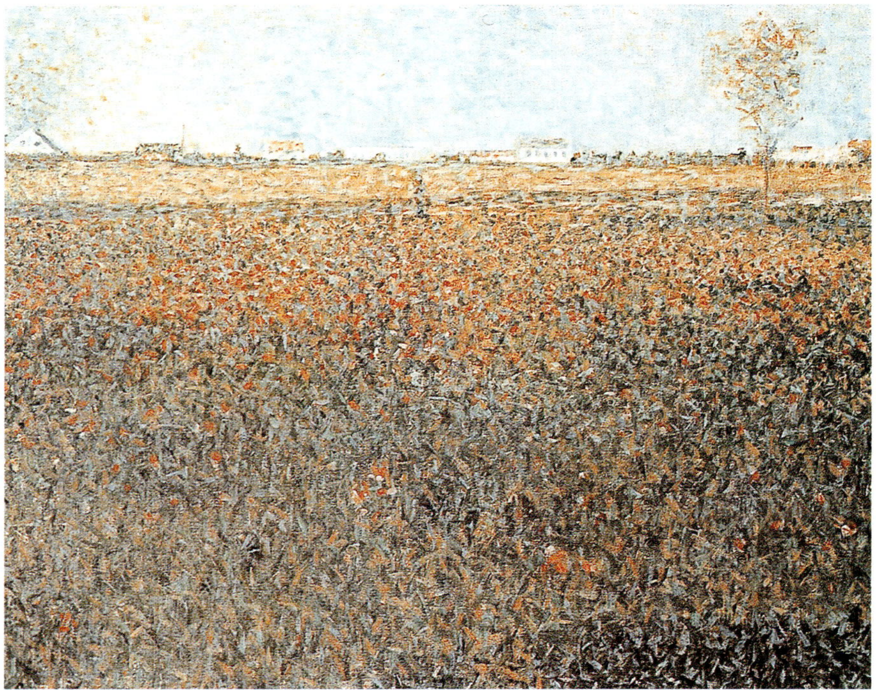

SEURAT
Alfalfa Field near St Denis
oil on canvas
1885. 65 × 81 cm
Seurat had been experimenting with Pointillism for several years when he painted this landscape. His teachers at the Ecole in Paris had found him hardworking, an essential quality for the painstaking technique he evolved.

month for Pissarro. In the Impressionists' first exhibition Pissarro's innovative landscapes were condemned along with the others. When the exhibition closed Pissarro was forced to appeal to Piette for help. Following his critical failure Pissarro's nine-year-old daughter, Jeanne, died the same month.

Pissarro was now almost forty-five years old. Fifteen years later in 1890 he wrote a letter to his niece, Esther Isaacson, summing up his career thus far: "I began to understand my feelings and know what I wanted in my forties – but only vaguely; at the age of fifty, in 1880, I conceived an idea of [artistic] unity without being able to render it; at sixty I am now beginning to see the possibility of rendering it." Pissarro's career was indeed a long and arduous search for the perfect method of expressing himself and his ideas. Until his sixty-second year when Durand-Ruel mounted a hugely successful retrospective of his work he was permanently in dire straits as his family continued to grow. Yet despite these pressures, he never begrudged anyone advice and encouragement. Younger painters, beginning with Cézanne in 1872, Gauguin in 1877, and later Matisse and Picabia sought him out. Cézanne revered him, saying he was like a father to him, "*un peu comme le bon Dieu*" ("a little like the good Lord"). Mary Cassatt thought he was such a good teacher he could have taught the stones to draw.

By the time of the last Impressionist exhibition in 1886 the great teacher was himself in an artistic crisis. The intervening years had seen him contribute to every Impressionist show and often cajole the other members of the group into accepting the works of younger artists such as Gauguin. He had been helped along by commissions from the successful patissier Eugène Murer, who had also bought a hotel room for him in Rouen where he spent considerable periods painting the cityscape. A printing partnership with Degas and Mary Cassatt had been successful, Durand-Ruel had supported him when and as he could, and so he had managed to get by. In 1884 the Pissarro family had moved to Eragny where they eventually bought the house they had leased (with the aid of a loan from Monet which Pissarro scrupulously repaid). Meanwhile Pissarro's interest in the human figure, especially the peasant women who were so much a part of the landscape, had come to dominate his work as a fundamental expression of his humanism. As Ralph Shikes observes:

> Often he paints the grubby kitchen gardens, quite understandably paintings of little appeal to a self-conscious middle class. His agricultural workers – members of the peasant family or day labourers – carry

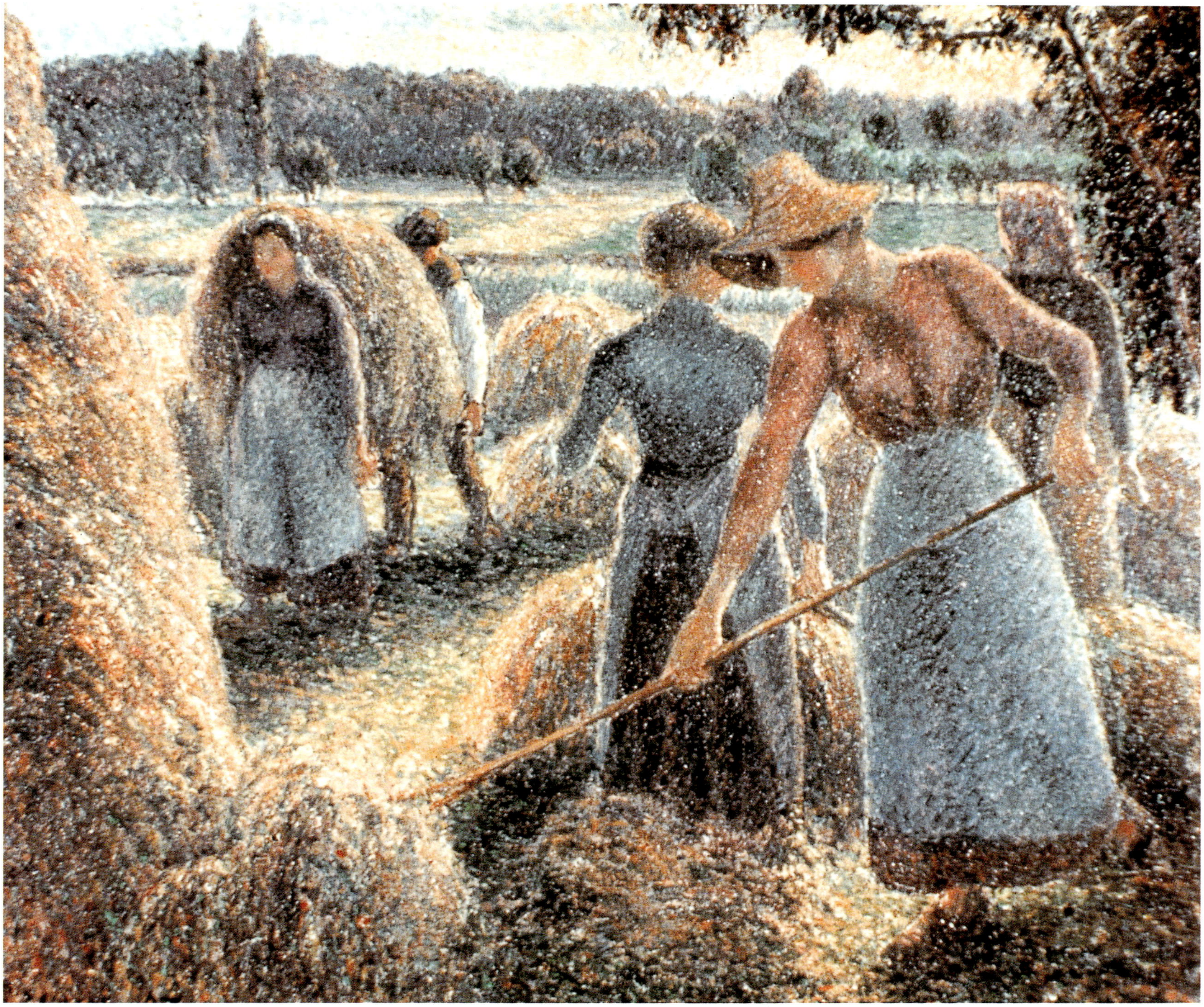

PISSARRO
Haymakers, Evening
oil on canvas
1893.
While retaining his familiar subject matter, which Seurat had also treated in small studies, Pissarro is now adapting Pointillism to his own style, and the woman in the foreground has lost the soft and natural posture of his earlier figures.

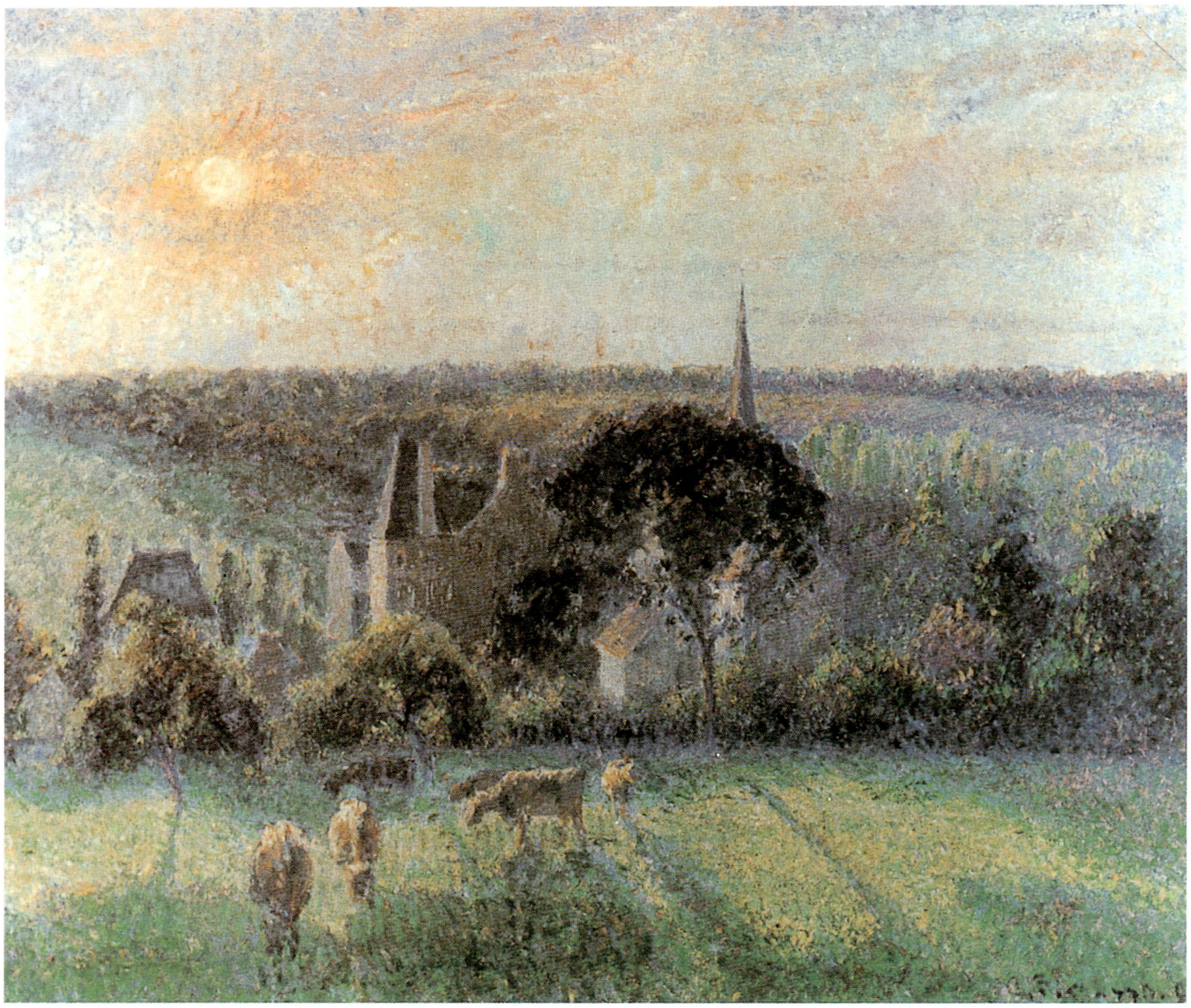

PISSARRO
Landscape at Eragny
oil on canvas
1895. 60 × 73.5 cm
Another example of Pissarro's late Pointillism. This is an afterthought – he had renounced the technique a few years earlier, and it has none of the dogmatic coldness seen in Seurat's works.

> buckets of water, herd the cows, feed the chickens. They are mostly women performing lowly chores. They are not heroic figures, but simple humanity observed in the cadenced rhythm of the seasons . . . as they perform their [daily] tasks.

But the method of expressing all this had become problematical. The web of comma-like brushstrokes which had now become his trademark seemed to have reached its logical conclusion and he was casting about for new ways of painting. A harder edge was called for. Impressionism seemed to have had its day; Renoir for example had recently found himself in a similar stylistic dead-end and was developing an overtly linear, Neo-Classical style; years before, Cézanne had abandoned a softer vision of the world and was absorbed in lines, volumes, and planes. In October 1885 Pissarro met the young Georges Seurat who was developing a new technique, Divisionism, based on several theories going back to Chevreul. Pissarro too had read the new colour theories proposed by the American colour theorists Charles Henry and

Ogden Rood, and with Paul Signac he found common cause in Seurat's juxtaposition of small dots of pure pigment to create the forms of a painting. "I am totally convinced of the progressive nature of this art," he wrote to Lucien, "and certain that in time it will yield extraordinary results. I do not accept the snobbish judgments of romantic Impressionists in whose interest it is to fight against new tendencies. I accept the challenge, that's all."

At the age of fifty-five Pissarro became a Neo-Impressionist; his anarchism had also become more fervent. Writing later to Lucien, he said: "I firmly believe that our anarchist philosophy is linked to our work and therefore disagreeable to current thought." Signac and Seurat were also sympathetic to the aims of anarchism, although it is difficult to see any concrete link between these amorphous aims and their work. In any case Pissarro's Neo-Impressionism was to last barely five years, and was resisted on the one hand by Durand-Ruel who refused to buy his Divisionist works and on the other by Impressionists who were loath to exhibit in the company of Divisionists. Nevertheless Pissarro secured what amounted to a separate Divisionist Room in the final Impressionist exhibition of 1886, where he, his son Lucien, Signac, and Seurat showed work which attracted both acclaim and horror.

The tedious physical process of painting in what was variously called the Neo-Impressionist, Pointillist, or Divisionist technique of dots took its toll on Pissarro and reduced the number of canvases (normally high) which he could finish. In May 1889 his mother died at the age of ninety-four. The same year Pissarro began to suffer from an eye infection, forcing him to work indoors, but not inhibiting his flow of work. He abandoned the limitations of Divisionism the next year and began a phase of painting urban and quayside landscapes in Paris, Rouen, Le Hâvre, and Dieppe, as well as in London. The years between 1889 and 1900 were perhaps the most productive of his life; in 1896 he was earning sufficient sums to begin paying back the money he had borrowed from Monet. Truly anarchic to the end, Pissarro became more committed to the cause as he approached his seventies. Back in the days of the Café Guerbois he had once suggested burning down the Louvre; now, in 1894, his

PISSARRO
Paris, Place du Hâvre
oil on canvas
1893. 60 × 73 cm
Dissatisfied with Pointillism, Pissarro looked instead for a different kind of subject and produced many cityscapes in his later years, most of them seen from the window of rooms high up above Paris, Rouen and Dieppe.

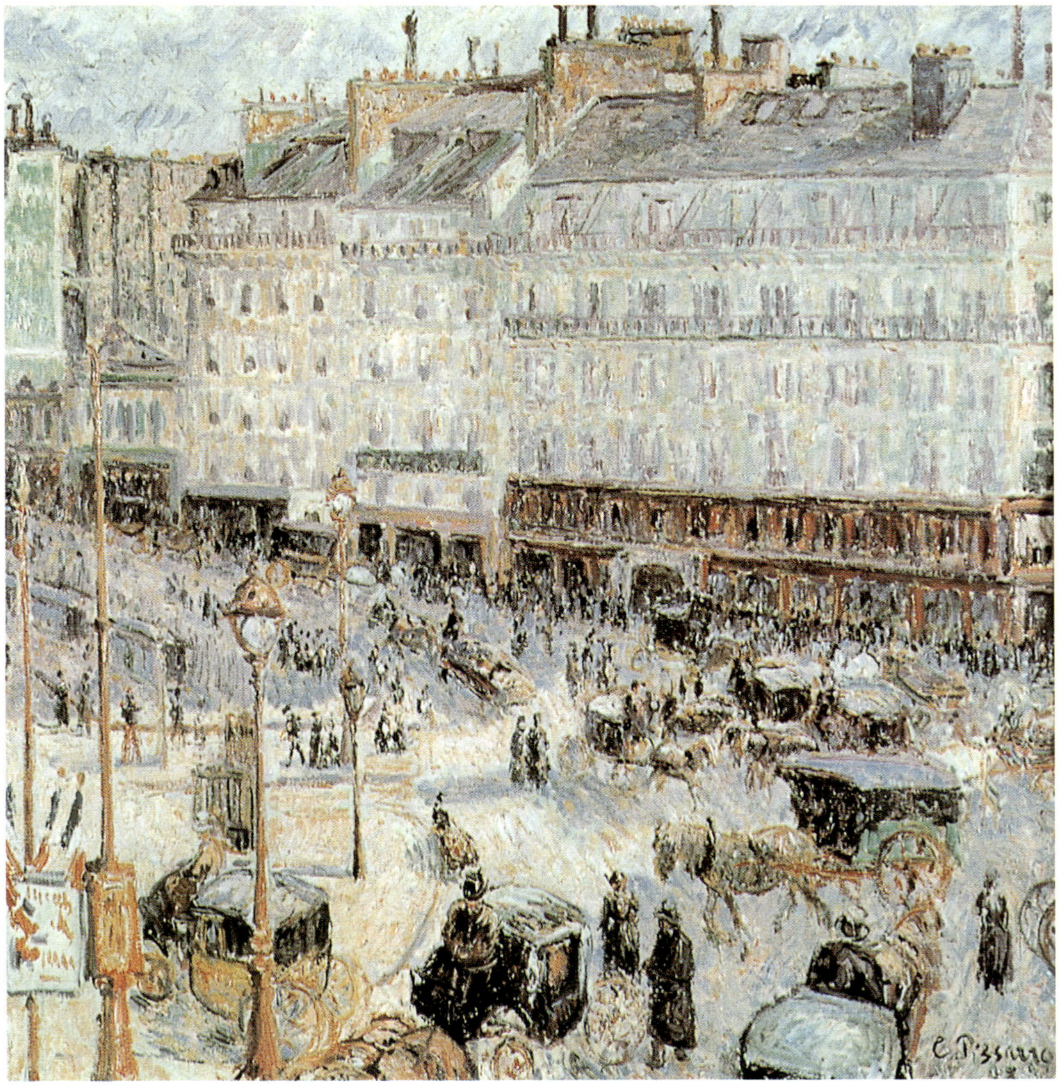

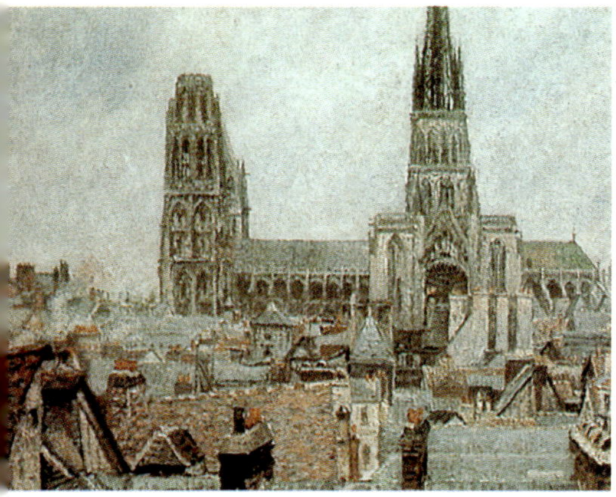

PISSARRO
Roofs of Old Rouen *(DETAIL)*
oil on canvas
c.1866–1902. 102 × 76 cm
ABOVE Closing the circle, the old painter, who died the following year, chose to re-work a painting executed when he was very much under Corot's influence.

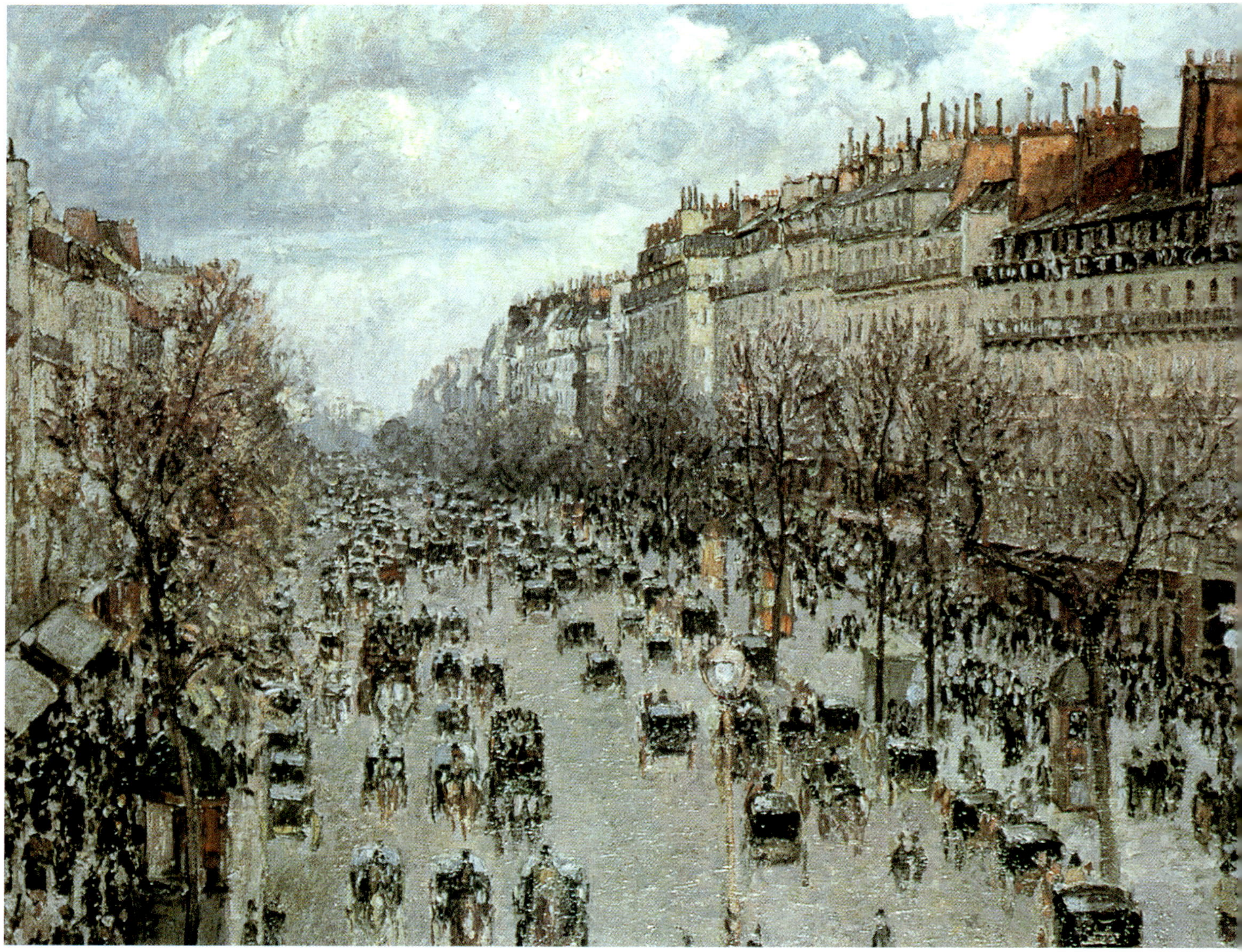

PISSARRO
Boulevard Montmarte, Paris
oil on canvas
1897. 72 × 91 cm
RIGHT Renoir was very critical of Pissarro's cityscapes. He might more justly have said that compared to Monet, Pissarro's style had not evolved as much. There is indeed no marked difference between some of Monet's cityscapes of 1876 and this painting, made twenty years later.

anarchist sympathies forced him to spend four months in Knocke, Belgium after the knifing to death of Président Sadi Carnot by an Italian anarchist. During the Dreyfus Affair, which practically tore *fin de siècle* France apart, he came out staunchly on Zola's side and against the entrenched anti-Semitism of the French military which had clumsily framed an innocent Jewish captain-of-the-guard and led to his exile and imprisonment.

Camille Pissarro died in Paris on 13th November 1903 of blood poisoning caused by an abscess of the prostate: his homeopathic doctor had attempted to cure it without an operation. His last years were marked by international honour and widespread public acclaim. Of all the Impressionists he was perhaps the best loved and respected by his friends, fellow artists, and protégés. After Pissarro's death Gauguin said of him, despite the severe criticism he had received from Pissarro: "*Ce fut un de mes maîtres. Je ne le renie pas.*" ("He was one of my masters. I cannot renounce him.")

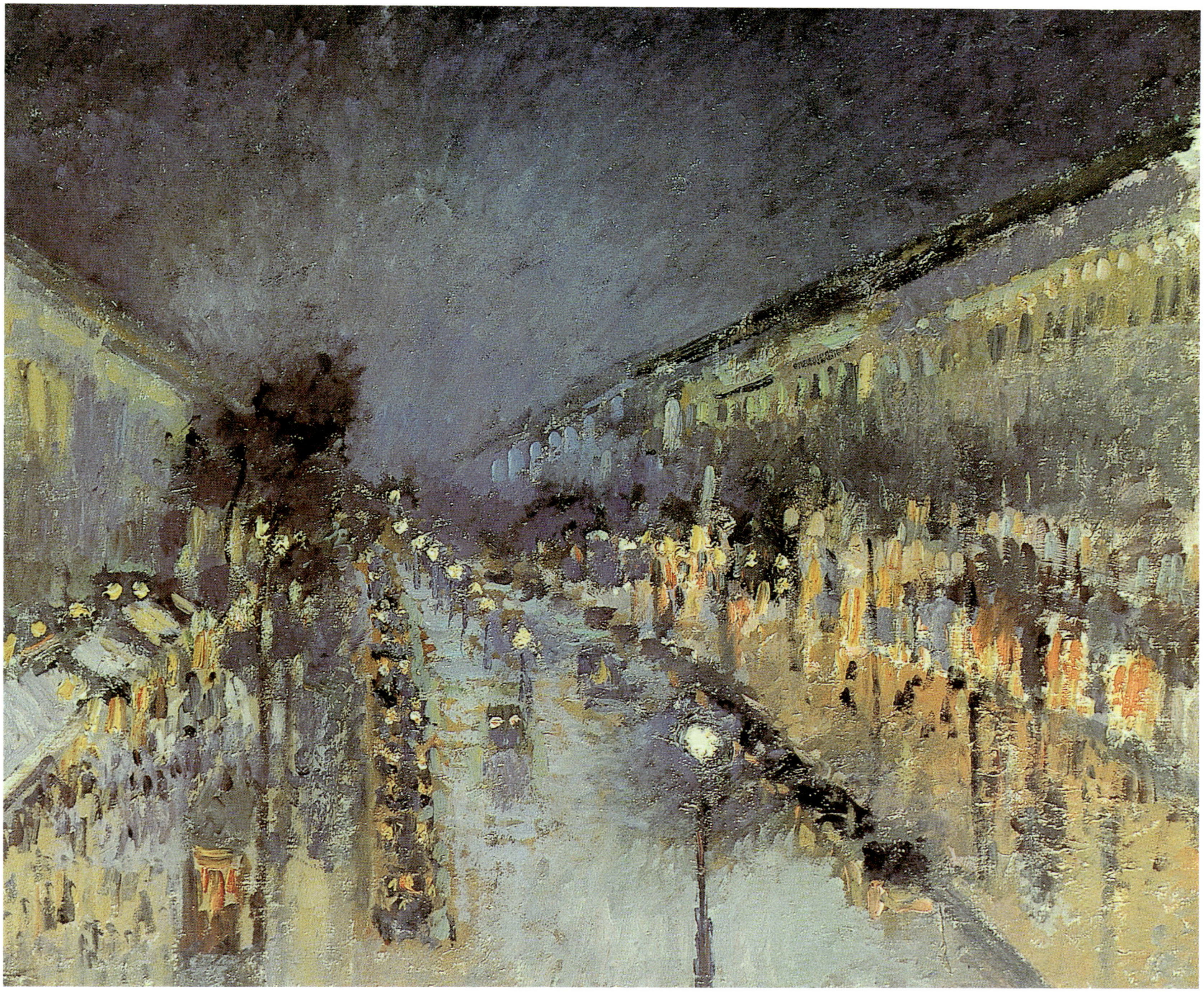

PISSARRO
Boulevard Montmarte by Night
oil on canvas
1897. 53.5 × 65 cm
Both pictures were painted from the Hôtel de Russie at the corner of the boulevard des Italiens and of the rue Drouot in Paris, in an area familiar to the Impressionist group. The night view presented a challenge which seems to have stimulated the artist, and Pissarro met it with great success, in a decidedly impressionistic way, giving life to the flicker of street lights and to the reflection of the rain on the pavement.

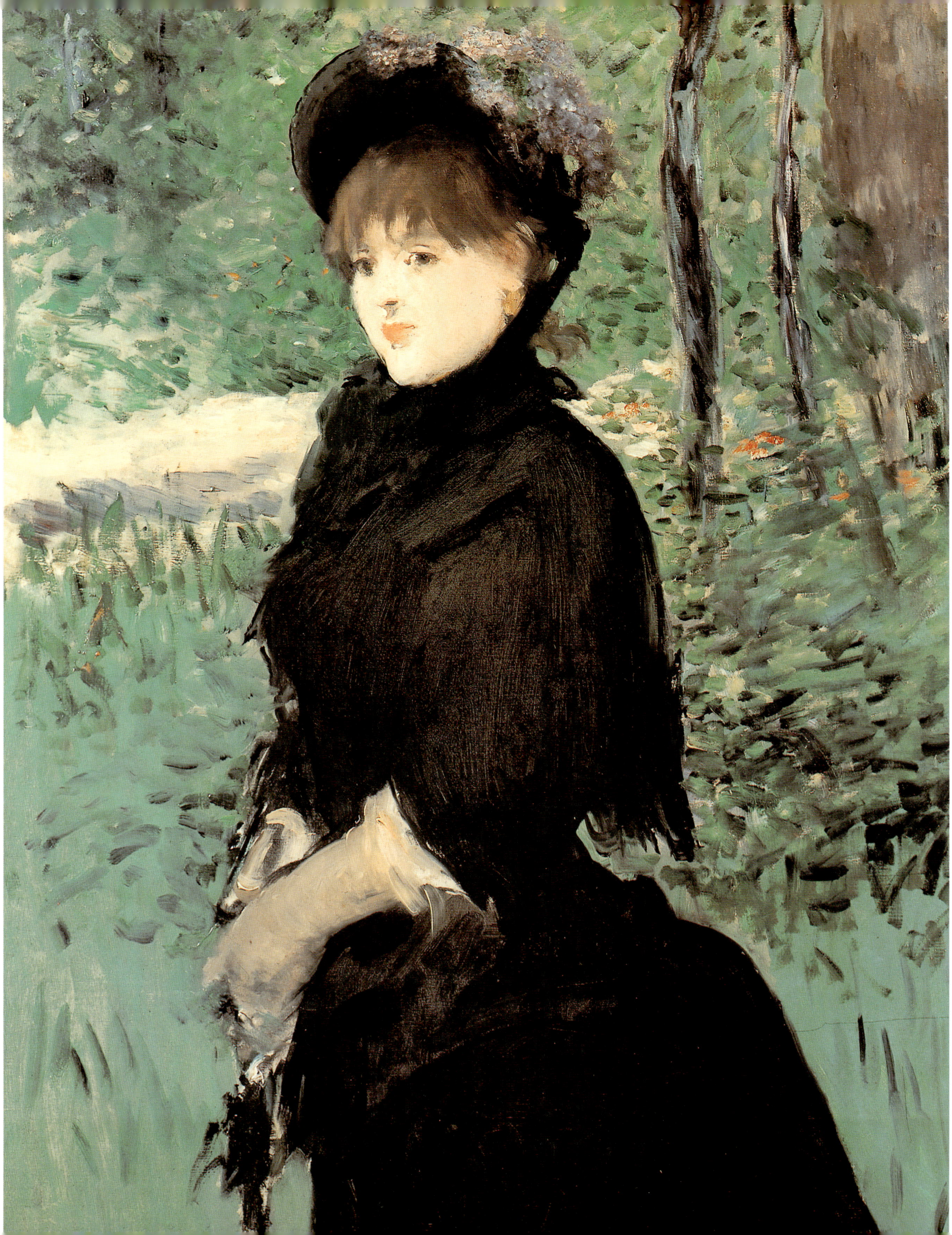

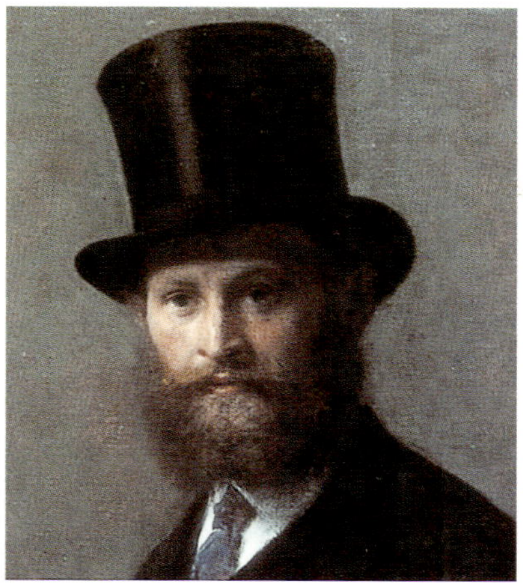

manet

Edouard Manet was the figurehead of a generation of artists who saw him as a champion of experimental and non-conformist art. As a conventional member of the bourgeoisie who desired nothing better than to be acclaimed by society at the Salon, Manet's career was marked by misunderstanding from both sides. As a friend of Baudelaire, he was at the very forefront of the artistic avant-garde, yet he remained personally conservative and eager to please. It was his ability to create something new from the most conventional of subjects that ensured his continuing fame as well as a deeply felt ambivalence amongst his critics, who until recently have expressed contradictory views that he was both a genius and lacking in imagination. His achievements lay in the ambiguity and unrivalled originality with which he portrayed the Paris of his day, as epitomized in the *Bar at the Folies-Bergère* and the *Corner in a Café-concert* – two paintings which more than any of his contemporaries' encapsulated impressions of an age of decaying and transitory brilliance.

EDOUARD MANET
By Fantin-Latour
1867
Above

MANET
The Walk
oil on canvas
c.1880. 92.5 × 70.5 cm
Opposite

Life and Works: Edouard Manet (1832–1883)

. . . a revolutionary painter who loved society and had always dreamt of the success only Paris can offer – the flattery of the ladies, the warm embrace of their salons, a life of luxury hurtling through admiring crowds.

Emile Zola

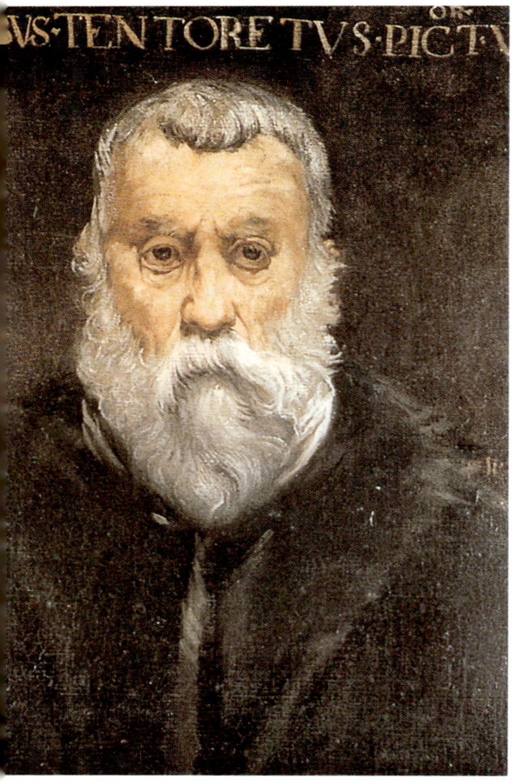

MANET
Copy of Tintoretto's Self-portrait
oil on canvas
61 × 50 cm
Above This is one of the numerous old masters copied by Manet. He was a registered copyist at the Louvre, but also worked in the Rijksmuseum of Amsterdam, and in Florence, Rome and Venice. Manet was a vital pivot in a long tradition which he sincerely acknowledged.

Edouard Manet was born in Paris on 23rd January 1832, the oldest son of August Manet, Head of Personnel at the French Ministry of Justice, and Eugénie Désirée Fournier, a diplomat's daughter.

Manet could have become a successful lawyer, which is what his father had in mind for him, but it was perhaps the influence of his artistic mother Eugénie and his uncle Edmond Fournier, a great connoisseur of art, that quashed the idea early on. From the age of fifteen Manet and his friend at the exclusive Collège Rollin, Antonin Proust, received special drawing lessons and were taken on instructive tours of the Paris museums by Edmond Fournier. At sixteen Manet rebelled against his father's wish to enter him in the Faculty of Law, declared his desire to be an artist, forced a compromise with his father (it was more of a ruse than anything) and joined the Navy. He failed the Naval entrance examinations but set sail nonetheless on 9th December 1848 at the age of sixteen as an officer cadet on the ship *Le Hâvre et Guadeloupe* bound for Rio de Janeiro.

On his return to France the next year Manet failed the Naval examinations once again and finally swayed his father to his artistic ambitions. The baggage Manet brought back from the Americas was crammed with drawings to prove his vocation.

In the Paris of the 1850s there were several independent ateliers where a budding artist could study, and Manet chose one of the most celebrated, that of Thomas Couture in the rue de Laval (now the rue Victor-Massé). Couture had beguiled the Salon of 1847 with his epic painting *The Romans of the Decadence* and was famous both as a painter and as a liberal teacher. Manet remained at Couture's from 1850 to 1856, studying the master's teaching, copying (amongst other things a Velazquez) at the Louvre and occasionally causing

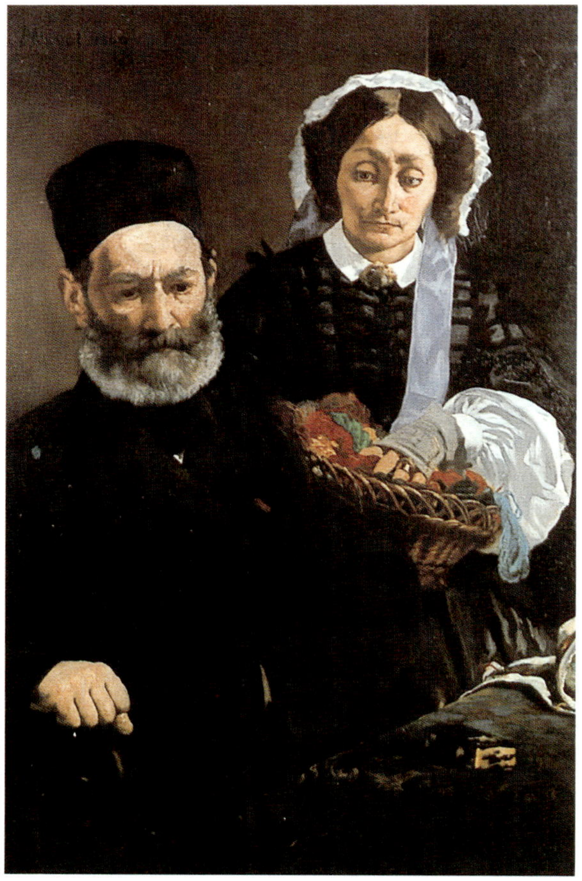

trouble in the atelier, as Antonin Proust remembered: "On Mondays, the day when a pose was to be struck for the rest of the week, Manet would invariably fight with Couture's models . . . Mounting the podium they would assume their traditional and exaggerated poses. 'Are you incapable of being natural?' Manet would cry, 'Is that how you stand when you're buying a bundle of radish at the greengrocer's?' " Proust described another incident which sheds some light on Manet's developing wit and his relationship with Couture: "One day Manet had managed to make Gilbert (a model) assume a natural pose, half dressed. Couture walked into the atelier and threw a fit in front of the clothed model. 'So you pay Gilbert to *keep his clothes on*? Who is responsible for this stupidity?' 'I am,' said Manet. 'Come now, my poor boy,' said Couture, 'you will never be anything but the Daumier of your time.' " Later Manet is supposed to have told Antonin, "The Daumier of my time! At least that would be better than being the Coypel of it." (Coypel was not a fashionable painter at that time.)

Despite these frivolities Manet was greatly indebted to Couture, an opponent of the all-pervading academic style and its constrictions. Couture's advice to his students was: "Make sure first of all that you have mastered material procedures; then think of nothing and produce with a fresh mind and hearty spirit whatever you feel like doing." This was exactly what Manet was to do, building on a complete mastery of technique and a deep appreciation of the old masters in order to make his revolutionary (or evolutionary) mark. A foretaste of what was to come is supplied by Antonin Proust, who remembered Manet drawing a picture in 1851 which showed the identification of bodies in the Montmartre cemetery, victims of the December *coup d'état* by Louis Napoleon. Manet was already a fierce republican; he had written to his father from Rio de Janeiro: "Try to keep a good republic for us against our return; I'm afraid Louis Napoleon is not a very good republican." How right he was; the corpses in Montmartre proved that Manet's fears for the Second Republic were well founded – it had lasted barely two years after his return from South America.

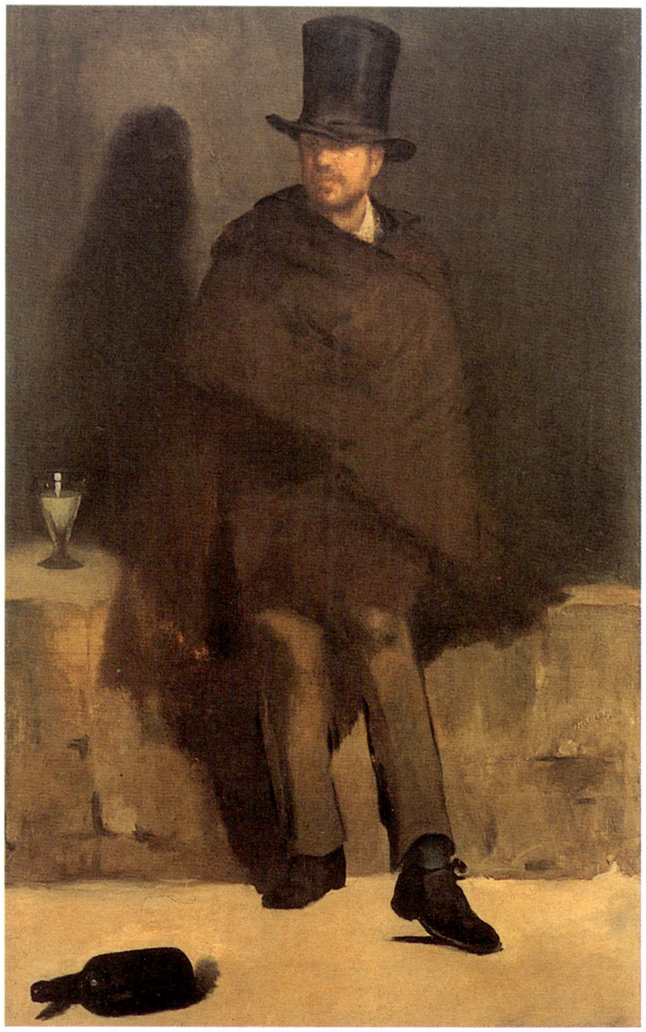

MANET
The Absinthe Drinker
1859. 177.5 × 103 cm
Left Absinthe had far too bad a reputation to be an acceptable subject for the Salon. Manet found his low-life models in the Batignolles area where he lived. The model here is the ragpicker Colardet.

MANET
The Parents of the Artist
oil on canvas
1860. 110 × 90 cm
Opposite The austere M. Manet does not indeed look like the sort of father a son could confide in about his illegitimate offspring. Manet never told his father about Léon, born to his twenty-year-old piano teacher Suzanne Leenhoff, and married only after his father's death.

In January 1852 a son, Léon, was born to Suzanne Leenhoff, Manet's twenty-year-old piano teacher with whom he had been having

MANET
Young Woman in Spanish Costume
oil on canvas
1862. 95 × 113 cm
RIGHT The pose is that of Goya's Maja. Whereas Goya painted both a nude and a dressed-up version, Manet chose to dress her as a torero. (DETAIL)

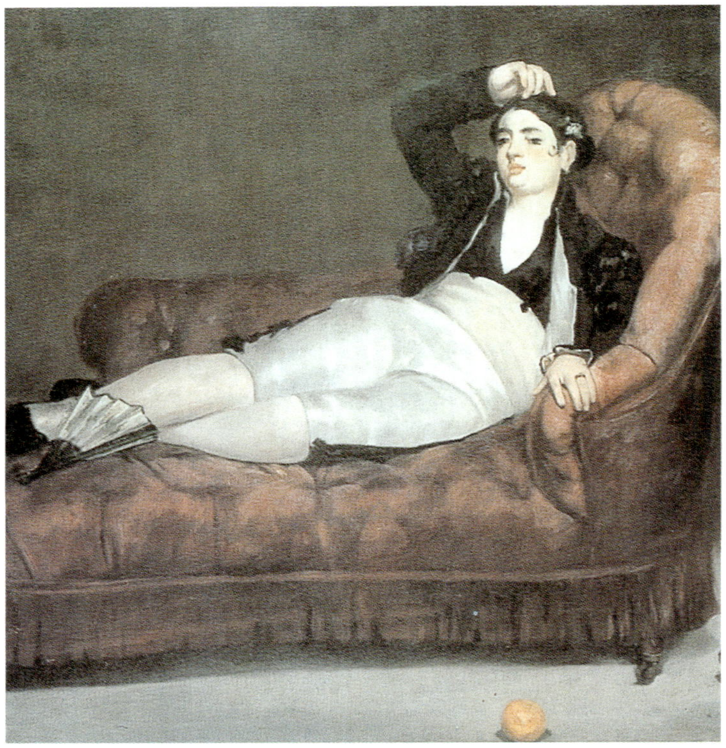

MANET
The Spanish Dancers
oil on canvas
1862. 61 × 91 cm
BELOW All things Spanish appealed to the French Romantics in ascendence during Manet's youth. Manet could not resist the opportunity of painting members of a ballet company that was touring Paris in 1862. The group in this picture includes Lola de Valence.

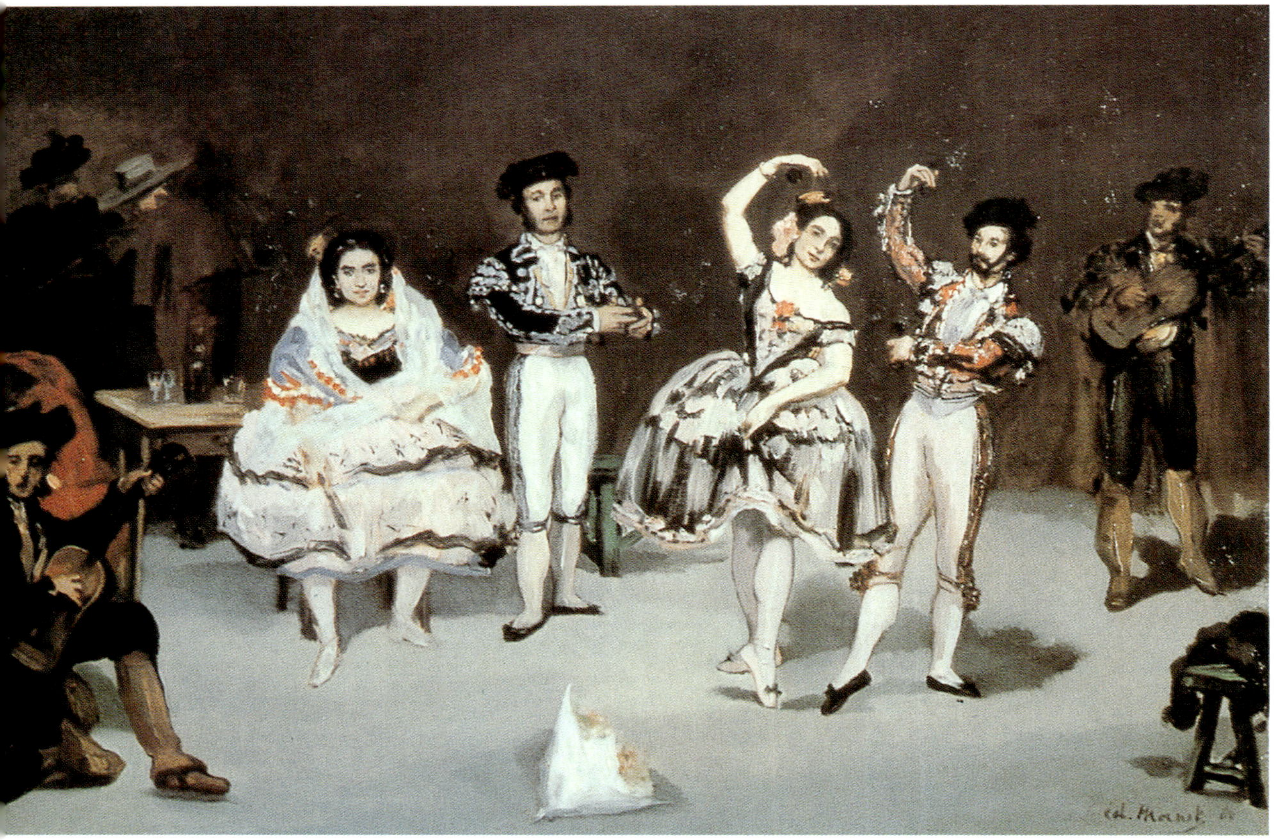

an affair since 1850. Eugénie Manet knew of the illegitimate birth, but she and Manet conspired to keep this from the austere and conservative Auguste Manet, passing the child off as Suzanne's brother and Manet's godson, even after Suzanne and Manet's marriage. Manet's strict adherence to form held sway, as it would in other matters, and Suzanne, like so many other mistresses, companions, and courtesans, was set up in an apartment to keep her out of harm's way until it was safe for her to emerge into society.

Manet left Couture's atelier around Easter 1856 and moved into a studio in the rue Lavoisier with another painter, Albert de Balleroy. He then made a tour of Holland, Germany, Austria, and Italy ending in Venice, visiting museums and studying the old masters. In 1859 Manet made his first submission, *The Absinthe Drinker* (*L'Absinthe*) to the Salon. It was summarily rejected on several counts, notably those of immorality and vulgarity; only Delacroix voted for it. The next year Manet made the acquaintance of the poet and art critic Charles Baudelaire, eleven years his senior, who had published his masterpiece, a collection of poems called *Les Fleurs du mal* (*The Flowers of Evil*) in 1857. The poems had caused outrage and several were banned. Flaubert's *Madame Bovary* had suffered a similar fate in 1856. The early years of Louis Napoleon's reign were difficult ones for literature and the avant-garde, of which Manet was rapidly becoming an important if somewhat reluctant member. He was now moving in two social milieux; upper middle-class salon society and the Bohemian demi-monde of Baudelaire and his friends where revolutionary new ideas were inspired and thrashed out. Baudelaire, with whom Manet became very close, died in agony of the

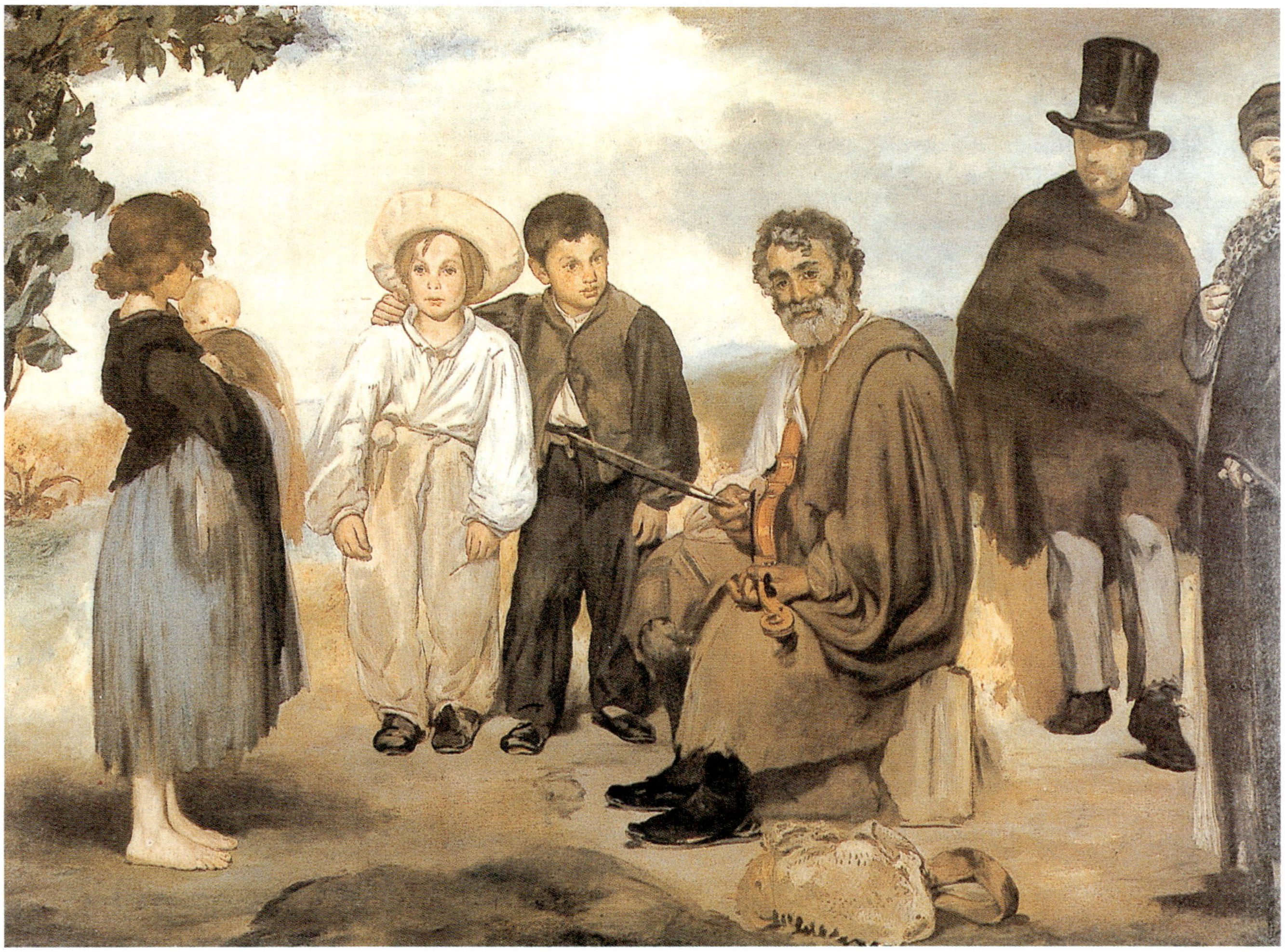

MANET
The Old Musician
oil on canvas
1862. 187.5 × 248.5 cm
This painting is a very large composition which retains a stillness typical of many of Manet's works. Again, he found his models near his home: he re-used the figure of The Absinthe Drinker, *who stands on the right, wearing a top hat. The old man was the gypsy Jean Lagrène. The cut-off figure along the right edge of the picture represents the Wandering Jew. All these people are poor, but Manet did not attempt to depict them in a romantic or sentimental manner, rather he displays the detachment from his subject matter which was later to bring accusations of coldness and impersonality.*

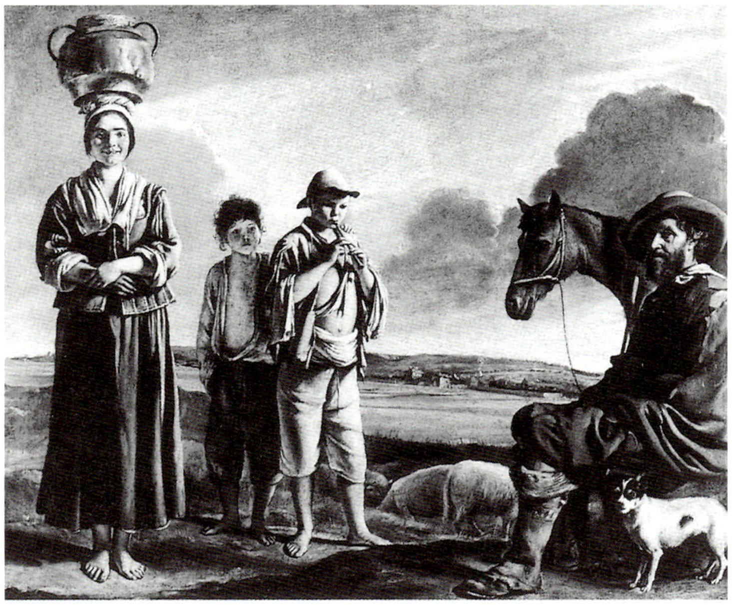

LE NAIN
Landscape with Figures
oil on canvas
c.1645. 54.5 × 67.5 cm
This painting was not in a public collection, but Champfleury, whom Manet knew, wrote about it in his book Les Frères Le Nain, *published in 1862. Manet is known to have worked from reproductions and he may have used this picture as the broad base of his own picture* The Old Musician.

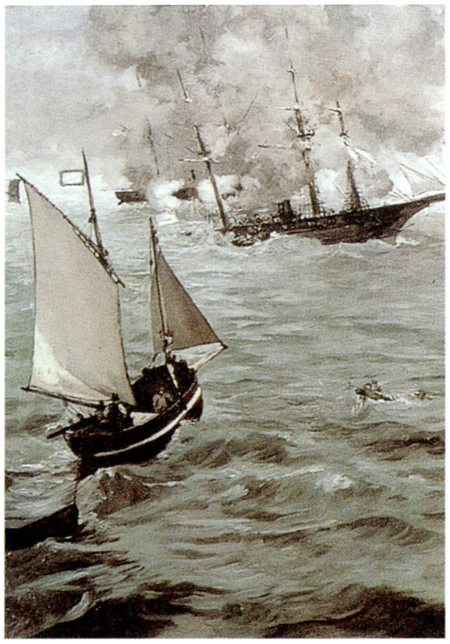

MANET
Battle of the *Kearsage* and the *Alabama*
oil on canvas
c.1865. 139 × 130 cm
ABOVE Always interested in current events and no doubt recalling his own days at sea before he became a painter, Manet painted two scenes of this remarkable episode in the American Civil War which took place off the coast of Boulogne. In the second picture, the Kearsage *is seen damaged and moored along the jetty.*

MANET
The Execution of the Emperor Maximilian
oil on canvas
1867–68. 35 × 26 cm & 89 × 30 cm; 190 × 160 cm; 99 × 59 cm.
RIGHT The first sketch, which Degas tried to piece together after Manet's death. Manet had acquired photographs of the execution which were available in Paris and noticed that the soldiers wore uniforms resembling that of the French army, except for the white gaiters. One of Manet's friends, the commandant of a local barrack, lent him a squad of soldiers as models.

effects of aphasia and syphilis in 1867. His anguished romanticism can be heard in these lines from *Les Fleurs du mal*:

– Ô douleur! ô douleur! Le Temps mange la vie,
Et l'obscur Ennemi qui nous ronge le cœur
Du sang que nous perdons croît et se fortifie!

– O agony, agony! Time eats away at life,
And the obscure Foe which gnaws on our hearts
Grows ever stronger on the blood we lose!

Manet's close friendship with Baudelaire inspired his art in other ways, however. It is noticeable that after *The Absinthe Drinker*, and Manet's encounter with the extraordinarily decadent Baudelaire, the artist avoided further images of rank dissolution. The less decadent side of Baudelaire, his penetrating art criticism and demand for an urban "painter of modern life", was of more interest, in fact, to Manet than the last torments of a dying genius.

Manet's early interest in politics did not abate and he remained keenly aware of current events throughout his life. In June 1864 he went to the port of Cherbourg to witness a bizarre incident of the American Civil War playing itself out. A corvette of the Union Navy, the *Kearsarge*, was attacking and pursuing a Confederate privateer, the *Alabama*, which had been detained in the French docks. Manet painted a gripping picture of the scene. Three years later he painted the first version of *The Execution of the Emperor Maximilian*. The painting was banned as being too sensitive a political subject for exhibition at Manet's pavilion in the place d'Alma during the 1867 Exposition Universelle. Indeed, from

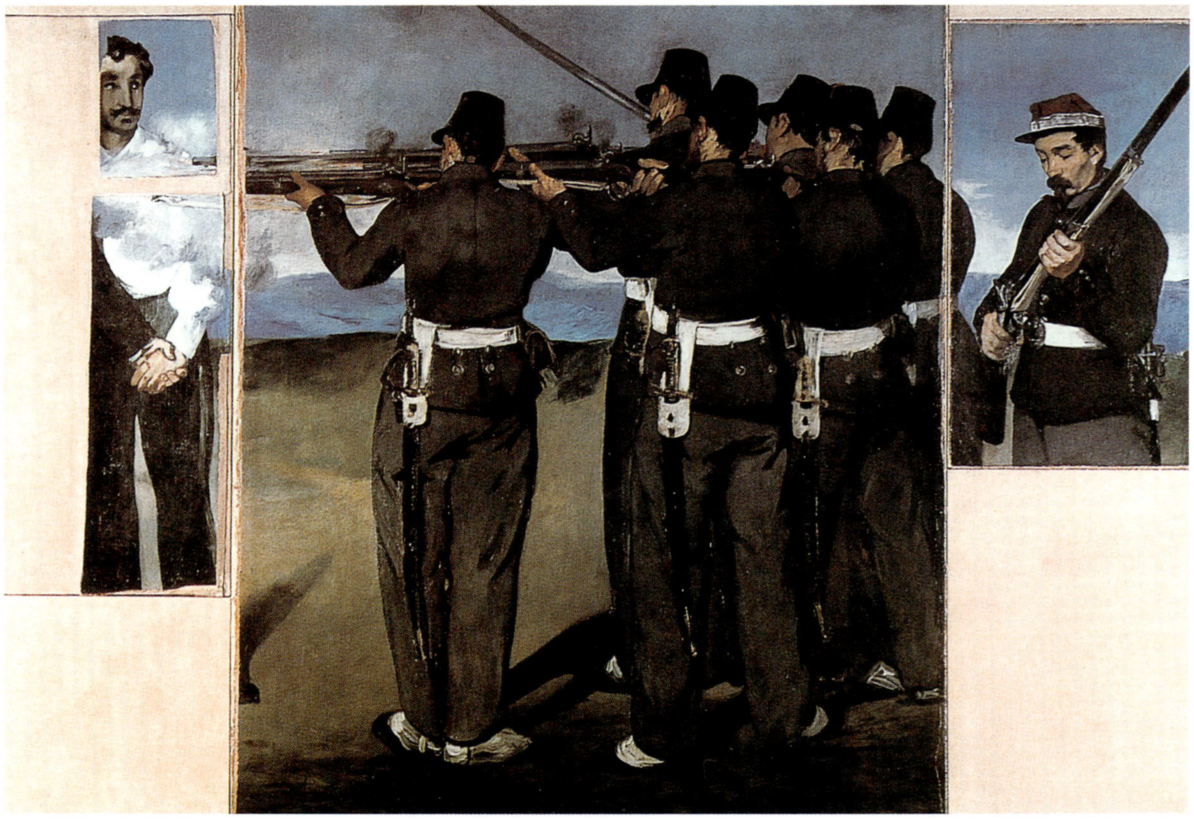

MANET
The Execution of the Emperor Maximilian
oil on canvas
1867. 195 × 259 cm
In this advanced study, the firing squad is wearing Mexican outfits and the faces of the victims are featureless. The news of the execution had just reached Paris and to Manet the incident illustrated all too well the bankruptcy of Napoleon III's regime.

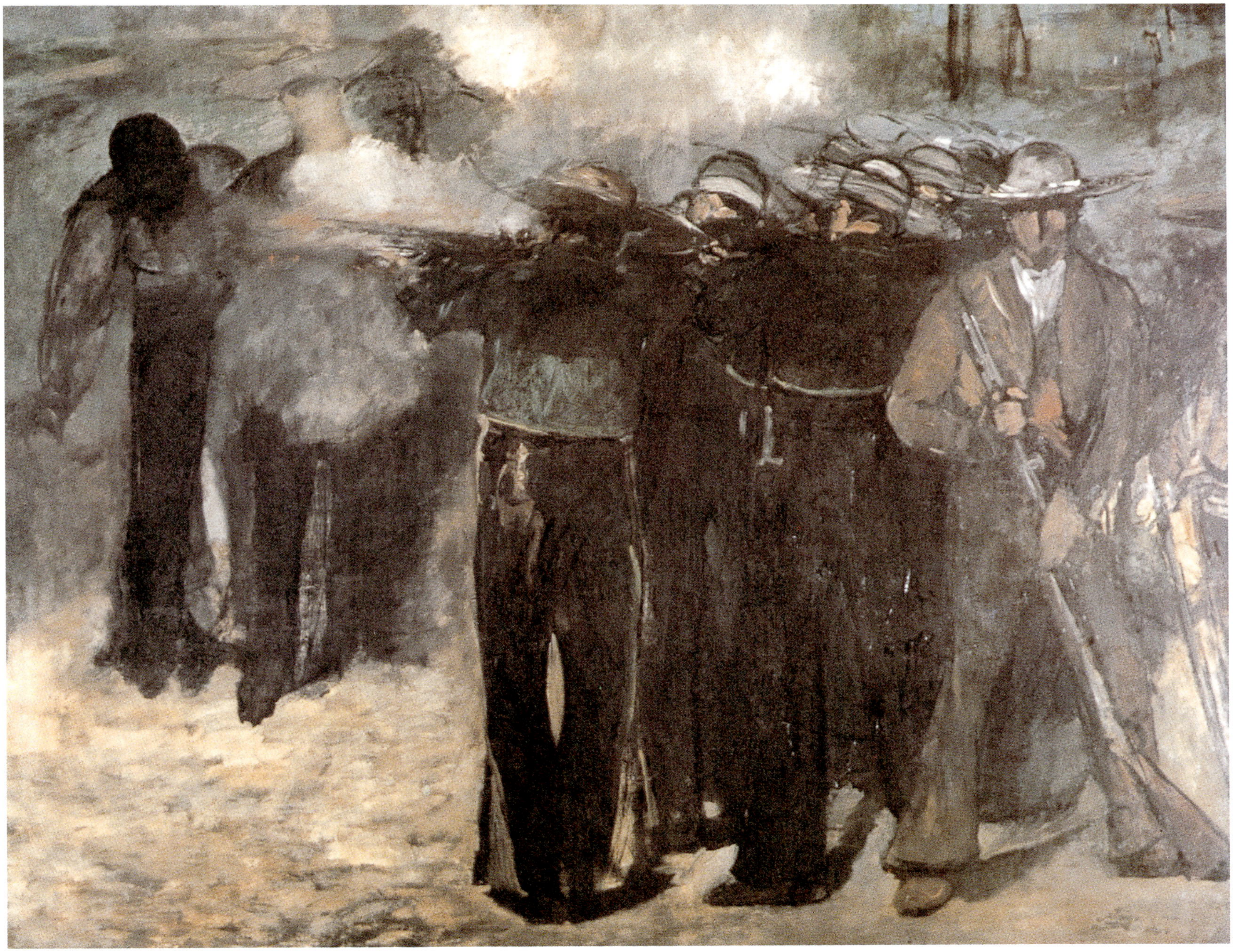

MANET
Olympia watercolour study
1863.
BELOW Manet undertook several studies for the scandalous painting.

MANET
Olympia
oil on canvas
1863. 130.5 × 190 cm
BELOW The older Courbet was critical of Olympia: "She looks like a Queen of Spades on a playing-card: not enough modelling." Manet, himself declared: "There is only one important thing: put down what you see the first time. If that's it, that's it." Manet painted with the light in his studio falling from behind him, which flattened the volumes of the figures in the painting and brought the artist violent criticism.

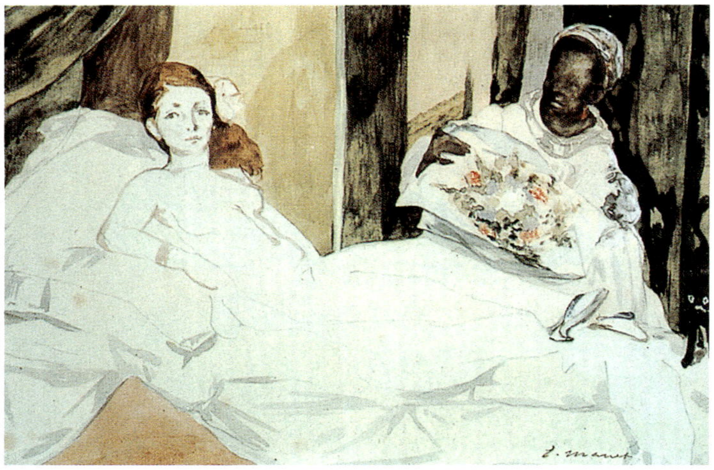

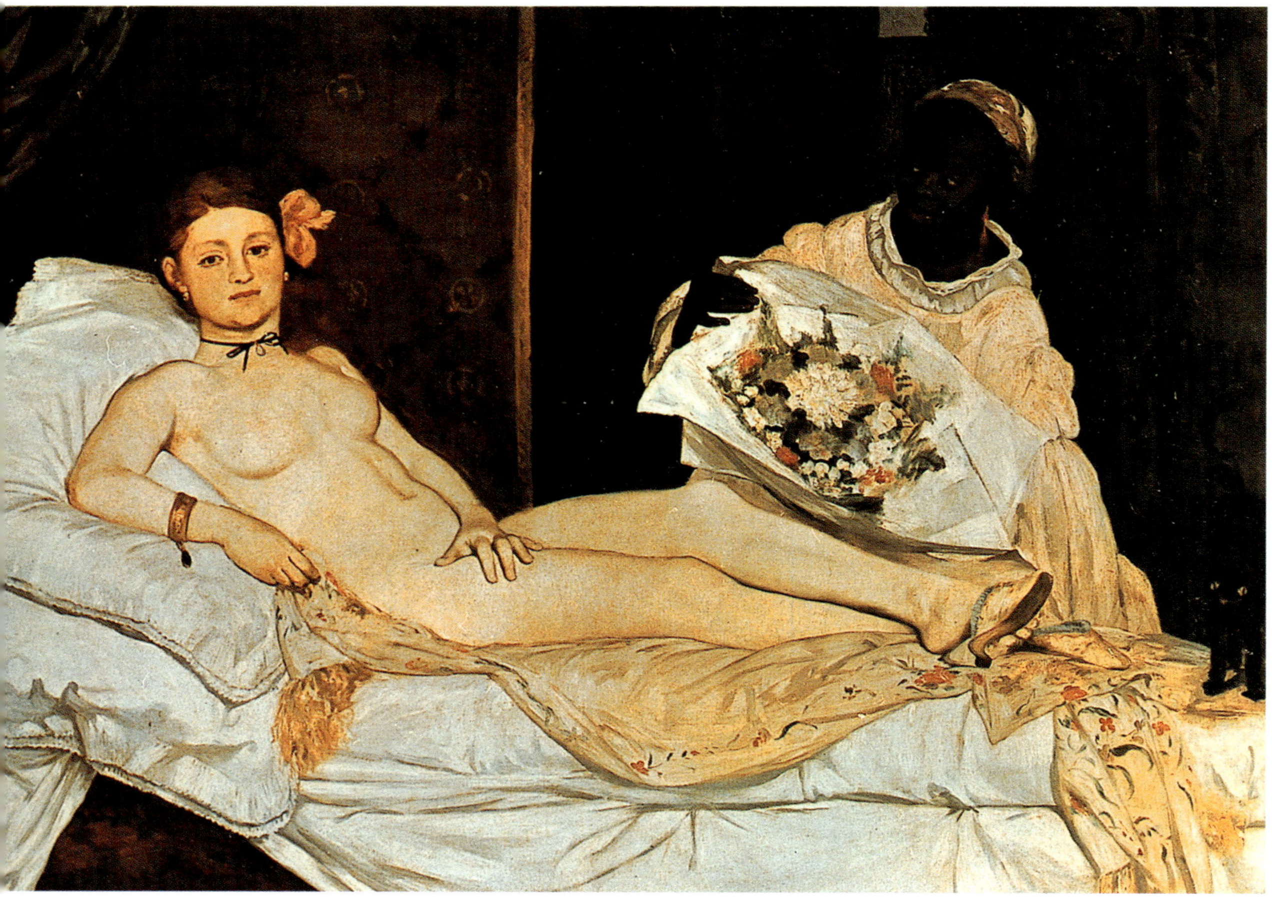

the scandal of *Luncheon on the Grass* at the Salon des Refusés of 1863 onwards Manet was constantly (and it must be said unwillingly) at odds with the authorities, both artistic and political. Manet's subject matter was at the forefront of modernity and strained the limits of the acceptable. He had side-stepped the social realism of Proudhon and Courbet and worked initially under the aesthetic veil of *l'art pour l'art* (Art for Art's Sake), as exemplified in its most frivolous literary form by these two stanzas from a poem by Théophile Gautier:

Que tu me plais dans cette robe
Qui te déshabille si bien,
Faisant jaillir ta gorge en globe,
Montrant tout nu ton bras païen!
Frêle comme une aile d'abeille,
Frais comme un coeur de rose-thé
Son tissu, caresse vermeille,
Voltige autour de ta beauté.

How you please me in this dress
Which undresses you so well,
Letting your breast burst forth,
Showing quite nude your pagan arm!
Fragile as a bee's wing,
Fresh as the heart of a tea-rose,
Its tissue, a vermillion caress,
Flutters about your beautiousness.

A une robe rose (*To a Pink Dress*)
FROM *EMAUX ET CAMÉES*, 1852

Apart from its concision – brevity was becoming Manet's own stylistic watchword – and its eroticism, *A une robe rose* also gives us a taste of just how small the Bohemian world of Paris was; the poem is dedicated to Apollonie Sabatier, delectable courtesane, and the *Présidente* of the infamous Club des Hashishins frequented by Baudelaire and Gautier, an object herself of extreme (and unrequited) passion from Baudelaire who immortalized her in a cycle of poems within *Les Fleurs du mal*. (She was also given permanent fame in other ways; the sculptor Clésinger made a cast of her body and then modelled it in marble to the delight of the 1847 Salon.)

The influence of Baudelaire's ideas in the early part of Manet's career can be seen in his painting, *Music in the Tuileries Gardens*, which answers the call for a painting of modern life by doing just that; depicting the bourgeoisie outdoors on a summer's day together with a smattering of Bohemians. Baudelaire and Gautier are among the strollers.

By 1865 *Olympia* had turned the art world upside down, and Manet was the focus of the younger artists' admiration. In that year he began to frequent the Café Guerbois, where contemporary accounts testify to Manet's *sang-froid* and incisive wit in the midst of his colleagues Bazille, Whistler, Nadar, Astruc, Renoir, occasionally Degas, Monet, Cézanne, and Pissarro. But his personality and his aims (if he had any other than simply to paint as well as he could) remain unclear. He was full

MANET
The Bullring
oil on canvas
1865–66. 90 × 110.5 cm
The public reaction to Olympia prompted Manet to travel abroad, and he went to Spain, where he continued to sketch. It was not until the mid-1870s and the influence of Monet and Berthe Morisot that Manet became an open-air painter. This work, like all the others, was done in his studio.

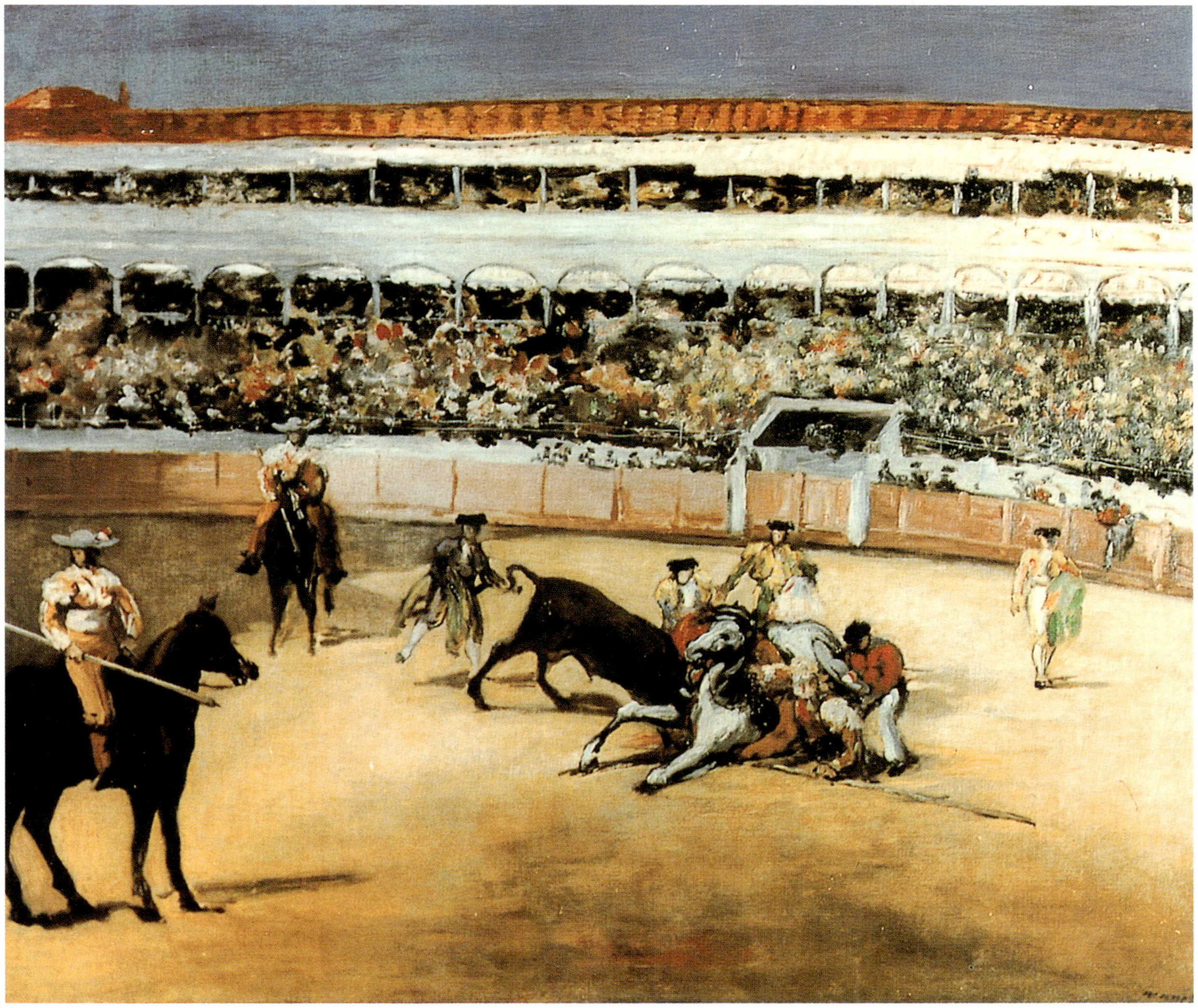

CHARDIN
Still Life with Plums
oil on canvas
c.1730. 45 × 50 cm
RIGHT The French writer Diderot praised Chardin's magical realism and colour harmonies. Others admired the varying effects of light on household objects, and scenes such as this one. It is easy to see how a diligent student and copyist of the classics like Manet would have been strongly influenced by work such as this.

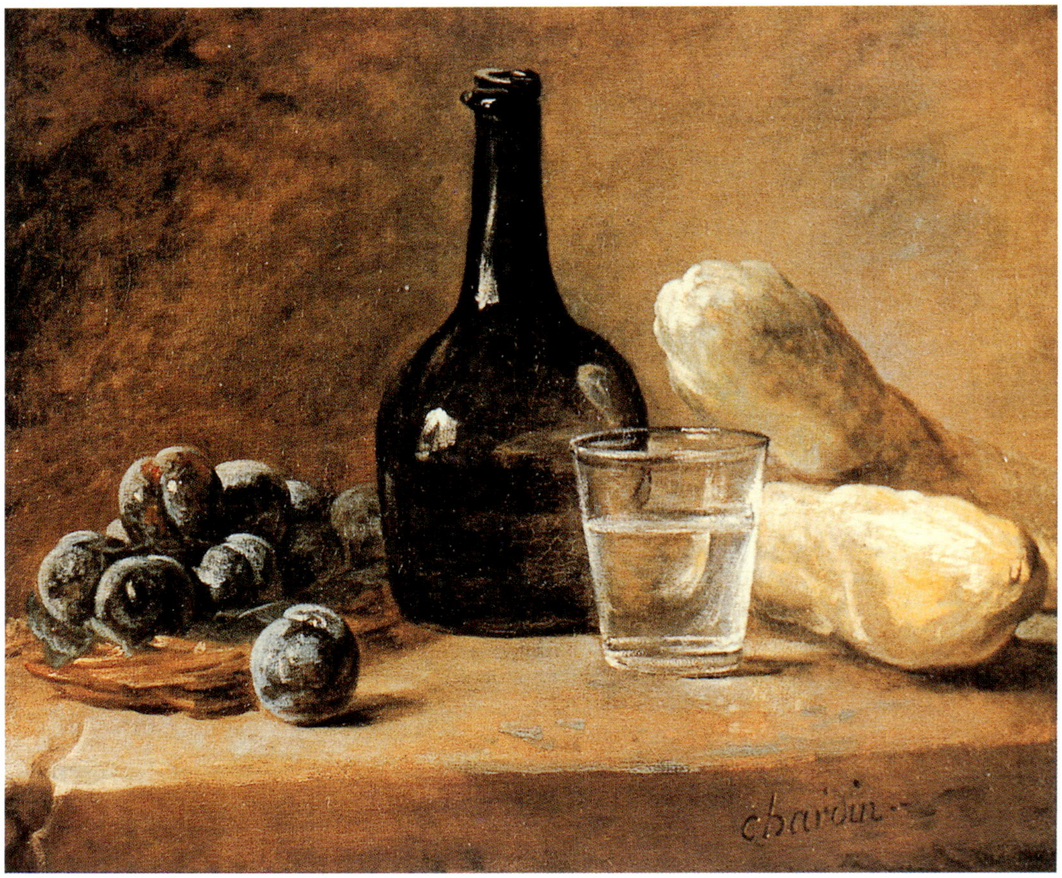

MANET
Still Life with Peaches and Melon
oil on canvas
1866. 69 × 92 cm
BELOW This again illustrates how attached Manet was to tradition. He painted a number of still lifes, some with oysters, which were one of the seventeenth-century Dutch artists' favourite subjects. Manet's work is never plagiaristic, no more than was Bach's borrowing of Vivaldi's musical themes.

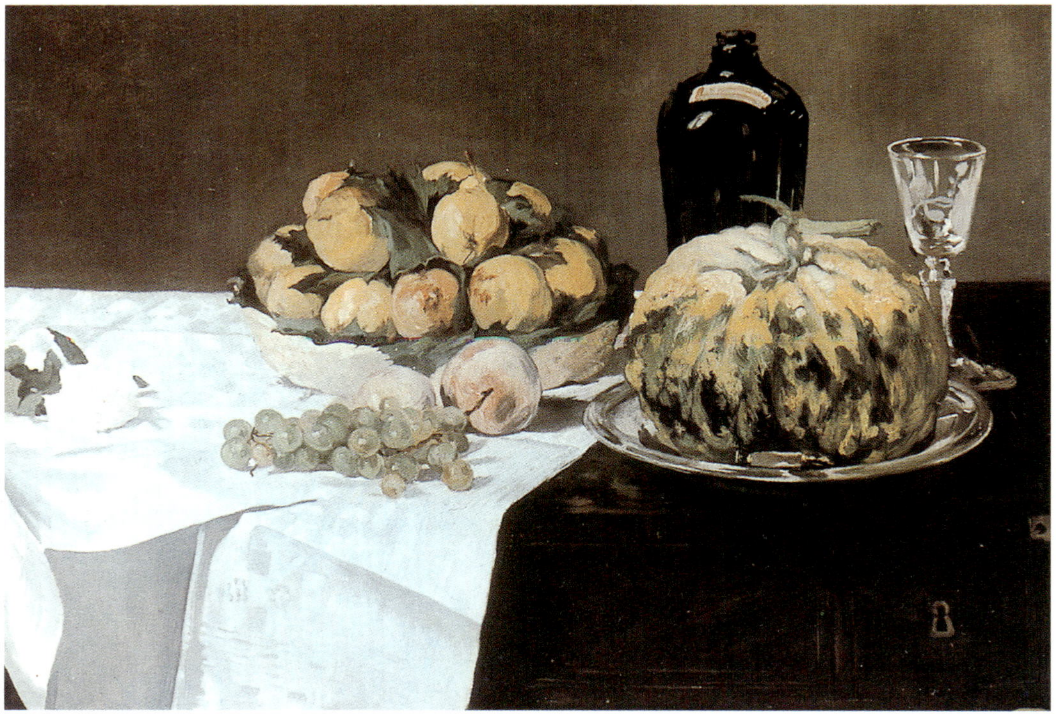

of disingenuous advice to younger painters along the lines of "paint what you see as soon as you see it," but his technique was in a class of its own. Few artists could wield a brush with as much nervous energy and accuracy as Manet; few artists (apart from Degas) would dare to choose the subjects he did; few artists had the thorough grounding of five years at Couture's and countless hours copying in the great museums of Europe; few artists had the leisure to paint (his father had left him a more than generous inheritance); ultimately few of his contemporaries (except Degas again) had the ineffable, ambiguous sense of a picture that Manet had. He was modest in triumph, self-effacing in defeat and did not have the inclination of a Pissarro to teach. What went through his mind is difficult to discern.

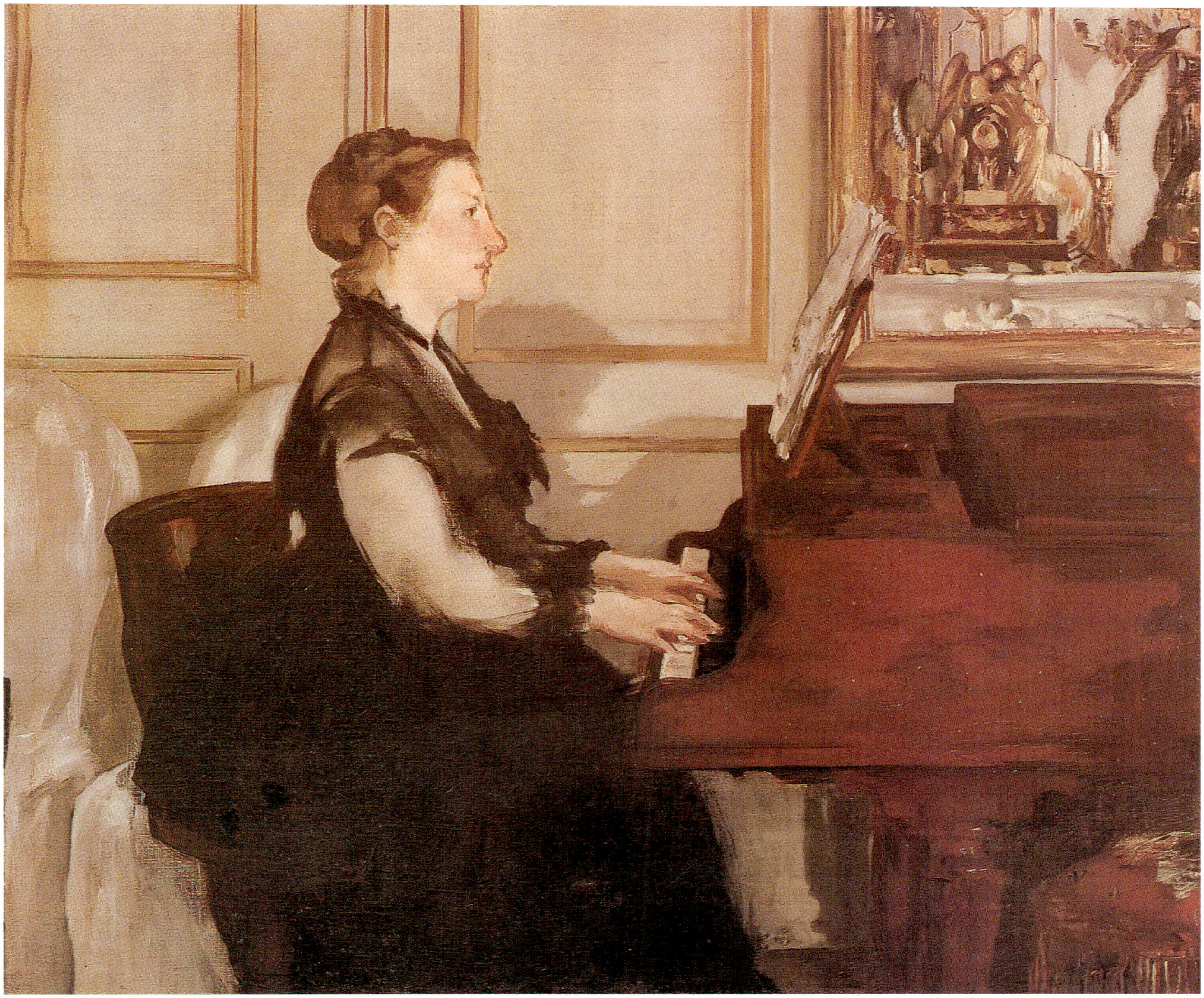

MANET
Madame Manet at the Piano
oil on canvas
c.1868. 38 × 46.5 cm
Mme Manet was an accomplished pianist and the couple often organized musical evenings with their friends. Now a bourgeoise, officially respectable since her wedding, she accepted her husband's passing affairs.

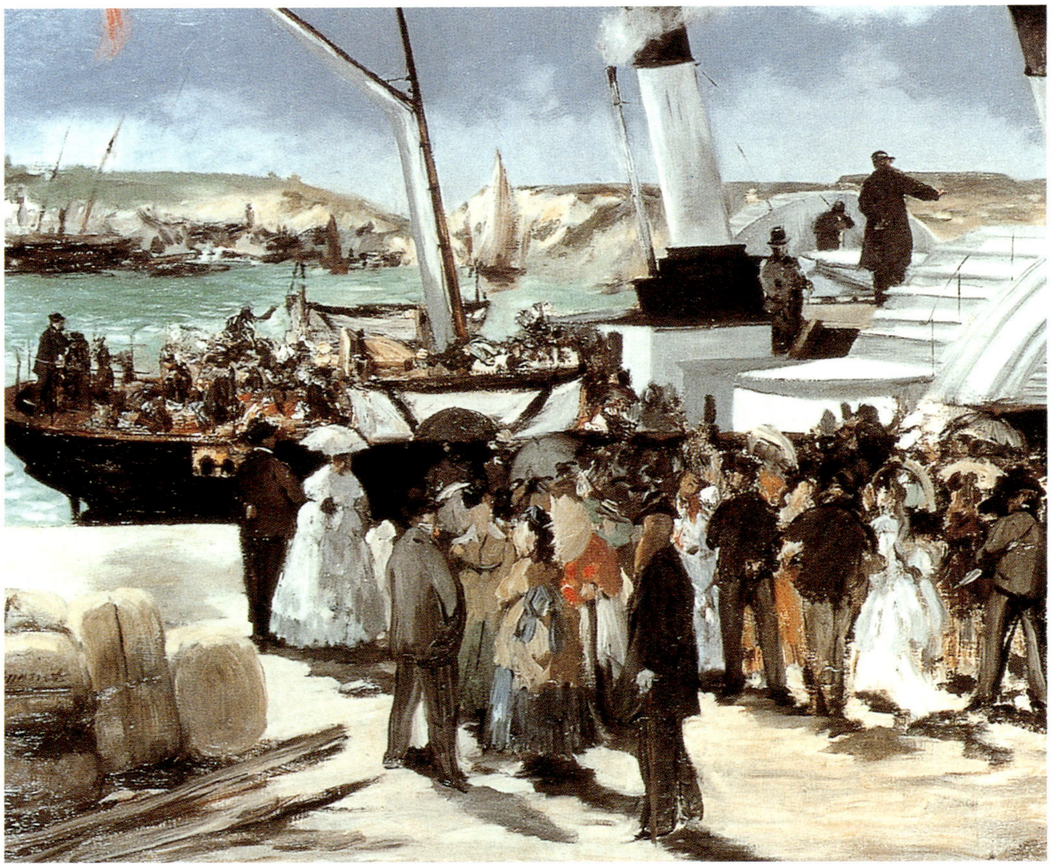

MANET
The Folkestone Boat, Boulogne
oil on canvas
1869. 60 × 73 cm
ABOVE Manet spent the summer in Boulogne with Degas, and painted six landscapes, the only ones he executed outside Paris in the 1860s. The scene shows passengers about to cross the English Channel.

However we do know that in some respects Manet was highly sensitive. In 1860 he moved his studio to the rue Victoire after the young boy who cleaned the brushes and scraped the palettes for him, the subject of *Child with Cherries* (*L'Enfant aux cerises*), hanged himself in the atelier, inspiring a short story from Baudelaire and sending Manet into depression. The artist had threatened to send the boy back to his parents, but had not foreseen the tragic effect of his reprimand. In the next two or three years as Manet's personal fame and ability to create scandal increased he found himself the subject of an irritable reprimand from Baudelaire. The poet had supported him loyally through the *Luncheon on the Grass* episode in 1863, but when the *Olympia* scandal erupted in 1865, Manet was at the end of his tether, desolated by the unheard of ferocity of the critics towards him. The year before Baudelaire had drawn the artist's attention to the fact that *Agnes at Christ's Tomb* depicted the Saviour's spear wound on the wrong side of his body. He wrote to Manet: "You will have to change the position of the wound before the exhibition opens. And don't give those spiteful people a chance to laugh at you." During the *Olympia* scandal Manet wrote to Baudelaire in despair:

> I wish you were here, my dear Baudelaire; they are raining insults on my head . . . I should have liked your sane verdict on my pictures, for all these cries have set me on edge . . . something must be wrong . . .

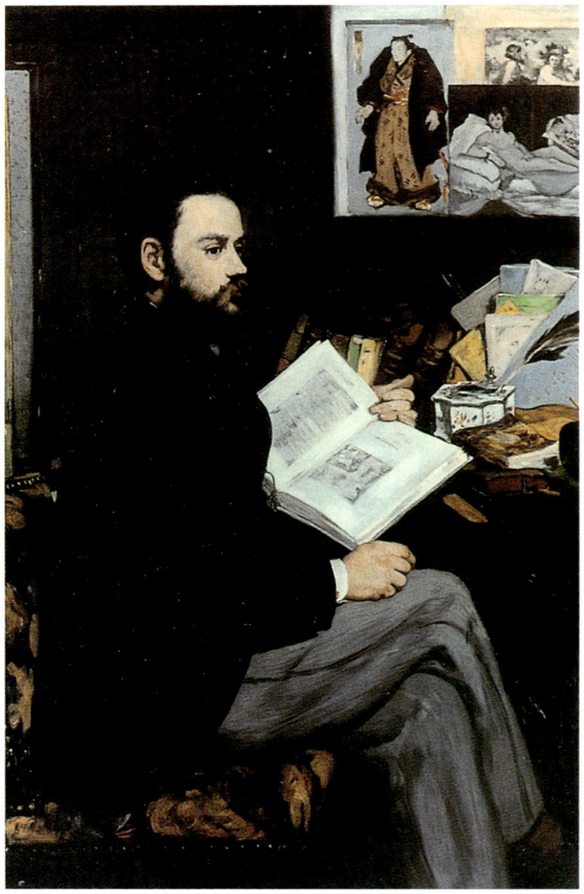

MANET
Madame Manet and Her Son Léon
at Arcachon
watercolour
1871.
RIGHT A sketch of peaceful domesticity, the soothing atmosphere Manet needed to restore his shattered spirits. The crushing of the Commune had been merciless and bloody, and most people in Paris were affected by these tragic events.

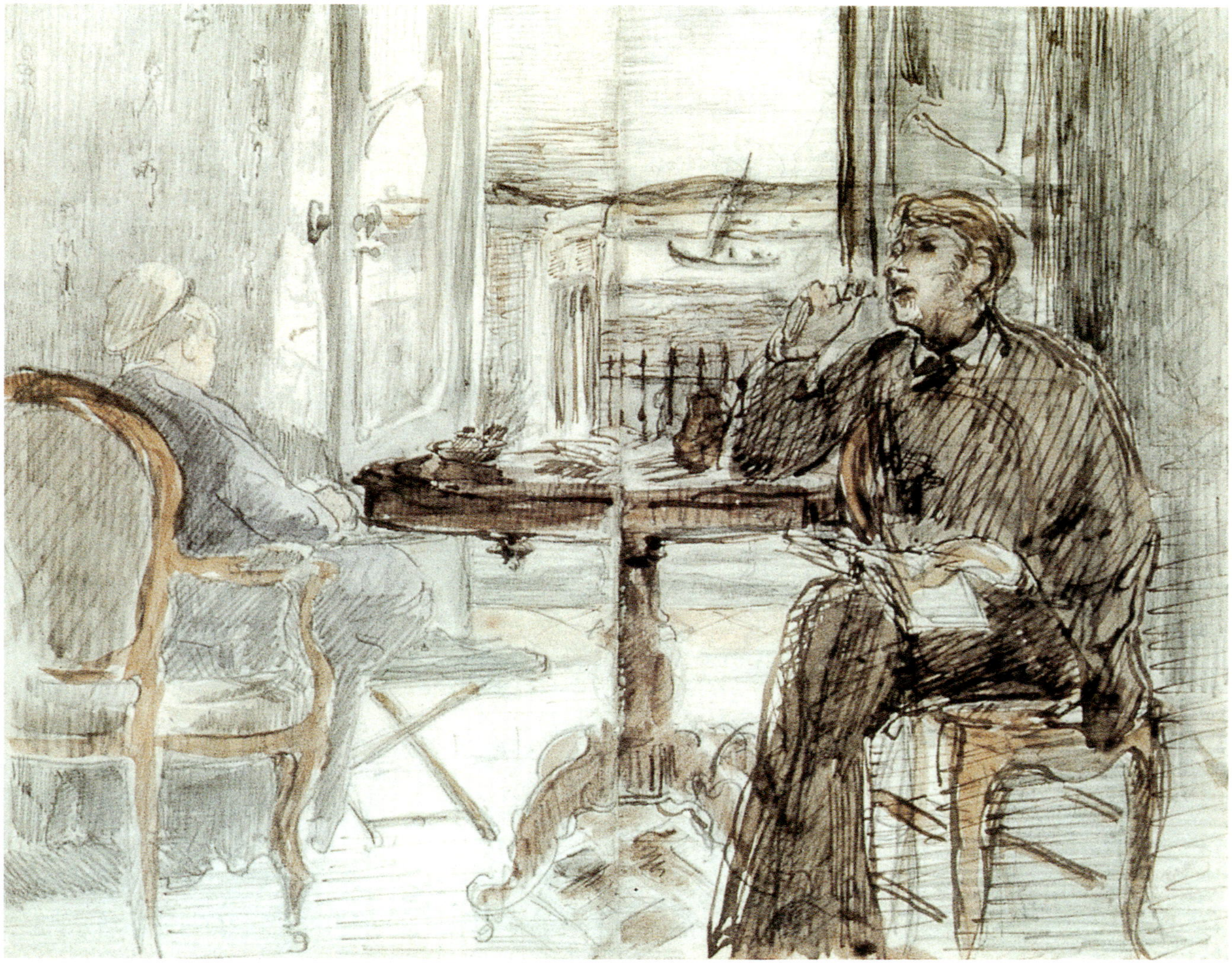

MANET
Emile Zola
oil on canvas
1868. 146.5 × 114 cm
LEFT Manet met the writer and journalist Zola, a childhood friend of Cézanne, in 1866. Zola was to become somewhat critical of Impressionism as he was the advocate of Realism. Zola wrote that: "The individual element, man, is infinitely variable. If temperament had not existed, all paintings would have of necessity to be simple photographs."

MANET
The Queue at a Butcher's Shop
During the War
engraving
1871. 23 × 16 cm
RIGHT

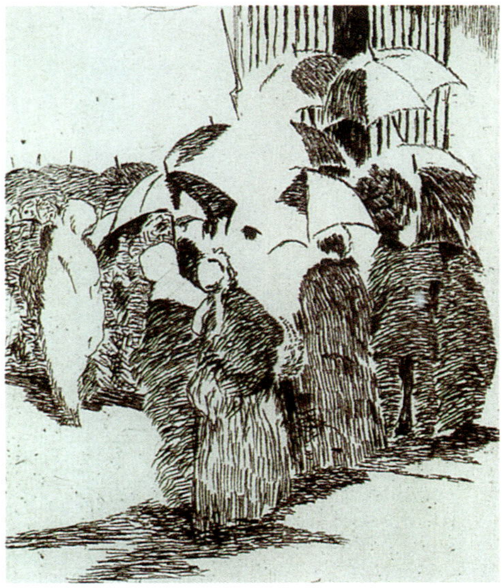

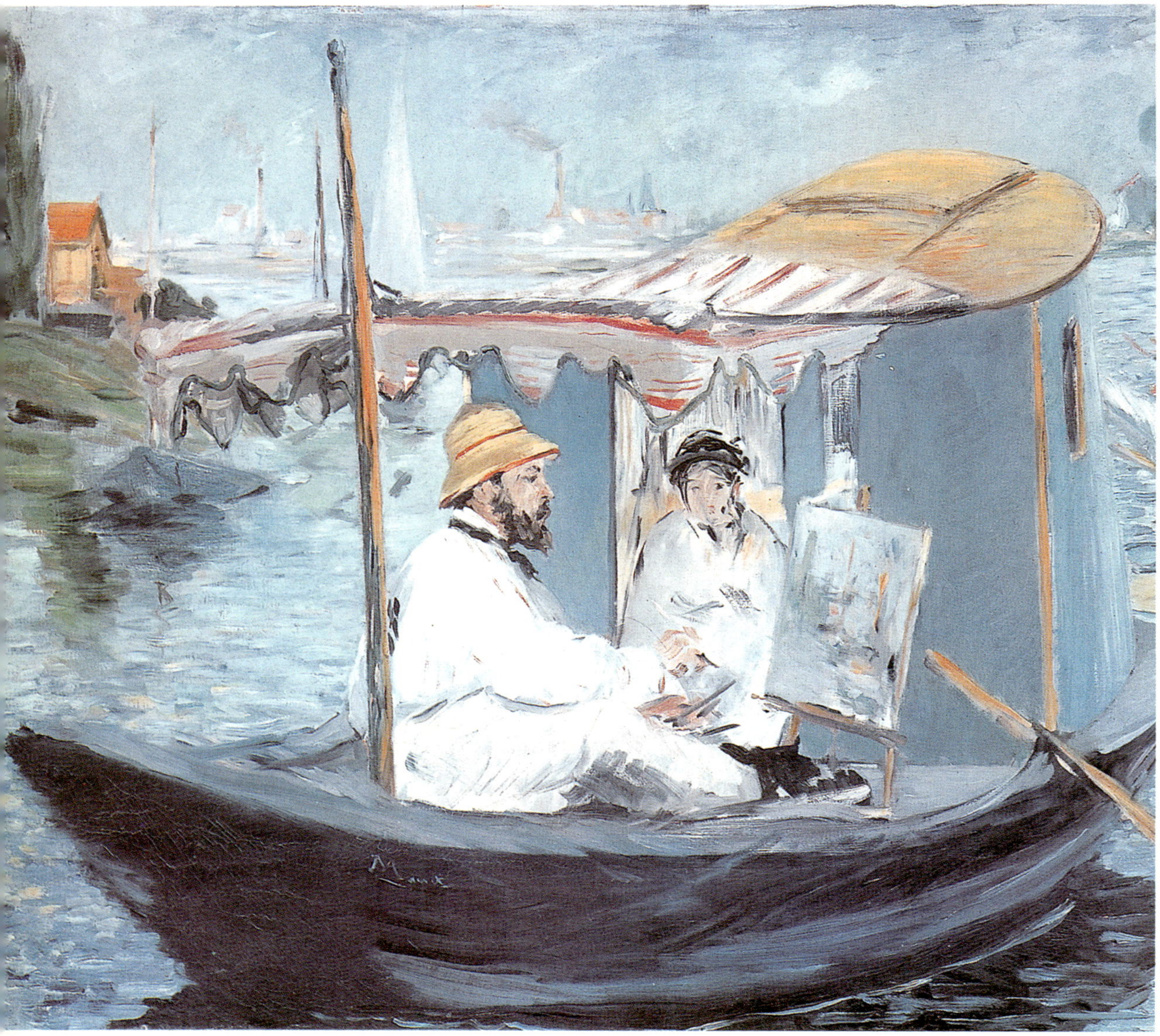

MANET
Monet Painting in His Studio Boat
oil on canvas
1874. 82.5 × 104 cm
Above Renoir and Monet spent the summer of 1874 painting at Argenteuil, then a small town along the Seine, not very far from Paris. Manet joined them and produced four boating pictures. It is certain that the younger Monet influenced his style.

Baudelaire's withering rejoinder reads:

> I am afraid I am again forced to speak to you about yourself. I shall have to apply myself to demonstrating to you just what your value is. What you ask is quite ridiculous. People are making fun of you, you say; their jokes set you on edge, etc, etc . . . Do you think you are the first man who has ever been in this position? Are you more of a genius than Chateaubriand or Wagner? Have people made fun of them, I wonder? They have not died of it. And in order not to inflate you with too much pride, I would add that these men are models, each in his own field, in a rich world, and that you, you are simply the foremost in the decrepitude of your art. I do hope you won't take this amiss. You know how dear you are to me. I wanted to have M. Chorner's personal impression [of *Olympia* and *Christ Mocked*], at least insofar as a Belgian can be considered a person . . . What he said tallies with what several intelligent men have said about you: "There are faults, weaknesses, a lack of aplomb, but there is an irresistible charm." I know all this, I was the first to understand it. He added that the picture of the nude, the Negress and the cat (is it really a cat?) was far superior to the religious picture.

Manet's technique, as poor M. Chorner observed, and Baudelaire knew, was the least of his worries. Since his years at Couture, when he would draw objects perfectly but upside down for fun, he had developed *peinture claire*, described by the art historian Bernard Denvir as

> A method of painting . . . which creates a high-key colour configuration by first

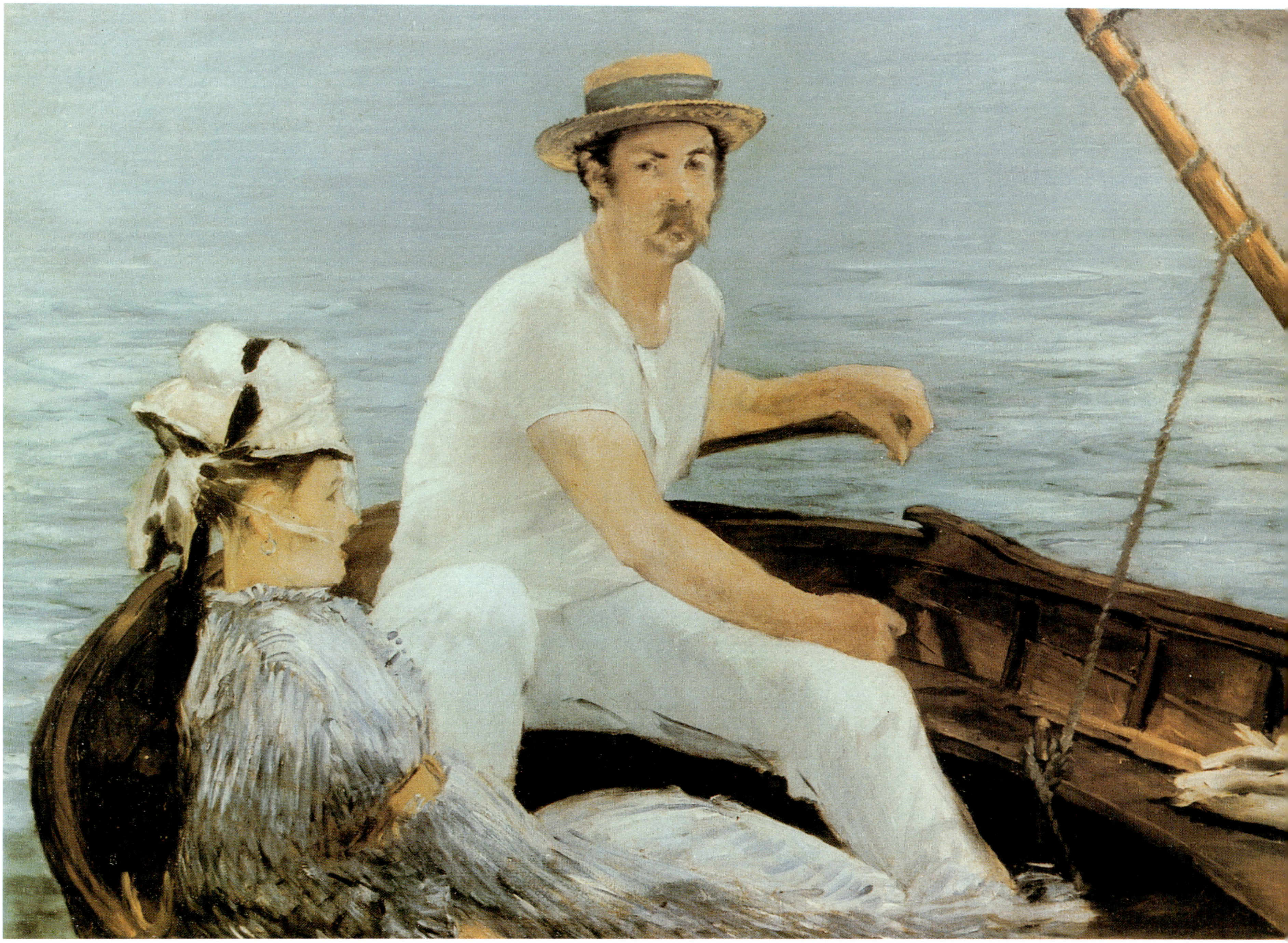

MANET
Couple Boating
oil on canvas
1874. 97 × 130 cm
The man is his brother-in-law Rodolphe Leenhoff, wearing the outfit of a fashionable sailing club. Manet showed the painting at the Salon of 1879.

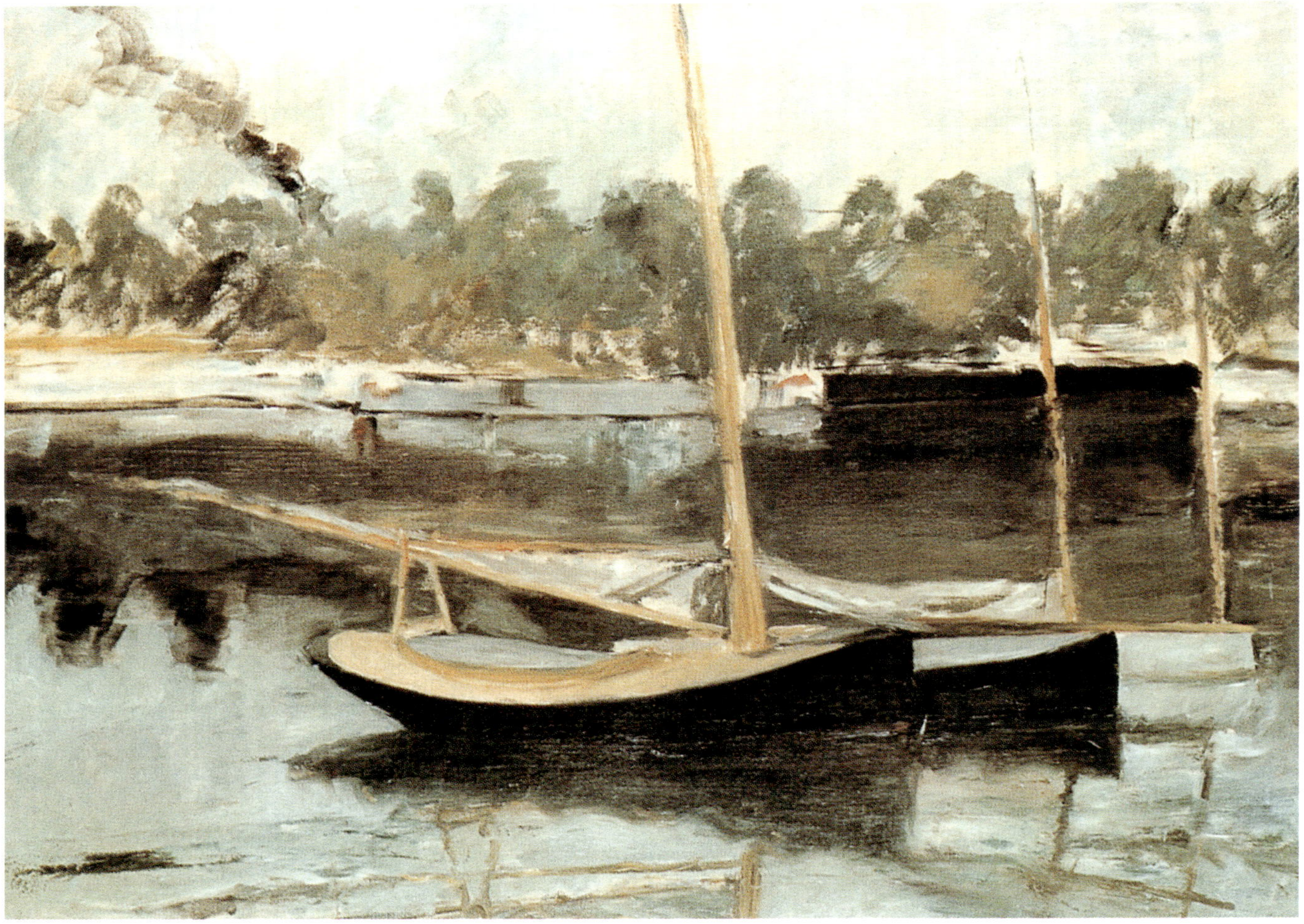

MANET
The River at Argenteuil
oil on canvas
1874. 61 × 100 cm
Right above Manet was much less interested in the effects of light than Monet and Renoir. Manet's brushwork is much smoother and more controlled than the other two artists'.

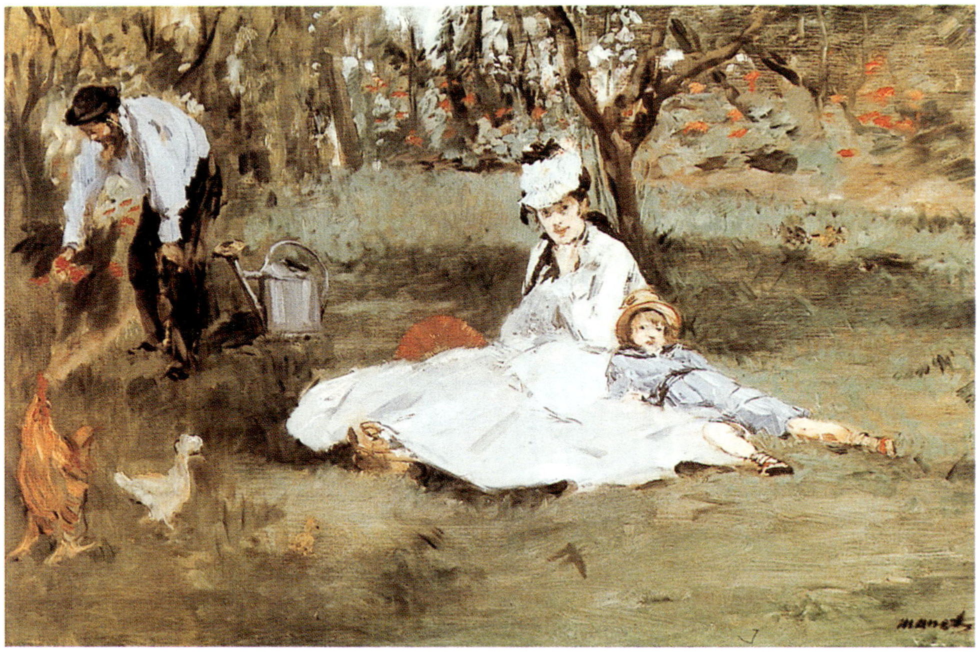

MANET
The Monet Family in Their Garden
oil on canvas
1874. 61 × 100 cm
Right The Monets received the Manets and the Renoirs during the summer of 1874, and both artists painted the Monets in their garden. Mme Monet and her son Jean have such similar poses that the pictures seem to have been done at the same time.

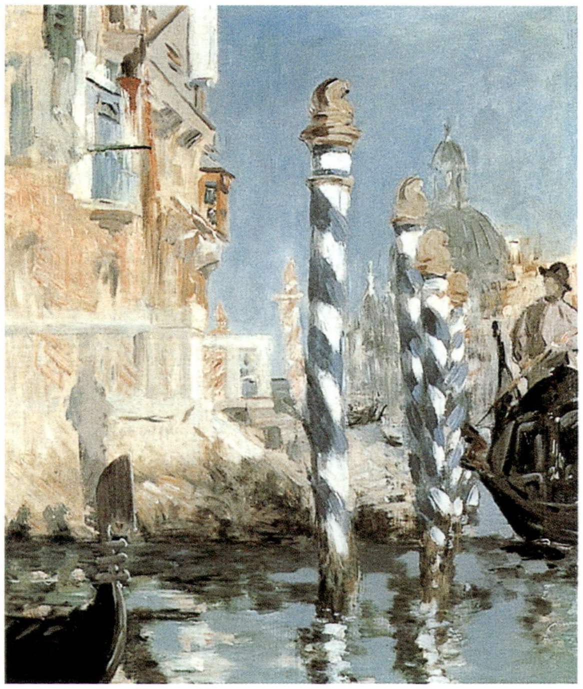

MANET
Venice, the Grand Canal
oil on canvas
1875. 57 × 48 cm
Left Manet went to Venice with Tissot, who had been enjoying great success with his elegant paintings in London since the war. Manet's style now shows the effect of his summer in Argenteuil the previous year and is much more impressionistic, with shorter, choppier brushstrokes and a heightened palette.

MANET
Nana
oil on canvas
1877. 150 × 116 cm
Below Nana did not scandalize the public as much as Olympia *had previously, but the painting was also refused by the jury of the Salon, for much the same reasons. The model was the actress Henriette Hauser, mistress of the Prince of Orange.*

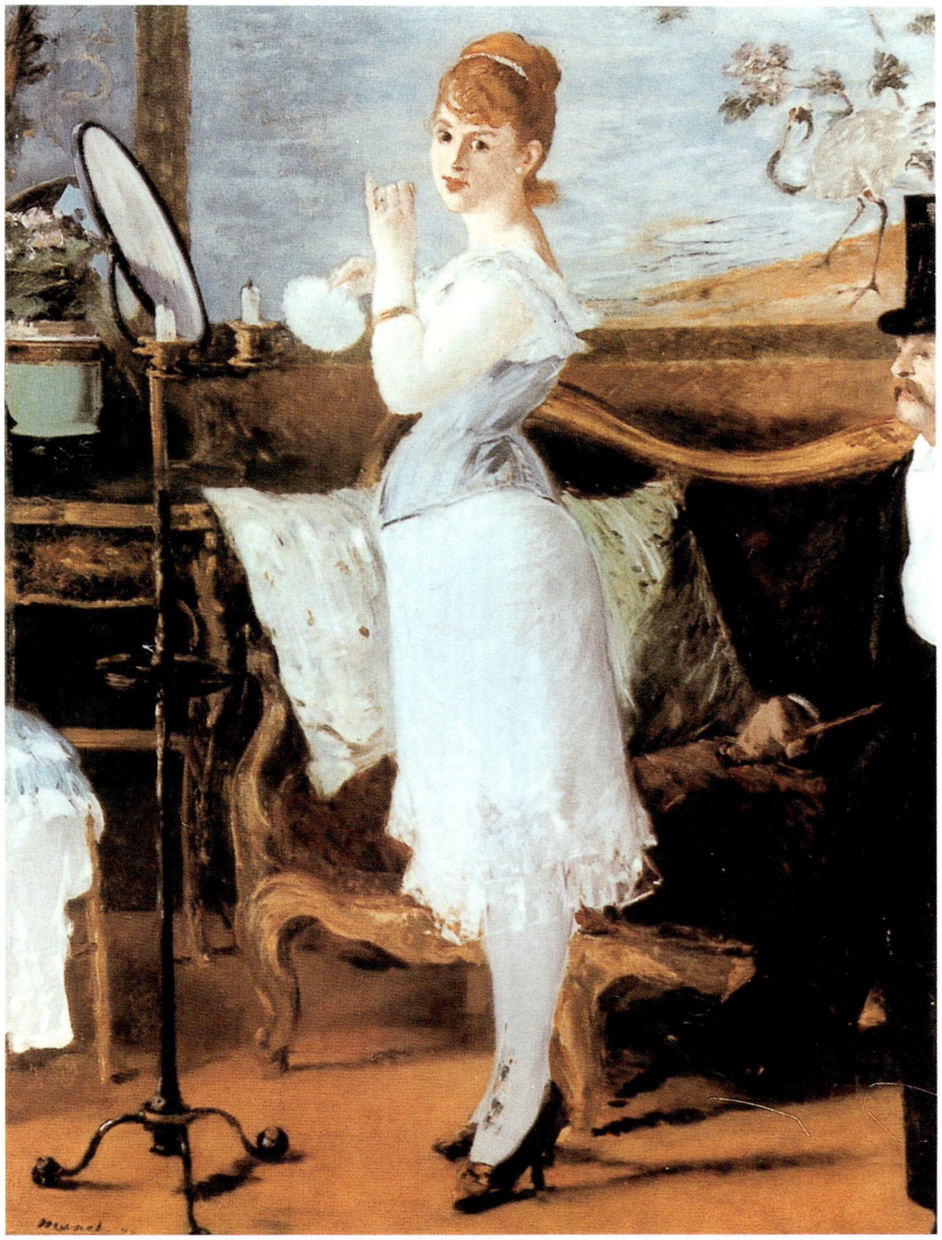

> applying loose-flowing and *grasse*, or fat, pigment onto the canvas, and then, whilst the paint is still wet, adding the half-tones and darker passages . . . the reverse of the accepted Academic process. The resulting effect is one of sparkle and vitality . . .

The problem for contemporary critics was that he had applied this bold and innovative technique to a fundamental reinterpretation of some of the icons of western art. By reinventing the nude in *Luncheon on the Grass* and *Olympia*, with explicit reference to past masters, he had appeared to rupture a series of seemingly inviolable traditions. To the budding Impressionists he was an iconoclast; to his own mind he was simply carrying on in the tradition he was falsely accused of breaking.

By the age of thirty-eight, and the outbreak of the Franco-Prussian War in 1870, Manet had painted several masterpieces and as Zola had said in 1866 in *L'Evènement*: "Our fathers

MANET
The Plum
oil on canvas
1878. 73.5 × 50 cm
RIGHT This young woman is holding an unlit cigarette and has ordered a plum in brandy. The picture shows the unique stillness of many of Manet's sitters. Various interpretations have been suggested, but she is probably just a working girl passing the time before she returns to her small lodgings.

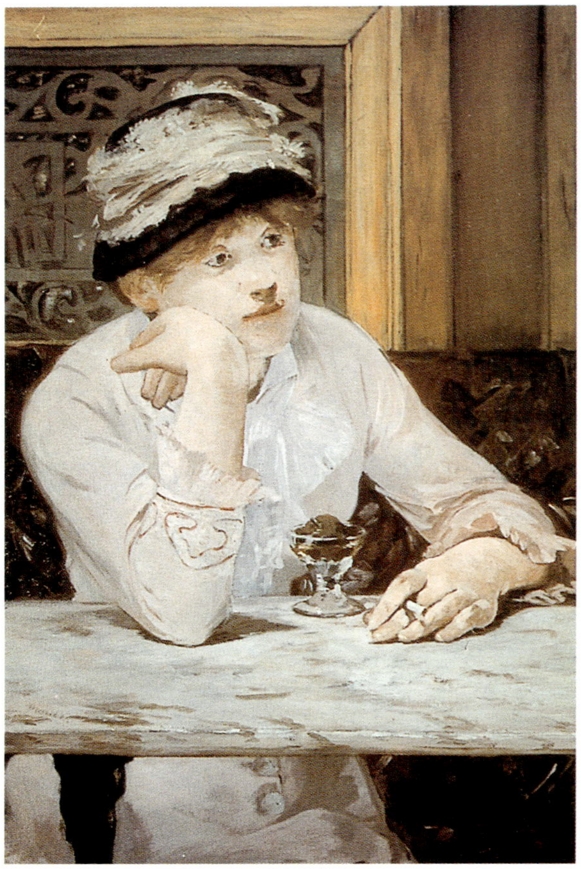

laughed at M. Courbet so we went into raptures over his work. Now it is we who laugh at M. Manet and it is our children who will be in raptures at his canvases." Manet was now probably the most famous (and infamous) artist of his day, but by the end of the Commune his nerves were shattered and he went to Boulogne in August 1871 to recover. Despite his ubiquitous fame he had sold very few paintings in the 1860s. This was scarcely a problem financially, but his self-esteem demanded buyers for his work, and success at the Salon. Durand-Ruel, the saviour of Monet, Pissarro, Renoir, and Sisley now stepped in and (with as great foresight as ever) bought 50,000 francs worth of paintings. Manet refused, however, to part with *Music in the Tuileries*, *Luncheon on the Grass*, *Olympia*, and *The Execution of Maximilian*, which Durand-Ruel had valued together at a total of 76,000 francs, an astronomical sum. *Olympia* was eventually purchased for the French nation by a subscription organized by Monet in 1890, seven years after Manet's death. For seventeen years the Louvre refused to hang the picture until Monet sought the aid of Président Clemenceau in 1907 and had it transferred from the Musée de Luxembourg to the Louvre – the whiff of scandal lingered around the painting for decades.

In December 1874 Manet's close friend Berthe Morisot married his brother Eugène. Thereafter there were no more languorous paintings of her pictured as she is in *The Balcony* (*Le Balcon*) or *The Sofa*. Whatever their relationship had been before – it had certainly been intense – she sat for him no more. In 1876 Manet met Méry Laurent, on whom Marcel Proust's character Odette

MANET
The Tub
pastel on canvas
1878–79. 54 × 45 cm
RIGHT Manet did not paint many nudes, and this one is reminiscent of the poses more familiar in his friend Degas' work, although the approach is quite different. The woman, like Nana *and* Olympia, *is aware of the gaze of either the viewer or the painter, whereas Degas's women are oblivious to any presence near them.*

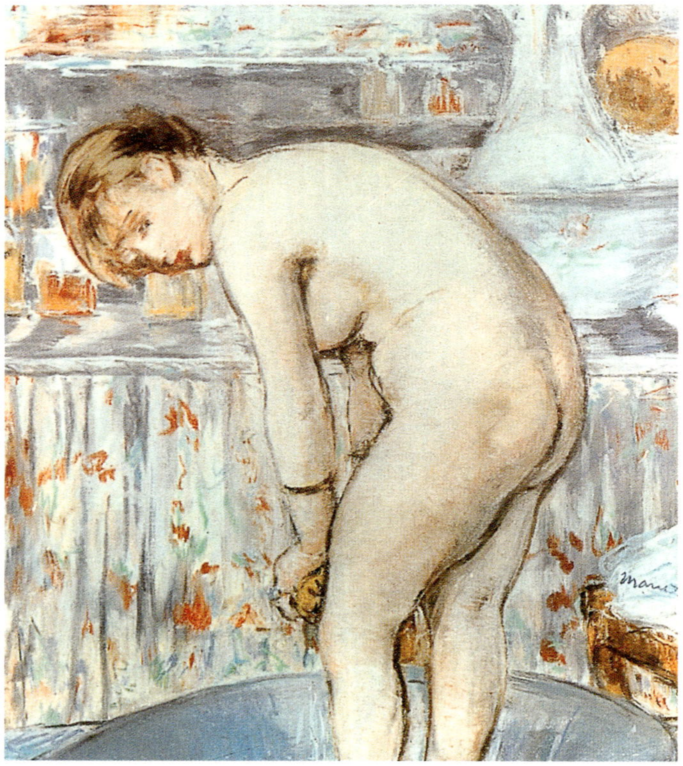

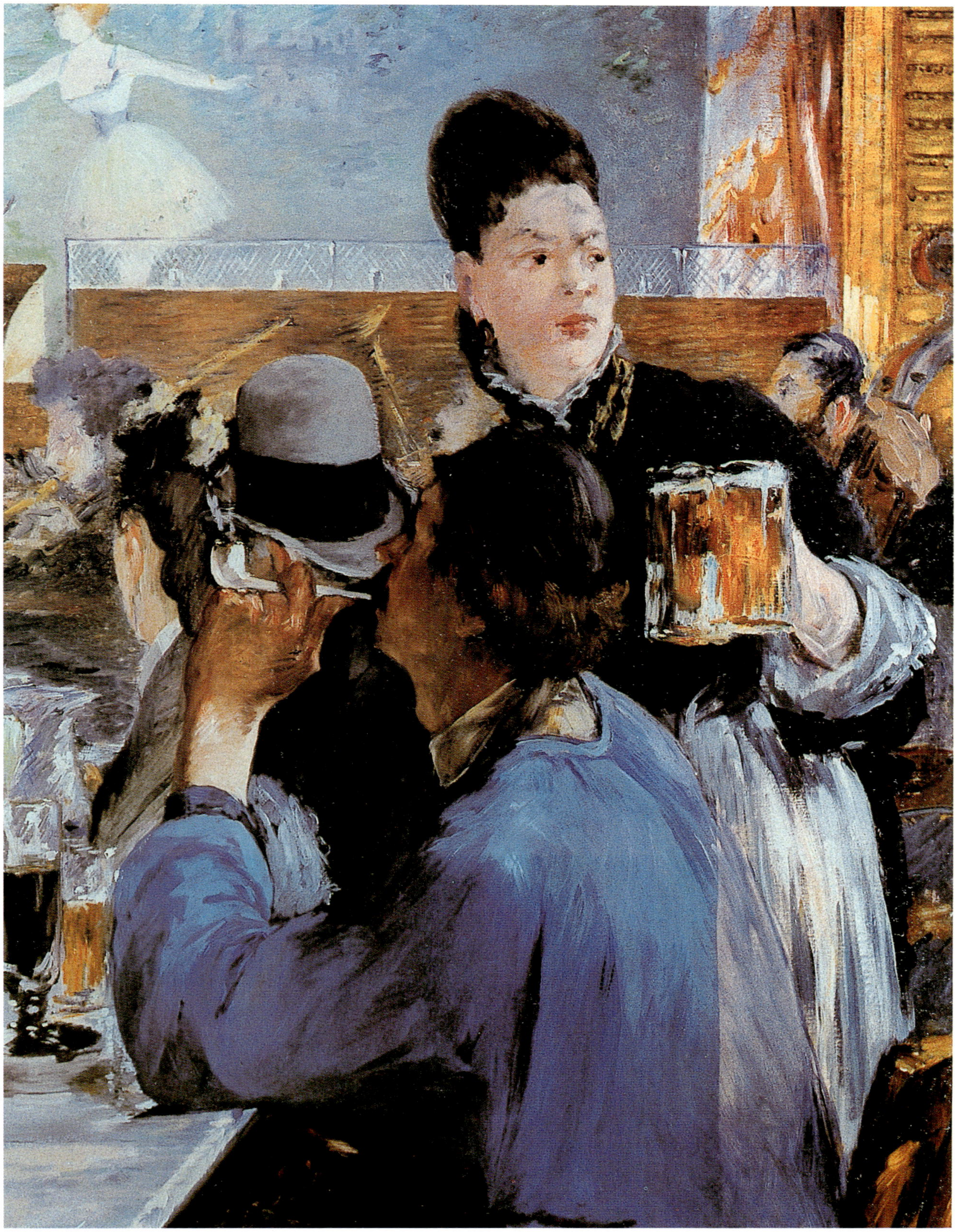

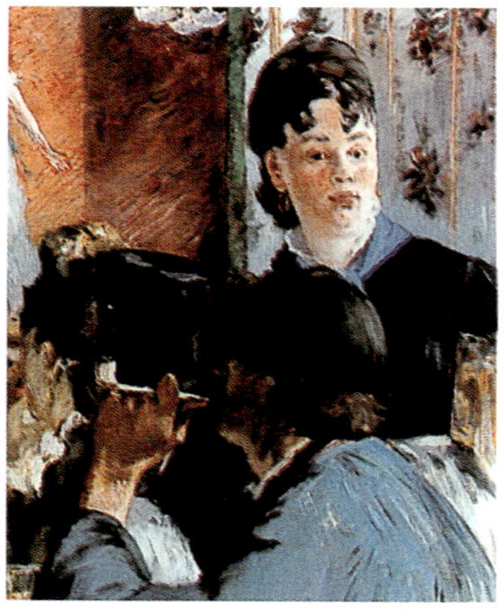

MANET
Study for the Beer Waitress
oil on canvas
1878–79. 77.5 × 65 cm
ABOVE The model is a waitress Manet knew, but she would only pose in the presence of her boyfriend, who is seated. In this study, the woman is also aware of an external presence, and looks at us.

MANET
The Beer Waitress
oil on canvas
1878–79. 97 × 77.5 cm
LEFT Manet has enlarged the composition to place the two sitters in a wider environment, and we can see more of the performer on stage. The setting was the cabaret Reichshoffen, on the boulevard de Rochechouart, but the painting was done in Manet's studio.

MANET
At the Café-concert
oil on canvas
1879. 47 × 39 cm
RIGHT Another café-concert scene with a young woman very similar to the sitter in The Plum, *who is also holding a cigarette. The man is like many characters of the time, not quite chic but of a relative bohemian elegance. We also find an example here of reflection in a mirror, which is most strikingly exploited in the later* Bar at the Folies-Bergère.

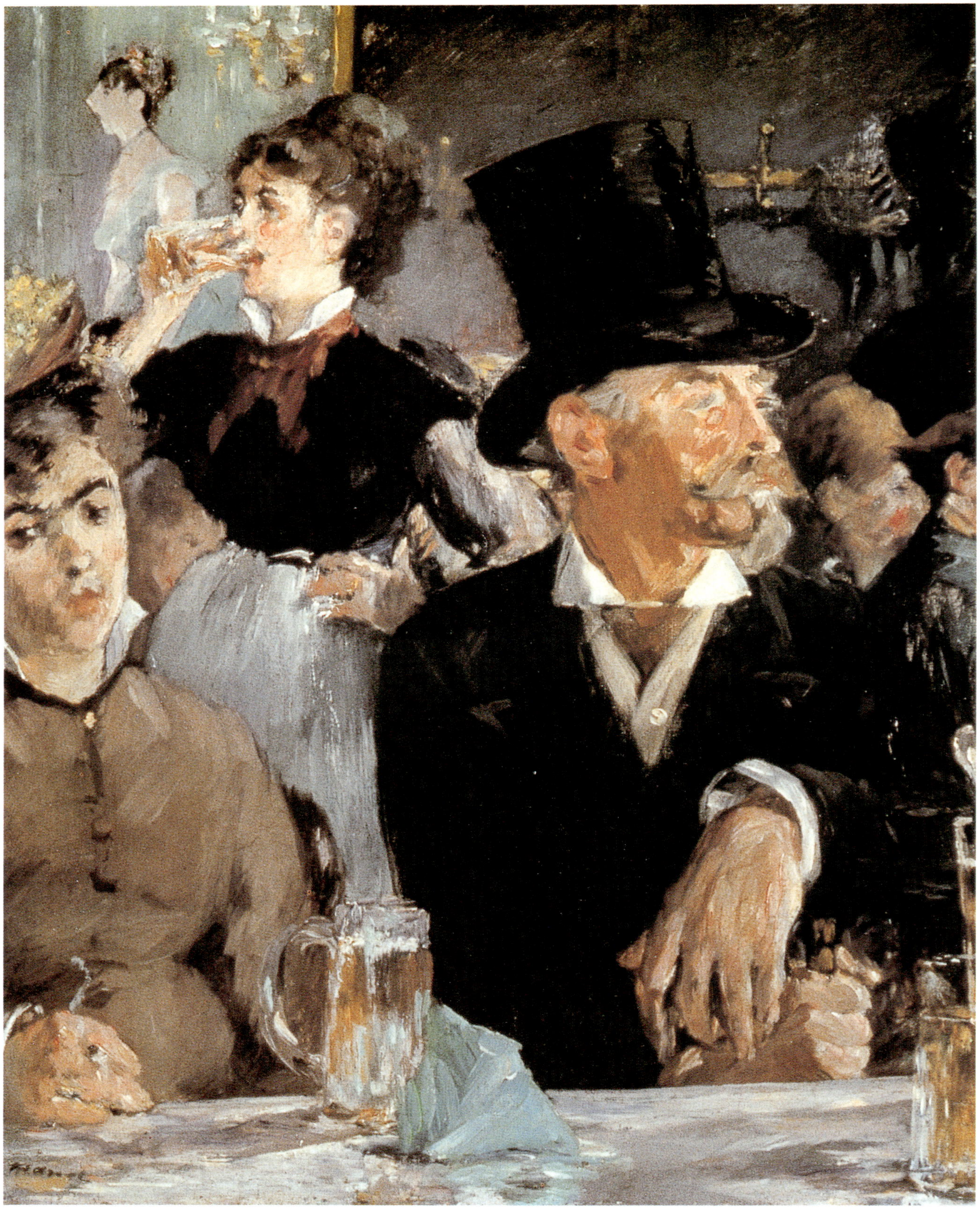

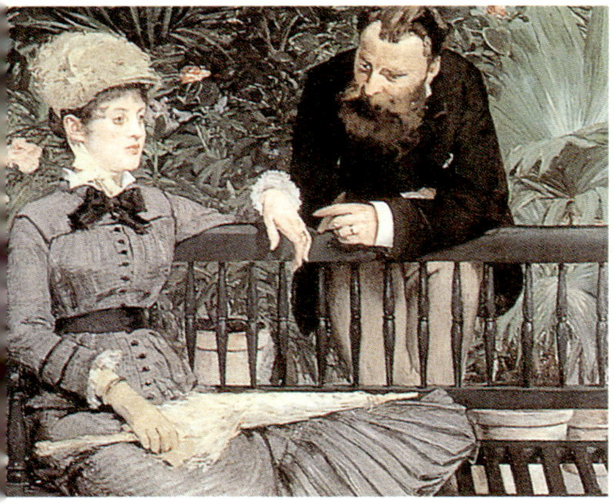

MANET
In the Winter Garden
oil on canvas
1879. 115 × 150 cm
ABOVE The sitters are Jules Guilleme and his American wife. Conservatories, which had first been fashionable among the very wealthy, were now adopted by the bourgeoisie.

Swann was based, a formidable courtesan and the lover of the poet Stéphane Mallarmé. It is possible that Manet had an affair with her; certainly they were devoted to one another in the last years of his life and she is the subject of his last work. The Symbolist poet Mallarmé and Manet had become friends in 1873 and developed a close and constant friendship to rival that with the late Baudelaire. Mallarmé was far removed from the decadence of Baudelaire (who was forced to borrow money from Manet and still owed him 500 francs when he died). He held salons on Tuesday nights crammed with the literary and artistic lions of his day, including Manet and the Impressionists. Manet's association with Mallarmé resulted in illustrations for the poet's translation of Edgar Allan Poe's *The*

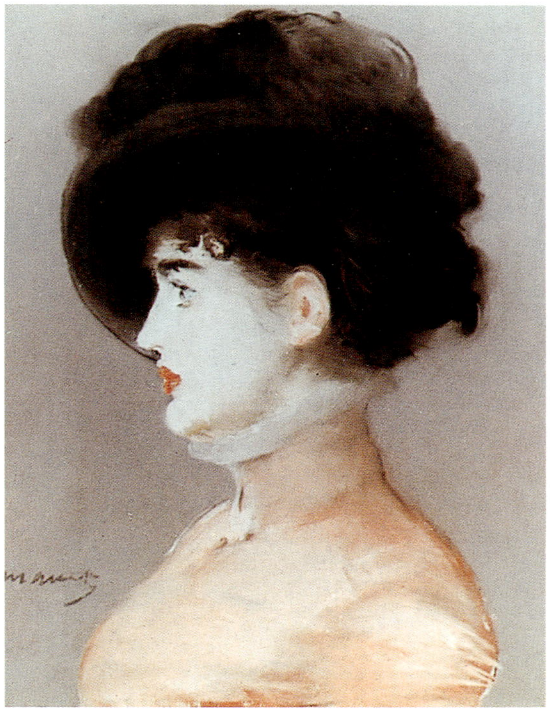

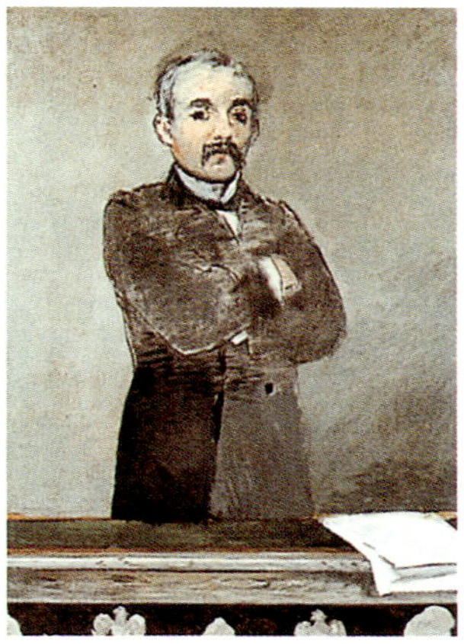

MANET
Georges Clémenceau
oil on canvas
1879–80.
ABOVE Gustave Manet, the painter's younger brother, was a friend of the famous French politician, then a deputy in the Parliament. Manet made two portraits of him and a pastel portrait of his wife.

MANET
Portrait of Irma Brunner
pastel on canvas
1882. 53.5 × 44 cm
LEFT ABOVE The sitter was of Viennese origin and was introduced to Manet by his friend Méry Laurent in 1882. Manet liked profile portraits of women wearing dark hats providing a strong background for the sitter's features.

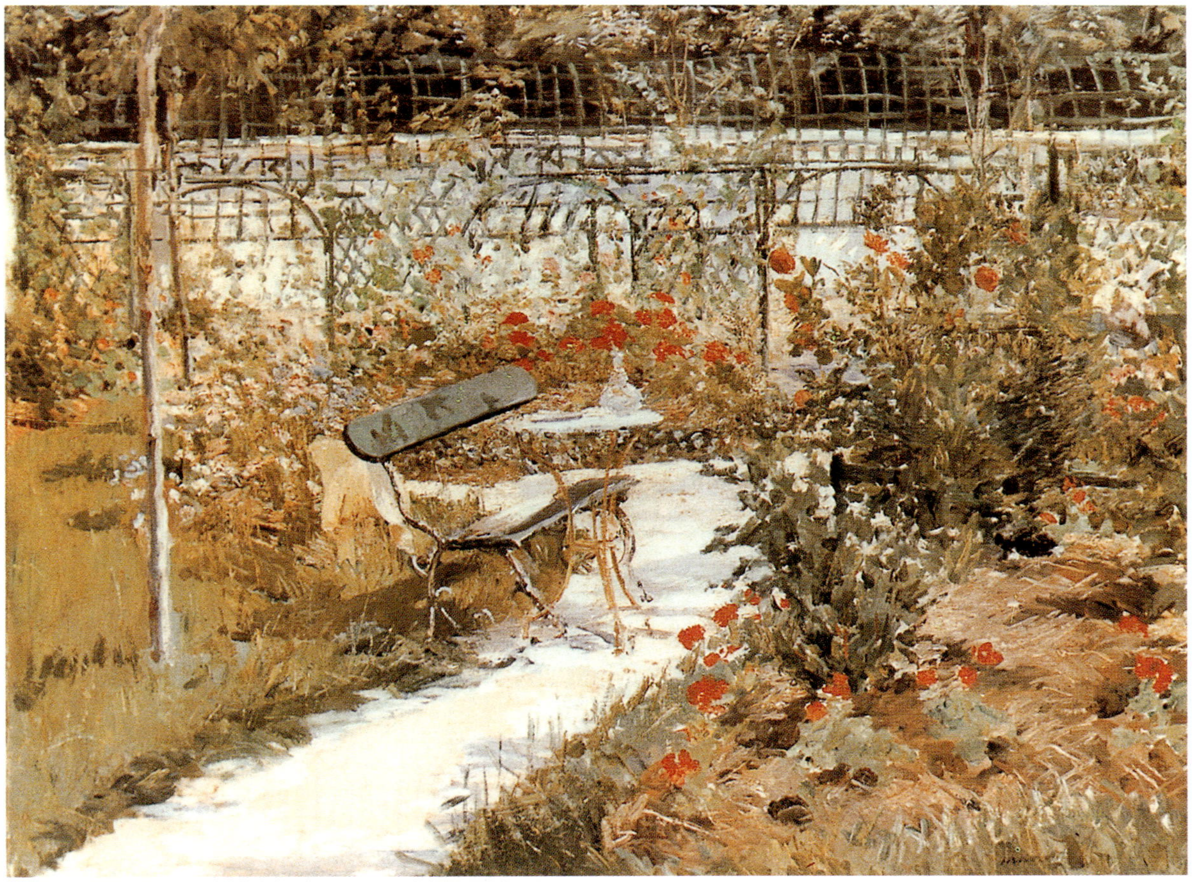

MANET
The Artist's Garden
oil on canvas
1881. 65 × 81 cm
LEFT BELOW In bad health, Manet rented a villa in Versailles during the summer of 1881, intending to paint the classical gardens of the castle, but he was not able to fulfil his project.

MANET
Autumn (Méry Laurent)
oil on canvas
1881. 72 × 50 cm
RIGHT The sitter was Méry Laurent, a "grande cocotte" he had met in 1876 when she came to see the show he had set up in his studio after two of his paintings had been turned down by the Salon. It was a huge success and people queued in the street to see. They were casual lovers and remained very good friends. This picture, commissioned by Antonin Proust, was to be one of four symbolizing the seasons, a theme which had been popular throughout the centuries, but Manet did not complete the series.

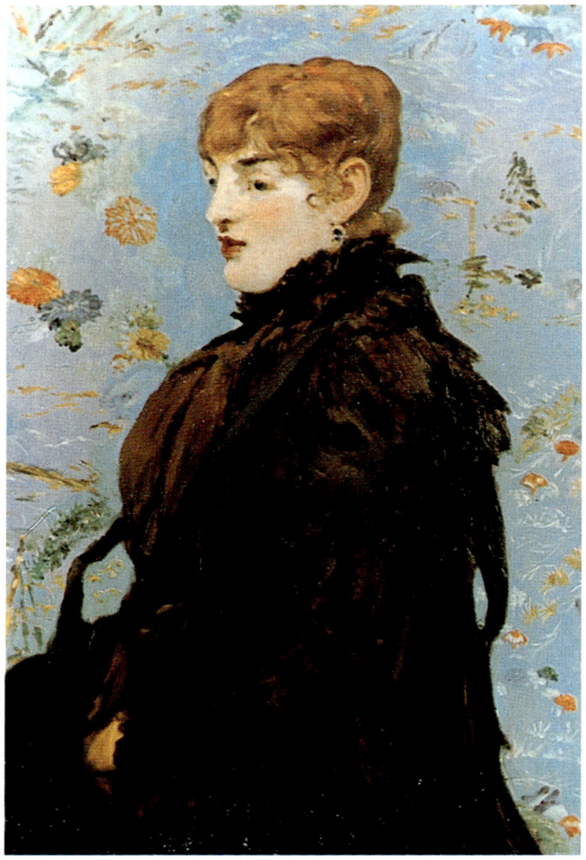

Raven as well as a remarkable portrait of Mallarmé which shows Manet under the increasing influence of his Impressionist friends. Indeed, the summer Manet had spent with Monet and his family at Argenteuil in 1874 had released his rather sombre style into a much more colourful, impressionistic idiom. His paintings of Monet, Camille, and Jean in the open air are some of the liveliest documents of the heyday of Impressionism. Manet's new-found interest in light and colour continued to produce sparkling canvases when he visited Venice the next year.

By the end of the 1880s Manet was beginning to feel the effects of the disease locomotor ataxia, which was to kill him before long. The official recognition he so strongly desired was still eluding him; yet he was still capable of causing a stir. In 1876 *Nana* had been rejected by the Salon on the grounds of impropriety and in 1881 he was damned with faint praise when the Salon awarded him a *seconde médaille* for his *Portrait of Pertuiset*. Finally his childhood friend Antonin Proust, who had risen to the rank of Arts Minister, secured Manet the *Légion d'Honneur*. Although he was working flat out on his last masterpiece, the *Bar at the Folies-Bergère*, he was in considerable pain, finding it increasingly difficult to hold a paintbrush. On 6th April 1883 he could no longer walk and was confined to bed. Two weeks later his left leg was amputated to stop the spread of gangrene. He died on 30th April and was buried in Passy cemetery on 3rd May.

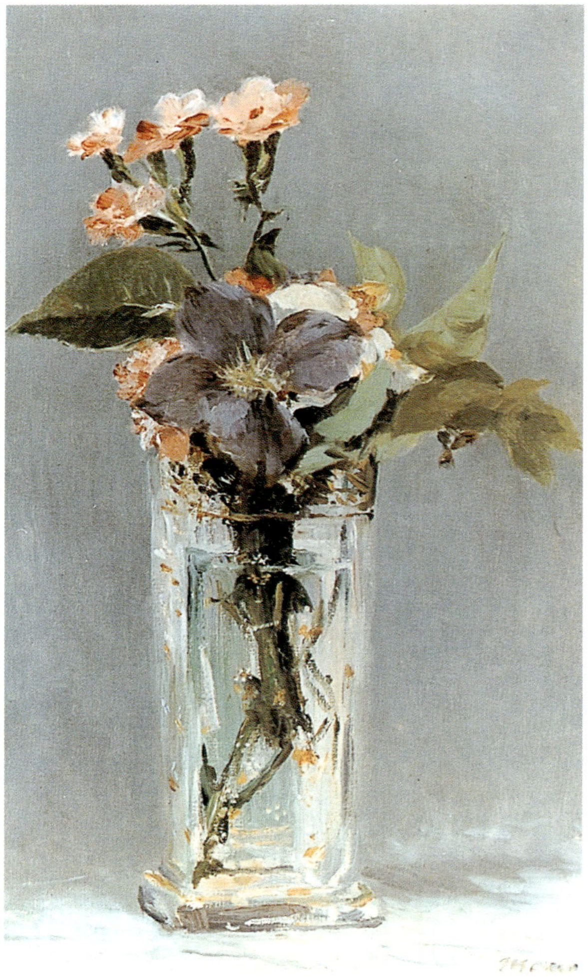

MANET
Still Life with Carnations and Clematis
oil on canvas
c.1882. 56 × 35.5 cm
FAR RIGHT Méry Laurent would send flowers to her dying friend Manet, and he used some of them in still lifes such as this one. Despite the appalling nature of his illness, which made it difficult for him to hold a pastel and almost impossible to hold a paint brush, Manet's technique remained remarkably controlled, and he did not reduce the size of his canvases.

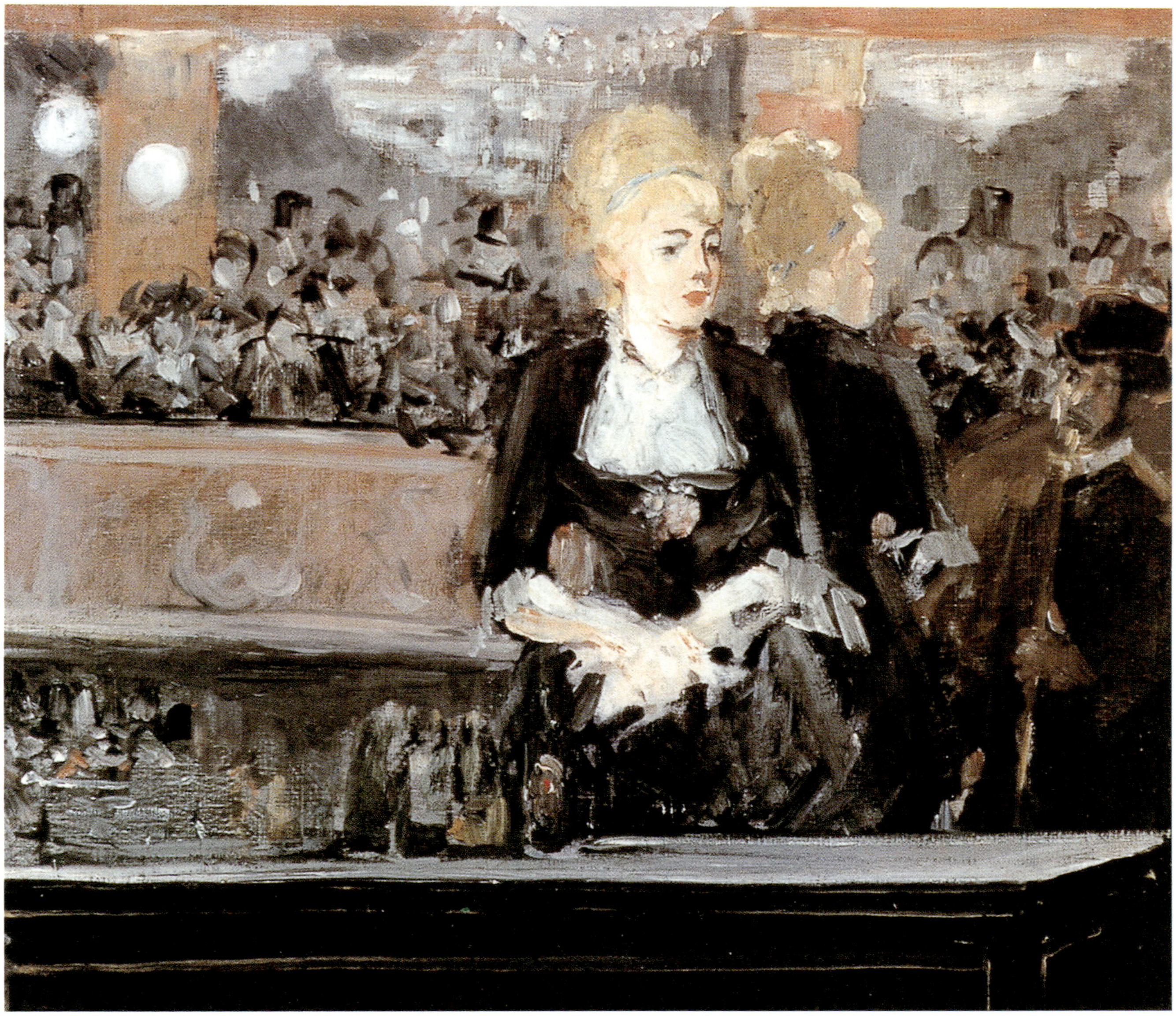

MANET
Study for Bar at the Folies-Bergère
oil on canvas
1881. 47 × 56 cm
LEFT In this large sketch, nearly half the size of the finished work, the waitress is off centre, looking sideways, and the mirror seems to be immediately behind her, while the male customer is very small.

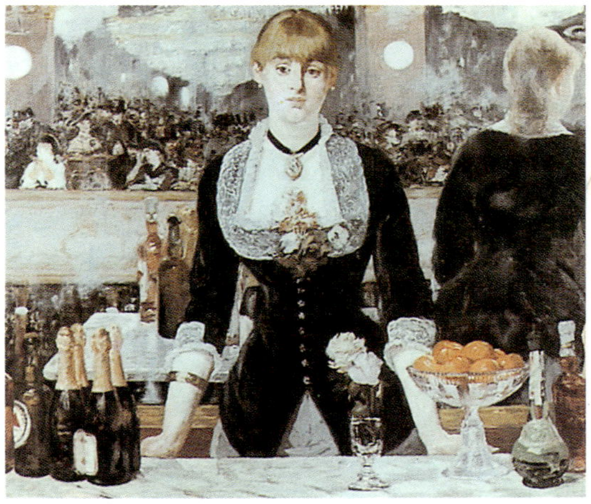

MANET
Bar at the Folies-Bergère
oil on canvas
1881–82. 96 × 130 cm
LEFT In the finished painting, Manet returns to his instinctive preferences and the waitress is facing us, but seems to look through us rather than at us. The foreground forms in itself a very beautiful still life, but Manet was much criticized for his handling of the woman's back and the customer reflected in the mirror. It is indeed inaccurate, but does it matter?

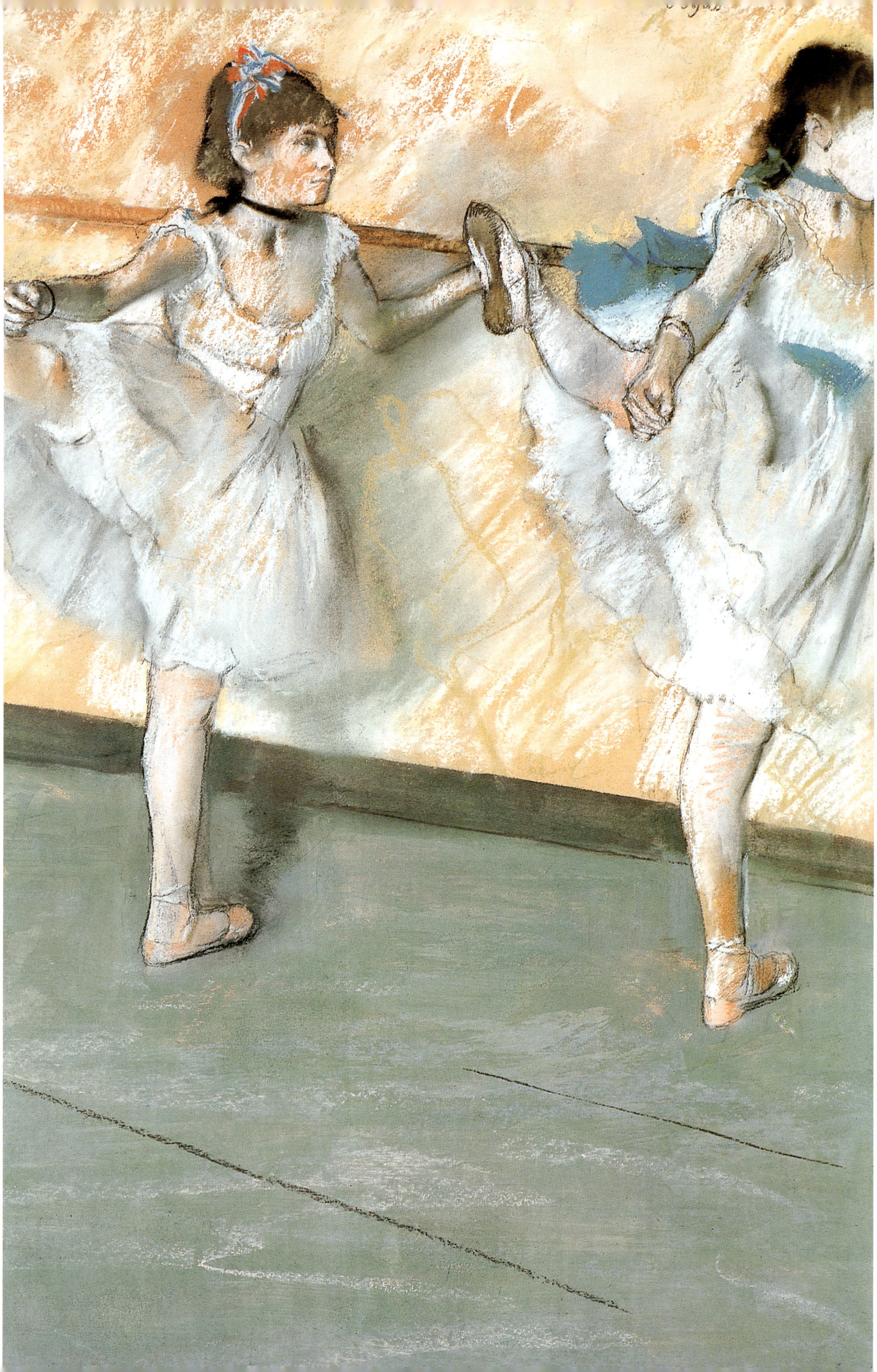

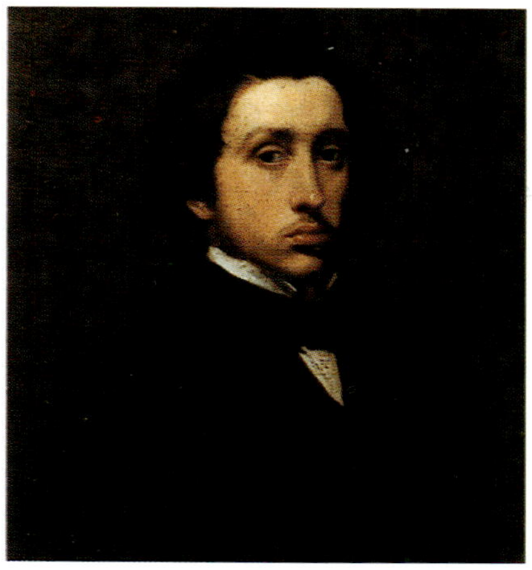

Degas

In a famous statement, Edgar Degas likened his art to the perpetration of a crime; "make counterfeits," he said "and add a touch of nature." Degas never painted *en plein-air* and had nothing but scorn for painters who did, preferring to make sketches of his subjects – primarily the human figure in motion – and use whatever means at his disposal, including photography, to ensure the accuracy of his observation before working in the studio. Thus, until his later experiments with pastel and gouache, Degas had very little to do with the Impressionism of Monet, Renoir, or even the later work of Manet. But, like Manet, his inspiration grew directly out of an intense admiration for past masters.

Despite his uncompromising refusal to espouse the style of his Impressionist colleagues, Degas was instrumental in the foundation of the *Société anonyme* and all the subsequent Impressionist exhibitions except one.

EDGAR DEGAS
Self-portrait
c.1855
Above

DEGAS
Dancers at the Barre
pastel on paper
c.1877. 66 × 51 cm
Opposite

Life and Works: Edgar Degas (1834–1917)

A painting is a thing which requires as much trickery, malice, and vice as the perpetration of a crime; make counterfeits and add a touch of nature.

EDGAR DEGAS

Edgar Degas, like Manet, was born into the higher echelons of Parisian society; in fact he came into the world on 19th July 1834 above a branch of his family's Neapolitan bank in the rue Saint-Georges. But unlike Manet, Degas did not have to fight his parents to become an artist. Amongst the Degas' friends were several eminently wealthy art collectors and government officials who encouraged Edgar, already self-taught, by allowing him to study and copy their art treasures. The Valpinçons, for example, owned Ingres' *Odalisque au turban*, a source of enduring delight and inspiration to the young Degas; and Achille Devéria, Keeper of the Cabinet d'Estampes, the Prints and Drawings Room at the Bibliothèque Nationale, allowed Edgar to peruse the collections and copy the works in them. By the time he was eighteen Degas had also obtained permission to copy at the Louvre. In a comfortable family environment, free of untoward pressure, with a father devoted to him (his mother died when he was fifteen), Edgar Degas was able to indulge his talents with the help of the finest public and private collections in Paris. In 1854 he was to visit wealthy uncles, aunts, and cousins in Naples and Florence where, as one biographer puts it, he undertook an orgy of museums and copying the old masters – Raphael, Mantegna, Bellini, Pollaiuolo, Botticelli, and Giotto. "Draw lines, young man, draw lines," Ingres is said to have advised his young devotee in 1855 when Edouard Valpinçon took Degas to visit the French master, and this he did, and continued to do.

By July 1856 Degas had finished his brief academic studies, having gained a place at the Ecole des Beaux-Arts the year before, studying with a disciple of Ingres, Louis Lamothe. Degas' ability was by now considerable; deep

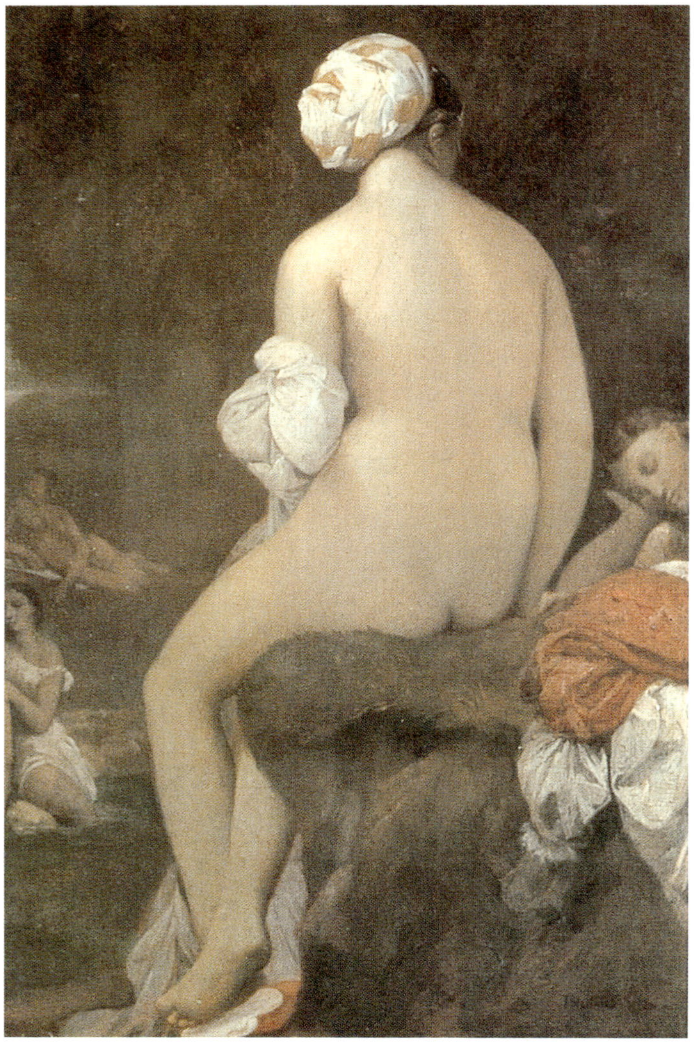

INGRES
Odalisque
oil on canvas
1826. 32 × 25 cm
This is the purity of line the young Degas admired. Friends of the Degas family had an odalisque similar to this which fascinated the young Degas.

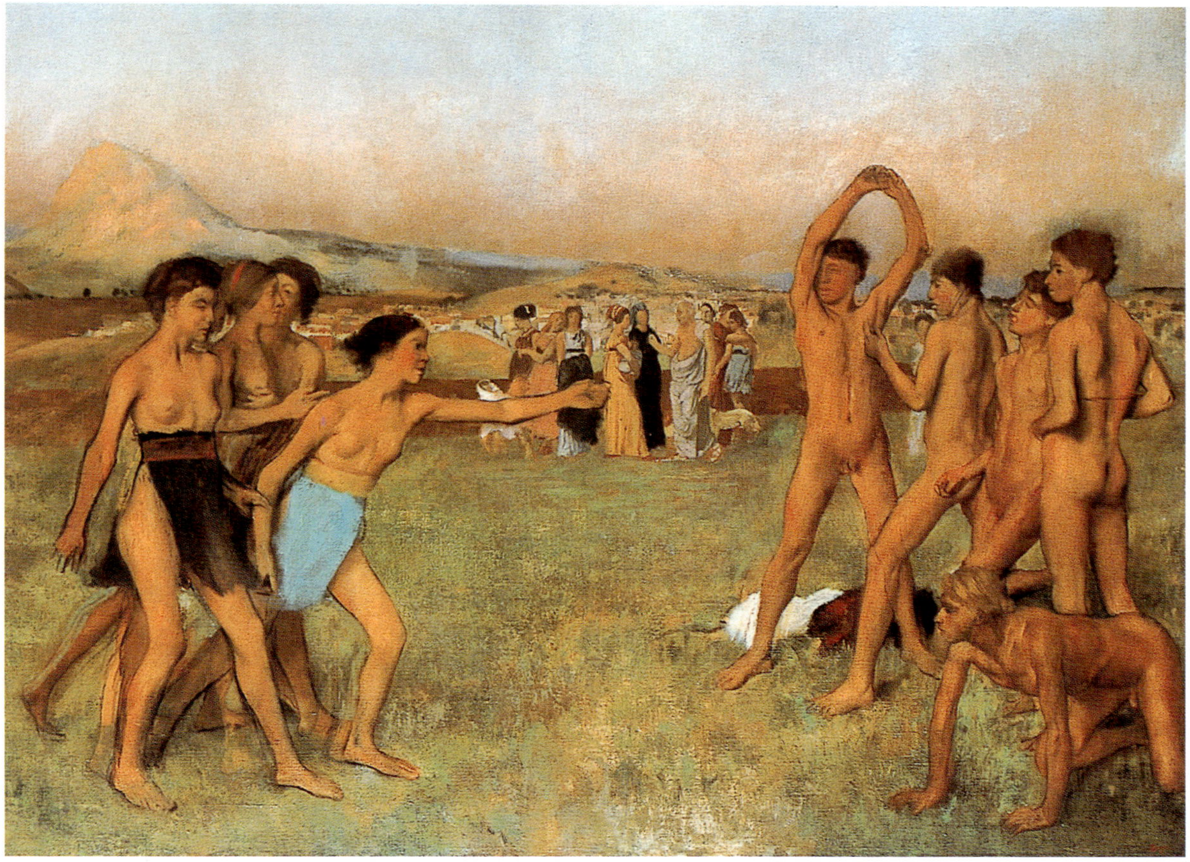

DEGAS
Young Spartans
oil on canvas
c.1860. 109 × 154.5 cm
Degas was inspired by his reading of classical authors for this unusual subject. In contrast to more academic painters he deliberately left out classical elements such as Greek buildings.

immersion in old masters of every conceivable school, but particularly the Italians, was producing polished results. He then set off for an extended tour of Italy which lasted until April 1859, where he continued to devour the old masters and paint family portraits. In November 1858 Degas' father Auguste, having just received a packing case from his son, wrote to him in Florence with some pride:

> I have unrolled your paintings and some of your drawings. I was very pleased, and I can tell you that you have taken a great step forward in your art; your drawing is strong, the colours are right. You have rid yourself of the weak, trivial, Flandrinian, Lamothian manner of drawing and that dull grey colour. My dear Edgar, you have no reason to go on tormenting yourself, you are on the right track . . . You have a great destiny ahead of you . . .

Auguste Degas seems to have had the measure of his son's potential; the portraits, self-portraits, genre paintings, copies of frescos and old masters produced in Degas' youth bespoke a solid if somewhat unexciting future for the artist. The abundance of self-portraits at such an early age testifies to Degas' single-minded obsession not only with art, but with himself; he resolutely remained a bachelor for the rest of his life.

On his return to Paris, Degas continued his steady self-improvement by copying in the Louvre, gaining permission to do so by listing his friend Emile Lévy as his fictitious master. That was where Edouard Manet first met him in 1862, interrupting him in the

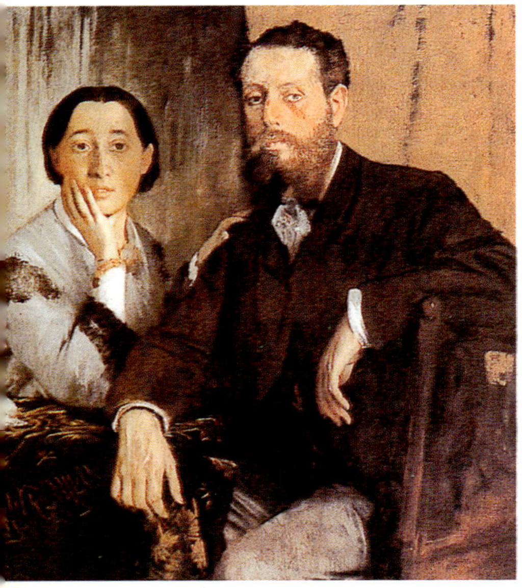

DEGAS
Edmond and Thérèse Morbilli
oil on canvas
c.1865. 117.5 × 90 cm
ABOVE Thérèse was Degas' sister; she had married her first cousin in 1863.

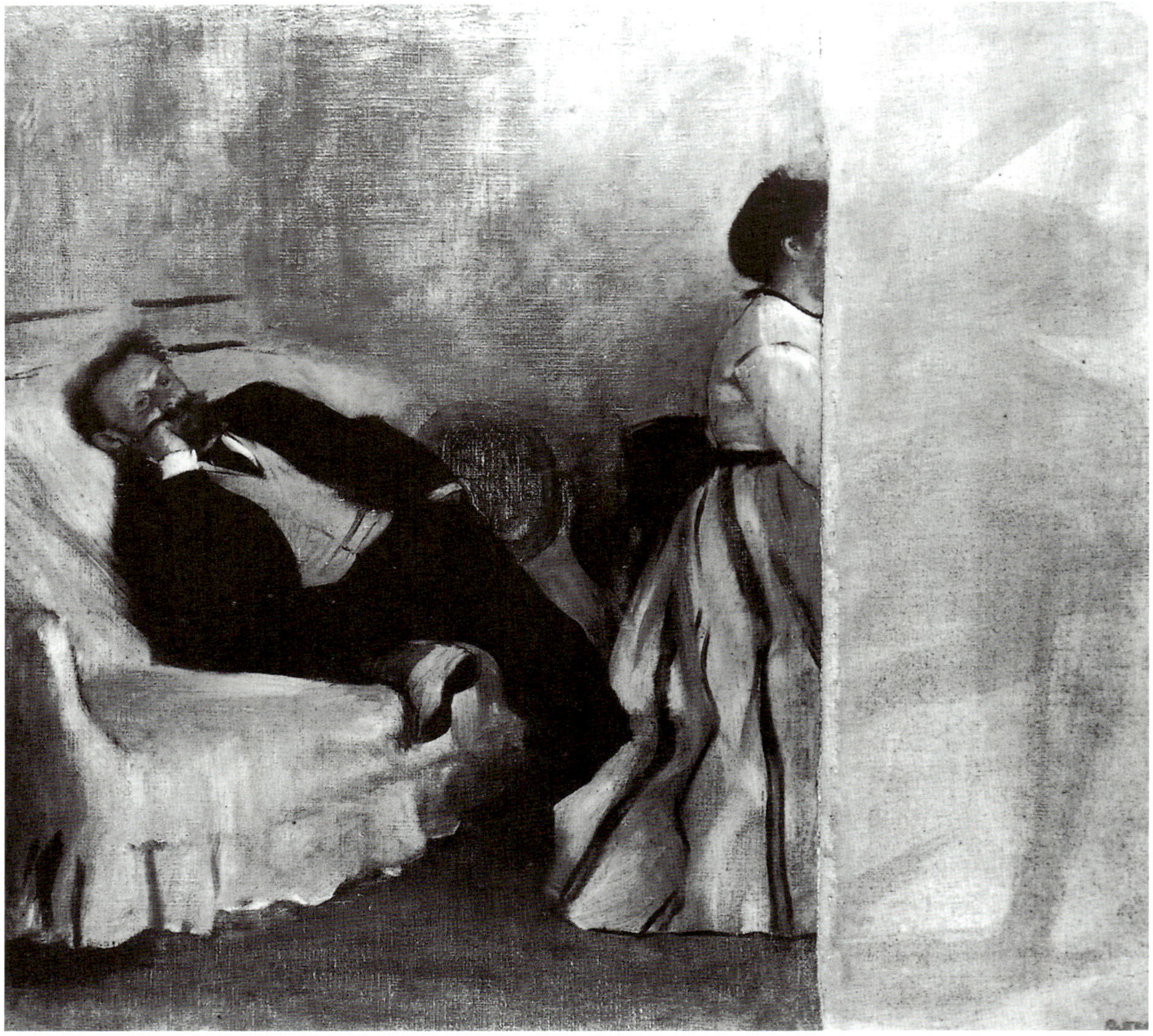

DEGAS
Manet Listening to His Wife Playing the Piano
oil on canvas
1865. 65 × 71 cm
RIGHT Manet did not like the way Degas had depicted his wife, Suzanne, in this double portrait, and cut part of the canvas off, much to Degas' horror. Degas intended to restore it but never did, perhaps because Manet executed a similar portrait later on.

DEGAS
On the Cliff-top
pastel on paper
c.1869. 30.5 × 45 cm
*OPPOSITE Although Degas was a virulent anti-*plein-airiste *he painted around a hundred landscapes in brief periods during the 1860s and the 1890s.*

process of copying Velazquez's *Infanta Margarita* onto a copper plate. At this time Degas was trying to finish his first important history painting, *Semiramis Building Babylon*, and, with the usual friendly rivalry which marked their relationship, Manet was to jest a decade later in the Café de la Nouvelle-Athène that "Degas was painting *Semiramis* when I was painting modern Paris." Manet had certainly completed *The Absinthe Drinker*, *Music in the Tuileries Gardens*, and the epochal *Luncheon on the Grass* by this time and was practically reinventing art, as his critics saw it, but Degas, only two years younger than Manet, was not far behind: *The Gentleman's Race: Before the Start*, with its highly original composition, dates from 1862.

The relationship between the two artists is described in several tantalizing anecdotes by their friends (and enemies), but remains clouded in a certain amount of mystery. We do know that they admired each other greatly and were in frequent contact; at one point in 1869, for example, Manet wrote to Degas asking for the return of two volumes of Baudelaire. One incident in particular tells us

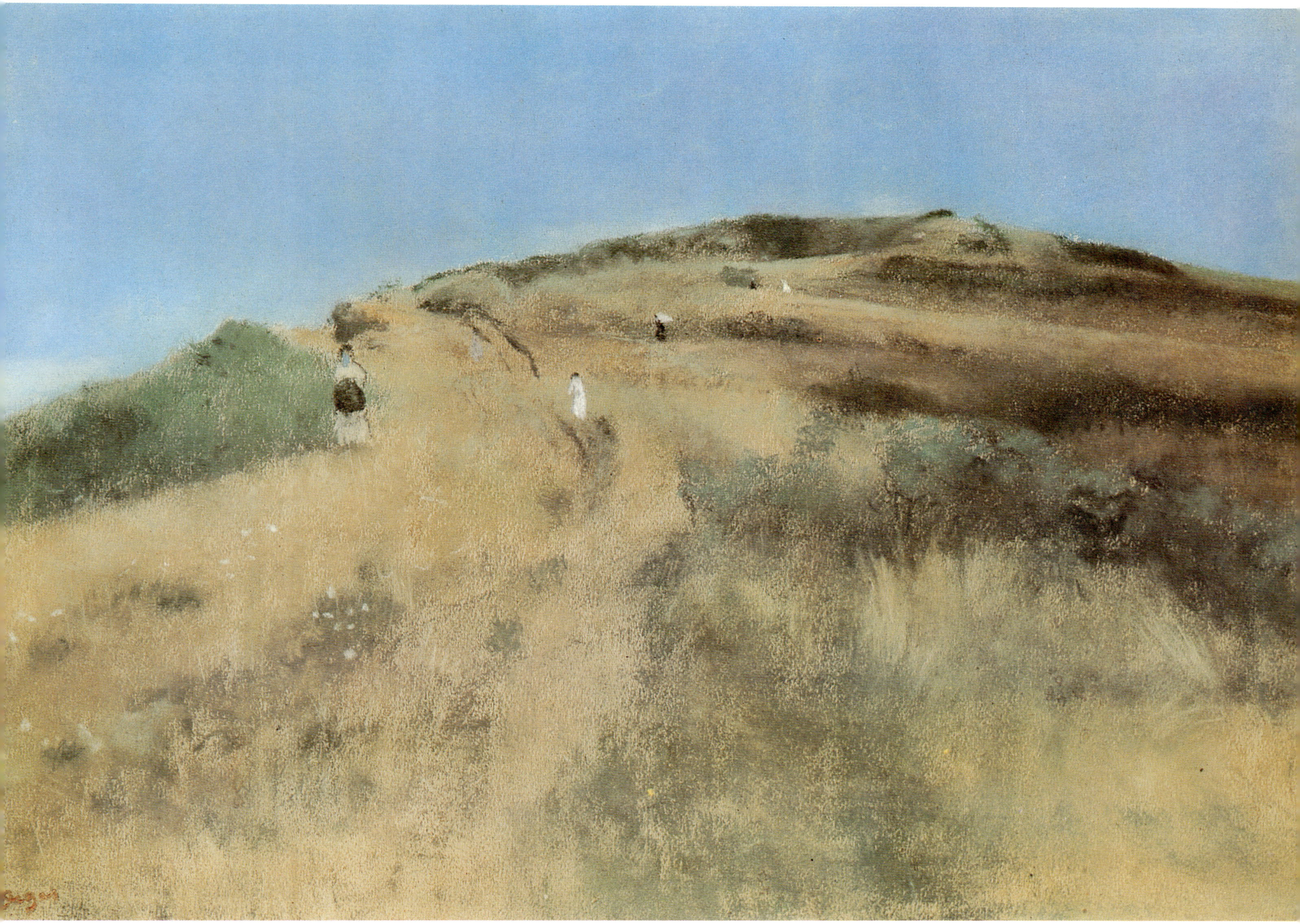

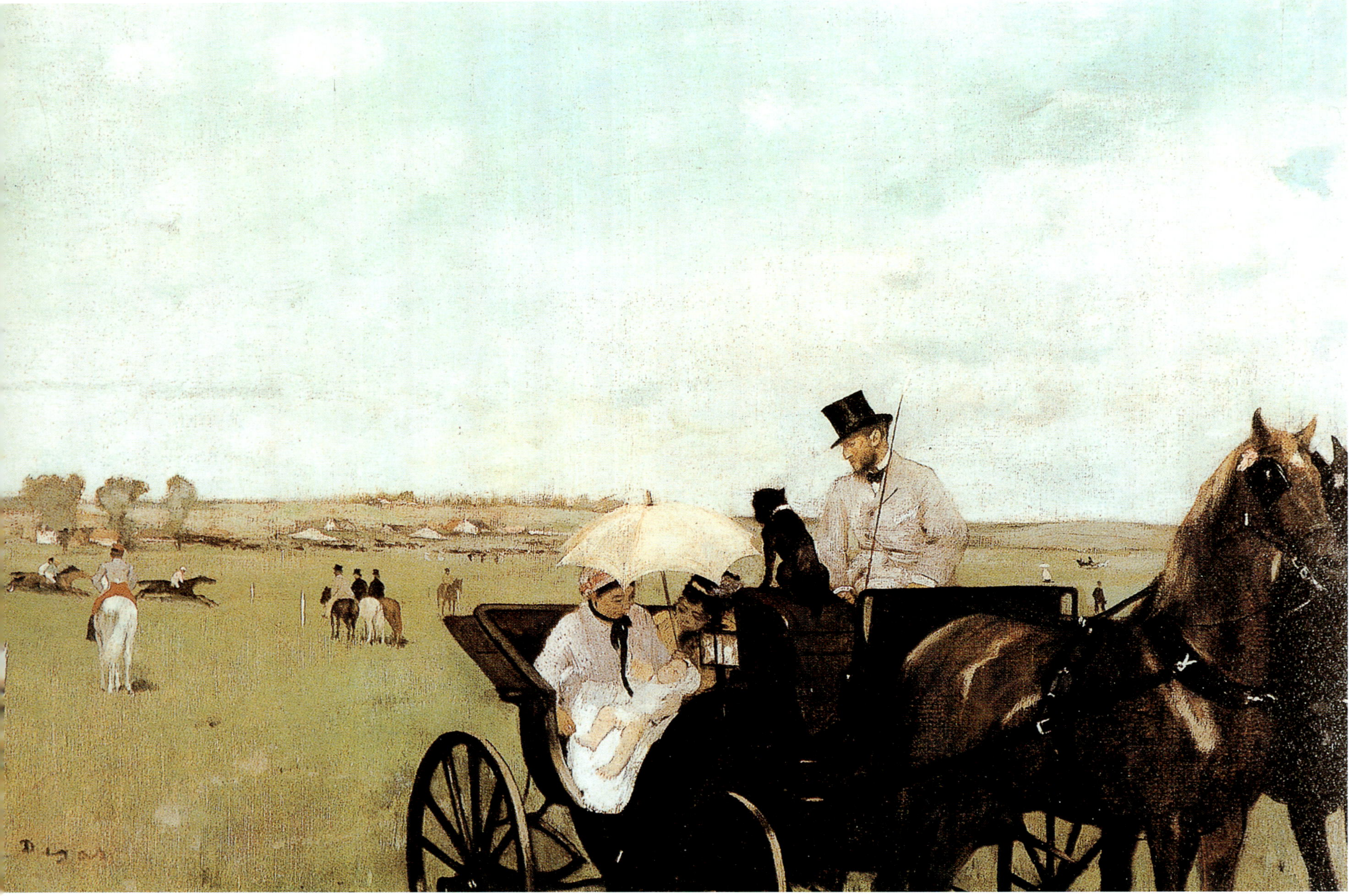

DEGAS
Races in the Country
oil on canvas
1869. 36.5 × 56 cm
This is a portrait of Degas' boyhood friend Paul Valpinçon, with his wife leaning over the nurse who holds their new-born son. Degas did several portraits of his friend and family, and often stayed with them in Normandy.

a great deal about their strange relationship. Between 1868 and 1869 Degas painted a double portrait of Manet with his wife, Suzanne, at the piano. It survives with a piece of canvas attached to the place where half of Mme Manet used to be before M. Manet slashed it off in a fit of pique. In 1924, with dubious accuracy, but with much wit, the dealer Ambroise Vollard recounted the tale Degas had told him in this way:

Vollard: Who slashed that painting?

Degas: To think it was Manet who did that! He thought that something about Mme Manet wasn't right. Well . . . I'm going to try to restore

DEGAS
Racehorses before the Stands
oil on canvas
1866–68. 46 × 61 cm

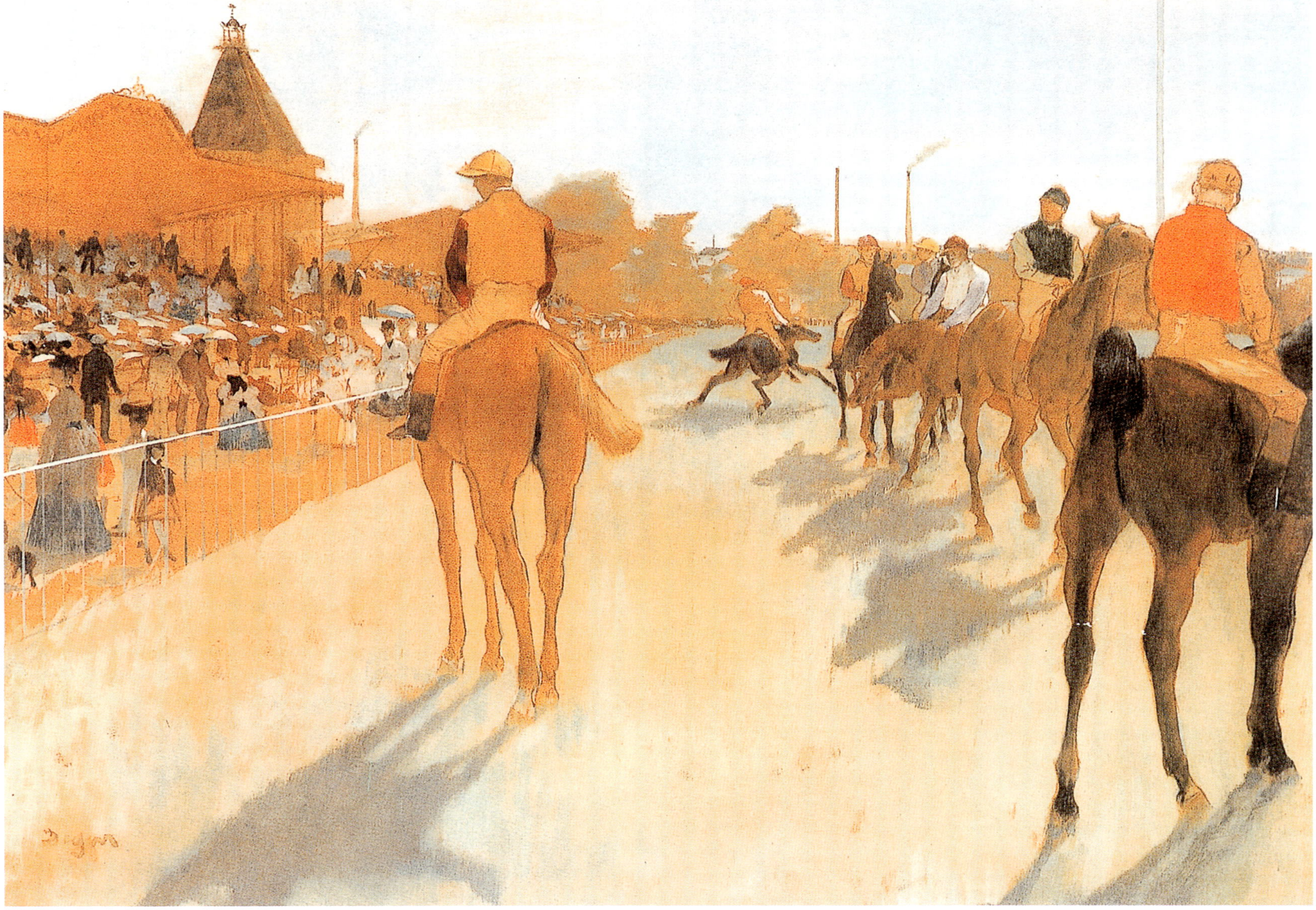

DEGAS
The Cotton Market
oil on canvas
1873. 73 × 92 cm
RIGHT The painting was executed while Degas was staying with relatives in New Orleans, and he thought it could sell in Manchester, a cotton-spinning centre. In fact it was exhibited in 1878 in the French southern city of Pau, which bought it for its museum.

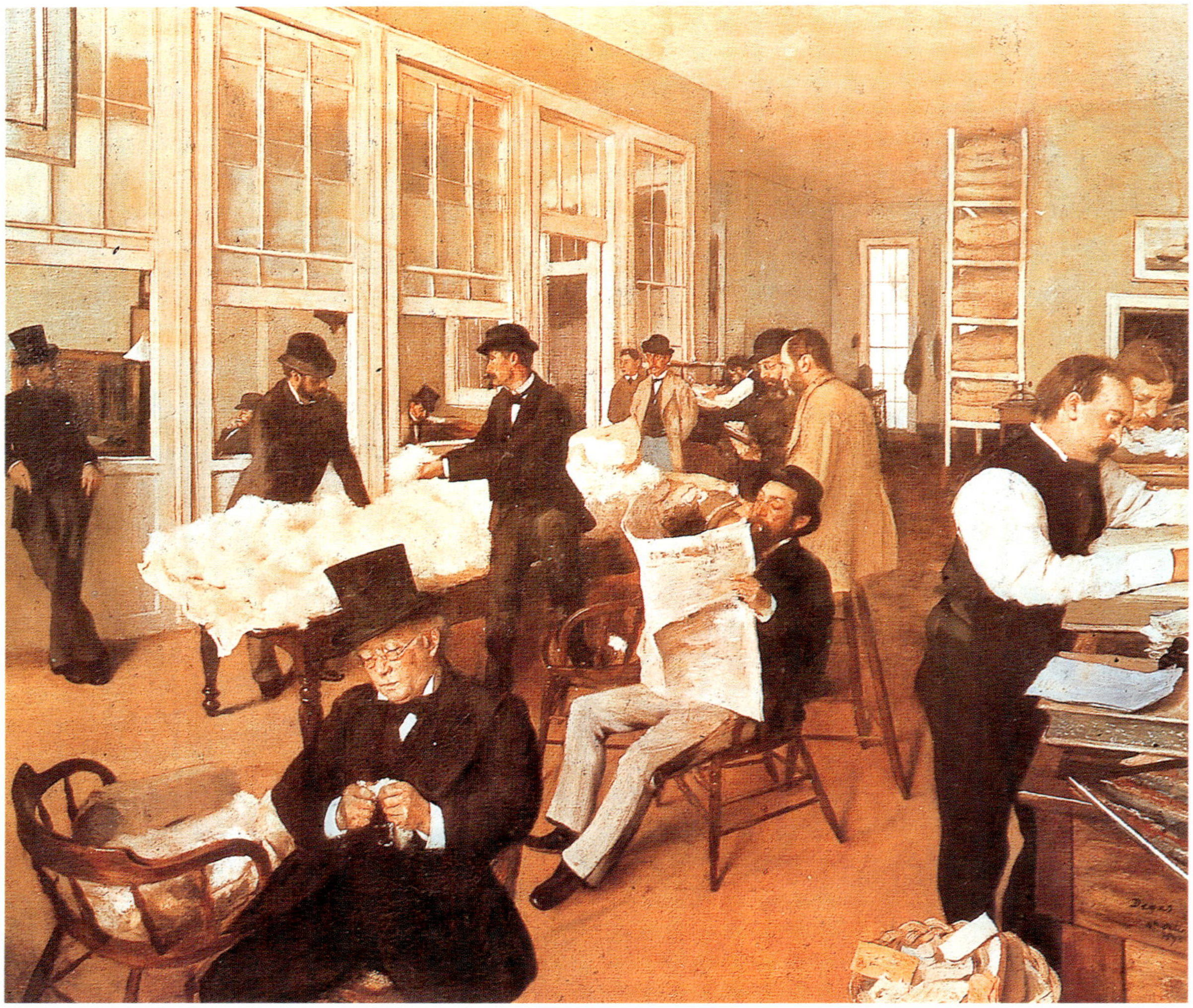

Mme Manet. What a shock I had when I saw it at Manet's . . . I left without saying goodbye, taking my picture with me. When I got home I took down a little still life he had given me. "Monsieur," I wrote, "I am returning your *Plums.*"

Vollard: But you saw each other again afterwards?

Degas: How could you expect anyone to stay on bad terms with Manet?

By the early 1870s Degas had emerged from his deep and intensive involvement in the past and its forms and, following the example of Manet, he was beginning to apply himself to painting the world of modern Paris, in particular its people (and horses) in motion. Unlike the Impressionists with whom he was to be deeply involved, Degas had shown little interest in landscape. Vollard remembers him wryly pronouncing: "If I were the government, I would have a squad of gendarmes to keep an eye on these people painting landscapes from nature. Oh! I don't wish anyone dead. I would, however, agree to spraying them with a little bird-shot, for starters!" But the landscapes he produced in the late 1860s are delicate, imaginary pastels done in the

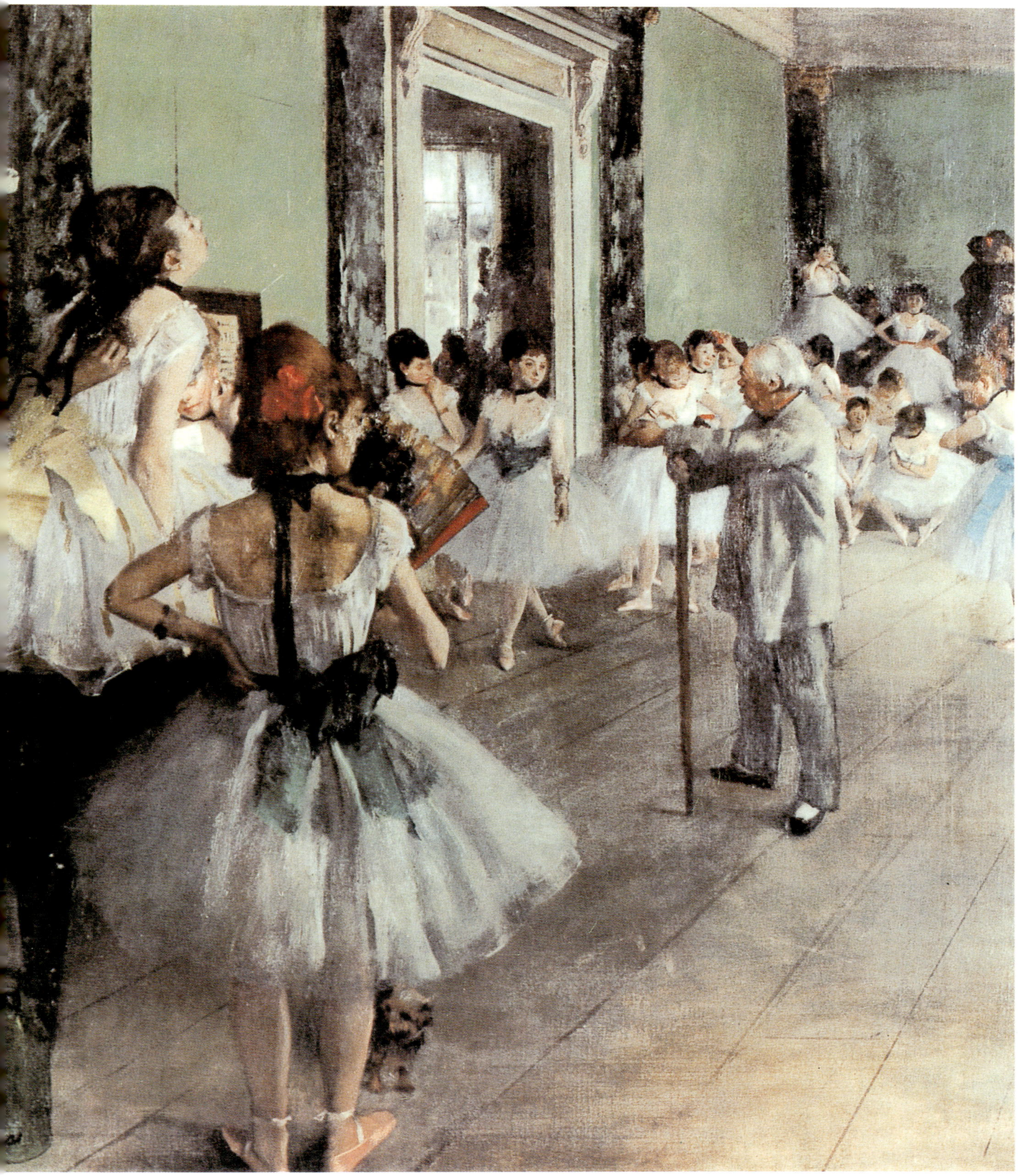

DEGAS
The Dancing Lesson
oil on canvas
1873–75. 85 × 75 cm
LEFT Degas' dance pictures are set in the old Opera House, which burnt down in 1873. He made numerous studies of the dancers.

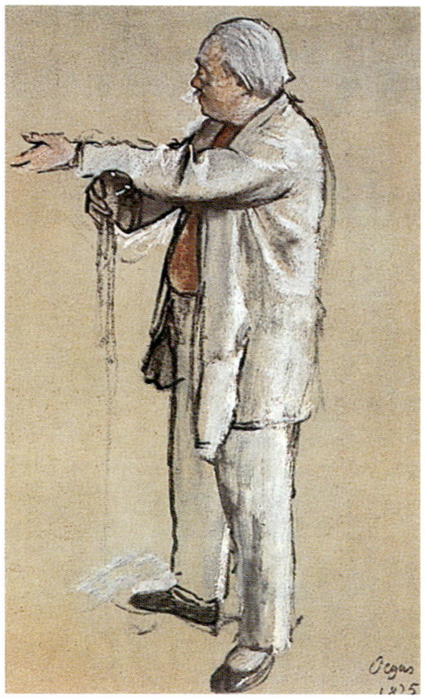

DEGAS
The Ballet Master Jules Perrot
oil on paper
1875. 48 × 30.5 cm
ABOVE Perrot, who retired when this picture was made, had been a star dancer and had taught for ten years in St Petersburg.

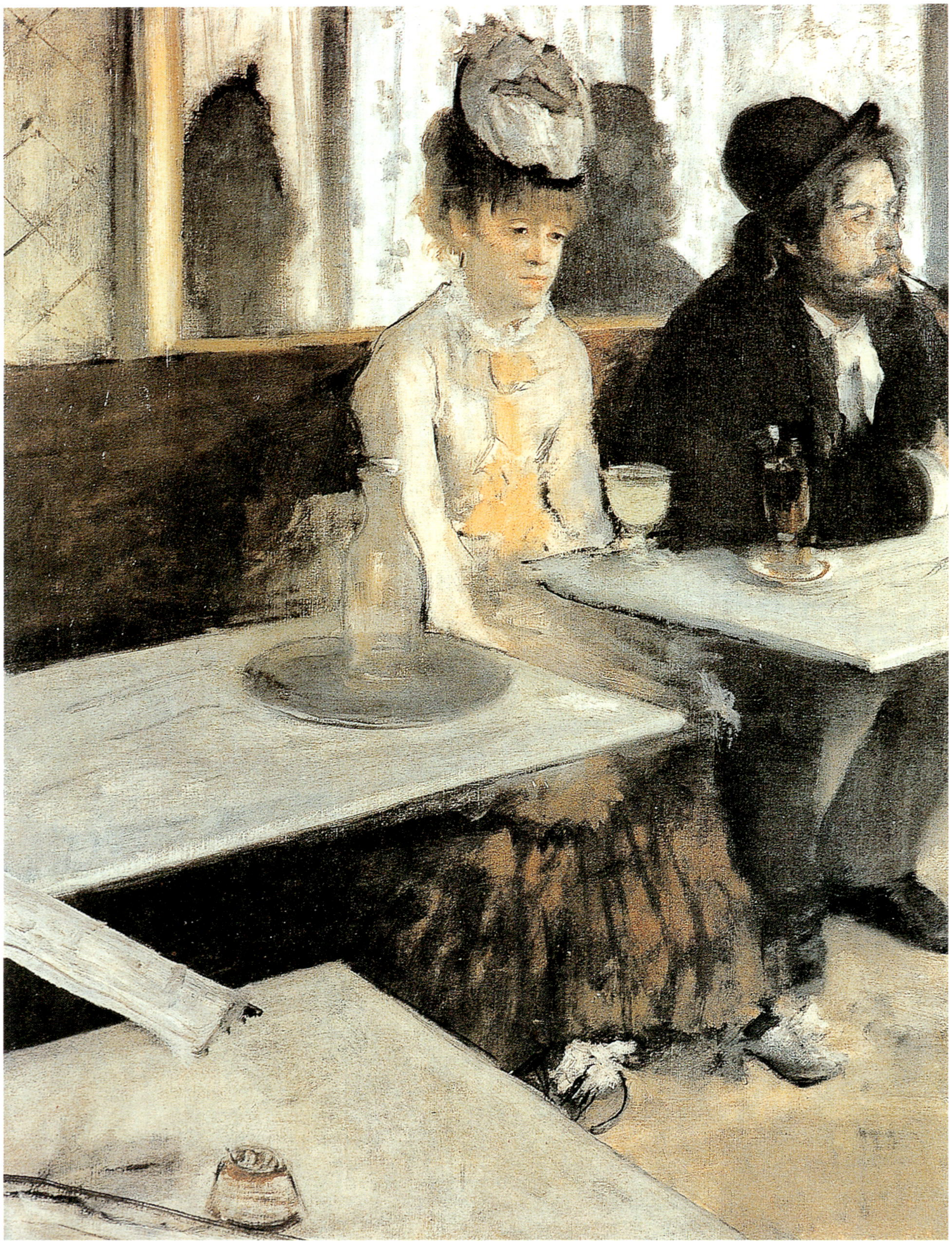

DEGAS
The Absinthe Drinker
oil on canvas
1875–76. 92 × 68 cm
LEFT The sitters are the actress Ellen Andrée and the painter Marcellin Desboutin, both friends of Degas. When Walter Crane saw it in 1893, he said it was a study in human degradation, male and female.

DEGAS
Dancer Bowing on Stage
pastel and gouache on paper
c.1877. 72 × 77.5 cm
RIGHT Strong sunlight affected Degas' eyesight, but he loved the effect of artificial light. He also liked to experiment with mixing different media, as in this picture.

DEGAS
Aux Ambassadeurs
pastel/monotype
1877. 37 × 27 cm
FAR RIGHT Degas started to make monotypes towards the mid-1870s. The process consists of applying greasy printer's ink or oil paint on a metal plate. The plate is then printed on paper and can be coloured with a variety of media, mainly oil or pastel. Café-concerts were a favourite haunt of Parisians and they varied in price and quality.

studio, whilst the monotypes of the 1890s are even more imaginary, appearing almost completely abstract.

The range of the subjects he tackled in the ensuing years is formidable: ballet dancers in rehearsal and before, during, and after performance; racehorses – before, during, and after the race; café-concerts and their singers in performance; the opera; acrobats; prostitutes; businessmen; milliners; a pedicurist, musicians; a billiard room. No nook or cranny of Paris in the 1870s and 1880s was immune from his fastidious gaze or his notebook. These notebooks, which have survived, allow us an important insight into the artist's mind. "Draw all kinds of everyday objects," reads a note from 1876, "placed, accompanied in such a way that they have in them the life of the man or woman – corsets which have just been removed, for example, and which retain the form of the body, etc, etc." Another note reads:

> On bakery, *Bread* – series on baker's boys, seen in the cellar itself, or through the basement window from the street – backs the colour of pink flour – beautiful curves of dough – still lives of different breads, large, oval, round, etc. Studies in colour of the yellows, pinks, greys, whites of bread . . . 2 panels on birth – delicate mother,

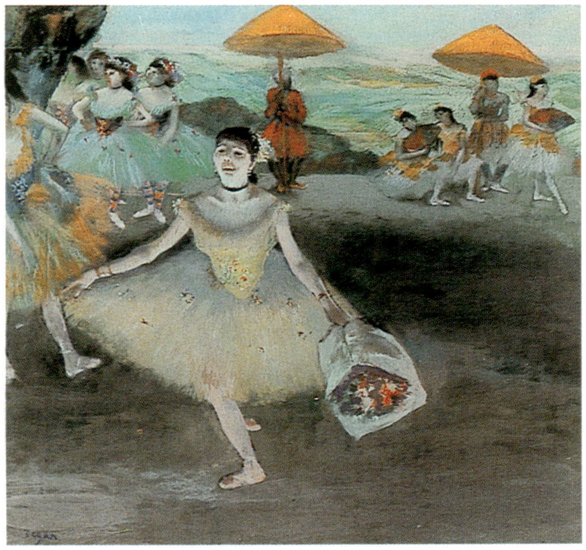

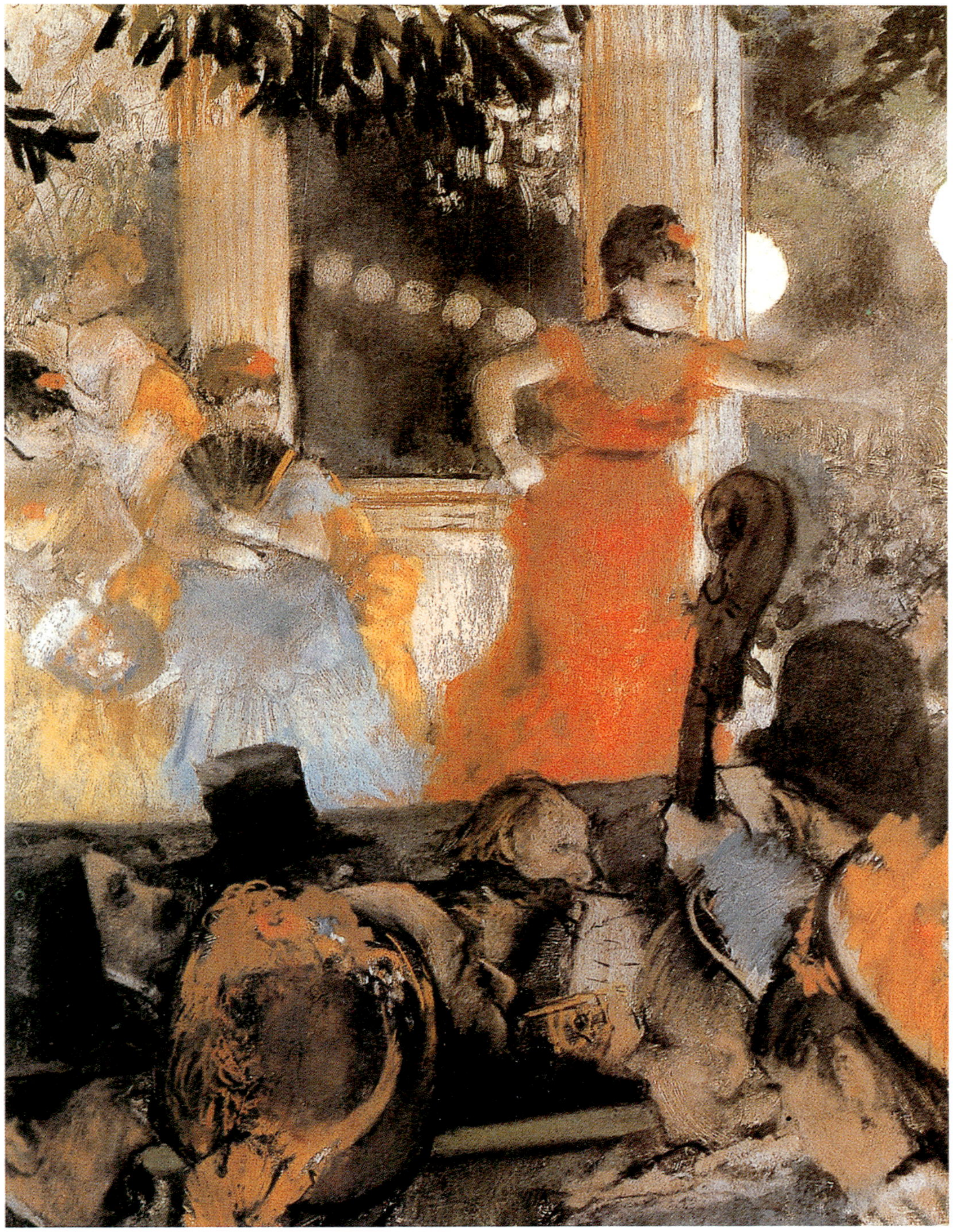

DEGAS
Portraits at the Stock Exchange
oil on canvas
c.1878–79. 100 × 82 cm
RIGHT Ernest May in the centre. He was a wealthy financier, patron and friend of Degas and had a collection of Corots and Impressionist works. The painting was exhibited at the Impressionist shows of 1879 and 1880, although it was not for sale.

DEGAS
The Name Day of the Madam
pastel/monotype
1876–77. 26.5 × 29.5 cm
BELOW It is easy to believe that Degas made these pictures for his own and his friends' amusement. The same was probably true of Picasso, who owned this picture.

fashionable – food – large wet-nurse – large behind – enormous ribbons. Lilac coloured dress fluted like a pillar . . .

He had inherited both the dark and corrupting Paris of Baudelaire with its accursed denizens –

You who wander, stoic, without complaint,
Across the chaos of the living city,
Mothers with bleeding hearts, courtesanes or saints,
Whose names in former times were on the lips of all . . .

(from *Les Fleurs du Mal*)

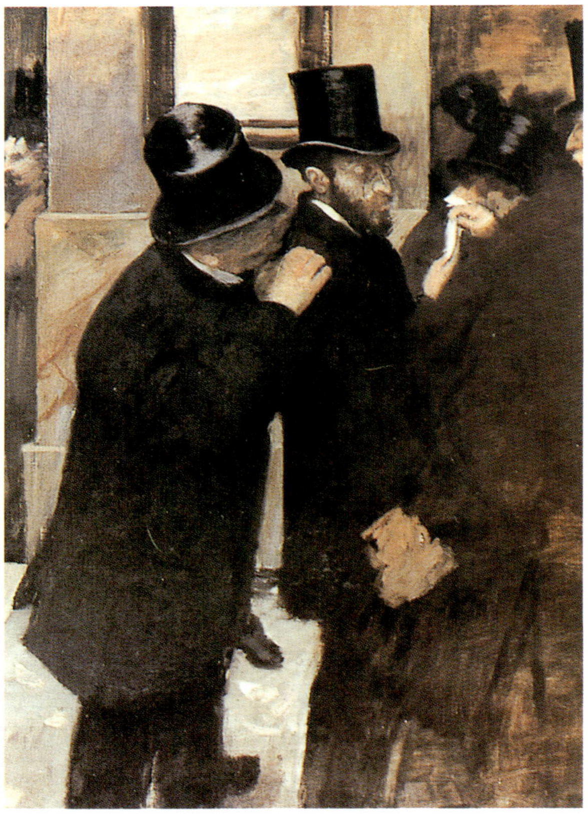

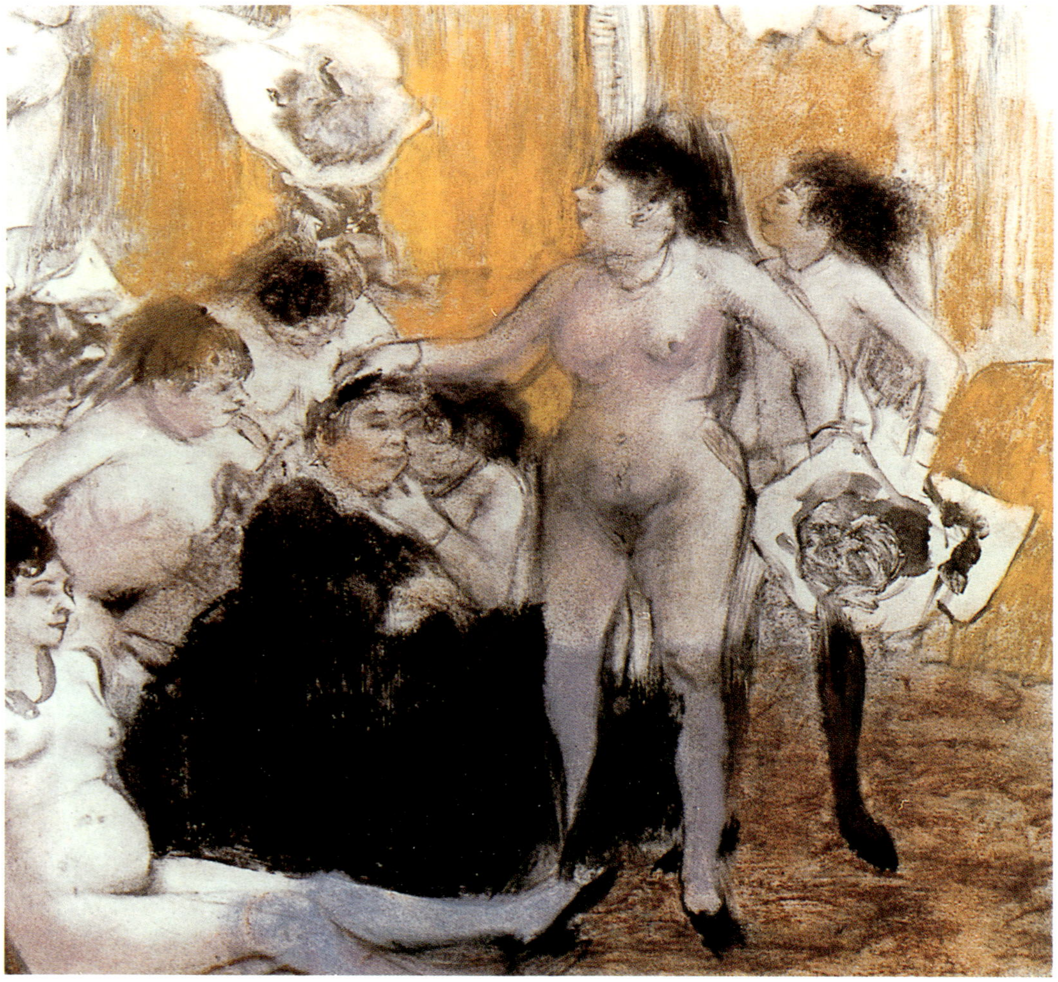

– and the sparkling life of *la ville lumière*, the only place he really felt at home, with its ordinary working people, its ever-increasing number of cafés, concerts, operas and ballets, stars and starlets.

Above all Degas was concerned with the female form: women dancing, women singing, women ironing, women before, during, and after the bath, women sleeping, combing and braiding their hair.

> Degas has another comprehension of life, a different concern for exactitude before nature. There is certainly a woman there, but a certain kind of woman, *without the expression of a face*, without the wink of an eye, without the décor of the *toilette*, a woman reduced to the gesticulation of her limbs, to the appearance of her body, a woman considered as a female, expressed in her animality . . .

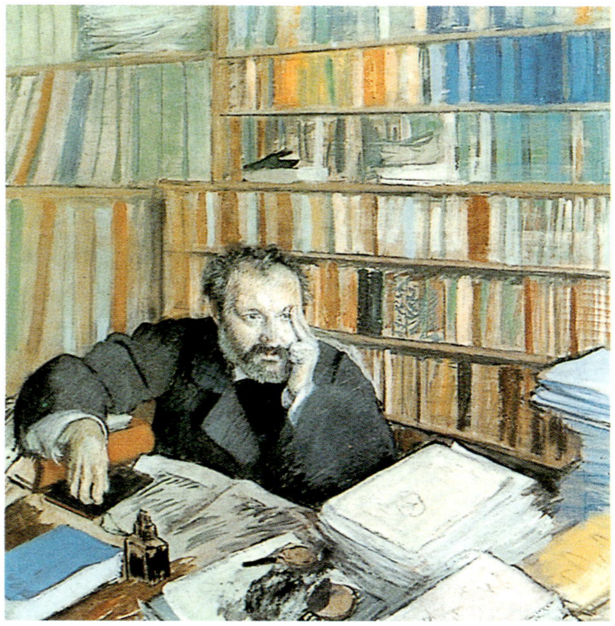

DEGAS
Edmond Duranty
pastel and tempera on paper
1879 101 × 100.5 cm
Duranty was a wealthy literary and art critic. Degas made three preliminary drawings for this picture, which was executed a year before Duranty's death.

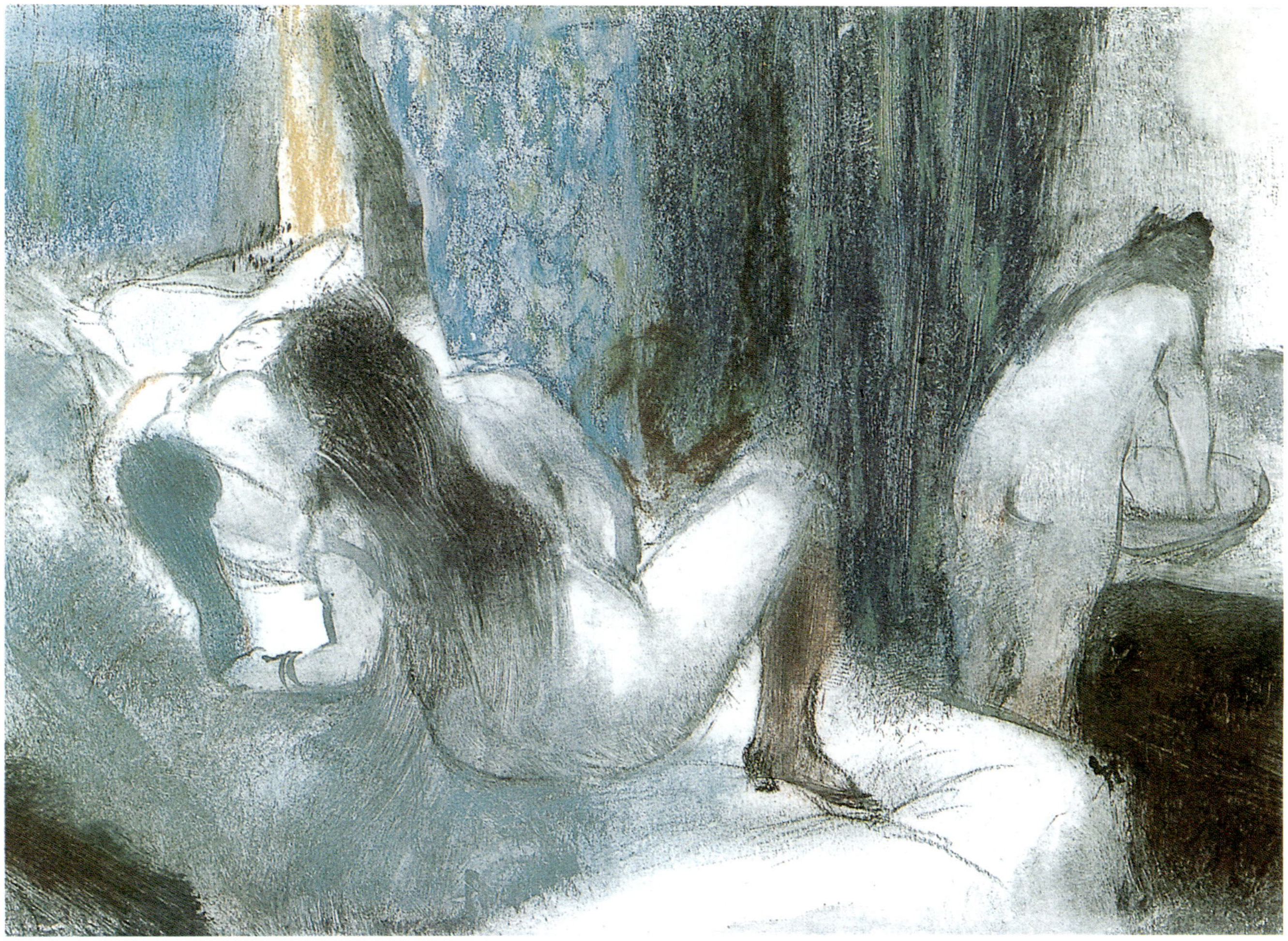

DEGAS
Brothel Inmates
pastel/monotype
c.1879. 14 × 20.5 cm
Degas did about fifty such works, which have always puzzled his admirers and critics as well as scholars, who offer various interpretations for this choice of subject and the manner in which it is treated.

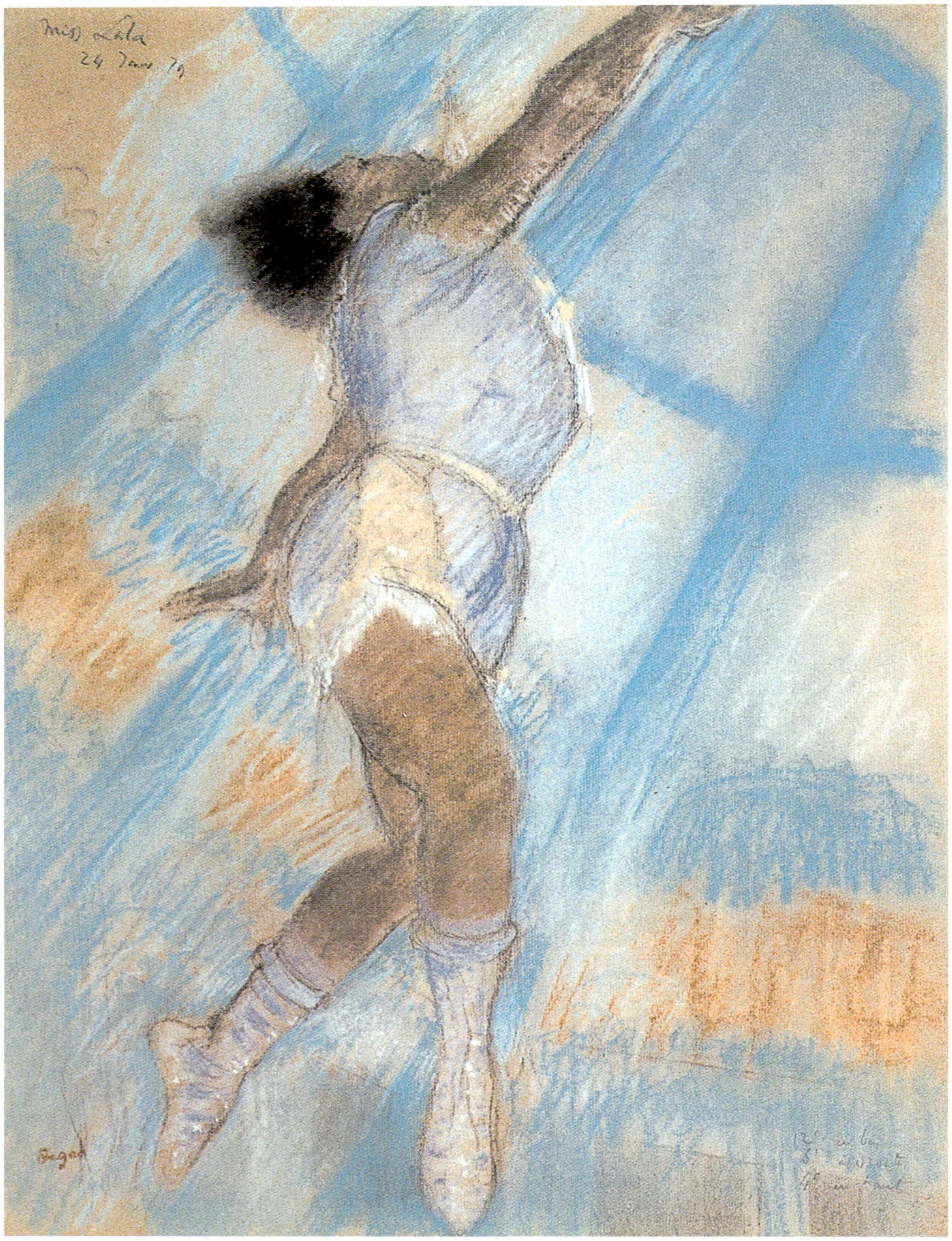

DEGAS
Study for Miss La La at the Cirque Fernando
pastel on paper
1879. 61 × 48 cm
Above Degas attended performances at the circus in January 1879, and made several studies, of which this is the last.

This is what the contemporary critic Gustave Geffroy thought of Degas' female subjects. It underlines the profound difference between Degas and Manet, who had presented the female nude and the semi-dressed *Nana* as provocations to accepted notions of art. Similarly Degas' late nudes bear only a passing resemblance to Renoir's in their rotundity. Renoir depicts his women "*with the expression of a face*", and all that implies. Increasingly Degas' women at their toilette are, as the 1890s wear on, studies of line and colour; indeed the coloured line, possible with pastels, opened up new avenues for experimentation. As he put it to Sickert, "They [his contemporaries, the Impressionists] are all exploiting the possibilities of colour. And I am always begging them to exploit the possibilities of drawing. It is the richer field." And none could draw with the mastery, and ultimately the abandonment, of Degas.

Degas' sheer energy, his urge to capture fleeting movement in its countless nuances resulted in a prodigious series of paintings, pastels, monotypes, drawings and eventually wax sculpture. Apart from the portraits it is almost impossible to find a Degas where movement and action are not inherent, yet his method was the exact opposite of the Impressionists. He did not attempt to capture the moment in a quick stroke of the brush – there is nothing impulsive about Degas. Everything is studied, planned and executed in the studio in controlled conditions – "I assure you no art is less spontaneous than mine. What I do is the result of reflection and study of the great masters. Of inspiration, spontaneity, temperament, I know nothing." On another occasion and on a slightly different note he said: "It is all very well to copy what one sees, but it is much better to draw what one remembers. A transformation results in which imagination collaborates with memory. You will reproduce only what is striking, which is to say, only what is necessary. That way, your memories and your fantasies are liberated from the tyranny of nature."

Degas approached his involvement with

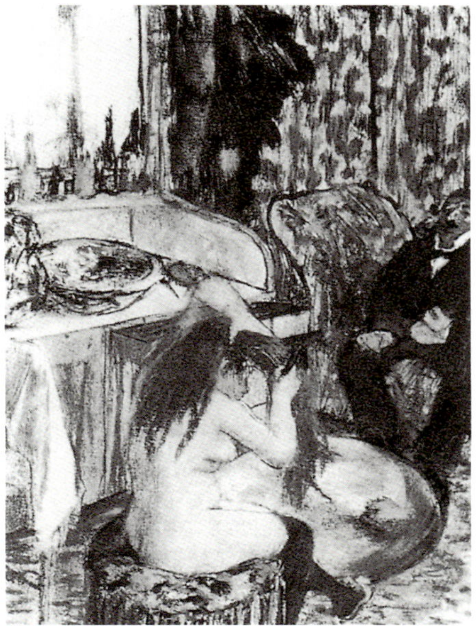

DEGAS
Nude Combing Her Hair
pastel/monotype
c.1877–79. 21.5 × 16 cm
Above It is indeed paradoxical that the admirer of Ingres' pure and idealized figures could produce such pictures.

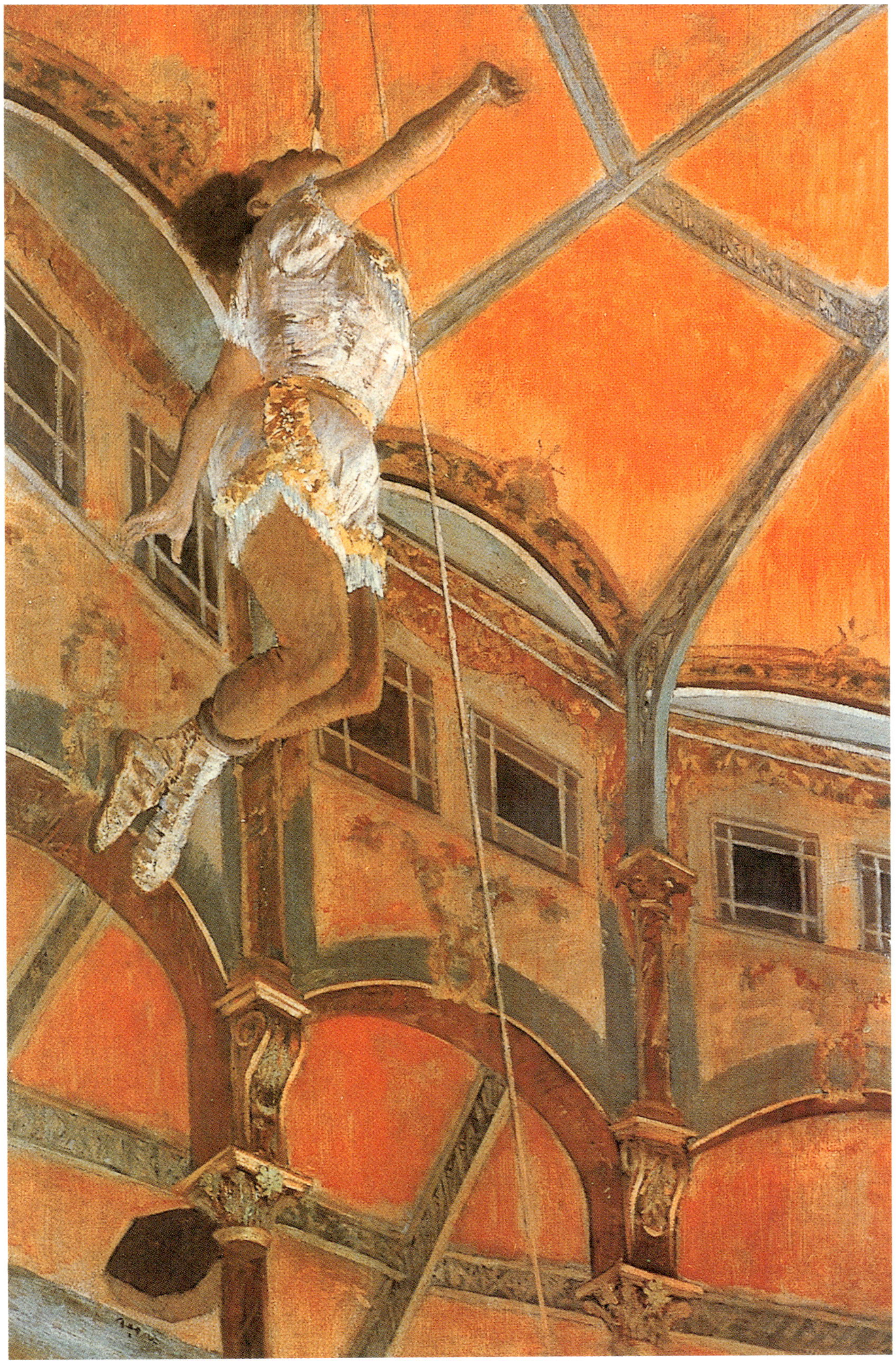

DEGAS
Miss La La at the Cirque Fernando
oil on canvas
1879. 117 × 77.5 cm
Left The cirque Fernando was located in Montmartre and later became the Medrano circus. As for Miss La La, she was renowned for the strength of her teeth.

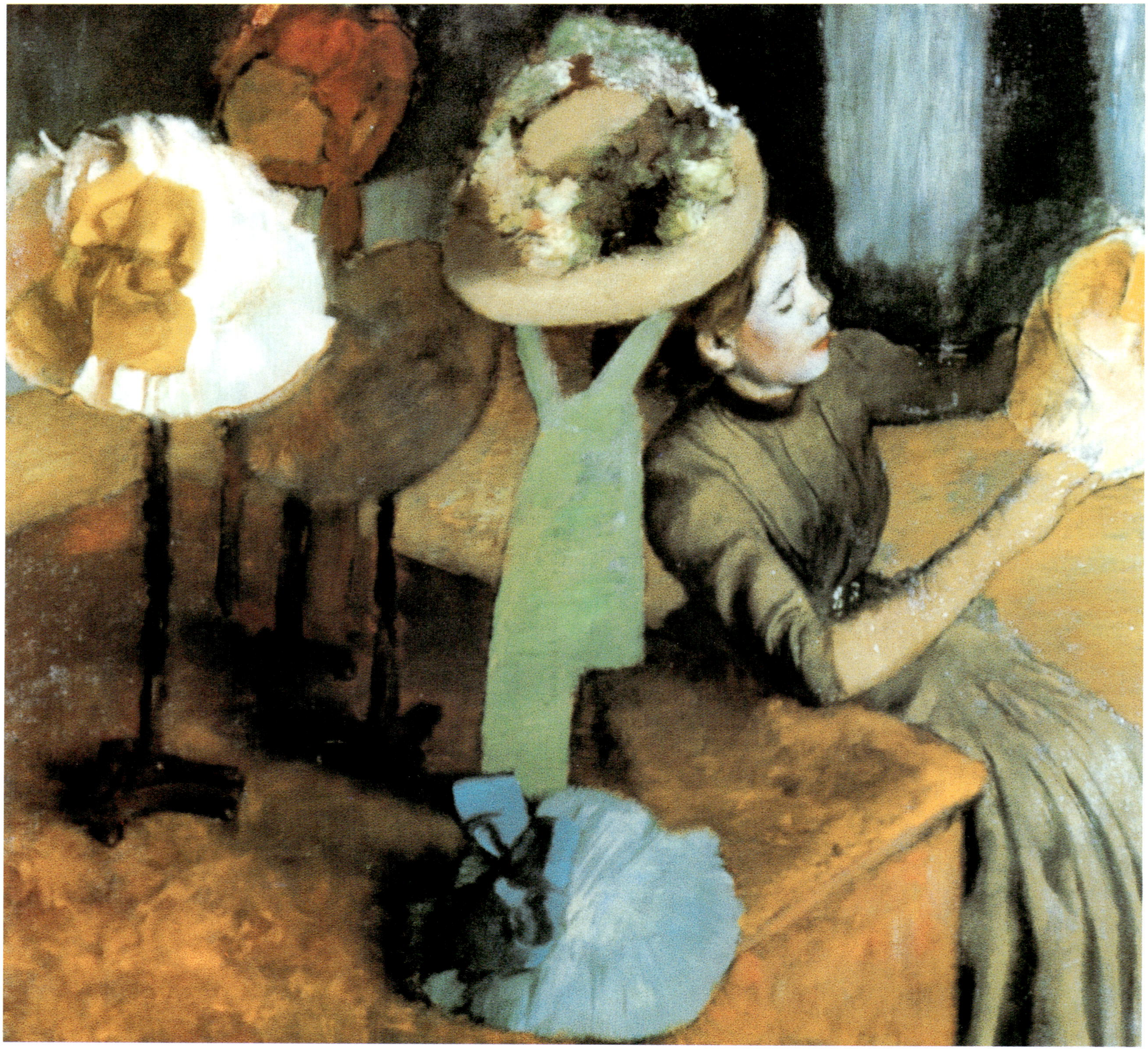

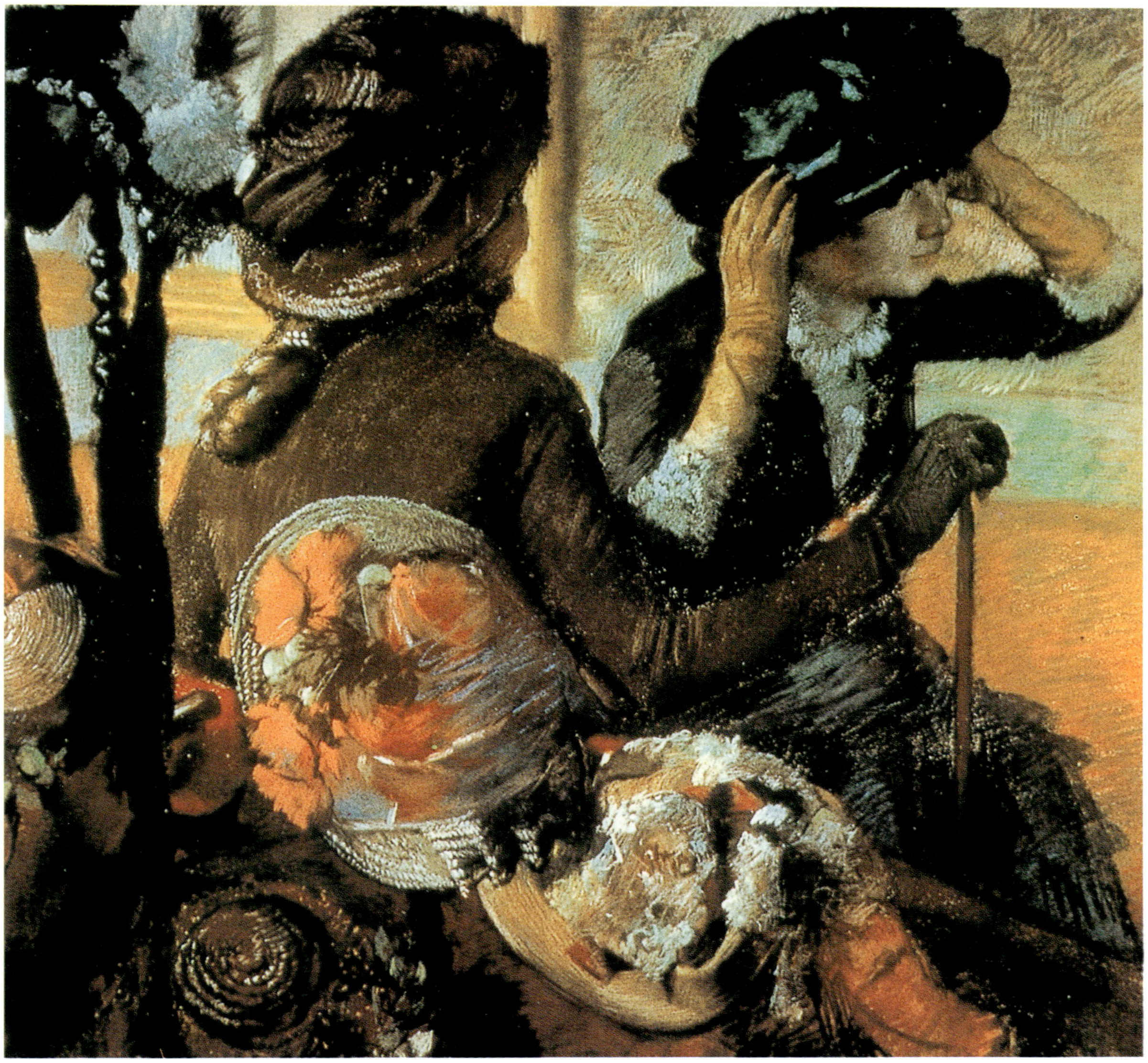

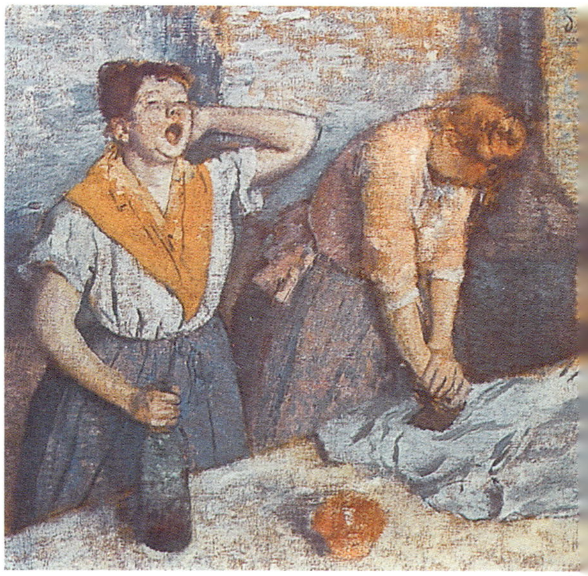

the Impressionists from the point of view of a Realist because he considered himself to be one and saw the first Impressionist exhibition in the rue des Capucines as an opportunity to promote what he called "a Salon of Realists." It should be noted that the terms Realism and Naturalism were confused and interchangeable at the time. Realists-Naturalists could also be Impressionists as far as the critics of the day were concerned; the term Impressionism subsumed a great deal that was deemed to be new or revolutionary. Thus Degas and Manet, by virtue of their age and status, were wrongly thought to be leaders of the Impressionist movement, when these titles have been awarded to Monet and Pissarro. It is clear that Degas had no interest in the *plein-airisme* being explored by Monet, Pissarro, Renoir, Sisley, and Morisot in the 1870s; his subjects were exclusively Parisian, from racehorses to prostitutes. Moreover, he was experimenting with new techniques and revitalizing neglected media such as pastel, gouache, and even distemper (used for painting scenery) in an attempt to transcend what were now appearing to be the limitations of oil paint.

DEGAS
Women Ironing
oil on canvas
c.1884–86. 76 × 81 cm
ABOVE The contemporary critic and friend of the Impressionists Georges Rivière wrote about Degas: "he is an observer, he never seeks exaggeration. The effect is always obtained from nature herself, without caricature. This is what makes him the most valuable historian of the scene he shows us."

DEGAS
At the Milliner's
pastel on grey paper
1882. 76 × 85 cm
LEFT This is probably the most attractive of a series of milliners drawn by Degas in the 1880s. The picture was shown by Durand-Ruel in 1882 in London, where it attracted little attention, apart from one good review from an unknown critic.

DEGAS
The Millinery Shop
oil on canvas
c.1882–86. 100 × 110.5 cm
OPPOSITE This is the largest of a series characterized by its unusual and ingenious compositions.

DEGAS
Dancer Massaging Her Ankles
pastel on paper
1882. 48 × 61 cm
Dancers were originally working-class girls chaperoned by ambitious mothers who also had a say in the choice of their daughters' "benefactors", wealthy men visiting the Opera backstage to choose pretty young girls for their pleasure.

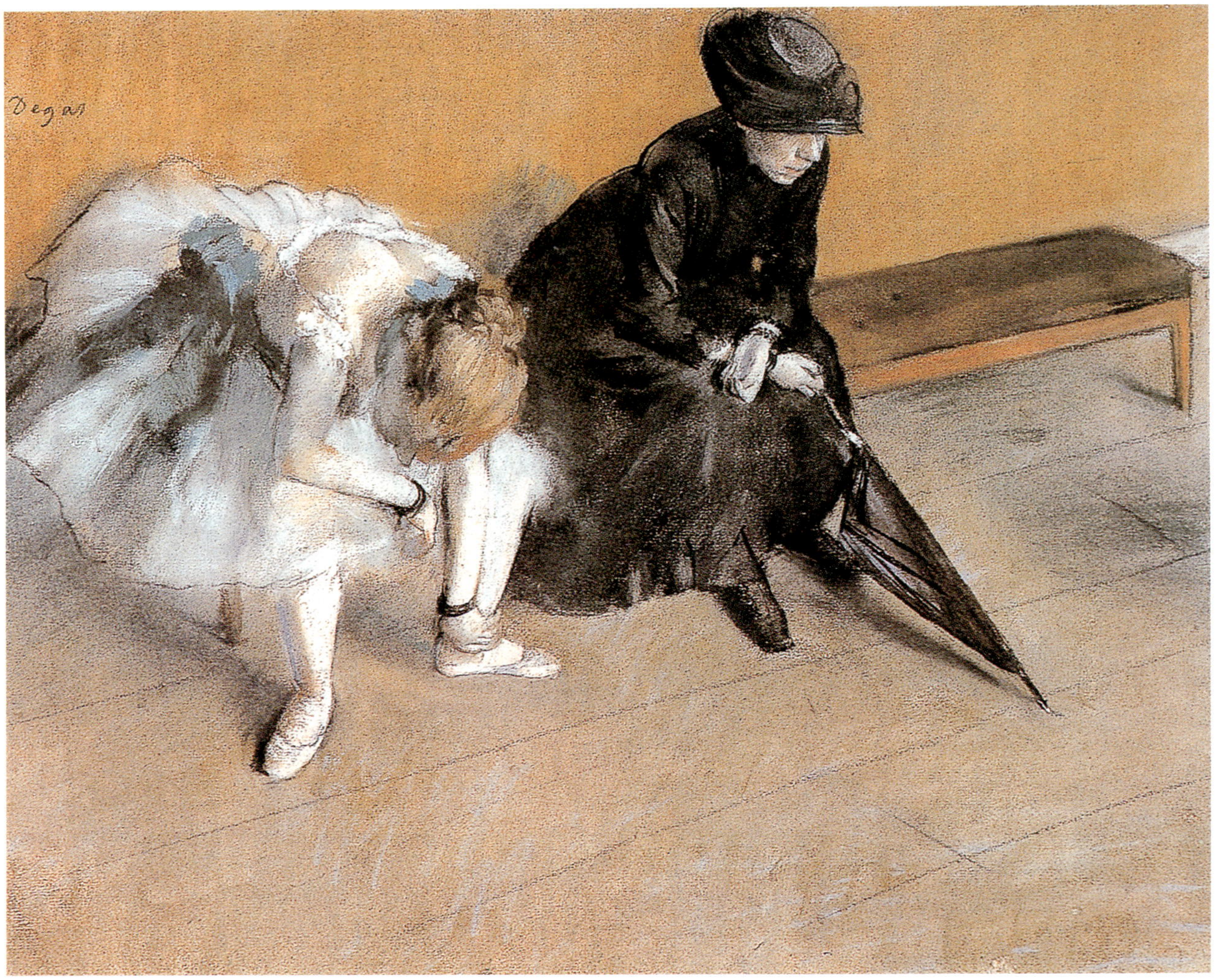

Abandoning oils meant he could paint rapidly on a paper support which could be infinitely extended by sticking separate pieces of paper together as required. In another vein he was experimenting with alternatives to the traditional gilt frames. Having revolutionized the framing of subjects within the composition, he now addressed himself to the immediate environment of the picture, even including the décor and lighting of the exhibition room itself.

Degas' interest in modern life embraced not only those who lived it but also the technological innovations of his day, from a new electric method of drypoint etching to Eadweard Muybridge's extraordinary photographic discoveries about the nature of human and animal locomotion. Degas himself was a keen photographer. Manet and the Impressionists had all been influenced to varying degrees by the new window on the world photography offered, but Degas, the scientific Realist, absorbed Muybridge's discoveries with particular relish.

In 1872 Muybridge, an Englishman working for the U.S. government, had begun to experiment with a photographic process which captured the movement of a horse in motion in order to discover whether all four hoofs left the ground simultaneously during

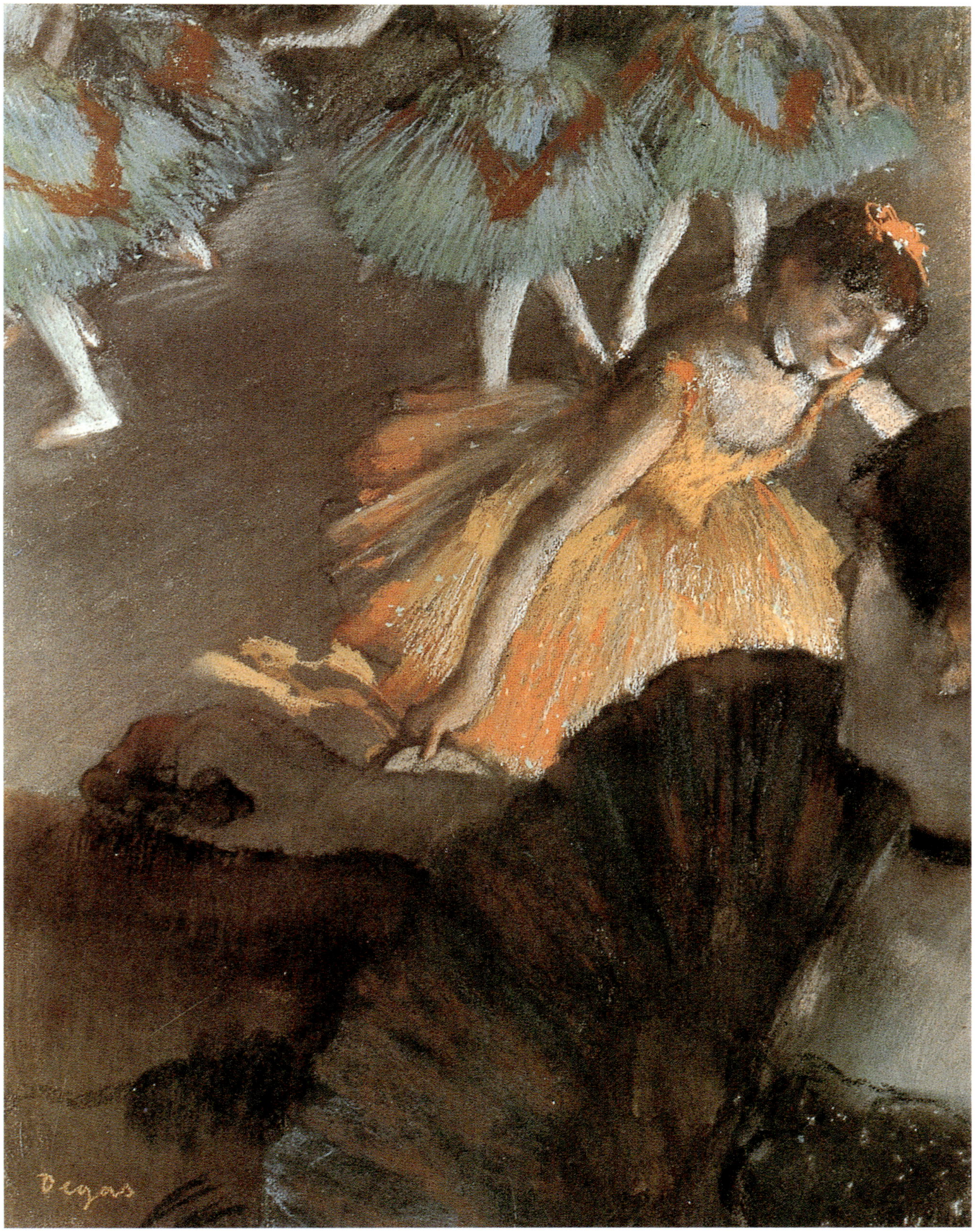

DEGAS
Ballerina and Lady with a Fan
pastel on paper
1885. 66 × 51 cm
Left This is a good example of Degas' sophisticated compositions: the woman in the foreground with her fan is in the shadow while the dancer is brightly lit. In the background, as in a framed photograph, fragmentary dancers rendered in subdued tones do not distract from the star.

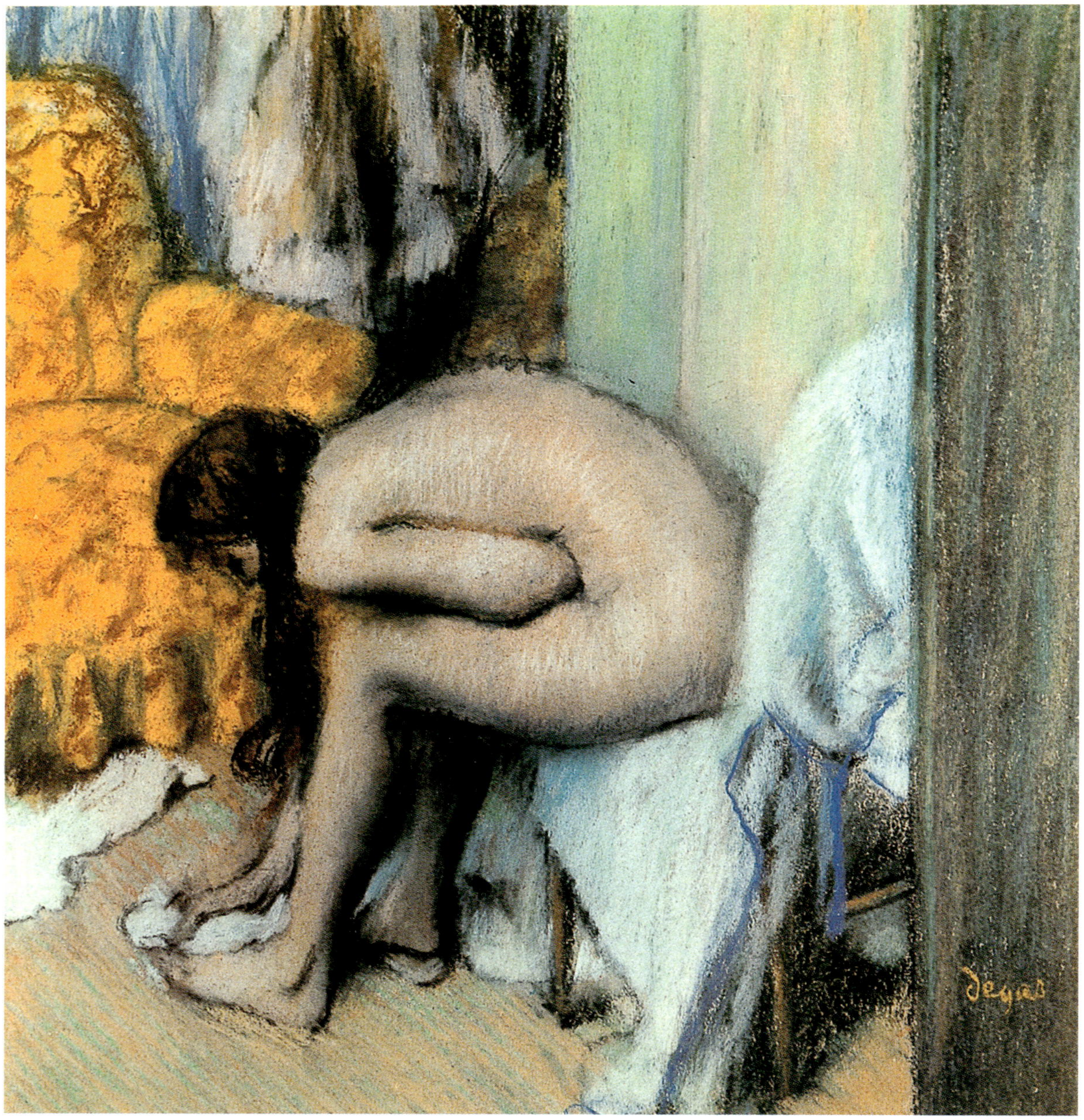

DEGAS
Woman Drying Her Foot
pastel on buff paper
c.1885–86. 54.5 × 52.5 cm
Left Degas painted numerous bathing scenes, and asked his models to adopt a great variety of poses. Of drawing, he said "Drawing is not form, it is the sensation one has of it." And: "Drawing is not what one sees but what one can make others see."

the trot, canter, and gallop. With the financial assistance of Leland Stanford, the Governor of California, Muybridge eventually succeeded, between 1877 and 1878, in using a battery of cameras and trip wires to expose frames at one thousandth of a second of a moving horse thus settling the argument once and for all. The first news of Muybridge's experiments had reached Paris as early as 1874 but until the publication of Muybridge's *Animal Locomotion* in 1887, the punctilious Degas was still drawing his horses' gait in the received manner, which is to say incorrectly. Degas set about studying and making pastel copies of Muybridge's photographs and after 1887 his horses all show the influence of the new information, including a series of wax sculptures of horses jumping and rearing.

DEGAS
Jockeys
oil on paper
c.1886–90. 26 × 36 cm
Opposite Race horses are a subject to which Degas frequently returned throughout his career. They are usually depicted just before or after the race itself, allowing for a variety of movement. Degas was an intense observer and had a well trained visual memory which enabled him to produce all these works in his studio, using notes made at the scene of the action.

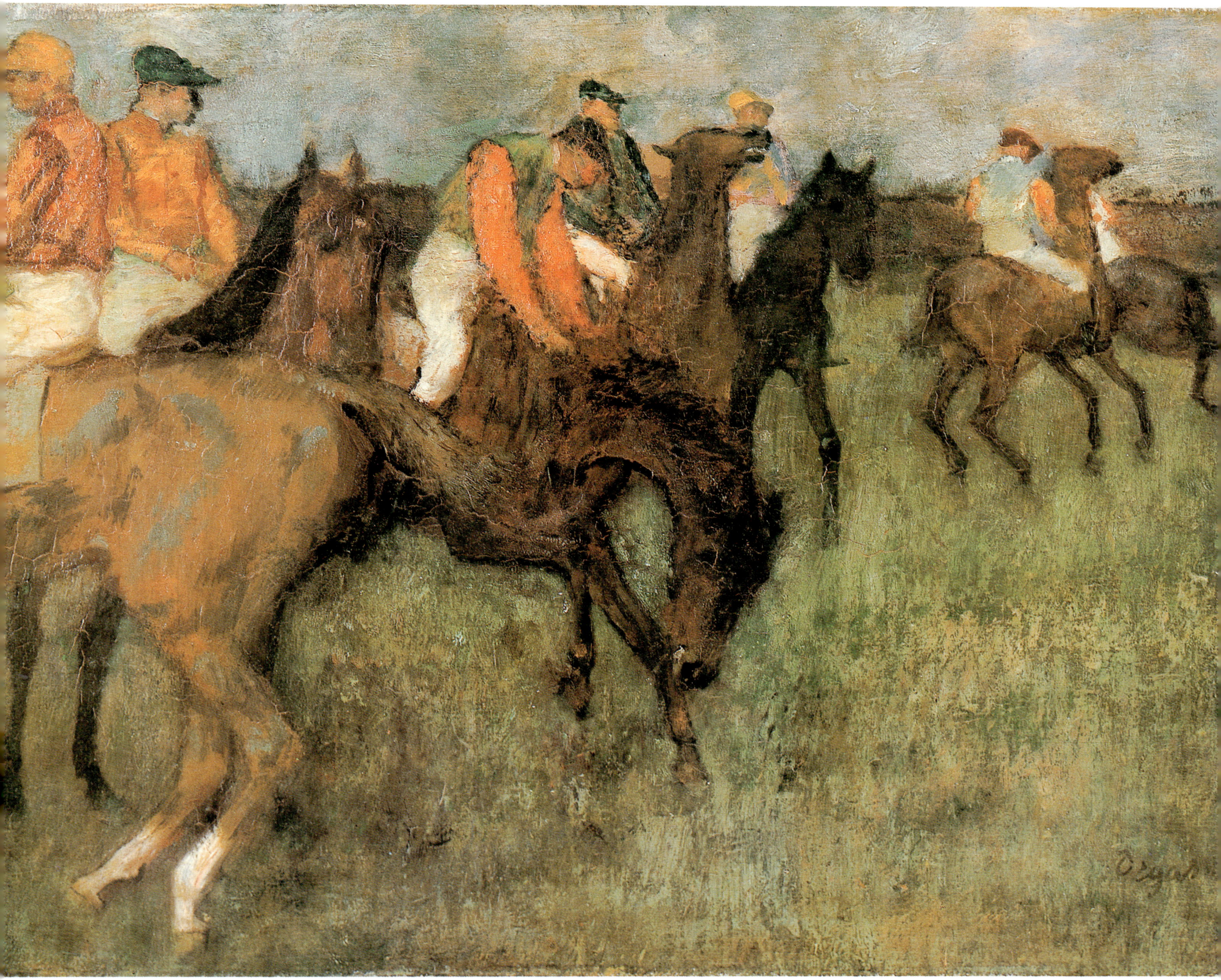

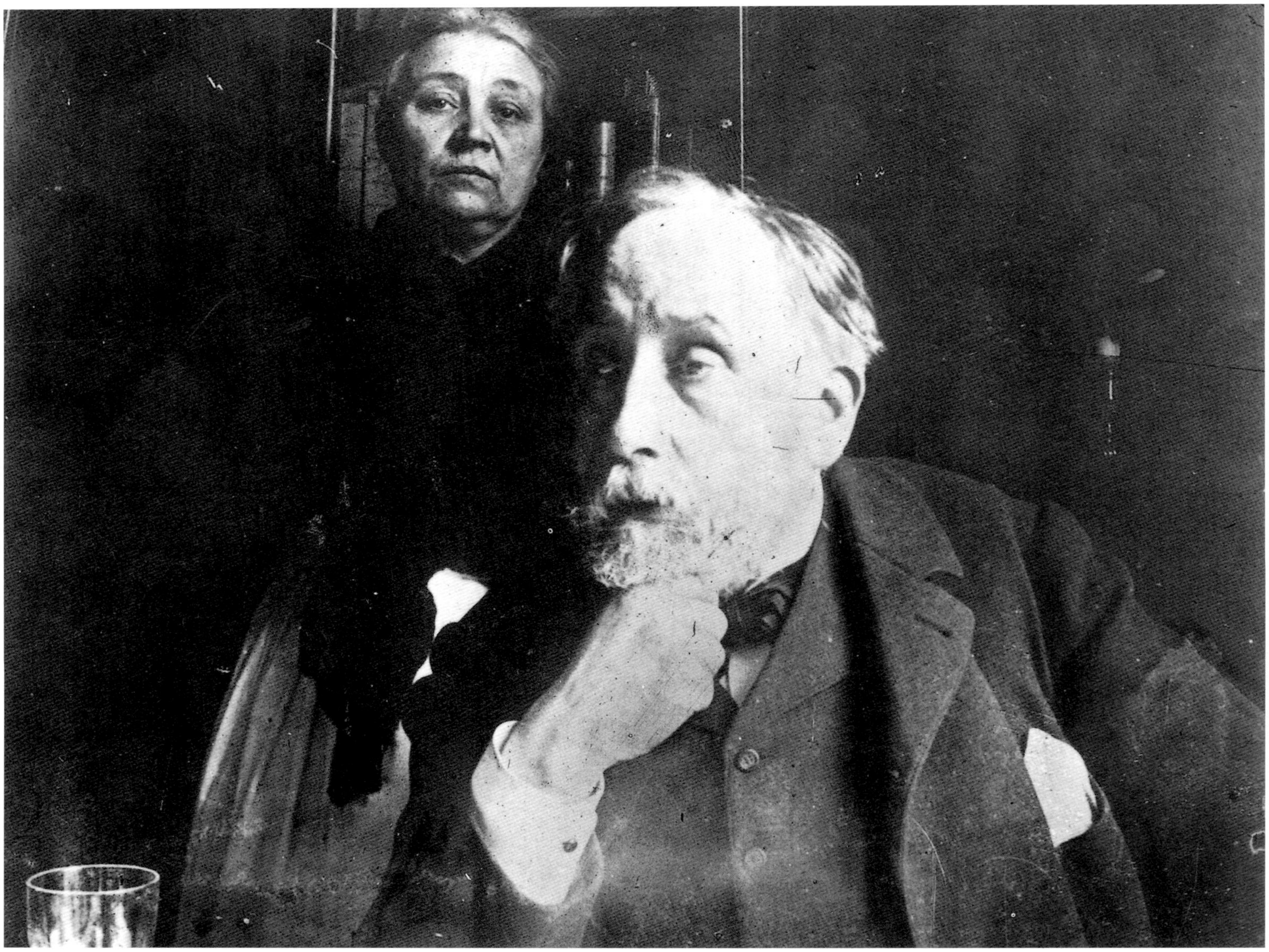

DEGAS
And His Housekeeper Zöe Closier
photographic self-portrait
1898–1900.
Degas had used photography for his work since 1865.

In his personal life Degas was a confirmed bachelor but a devoted friend to those who could conquer the barrier of prickliness he erected around himself. His relationship to the Impressionists was marked by an energetic involvement in their cause, even though he himself was uninterested in *plein-airisme* as such. Like Renoir, he was profoundly anti-Semitic and sided vociferously with the anti-Dreyfusards, even though he worked closely with Pissarro and his childhood friend, the novelist and dramatist, Ludovic Halévy. In his last years his eyesight, which had troubled him all his life, began to fail. "Since my eyesight has diminished further my twilight has become more and more lonely and more and more sombre. Only the taste for art and the desire to succeed keep me going," he wrote in the last years of the century. He kept going until his death on 27th September 1917, turning increasingly to sculpture to express himself and producing, ironically, in his last years, his most impressionistic and colourful works in pastel.

DEGAS
Three Russian Dancers
pastel on paper
c.1910. 62 × 67 cm
Degas produced a series of about seventeen Russian dancers, of which this is probably a later example. Some of the others are more colourful.

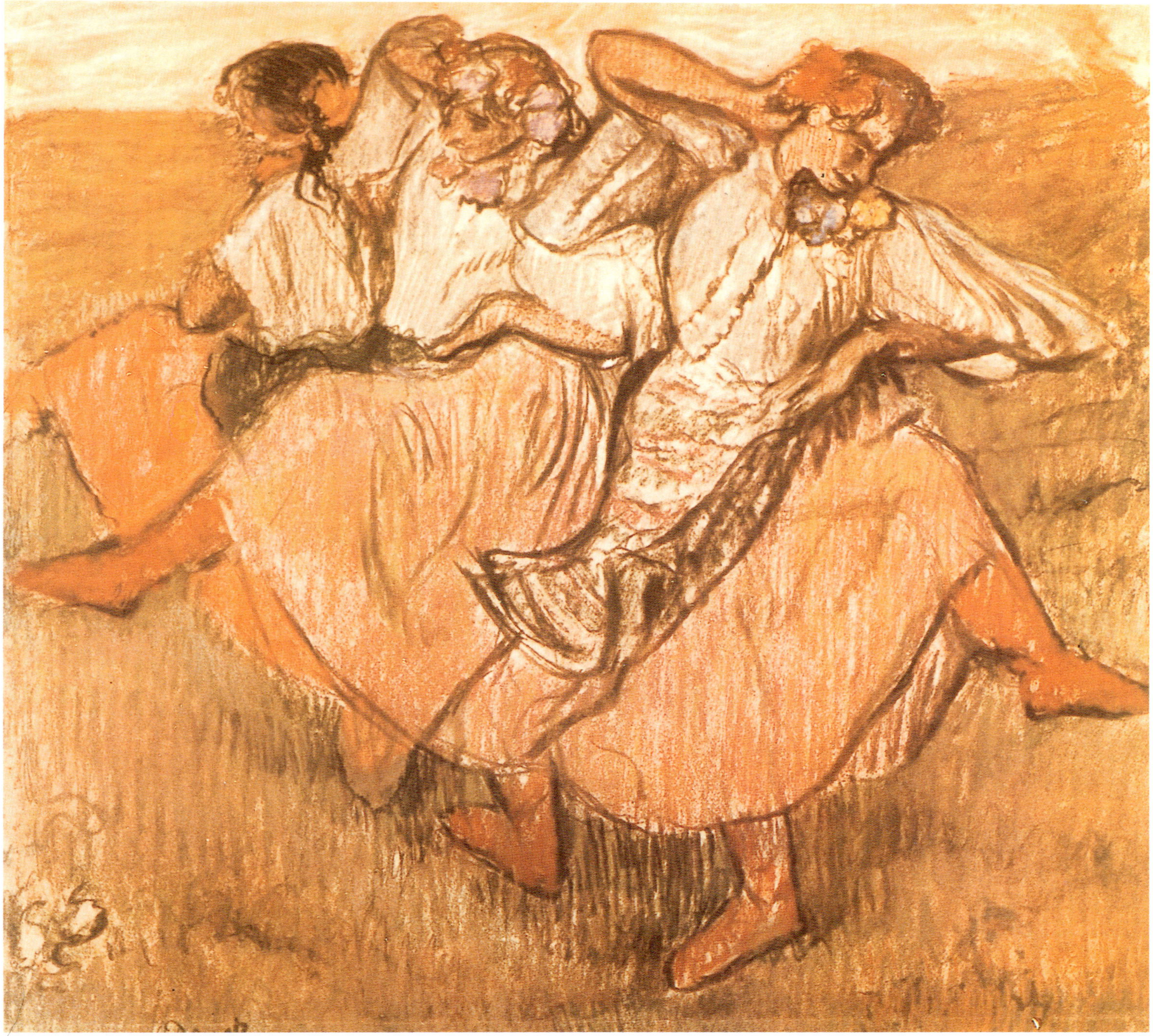

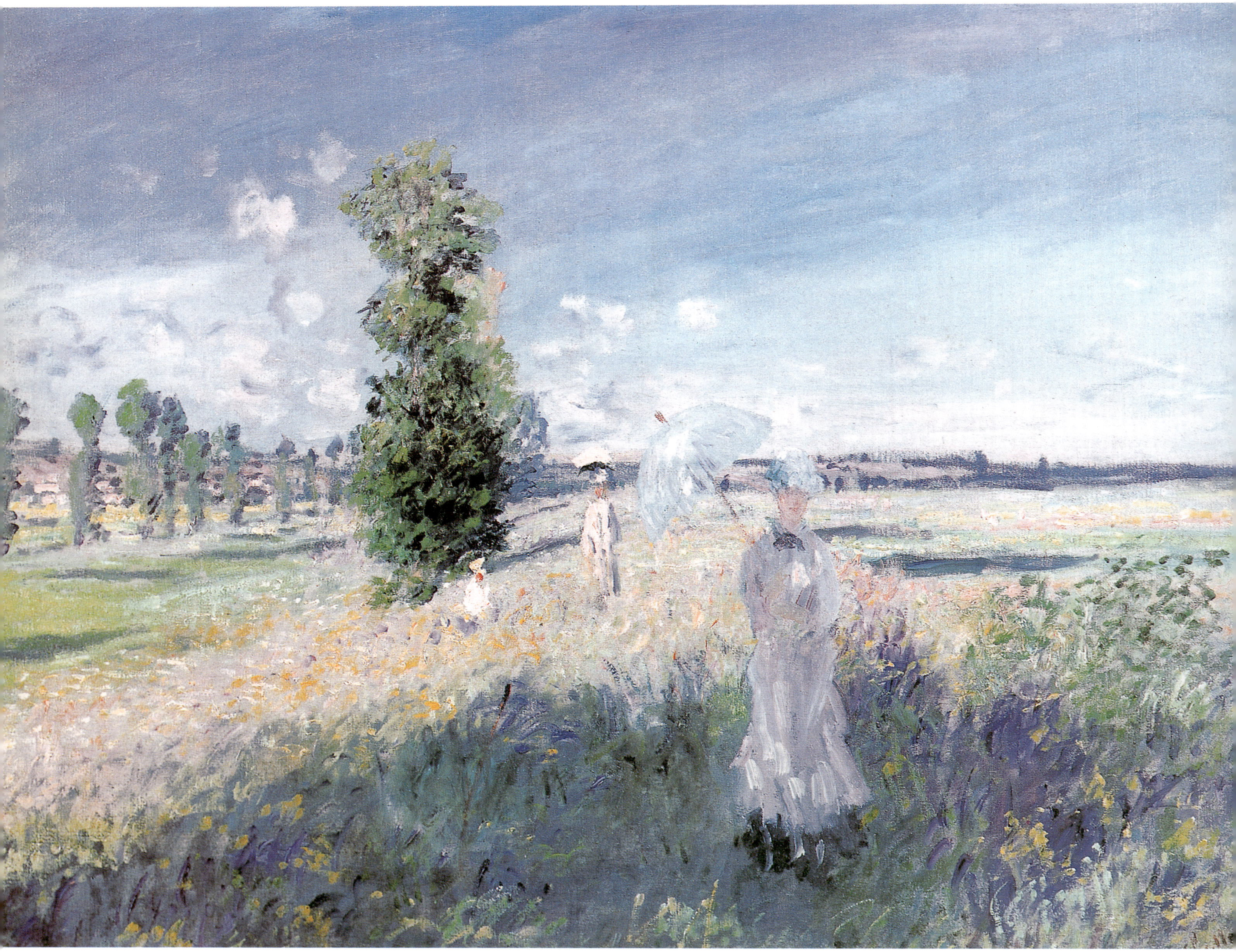

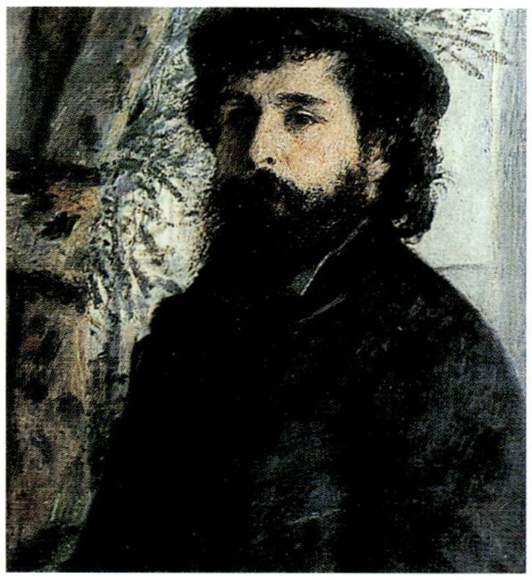

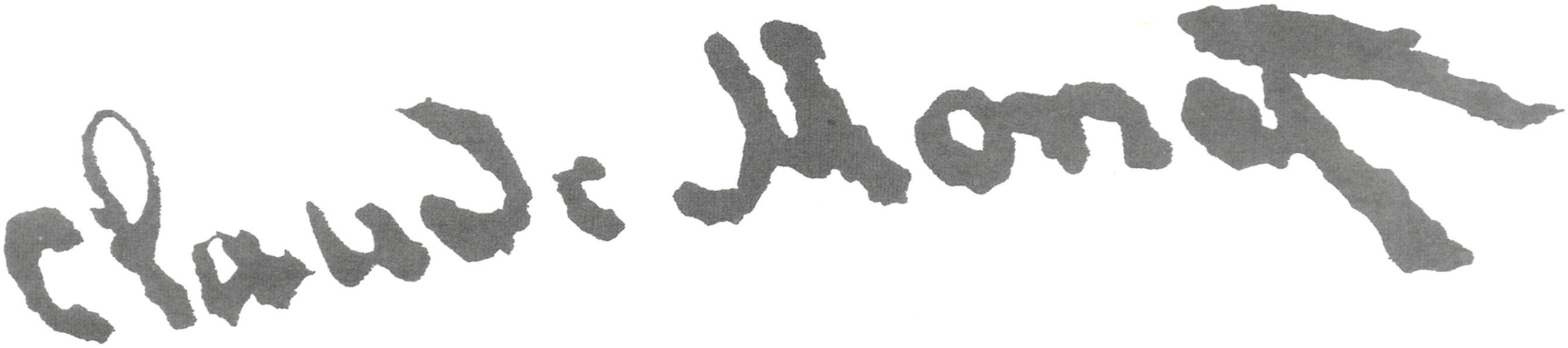

THE NAMES OF Claude Monet and Impressionism are nearly synonymous. It was, after all, one of his paintings that gave the movement its title, and he was the most consistent, the most prolific and the most uncompromising of his generation in the struggle to capture the transitory effect – the attempt to depict the totality of the motif before him. There was never enough of anything for him: enough of the right quality of light, enough money, enough time, enough appreciation. To be a friend of Monet in the early days meant a drain on one's financial and emotional resources, as the kindly Bazille discovered. However, in the last few decades of worldwide success and lionization, the once impecunious painter of "tongue-lickings" was fetching thousands of dollars for a painting of a grain-stack, and he made sure that he was not undercut, juggling dealers to get the right price.

CLAUDE MONET
By Renoir
1875
Above

MONET
Walk in the Country
oil on canvas
1875. 60 × 80 cm
Opposite

LIFE AND WORKS: CLAUDE MONET (1840–1926)

. . . the more I go on, the more I see that a lot of work has to be done in order to render what I seek: "instantaneity", above all the enveloppe, *the same light spreading everywhere, and more than ever I am disgusted by easy things that come without effort . . .*

LETTER FROM MONET TO GUSTAVE GEFFROY, 21ST JULY 1890

Claude Oscar Monet, the youngest of two sons, was born on 14th November 1840 in Paris. Five years later Adolphe Monet took his family to live in Le Hâvre, a seaport on the Normandy coast, where he joined the busy firm of wholesalers and ship's chandlers run by his relations, the Lecadres. At an early age Claude showed an aptitude for drawing and when he was old enough to attend the Collège du Hâvre he began to study under the eye of Charles Ochard who himself had studied under the great Neo-Classicist, and painter-advocate to Emperor Napoleon I, Jacques-Louis David.

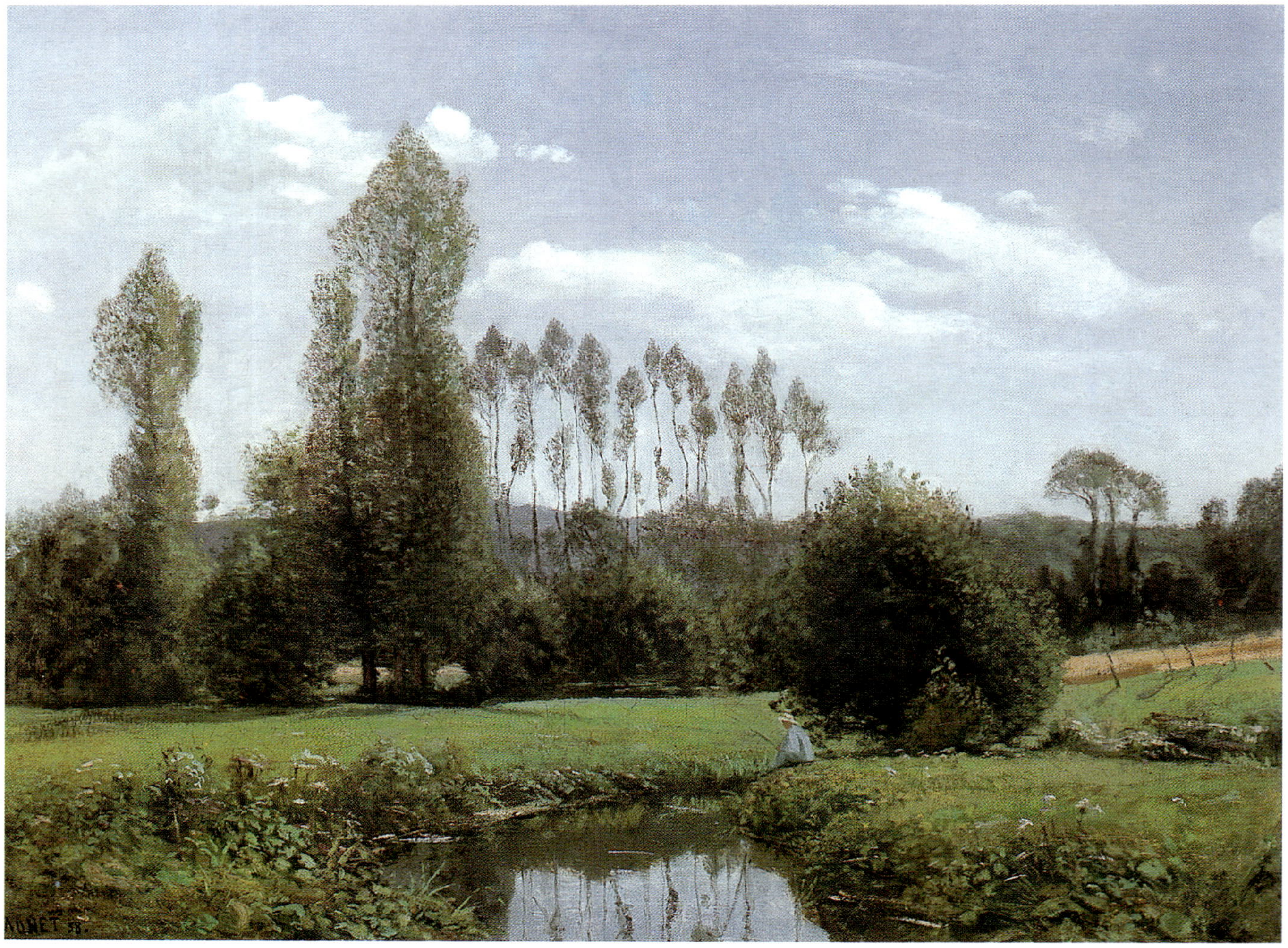

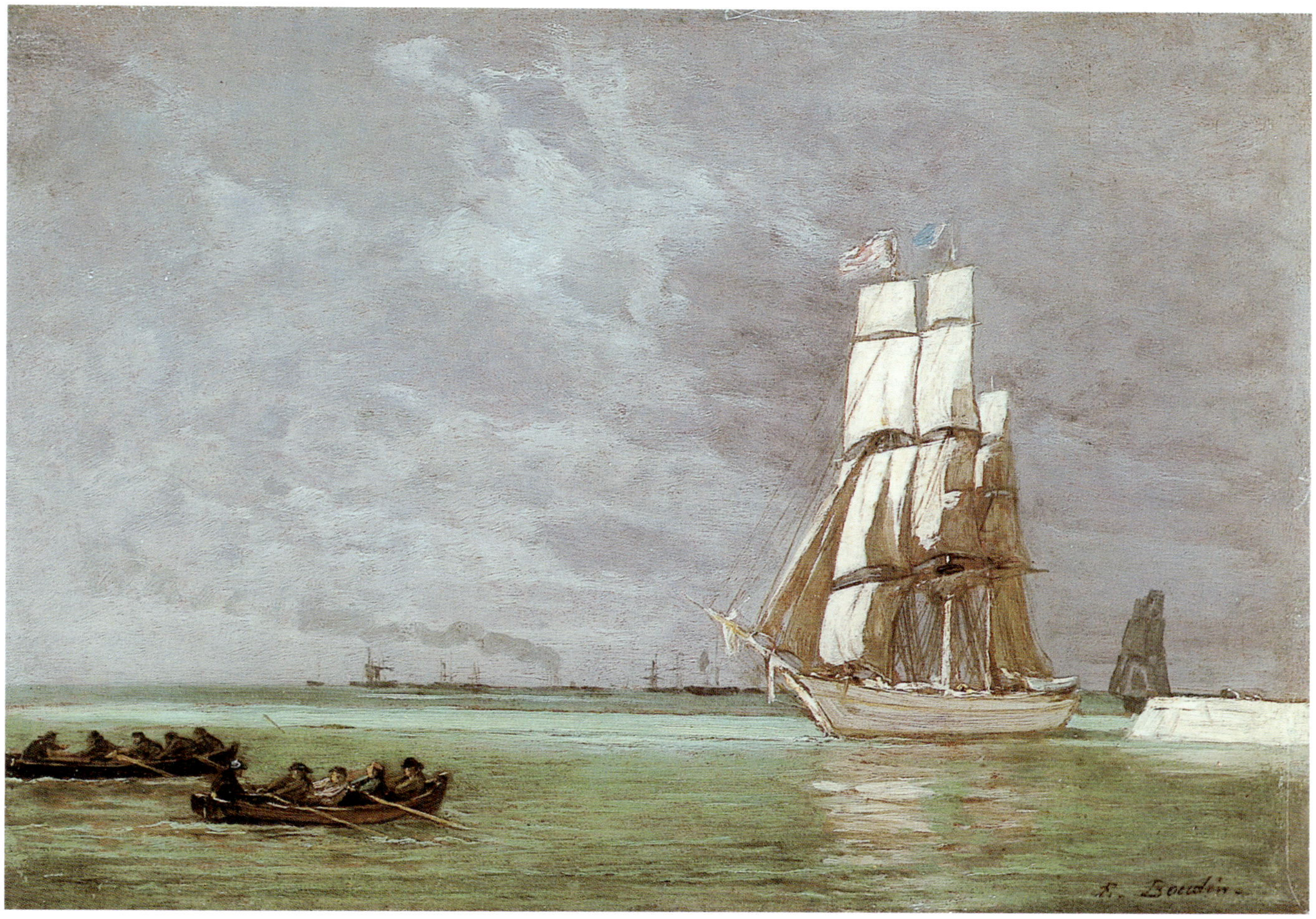

BOUDIN
Honfleur, the Port, Stormy Weather
oil on wood
c.1852–55. 26 × 37.5 cm
This painting does not have the light touch more familiar in Boudin's other work, but it has a simplicity of style and a sense of light characteristic of this artist, who rarely ventured far from the sea.

"I more or less lived the life of a vagabond," said Monet in 1900 recalling his early years. "By nature I was undisciplined; never, even as a child, would I submit to rules. It was at home that I learned the little I know. School seemed like a prison and I could never bear to stay there, even for four hours a day, especially when the sunshine beckoned and the sea was smooth." By the age of fifteen Monet was by his own account known all over Le Hâvre as a caricaturist, a pastime he had developed by drawing caricatures of his teachers "in the most irreverent fashion." However the more serious side of his talent was encouraged by his aunt, Mme Lecadre, an amateur painter who took Claude's artistic development to heart, especially after the death of his mother in 1857. Monet's devotion to art worsened his relationship with his father who wanted Claude to stay at school and take his baccalaureate. Mme Lecadre was acquainted with the painter Armand Gautier and together they persuaded the reluctant Adolphe Monet to let his son pursue a career in art. Thus the young Monet got his own way and skipped the examination, leaving school with no qualifications save an abundance of energy and an uncompromising belief in himself.

Monet's talents needed to be channelled in the right direction, however; he could not be expected to progress in the art world without formal training of some sort, although this was much against his nature. An early turning

MONET
View of Rouelles
oil on canvas
1858. 46 × 65 cm
OPPOSITE Believed to be the first of Monet's landscapes. We find in this corner of Normandy some of the themes which would later dominate Monet's work: water, poplars and a good deal of sky. Boudin had introduced him to open-air painting about two years previously.

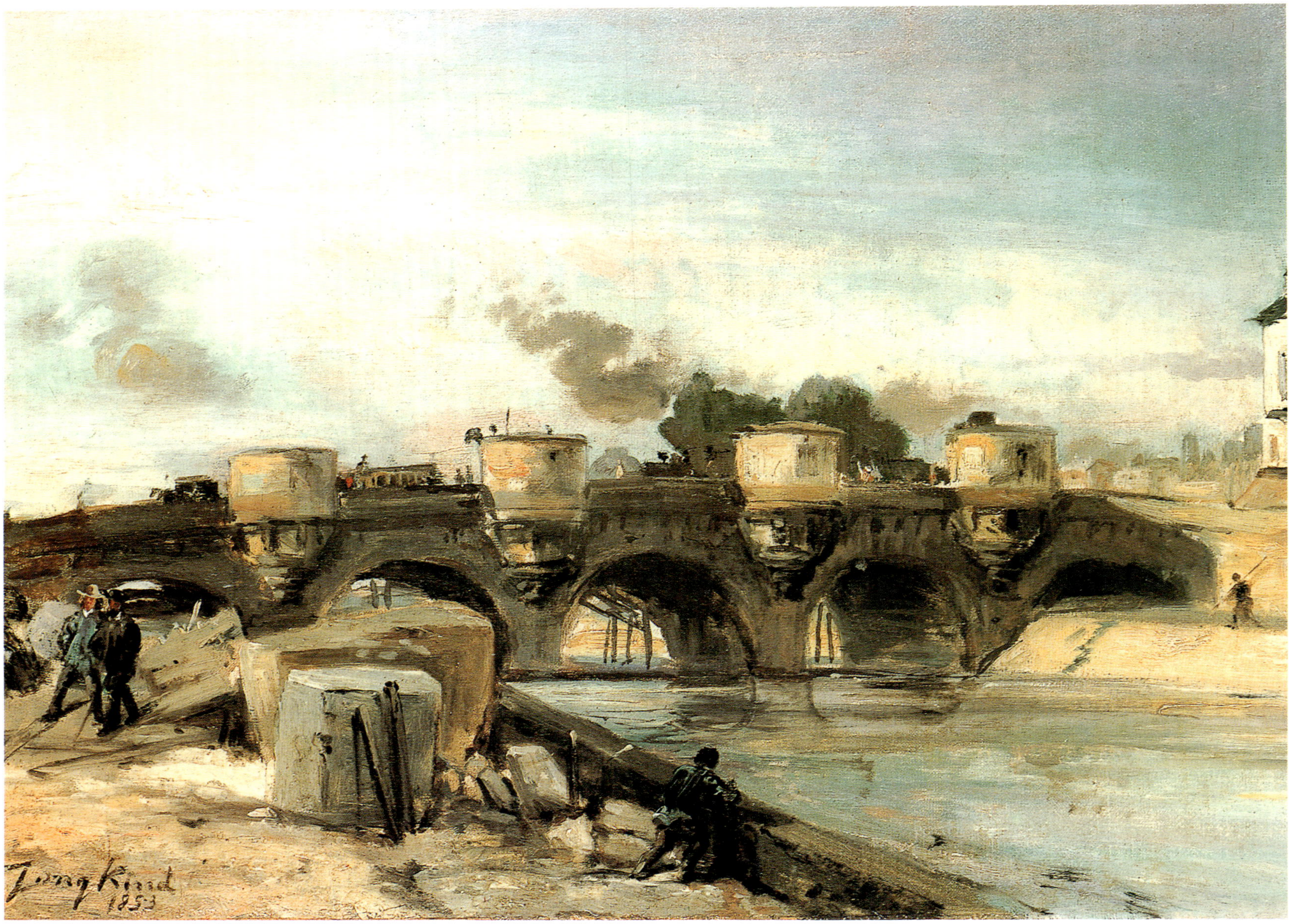

JONGKIND
Fire on the Pont Neuf, Paris
oil on canvas
1853. 27.5 × 40.7 cm
Jongkind and Boudin were Monet's real masters and the younger painter was not in the least shaken when both were rejected by the Salon.

point came when Gravier, the frame-maker, in whose shop Monet often displayed his drawings, introduced him to the local landscapist Eugène Boudin. Monet had been avoiding this meeting – he thought Boudin's landscapes were "horrible, used as I was to the false and arbitrary colour and fantastic arrangements of the painters then in vogue" – but Boudin eventually persuaded Monet to accompany him on a landscape expedition. It was a revelation: "I understood," said Monet, "I had seen what painting could be, simply by the example of this painter working with such independence at the art he loved. My destiny as a painter was decided."

Having failed to obtain a grant to study art in Paris from the municipal authorities in Le Hâvre, Monet gathered up his savings – income from the caricatures – and went to Paris in the spring of 1859 armed with letters of introduction from Boudin to several artists including Troyon and Gautier. Troyon thought Monet showed promise and advised him to enrol at Thomas Couture's atelier (where Edouard Manet had studied). Monet dismissed this idea out of hand, even though Couture was known to be one of the more enlightened masters in Paris at the time, and returned to Le Hâvre. He was back in Paris again the next winter drawing the models at the free Académie Suisse, where his first encounter with Pissarro took place.

In 1861 Monet was called up for military service (which normally lasted seven years).

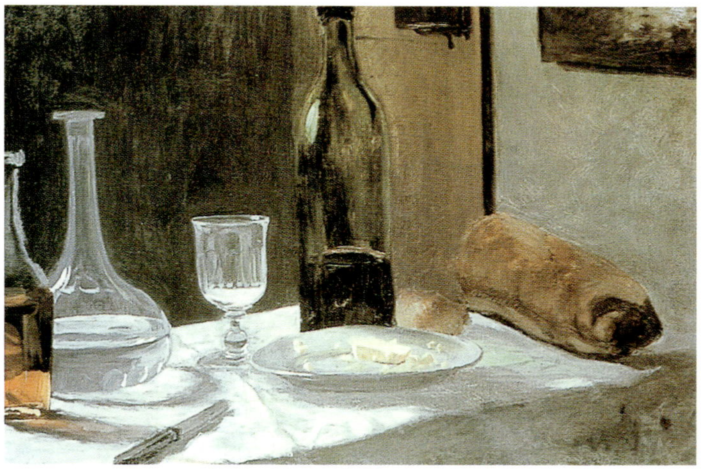

MONET
Still Life with Bottles
oil on canvas
1859. 41 × 60 cm
Still lifes and nude studies were very much part of an artist's training and Monet, who rarely depicted this kind of subject, shows that he could already produce solid if not exceptional studies. A short while later, Troyon encouraged him to practise drawing.

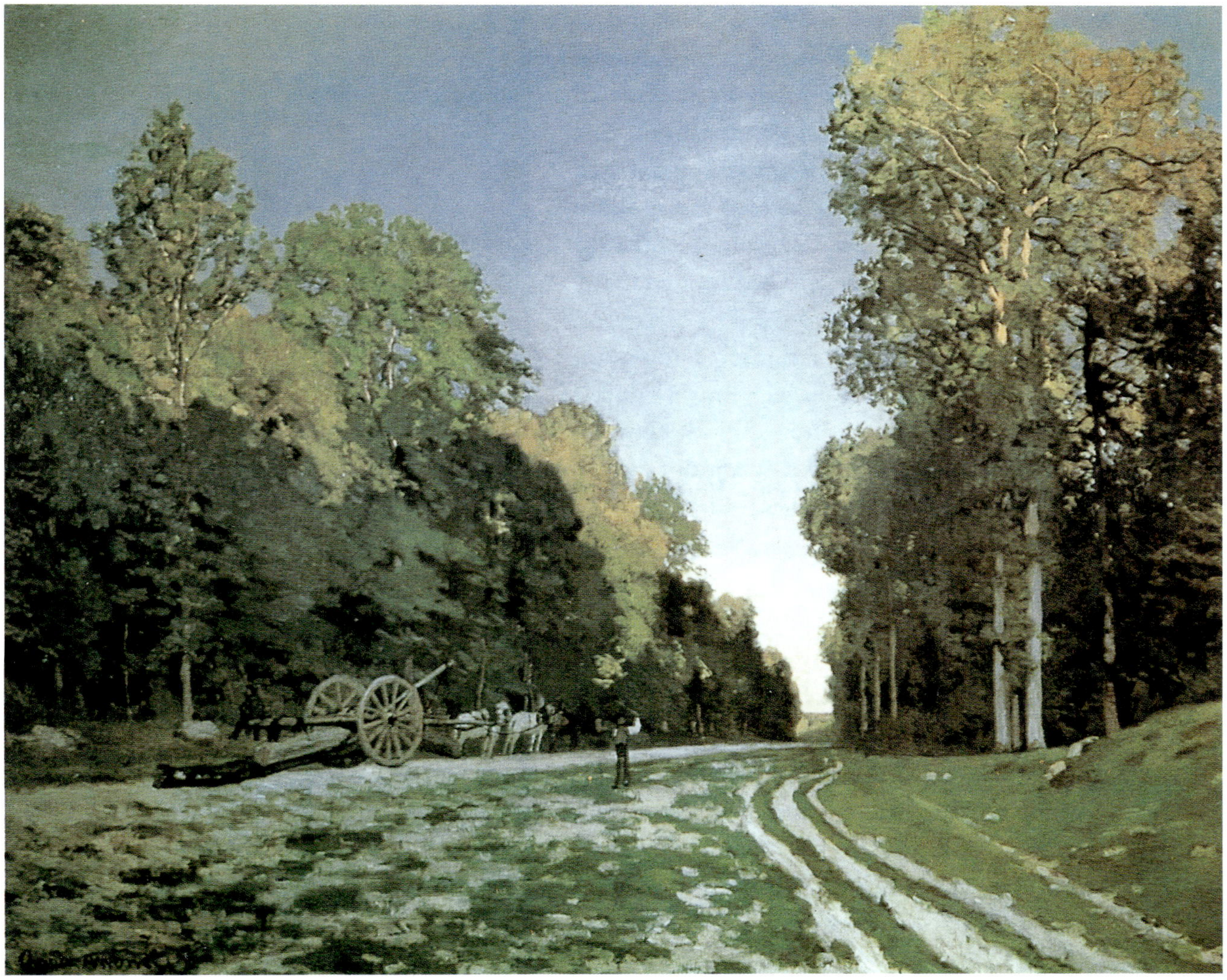

MONET
Route de Chailly, Fontainebleau
oil on canvas
1864. 98 × 129 cm
Chailly was a village near Barbizon, dear to the landscapists of the previous generation such as Corot, Courbet, and Daubigny. Monet wrote to Bazille about one of his Fontainebleau landscapes, saying that it might remind people of Corot, but insisted that it was not a deliberate attempt to copy the style of the older artist.

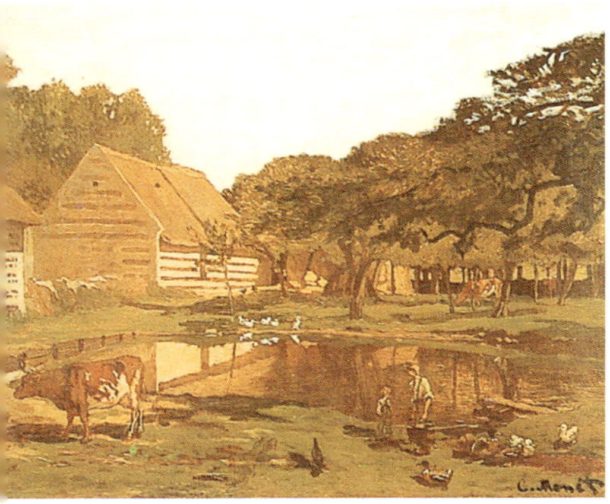

MONET
Farmyard in Normandy
oil on canvas
1864. 65 × 81.5 cm
ABOVE In the summer of 1864, Monet travelled with Bazille down the Seine to Normandy, where they rented cheap lodgings and worked on landscapes before joining Jongkind and Boudin at Honfleur.

MONET
Luncheon on the Grass
oil on canvas
1865–66 (fragments).
150 × 42 cm; 248 × 217 cm
RIGHT and OPPOSITE Spurred by Manet's recent and infamous Luncheon on the Grass, *Monet decided to paint his own version of the subject, which he did as a plainly contemporary scene, using his friends as models, including his girlfriend Camille. We see the concern of the artist for clothes, but mainly for light, which falls from behind the figures and is rendered in bold patches. Monet said later that this picture marked the beginnings of his experiment with the principle of the division of colours, working at effects of light and colour which ran counter to accepted conventions.*

Young men had to submit their names and be selected by chance. Families with the means, however, could buy their sons out of the lottery. Adolphe offered to do this if Monet would renounce art and join the family business. Instead, Monet defiantly enlisted. He joined the Chasseurs d'Afrique in the French colony of Algeria (where he was deeply impressed by the qualities of light and space), but was home within a year suffering from typhoid. It was then that he met his first "true master . . . the final education of my eye," Johan Jongkind, a Dutch land- and seascapist who was to prove a seminal influence.

Mme Lecadre, who was convinced of Monet's potential, offered to buy him out of the army and a deal was struck with Adolphe whereby Monet would go to Paris with an allowance to study art on the condition that he joined a recognized atelier and undertook formal tuition. Monet agreed and chose Charles Gleyre's atelier. Gleyre was noted for his interest in landscape and had trained many students for the Prix de Paysage Historique. He also charged only for models and equipment, not his teaching, which was an added incentive to Monet, whose father thought him irresponsible with money and was keeping him under tight financial reins.

Thus it was in 1862 that he began his studies at Gleyre's atelier and met Renoir, Bazille, and Sisley and within months was leading them off on landscape painting expeditions to the Fontainebleau Forest and the countryside around Paris. By 1863 French art was in turmoil; Edouard Manet had outraged visitors to the Salon des Refusés with his *Luncheon on the Grass* (*Déjeuner sur l'herbe*). Unknown and unnoticed Monet was forging ahead with his own programme of energetic self-improvement, having rejected Gleyre's

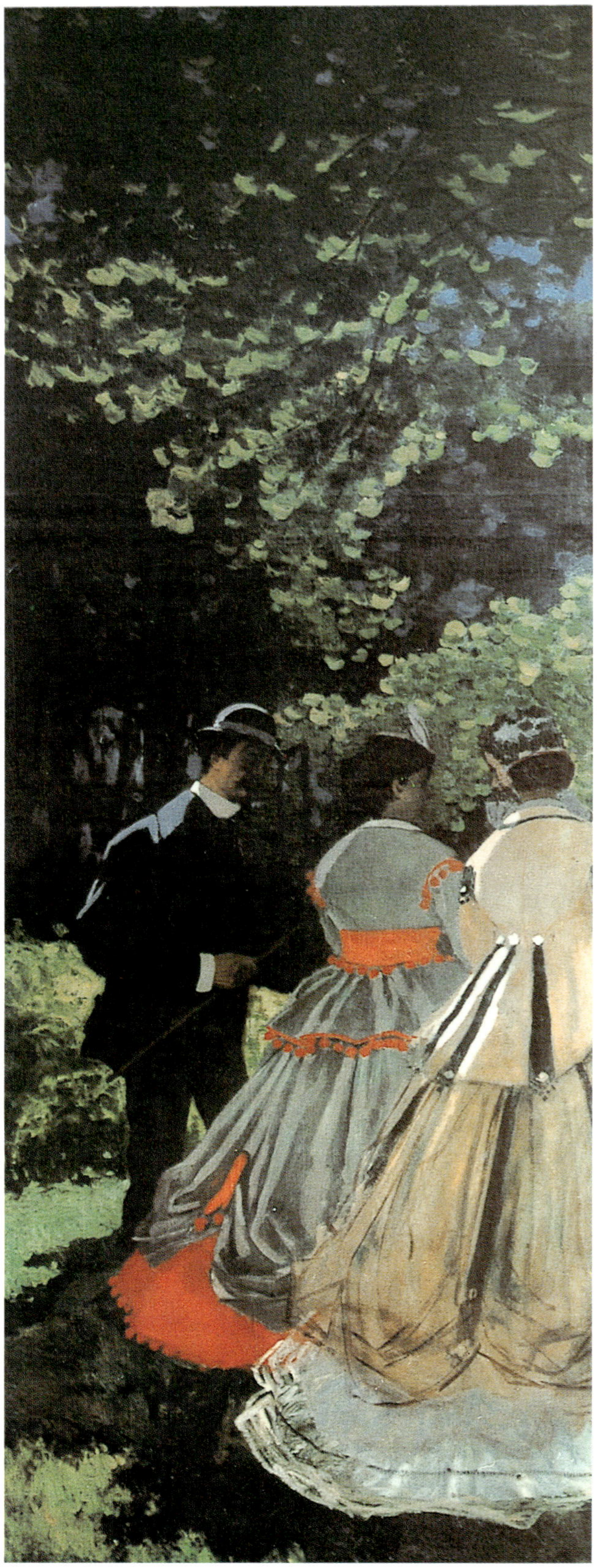

teaching. When Gleyre was forced to retire in 1864 Monet was twenty-four and at liberty to pursue his career as he saw fit, though still at the mercy of his father on whom he relied greatly for financial support. Bazille began to help out with money, companionship and by sharing a studio with him between 1865 and 1866, in the rue Furstenberg. Bazille's untimely death in the Franco-Prussian War was a grave blow to Monet.

By the Salon of 1865 Monet had enjoyed some limited success and gained a few commissions. That year the Salon accepted and exhibited two of his landscapes to a mixed reception. One critic thought him "a young Realist who promises much," another compared his work to a child's scrawl. Despite the critics, the artist's intense engagement with the effects of light and colour was clearly emerging as Monet's focus: he was still under the influence of Boudin, Jongkind, Manet, and even Courbet, although his work showed no sign of turning into overt Realism. Monet's experiments with large-scale figure paintings at this time are the beginning of the end of his interest in people as a subject for painting. His own *Luncheon on the Grass* which was never completed was to have been a major integration of light effects and figures in a total composition which would, as Forge says, "monumentalize the language of a *plein-air* sketch."

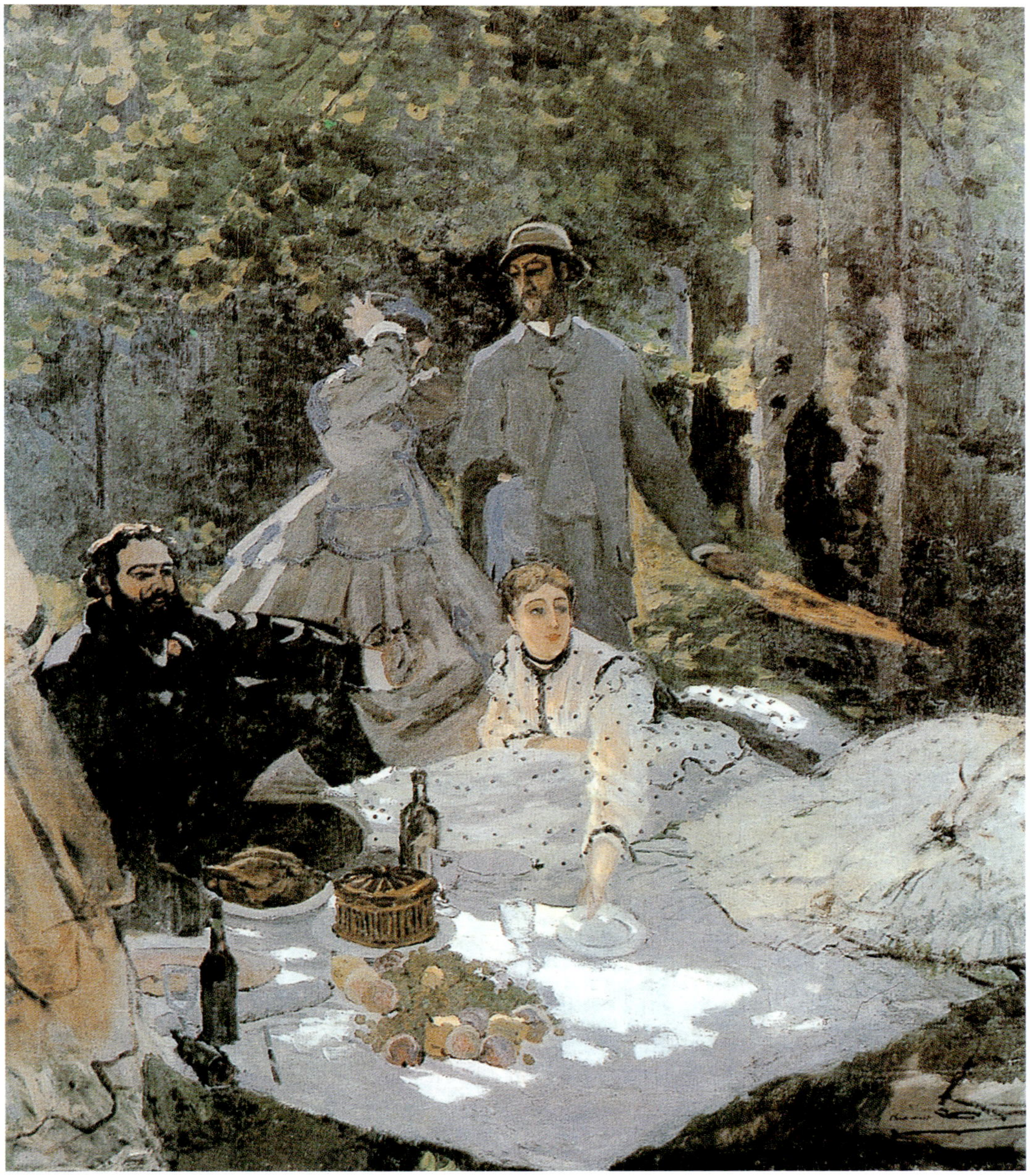

It was an audacious attempt doomed perhaps to failure. Monet had neither the time, the studio space nor the money to devote himself to its completion. In 1865 he had injured his leg and was laid up for some time, unable to work on the painting. Bazille, who had abandoned his medical studies to become a painter, made good use of his medical skills and rigged up a contraption which dripped water onto Monet's leg to ease the pain. A touching portrait by Bazille shows an irritated Monet lying in bed at the Cheval-Blanc Inn in Chailly where he had spent the summer working on the ambitious picture, impatient for Bazille to come and model. Bazille's *Monet after His Accident* (*Monet après son accident*) is also an eloquent testimony to the devotion of Bazille to his awkward friend.

Monet was in increasing trouble with his father and Aunt Lecadre. He had a girlfriend, Camille-Léonie Doncieux, who had posed for several figures in *Luncheon on the Grass* and a new large-scale picture, which was ultimately rejected by the Salon, *Women in the Garden* (*Femmes dans un jardin*). The lovers fell foul of their respective parents. In 1867, Monet was being chased by creditors, Camille was pregnant and the 800 francs Monet had made from the Salon of 1866 had long since run out. Aunt Lecadre, in league with Adolphe Monet, forced Claude to retreat to Sainte-Adresse on the Normandy coast. In his absence Monet's son, Jean, was born that July in Paris. We know from a letter Monet sent to Bazille in May 1867 that Camille herself was "ill, bedridden and penniless" and that he did not know what to do, except remind his friend he owed him fifty francs by the first of the month. Bazille had come to Monet's rescue by buying *Women in the Garden* for 2,500 francs to be paid in monthly instalments. In June he was asking Bazille for 100 or 150 francs; by August he was writing a pitiful letter to Bazille saying how much it pained him to think of his child's mother having nothing to eat. The letter ends on a desperate demand from Monet – "Really, Bazille," he says, "there are things that can't be put off until tomorrow. This is one of them and I'm waiting."

The enforced sojourn at Sainte-Adresse enabled Monet to produce several beach scenes

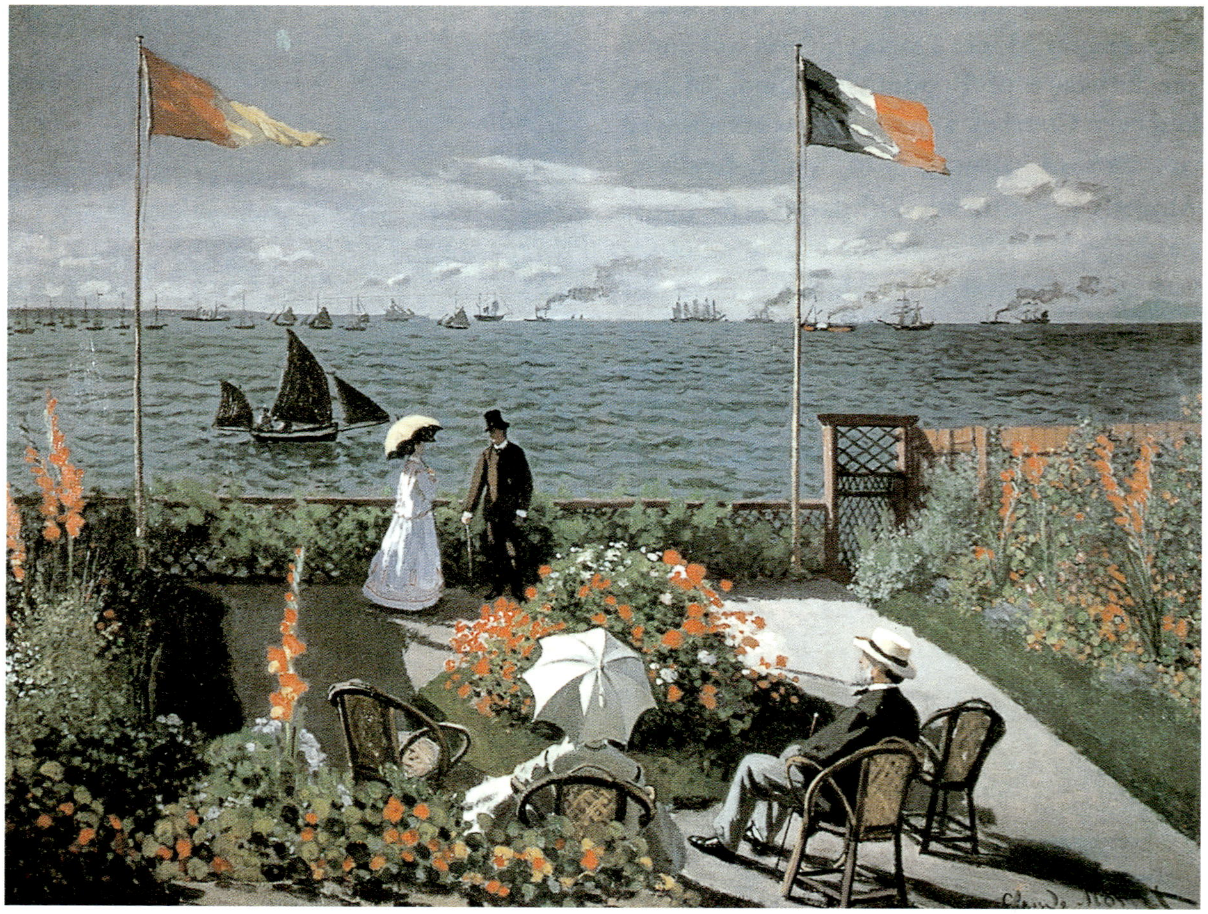

MONET
Terrace at Sainte-Adresse
oil on canvas
1866–67. 98 × 129 cm
In 1866 Monet was forced to leave Camille and go to his aunt's summer house at Sainte-Adresse, where he painted this view from a first floor window. His aunt is barely seen under her parasol and his father sits on the right. His cousin Jeanne-Marguerite stands with a friend by the trellis. Monet has left most of the sea empty to suggest depth, leaving a variety of ships to furnish the horizon.

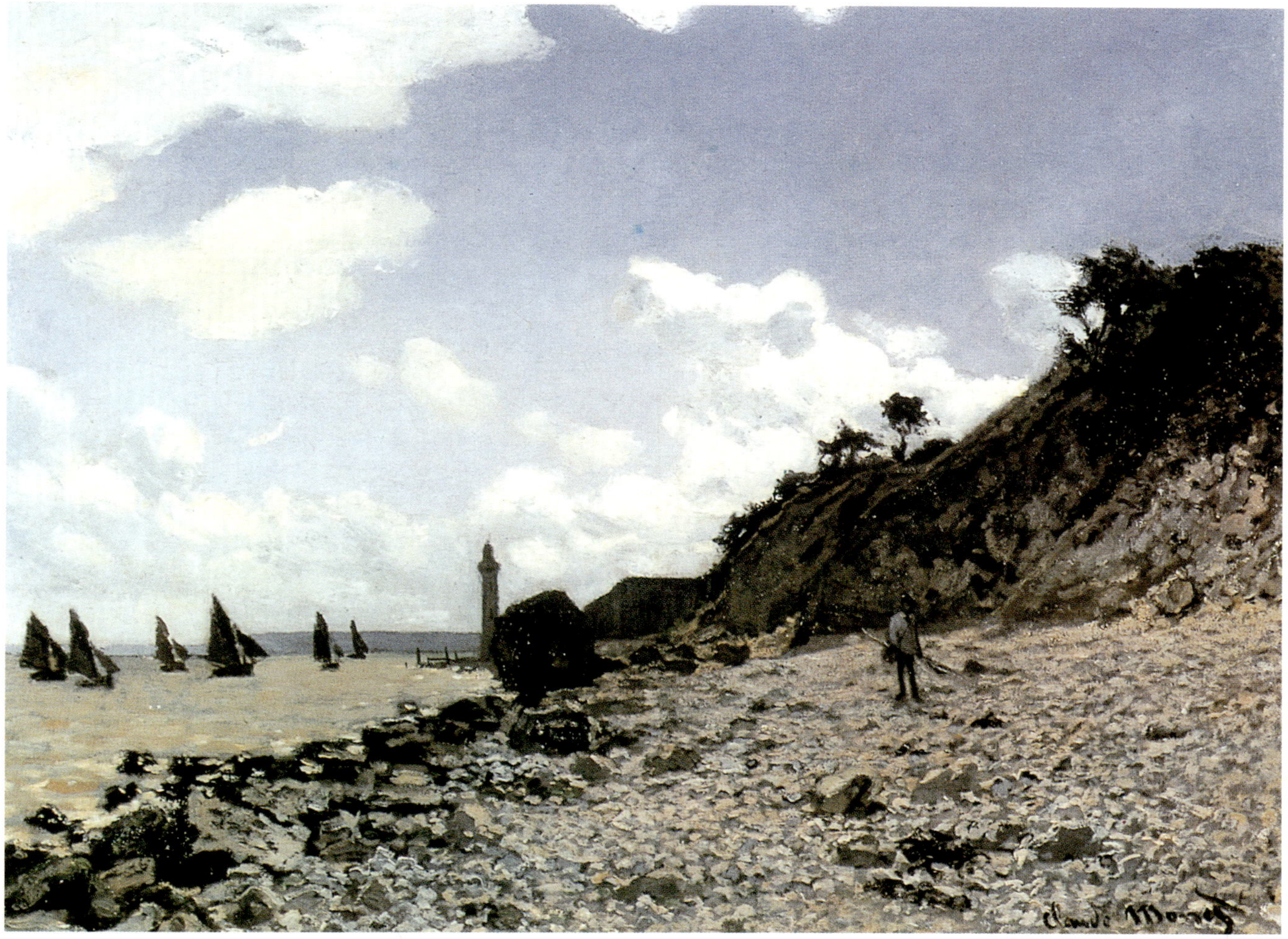

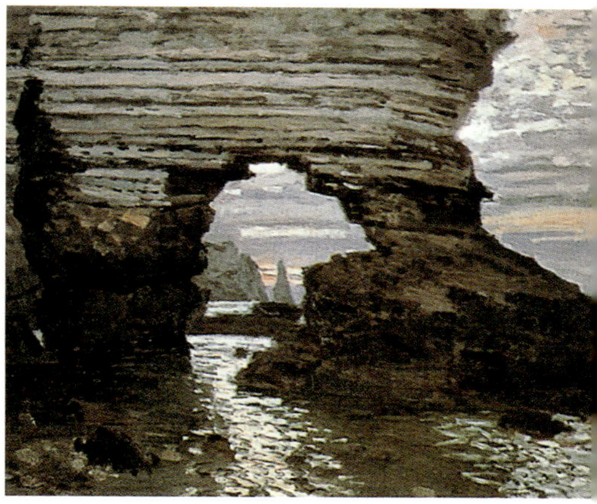

MONET
Cliffs at Etretat
oil on canvas
c.1868. 81 × 100 cm
ABOVE Etretat is further down the coast and was to become one of Monet's favourite subjects. He painted this particular stretch of cliff, called the Needle, many times. In this early example, Monet parallels the strata of the stone with those of the sky.

MONET
Beach at Honfleur
oil on canvas
c.1867. 60 × 81 cm
LEFT Monet took full advantage of this summer to travel down the coast painting a series of beach scenes in which one of his main preoccupations was the variable aspect of the light on the sea and in the sky. It is now impossible to mistake his work for that of Boudin, Jongkind or any other painter.

which showed an increasing maturity of vision. Sadly the whole episode contributed to more disaster. In the autumn Monet was suffering from eye-strain caused by the brilliant sunlight at Sainte-Adresse and was obliged to stop painting during that season. The next year, despite selling a full-length (and very sober) portrait of Camille called *Woman in the Green Dress* (*Femme en vert*) to the editor of *L'Artiste*, Arsène Houssaye, as well as a commission for a portrait of Mme Gaudibert, the wife of a Le Hâvre notable, Monet had his paintings seized by creditors at an exhibition in Le Hâvre. The strain on his relationship with Camille, who had a new baby to look after, must have been severe. The bad times rapidly alternated with the good. In June 1868 Monet, Camille, and Jean had been thrown out of a country inn; Monet had attempted suicide and said so to Bazille in a letter. Whether the hardy Normand was capable of suicide is obscure – his liberal use of bathos in all his begging letters to Bazille is obvious. By December Monet was ecstatic; he wrote to Bazille from Etretat on the Normandy coast where he and his family were installed in a little cottage thanks to the patronage of M. Gaudibert, saying how happy he was surrounded by his family and able to work in peace. He adds with reference to his

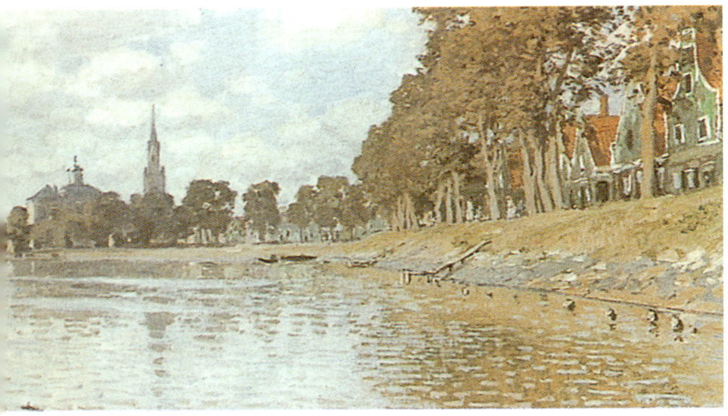

MONET
Zaandam
oil on canvas
1871. 40 × 72 cm
ABOVE Leaving London, Monet went to The Netherlands, where he painted a series of landscapes in Zaandam and other sites. Holland was a natural choice for an artist so fond of water.

work: "The further I get the more I realize that no one ever dares give frank expression to what they feel."

In the summer of 1869 this is exactly what Monet began to do in earnest when, working in the company of Renoir at La Grenouillère on the Seine, he produced what are the first truly Impressionist paintings. Monet called them "rotten sketches" but signed them nonetheless. They were indeed sketches for a finished work which is now lost (but survives in a rather indistinct photograph) and which appears to show the existing Grenouillère pictures are not dissimilar to the completed version. At this point in the history of Impressionism in general, the distinction between sketch and completion was beginning to lose its importance. Monet was now using paint with increasing confidence in swift, bold brushstrokes, painting wet-in-wet in places to create fluid and subtle mixtures of colour. This technique was developed in the work produced the next summer in Trouville on the Normandy coast, and reached new heights during his exile in London of 1870–71 and his subsequent trip to Holland.

Monet had just married Camille when he had to flee to London to avoid being called up to fight the Prussians. Although his time in London was fraught with difficulties – "I endured much poverty," he recalled in 1900 – it meant he was in the company of Pissarro,

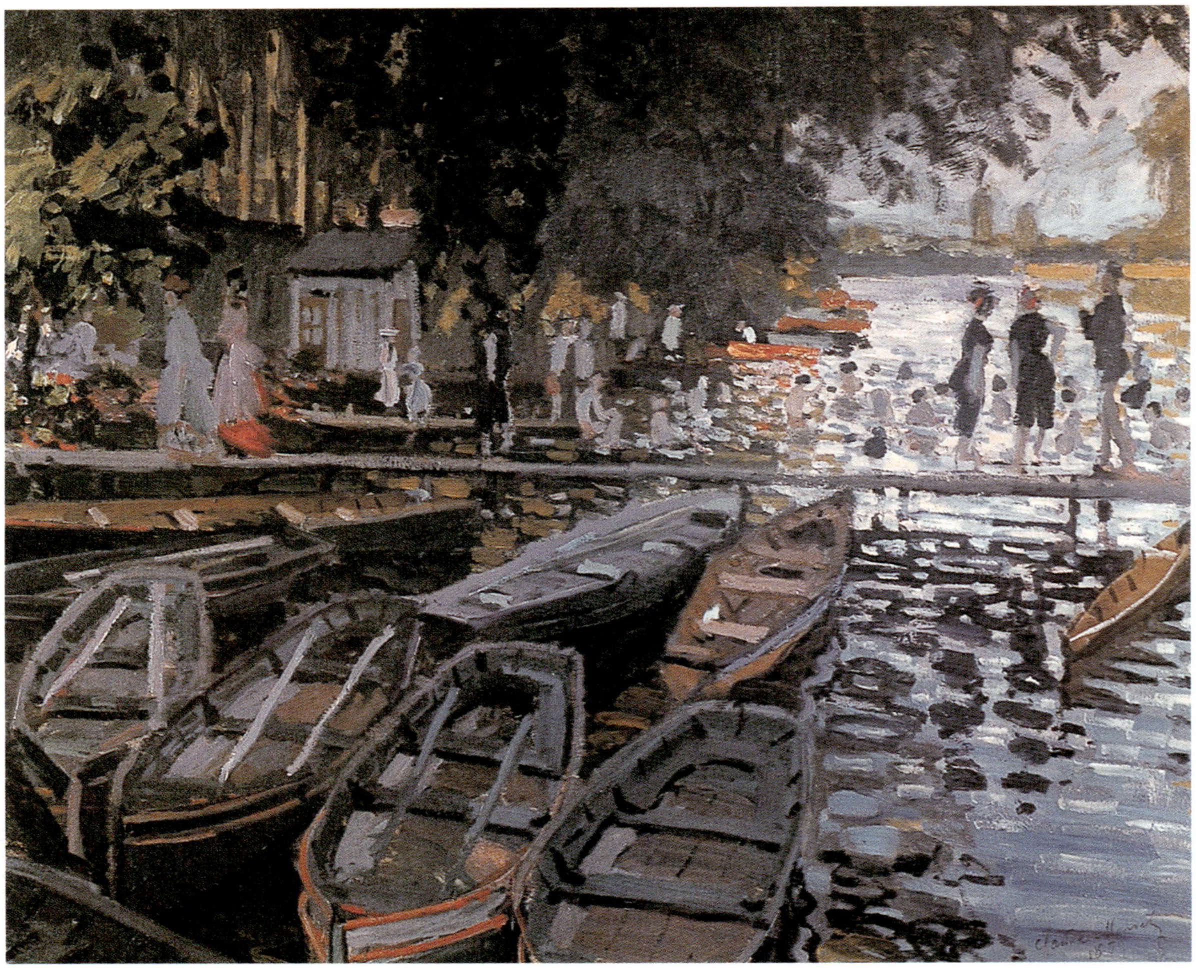

MONET
Bathers at La Grenouillère
oil on canvas
1869. 73 × 92 cm
RIGHT La Grenouillère was so popular that even the Imperial couple once stopped to visit it. Set on a small island on the Seine, it consisted of two barges moored under trees and roofed with awnings. Gangplanks linked the barges to a tiny artificial islet nicknamed the "camembert". The series of paintings of La Grenouillère marks a turning point in Impressionism, although Monet thought that he had only produced "rotten sketches".

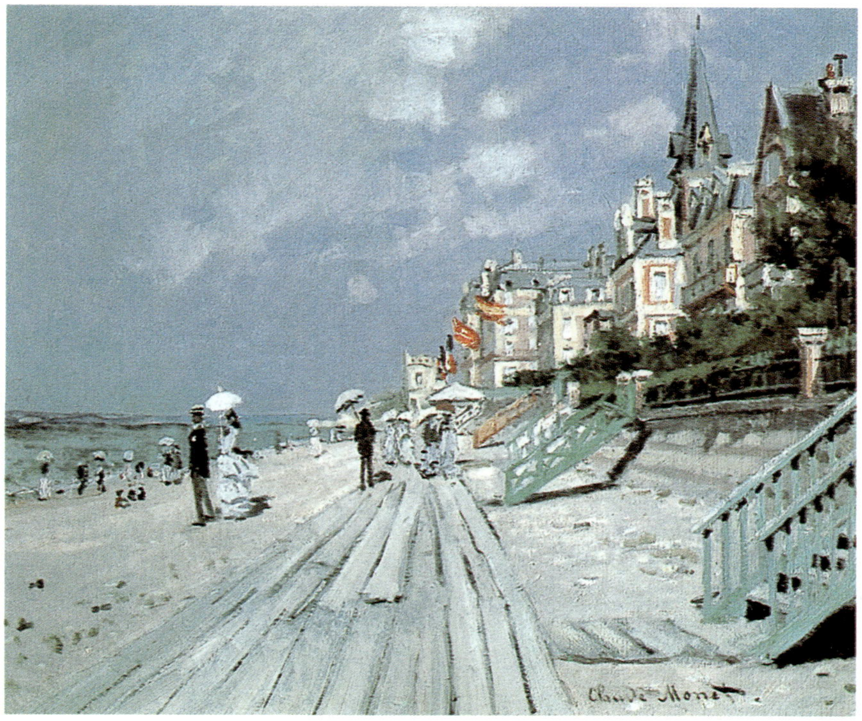

MONET
Beach at Trouville
oil on canvas
1870. 52 × 59 cm
LEFT The Hôtel des Roches Noires was one subject which he treated several times. As the railway had made the Normandy coast easy to reach, elegant vacationers needed hotels such as this one, which had 150 rooms as well as entertainment rooms. The Monets were not, however, in this financial league and they stayed in a modest hotel in a back street.

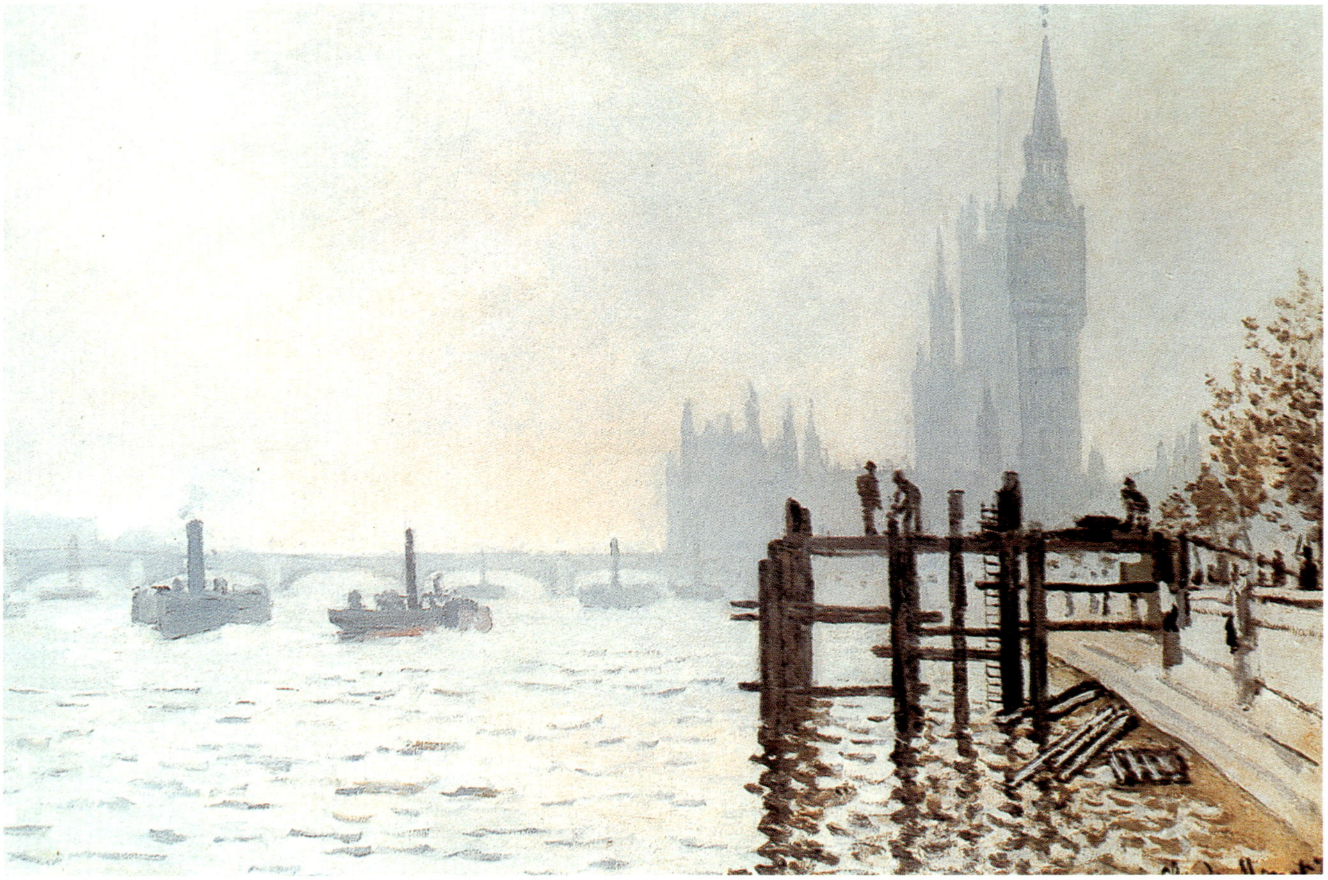

MONET
The Thames below Westminster
oil on canvas
1871. 47 × 72.5 cm
LEFT During the war Pissarro busied himself in the area south of the Thames where his mother lived. Monet stayed in town, painting views of the parks but mainly the Thames, to which he often returned in later years, especially in the winter. He was fascinated by the effect of light and fog unique to London and said that London would be ugly without it. While he was there, he tried to exhibit at the annual show of the Royal Academy, but was rejected.

Daubigny, and the dealer Paul Durand-Ruel, all exiles from the war. The all-important business relationship he struck up there with Durand-Ruel was to last the rest of his life despite many ups and downs. London itself – its mercurial climate, prodigious mists and fog, its river, parks and buildings – provided a new set of atmospheric problems for Monet to solve. He was to rediscover the vagaries of English weather to his delight and horror when he returned to London over thirty years later.

In 1871, after the war and the Commune, Monet returned to France and set up home with his family in Argenteuil on the Seine near Paris. There they remained in occasionally frugal stability for seven years. Settled in the

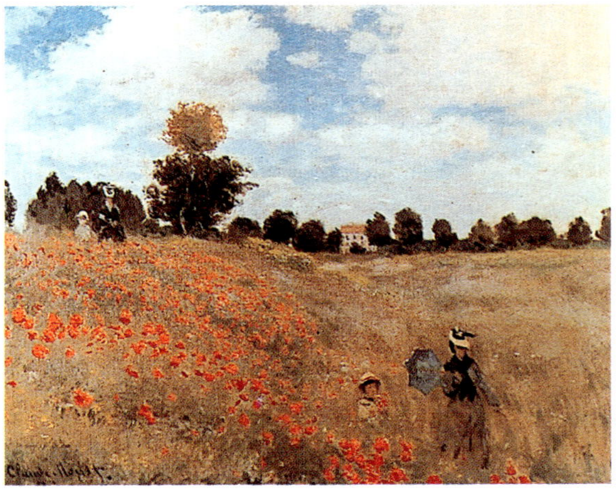

MONET
Poppy Field
oil on canvas
1873. 50 × 65 cm
RIGHT ABOVE This is almost certainly Camille and Jean walking in the tall grass of a field not far away from their home. Argenteuil and the surrounding localities were undergoing dramatic changes since the railway made them so accessible from Paris. This is the archetypal Impressionist painting – atmospheric, sketchy, lively, and full of light.

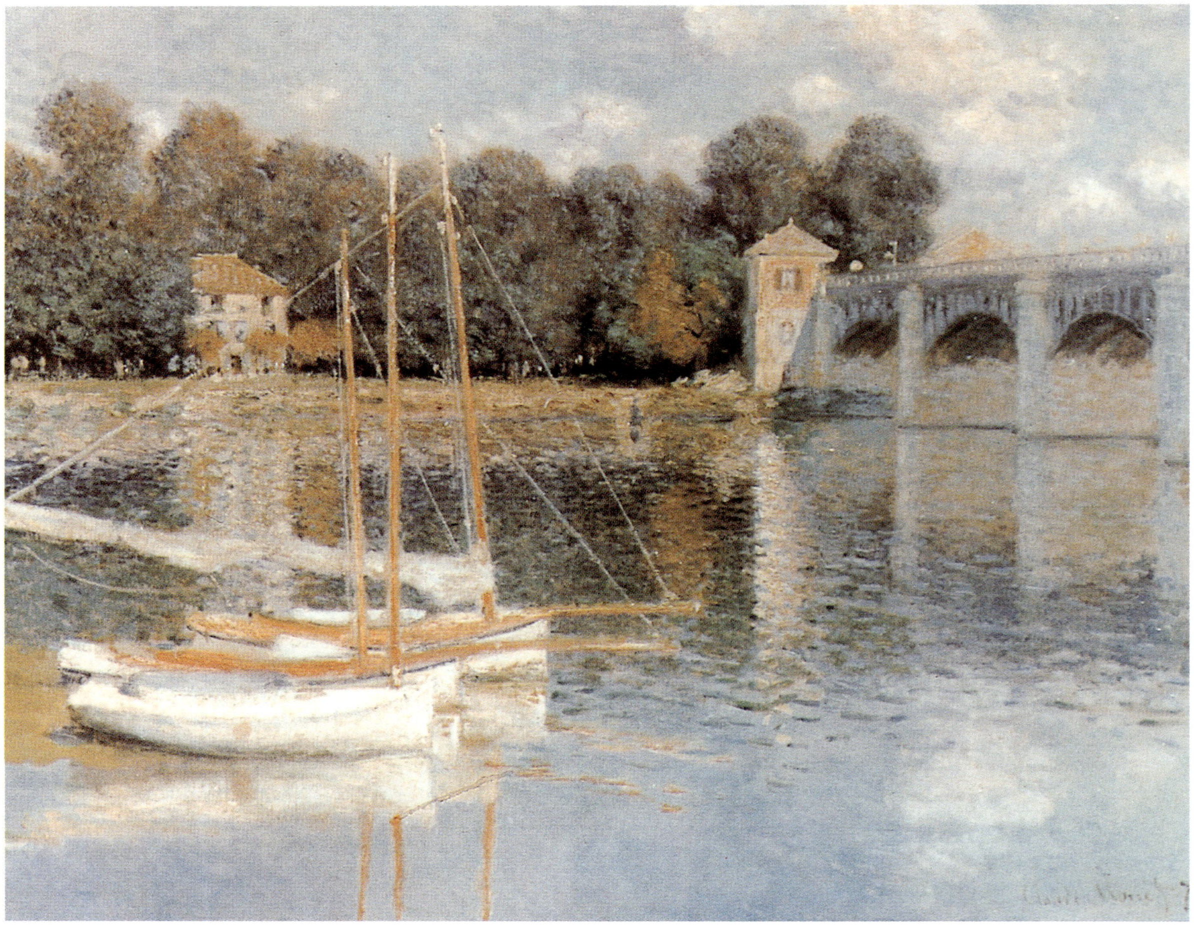

MONET
The Bridge at Argenteuil
oil on canvas
1874. 60 × 81 cm
RIGHT Argenteuil had much to offer a painter like Monet: open country, a garden full of flowers, the Seine with its pleasure boats. The new bridge, rebuilt after the war, and the train, were modern elements which interested the Impressionists, in contrast to the Barbizon landscapists of the previous generation.

MONET
Train in the Snow
oil on canvas
1875.
OPPOSITE BELOW Monet's house was opposite the station at Argenteuil, and he pictured it several times. This is one of many snow scenes, a subject he never tired of depicting, even if he had to endure the most appalling conditions.

growing but as yet rural town of Argenteuil, but near enough to Paris to make possible frequent trips there on the railway, Monet could now concentrate on transferring to the canvas the *enveloppe* which his unique vision disclosed. The subjects that now fell within his view ranged from Argenteuil and Paris streets, to the river and the railway, as well as his house and the surrounding countryside. Working out of doors whenever possible, Monet began the system which was to serve him until his death of having several canvases on the go at once, always ready to capture some fleeting atmospheric effect. He began to

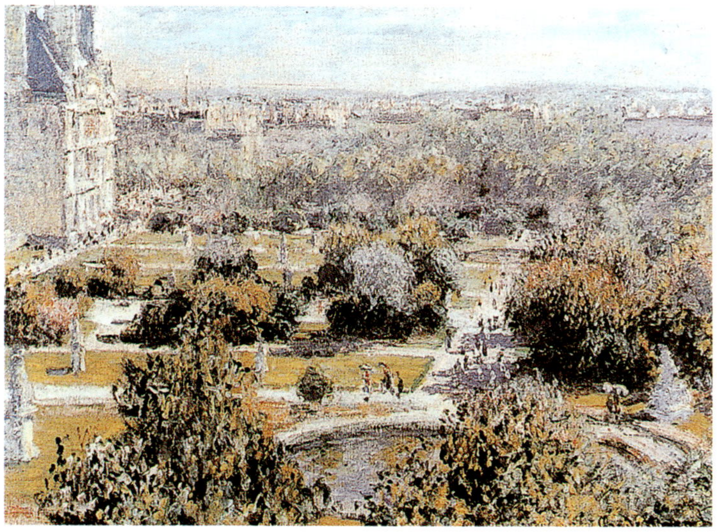

MONET
The Tuileries Gardens
oil on canvas
c.1876. 53 × 72 cm
LEFT The arrangement of the Tuileries gardens, which had been burnt down during the Commune, had been much altered, and Monet, "borrowing" a window from his friend the collector Victor Chocquet, was able to paint four pictures showing the ponds and the symmetrical design. Pictures of new Parisian vistas were likely to sell, a consideration Monet could not ignore, but they also provided a diversion from country and garden scenes.

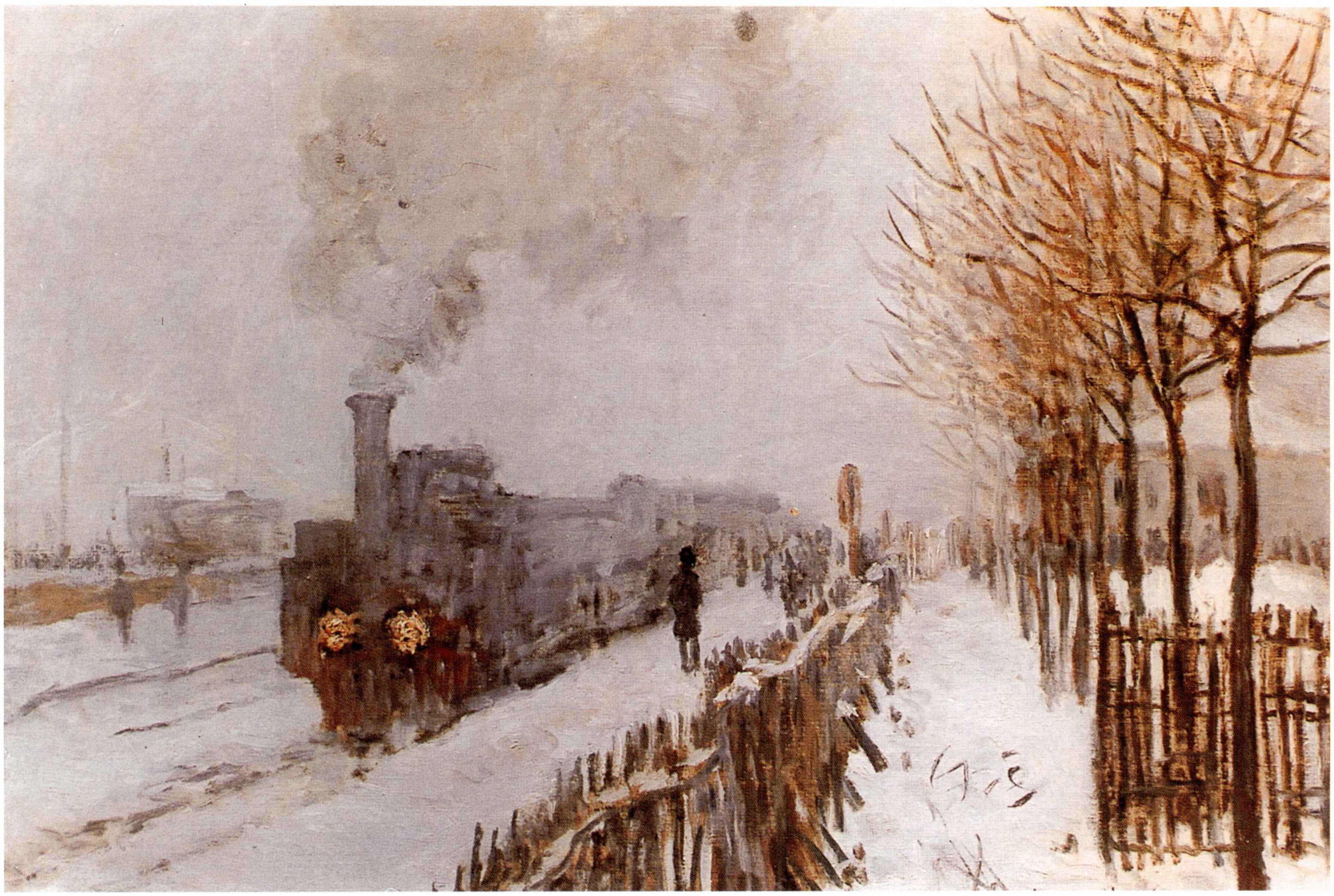

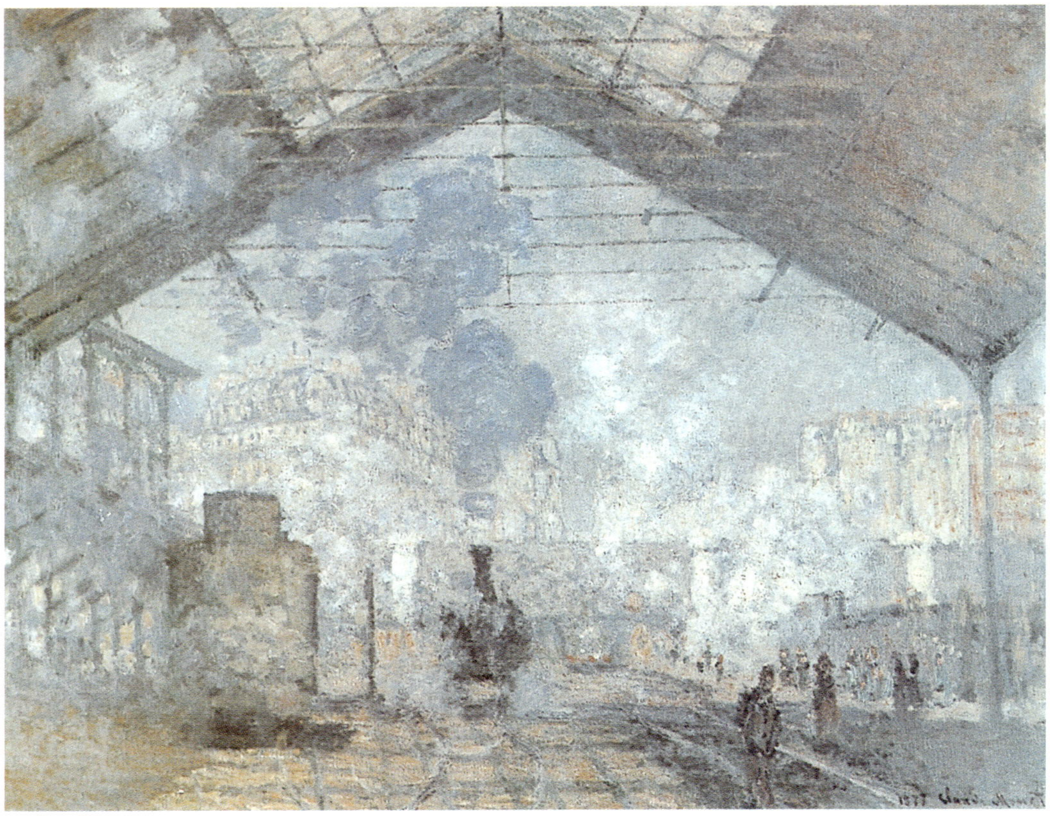

MONET
Gare St Lazare
oil on canvas
1877. 75.5 × 104 cm
Another view of the station, with the Pont de l'Europe in the distance.

produce more varied views of the same subject as seen in different weather conditions. These culminate in his last Paris pictures – the series of Gare St Lazare paintings which treat the station, its massive structure and swirling clouds of steam as intricate webs of colour, truly urban landscapes.

It is perhaps fitting that it was a picture by Monet, *Impression, Sunrise*, which gave the Impressionists their name, for during the 1870s he forged tirelessly ahead and came to exert a powerful influence on his fellow artists. Edouard Manet's summer season at Argenteuil alongside Monet resulted in Manet's decisive shift towards the Impressionist style of swiftly applied bright pigment. Renoir and Pissarro were also visitors to Argenteuil. For a relatively brief period Monet was at the heart of the Impressionist enterprise, contributing to the Impressionist exhibitions, joining in the discussions at the Café Guerbois in Paris, borrowing money from an increasing circle of friends – including Manet and Zola. The substantial amounts he was now earning were spent on, amongst other things, servants for the large house at Argenteuil. Monet also made important contacts with patrons such as Hoschedé and Chocquet.

In the end circumstances and the solitary, ambitious nature of Monet's personal endeavour drew him further away from the other Impressionists. The fall of his patron Hoschedé, a decline in Monet's modest fortunes, Camille's second pregnancy and, soon after, her worsening illness, led to the two families living together in a new home in Vétheuil, further along the Seine from Argenteuil. Eventually Ernest Hoschedé left the Monet-Hoschedé household, and, after the death of Camille in 1879, Monet, Jean, Camille's new baby Michel, Alice Hoschedé and her six children were left to carry on with life together as best they could.

The turmoil in his personal life, the real threat of poverty with a family of nine to support, and the withering of Monet's links to the other Impressionists, formed an inauspicious start to the 1880s. He had been too poor and depressed by the time of the fourth Impressionist exhibition in 1879 to want to exhibit, however, and the good Caillebotte, who had rented the studio where Monet had finished the Gare St Lazare pictures, had himself collected twenty-nine works from Monet and sent them in for him. The next year Monet absented himself from the fifth Impressionist show. To the extreme disgust of Pissarro and Degas, Monet decided instead to submit to the Salon for the first time in many years.

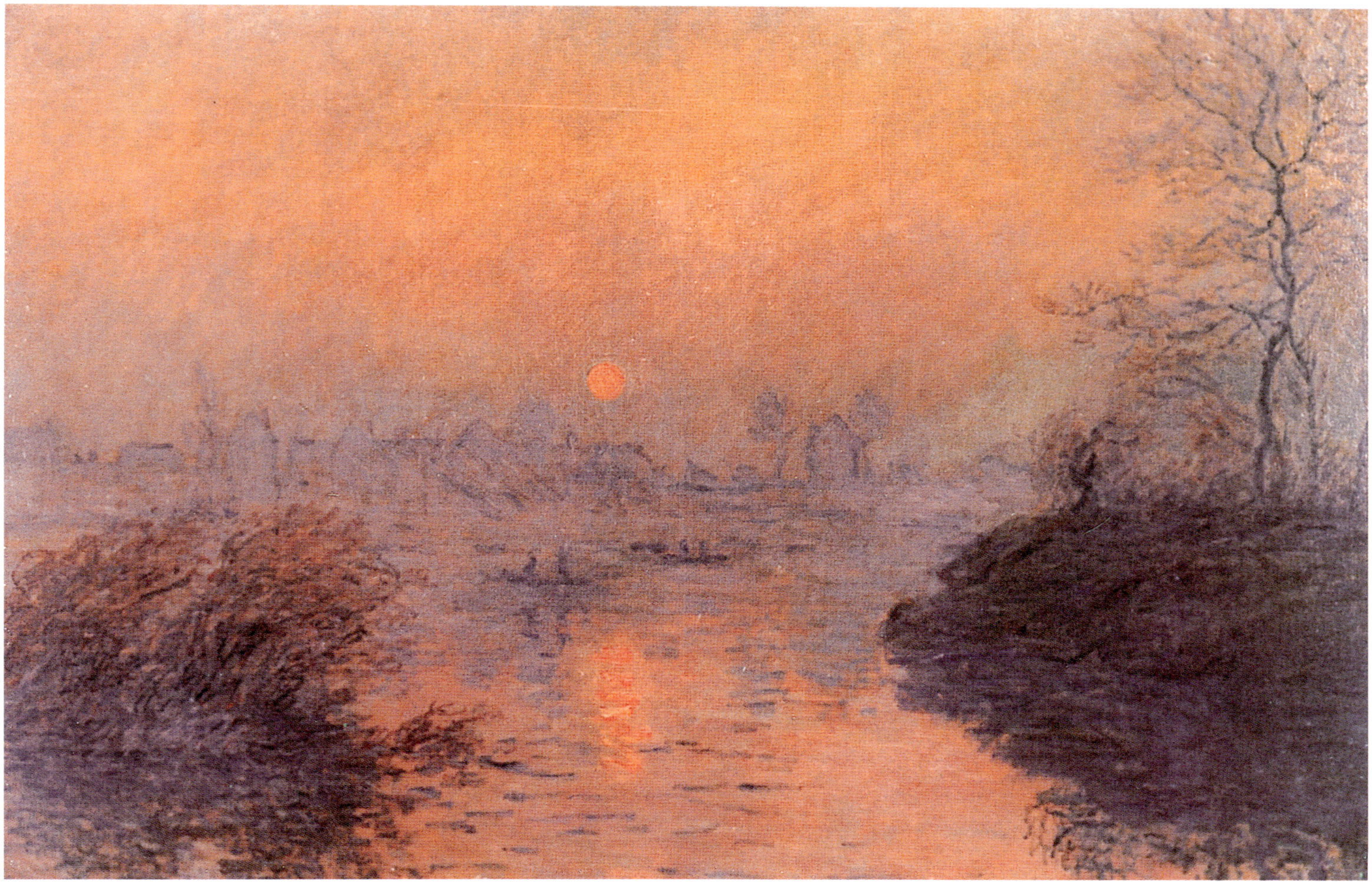

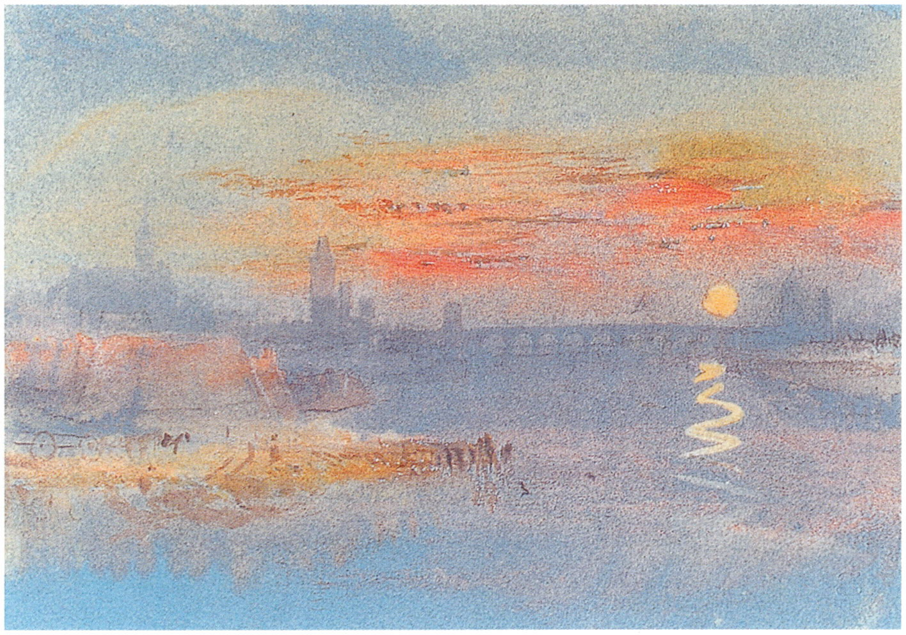

TURNER
Tours, Sunset on the River Loire
watercolour on blue paper
c.1832. 13.5 × 19 cm
LEFT During his stay in London, Monet naturally went to visit the National Gallery, where a set of watercolours by Turner was on show. It has been established that this particular work was probably on show in 1870–71. This watercolour of a French river, not particularly typical of Turner's style, is startlingly impressionistic, some forty years before the first Impressionist exhibition was held in Paris. If Monet did indeed see it, it would certainly have found its way into the artist's subconscious.

MONET
Sunset at Lavacourt
oil on canvas
1880. 101.5 × 150 cm
ABOVE This picture forms a sequel to the famous Impression, Sunrise.

MONET
The Artist's Garden at Vétheuil
oil on canvas
1881. 150 × 120 cm
RIGHT Here, we see the same blue and white jars first seen in the garden at Argenteuil, but we do not see the road between the garden and the house, a topographical oddity also present in Giverny, nor do we see the Seine behind the painter, at the bottom of the garden.

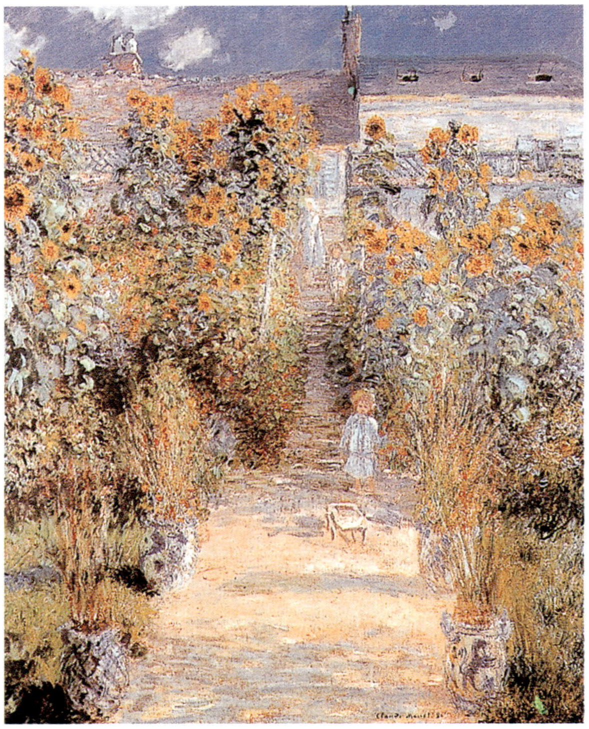

MONET
Cliff Walk, Pourville
oil on canvas
1882. 65 × 81 cm
BELOW Monet frequently went to the same coastline of Normandy to paint, usually alone. Monet stayed nearly six months in the area, experimenting in depicting the changing light with increasing accuracy. He had started to use boxes specially made for him, capable of holding freshly painted canvases.

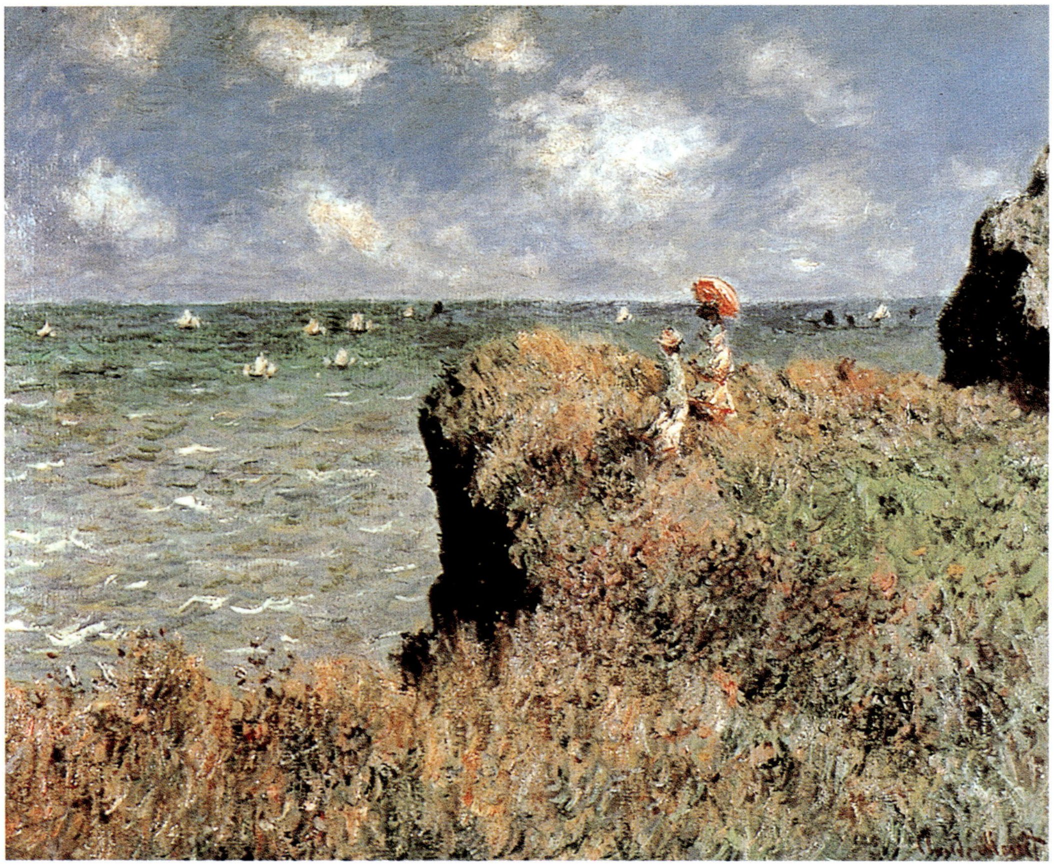

Monet's relationship to Durand-Ruel now took on a new importance. Durand-Ruel had found him reasonably bankable in a time of economic depression and Monet was the first of the Impressionists to have a one-man show at the dealer's gallery in 1883. During the 1880s Monet at last began to make a comfortable income from his work and in 1883 he was able to move to Giverny, his last home. But his dedication to expanding his vision was untrammelled.

The search for new inspiration now took him on a series of extended travels in search of problematical landscapes. He went first to the Normandy coast, usually leaving Alice and the children behind, and then to more distant climes – the south of France, northern Italy and Norway. The intrepid artist often found himself battling with the elements. A letter to Alice from Etretat in 1885 recounts how he was working at the Manneporte, a spectacular rock formation off the northwestern coast and the subject for several paintings, when he failed to observe a huge wave which smashed him against the cliff and dragged him down in its undertow: "My first thought was that I was done for . . . My boots stockings and coat were soaked through . . . the palette . . . had hit me in the face and my beard was covered in blue and yellow, etc . . . the worst thing was that I lost my painting which soon disintegrated along with the easel."

For an artist such as Monet who had developed an incredible sensitivity towards colour in a northern French landscape, which is subdued at the best of times and in the winter mournfully so, one might well imagine what the intense Mediterranean sun and landscape could unleash in his mind. The bright blues of the sea and sky were at first, he said, "appalling" and "beyond me": in the end of course he mastered them. During the 1880s Monet's palette was finally liberated from any lingering attachment to naturalistic colour; the *Rocks at Belle-Île* (*Rochers à Belle-Île*), and the *Poppy Fields at Giverny* (*Champs de pivots à Giverny*) are worked and re-worked (in the studio) with thick, startlingly livid pigment. They go beyond the mere *impression* of colour values and have now become a mode of *defining* the complex emotional relationship of the artist to the scene in terms of colour.

In 1892 Ernest Hoschedé died, enabling Monet and Alice to marry. The artist had now cut down on his travels and began to devote himself once again to the landscape around his home. Continually searching for a way to paint the elusive moment, the "fugitive effect," as he put it, Monet had embarked on a multi-canvas series of subjects, the first of which, the *Meules* or *Grain Stacks* (not "hay-stacks", they are stacks of wheat or oats), was begun in the mid-1880s. When the series was due to be exhibited at Durand-Ruel's gallery in 1891 Pissarro was moved to complain to his son Lucien: "All people want at the moment is Monets, apparently he can't paint enough to meet the demand. The worst thing is that they all want grain stacks at sunset! Always the same story, everything he does goes to America at prices of four, five, and six thousand francs."

The series of *Meules* was thus a stunning success, both financially and artistically. The concept of a group of pictures on one subject, which had been seen as a whole, reflected Monet's method – to work on several canvases at once, waiting for the light to change to the correct quality for a particular picture. Moreover, the series now represented a record, in a disturbing totality, not only of the

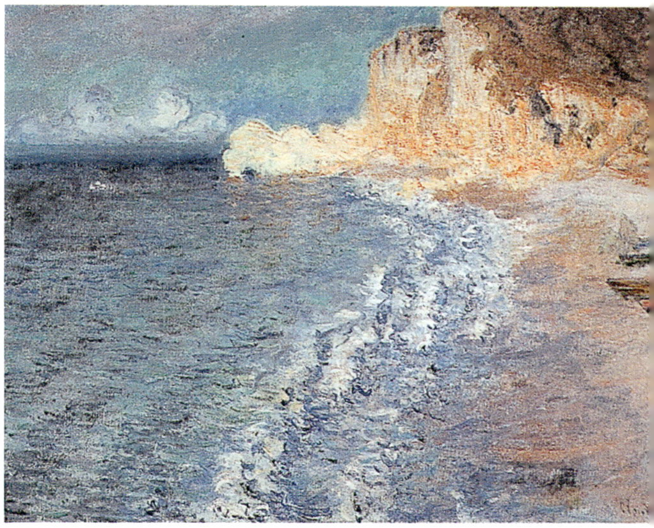

MONET
Morning, Etretat
oil on canvas
1883. 63 × 81 cm
ABOVE Monet spent part of the summers between 1883 and 1886 at Etretat, painting the various uniquely arched cliffs.

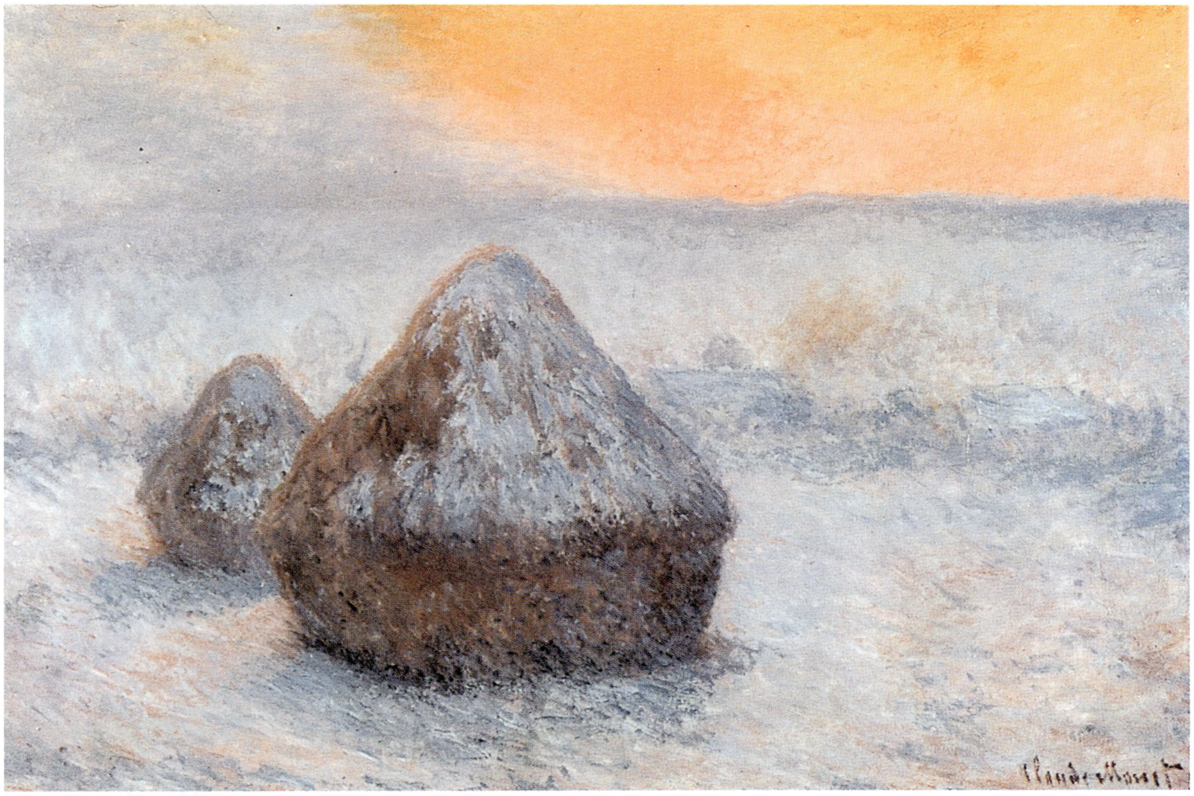

MONET
Grain Stacks, Sunset
oil on canvas
1891. 65 × 100 cm
LEFT The Neo-Impressionists found Monet's works "old hat" by now, because he was merely evolving rather than radically changing direction.

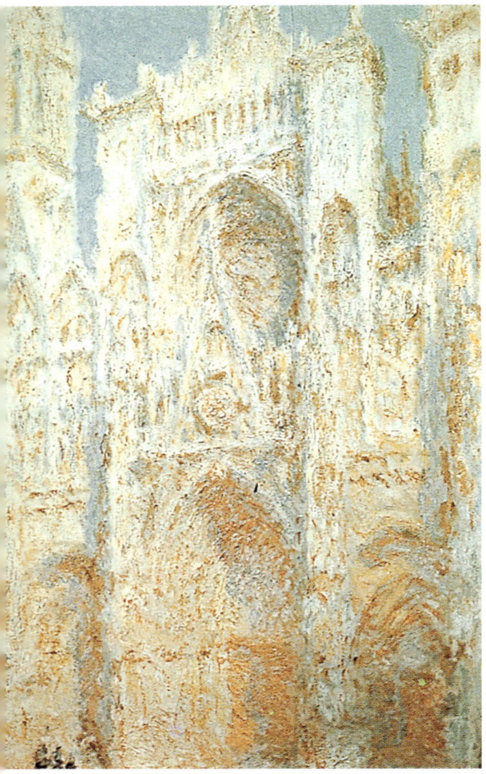

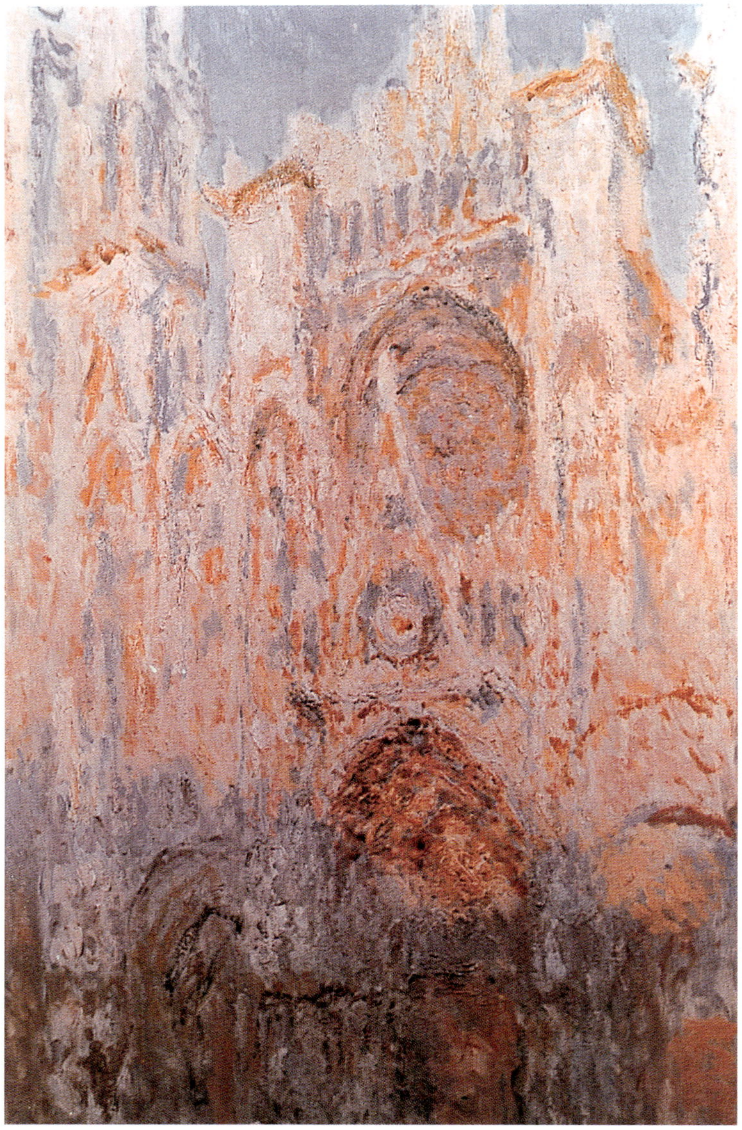

MONET
The Cathedral, Bright Sun
oil on canvas
c.1894. 107 × 73 cm
Above

MONET
Rouen Cathedral
oil on canvas
1894. 100 × 65 cm
Right

MONET
Rouen Cathedral, Albany Tower
oil on canvas
c.1894. 106 × 74 cm
Far right

subject under varying conditions, but Monet's response to it over time. Speaking of the *Meules* series, which he saw in 1895, the painter Wassily Kandinsky said: "Painting took on a fabulous strength and splendour, and at the same time, unconsciously, the object was discredited as an indispensable element of the picture." True enough, contemporary viewers were initially perplexed by the need to see the whole through its parts. The "discredited object" – in other words making the object abstract by repeating it in various states – is a major consequence of Monet's series paintings. The *Poplars* series of 1891, the Rouen Cathedral series of 1894, and the *Mornings on the Seine* of 1896–97 continue this serial preoccupation. In the late 1890s and early 1900s Monet went on his last travels to London (where he had painted over 100 views of the Thames by 1904) and his last expedition to Venice in 1908.

As Monet's work was now selling for substantial amounts he could afford to realize his dream of creating a large flower and water garden, achieved by buying a plot adjacent to the house, diverting the stream which ran through the land and forming a water-lily pond with a Japanese bridge over it. It was in this garden that he spent the last decades of his life. Over the years the garden expanded into a wonderland of flowers of all varieties.

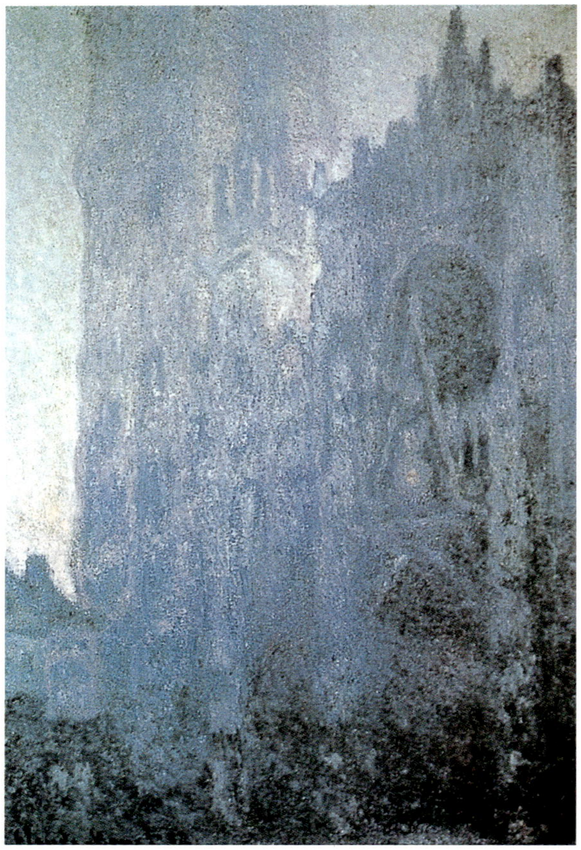

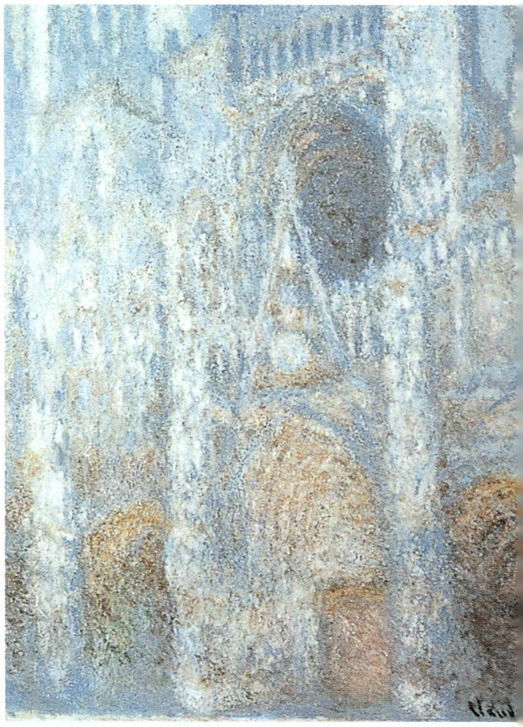

MONET
The Cathedral, Sunlight
oil on canvas
1894. 107 × 73 cm
Above

MONET
The Cathedral Fog
oil on canvas
1894. 106 × 72.5 cm
Left Monet started his series on the cathedral of Rouen in the late winter of 1892–93 and the following year, set himself up in the window of a shop from where he could follow the changing light on the medieval façade.

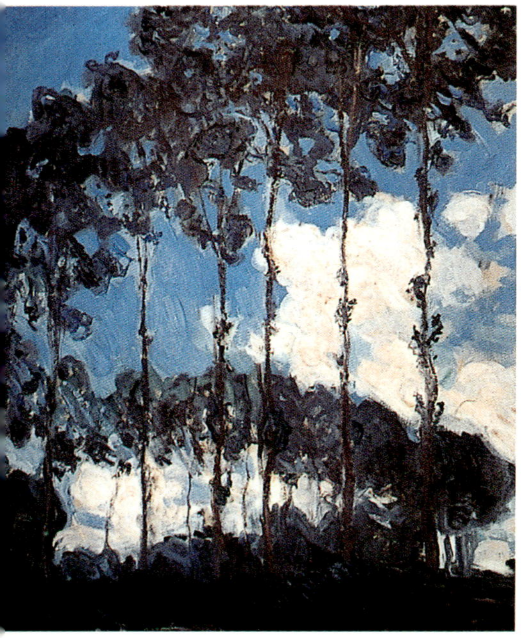

MONET
Poplars on the Epte
oil on canvas
1891. 92.5 × 73.5 cm
Above Monet was particularly fond of this quick study, perhaps because it is both a bold and stylized picture, in which the effect is achieved with far less nuances than in most of his other pictures.

MONET
Poplars
oil on canvas
1891. 101 × 66 cm
Right The series of poplars followed immediately after the grainstacks, and was shown at Durand-Ruel in 1892. By then, Monet's eyesight was deteriorating.

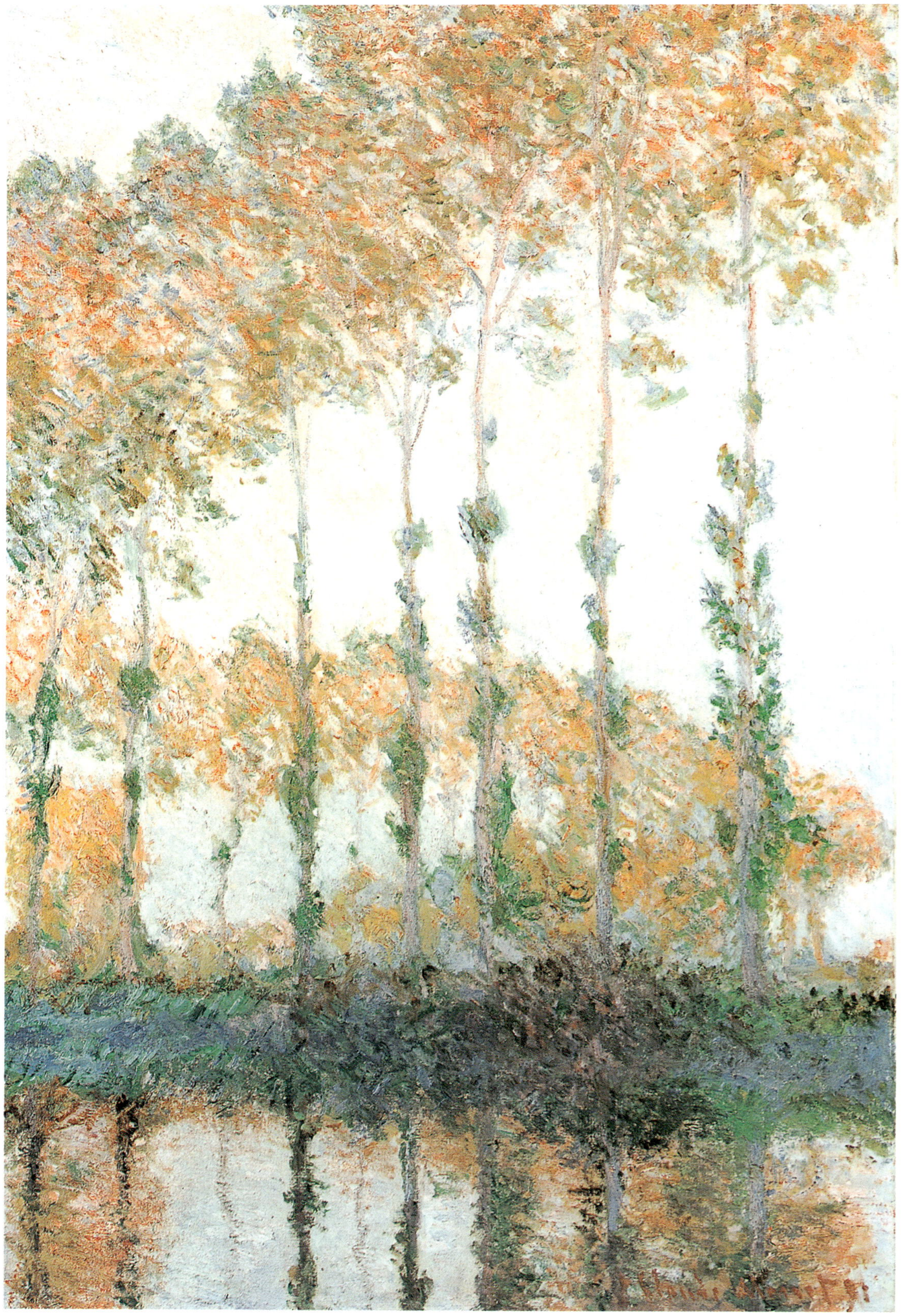

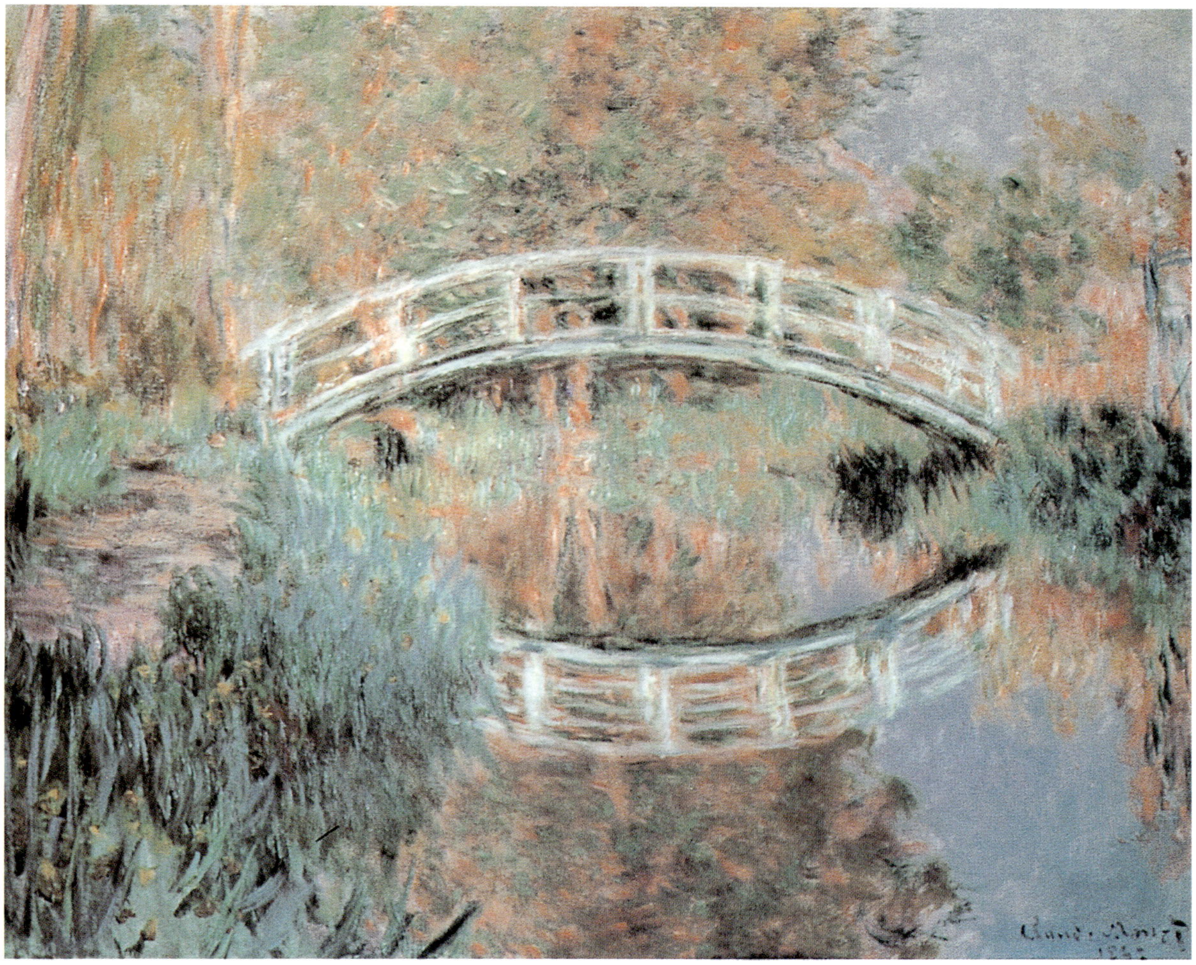

MONET
The Japanese Bridge at Giverny
oil on canvas
1893. 97 × 117 cm
Monet had a Japanese-style bridge built over a pond he created by diverting a tributary of the local river Epte. He had already undertaken a great deal of gardening, but no water lilies are growing in the pond, although he had intended to grow them even before he was authorized to divert the course of the river. Monet depicted this pond tirelessly until his death in 1926.

"What I need most of all are flowers, always, always," he said. His artistic attention now turned to the waterscape offered by the lily pond. A prodigious series of *Nymphéas*, or *Water Lilies*, now followed, taking Monet into new realms of vision. As he told Geffroy in 1908: "These landscapes of water and reflections have become an obsession. It's quite beyond my powers at this age, but I need to succeed in expressing what I feel." The consequence of this obsession was the *Nymphéas, paysages d'eau* (*Water Lilies, Waterscapes*) a series of forty-eight canvases exhibited at Durand-Ruel's in 1909. This later became a monumental concept for a huge *décoration* to be donated to the State and installed in a public building in Paris. The plan, encouraged by the politician Georges Clemenceau, was audacious and at times it seemed as though it would never happen. In 1911 Alice Monet had died and to add to his grief his son, Jean, died in 1914. Cared for by his step-daughter Blanche Hoschedé-Monet and with the support of Clemenceau, the seventy-four-year-old artist was able to persevere with the project for the massive *décorations*.

To realize the *décorations* Monet proposed the building of a new studio specially to house the work in progress. As World War I raged around him, Monet supervised the construction of the studio and worked on the *Nymphéas* in the old studio. He had developed

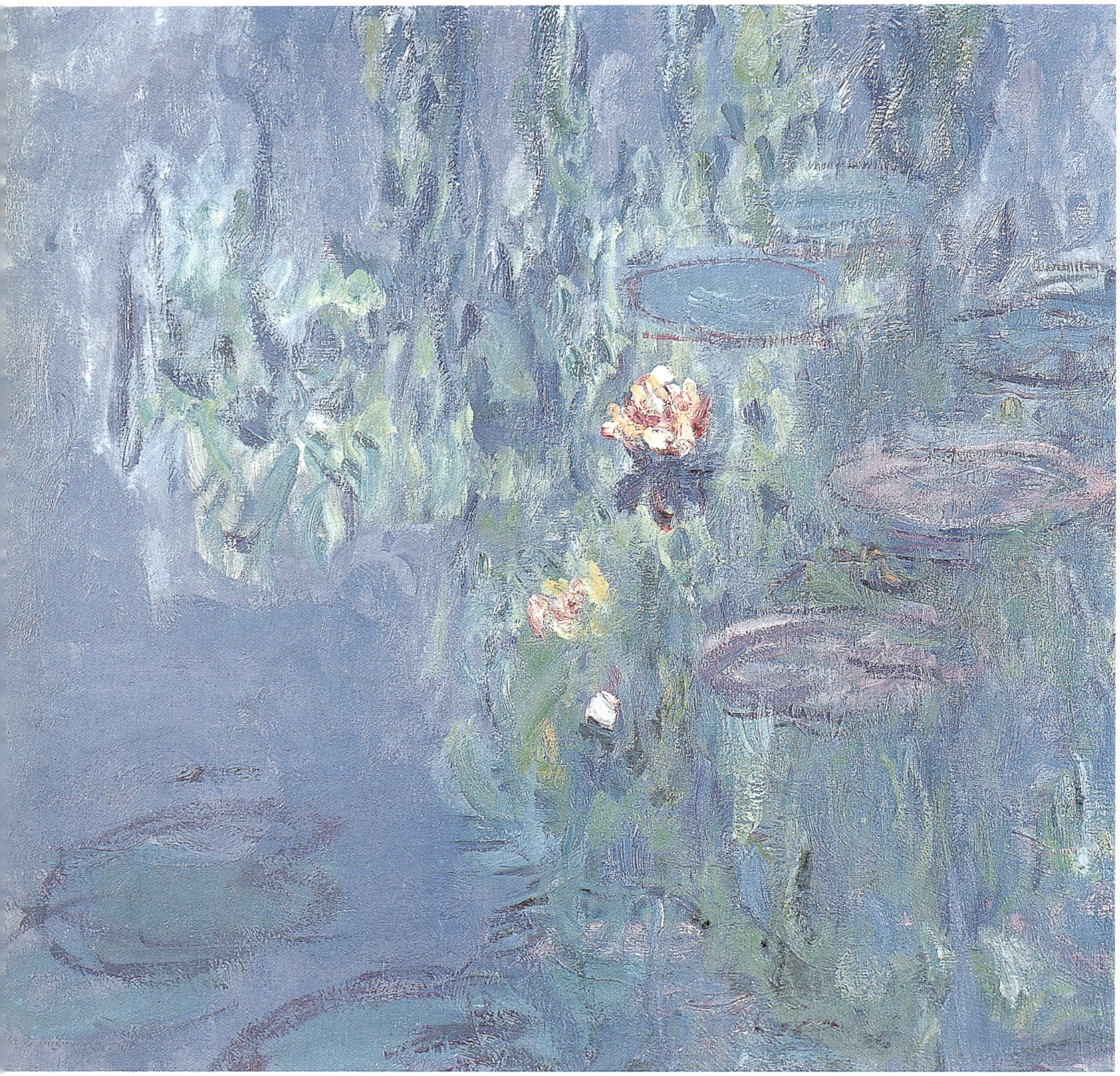

MONET
Nymphéas *(Detail)*
oil on canvas
undated. 132 × 84 cm
Monet painted hundreds of pictures of this pond or parts of it.

cataracts which made it increasingly difficult for him to discern colour, yet he carried on remorselessly. When the new studio was finished in 1916 he began what was almost a decade of unremitting work on the *décorations*. His failing eyesight meant he was frequently uncertain of what he was doing and, in despair, he destroyed several canvases. An operation in 1923 eventually restored enough of his sight for Monet, now eighty-three and dying of cancer caused by habitual cigarette smoking, to near completion of the *décorations*. The immense work was designed to be housed in a circular or oval room and to this end the Orangerie near the Louvre was designated to house it, but not without political and personal complications on a huge scale.

Monet died on 5th December 1926, a month after his eighty-sixth birthday, with Clemenceau at his side. He had lived just long enough to see the completion of the *décorations*, his troublesome masterpiece of a gift to the French nation. As Gustave Geffroy said of the lily pond, the inspiration for his last great works:

> There he found, as it were, the last word on things, if things had a first and last word. He discovered and demonstrated that everything is everywhere, and that after running round the world worshipping the light that brightens it, he knew that this light came to be reflected in all its splendour and mystery in the magical hollow surrounded by the foliage of willow and bamboo, by flowering irises and rose bushes through the mirror of water from which burst strange flowers which seem even more silent and hermetic than all the others.

Monet was famed throughout the world and his work fetched enormous prices; his persistence and stubborn devotion to his art had made his fortune. He had also outlived two wives, a son, the Second Republic, the Second Empire and all of his contemporaries including Pissarro, Degas, and Renoir.

Six months before his death he wrote: " . . . in the end the only merit I have is to

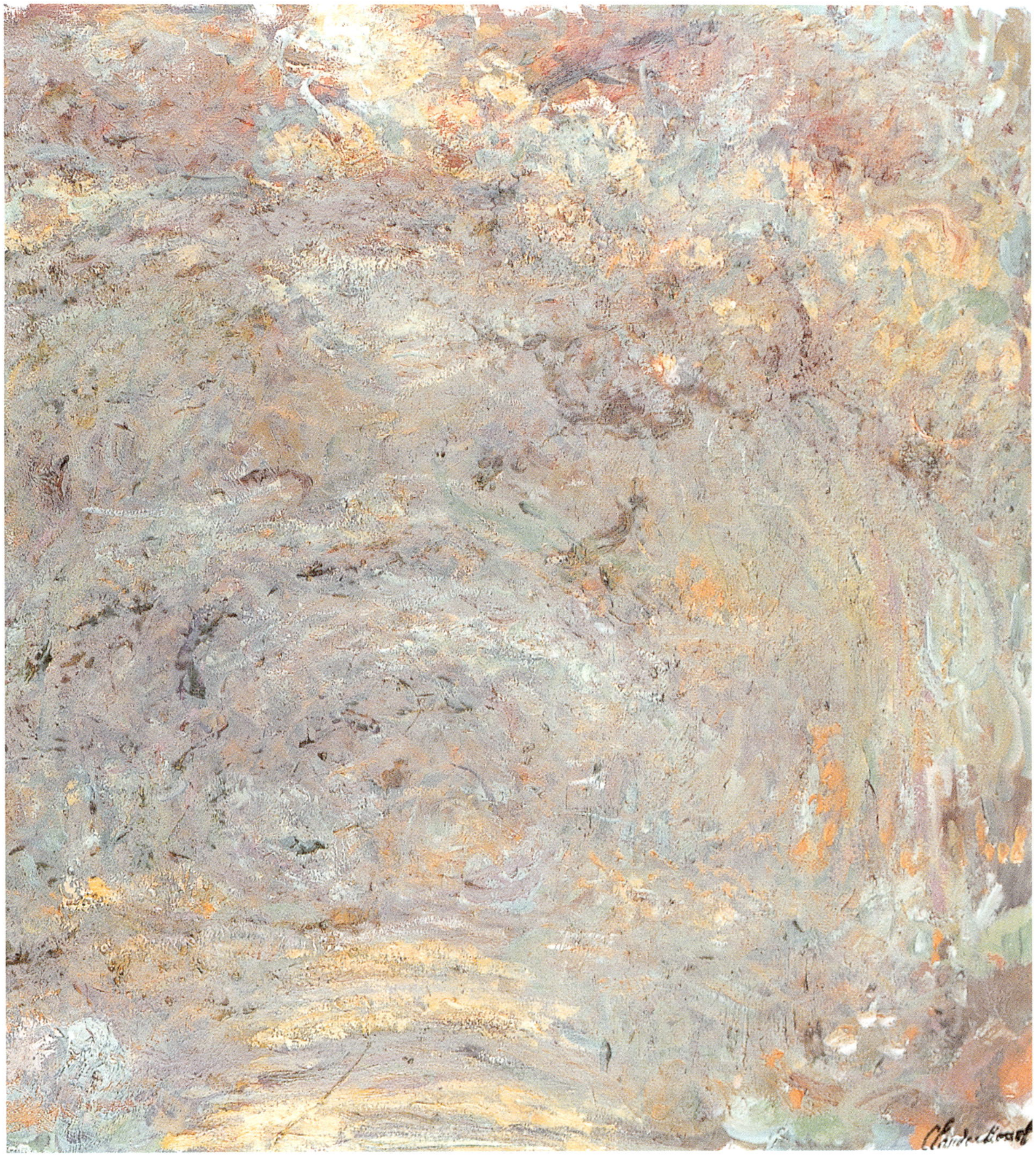

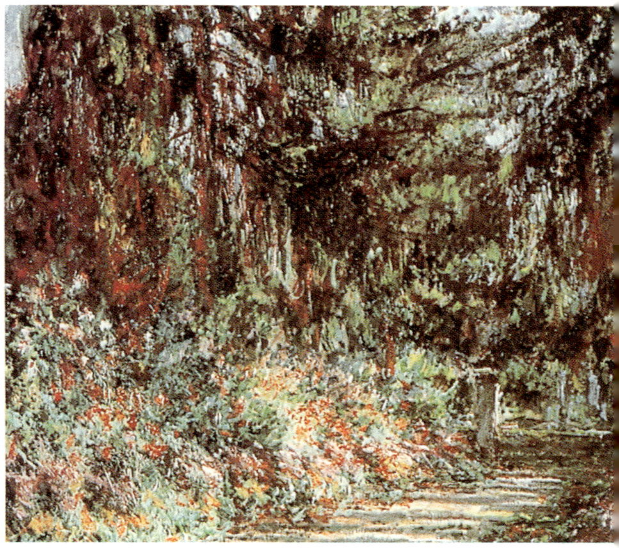

MONET
An Alley at Giverny
oil on canvas
1902. 79 × 90 cm
ABOVE The garden at Giverny is vast and arranged in several parts.

MONET
Alley in Giverny
oil on canvas
c.1920. 89 × 100 cm
LEFT Monet's bad eyesight cannot entirely explain the semi-abstract style he had now reached. It often happens that ageing artists lose their stamina and produce works which do not compare favourably to their earlier ones. With Monet, this was not the case.

have painted directly from nature before the most fugitive effects, and it still upsets me that I was responsible for the name given to a group, most of whom had nothing Impressionist about them . . . "

A series of paintings of the Japanese bridge and the garden at Giverny are among Monet's last works apart from the *décorations*. The last canvases are covered by violent, feverish brushstrokes with an inferno of colour; the last challenges to sunlight of one of the first great Impressionists.

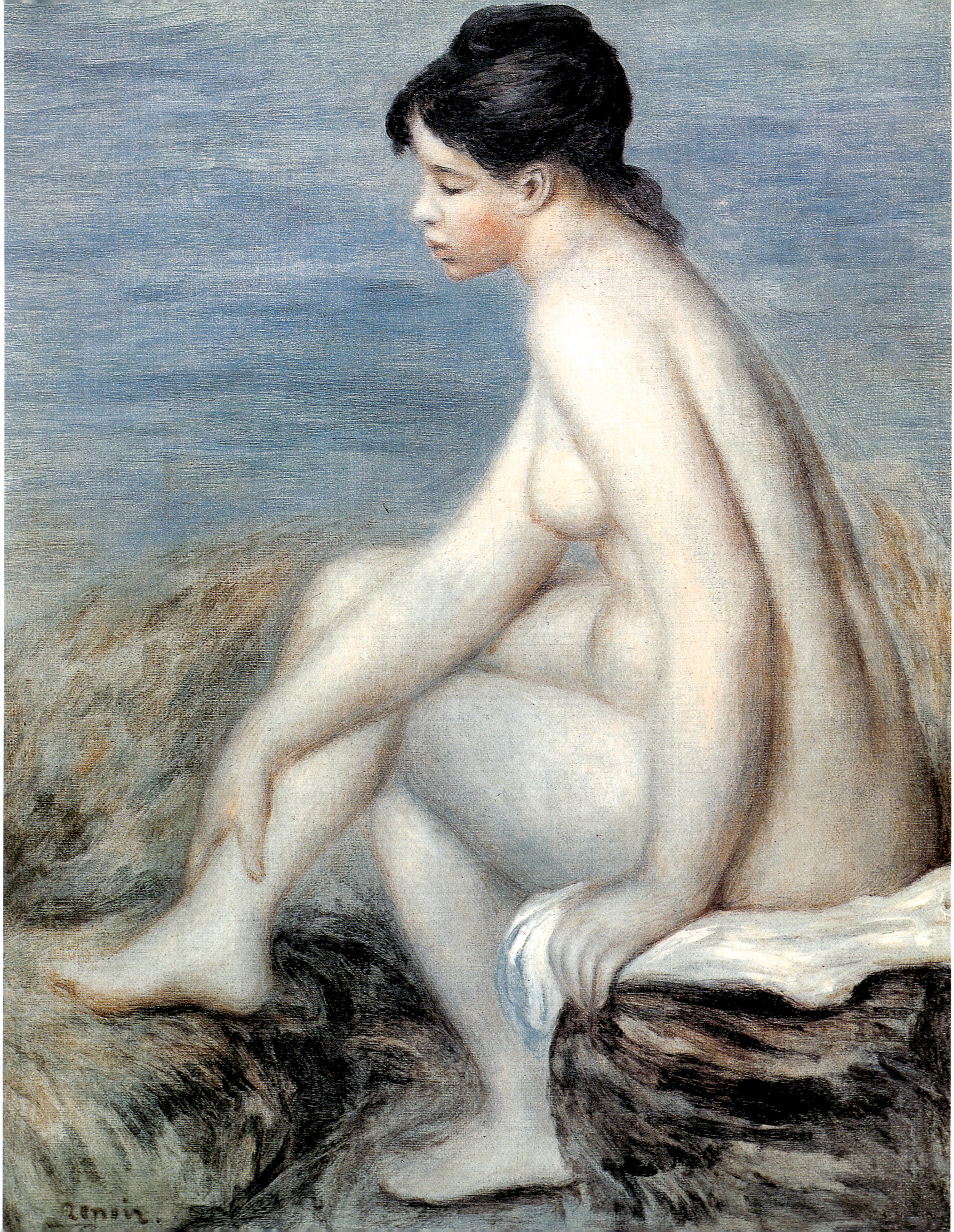
Renoir.

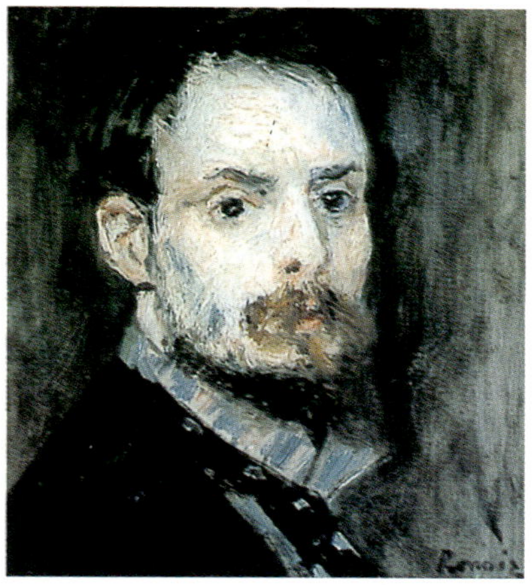

Renoir

George Moore, an English writer who was reasonably close to the Impressionists during the Batignolles days, thought Pierre-Auguste Renoir possessed a certain "vulgarity", a feeling expressed, though not of course explicitly, by Renoir himself, whose eventual fame sat uneasily on the head of a self-confessed artisan. Although his ambivalent social position gave him much to be nervous about, Renoir was existentially nervy, a source of perpetual motion who would whistle incessantly whilst painting and fall into utter moroseness and depression when idle.

As an iconoclast of his own work, his dissatisfaction with the extraordinary surface effects of his "high Impressionist" period culminated in a search for classical simplicity in line and volume which lead him back to the work of Raphael, and sideways to the experiments of Cézanne. In the end he found his métier in the female figure. Even when his eyesight and rheumatic hands began to fail him, he branched out into sculpture, using an assistant, as well as tapestry design and ceramics – he had after all begun his career as a porcelain-painter.

PIERRE-AUGUSTE RENOIR
Self-portrait
c.1875
Above

RENOIR
Seated Bather
oil on canvas
c.1885. 54.5 × 42 cm
Opposite

Life and Works: Pierre-Auguste Renoir (1841–1919)

Artists do exist. But one doesn't know where to find them. An artist can do nothing if the person who asks him to produce work is blind. It is the eye of the sensualist that I wish to open.

Pierre-Auguste Renoir

RENOIR
Bazille at Work
oil on canvas
1867. 105 × 73.5 cm
Below Renoir has produced an honest and forthright portrait of his close friend. The rendering is fluent but the artist has not yet found the style to which he owes his fame.

Pierre-Auguste Renoir's father Léonard "Raynouard", as the land register of the time called him, was a tailor from Limoges who had moved to Paris in 1844 with his family. Renoir's mother, Marguerite was a dress-maker and Pierre-Auguste, born on 25th February 1841, was the sixth of seven children, two of whom died in infancy. At the age of fourteen Renoir was apprenticed in the traditional way to M. Levy, a porcelain-painter. To improve his skills he also studied drawing at a free school and when Levy's firm could no longer compete with the machine-produced porcelain-ware taking over the market and closed down in 1858, Renoir then painted fans for his brother, Henri, copying the work of Watteau, Lancret, Boucher, and Fragonard, and blinds for a M. Gilbert until he entered Charles Gleyre's atelier in 1861. A year later he met Monet, Bazille, and Sisley there. His capacity for self-improvement was formidable, and in 1862 he won a place at the Ecole des Beaux-Arts where he studied as a pupil of Gleyre's until 1864. He had also gained permission to copy in the Louvre and the Cabinet d'Estampes. In later years, when he and his friends were famous, Renoir was the only one to recognize the efforts of the good Charles Gleyre: "It was under Gleyre that I learnt my trade as a painter," he said, and in the 1880s he was to return to the techniques Gleyre had taught him. At the time, however, his relationship with Gleyre had its humorous moments. On one occasion Gleyre inspected some of Renoir's work and wryly advised him that painting shouldn't be done for one's own amusement, to which the plucky Renoir replied "If it didn't amuse me I wouldn't paint."

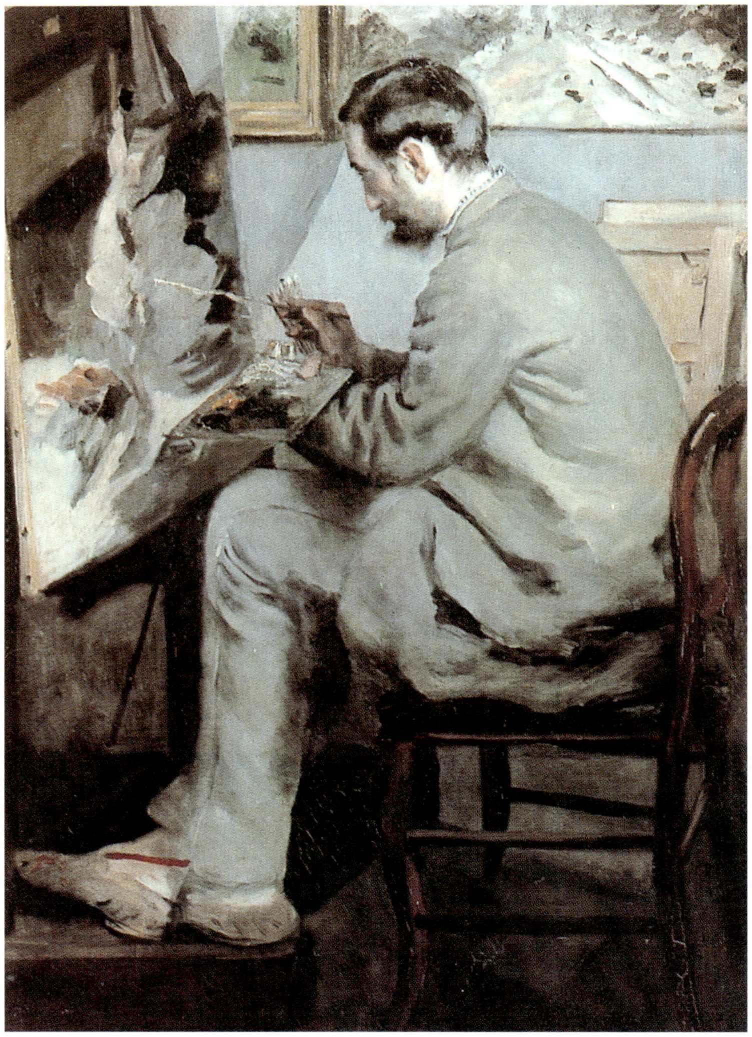

Renoir's career at the Ecole des Beaux-Arts

was hardly spectacular; on one occasion he came fourth with an honourable mention in the perspective drawing examination, but generally his results were undistinguished. Not so his formative relationship with the other Gleyre students. In 1862 he was already accompanying them on landscape painting expeditions to the Fontainebleau Forest. "When I was young," he said nostalgically many years later, "I used to go to Fontainebleau with Sisley, with just my paint-box and the shirt on my back. We would wander round until we found a village, and sometimes come back a week later when we had run out of money." Monet, Bazille and Sisley had soon become important allies. They were all from the prosperous middle class, though Renoir, from the skilled working class, an *ouvrier de la peinture* as he called himself, had to earn a living by undertaking decorative work. As the art historian John House observes in his study of "Renoir's Worlds", when Bazille, comfortably supported by his parents, shared his studio with his friends, Monet played the role of a bohemian who had rejected parental authority, whereas Renoir simply had to seek the cheapest way he could find to live. Renoir strove to become a *bourgeois* through his art and his friends. His first successful submission to the Salon in 1865 was a portrait of Sisley's wealthy father, and the greater part of his career was to depend on patronage by and portraiture for the bourgeoisie. Yet the question of class troubled him throughout his life; his later affair with and marriage to a laundress, Aline Charigot, was kept secret from his friends – Renoir was terrified that they might think of her as a lowly peasant.

By nature Renoir was a restless soul and in this respect he was later to be compared to Watteau, one of his early influences. He was also highly impressionable. Unsympathetic analyses of his work held up the considerable influence of his contemporaries, firstly Monet and later Cézanne, as proof that he was ambivalent and confused as to his own identity as an artist. To a certain extent this is true, but his talent was both convincing and original, chiefly in his portrayal of the modern life of Paris for which he is most admired.

In 1868 Renoir and Bazille moved into rooms with a studio in the Batignolles quarter of Paris. As a member of the group of future

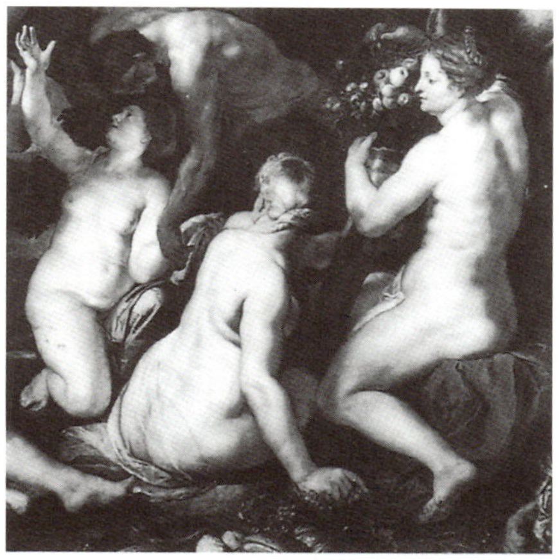

RUBENS
An Allegory of Fruitfulness *(Detail)*
Above These were women after Renoir's own heart, miles away from the cold and polished beauties praised by the Salon.

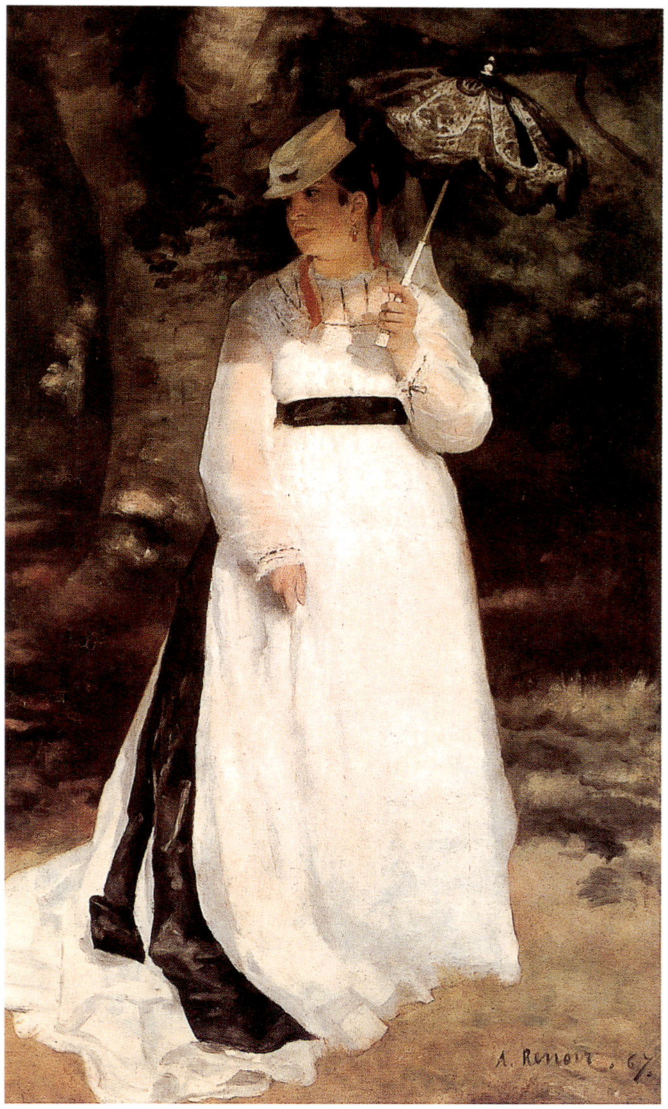

RENOIR
Lise
oil on canvas
1867. 181.5 × 113 cm
Left Painted in 1867, the portrait of the artist's mistress was exhibited at the Salon the following year.

Impressionists who had gravitated towards the Batignolles and the Café Guerbois where Edouard Manet held court, Renoir was now becoming involved in the struggle for recognition. Following the Salon's rejection of his painting *Diana the Huntress* (*Diane chasseresse*) in 1867, he had signed a petition calling for another Salon des Refusés and was soon to be a prominent member of the *Société anonyme* which launched the first Impressionist show. In 1868, he received considerable acclaim at the Salon for his painting *Lise with a Parasol* (*Lise au parasol*), which Zola thought "a successful exploration of the modern". The critic Duret had bought a previous *Lise*, also known as *The Gypsy Girl* (*La Gitane*), and Renoir's name was increasingly to be heard mentioned in connection with the avant-garde whilst his style remained subtly tailored to the Salon. Lise Tréhot, the subject of *Lise* and many more paintings to come, was the sister of Clémence Tréhot, the mistress of Jules Le Coeur, a painter and close friend of Renoir and Sisley. In 1865 Le Coeur had bought a house at Marlotte in the Fontainebleau Forest where Renoir, Sisley, and the Tréhot sisters would frequently spend the summer months. Nearby was the famous Cabaret de la mère Anthony, a country inn frequented by artists, writers, and bohemians of every hue. The Cabaret is the subject of an early picture which Renoir remembered with great pleasure. "It is not that I find the picture itself particularly exciting, but it does remind me of good old Mother Anthony and her inn at Marlotte. That was a real village inn!"

During the late 1860s Renoir's style was at a crossroads. The rapidly executed *Skaters in*

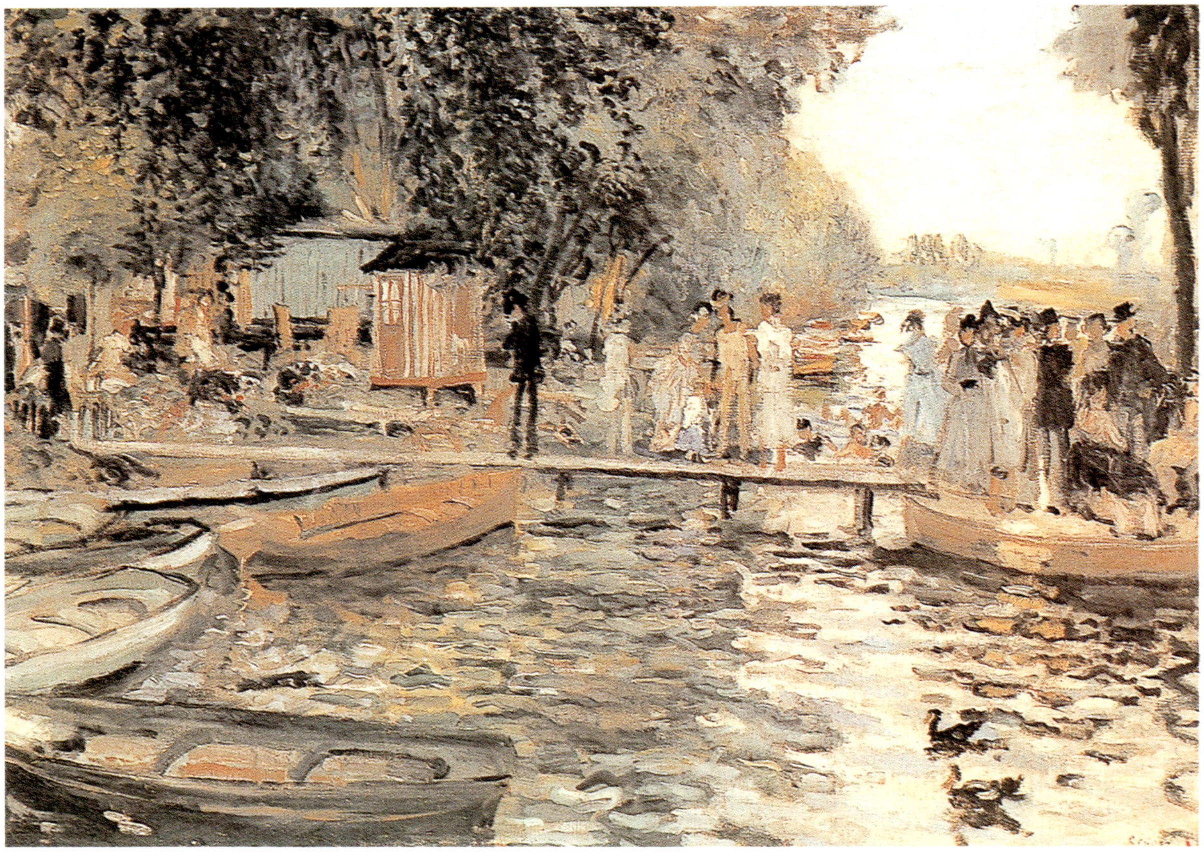

RENOIR
La Grenouillère
oil on canvas
1869. 65 × 93 cm
RIGHT Here we see people standing on the gangplank between the bank and the "camembert" from which they could watch the bathers. Renoir's brushstrokes are lighter and lack Monet's bravura handling.

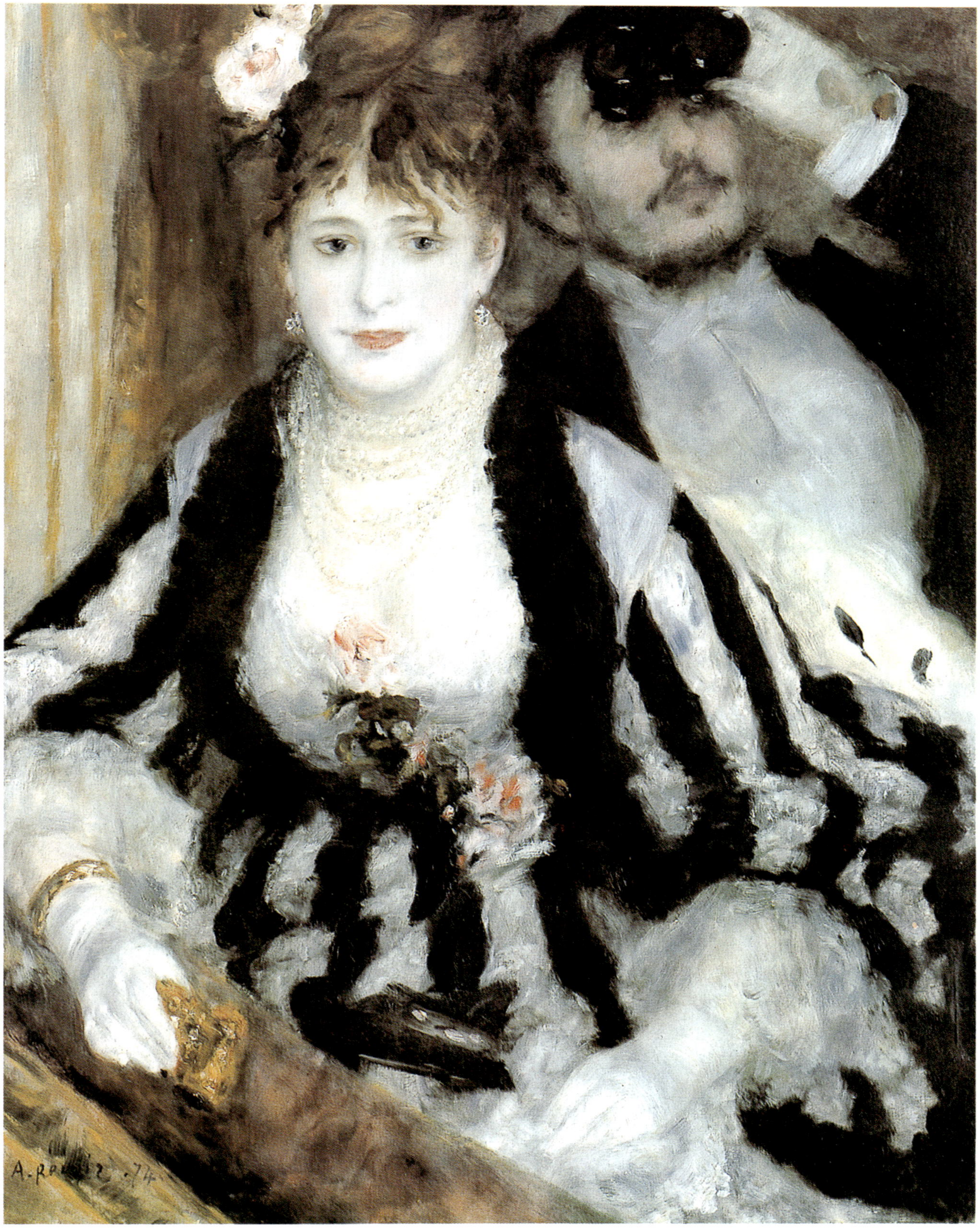

RENOIR
La Loge
oil on canvas
1874. 80 × 64 cm
This now famous picture passed unnoticed at the first Impressionist exhibition, as did the artist's other works, although it was the first Impressionist treatment of this subject. It has since been acknowledged as a masterpiece. A work of charm and candour, the mismatching of the sitters to the setting adds to the painting's appeal. The woman was the model Nini Lopez, who does not have the allure of a high society woman. The man was Renoir's brother, Edmond; willing accomplice in many of the artist's works.

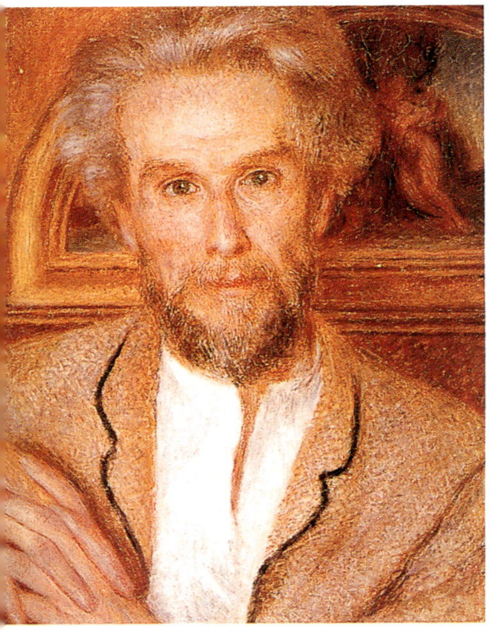

RENOIR
Victor Chocquet
oil on canvas
c.1876. 46 × 36 cm
ABOVE Chocquet, a modest civil servant with a small private income, was a compulsive collector of paintings.

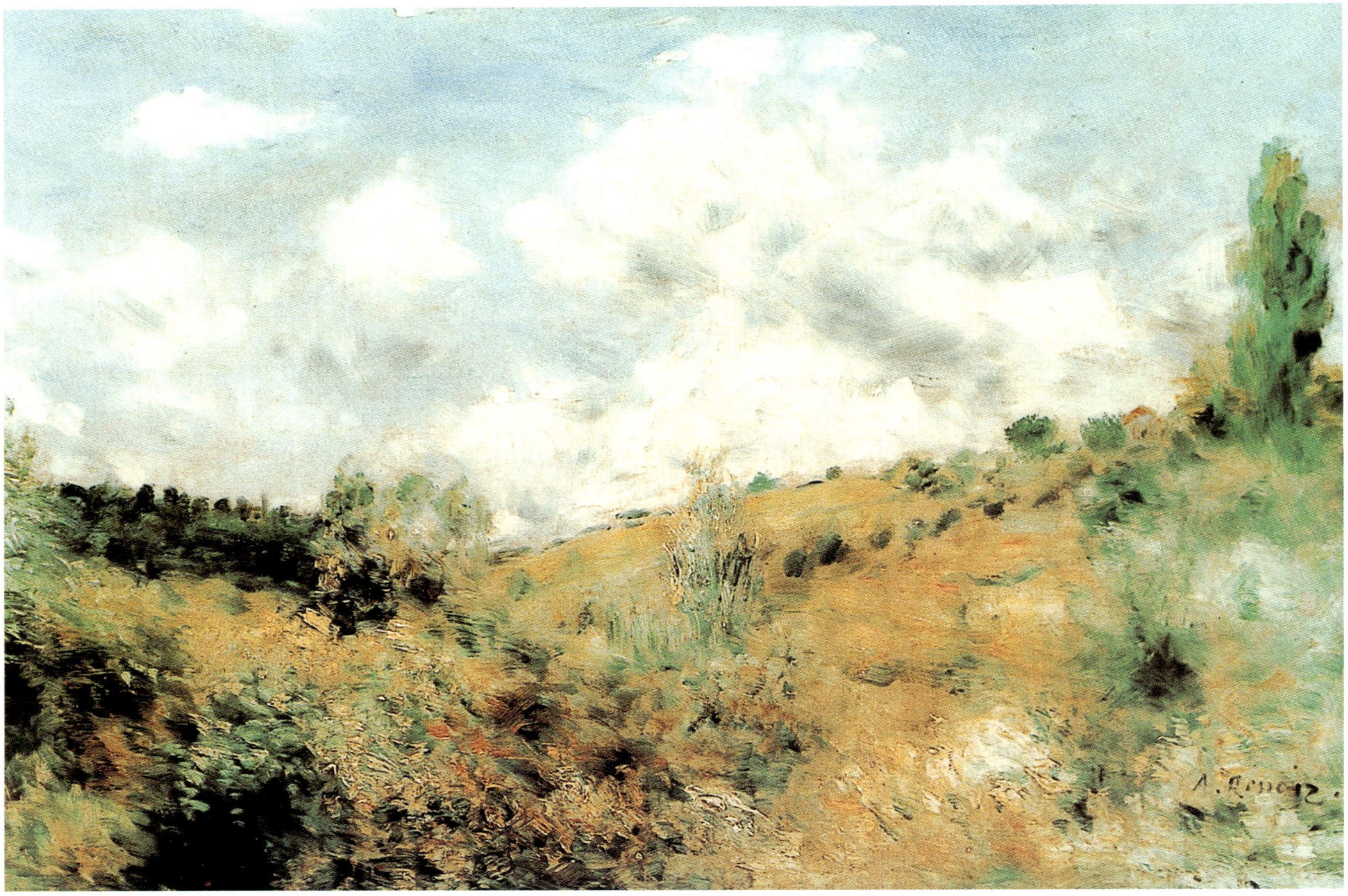

RENOIR
The Gust of Wind
oil on canvas
c.1872. 52 × 82.5 cm
RIGHT ABOVE Renoir has abandoned his emulation of Monet's boldness, as in the Grenouillère pictures, and is now attempting to capture the effect of a windy day and the movements of the clouds with a light brush.

the Bois de Boulogne (*Patineurs au Bois de Boulogne*) of 1868 showing the marked influence of Monet, contrasts with the sobriety of the touching double portrait of Sisley and his wife-to-be, *The Engaged Couple* (*Les Fiancés*) of the same year. In 1869 Renoir spent the summer living with his parents in Louveciennes. Nearly every day he travelled the few miles up the river to Bougival where Monet was living and together they went to paint at the popular bathing establishment known as La Grenouillère (The Froggery) on the Île-de-Croissy in the Seine. To many minds this is where Impressionism was born. The two artists worked side by side at the same views with practically the same palette and brushstrokes. A comparison of the results of that summer shows that Renoir had tried to apply a great deal of Monet's approach. The short, rapid brushstrokes and high-keyed colours employed by Monet are echoed by Renoir, but in a more uncertain fashion. Renoir's approach to the subject concentrates more on the crowd of figures in the scene.

With the outbreak of the Franco-Prussian war in July 1870, Renoir joined the Tenth Cavalry Regiment and was posted to Libourne in the Bordeaux region. There he succumbed to a severe attack of dysentery and was rescued by his uncle who took him to the town of Bordeaux to recuperate. By the end of February 1871 he was back with his regiment and his record states that he "conducted himself well for the duration of the war." By the time in April when he had been demobilized and returned to Paris, the

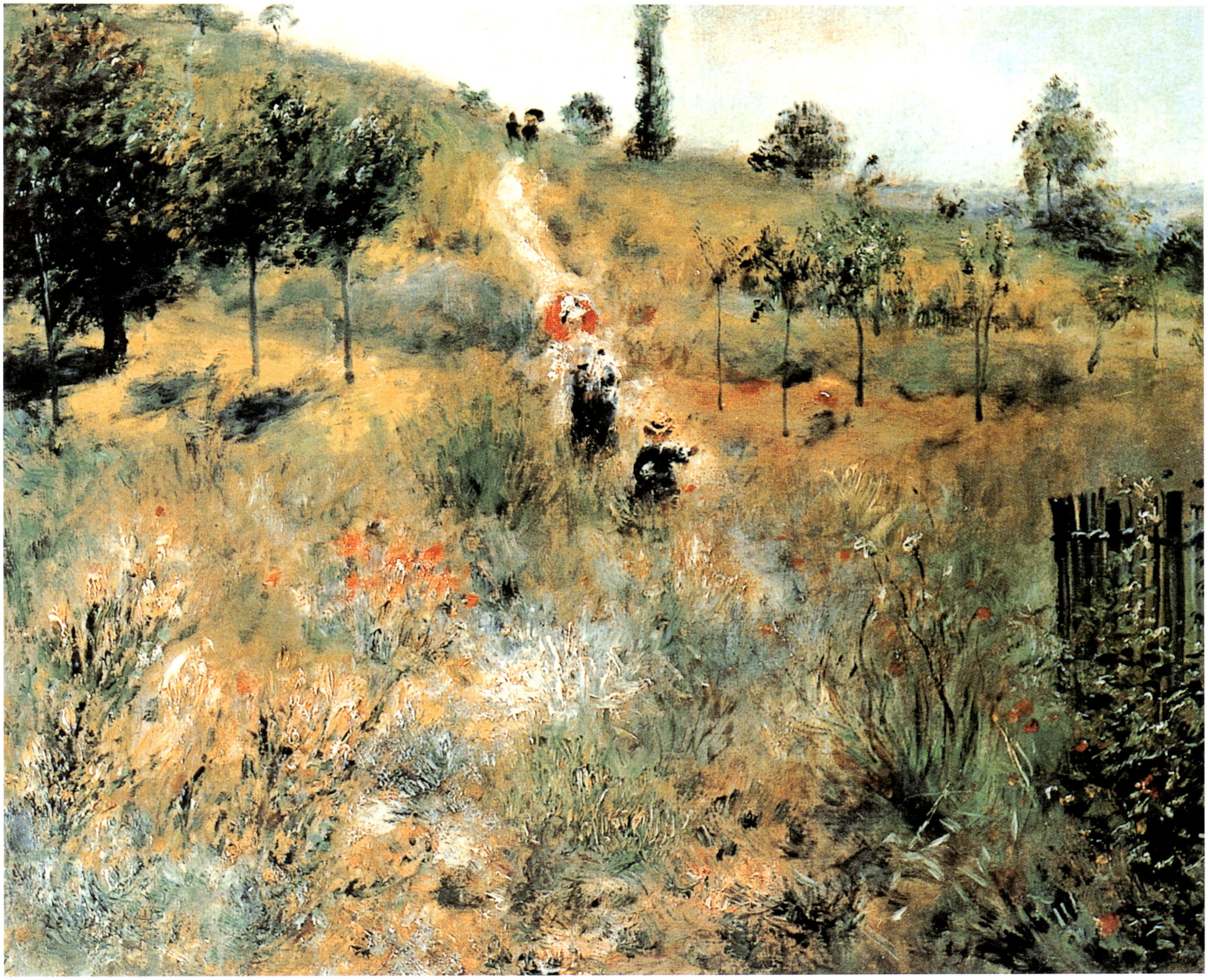

RENOIR
The Path in the Grass
oil on canvas
c.1875. 60 × 74 cm
The composition of this painting is reminiscent of the Poppy Field *painted by Monet two years previously; though Monet's work includes a greater depth of sky and his horizon is firmly marked by a row of trees. Here, the path is clearly the axis of the picture, balanced by the vertical tree off centre. The vegetation is detailed in Renoir's own fluttering style.*

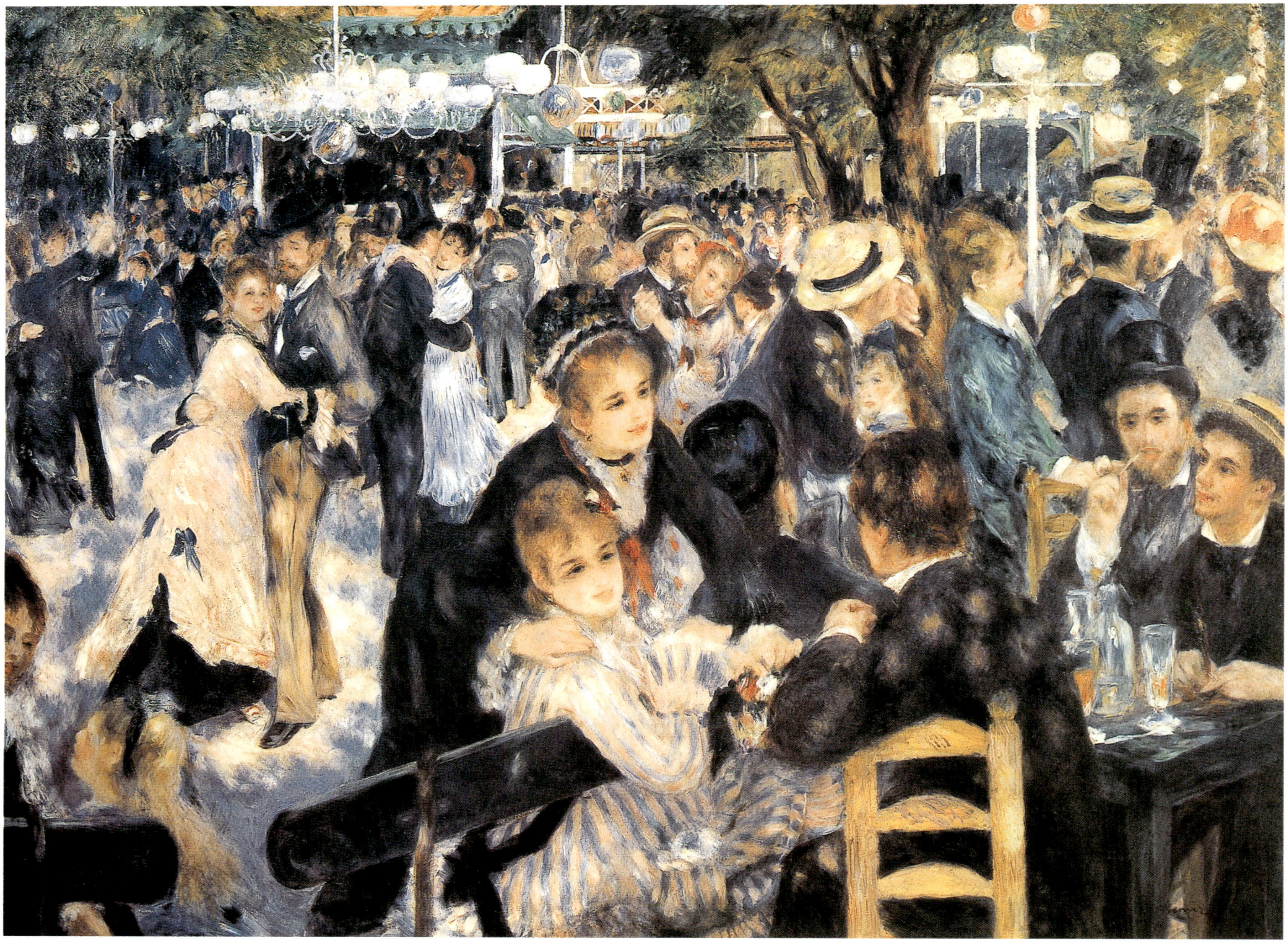

RENOIR
Ball at the Moulin de la Galette
oil on canvas
1876. 131 × 175 cm
In order to paint this composition, Renoir called on some patient friends. The three men on the right are Pierre Franc-Lamy and Norbert Goenette, both painters, and the writer Georges Rivière. On the bench are two sisters, Estelle and Jeanne, the latter was Renoir's new model, who also posed for The Swing. *The dancer in pink is Margot (Marguerite Legrand) with the Cuban painter Solarès. The girls were all from the working classes and the men were younger friends of the artist.*

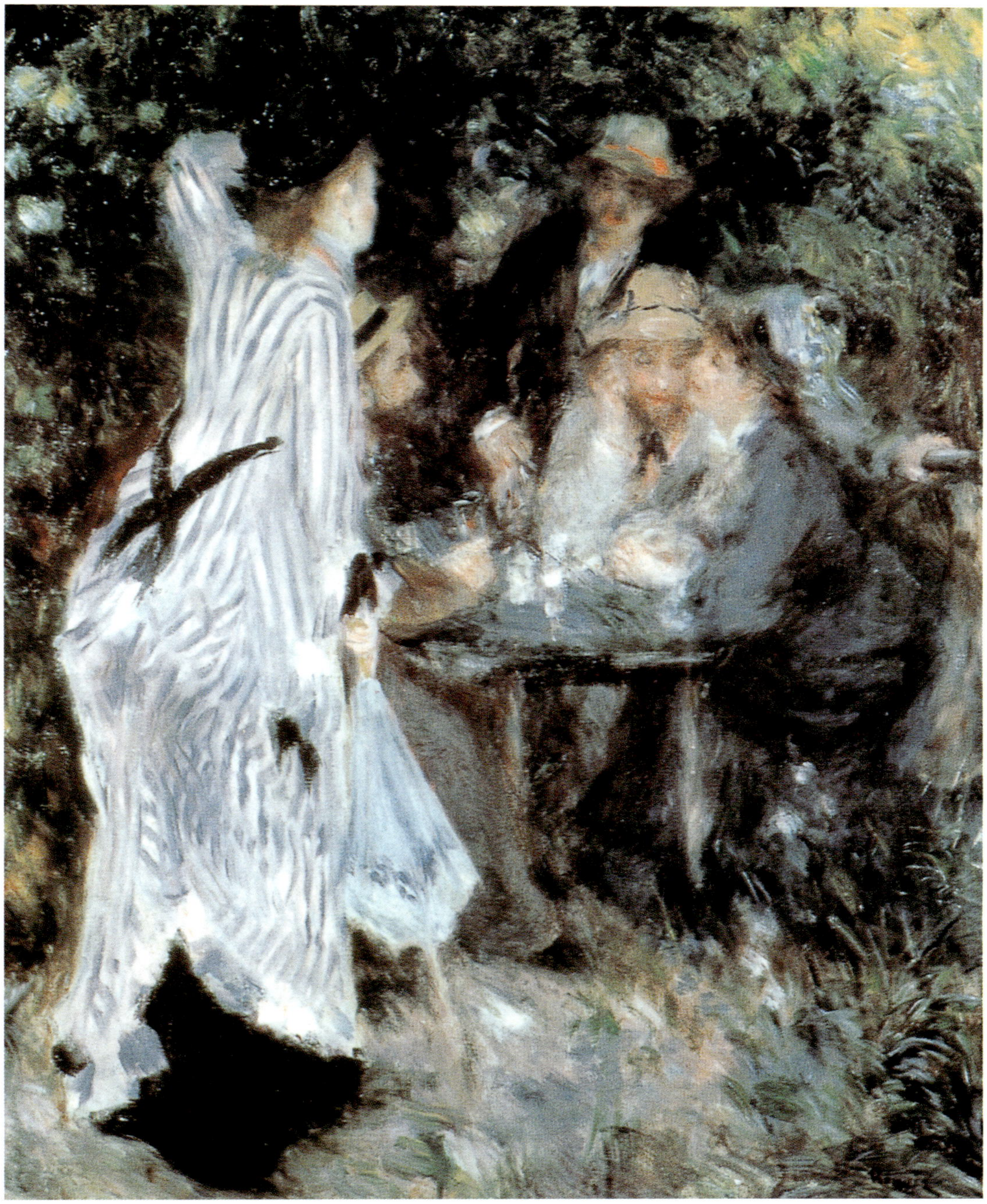

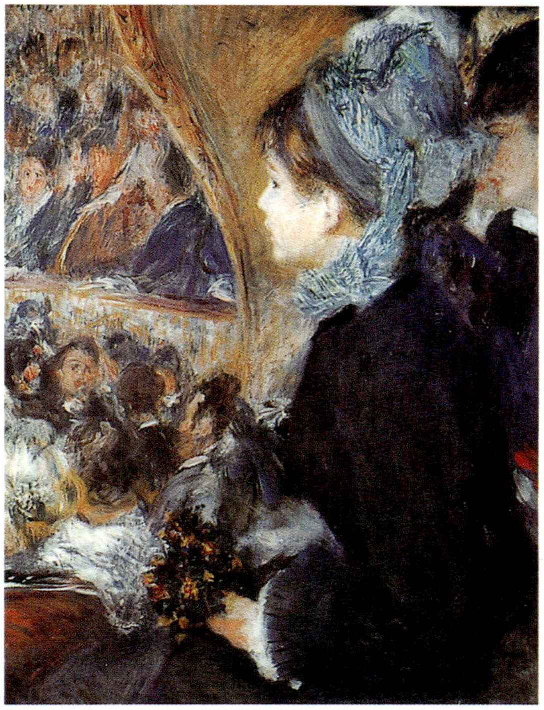

RENOIR
The First Outing
oil on canvas
c.1876–77. 65 × 49.5 cm
ABOVE Two years after La Loge, *the atmosphere of this picture is very different. The girl is a young and unsophisticated figure. It has been recently discovered that Renoir had originally painted a male figure in profile, which occupied most of the space now taken by the distant boxes, and that the blue garment left of centre was part of this man's jacket.*

RENOIR
Under the Arbour, Moulin de la Galette
oil on canvas
1876. 81 × 65 cm
It is a sunny Sunday, the characters are all younger than the artist, and life has no more weight on this leisurely afternoon than it has in the works of the eighteenth-century artists.

Commune was in power and the city was under siege. Nothing could stop him painting though, and he obtained a pass from the Prefect of Police and was able to leave Paris on painting expeditions and to visit his parents in Louveciennes.

Between 1871 and 1874 Renoir continued his close association with Monet, visiting him at Argenteuil during the summers, as well as becoming more intimately involved in the fledgling *Société anonyme*; he now had a studio in Montmartre in the rue Saint-Georges where the *Société anonyme* often met in 1873 to plan its first exhibition. His style was beginning to mature; his view of the *Pont Neuf* of 1872, though the choice of the subject was influenced by Monet, presents a highly original use of colour and contrasts strongly with a rather dour view of a similar subject, the *Pont des Arts*, done in 1867. Renoir's brother Edmond, a journalist, had an interesting anecdote about how the *Pont Neuf* was painted. The two brothers would take up residence at a little café and for ten centimes each they could sit with two coffees for hours. Whilst Auguste painted, Edmond scribbled, occasionally venturing onto the bridge to engage passers-by in conversation so that Auguste could sketch them *in situ*. In another vein the *Morning Ride in the Bois de Boulogne* (*L'Allée cavaliére au Bois de Boulogne*) of 1873, an enormous canvas eight and a half by seven and a half feet, is an attempt by Renoir to paint a large-scale work with the Salon in mind. Despite this ambition, it was rejected and appeared at the Salon des Refusés.

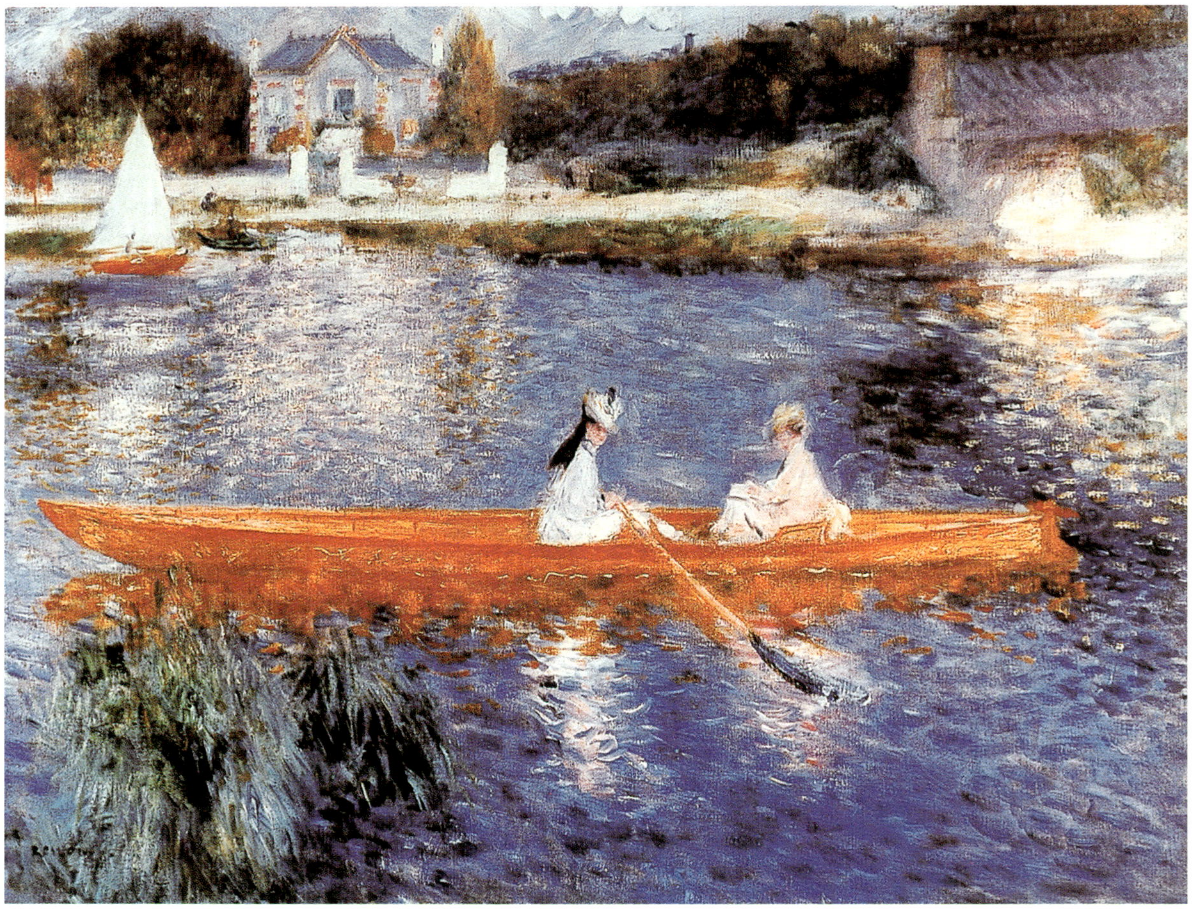

RENOIR
The Seine at Asnières (The Skiff)
oil on canvas
c.1879. 71 × 92 cm
Victor Chocquet bought this painting, one of a series of boating scenes which Renoir painted between 1879 and 1880. Renoir succeeded in rendering the flickering of light dancing on the river, using small brushstrokes to depict the water. In the background a train advances from behind a hedge. This is the archetypal rainbow palette.

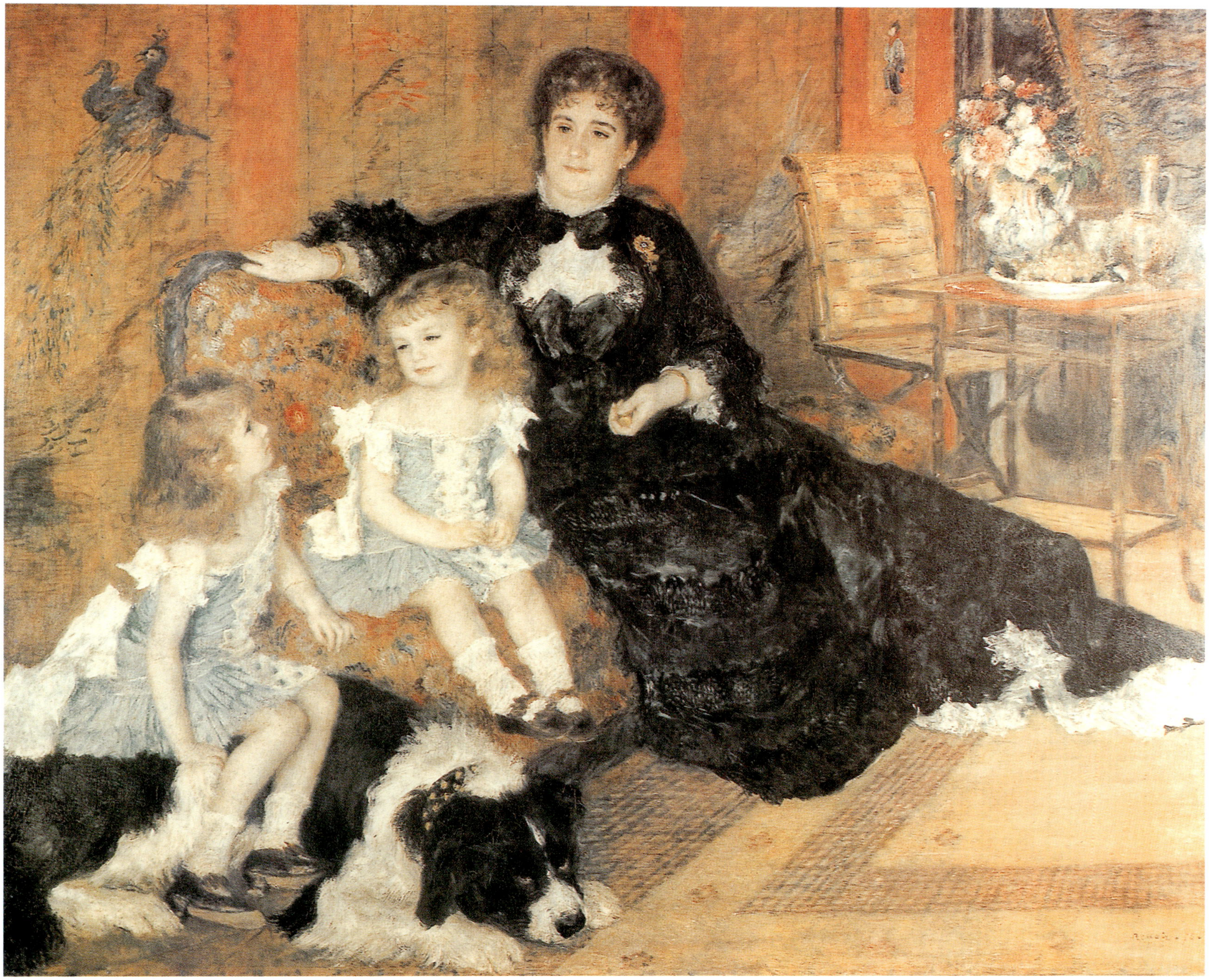

RENOIR
Madame Charpentier and Her Children
oil on canvas
1878. 154 × 190 cm
In 1876, Renoir had the good fortune to meet the Charpentiers, a wealthy and influential couple. Marguerite commissioned her own portrait and, using her connections, made sure that it was prominently displayed at the Salon. However, this did not spare the work from criticism, some of which could be applied to much of Renoir's work: a gifted colourist but lacking in draughtsmanship.

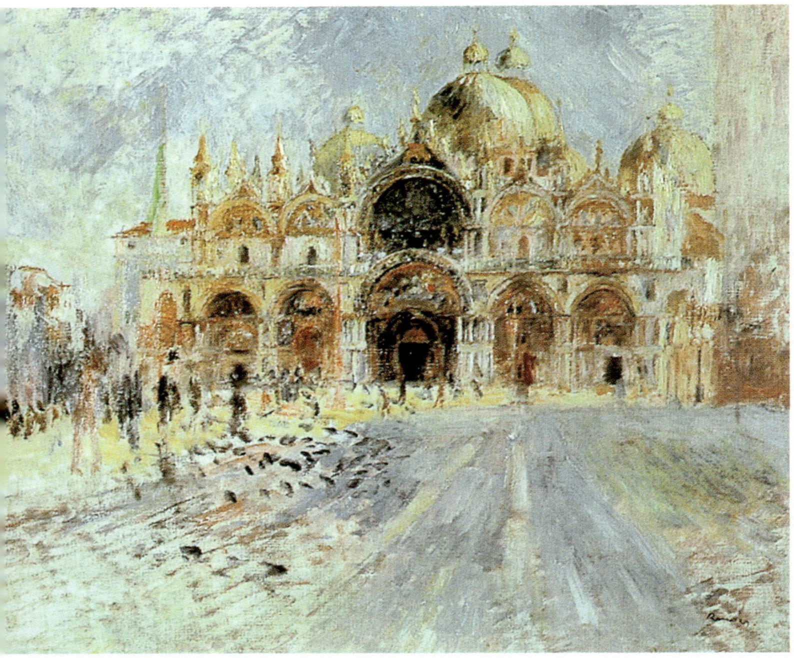

RENOIR
Venice, Piazza S. Marco
oil on canvas
1881. 64 × 81 cm
ABOVE This lively picture is unfinished and Renoir's dealer, Durand-Ruel, declined to purchase it although it has glowing qualities and the rendering of the basilica itself is complete. The ultimate purpose of this trip was to study the works of the Italian old masters at a time when he was seeking to improve his technique.

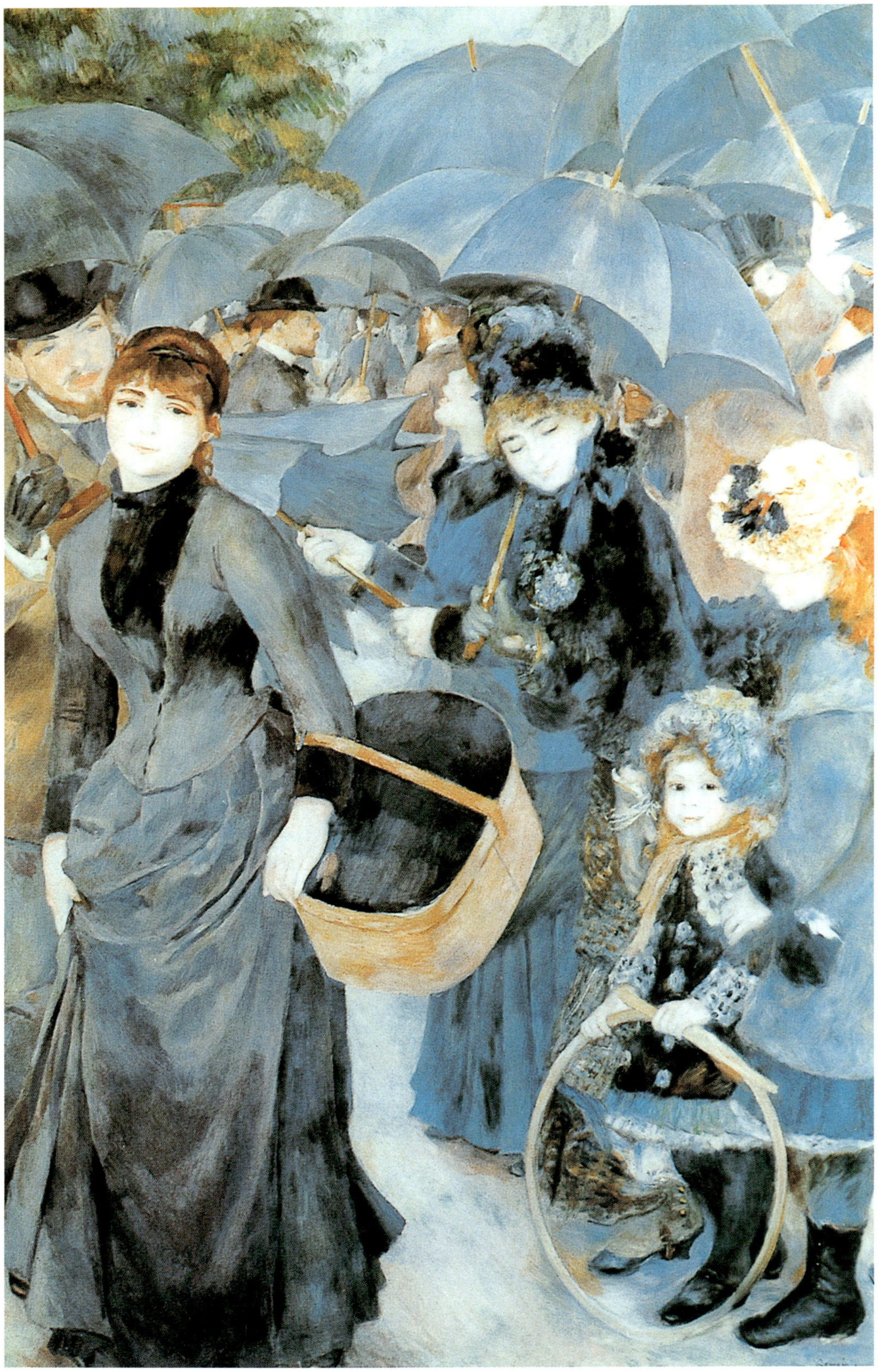

RENOIR
The Umbrellas
oil on canvas
c.1885. 180.5 × 115 cm
RIGHT Many artists begin with a tighter style which becomes somewhat looser as they gain experience and self-confidence. The opposite was true in Renoir's case: he felt he had reached a dead-end and his observation of the neat contours and finish of painters such as Raphael prompted him to work with more discipline and care.

When the accounts for the first exhibition of the *Société anonyme* were drawn up after the disastrous exhibition of 1874 each member of the society owed 184 francs 50 centimes; few paintings had been sold, although Renoir had managed to avoid most of the hysterical criticism aimed at colleagues such as Monet, Pissarro, and Degas. One of the pictures Renoir exhibited, *La Loge*, the first of several paintings on this theme and now considered an icon of Impressionism, was later bought by Père Martin, a rather dubious small-time dealer, for the sum of 425 francs. This was not an insubstantial amount for an impecunious artist – in any case Renoir owed it in back rent – but a Salon picture by Meissonier, for example, could fetch 40,000 francs. In December the *Société* terminated, with Renoir as the chairman. The next year, resourceful as ever, he had the idea of a joint auction with Monet, Sisley, and Morisot to be held at the Hôtel Drouot. The newly named Impressionists were by now so infamous that there were demonstrations when the paintings went on show in March. Renoir sold twenty works for an average of 112 francs, with some going for as little as 50 francs. Thankfully Renoir's precarious position was now helped by the fortunate arrival on the scene of the collector Victor Chocquet who commissioned several portraits of his family which kept the artist financially afloat.

In 1875 Renoir had rented for a hundred francs a month the dilapidated outbuildings of

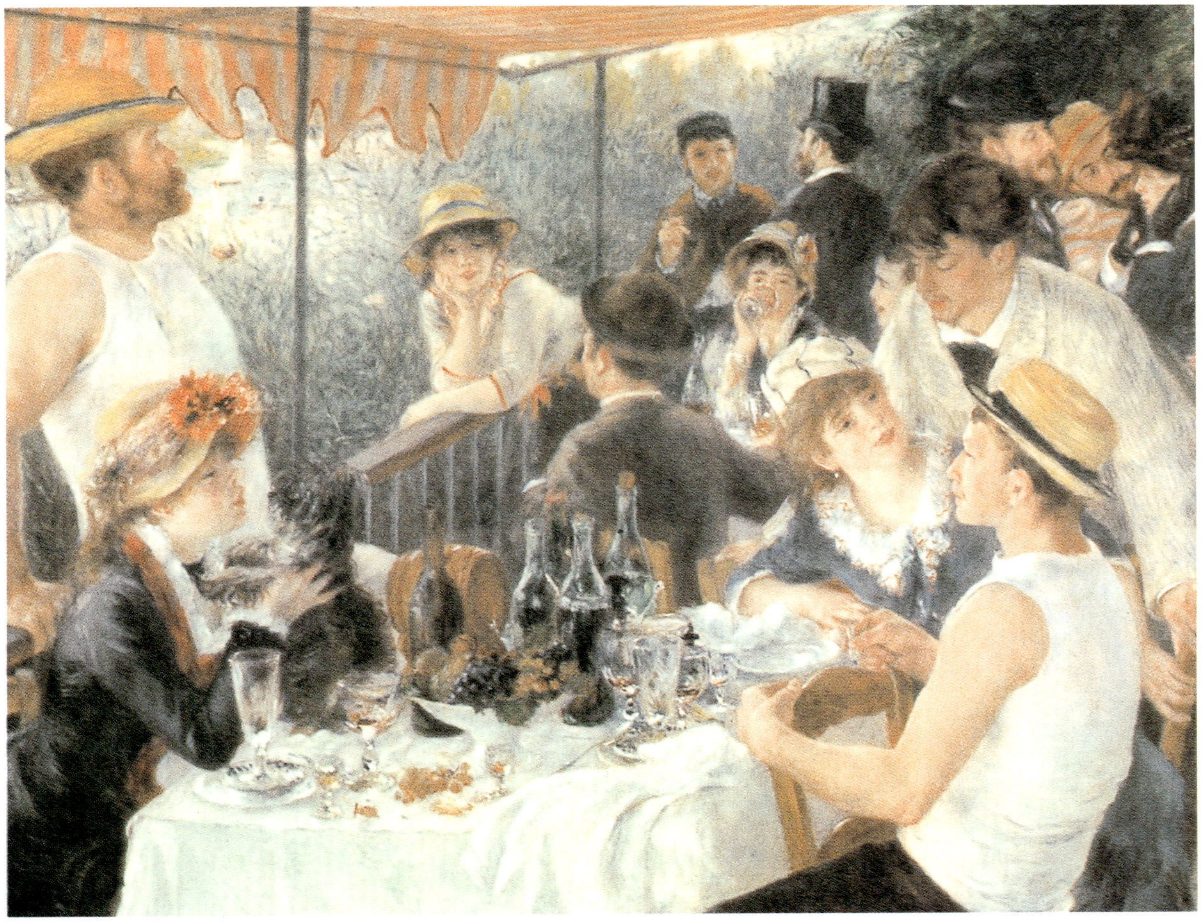

RENOIR
Luncheon of the Boating Party
oil on canvas
1880–81. 130 × 173 cm
On the left, holding a small dog, is Aline Charigot, Renoir's future companion and wife. Alphonse Fournaise, son of the establishment's owner, stands next to her. The girl leaning on the balustrade is a model. The man wearing a top hat is Charles Ephrussi, a wealthy writer and collector. Angèle, another model, is seated, drinking. The painter Lhote leans forward to talk to the actress Jeanne Samary, and the painter Caillebotte, another close friend of Renoir's, wearing a singlet and a straw hat, is seated in the foreground. This was the last of Renoir's crowd scenes, and one of his most popular works ever.

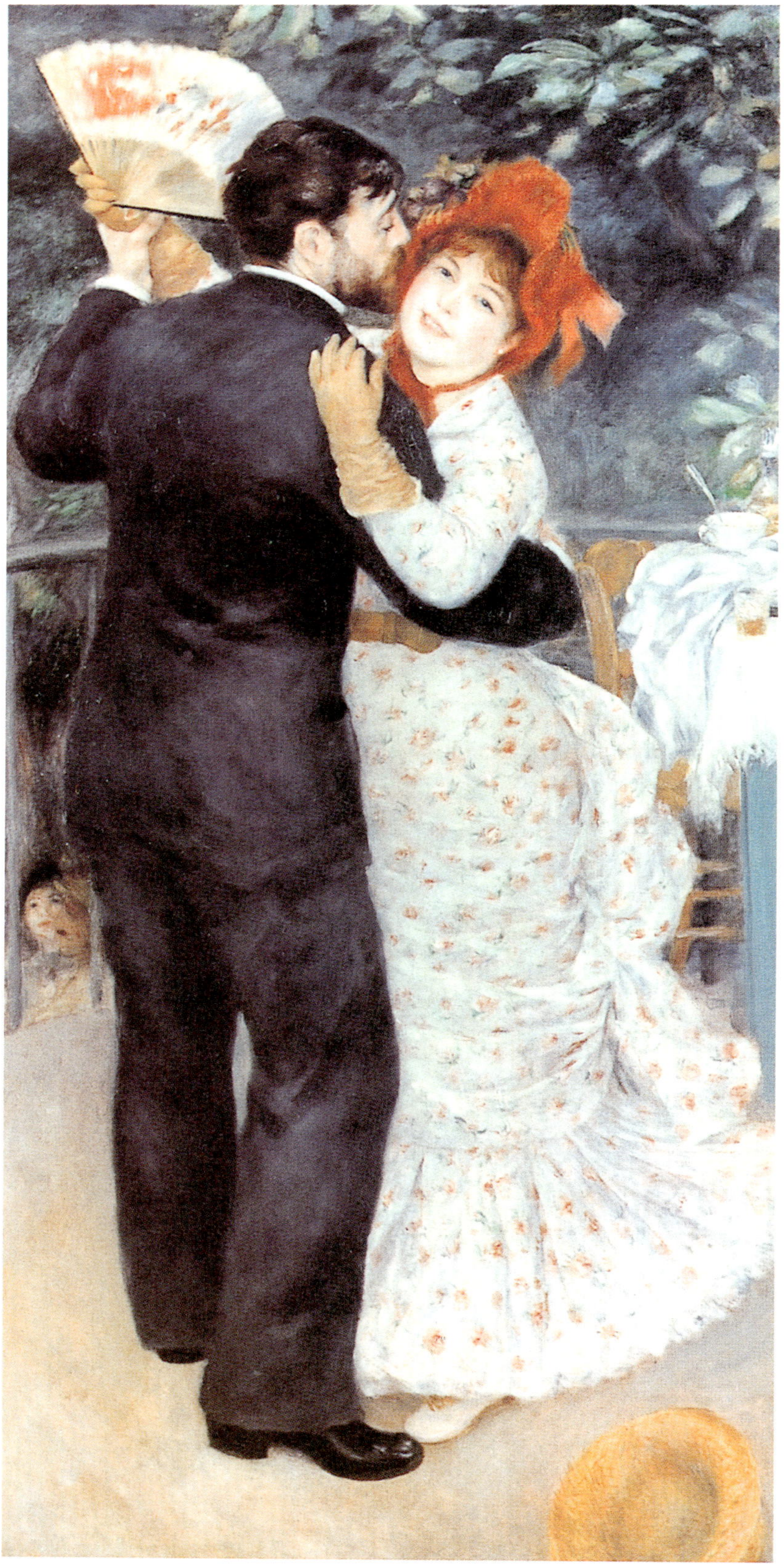

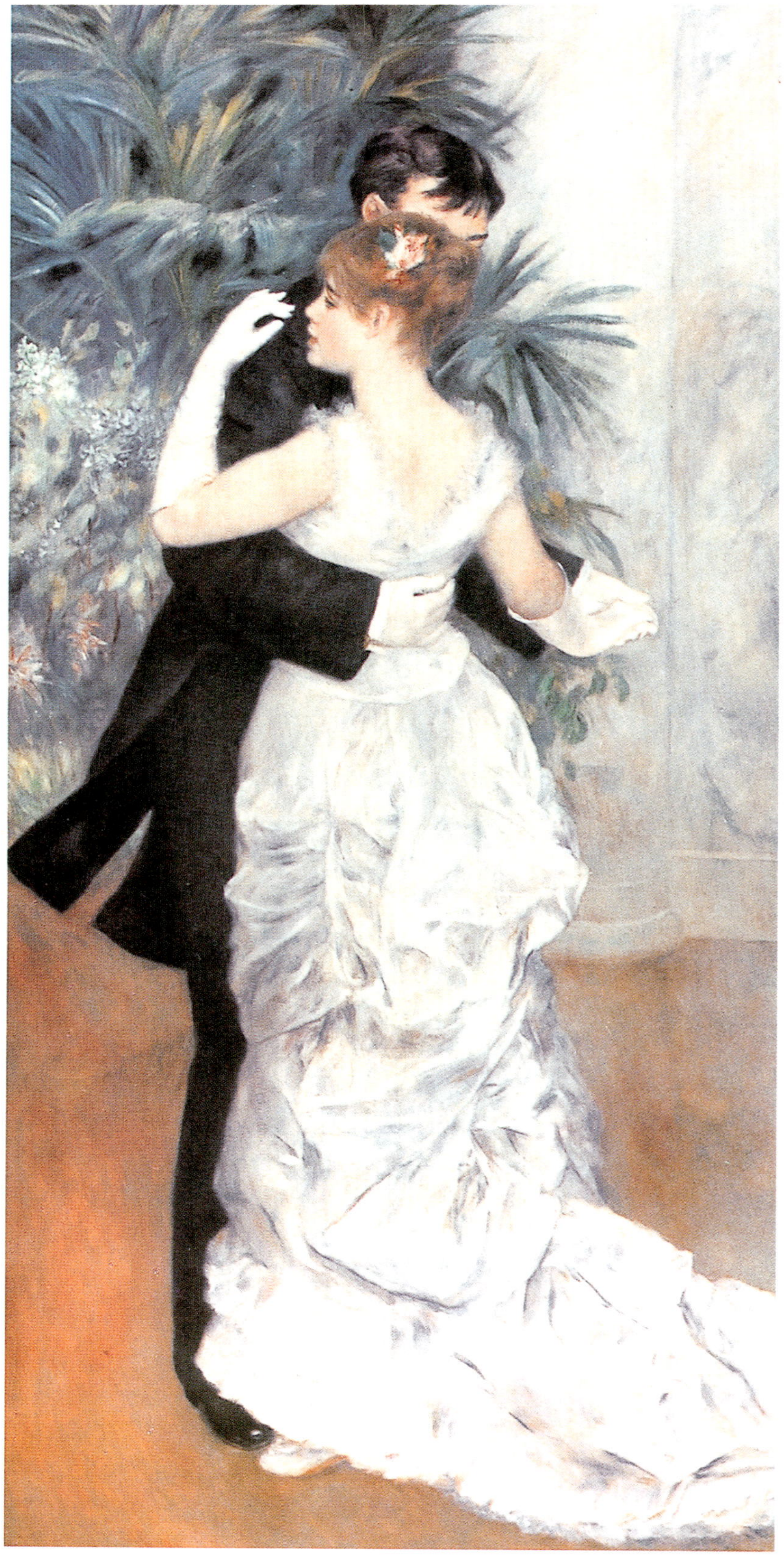

RENOIR
Dance in the Country
oil on canvas
1882–83. 180 × 90 cm
Opposite left Renoir painted three nearly life-size dancing couples between 1882 and 1883. The differences are quite marked between the relaxed and happy Aline in Dance in the Country, *who was putting on weight, and the more composed, elegant couple of* Dance in the City, *for which the young model Maria Clémentine (later known as the painter Suzanne Valadon) was the model. Renoir's old friend Lhote, who had posed for several other pictures, is the partner in both panels.*

RENOIR
Dance in the City
oil on canvas
1882–83. 180 × 90 cm
Opposite right

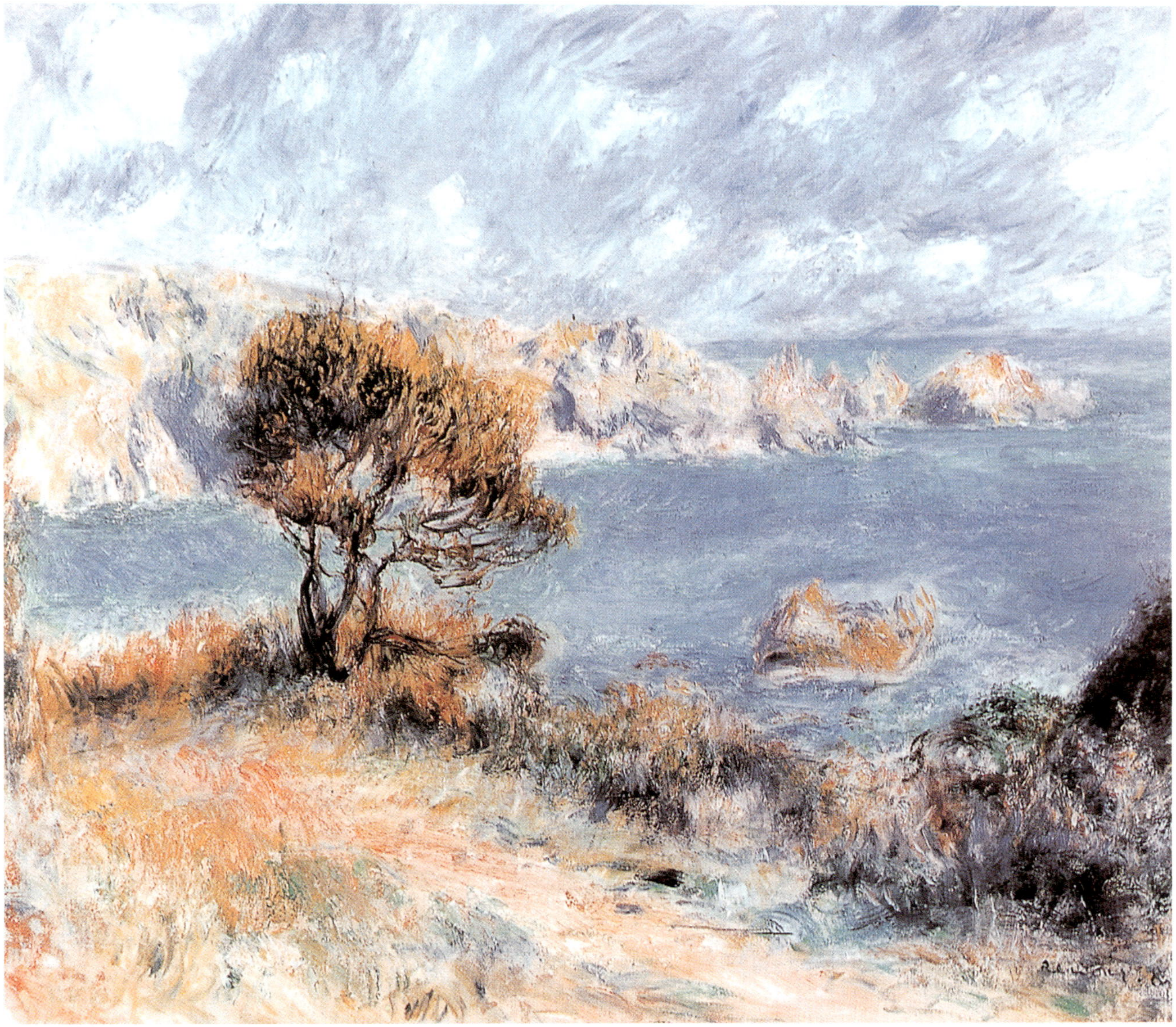

RENOIR
Landscape at Guernsey
oil on canvas
1883. 46 × 56 cm
Left Renoir and his family spent a month on the Channel Island of Guernsey in the late summer of 1883, where he painted around fifteen pictures, many of them intended as sketches to be used for studio compositions later on.

an old folly with a garden in the rue Cortot as a studio. The next summer his friends Pierre Lamey, Frédéric Cordey, and Georges Rivière often joined him in outings to a popular haunt, the Moulin de la Galette – a dance hall and café beneath one of the last remaining windmills of Montmartre. According to Georges Rivière, in the mornings he and the others would help Renoir carry his canvas and easel round the corner to the dance hall where the artist spent the summer painting a large scene of the crowds there now known as the *Ball at the Moulin de la Galette* – one of several masterpieces he was to produce that summer. Although he certainly worked on it *in situ*, posing his friends and acquaintances, including Rivière, it was prepared with sketches and finished in the studio in the rue Cortot. Nevertheless, it is Renoir's first large-scale figure painting to deploy the swift technique he had been perfecting since the summer of 1869 at La Grenouillère with Monet. The dappled sunlight is a particular feature of this period, as is the abandoned use

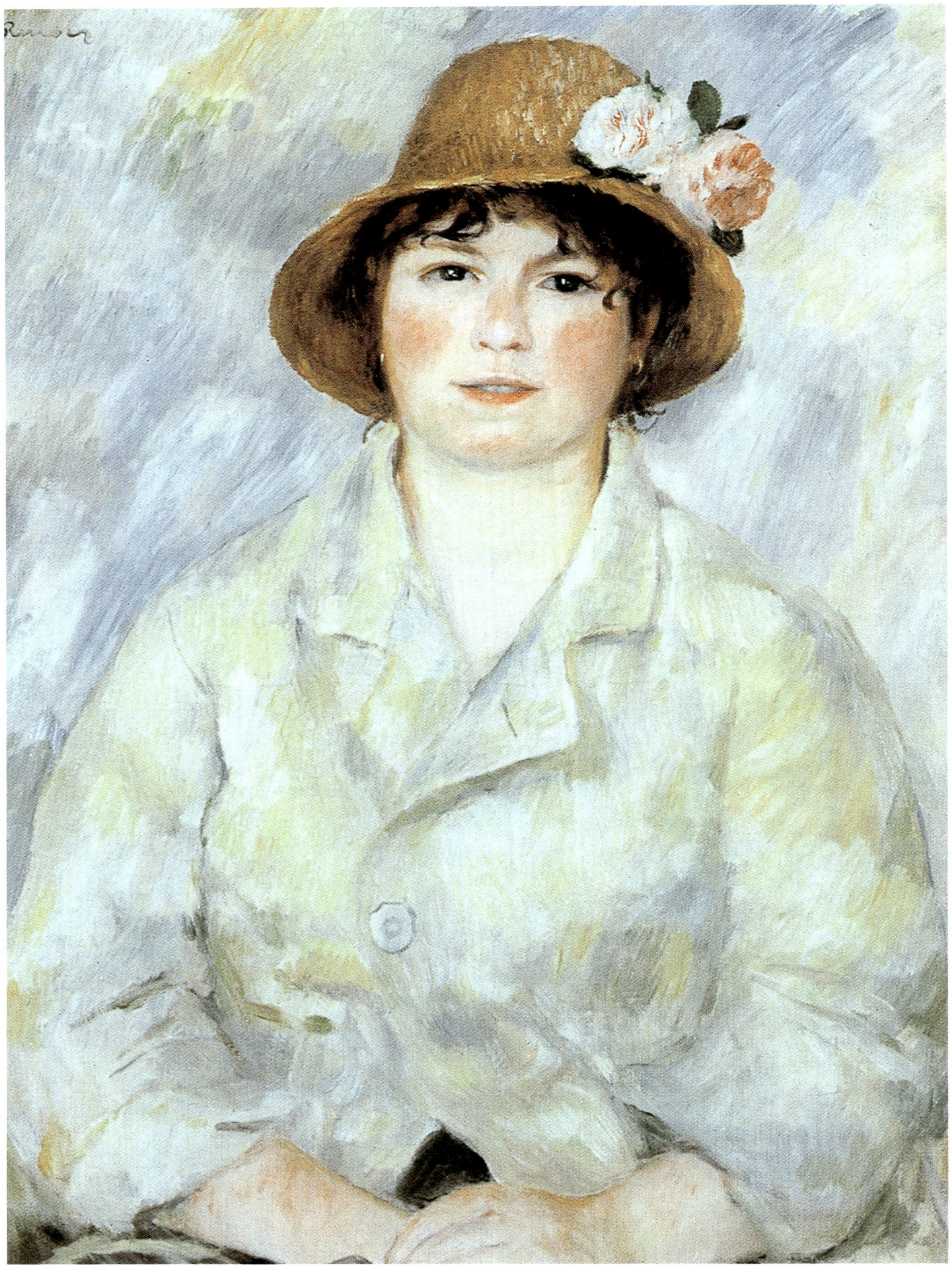

RENOIR
Aline Charigot
oil on canvas
c.1885. 65 × 54 cm
ABOVE The rendering of this portrait, which Renoir kept all his life, evokes the diagonals of Cézanne.

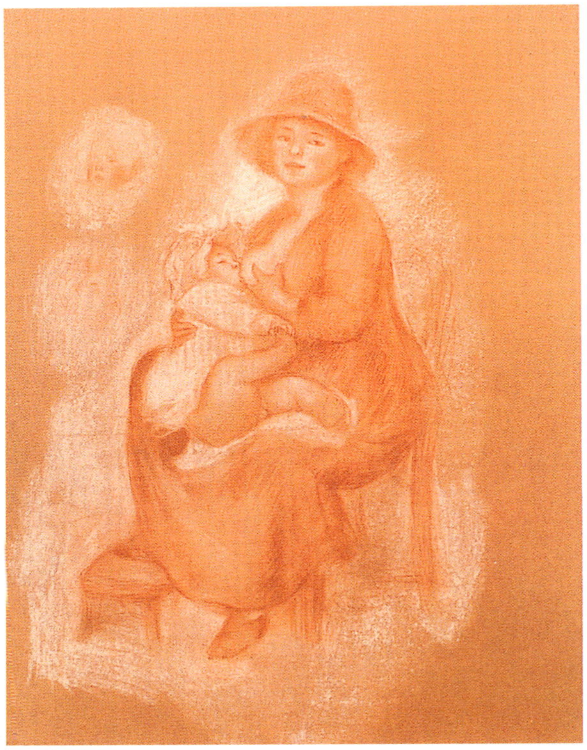

of colour in the shadows. The painting was shown at the third Impressionist group exhibition the next year when a critic under the pseudonymous name of Flor O'Squarr said of Renoir's painting:

> The painter had caught perfectly the raucous and slightly bohemian atmosphere of this open-air dance hall, perhaps the last of its kind in Paris . . . The harsh sunlight is filtered through the greenery, sets the blonde hair and pink cheeks of the girls aglow and makes their ribbons sparkle. The joyful light fills every corner of the canvas and even the shadows reflect it. The whole painting shimmers like a rainbow and makes one think of the dainty Chinese princess described by Heinrich Heine: her greatest pleasure in life was to tear up satin and silk with her polished jade-like nails and watch the shreds of yellow, blue, and pink drift away in the breeze like so many butterflies.

RENOIR
Maternity
sketch in red chalk
1885.
OPPOSITE RIGHT Renoir made a number of sketches and three paintings of Aline with their first son, Pierre. The artist, who already complained of being old when he was forty, and who was forty-four at the time of his son's birth, was very moved by the birth of his children.

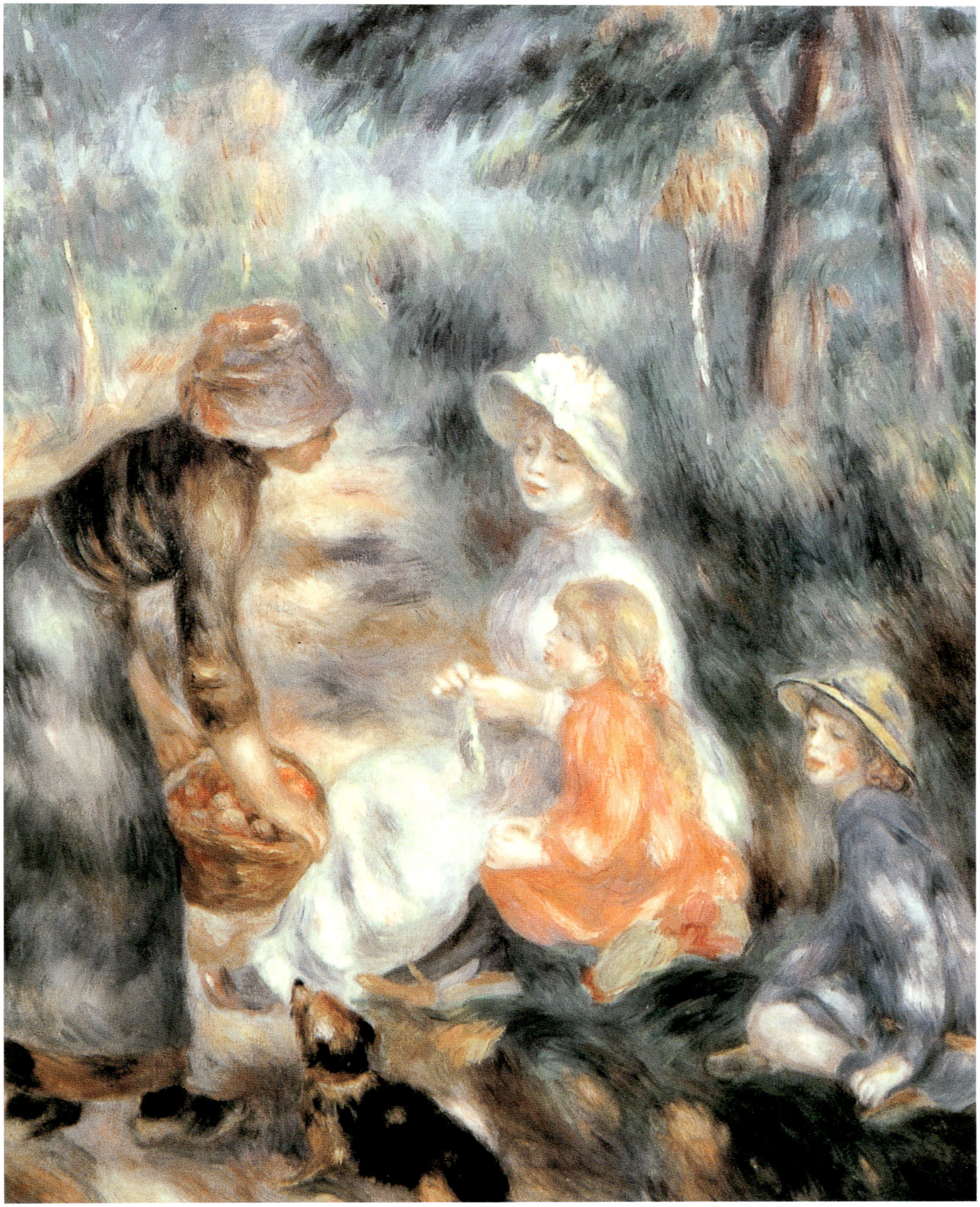

RENOIR
The Apple Seller
oil on canvas
c.1890. 66 × 54 cm
In this rustic scene, Aline poses with a young girl and probably her son, Pierre, seated to the right. This is the most elaborate of three pictures Renoir painted on the same theme.

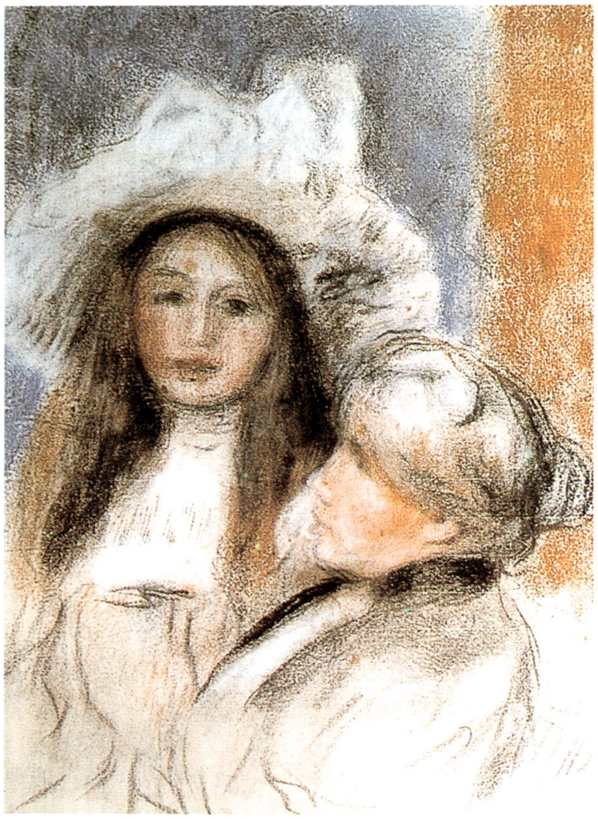

RENOIR
Berthe Morisot and Her Daughter, Julie Manet
pastel on paper
1894. 59 × 45 cm
In his later years, Renoir had become close to Berthe Morisot and Degas. Distressed by the death in 1892 of her husband Eugène Manet, Morisot had aged rapidly. She is seen here with her fifteen-year old daughter, Julie, who fills most of the space and attracts the eye, perhaps subconsciously because Renoir was essentially a painter of youth, though the balance between the two sitters is somewhat restored in the oil portrait.

This summer also produced the equally famous *The Swing* (*La Balançoire*), thought to have been painted in the garden at the rue Cortot. A young woman from the neighbourhood, Jeanne, posed on the swing (and is also present in *The Ball*). The same dappled light is more intensely expressed here and imbues the picture with that insouciant charm of which only Renoir (who had of course once copied Watteau for a living) was capable. Zola was so taken with the painting that he used it in his novel *Une Page d'amour* of 1878, where the heroine is "standing on the very edge of the swing and holding the ropes, with her arms outstretched . . . she was wearing a grey dress decorated with mauve bows . . . That day the sunlight was like light-coloured dust in the pale sky . . . "

Towards the end of the 1870s Renoir began to be less involved with the Impressionists as a group. After the third Impressionist exhibition in 1877 he forsook the group and began to concentrate on the Salon as an outlet for his work. His new patrons the Charpentiers were now beginning to commission portraits as well as decorations for their town house in Paris, and Renoir scored a relative success at the Salon of 1879 with the *Portrait of Madame Charpentier and her Children*. Marcel Proust includes a long description of the painting in *Le Temps retrouvé* (*Time Regained*) and likens it to "Titian at his best". The most favourable reviews concentrated on Renoir's use of colour, which was by now quite brilliant. The steady development of what became known as his rainbow palette can be seen in perhaps its most scintillating and impressionistic form in *Boating on the Seine* (*Canotage sur la Seine*), (also known as *The Skiff*, or *The Seine at Asnières*, though it was probably painted at Chatou), produced around the same time as the Charpentier portrait. The painting shows an almost textbook application of Chevreul's principles of simultaneous colour contrast. Renoir uses only seven pigments and white, applying them to the canvas in bold, practically unmixed patches to convey an impression of sheer luminosity.

It is ironic and typical of Renoir's nature that at a time he was producing veritable icons of Impressionist art he was also beginning to have serious doubts about his own ability. The financial need to paint an increasing number of society portraits no doubt aggravated the strain on his own artistic judgment of himself. To make matters worse, in 1880 he and Monet had fallen out with Degas, who they suspected was highjacking the Impressionist exhibitions and populating them with his protegés. A trip to Algiers, his first abroad, in the spring of 1881 reassured

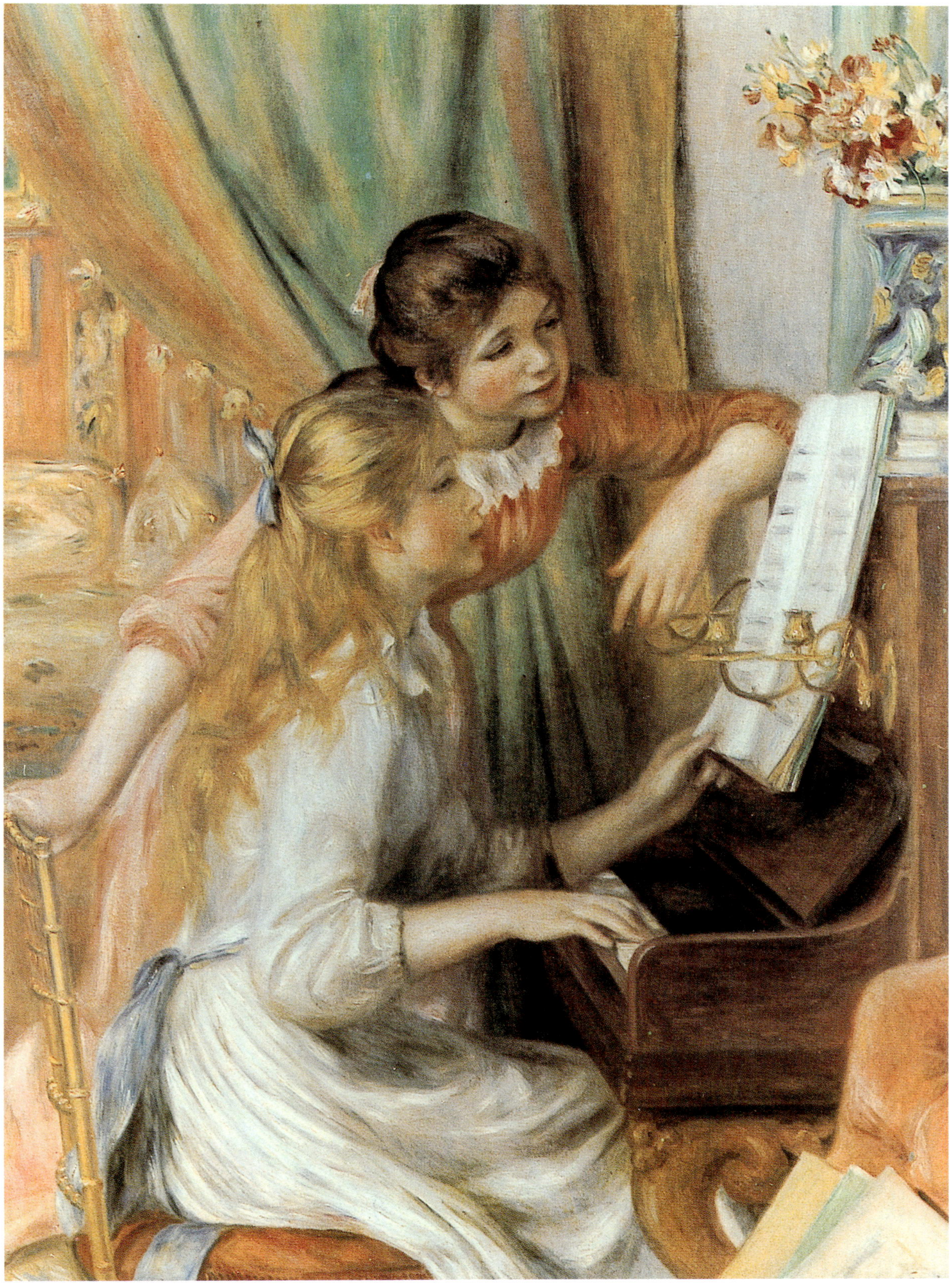

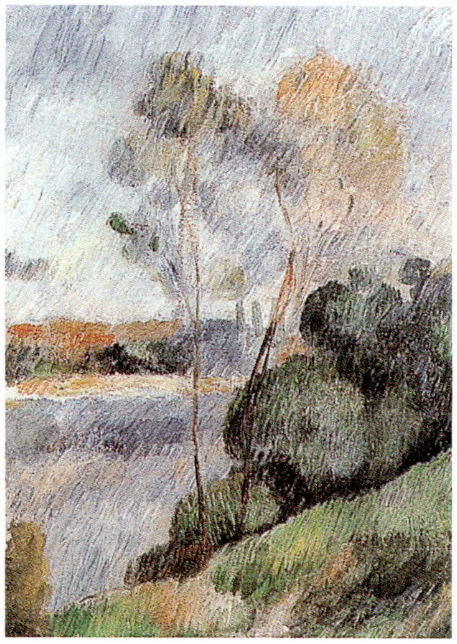

RENOIR
Landscape
oil cn canvas
c.1895. 46 × 33 cm
Above Renoir was deliberately trying to adapt Cézanne's diagonal brushstrokes to his own style and to adapt his colour harmony. This is an atypical work, more vigorous than his usual pictures.

RENOIR
Girls at the Piano
oil on canvas
1892. 116 × 90 cm
Left Renoir, at last an established artist, was asked by the French government to provide a substantial painting for the national collection, for which he was to be paid 4,000 francs.

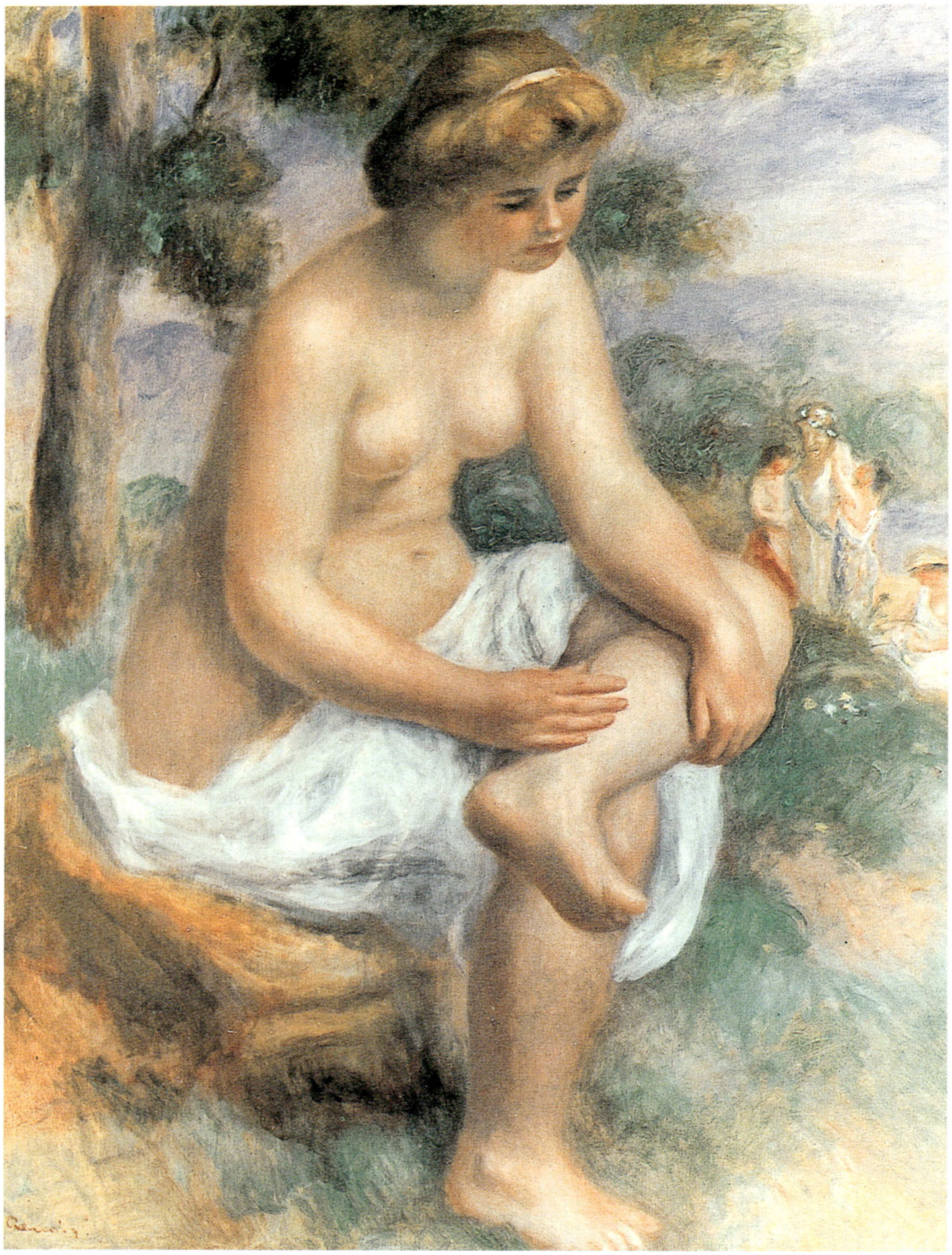

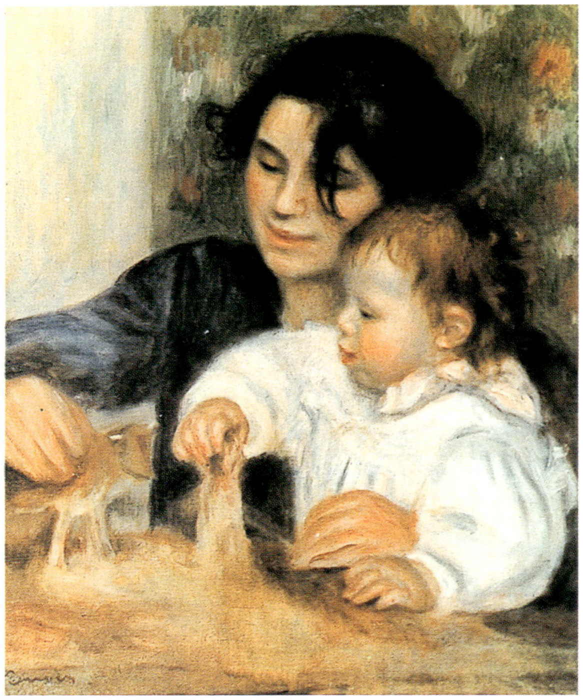

him of the direction he was taking as an Impressionist and he was soon back in France at Chatou and Bougival painting masterpieces such as *Luncheon of the Boating Party* (*Le Déjeuner des canoteurs*) with rekindled vigour. But by October he had left for Italy, writing to Mme Charpentier: "I have suddenly become a traveller and I am in a fever to see the Raphaels . . . "

Renoir had gone to Algeria in the Romantic footsteps of Delacroix, but he now approached Italy seeking the formal classicism of Raphael, which he was to find in the great decorations at the Villa Farnesina. He was also profoundly influenced by what he called "the grandeur and simplicity" of the ancient Pompeian wall paintings in Naples. It was some time, however, before these new influences could reconcile themselves in his work: " . . . it's all a mess. I'm still making a mess and I'm forty years old," he wrote to Durand-Ruel from Italy in November 1881.

Renoir returned to France in January 1882

RENOIR
Bather, (Eurydice)
oil on canvas
1895–1900. 116 × 89 cm
FAR LEFT This nude is not any nude, it is Venus in the nude. Here, four tiny figures in the background provide a pretext for the title. Renoir had by then completely returned to his "soft" style, which he attempted to control only when he was painting commissioned portraits.

RENOIR
Gabrielle and Jean
oil on canvas
1895–96. 65 × 54 cm
LEFT The Renoirs' second son, Jean, was born in September 1894, shortly after Gabrielle, a distant relative of Aline's, came to live with them as a housekeeper. She stayed more than twenty years with the family and became a frequent model for Renoir.

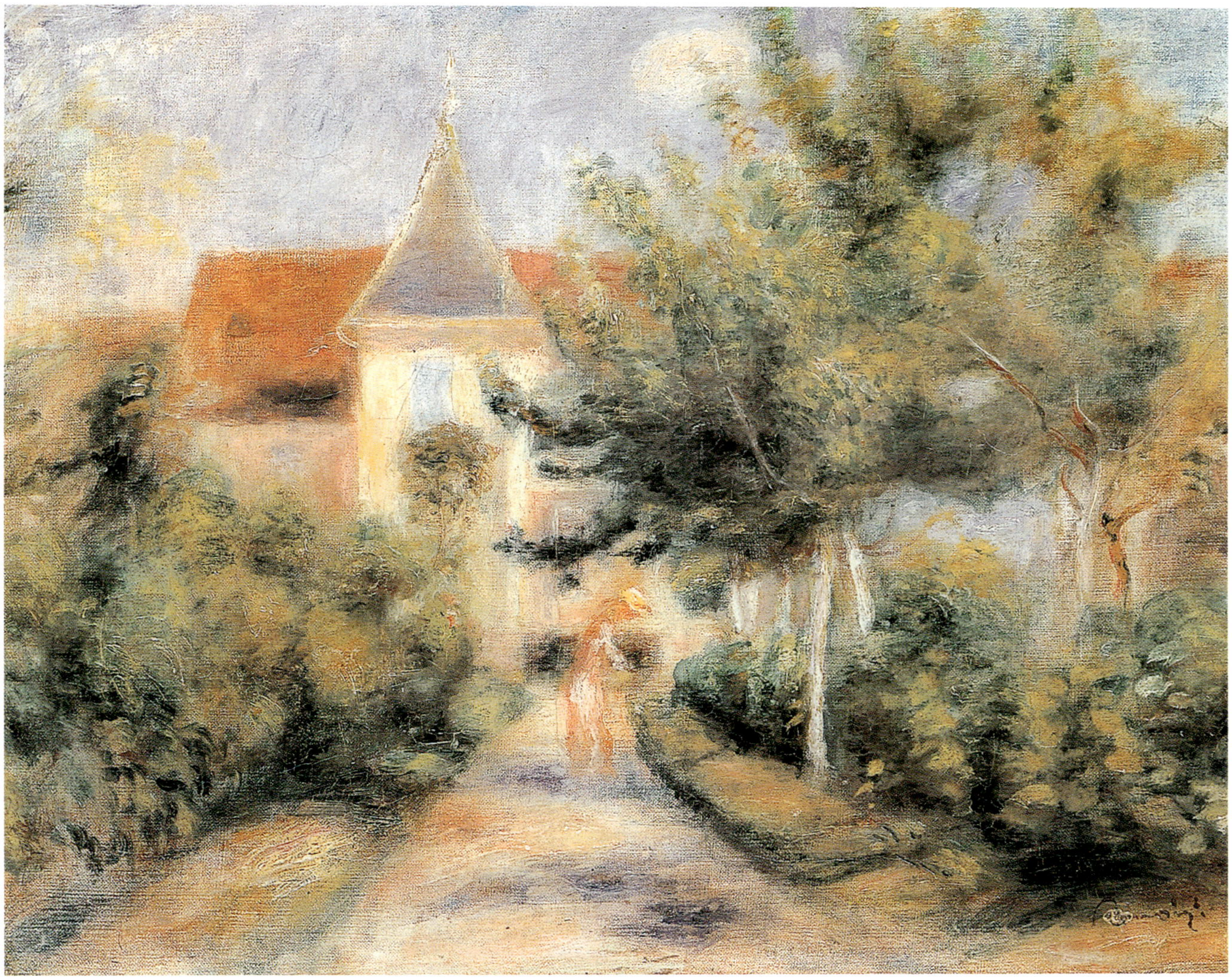

RENOIR
The Artist's House at Essoyes
oil on canvas
1906. 31 × 40 cm
RIGHT Renoir's late style became increasingly loose, which is partly explained by his failing eyesight and the crippling arthritis which in the end confined him to a wheelchair.

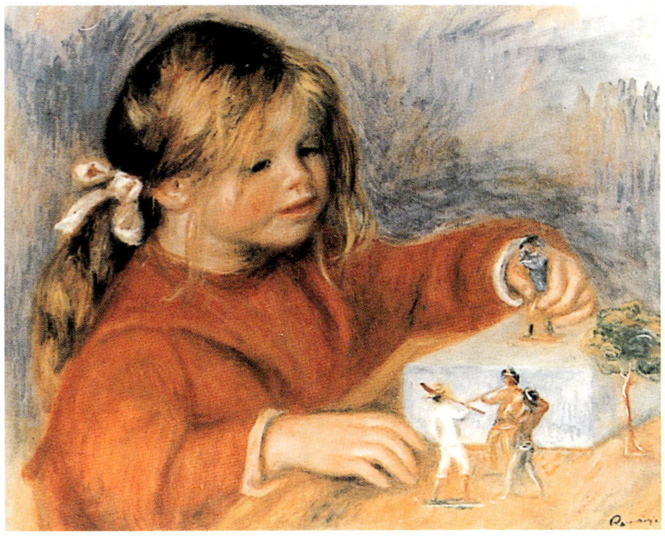

RENOIR
Claude Renoir Playing
oil on canvas
1905. 46 × 55 cm
RIGHT BELOW Renoir liked to portray children, particularly his own, and his style is well suited to their tender features.

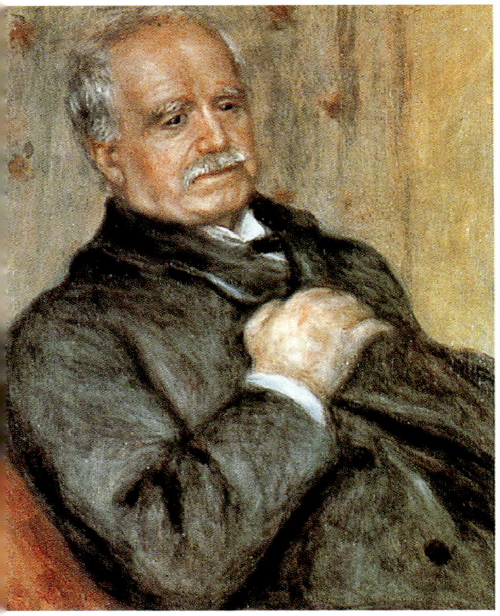

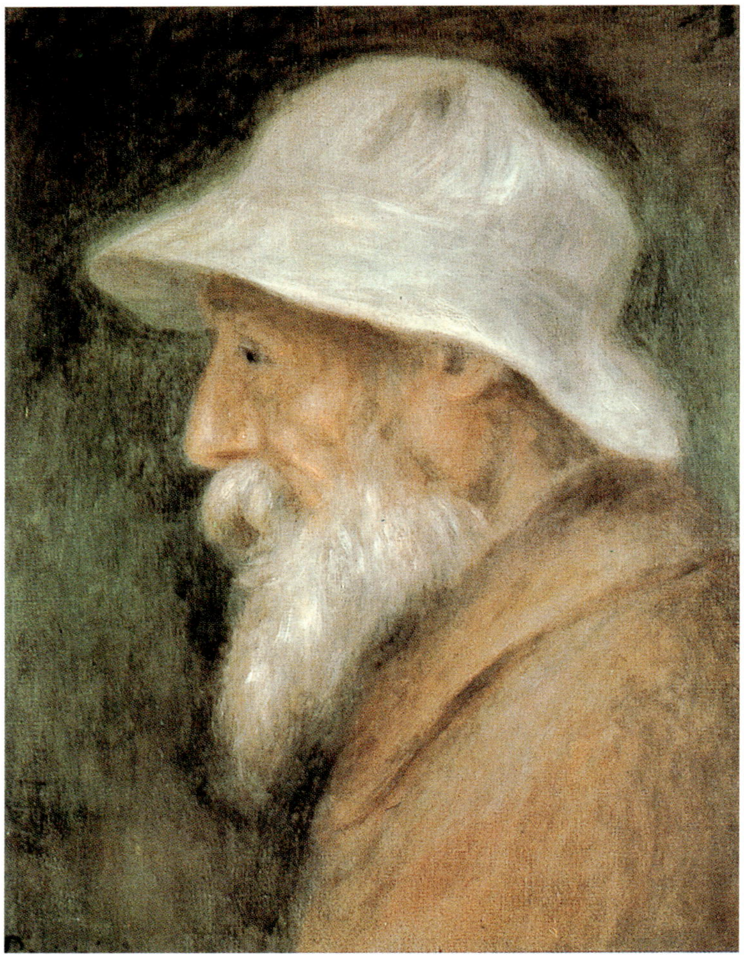

RENOIR
Portrait of Durand-Ruel
oil on canvas
1910. 65 × 54 cm
ABOVE Surprisingly, Renoir did not paint his longtime dealer and friend before 1910.

RENOIR
Self-portrait
oil on canvas
1910. 42 × 33 cm
RIGHT In this honest work, the artist has depicted himself at the age of sixty-nine.

and joined Cézanne at L'Estaque in the south of France where the two went on landscape expeditions and Renoir caught pneumonia. He had also caught something of Cézanne's vision of the hidden structure of planes and lines in nature. The confluence and confusion of the diverse influences at work on Renoir can be seen in *The Umbrellas* (*Les Parapluies*), which shows him struggling to reconcile a linear style with Impressionist brushwork. More importantly, in the mid-1880s there is a new concentration on the female nude as a vehicle for expressing light, colour and form. He told Berthe Morisot that, "the nude seemed to be one of the most essential forms of art." Renoir's fellow Impressionists and the dealer Durand-Ruel were mystified by the new linear style and said so, but Renoir persisted in his experiments with a series of *Bathers*, culminating in the monumental *Bathers* (*Baigneuses*) of 1887. His interest in the female form had also taken a new turn in 1885 when his mistress, Aline Charigot, bore his first son Pierre, prompting the artist to produce the Raphael-inspired *Maternity*, developing the simplified theme of the *Bathers*.

Renoir's "*manière aigre*" ("sour period") as he called it, came to an end in the late 1880s. After a trip to Spain in 1892 he drew new inspiration from Velazquez. The work of the eighteenth-century French painters Watteau and Fragonard which he had copied onto fans in his youth also came to influence him and he rediscovered the delicate virtues of Corot whose work was now much in demand by collectors. The insistence on line gradually softened but his humanistic concern with the figure remained overwhelmingly important.

In 1902 Renoir and Aline moved to the south of France where the warm climate eased the severe arthritis which was making it difficult for him to paint. He could now "only paint broadly" as he put it, and the nerve in his right eye was partially atrophied. Undaunted by his illness he embarked on a series of sculptures echoing the nude figure paintings, though he had to use the hands of an assistant to model them.

Aline died in 1915 of a heart attack caused by overweight; she was a compulsive eater. Renoir died on 3rd December 1919 and was buried next to her in Essoyes.

In 1900 he had been made a Knight of the Légion d'Honneur and in the last year of his life, he became a Commander of the Légion d'Honneur, a triumphant honour for a humble "*ouvrier de la peinture*".

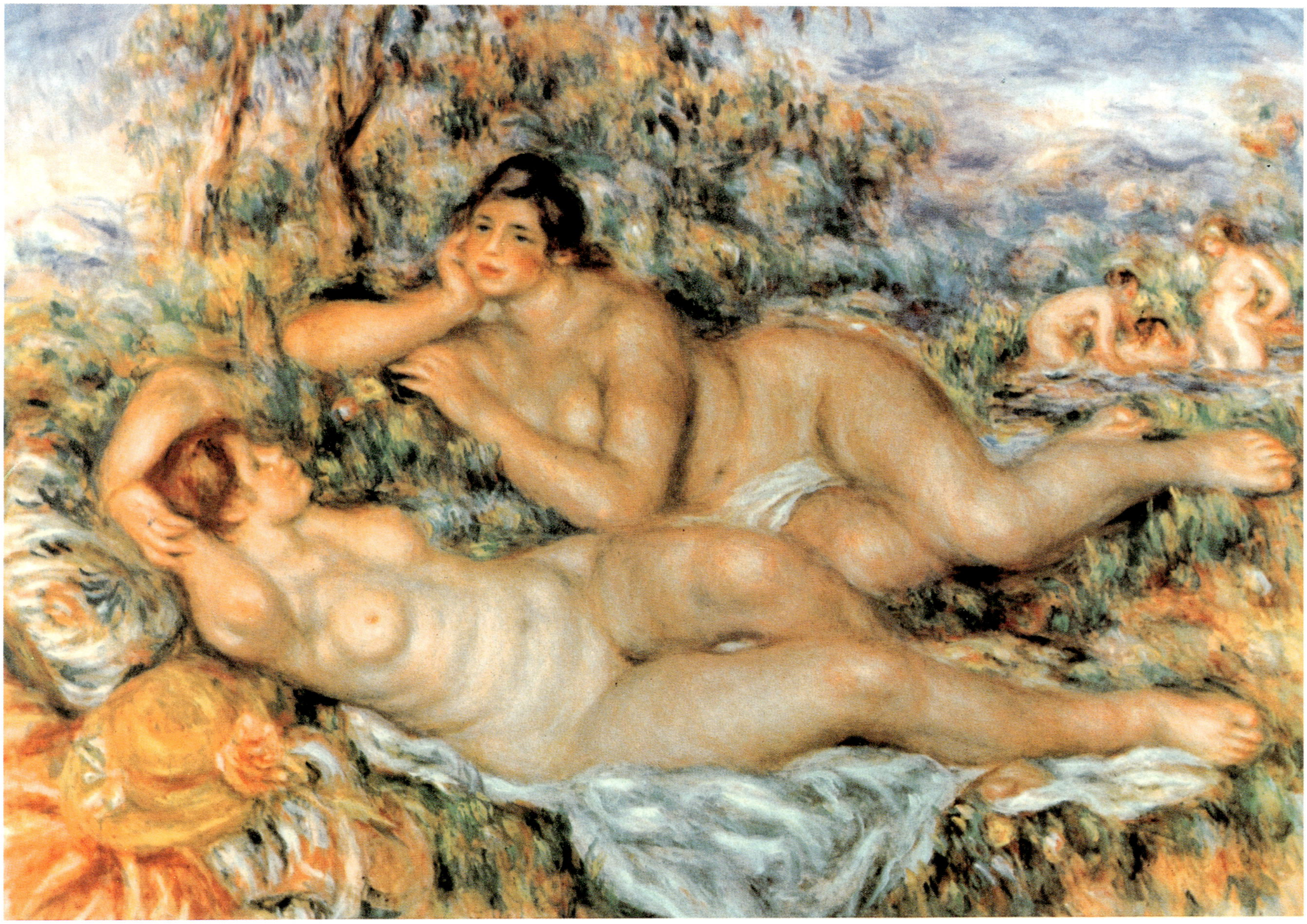

RENOIR
The Bathers
oil on canvas
c.1918–19. 110 × 160 cm
With this work, the ailing painter was determined to make a final statement, showing nude women in a landscape, two of his favourite subjects. Crippled by illness, he had the easel set up in such a manner that he could reach any part of this large canvas. Pain sometimes interrupted his work. His son, Jean, stated that his father "considered it as a final achievement. He thought he had summed up in it the research of his whole life", though to many people the painting is more often seen as the final work of a weakening artist. Georges Duthuit probably echoed the modern public's feeling when he wrote that "Renoir's late work was short of imagination, and deprived of any dramatic sense . . . so that one finds something slack and overblown."

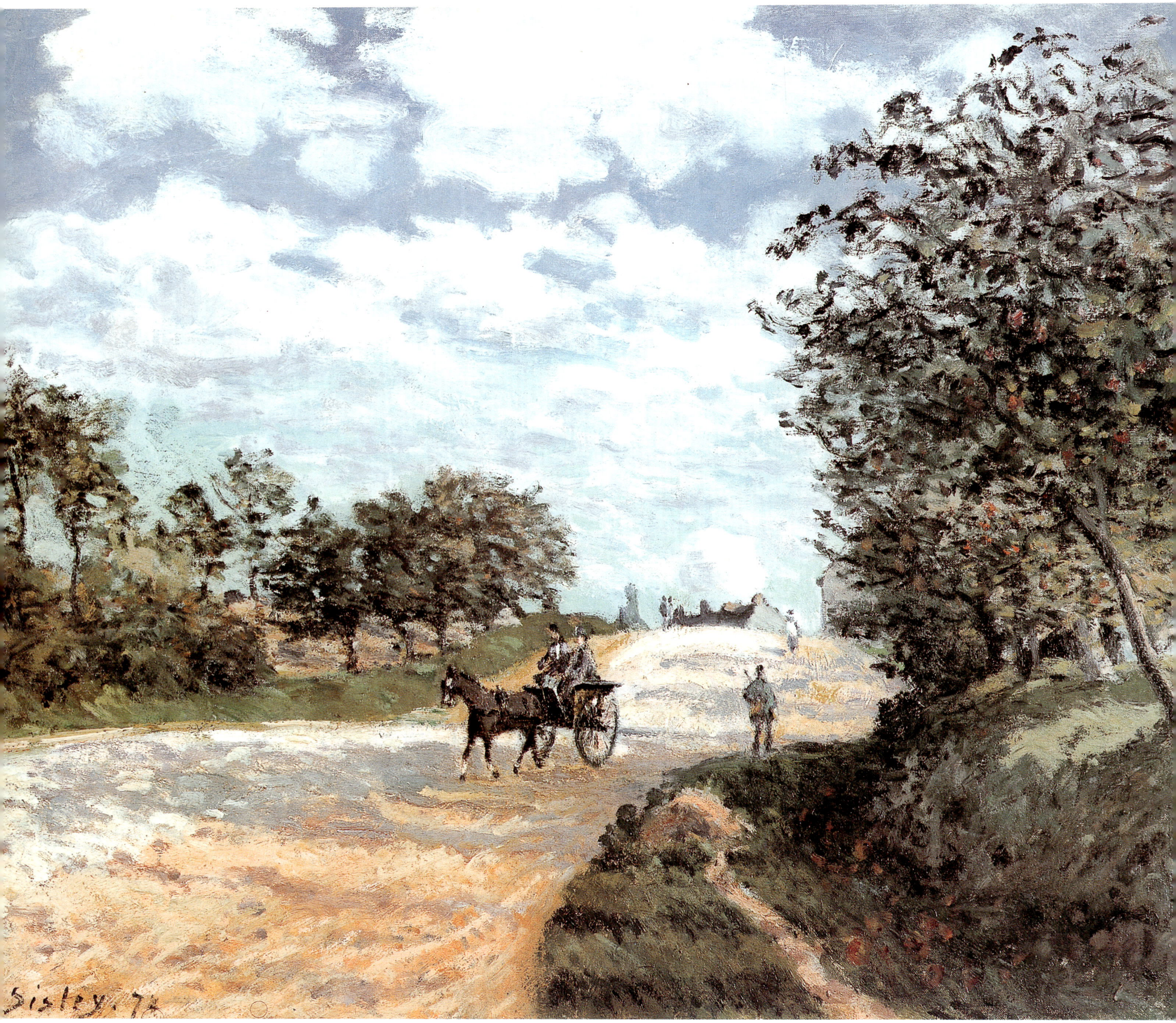
Sisley.

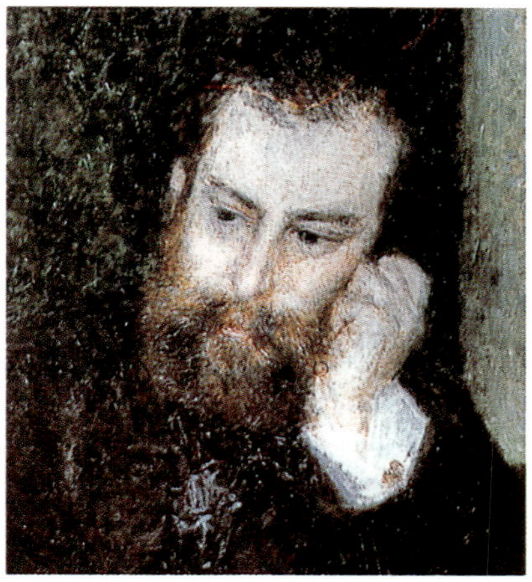

ALFRED SISLEY
By Renoir
1874
Above

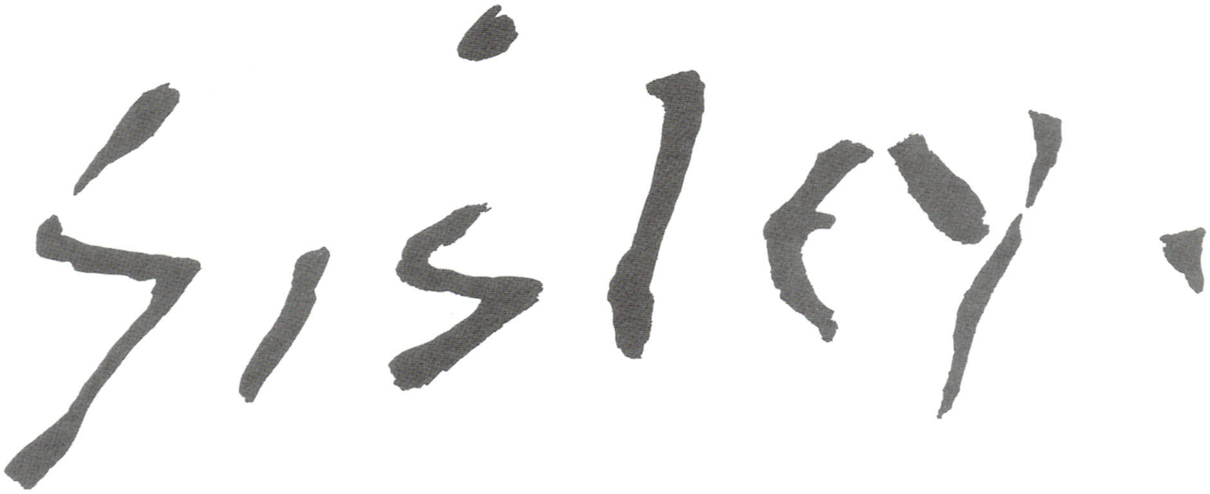

FROM COMFORTABLE BEGINNINGS as the son of a successful English businessman in Paris, Alfred Sisley's story is one of tragic decline and late success. After the crash of his father's firm in the Franco-Prussian War, Sisley and his family were reduced to a state of penury which persisted almost to the end of his life when cancer of the throat killed him at the age of sixty.

Part of Sisley's lack of wordly success is undoubtedly due to the subdued and comparatively unspectacular nature of the landscapes which were his almost exclusive preoccupation. Had he been interested in the colourful effects of dazzling sunlight or violent seascapes he may have enjoyed more attention than the belated admiration of a small number of collectors and connoisseurs. Yet his work is dramatic and powerful in its own way and his snowscapes, especially, convey something of the unremitting sadness which plagued him.

SISLEY
The Road from Mantes to Choisy-le-Roi
oil on canvas
1872. 46 × 55 cm
Opposite

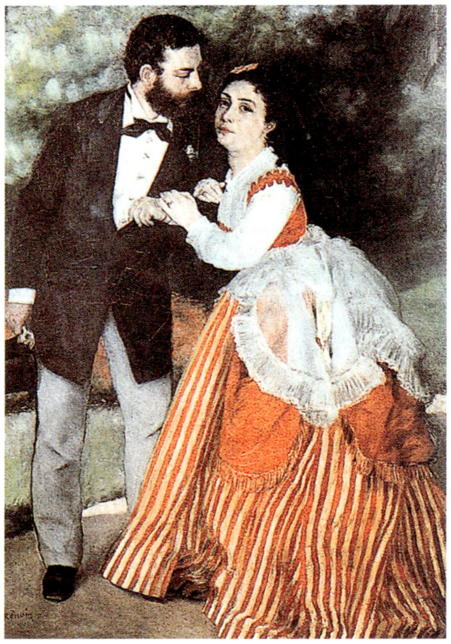

Life and Works: Alfred Sisley (1839–1899)

The light of glory will never shine on his work in his lifetime.

Gustave Geffroy on Sisley, 1894

Alfred Sisley was born in Paris on 30th October 1839 to affluent English parents. His father, William, ran a business exporting artificial flowers to South America and his mother, Felicia, was well known as a society lady interested in the arts and music. At the age of eighteen Alfred was sent to London to prepare for a career in business, but his four years there were not solely devoted to the commodities market; he spent a great deal of his time in the art galleries and museums dreaming of being an artist. The works of Constable and Turner attracted him especially, and it was in landscape that he was to make his name.

In 1862 Sisley returned to Paris from a trip and persuaded his parents to consent to his pursuing a career as an artist and in October he joined Gleyre's atelier. By December he was enjoying a dinner party given by Bazille

RENOIR
Sisley and His Wife
oil on canvas
1868. 106 × 74 cm
Above Although this picture is usually accepted as being the Sisley couple, it is possible that Renoir used his mistress Lise Tréhot since he wrote to Bazille that, "I put Lise and Sisley on show at Charpentier and shall try to get a hundred francs out of him".

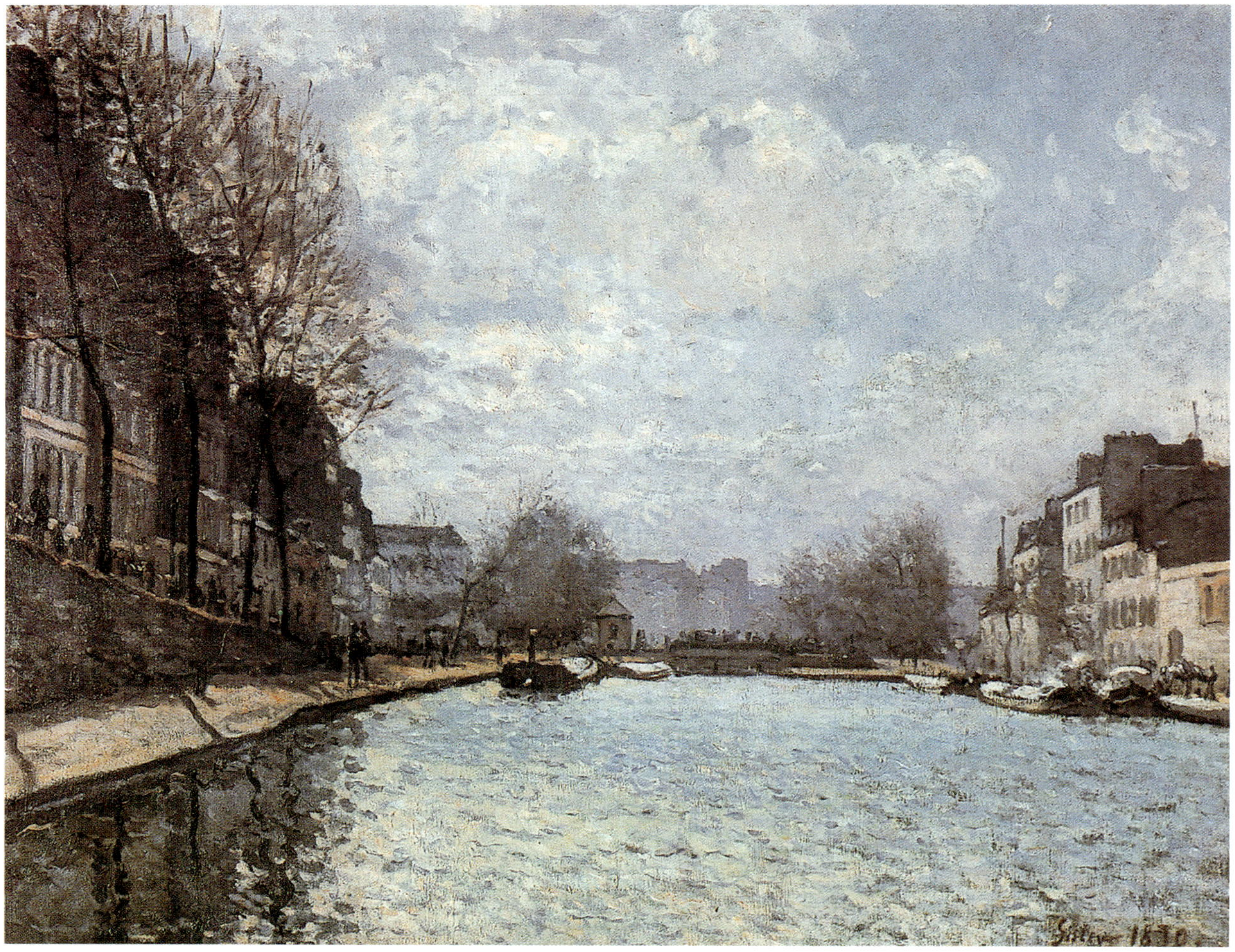

SISLEY
St Martin Canal, Paris
oil on canvas
1870. 50 × 65 cm
Right Sisley, like most of his Impressionist friends, was interested in depicting water and sky, the two elements which best suited their stylistic research, and amongst the most difficult to render.

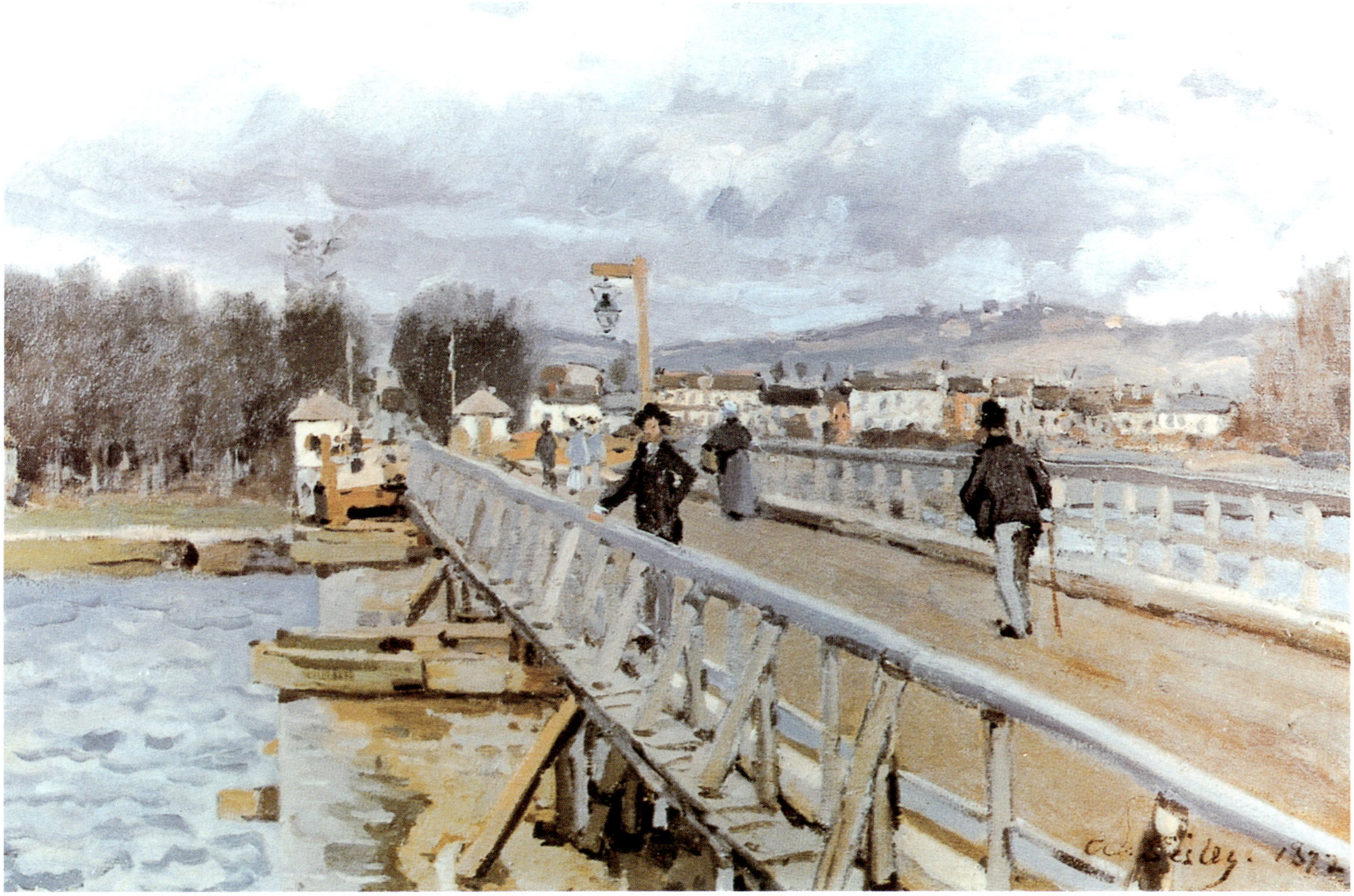

SISLEY
The Bridge at Argenteuil
oil on canvas
1872 39 × 60 cm
Above Argenteuil is closely associated with Monet, who lived there and made well over 175 pictures of the area.

at which the other guests included Monet and Renoir. By the next Easter the budding Impressionists had all left Gleyre's, and Sisley and his friends were to be found on the edge of the Fontainebleau Forest at Chailly painting landscapes *en plein-air.* And this is what Sisley was to concentrate on for the rest of his life, combining the English tradition of landscape painting with the new techniques evolving amongst the young Impressionists.

By 1866 Sisley was exhibiting two works at his first Salon. He had been working in close contact with Monet, but unlike Renoir, who was to incorporate much of Monet's technique into his early work, Sisley had already developed a more subdued palette, which in many ways suited his calm and reserved temperament. Shortly after the 1866 Salon he married a young Parisienne, Marie Lescouezec, who was to bear him two children, Pierre and Jeanne. Two years later, when the Sisleys were living in the rue de la Paix in the Batignolles, Renoir painted a large-scale double portrait of them which conveys something of the gentleness of Sisley and his devotion to his wife. In the late 1860s Sisley was increasingly part of the Batignolles Group meeting in the Café Guerbois, and like Bazille he was essentially a man of leisure, painting when and as he liked and under no pressure to achieve financial success with his work. Nevertheless he was to be a founding

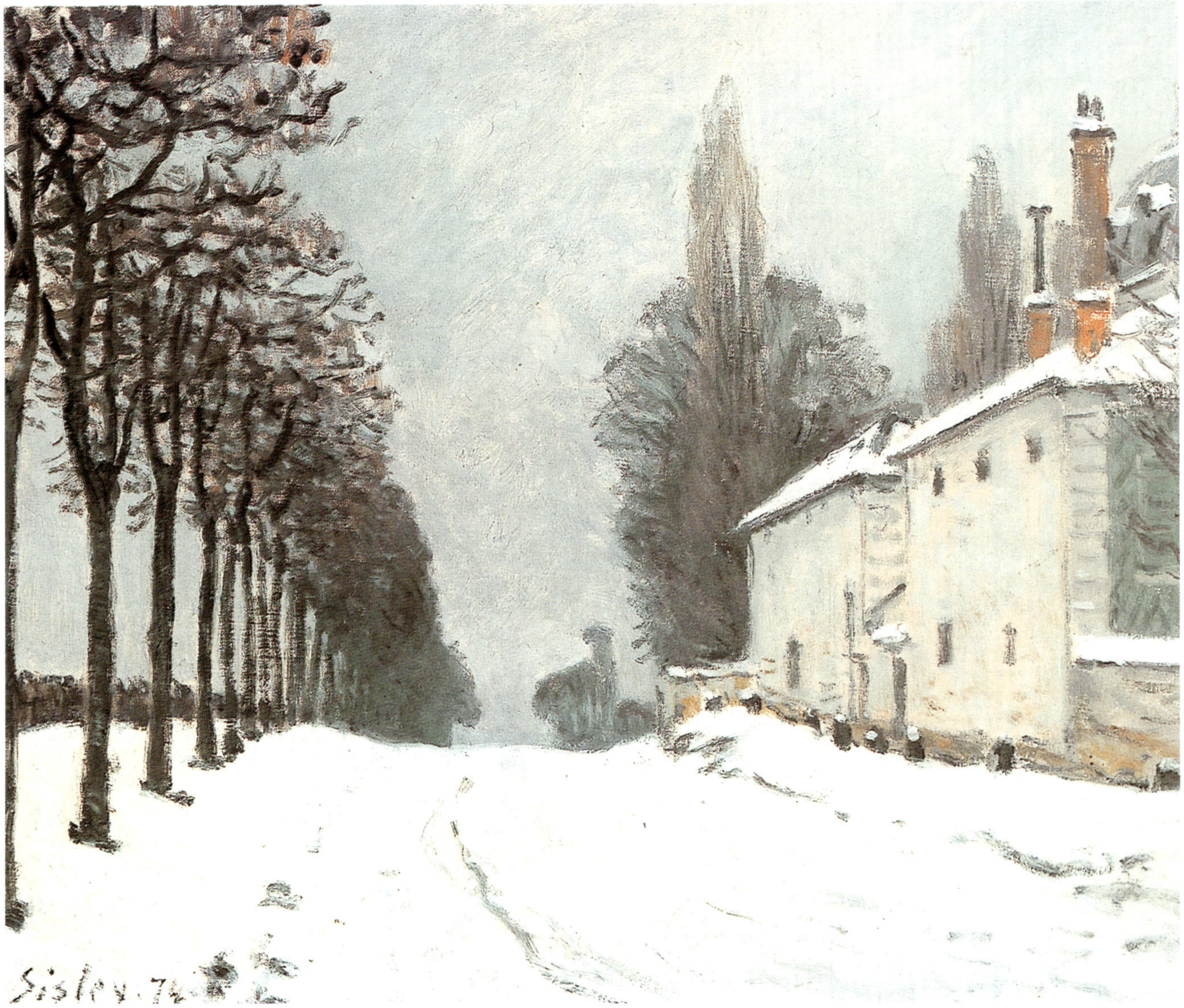

SISLEY
The Road at Louveciennes, Winter
oil on canvas
1874. 38 × 46.5 cm
As with Pissarro and Monet, Sisley liked to paint snowy landscapes, and indeed his style at the time was close to that of Pissarro and Guillaumin, plain and simple compared with most of Monet's works.

SISLEY
The Aquaduct at Marly
oil on canvas
1874. 54 × 81 cm
RIGHT The castle was destroyed, but the aquaduct which brought the water for the basins and fountains of the castle was restored by Napoleon III in 1858.

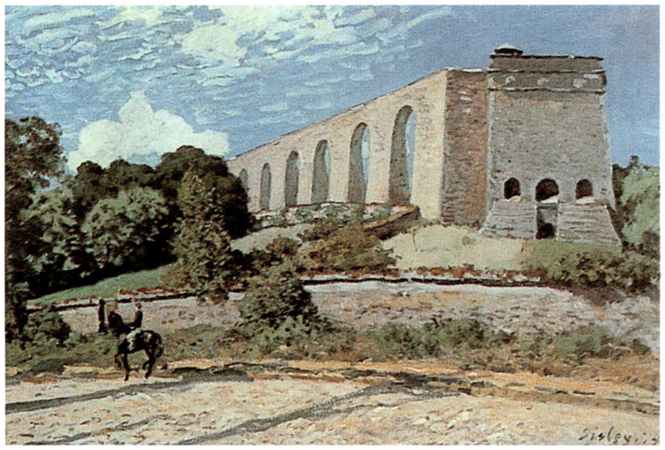

member of the *Société anonyme* in 1873, by which time his life had taken a drastically different course.

The Franco-Prussian War of 1870–71 proved to be the downfall of William Sisley and inaugurated a long period of struggle for his son, Alfred, and his young family. Sisley's father had been taken ill and his business had crumbled; when he died in 1871 the family was ruined and Sisley was now forced to paint for a living. Fortunately Monet and Pissarro, who had met the sympathetic dealer Durand-Ruel in London during the war, introduced him to Sisley in 1872 and he was assured of a moderate number of sales, but not enough to regain his previous leisured lifestyle. Sisley's post-war output increased exponentially as he painted the landscapes around his home in Louveciennes.

When the first Impressionist exhibition opened in 1874 Sisley was represented by five paintings. Perhaps fittingly, for Sisley did not court scandal, they were overshadowed by the "tongue-lickings" of Monet and the other "scandalous" paintings. Monet's influence was in fact discernible in Sisley's work; he was beginning to use brighter pigment in the broken patches which characterized the work of Monet, Renoir, and Pissarro during the 1870s and early 1880s. A trip to England in July 1874 produced some of Sisley's most colourful views of the Thames and the regattas at Hampton Court.

Sisley continued to exhibit with the Impressionists in 1876, 1877, and 1882. Between 1874 and 1877 he lived with his family at Marly-le-Roi, and it was here that he produced a series of his finest paintings of the floods which periodically inundated the area. The critic Georges Rivière, writing in the influential, short-lived, Impressionist organ

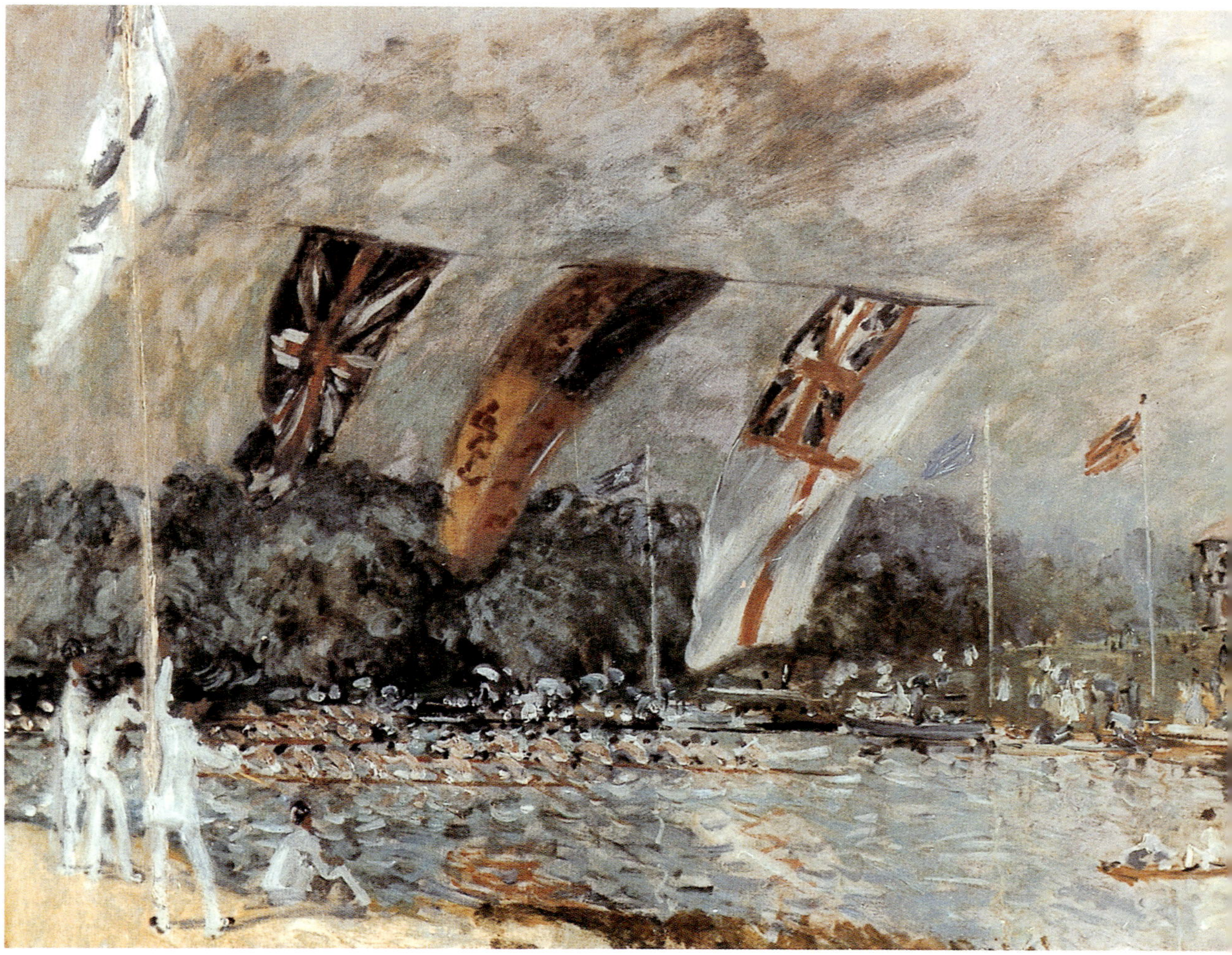

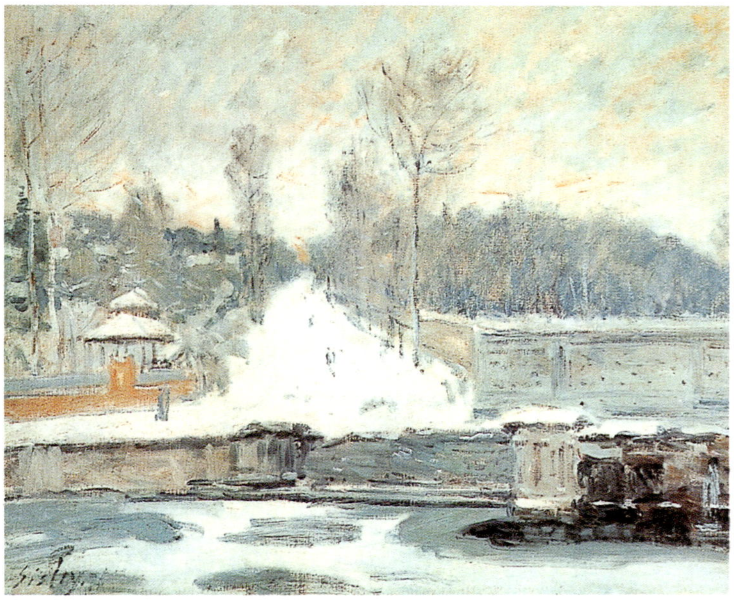

SISLEY
Regattas at Molesey
oil on canvas
1874. 66 × 91.5 cm
ABOVE During a trip to England, Sisley painted pictures similar to Monet's work at Argenteuil.

SISLEY
The Watering Place, Marly
oil on canvas
1875. 49.5 × 65.5 cm
LEFT This work was quite understandably quickly executed in the cold weather, and retouched at home later on.

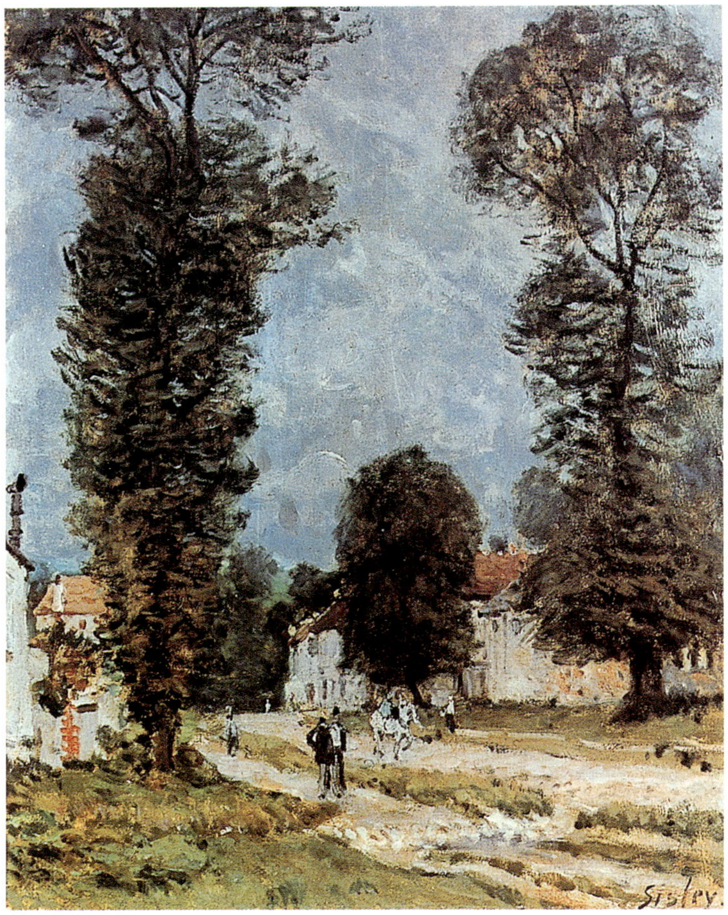

SISLEY
The Road to Versailles
oil on canvas
1875. 47 × 38 cm
Right This road, linking Marly to Versailles since the seventeenth century, was a favourite theme for Pissarro, Renoir, and Sisley.

l'Impressionniste, said of Sisley: "In all his [canvases] one discovers the same taste, the same finesse, the same tranquillity . . . " The effects of light reflected by water under a dull grey sky and the melancholy aspects of the snowscape characterize Sisley's own depressed state of mind at this time. He was in permanent financial crisis, alleviated only by Durand-Ruel and the patrons that the prospering Renoir had cultivated, the wealthy Charpentiers, and the *pâtissier* Eugène Murer, who invited Sisley and his wife to his restaurant every Wednesday along with Guillaumin, Renoir and the famous colour merchant Père Tanguy.

By the end of the 1870s Sisley was still as desperate as ever for money. Several arrangements whereby he would be paid in advance for a number of canvases helped him eke out a living, but in 1879 he decided to renounce the Impressionist exhibitions and try his luck with the Salon once again. "I am tired," he wrote to Théodore Duret, "of vegetating as I

SISLEY
The Path of the Old Ferry at By
oil on canvas
1880. 50 × 65 cm
Right Sisley desperately tried to paint commercial pictures but was unsuccessful all his life. Sisley tried to emulate Monet's compositions and even his style, hoping that he, too, might be rewarded for his efforts.

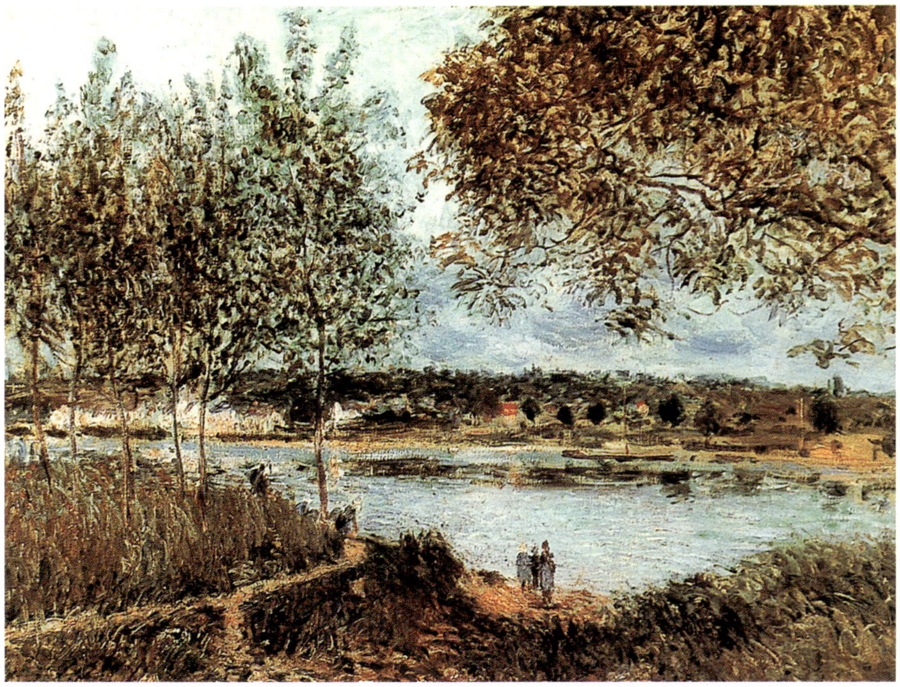

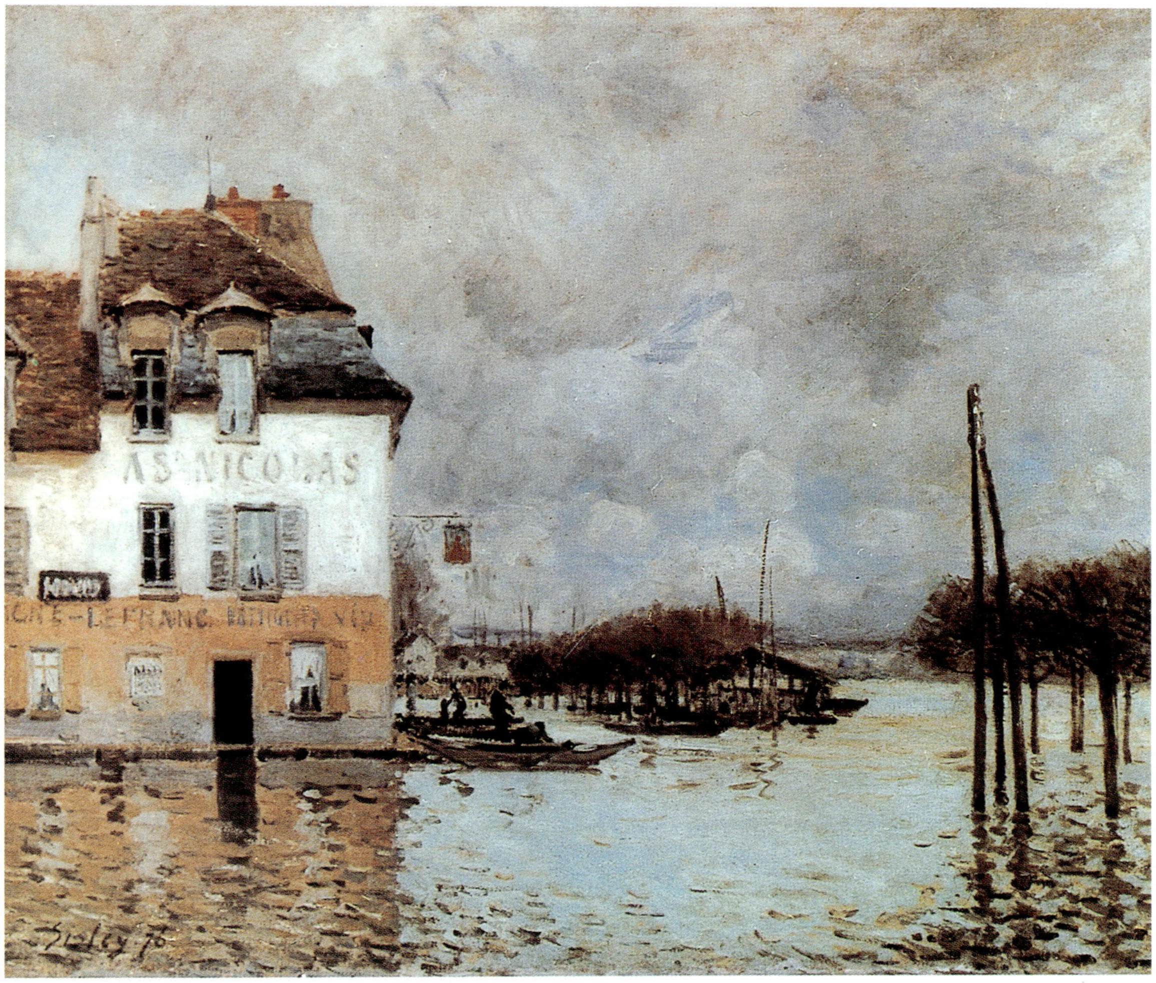

SISLEY
Flood at Port Marly
oil on canvas
1876. 60 × 81 cm
LEFT One in a series, this is not an alarming scene of distressed people trapped in their homes but a peaceful and bucolic one in which the water is seen as a soothing element in which the houses are reflected.

have been doing for so long. The moment has come to make a decision. It is true that our exhibitions have served to make us known, and as such they have been very useful, but I think we ought not isolate ourselves much longer. The time is still far off when we can do without the prestige which the Salon offers. Thus I have resolved to submit to the Salon. If I am accepted, and there is still a chance this year, I think I will be able to get things sorted out . . . "

But Sisley was rejected by the Salon and then evicted from the house in Sèvres where the family had been living since 1877. With the help of Charpentier other lodgings were found and throughout the 1880s, when the

SISLEY
Spring at Veneux
oil on canvas
1880. 73 × 90 cm
BELOW Sisley's pictures were not as strongly individual as those of the other Impressionist painters.

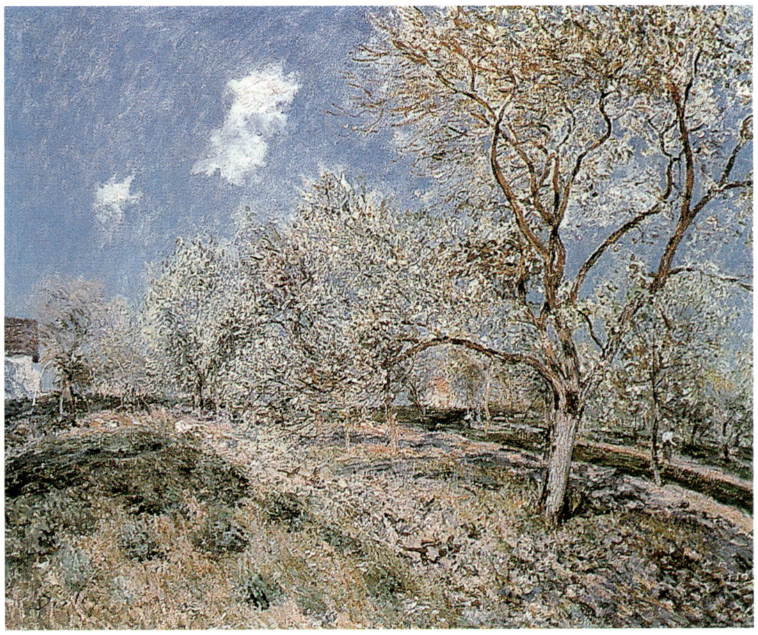

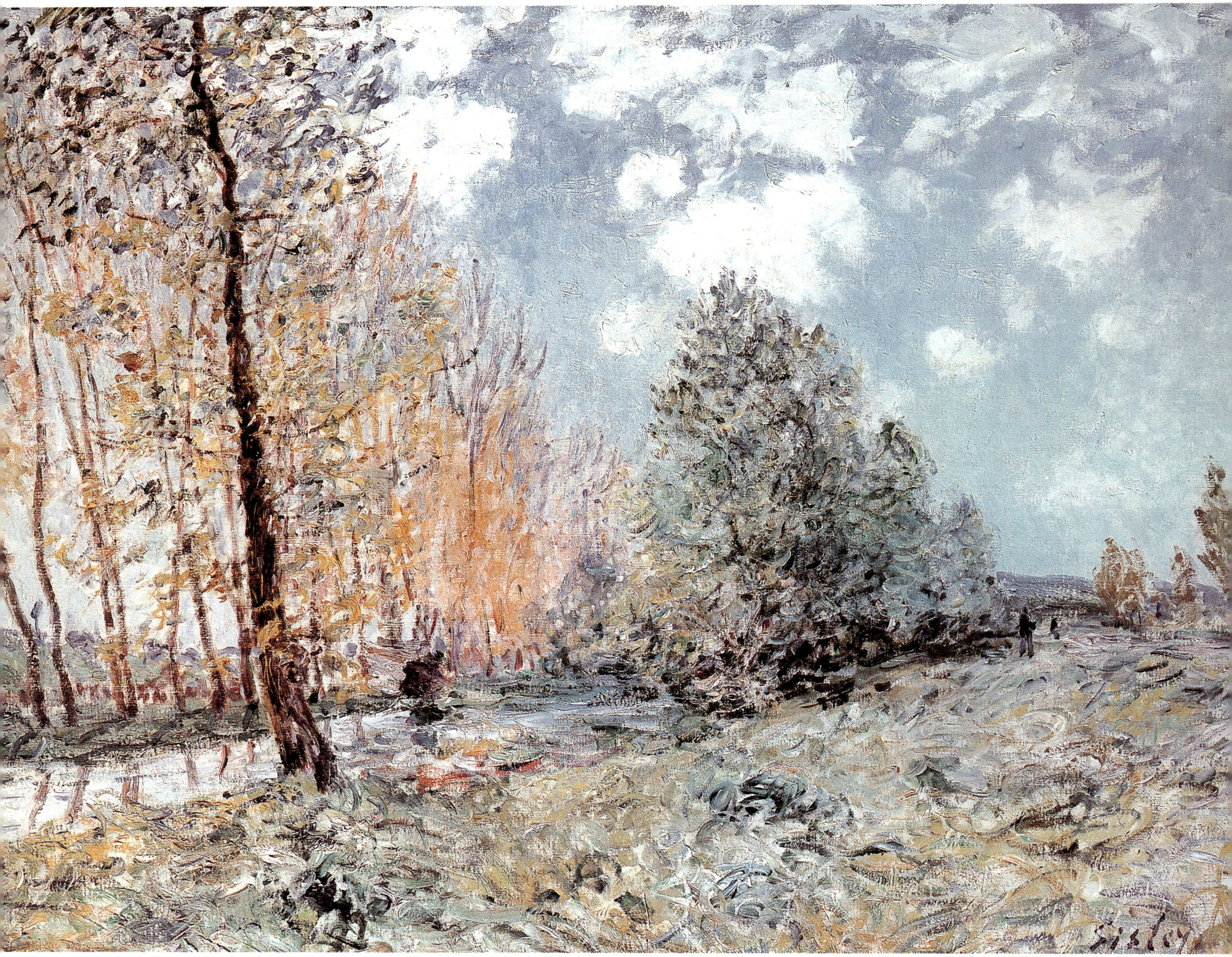
Sisley

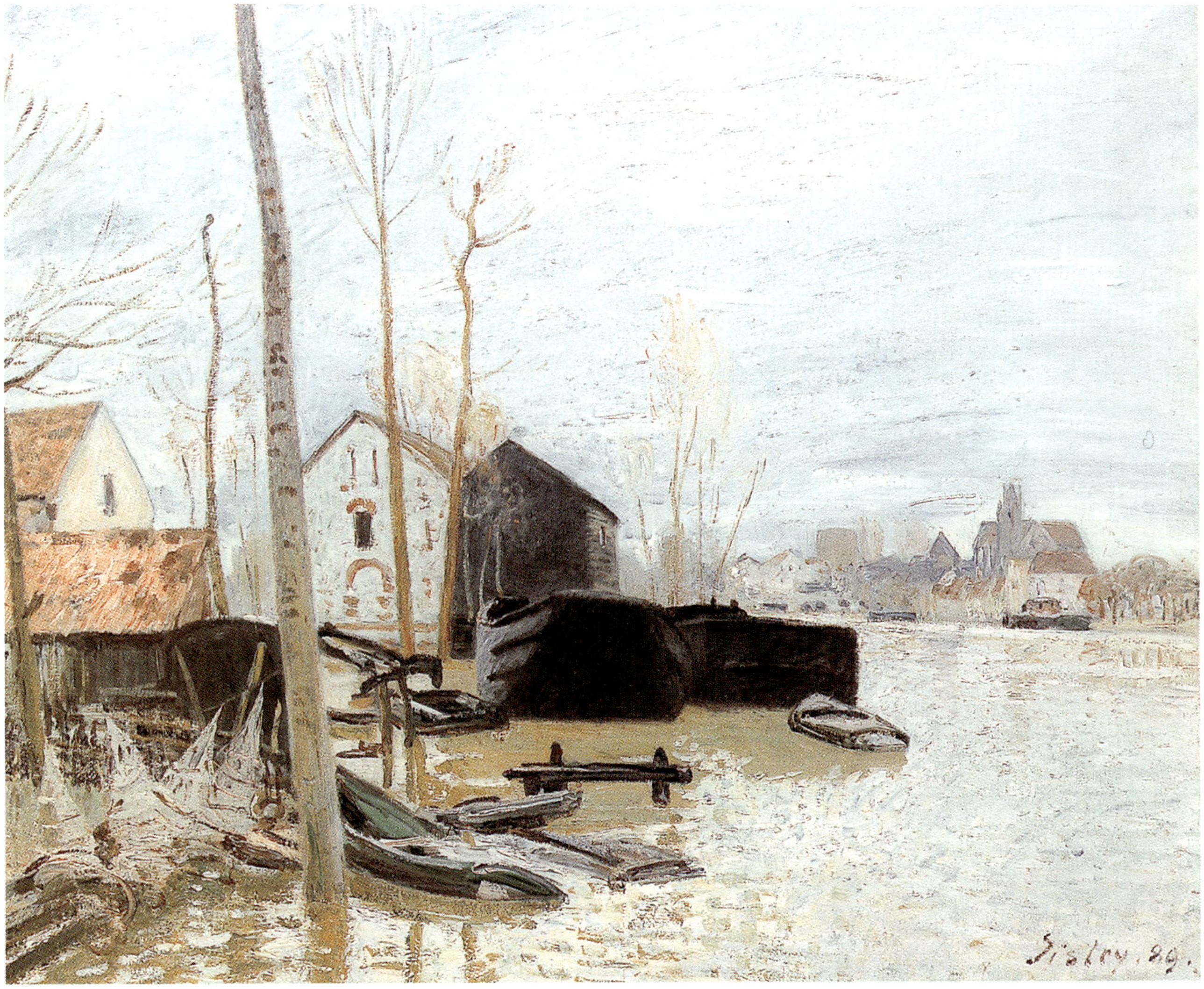

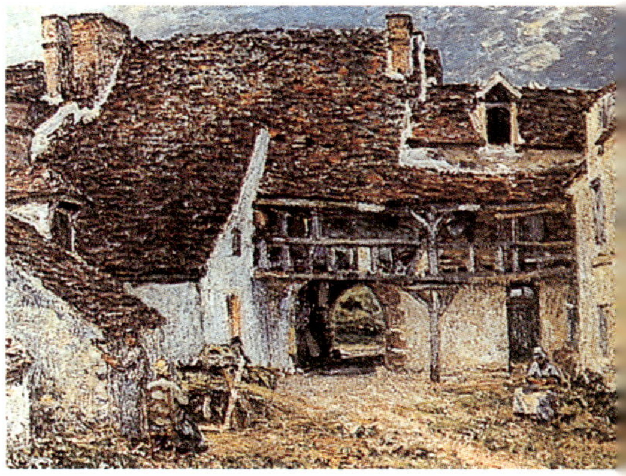

SISLEY
Farmyard at St Mammet
oil on canvas
1885. 73 × 93 cm
Above His style is more compact than in his other landscapes of this period but he still uses short strokes to suggest the texture of the ground and of the tiled roof.

SISLEY
Flood at Moret-sur-Loing
oil on canvas
1889. 64.5 × 81 cm
Left This is a rather extreme example of Sisley's return to his more spontaneous style, in which the brushstrokes blend to produce the more plain effect of his earlier years.

Sisley's lived in the Fontainebleau area, the artist's fortunes slowly began to revive. Never very keen on self-promotion, Sisley had worked quietly in the country. His landscapes were, however, greatly admired by his friends and critics, as well as several dealers; and by the early 1890s he was able to find a growing, if modest market for his work. This now featured series of paintings of the same subject, particularly the church at Moret where the family finally settled. In the mid-1890s, when Monet and Renoir were selling at huge prices, Pissarro in fact complained to his son Lucien: "Doesn't Monet sell at a high price, and Renoir and Degas too? But Sisley and I are still bringing up the rear of the Impressionists."

In 1897, despite severe rheumatism brought on by long hours painting snow-scapes *en plein-air* – some of his most beautiful works – Sisley set out on a tour of southern England and Wales, producing several landscapes; but on his return to Moret another, fatal illness began to take hold of him. He was dying of throat cancer. On 31st December 1898 he wrote to his doctor: "I have given up, my dear Friend, I have lost all my energy; I can barely get into my armchair so they can

SISLEY
Landscape with a River
oil on canvas
1881. 54 × 73 cm
Opposite The light, lively brushstrokes in this landscape were not typical of Sisley's style and show his attempt at diversity.

SISLEY
Lady's Cove, Langland Bay
oil on canvas
1897. 65 × 81 cm
OPPOSITE Two years before his death Sisley's style had become more hesitant, mixing small brushstrokes with a broader rendering, especially in the sky.

SISLEY
The Loing Canal
oil on canvas
1892. 73 × 93 cm
RIGHT Sisley painted at least ten views of the canal, which was not far from his home at Moret.

SISLEY
The Church at Moret
oil on canvas
1894. 100 × 82 cm
RIGHT BELOW In this picture, one of a series echoing the famous Rouen cathedrals painted by Monet the same year, Sisley has also chosen the medieval façade of his local church to render the effect of light and shade.

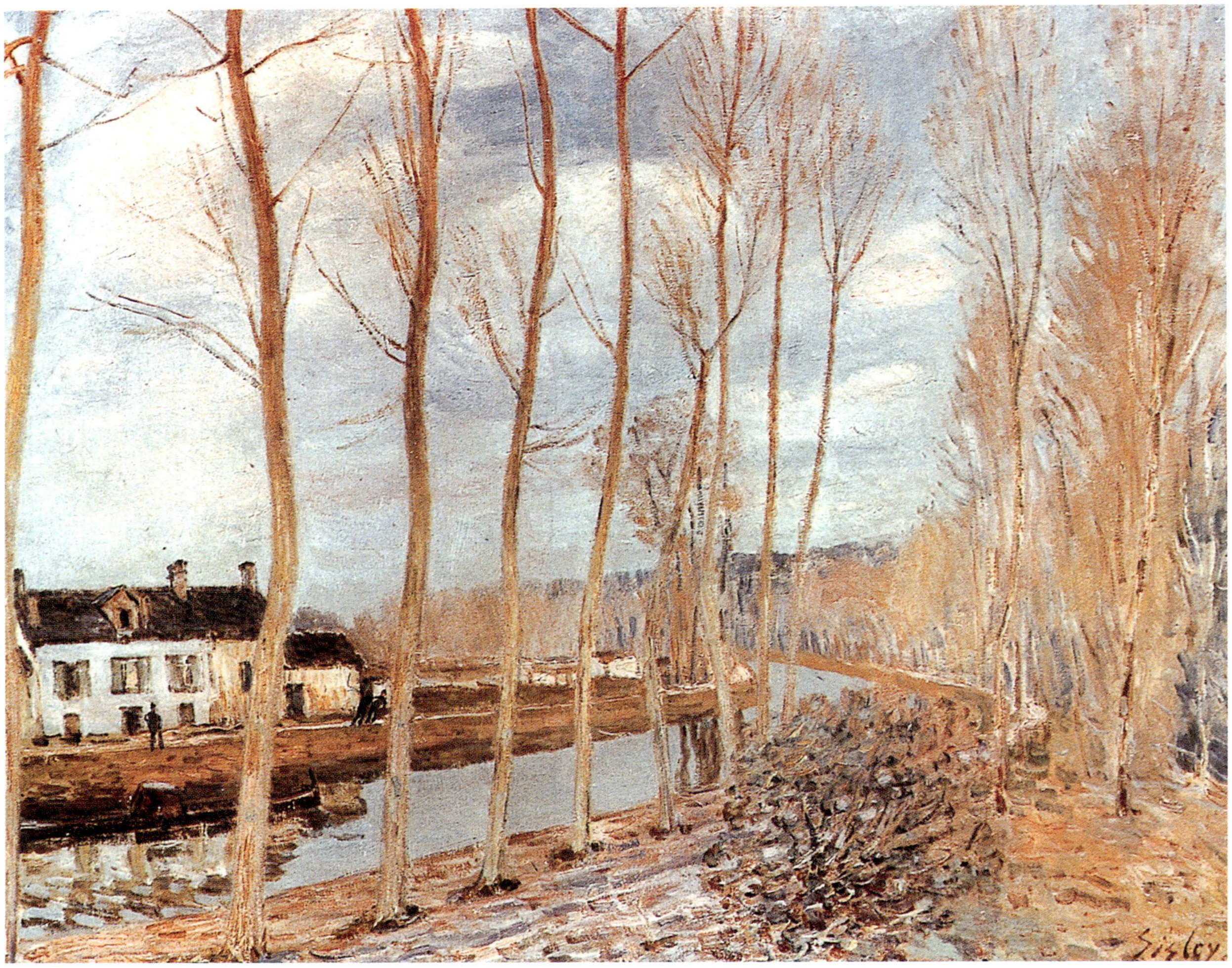

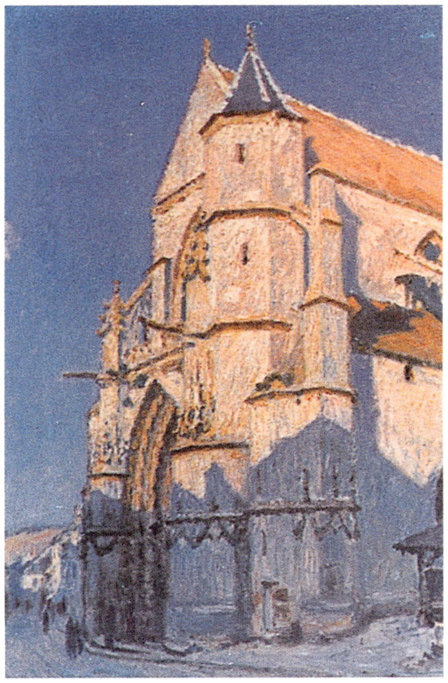

make the bed. I can't move my head anymore because of the swelling in my neck, my throat, and around my eyes. I don't think this can go on much longer. However, if you know of someone you can trust and who won't charge me more than 100 or 200 francs, I will see him . . . " A brief remission followed in the new year. However, a week before his death Sisley summoned Claude Monet to take his leave and to entrust his affairs to him. The artist whom Pissarro had called "a great and beautiful painter" died on 29th January 1899 and was buried on a cold grey day in the cemetery at Moret-sur-Loing; the ceremony was attended by a few friends including Monet and Renoir.

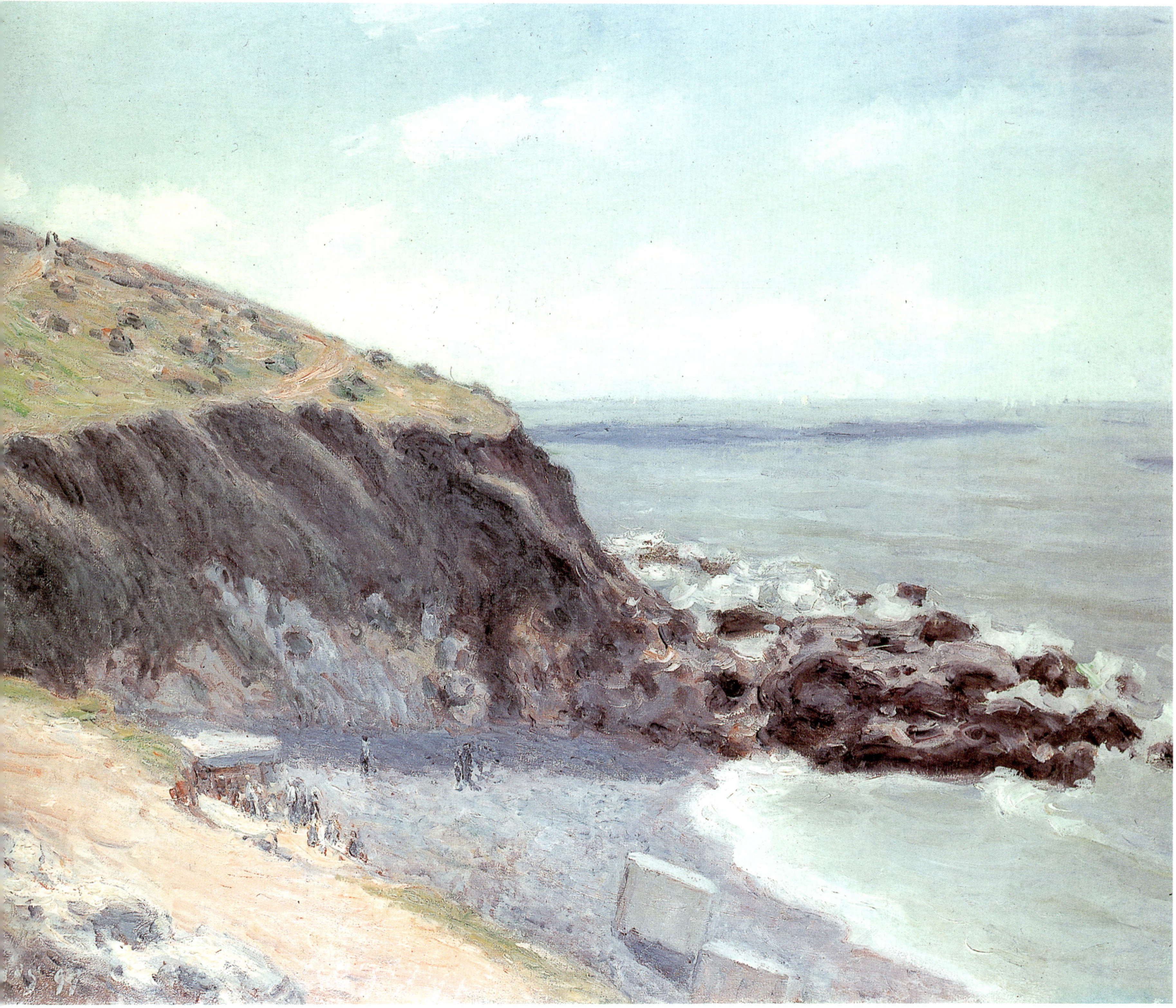

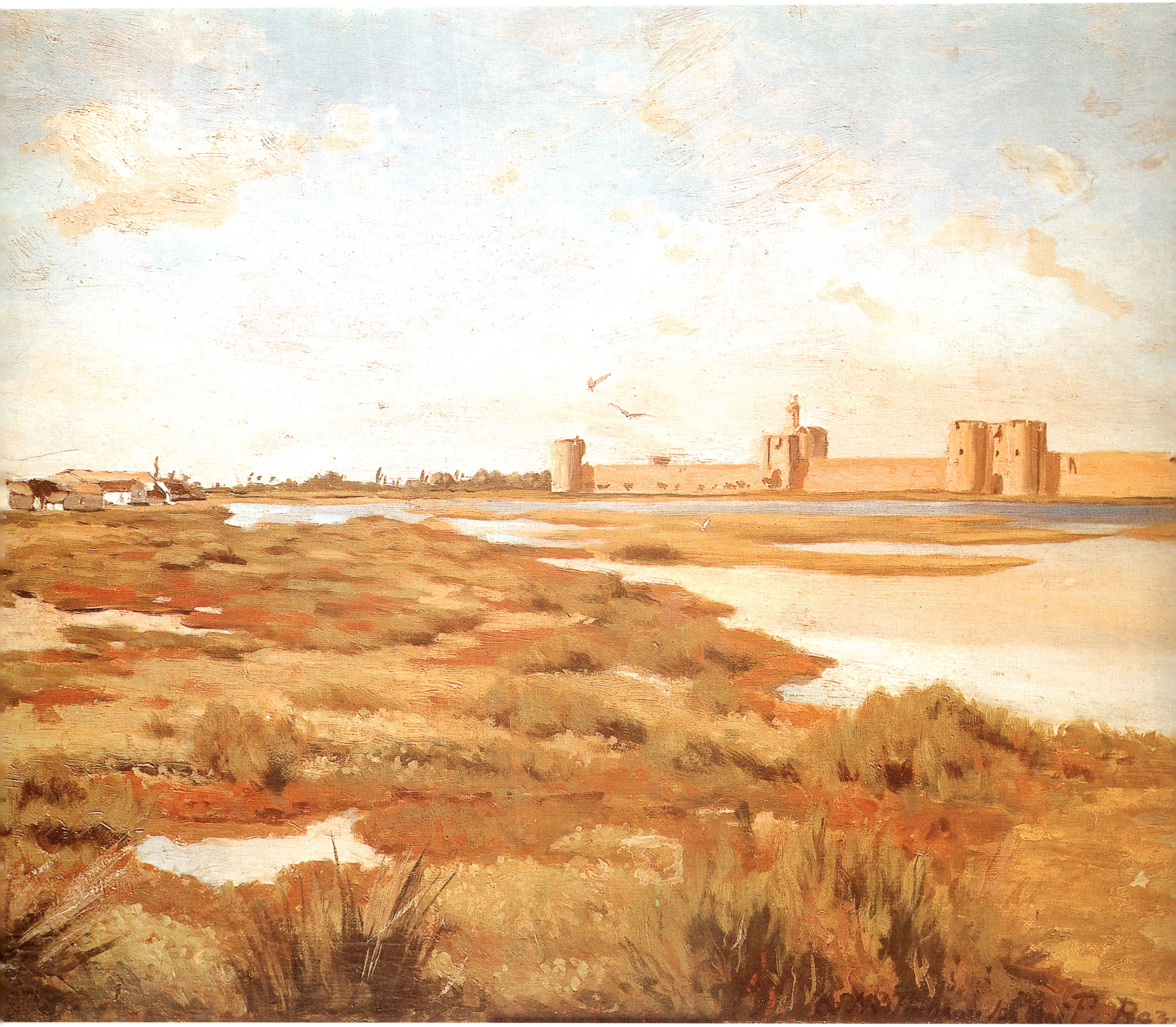

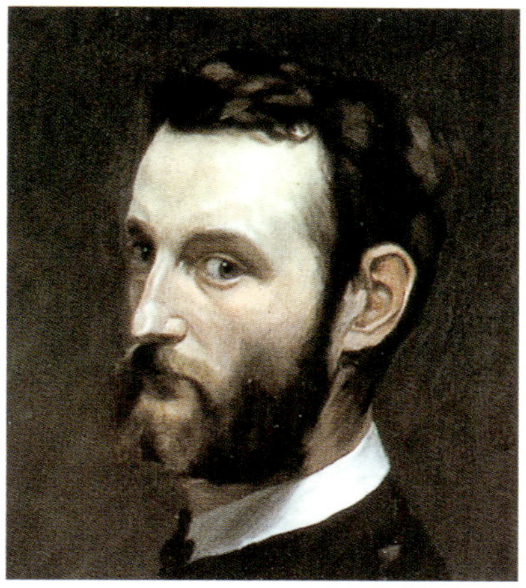

Bazille

THE FRANCO-PRUSSIAN WAR of 1870–71 robbed the young Impressionist movement of the talents of Frédéric Bazille. Bazille's role in the history of Impressionist art rests largely on a very few paintings which were highly regarded by his contemporaries. Without Bazille's generosity and care the early careers of Monet and Renoir, in particular, would have been immeasurably more difficult then they undoubtedly were. Bazille was genuinely pleased to be able to report to his parents in 1867 on moving into a new studio that, "counting Renoir, I am housing two hardworking painters." On the untimely death of the young artist his close friend Edmond Maître said of Bazille that he "was the most gifted, the most lovable in every sense of the word", and none of his contemporaries denied it.

FRÉDÉRIC BAZILLE
Self-portrait
1865
ABOVE

BAZILLE
The Ramparts at Aigues-Mortes
oil on canvas
1867. 46 × 55 cm
OPPOSITE

Life and Works: Frédéric Bazille (1841–1870)

Bazille, unlike Monet, did not seek the trembling visual moment . . . His profound originality was to "live his painting and paint his life."

François Daulte

Frédéric Bazille was born in Montpellier on 6th December 1841. He was killed on 28th November 1870 at Beaunes-la-Rolande near Orléans in the last days of the Franco-Prussian war. Renoir remembered him as, "that gentle young knight; so pure in heart; the friend of my youth." His untimely death meant the loss of a promising young artist as well as a severe blow to the friends he had met at Gleyre's atelier in 1862 – Monet and Renoir – who had relied on him to support them in many hours of need.

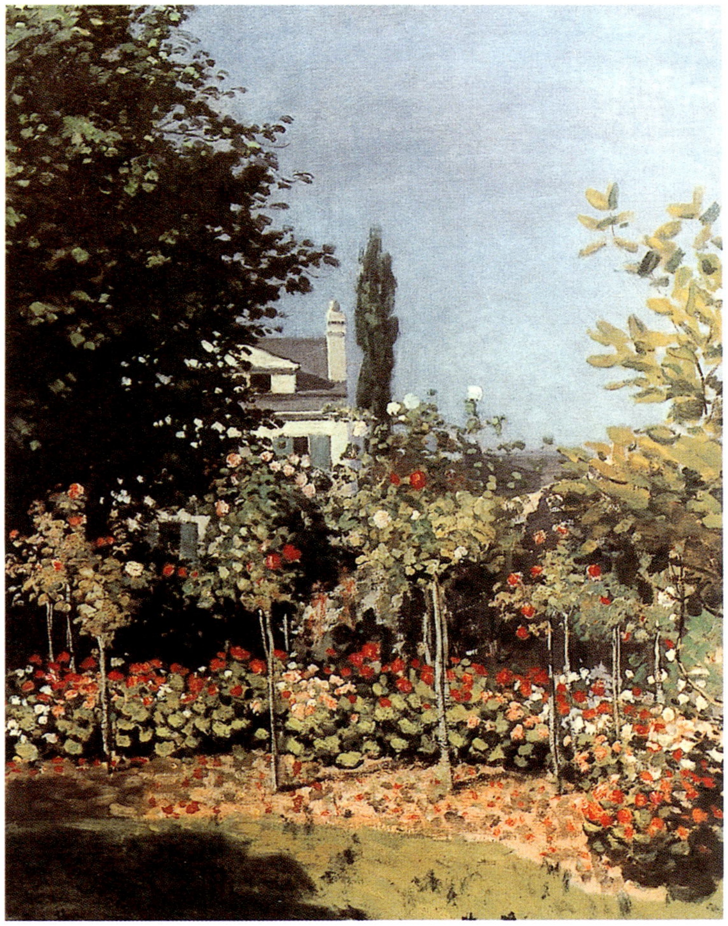

MONET
Garden in Full Bloom
oil on canvas
c.1866. 65 × 54 cm
Bazille admired Monet's style as early as 1866 when the artist was still so influenced by Corot.

Born into a wealthy family of wine-growers from Montpellier, Frédéric Bazille, like Manet and Degas, had the world at his feet. Encouraged in his painting by Alfred Bruyas, the great patron and collector of Courbet's work, Bazille had nevertheless followed his father's wishes and entered the medical academy at Montpellier where he studied for three years. In 1862 he arrived in Paris to continue his medical studies and at the same time enrolled in Gleyre's atelier. Eventually, medicine fell by the wayside and he began to devote himself to being an artist.

Bazille's new friends at Gleyre's were mentioned in his letters home. On one occasion he wrote that Monet was "quite good at landscapes; he has given me advice which has helped me very much." For his part, the wealthy Bazille became a vital source of financial and practical support for Monet and Renoir, who lived precarious existences in the early days. Bazille's generosity was legendary. When Monet injured his leg in 1865 it was Bazille who put his medical studies to good use by rigging up a contraption to ease the pain; when Monet was in trouble Bazille would lend him money and buy his paintings in instalments; when Monet needed a model Bazille would oblige; when Monet and Renoir needed a studio, Bazille would offer his.

Between 1865 and 1866 Bazille shared his Paris studio in the rue Furstenberg with

Monet. After the arduous summer of 1865, when Monet was hard at work on his own huge version of *Luncheon on the Grass* (*Déjeuner sur l'herbe*), suffering from a damaged leg, penniless, and demanding that Bazille should drop everything he was doing to pose for him in Chailly, we may well imagine that Bazille's patience and generosity were somewhat stretched. In January the next year, Bazille threw a fancy-dress party in his studio at which he appeared in the uniform of a cavalry officer and Monet typecast himself as a Normandy fisherman. The party was a stunning success, but the other tenants in the building complained so that Bazille and Monet had to move. Bazille took an apartment on his own; the irrepressible Monet had taken his toll. As Bazille wrote to his brother, Marc, in February 1866, shortly after moving to a new address in the rue Godot-de-Mauroy: "I must admit that I won't mind living alone for a little while; sharing with someone has its drawbacks, even if you get on well together."

This isolated spell was very short-lived; Monet and Renoir were soon sharing various studios that Bazille acquired and then left. The penultimate studio, in the rue de la

BAZILLE
The Terrace at Méric
oil on canvas
1867. 55.5 × 91.5 cm
This painting shows Monet's influence, with well defined areas of light and shade.

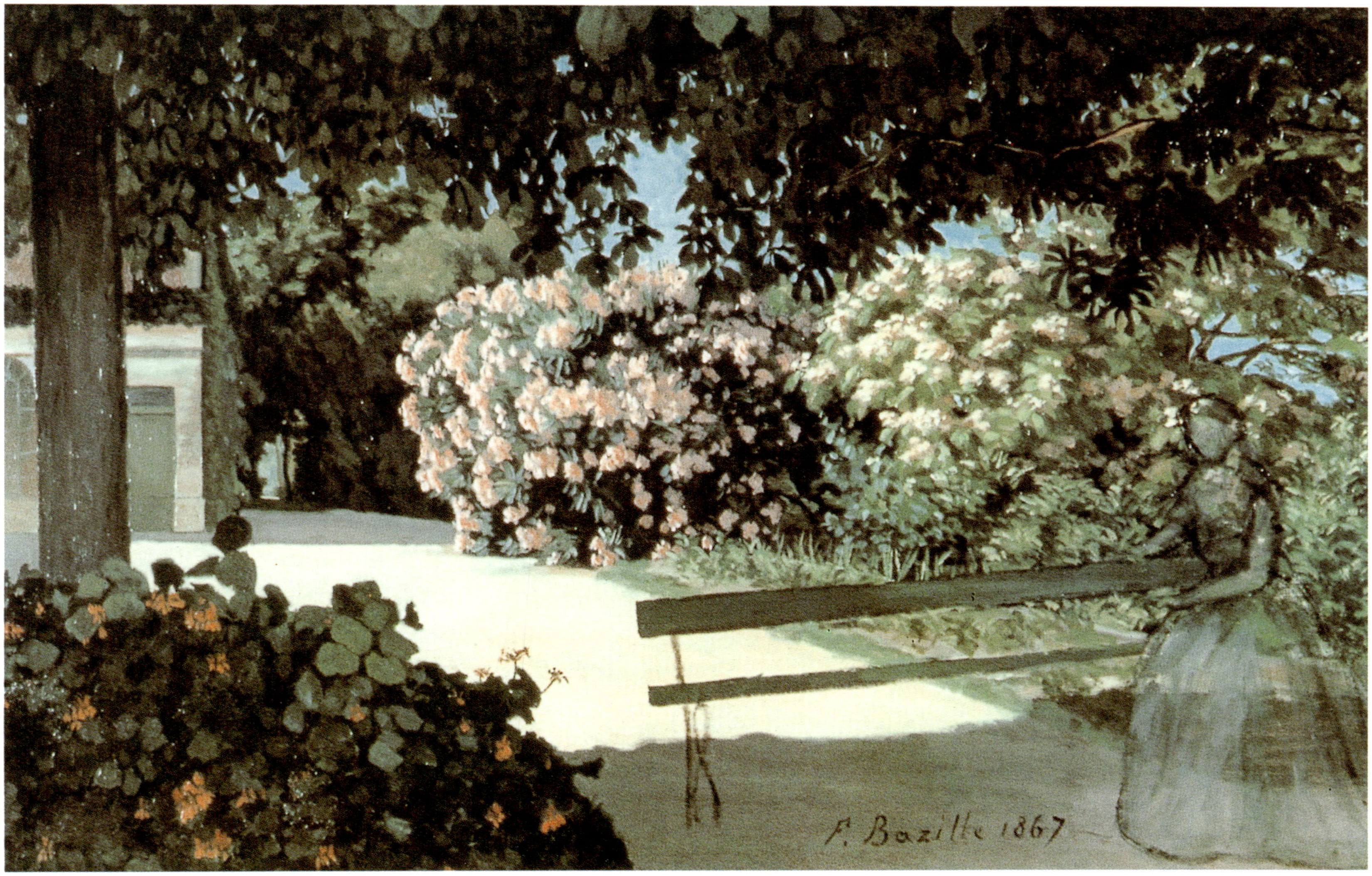

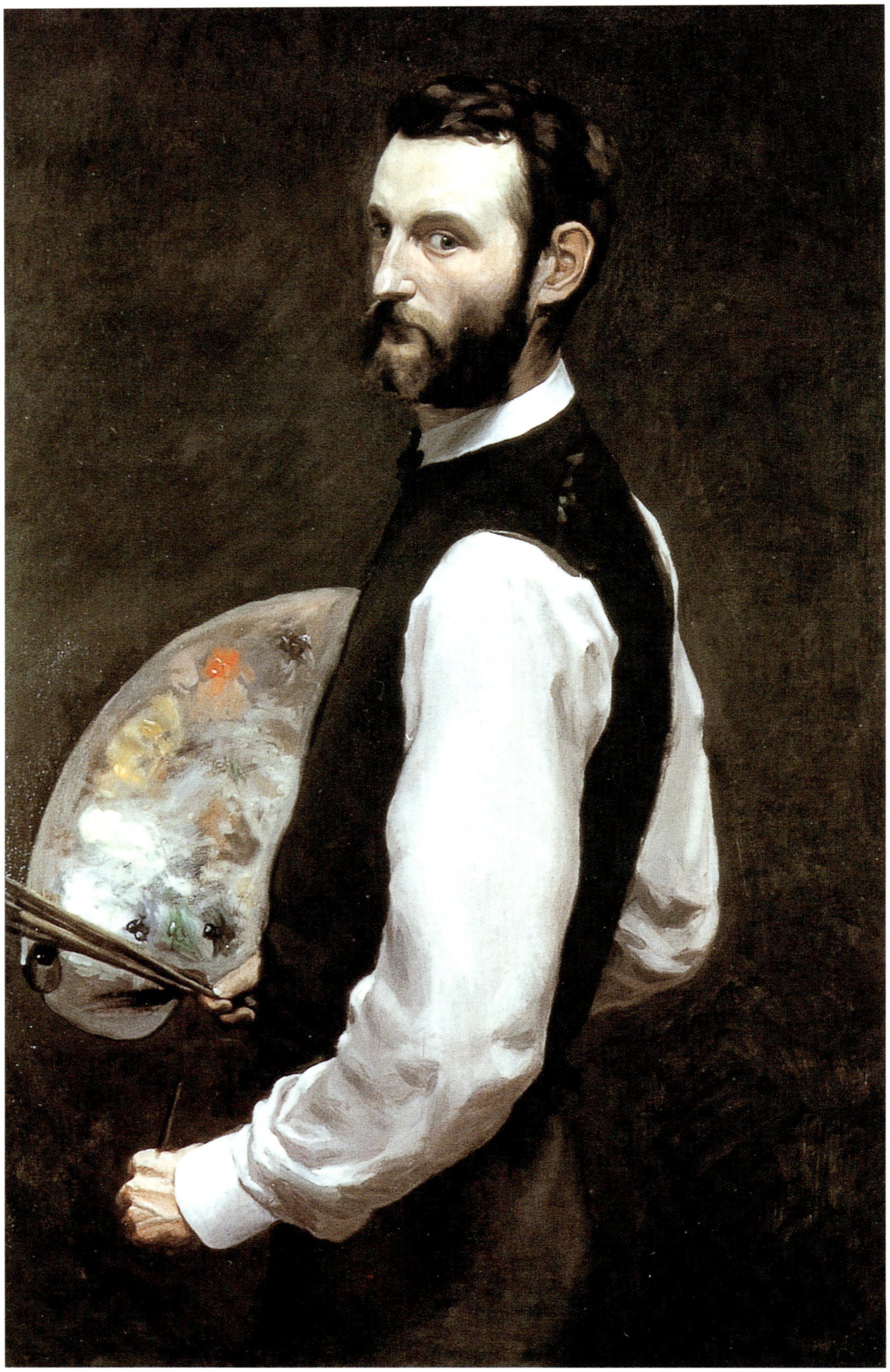

Condamine, is the setting for a group portrait of some of his friends including Monet, Manet, and Zola. By nature Bazille was sociable and by class a socialite; his friends ranged all the way up the social and artistic scale – from the struggling Monet and Renoir, via Manet and his circle, to the composers Fauré, Saint-Saëns, and Chabrier. His class allowed him entry to the most respectable salons of Paris and he made good use of them, but he was also a frequent participant in the artistic gatherings at the Café Guerbois. It was there that the first ideas for an independent exhibiting society would have been thrashed out, seven years before the *Société anonyme* staged its show in the boulevard des Capucines, by which time Bazille had been dead for four years. In a letter to his parents of 1867, Bazille mentions the idea of renting a large studio where the nascent group would exhibit as many of their pictures as they wished, and not be at the mercy of the Salon. "With these people [Courbet, Corot, Diaz, Daubigny] and Monet, who is stronger than all of them, we are sure to succeed." (In the end the older generation of *plein-airistes* and the Realist Courbet did not participate, and neither, of course, did Bazille.)

The Franco-Prussian War of 1870 interrupted the evenings at the Café Guerbois; the future Impressionists who had met at Gleyre's dispersed – Monet and Pissarro moved to London, Renoir was mobilized to the South, and Bazille joined the Zouaves regiment, soon reaching the rank of second lieutenant. From the start of the war the French armies were in disarray and the Prussians made swift advances. Bazille's regiment spent its time marching up and down the country. He wrote to his parents in October 1870 describing his experiences: "We're a stone's throw

BAZILLE
Self-portrait
oil on canvas
1865. 109 × 72 cm
OPPOSITE The tall Bazille was known for his kindness and generosity towards his friends. This self portrait, executed three years after he had started to paint, is evidence of his early promise. When Bazille arrived in Paris in 1862, he soon befriended Cézanne and Zola (both from the south of France like himself), Sisley, Guillaumin and in particular Monet, whom he much admired.

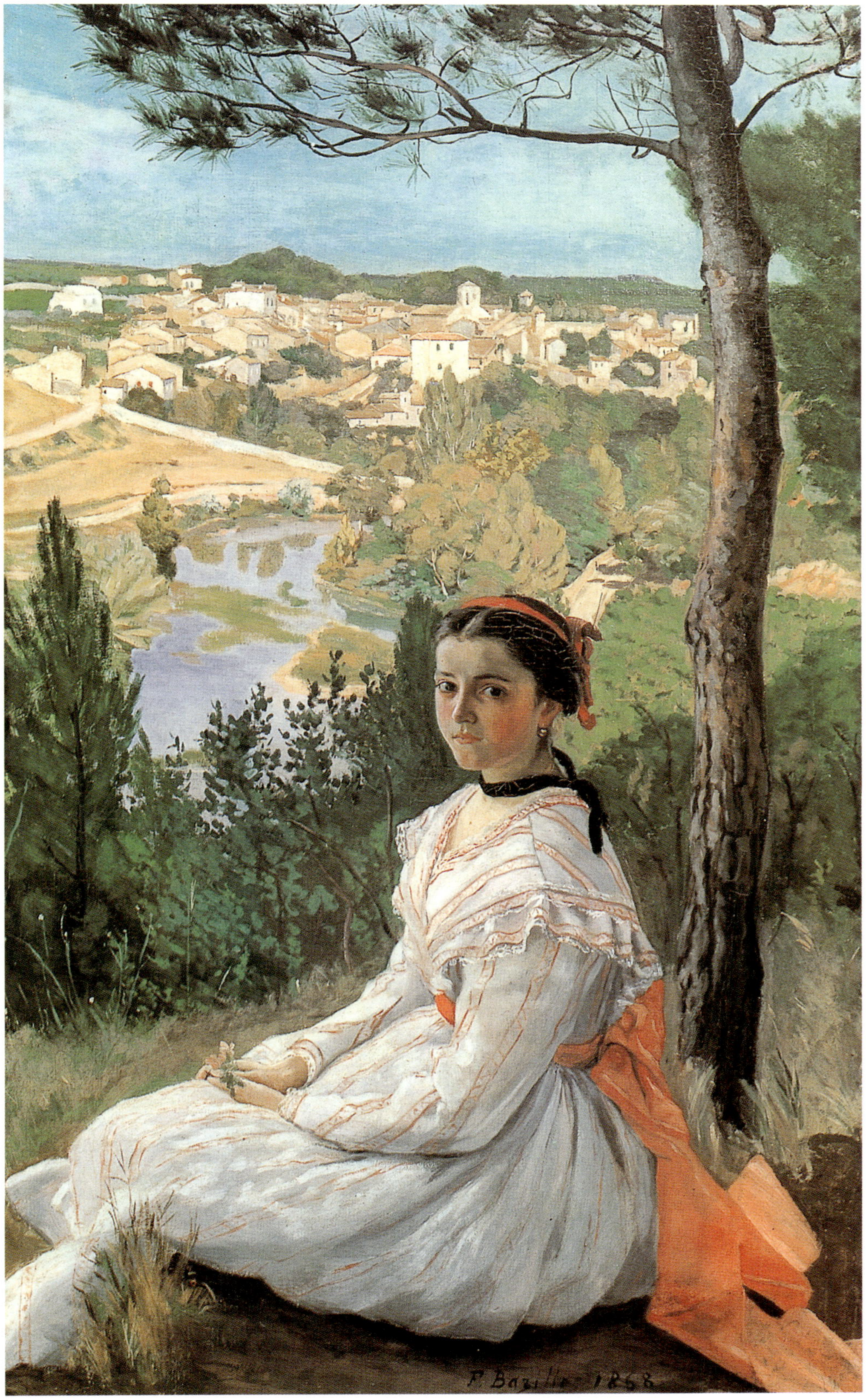

BAZILLE
View of a Village (Castelnau)
oil on canvas
1868. 130 × 89 cm
This painting, exhibited at the Salon of 1869, is a much improved version of The Pink Dress *of 1864. Elegantly rendered, the earlier stiffness has disappeared and the figure of the girl sitting on a parapet overlooking the southern village below is very attractive. In her comments on the Salon of 1869, Morisot praised the* View of a Village *highly.*

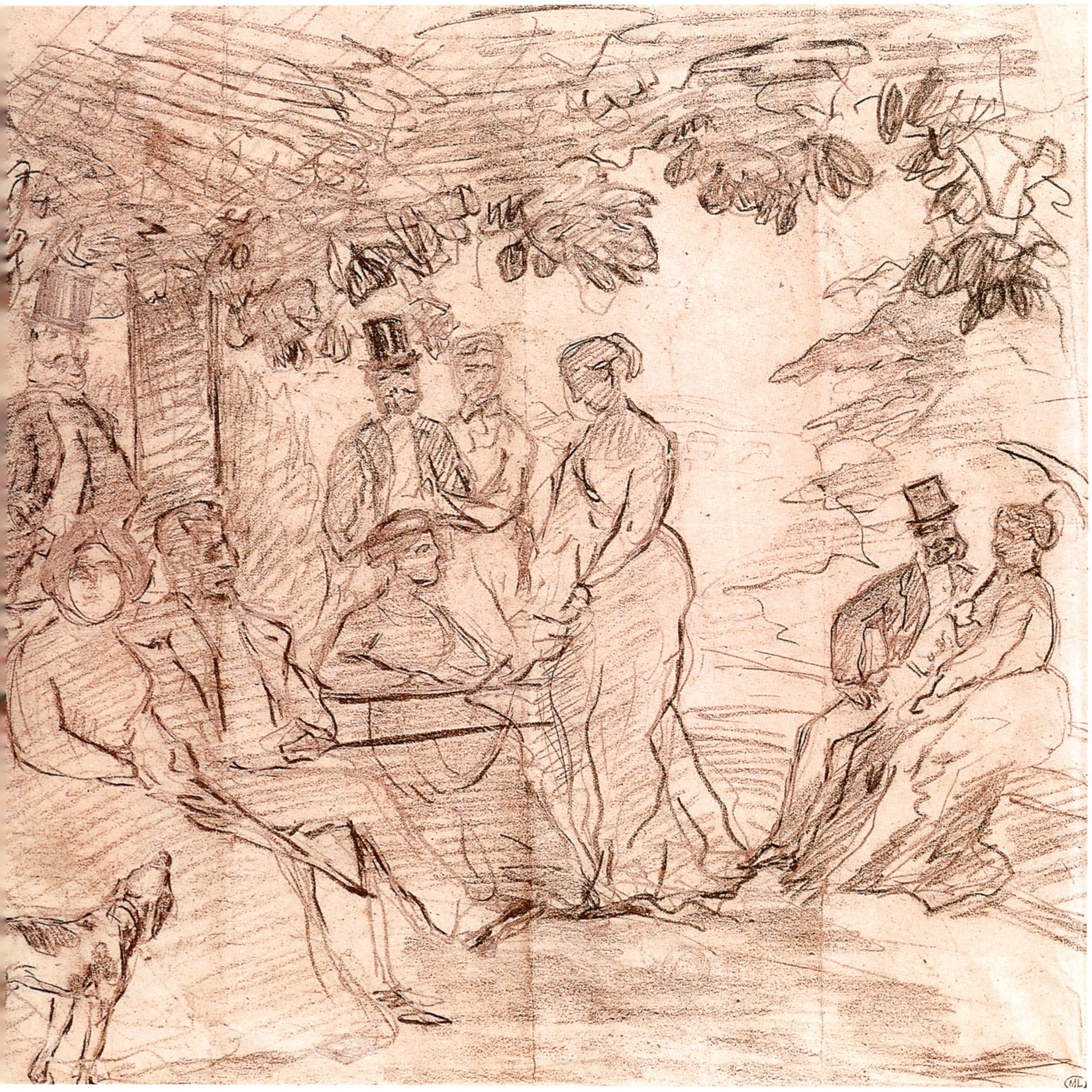

BAZILLE
The Family Reunion
Charcoal on paper
1867.
This study highlights Bazille's inferior draughtsmanship in comparison to the skilful sketches of Degas.

from Besançon, wandering about aimlessly from camp to camp . . . the short marches and manoeuvres they make us do tire the men and sap their morale . . . Always this monotonous rain, cold feet. I'm bored and I never thought I'd suffer from that in wartime." Another letter reads; "The grass in the meadows we pass is losing its colour; we are doing as much damage as the Prussians." A month later on 28th November Bazille's company received orders to march on Beaunes-la-Rolande near Orléans. François Daulte, Bazille's biographer, describes the young artist's last moments:

> The company halted on the top of ridge overlooking Beaune. It was greeted with a hail of Prussian bullets. The first of the men advancing towards the town fell like flies . . . In the general chaos women and children were escaping from the town and running towards isolated farm buildings which would offer some protection . . . Bazille's turn came and he charged, crying: "Don't shoot! Women and children!" He was hit by two bullets to the arm and chest. He fell, face down in the earth, fifty metres from the château where Corot had painted one of his masterpieces.

Bazille was buried in the snow. Six days later his father came to dig up the body and take it back to Montpellier.

In his brief time, Bazille was at the very heart of the growing Impressionist movement and his prematurely curtailed oeuvre proves that he had considerable talent, especially for the figure, portrait, and serene landscape. His career in the Salon, for example, was not undistinguished. His *Family Reunion*, a frozen and static work, highly

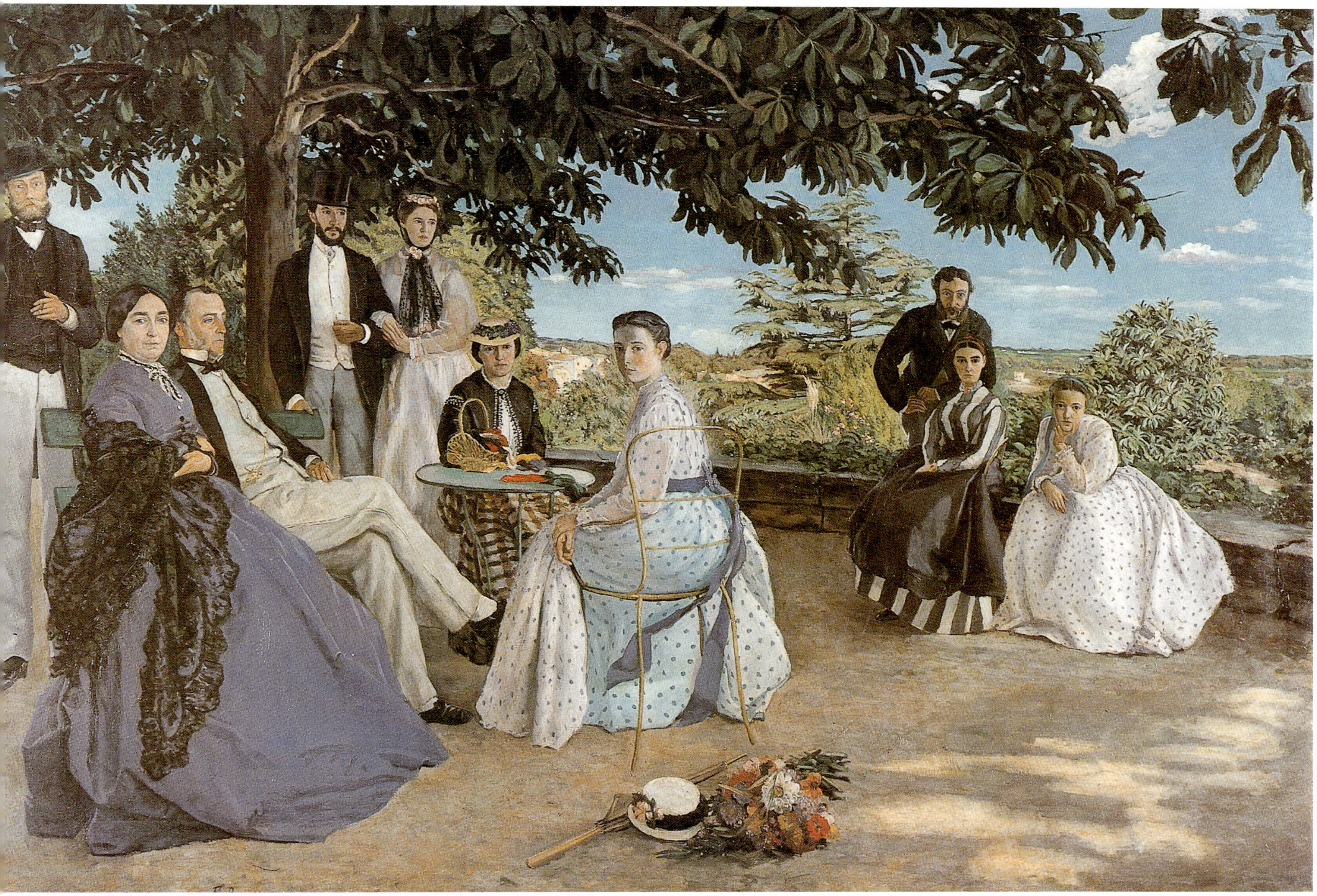

BAZILLE
The Family Reunion
oil on canvas
1867. 152 × 230 cm
Bazille has altered his original composition for the better: the standing woman is now seated; he has given more depth to the picture, which allows him to place the group of three figures near the parapet on the right. The dog has disappeared, and he has filled the foreground with a well-rendered bunch of flowers and a straw hat over a folded umbrella. The figures appear rather formal, as if they are posing for a photograph, though the general atmosphere of genteel bourgeoisie in the light and shadow of a summer day is well evoked.

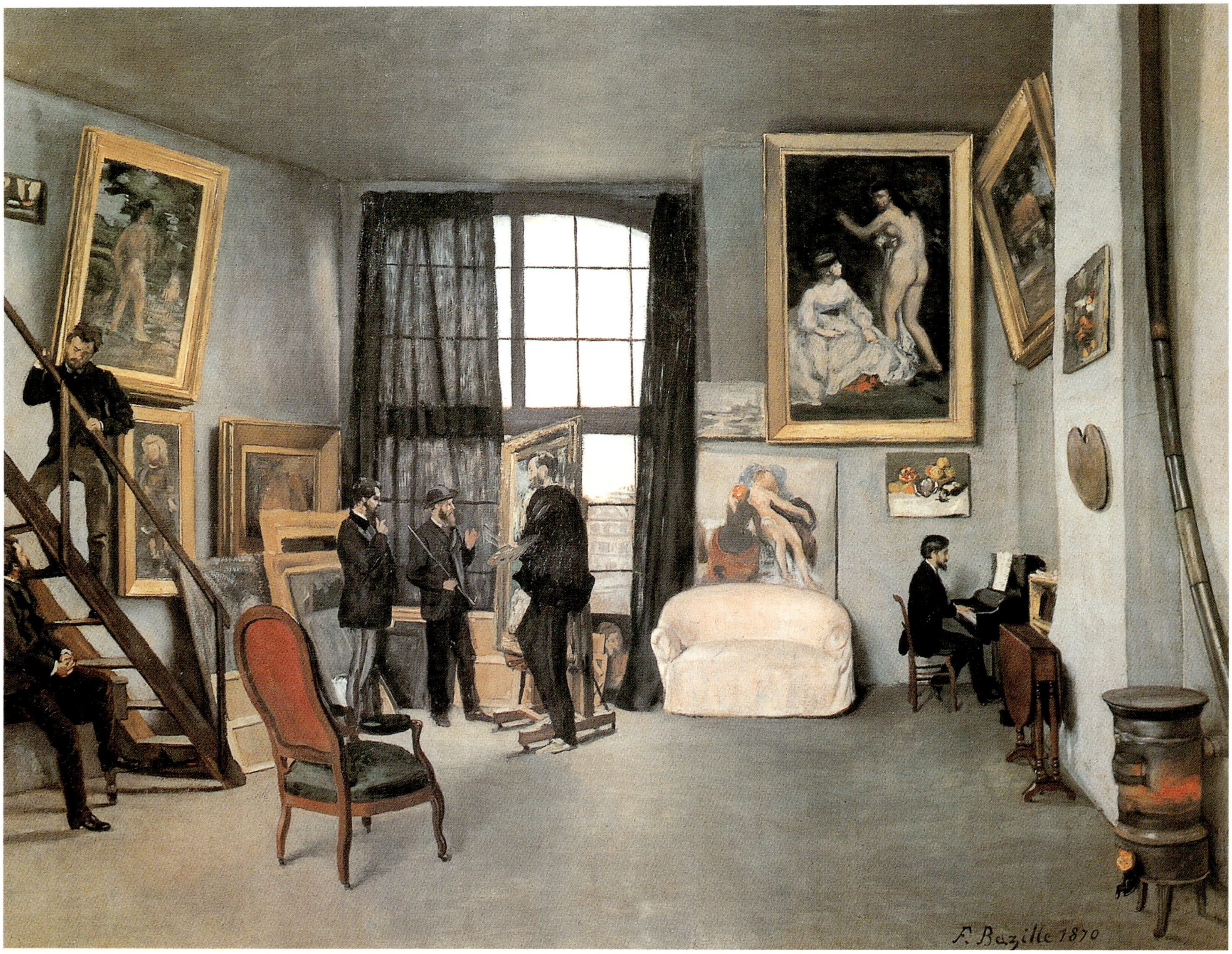

BAZILLE
The Studio Rue de la Condamine
oil on canvas
1869–70. 98 × 128.5 cm
ABOVE This picture was painted shortly before Bazille was killed during the war of 1870, and it is more interesting as a document than as a work of art, because we see his surroundings and some of his close friends: Zola leans on the railing of the steps, talking to Renoir, seated below; Manet is looking at the painting on the easel and Monet stands behind him. As for Bazille himself, he is the tall, disproportioned figure standing alongside the easel. Manet painted this, exaggerating his friend's height. Bazille's studio was a welcome refuge for penniless friends such as Renoir and Monet.

BAZILLE
Verlaine as a Troubadour
oil on canvas
1868. 45 × 37.5 cm
RIGHT This is an evocative and thoughtful portrait of the tormented poet and absinthe drinker. Bazille has movingly framed the sitter's pensive looks and sensitive features with the colourful fancy beret.

influenced by photography, enjoyed some success at the Salon of 1868, and when in 1870 his *Toilette* was accepted and hung in a decent position, he wrote to his parents: "I am delighted . . . my picture is very well placed. Everyone can see it and is talking about it . . . Judgements on it have been various; some people have laughed, but I've also received some hyperbolic eulogies, which modesty forbids me to set down in writing." (The Salon in the Palais de l'Industrie was so vast that many pictures were skied high up on the walls – to get one's work hung at eye-level was a great achievement, as Berthe Morisot discovered.)

Bazille's early landscapes are lost, so it is impossible to determine how much Monet did help him, as he wrote, in this respect. Some later views by Bazille of the Aigues-Mortes from varying distances and angles show that he was an accomplished landscapist, but far from the vein of Monet. His view is one of stillness and tranquillity: no "fugitive effects" are captured in Bazille's work. Indeed it is doubtful whether Bazille would have ever developed into the Impressionism of Monet, Pissarro, or Sisley. This, as Daulte believes, is partly because Bazille "is a son of the Midi, of the land where men have always been 'gatherers of form'. The light of southern France does not lend itself to the interpretation of landscape in the manner of Monet, Sisley, or Pissarro. It carves objects up rather than joining them together. It tends towards the expression of planes and contours . . . "

"Bazille," Daulte concludes, "unlike Monet, did not seek the trembling visual moment . . . His drawings, like his sketches and his paintings, follow his life . . . His profound originality was to 'live his painting and paint his life'."

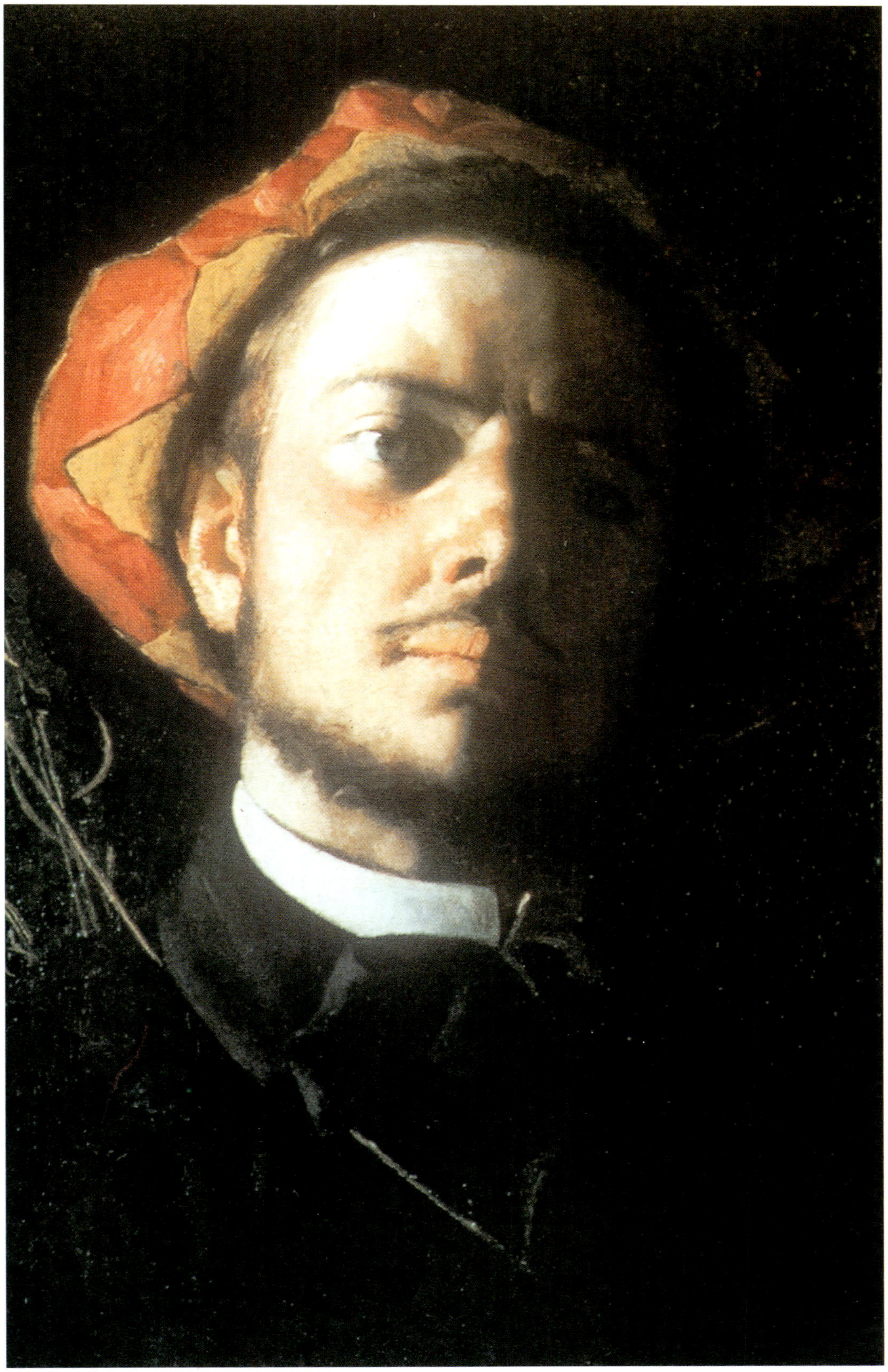

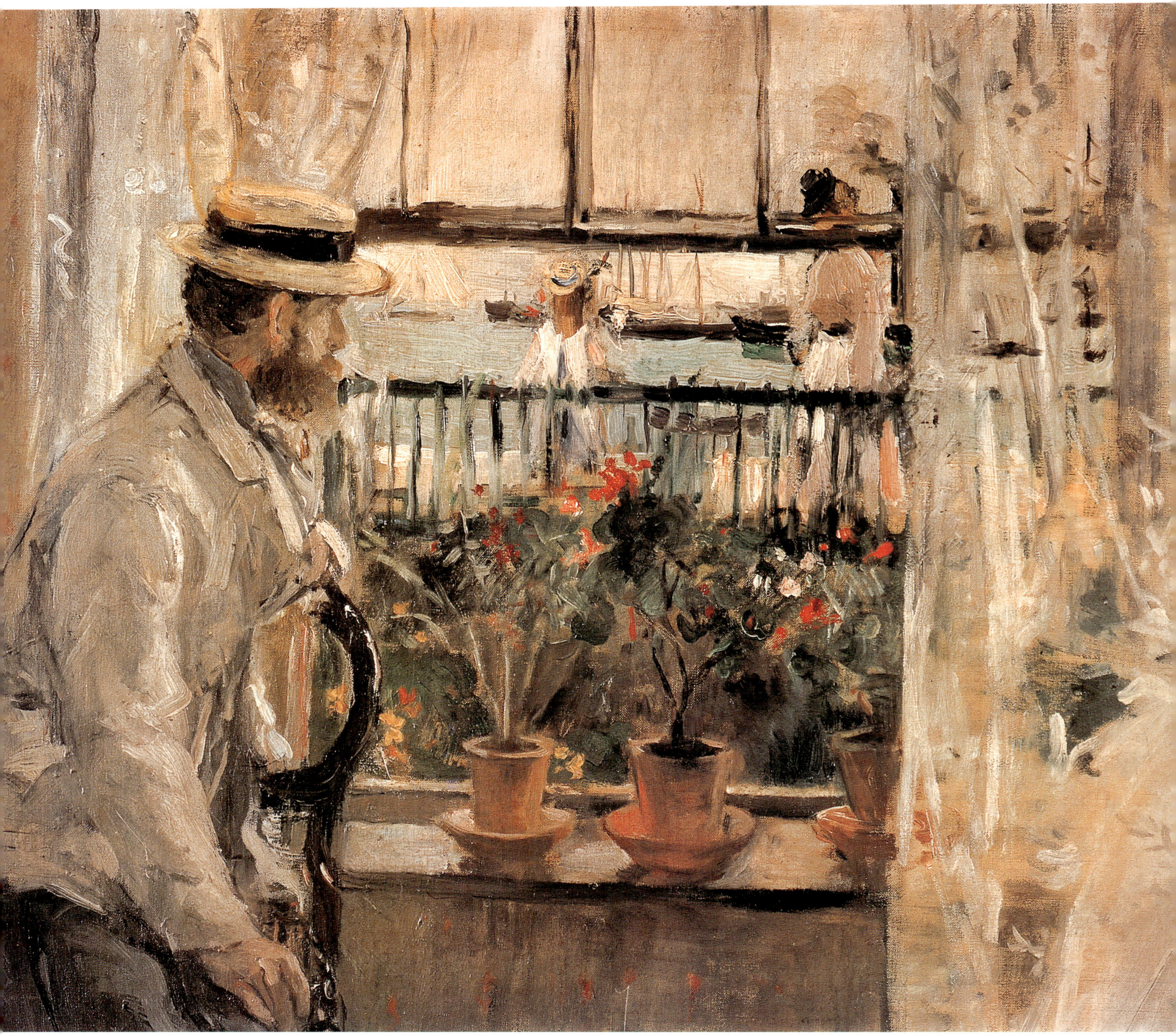

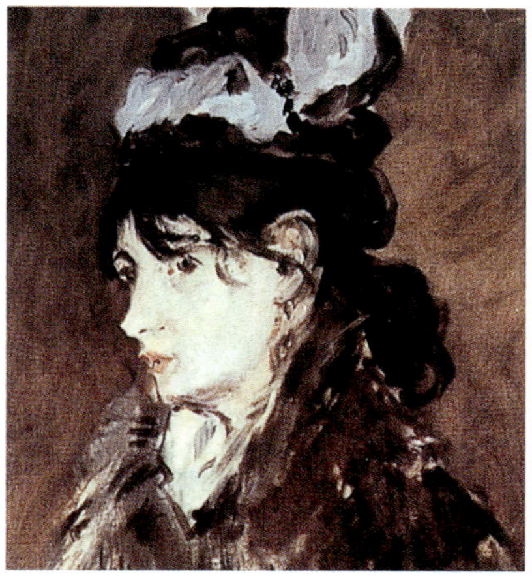

Berthe Morisot

BERTHE MORISOT
By Manet
c.1869
Above

Writing in *Le Temps* in 1877, the perceptive critic Paul Mantz called Berthe Morisot, "the one real Impressionist". The work of Monet, Pissarro, Renoir, and Sisley notwithstanding, Berthe Morisot was a major exponent of the popular style of Impressionism, with a uniquely delicate and controlled vision of her environment; an environment, however, bounded by the severest restrictions.

Morisot painted the life in her home, her daughter, her sister Edma and her women friends, attacking her subjects with a vitality and originality which was put down to "feminine charm" by most critics, but appreciated by her contemporaries in the Impressionist movement for what it was. Most histories of Impressionism relegate Morisot, along with Cassatt, to the sidelines as a picturesque adornment to the main body of Impressionist work. Not only did Morisot achieve consistent success at the official Salon, but as a regular contributor to the Impressionists' exhibitions, she was a major figure in the development of the movement.

MORISOT
Interior at the Isle of Wight
oil on canvas
1875.
Opposite

Life and Works: Berthe Morisot (1841–1895)

Poor Mme Morisot, the public hardly knows her.
Camille Pissarro in a letter
to his son Lucien, 1895

Berthe Morisot and her sisters Edma and Yves were born into the wealthy and respectable household of a top civil servant who had retired to the exclusive Parisian suburb of Passy – in the nineteenth century, a rustic suburb at the edge of the bustle of the growing city. Here they were brought up with a host of cultural accomplishments, including the art of conversation, music, and drawing. In a comfortable establishment like the Morisot's, the talents of young women were nurtured for the benefit of their mortal souls, their parents and ultimately their husbands. A modest and respectable *bourgeoise* was expected to be a cultured, but not over-cultured, adornment in a male-dominated society which valued above all grace, charm, and sociability in its wives and mothers.

The education of Berthe Morisot and her sisters was in this respect quite normal – an English governess, an exclusive school and of course drawing lessons from a respectable professional artist, in this case Joseph-Benoît Guichard – a follower of Ingres and Delacroix. The aim was to engender in the young ladies the skills of an appreciative amateur, not to make them into artists. During the nineteenth century there had been dangerous precedents which the bourgeoisie did not at all costs wish their daughters to emulate. In the field of literature, for example, the prodigious, immensely popular woman novelist

BOUCHER
Pan and Syrinx
oil on canvas
1759. 32.5 × 42 cm
Below Boucher was one of the old masters Morisot used to copy in the Louvre around 1858.

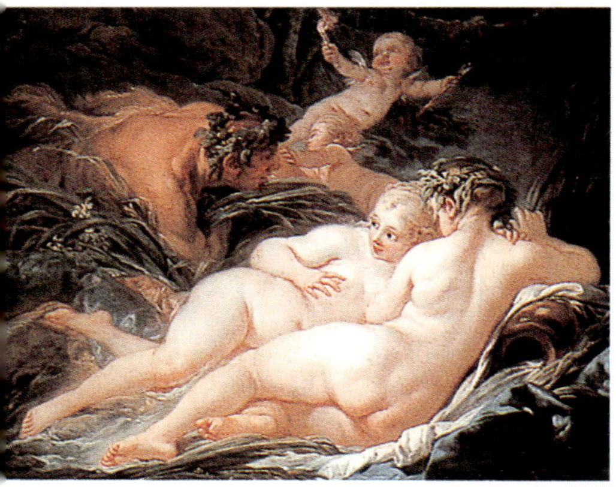

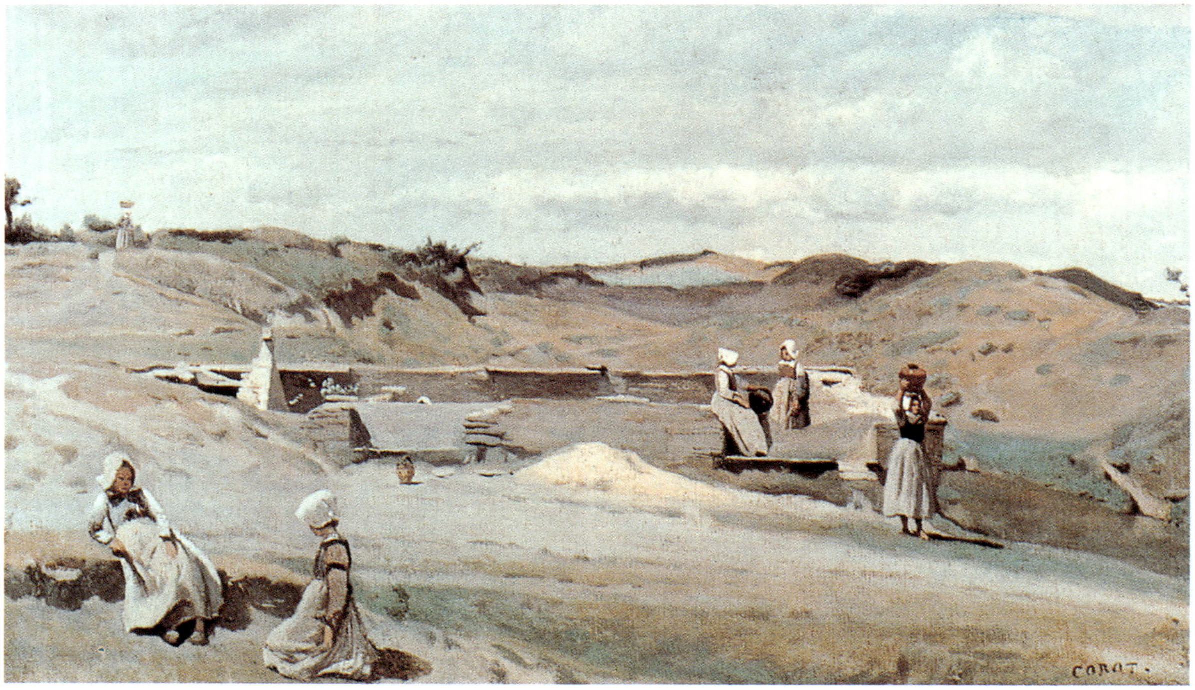

COROT
Mur, Côtes du Nord
oil on canvas
c.1855. 33 × 56 cm
Right At about the same time, Morisot met the much older Corot.

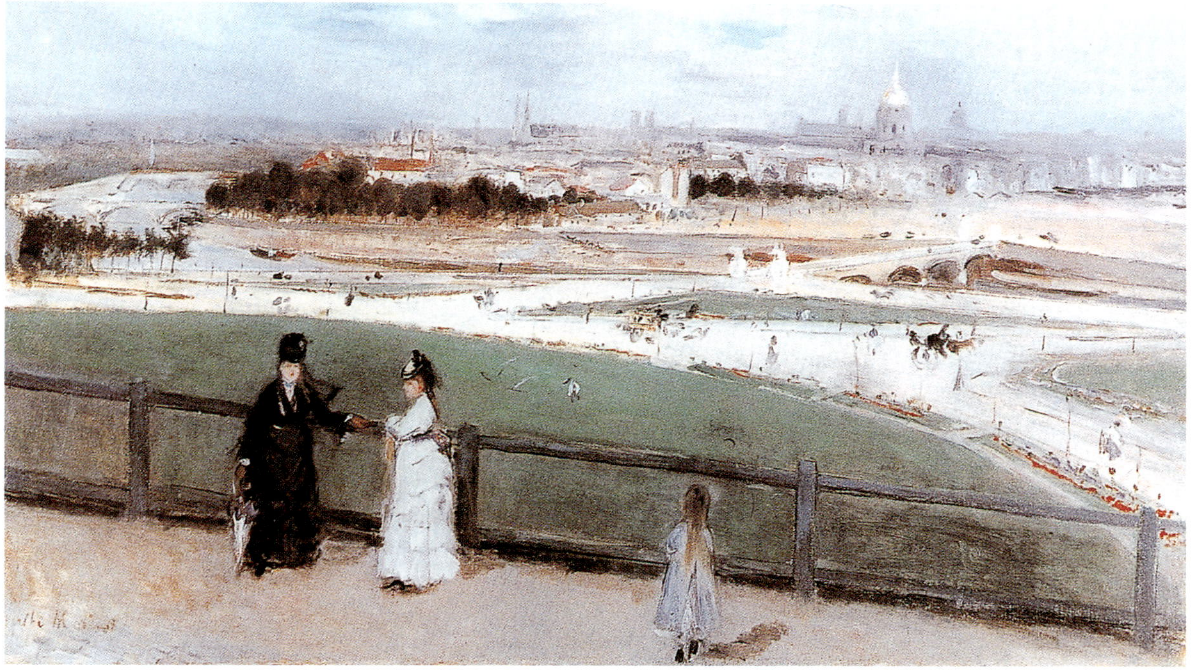

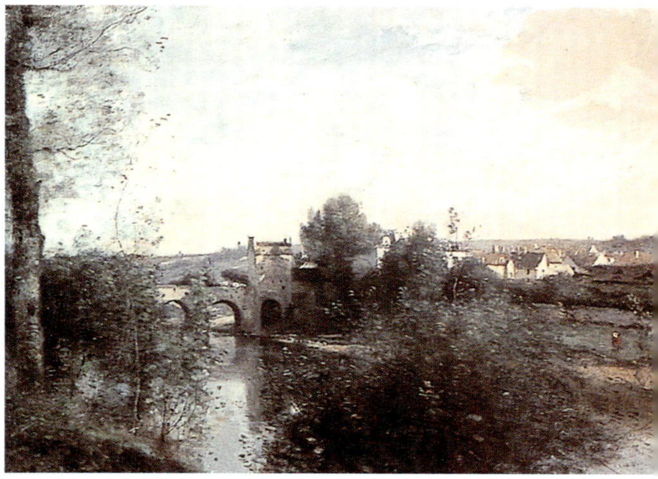

COROT
Limay
oil on canvas
1870–72. 41 × 66 cm
Above

MORISOT
View of Paris from the Trocadéro
oil on canvas
1872. 46 × 81.5 cm
Left Above This panorama is unusual for Morisot. It shows the continuing influence of Corot. Morisot opted more and more for intimate domestic scenes which were more practical subjects for her to work on.

and playwright George Sand had scandalized respectable society both by being a free literary spirit and by proclaiming her freedom to move about society wearing men's clothes. Her novels centred on the right of women to choose their loves, if not their lives, and were profoundly shocking, but also entertaining. When Berthe and Edma began to take more than a moderate interest in their art studies, the vain Guichard lost no time in warning Mme Morisot of her daughters' dangerous inclinations: "Considering the character of your daughters," he is reported by Berthe's brother Tiburce to have said to Mme Morisot, "my teaching will not endow them with minor drawing room accomplishments: they will become painters. Do you realize what this means? In the *haute bourgeois* milieu to which you belong, this will be revolutionary, I might almost add catastrophic. Are you sure that you will not curse the day when art, having gained admission to your home, now so respectable and peaceful, will become the sole arbiter of the fate of your two children?" Perhaps Guichard feared that before long they might be wearing trousers and standing on the Pont Neuf, quite unchaperoned, save for an easel.

Thankfully Mme Morisot trusted in her better judgment and allowed her daughters' talents to flourish. She and her husband were, in any case, friendly with the respectable artistic circles of Paris (to which even the dangerous Manet belonged, thanks to his otherwise impeccable social status). Berthe and Edma soon outstripped what Guichard could teach them and came under the tutelage of his illustrious friend Corot, who began to join the Morisots for dinner on Tuesdays when he was in Paris. In the summer of 1861 the sisters persuaded their parents to decamp to Ville d'Avray to be near Corot and continue their studies. Early on it was clear that, following in the footsteps of Corot who influenced so many of the Impressionists, Berthe was going to be a keen *plein-airiste*,

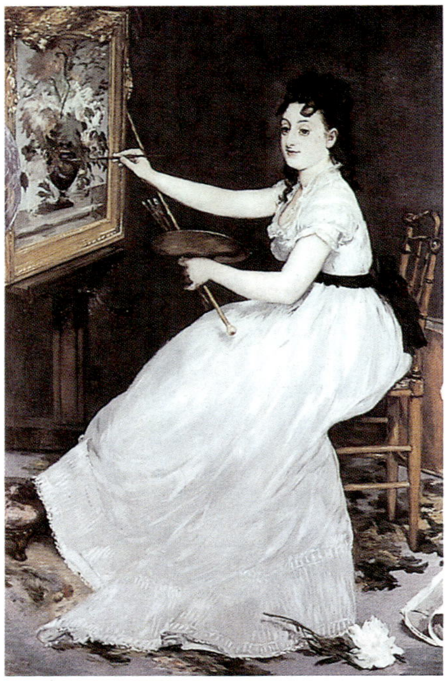

BAZILLE
Eva Gonzalès
oil on canvas
1870. 191 × 133.5 cm
ABOVE Eva Gonzalès was Manet's only pupil, and Berthe felt quite jealous of someone she saw as an unwelcome rival.

MANET
Berthe Morisot
oil on canvas
c.1869. 74 × 56 cm
RIGHT This is a sketchy picture, but it has the light touch and the liveliness of Morisot's brush in contrast to the darker rendering of Manet.

and she was later to become one of the most atmospheric and impressionistic of her contemporaries, having developed a swift, fluid technique using broken patches of bright colour.

By 1864 she had two paintings accepted at the Salon, *On the Banks of the Oise*, and *The Old Path at Auvers*; the next year she was again successful with a landscape and a still life. This success brought her to the attention of admiring critics, although many thought her work a "charming", or "feminine" aberration. During the 1860s Morisot had, in common with her contemporaries, been an assiduous copyist at the Louvre, studying the old masters and developing her drawing technique. Then in 1868 she was introduced by Fantin-Latour to the *infamous* Edouard Manet who took an immediate liking to her artistic talent and her beauty. He included her in *The Balcony* (*Le Balcon*) which he produced in the autumn of 1868, and she reciprocated by giving him her painting *The Harbour at Lorient* which shows Edma sitting on the harbour wall with a parasol.

The fact that Manet painted Morisot's portrait on more than one occasion, but that Morisot never painted his, is of more than passing interest. A respectable woman and a female artist in the higher echelons of society could not receive a lone gentleman, or any sort of man for that matter, in her studio without causing comment. A male artist, on the other hand, was expected to paint the portraits of society women. And by the 1870s they could also pass freely through brothels, low-life cafés, theatre dressing rooms – anywhere indeed they chose in the effort to capture Baudelaire's bustling "Modern Life". Baudelaire, Manet, and Degas were all *flâneurs*, strollers through the life of Paris.

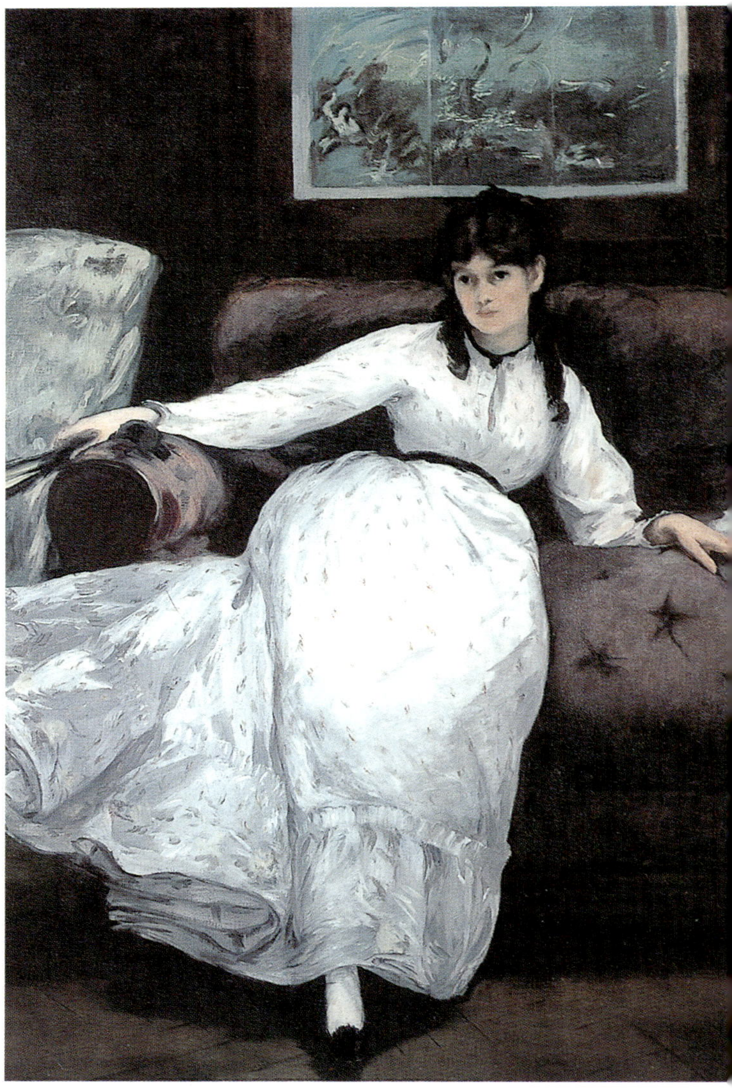

As Griselda Pollock has recently demonstrated in an essay called "Modernity and the Spaces of Femininity", women artists in nineteenth-century Paris could not be the "Painters of Modern Life" (such as Manet and Degas) that Baudelaire sought. The space in which they could move was both literally and symbolically limited to a set of places which were the realm of bourgeois women and which they could safely depict; dining-rooms, drawing-rooms, bedrooms, private gardens, verandas and balconies. Outdoors they could paint scenes in the park and the

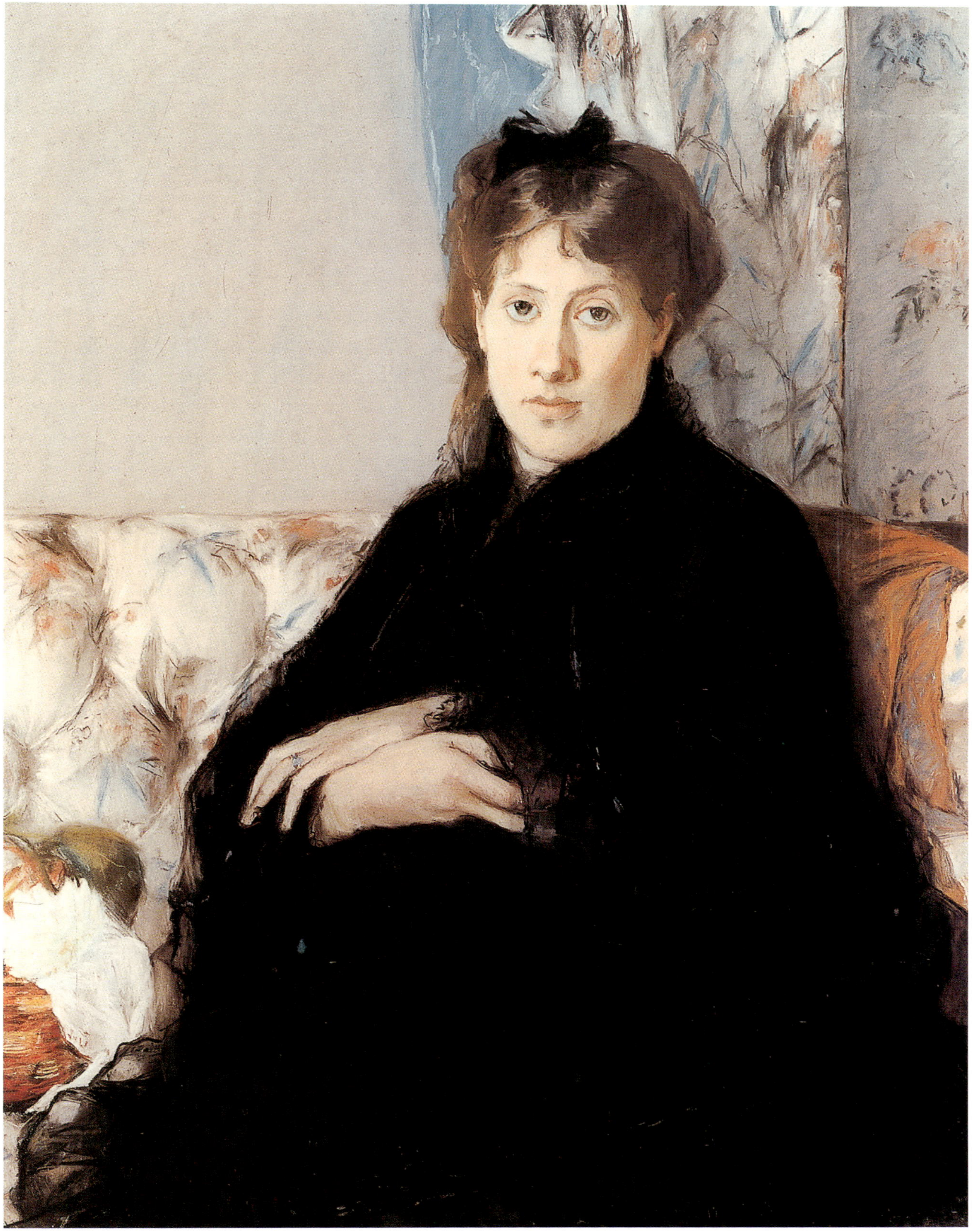

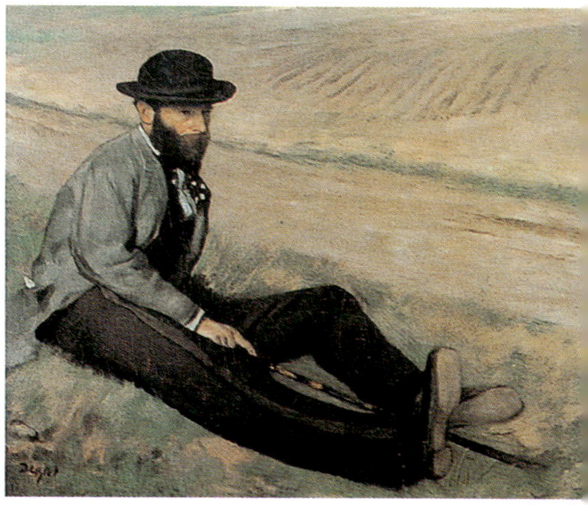

DEGAS
Eugène Manet
oil on canvas
1874. 65 × 81 cm
ABOVE When Manet was painting Berthe's portrait in 1872, he suggested that she should marry his brother Eugène, which she did two years later.

MORISOT
Madame Edma Pontillon
pastel on paper
1871. 81 × 64.5 cm
LEFT The young woman is Berthe Morisot's sister. The portrait shows Manet's influence on Berthe Morisot's style with its sober stillness.

MORISOT
Summer
oil on canvas
1878. 76 × 61 cm
RIGHT This swift, lively rendering is typical of the mature Morisot.

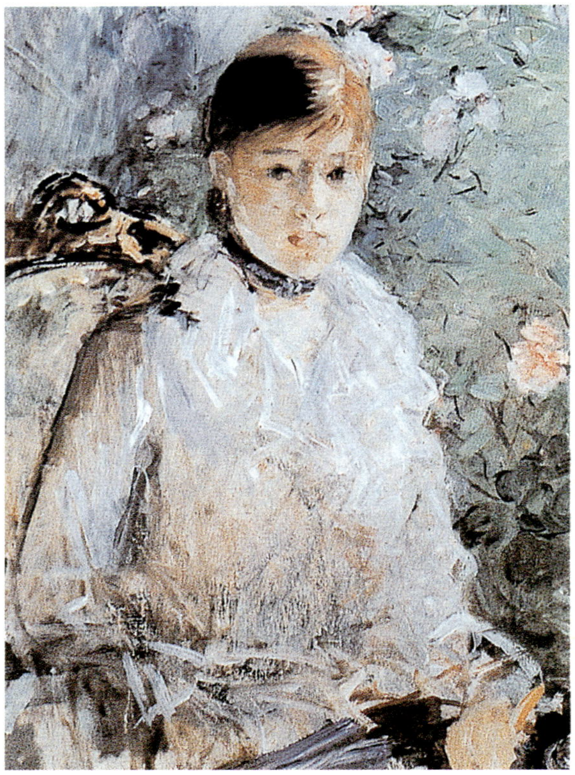

MORISOT
Summer's Day
oil on canvas
c.1879. 45.5 × 75 cm
BELOW This painting was shown in the fifth Impressionist exhibition of 1880.

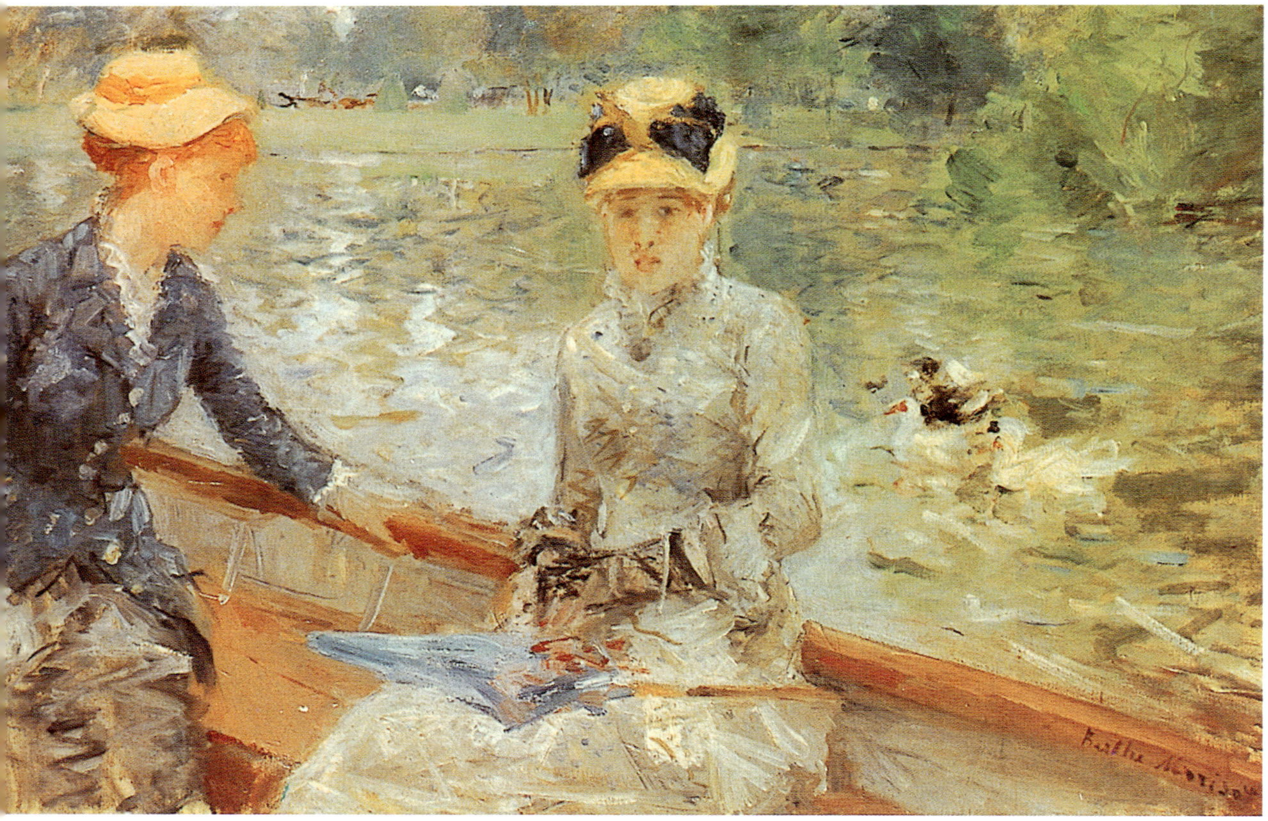

private box in the theatre, as long as they showed young women chaperoned; a respectable young women could not under any circumstances be seen alone in public. An artist contemporary with Morisot and Cassatt in Paris, Marie Bashkirtseff, described the enormous restrictions placed on her in a diary entry for January 1879:

> What I long for is the freedom of going about alone, of coming and going, of sitting in the seats of the Tuileries, and especially in the Luxembourg, of stopping and looking at the artistic shops, of entering churches and museums, of walking about old streets at night. That's what I long for, and that's the freedom without which one cannot be a real artist. Do you imagine that I derive much benefit from what I see, chaperoned as I am, and when, in order to go to the Louvre, I must wait for my carriage, my lady companion, my family?

These restrictions were being eroded, but not fast enough for Morisot to break free of them, even if she had wanted to, and there is no reason to believe that she did.

The subjects available for Morisot to paint were thus centred around motherhood, child-rearing, domestic labour, female companionship, in short the world of the bourgeois woman with all its rituals – a rich enough field, but one that had hitherto been condemned to the lowly status of genre painting. Until Morisot, Cassatt, and Marie Bracquemond (who, like Cassatt, first showed with the Impressionists in 1879) began to paint scenes from their daily lives in a new way (in their version of Baudelaire's "Painting of Modern Life"), women and children were generally either the subjects of

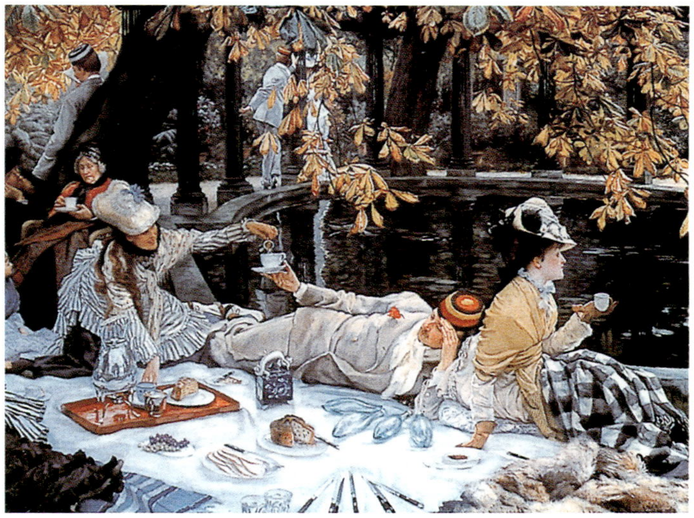

TISSOT
Holiday
oil on canvas
c.1876. 76 × 99.5 cm
Left In contrast to Morisot and the other Impressionists, Tissot depicts scenes with great precision, in which no detail is left out.

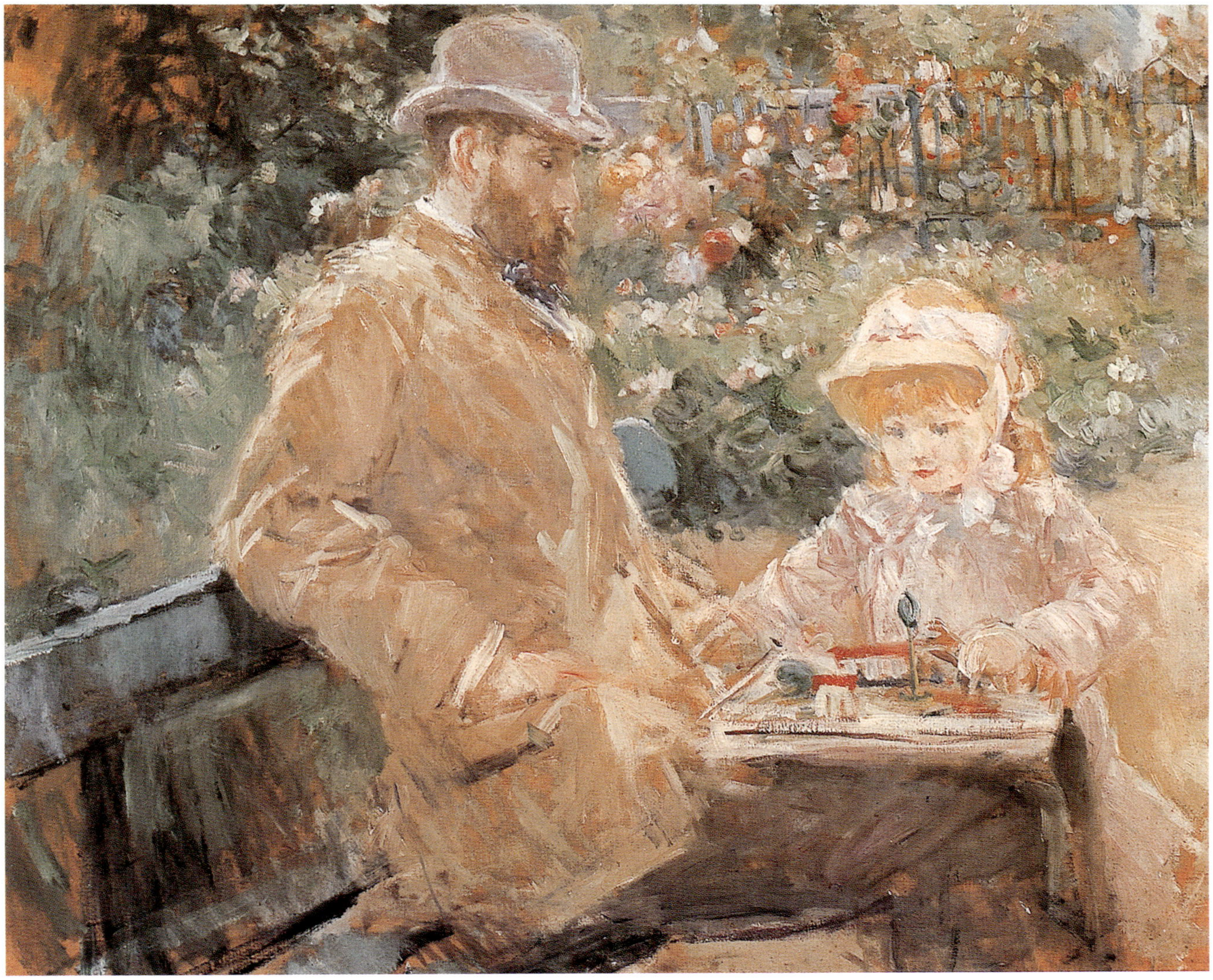

MORISOT
Eugène Manet and His daughter Julie at Bougival
oil on canvas
1881. 73 × 92 cm
Left below Charles Ephrussi said of Morisot's paintings that "One step further and it will be impossible to distinguish or understand anything at all."

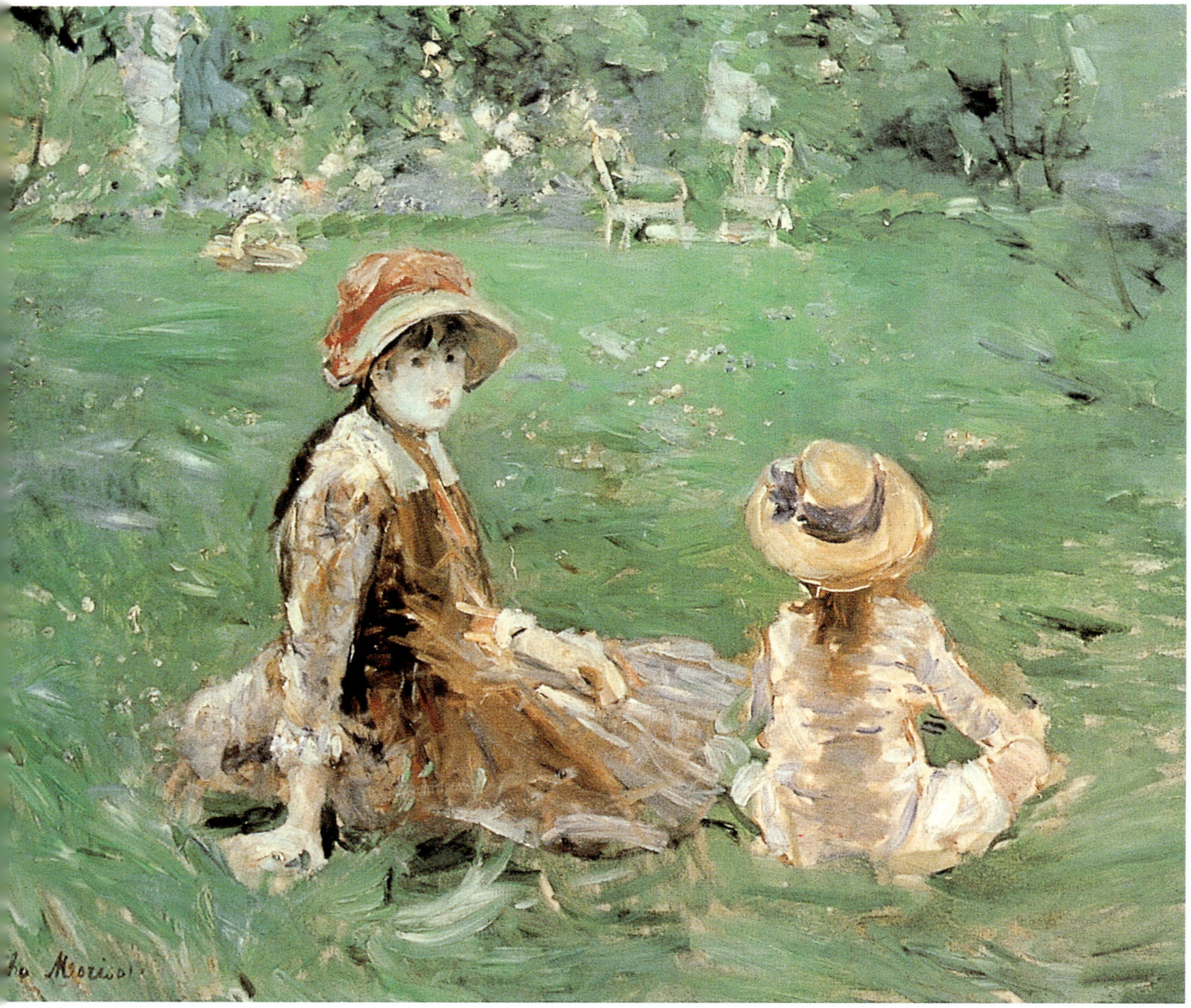

MORISOT
In the Garden, Maurecourt
oil on canvas
1884. 54 × 65 cm
Above Morisot painted several pictures set in the park-like garden.

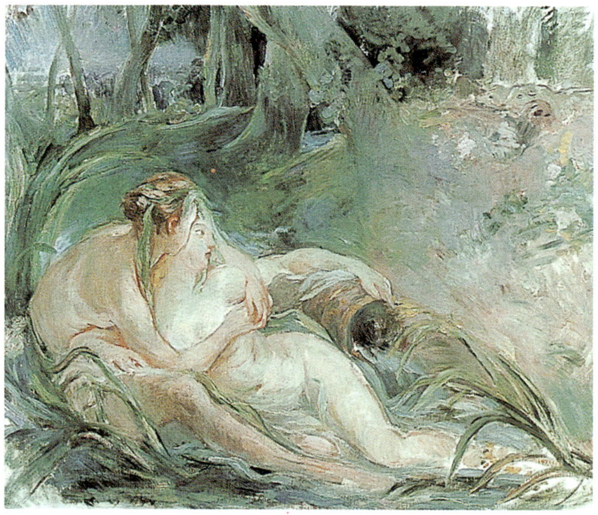

MORISOT
Copy of Apollo and Latone
after Boucher
oil on canvas
c.1885. 63.5 × 79 cm
Right Towards 1885, Morisot was prompted to make more studies and draw more nudes, following the example of Renoir.

documentary portraiture or appeared translated into mythic or religious symbols, as Madonnas or cherubs. Though Morisot did not transgress the social and personal norms of the day, she did achieve an evocation of her life, in her own artistic terms, which had not hitherto been possible.

Yet the problem for the critics of her day remained the fact that she was a gifted artist and a woman. The two could not easily be reconciled – there was no tradition (acceptable to men) of women in art, and all the critics and judges were men – and so her paintings were damned with faint praise for their freshness, delicacy, sensitivity, and femininity, and simply damned outright for betraying, as Joris-Karl Huysmans put it, "hysteria". Typically the critic Albert Wolff, arch-enemy of the Impressionists, had trouble coming to terms with Morisot's gender and her obvious talent. In his vitriolic denunciation of the second Impressionist exhibition in 1876 he wrote, "There is also a woman in this group, as there almost always is in any gang; she is called Berthe Morizot [sic], and she makes an interesting spectacle. With her, feminine grace is retained amidst the outpourings of a mind in delirium." Although he dismisses Morisot in two sentences, he centres on a problem in art history and criticism which has persisted to this day.

"Above all else," writes one historian of Impressionism, "she provided a social and inspirational centre for the Impressionists." It is true that Morisot was at the very centre of the Impressionists, a regular contributor to the group's exhibitions, loved and respected by Manet (whose brother Eugène she married), Degas, Renoir, Monet, Pissarro, Whistler, and the poet Mallarmé (who became the guardian of her only child, Julie,

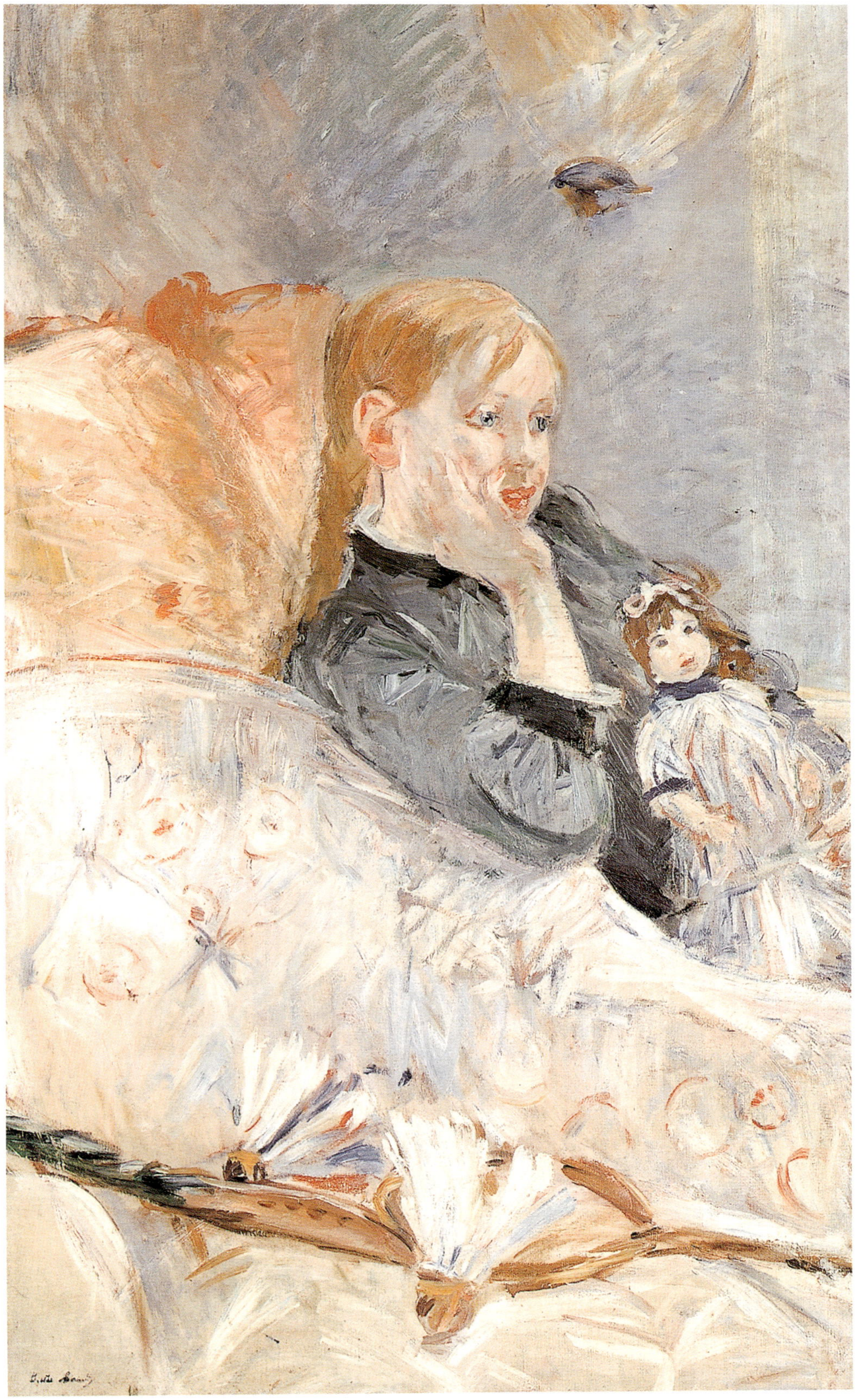

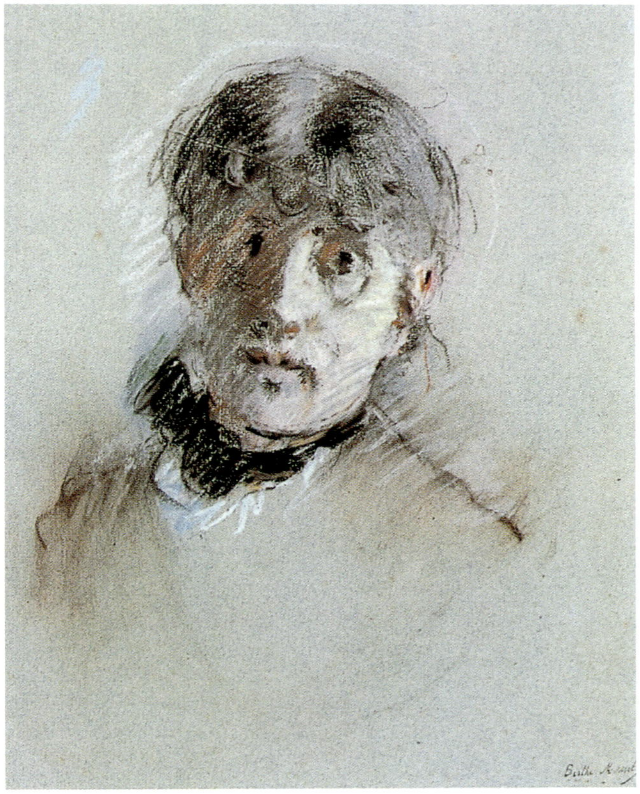

MORISOT
Self-portrait
pastel on paper
1885. 46 × 36 cm
ABOVE In spite of the fluttering lines, the style of this portrait is greatly influenced by Manet, who had died two years previously.

MORISOT
Young Girl with a Doll
oil on canvas
1886. 97 × 58 cm
LEFT This young girl is probably her daughter, Julie Manet, who was born in 1878. Morisot liked to paint and draw children, even if they were impatient.

MORISOT
Young Girl with a Basket
pastel on paper
1891. 58 × 61 cm
Below Morisot always managed to represent children in natural, unaffected poses.

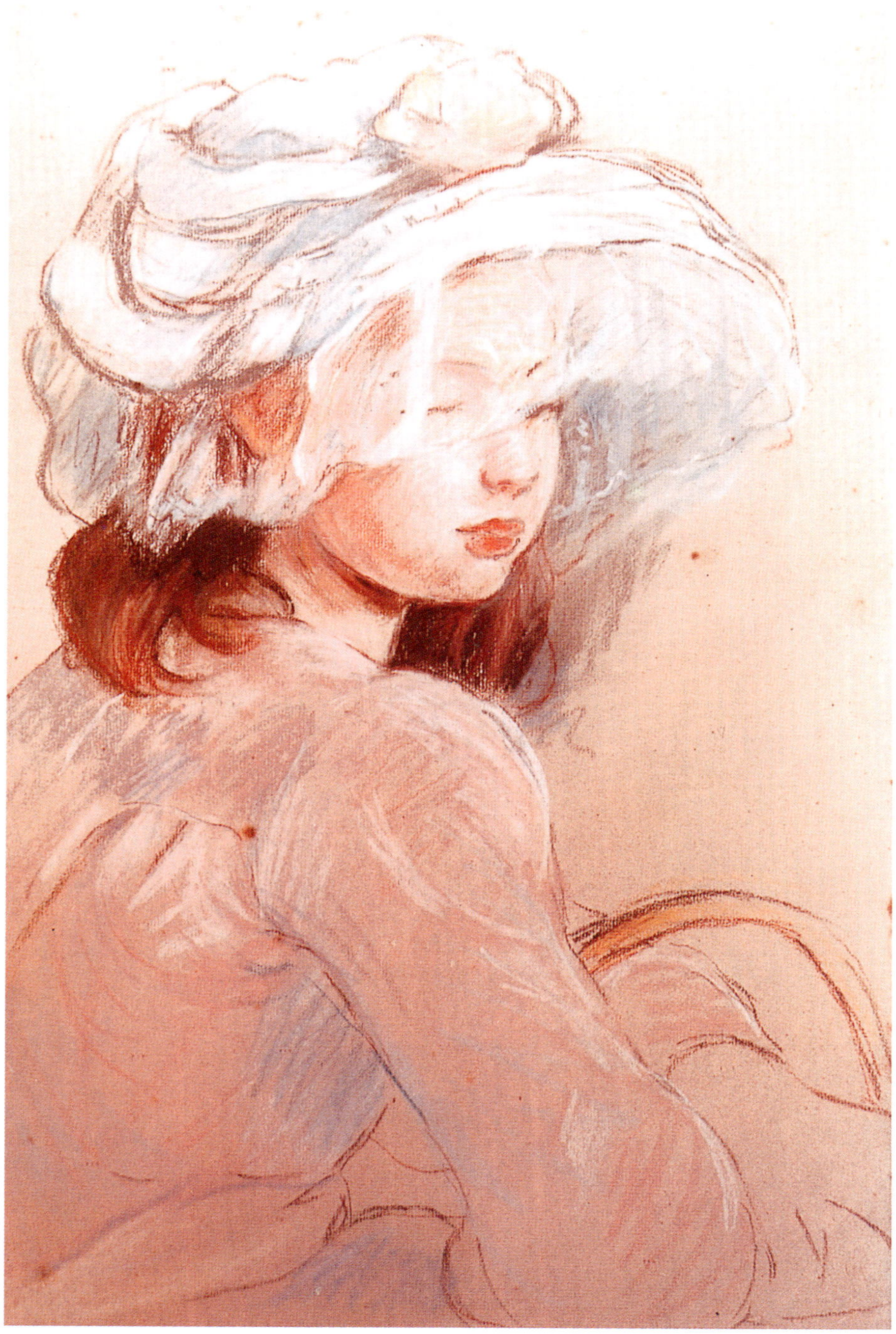

after her death), but she could do no more than play out her predestined role as a society hostess, even if it was as one of the most select group of artistic revolutionaries. She could not join in the discussions in the cafés and, symbolically, she is not in Bazille's or Fantin-Latour's portrait of the Batignolles Group of which she was an important part.

It is only in the last twenty years that a critical debate has arisen which treats her work and that of her female contemporaries as the product of original minds working in a restrictive system, as producers of art, rather than women artists, and this has opened up new ways of seeing Morisot's oeuvre. Griselda Pollock, for example, has delved into the important complexities inherent in the representation of space in Morisot's paintings and the relationship between the bourgeois female figures in them to the world depicted outside the salon and beyond the balcony.

In 1896, on the first anniversary of Morisot's death, Durand-Ruel mounted a retrospective which had Monet, Degas, Renoir, and Mallarmé fighting over where to hang which picture. Each thought they knew best, just as twenty years before that Edouard Manet had known what was best for Morisot's intense painting of her mother and sister. Morisot wrote after the incident: "He cracked a thousand jokes, laughed like a madman, handed me the palette, took it back and finally by five o'clock in the afternoon we had made the prettiest caricature that was ever seen . . . I am left confounded . . . Mother thinks the episode is funny, but I find it agonizing."

In her diary Morisot's daughter, Julie, described the effect of her mother's posthumous retrospective: "Everyone is astonished on entering the room, exclaiming 'I would never have believed she did so much work!' They say that Maman never showed all these drawings, that she hid part of her work. Today it comes as a revelation." Or as Pissarro said, "Poor Mme Morisot, the public hardly knows her."

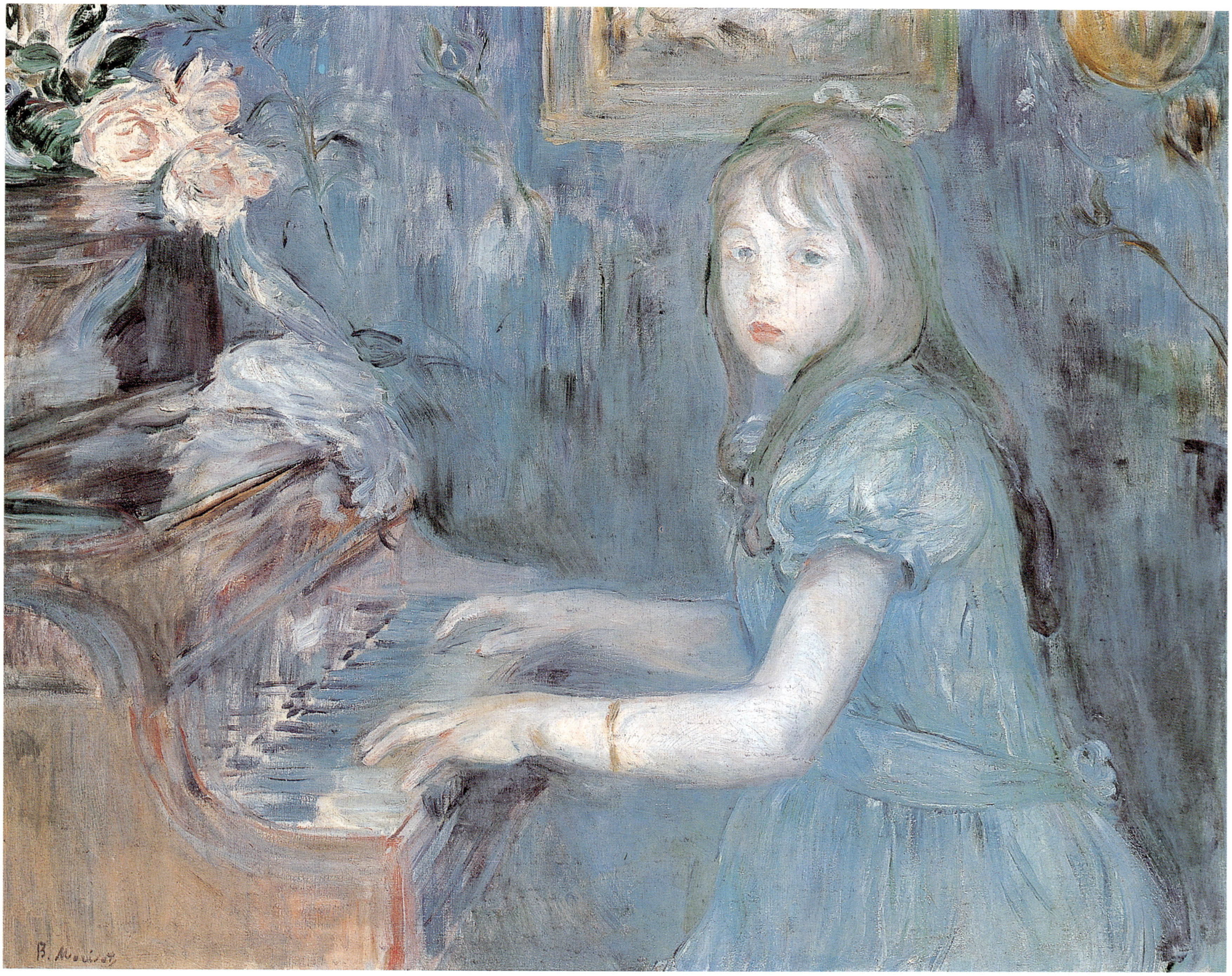

MORISOT
Lucie Léon at the Piano
oil on canvas
1892. 65 × 80 cm
The peacock pattern of the wallpaper is blended in the background so as not to draw our attention from the morose-looking adolescent.

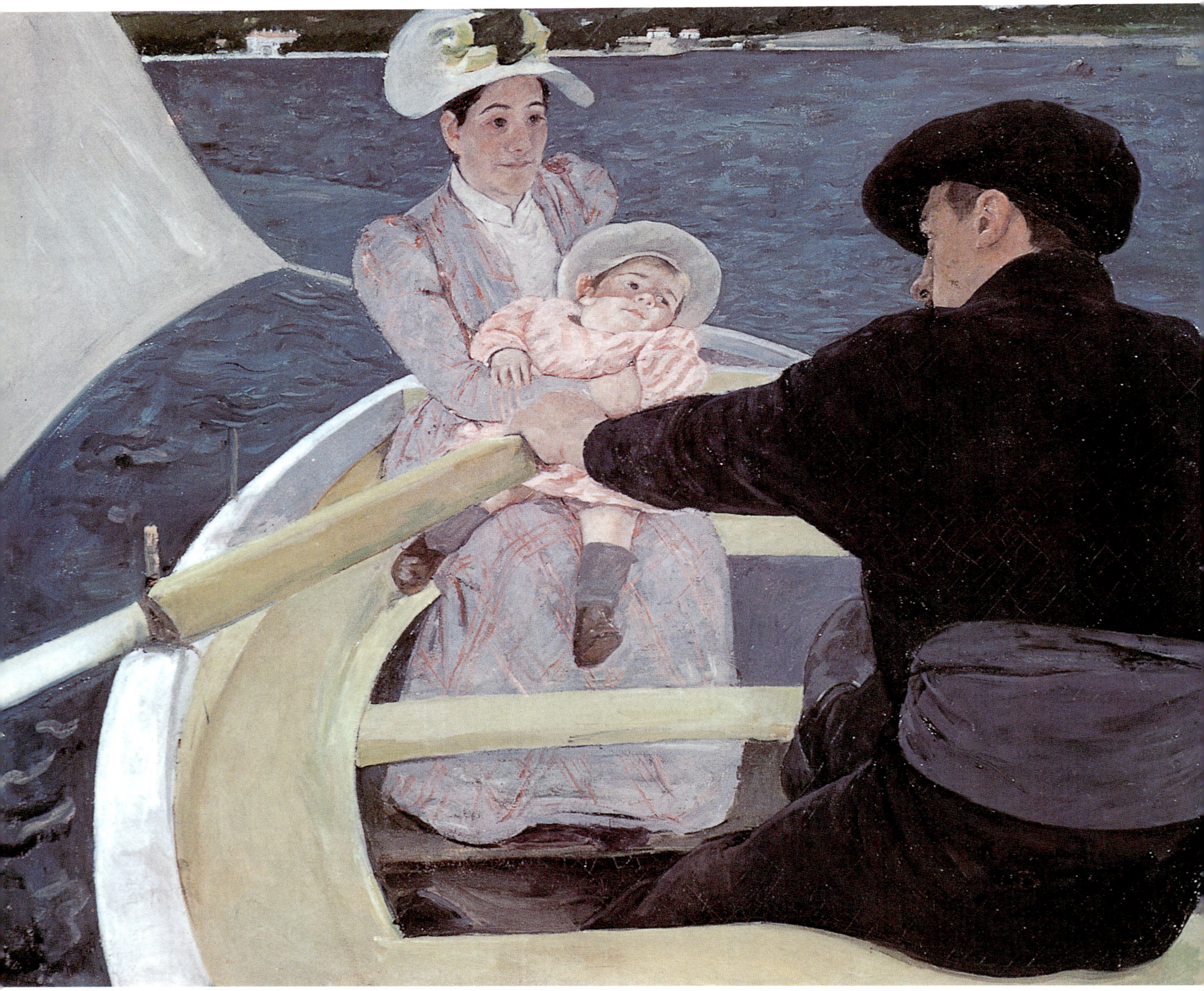

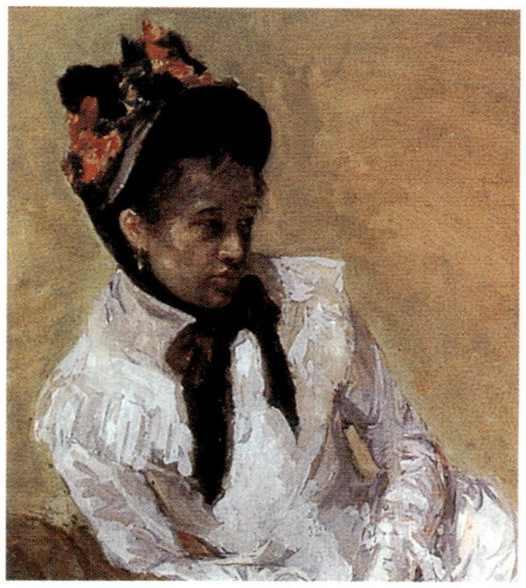

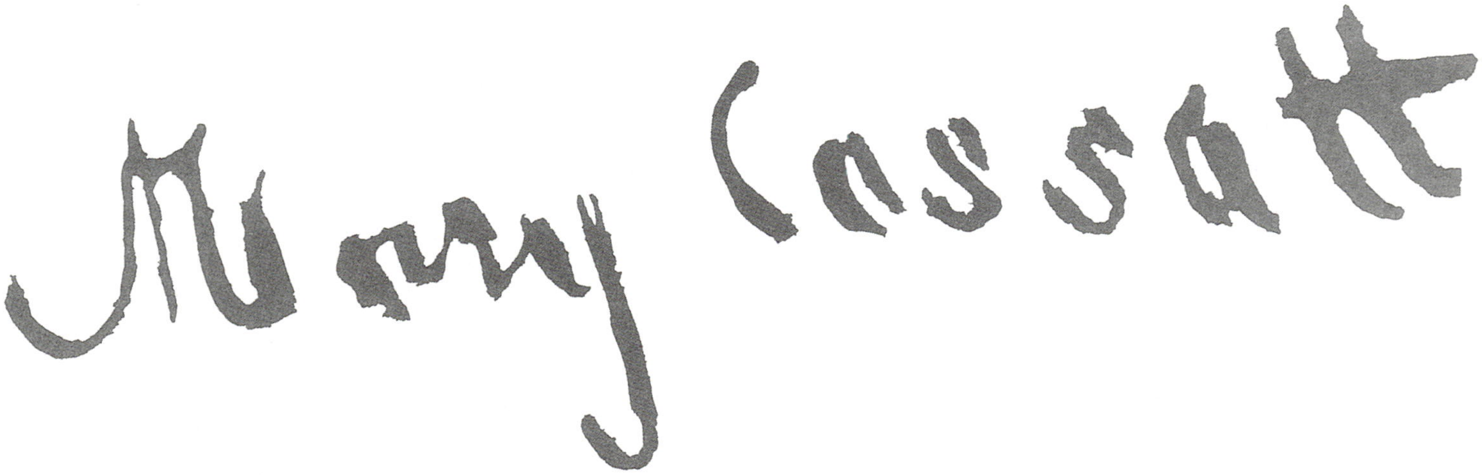

Mary Cassatt spent most of her life in France and together with Whistler and Sargent formed part of the great triumvirate of American expatriates working in Europe. From her earlier paintings we can see that in part Mary Cassatt inhabited a Jamesian world of endless afternoon teas, gentle conversation and hushed admiration in the long halls of the Louvre (where Degas pictured her in an etching), punctuated by the occasional excitement of the theatre. These pictures do indeed offer us a keenly observed insight into the strictures and rituals of a bourgeois gentlewoman in late nineteenth-century Parisian society, but her most impressive work shows us women at work – her sister Lydia at work on her tapestry frame, Lydia crocheting in the garden, a woman bathing her daughter – and these images tell us as much about Cassatt's concern to depict the reality of modern life for women as the eternally poised *Cup of Tea*.

MARY CASSATT
Self-portrait
c.1895
Above

CASSATT
The Boating Party
oil on canvas
1893–94. 95 × 117 cm
Opposite

Life and Works: Mary Cassatt (1844–1926)

What drawing! What style!
Edgar Degas on Mary Cassatt's
Girl Arranging Her Hair

Mary Cassatt was born in Allegheny City, Pennsylvania, on 22nd May 1844. When she was ten the family moved to Paris on the advice of doctors who thought Europe would provide a cure for their ailing son, Robbie, the second of two sons. A year later they quit Paris and arrived in Germany where the oldest son, Alexander, continued his engineering studies. Europe was to no avail and Robbie died, so the Cassatts went back to America in 1855. There Mary Cassatt studied art at the Pennsylvania Academy of Fine Arts where the teaching mirrored that of its French counterparts and included the same rigorous drawing exercises from plaster casts that had served would-be artists for generations.

MANET
The Reading
oil on canvas
1868. 60.5 × 73.5 cm
Cassatt chose the most traditional artists of the Impressionist group, those who in fact were the least Impressionist in style, to emulate.

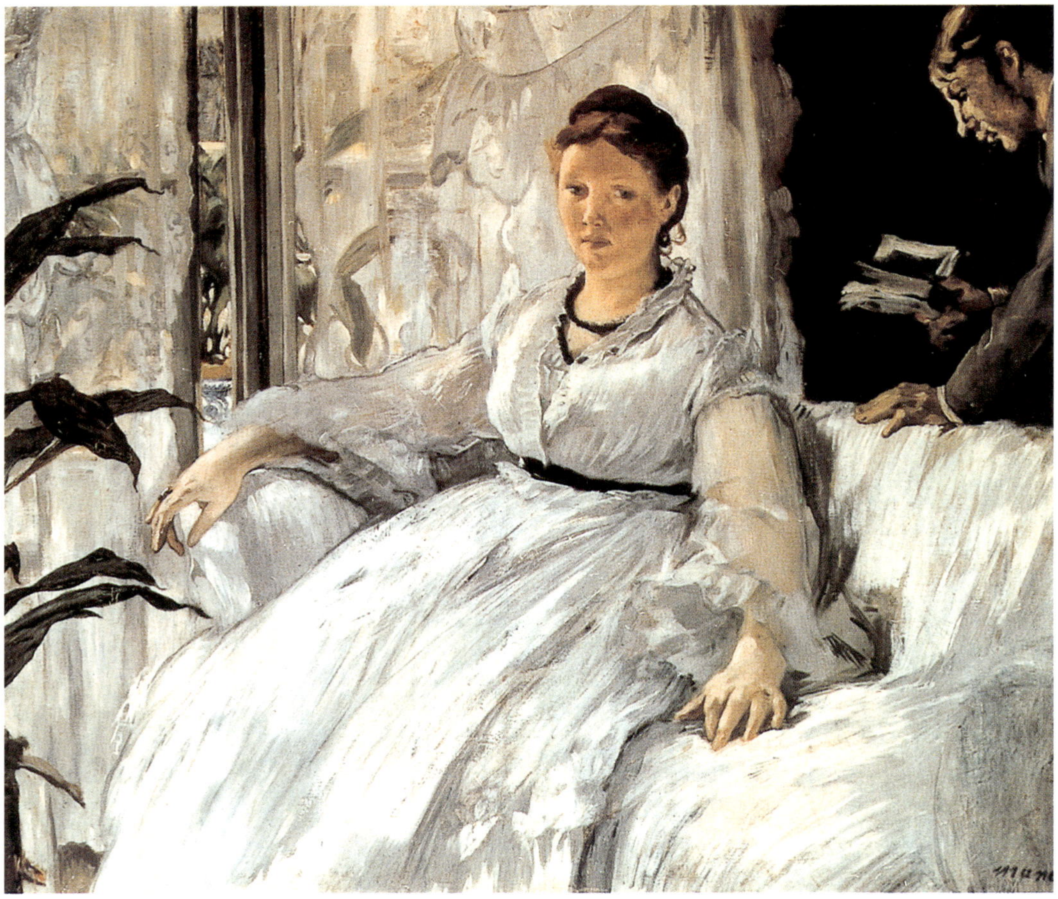

Two years later, despite the profound misgivings of her father, who said he would rather see her dead than an artist, Cassatt returned to Paris and began to study under Gérôme and Chaplin. In 1868 she had her first work *The Mandolin Player* accepted at the Salon, but two years later she was back in Pittsburgh as the Franco-Prussian War, and later the Commune, devastated Paris. In 1872 she continued her European travels, studying the work of Correggio and Parmigianino, as well as printmaking,at the academy in Parma, followed by a tour of Spain, Belgium, and Holland before resettling in Paris. Cassatt's *Portrait of Madame Cortier* shown at the 1874 Salon drew her to the attention of Degas, who conceived a liking for her work. Her own encounter with Degas' work was crucial. She described "seeing for the first time Degas' pastels in the window of a picture-dealer on the boulevard Haussmann. I used to go and flatten my nose against that window and absorb all I could of his art. It changed my life. I saw art then as I wanted to see it." For his part Degas said of her, "Here is someone who feels as I do." In 1877 Cassatt's parents and her sister Lydia, who was to feature as a model in many of her paintings, arrived in Paris to settle there permanently.

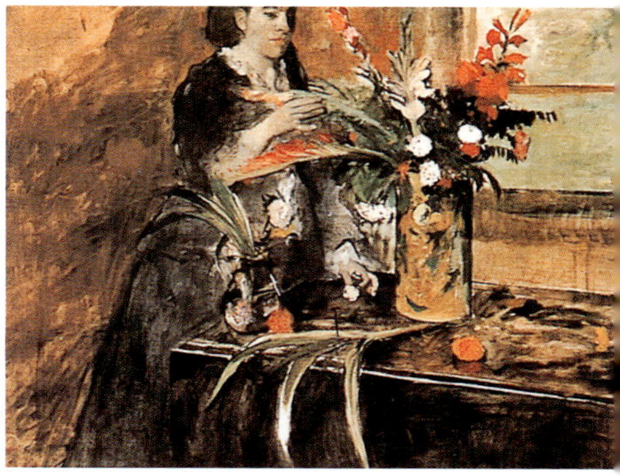

DEGAS
Estelle Musson
oil on canvas
1872. 94.5 × 129.5 cm
ABOVE This is a scene of quiet domestic simplicity, close to Cassatt's own style. Here, though, the bouquet shares the centre of the composition with the sitter, who is eclipsed by the brightness of the flowers.

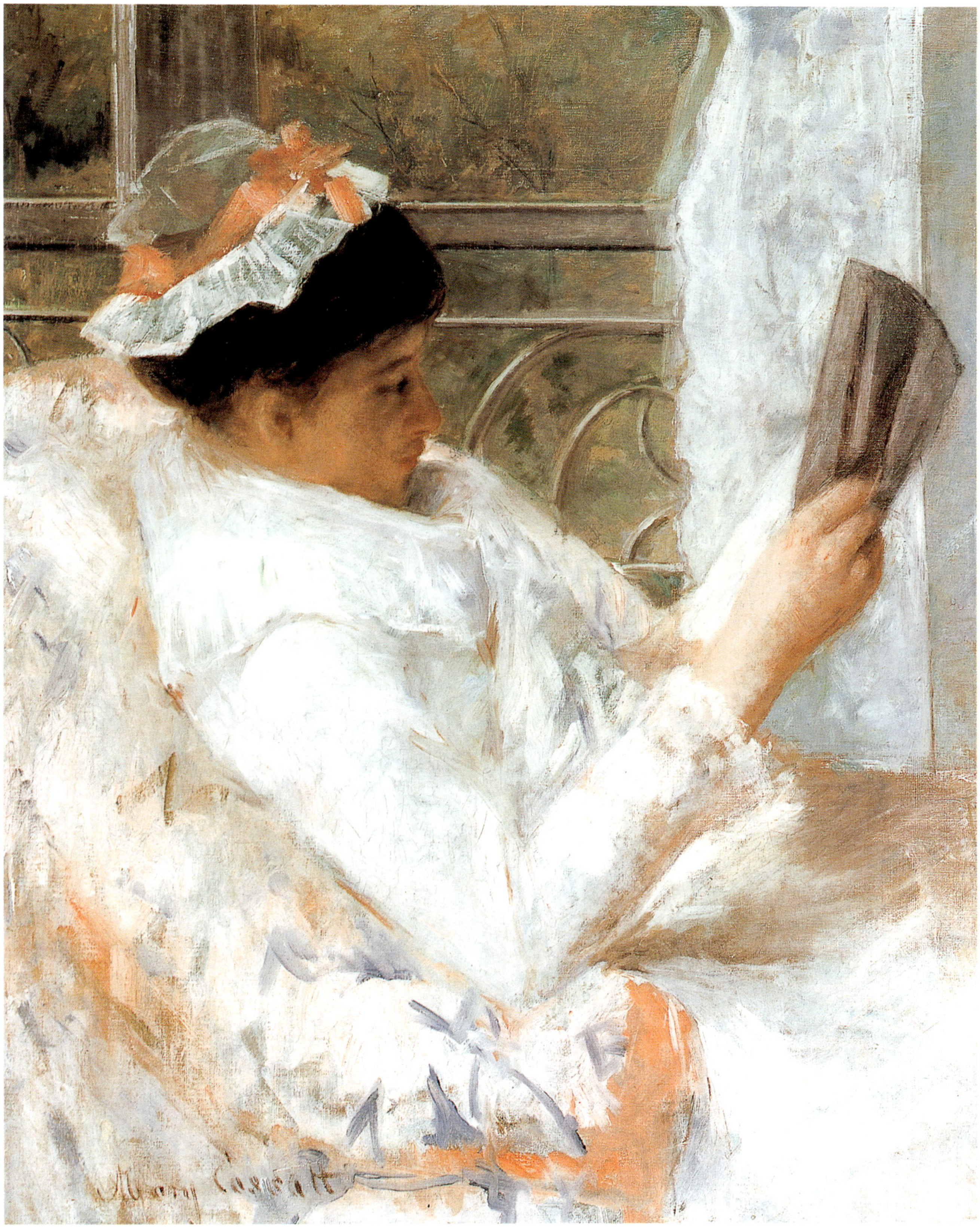

CASSATT
Lydia
oil on canvas
c.1878. 81.5 × 65 cm
LEFT Cassatt found most of her models from amongst her close relatives. This is a natural and relaxed portrait of her sister, Lydia.

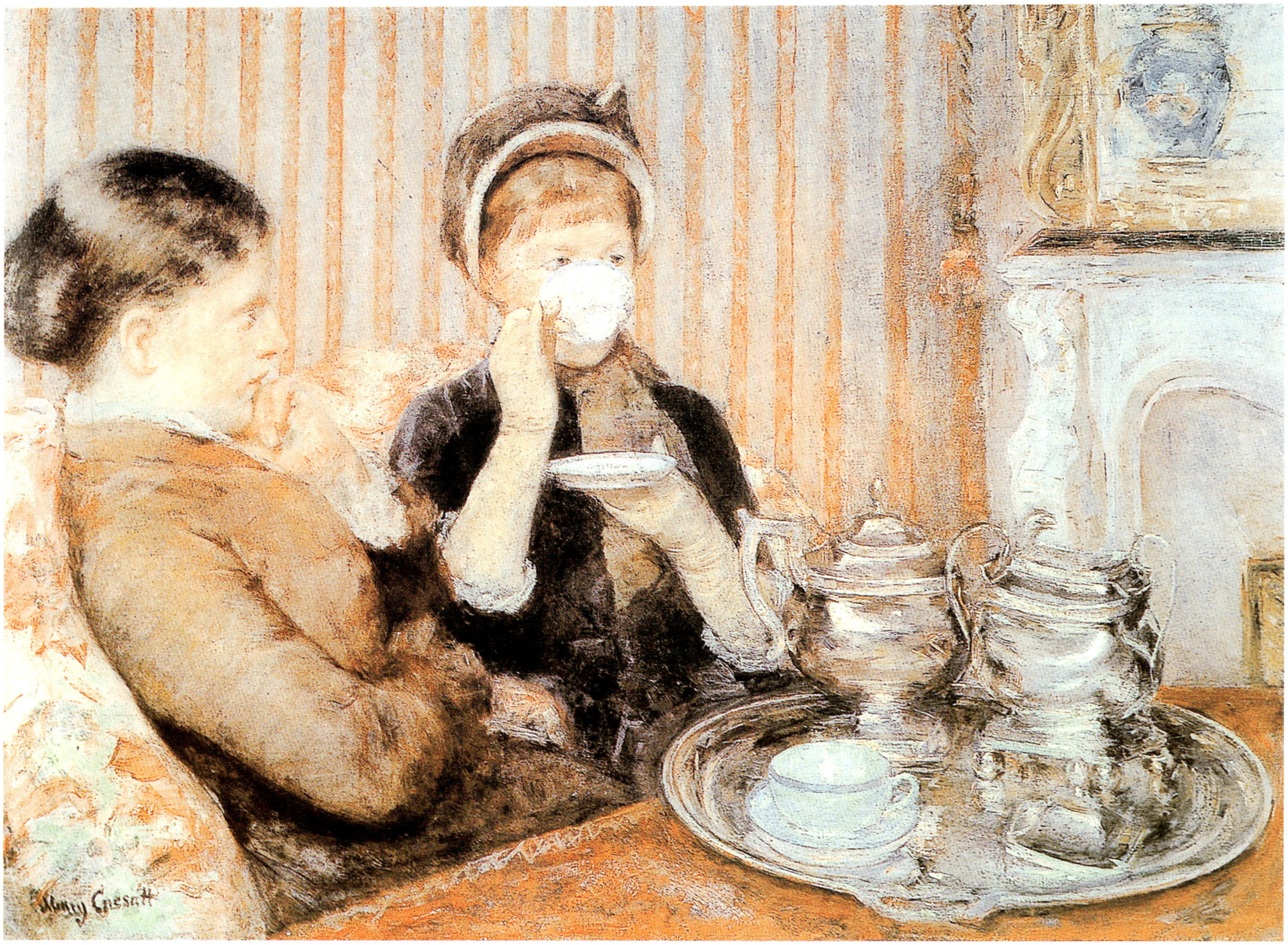

CASSATT
The Cup of Tea
oil on canvas
1880. 64.5 × 92.5 cm
Lydia Cassatt poses with the tea-cup. This is a rather formal scene which is matched by the artist's highly controlled style.

As a protégée of Degas , Cassatt became a regular contributor to the Impressionist exhibitions. She was represented in the shows of 1879, 1880, 1881, and 1886, but her close alliance with Degas meant her absence from the contentious penultimate exhibition which featured Monet, Renoir, and Sisley, who would not exhibit with Degas or his followers. Despite the influence of Degas, Cassatt's work was as individual as her character; the early period of her work is marked by airy compositions, many on the theme of domestic life reminiscent of Berthe Morisot's paintings. And as we have seen in the case of Morisot, there was little else Cassatt could legitimately paint without breaking the bounds of convention; she was limited in scope, but not in vision, to her immediate surroundings. As her painting of 1878 *Young Girl in a Blue Armchair* shows, Cassatt had

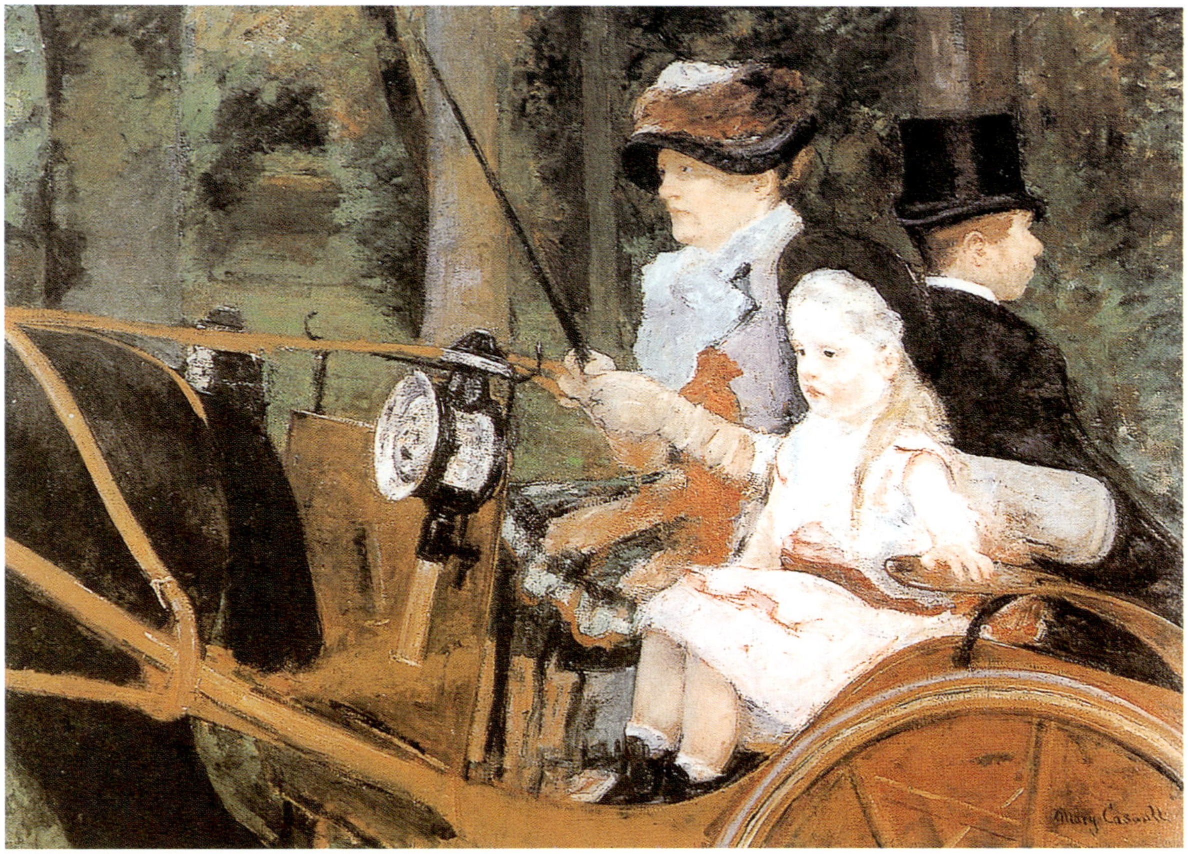

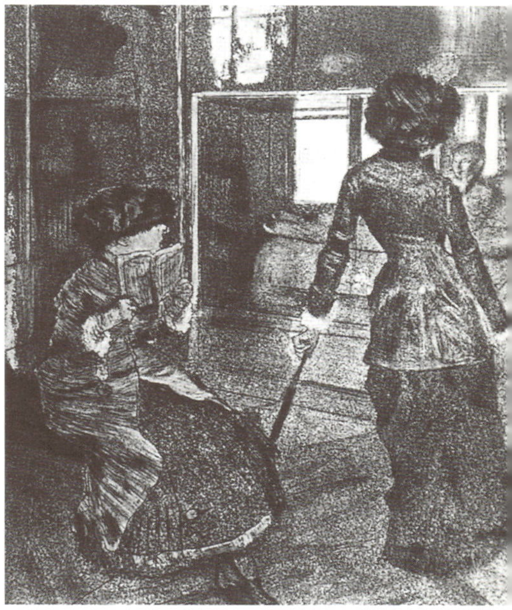

DEGAS
Mary Cassatt at the Louvre
etching, aquatint and drypoint
after a pastel
1880. 26.7 × 24.5 cm
ABOVE Degas was a supporter of Cassatt, whom he had invited to show at the first Impressionist exhibition.

CASSATT
Woman and Child Driving
oil on canvas
1881. 89.5 × 131 cm
LEFT The picture is no more Impressionist in style than most of Degas' work, especially in the handling of the background, in which the light plays no part.

made the subject of children comfortably her own, and although Degas is believed to have worked on the painting, particularly the background, the painting evokes the strange perspective that children have on the world to great effect. The distortions of space in the foreground and the plunging perspective to the back of the room with its huge, solid armchairs show Cassatt applying her classical training to an intensely personal vision of the world, seen simultaneously from the point of view of a child and an adult.

One of Cassatt's most famous paintings, shown at the fifth Impressionist exhibition in 1880, is *The Cup of Tea*. This, and a work such as Morisot's *The Artist's Mother and Sister* provide a powerful insight into the common-place, immensely dull, but powerful rituals of the bourgeois woman at the time. The sense of time passing with excruciating languor is as tangible as the oppressive atmosphere of the rooms in which it passes.

In the 1880s Cassatt began to move away from a style which was never as loose and impressionistic as Berthe Morisot's, cleaving as it did more to the example of Degas and Manet, and became strongly influenced by Japanese art, particularly in her own attempts at the problematic process of colour print-making, in which she managed to reconcile line and colour with unrivalled results.

Although she joined the Impressionist group at a point when it was beginning to splinter, Cassatt was highly respected by all sides and did much to foster a sense of common purpose, working for example with Pissarro and Degas between 1879 and 1880 on the ill-fated journal of prints *Le Jour et la nuit*.

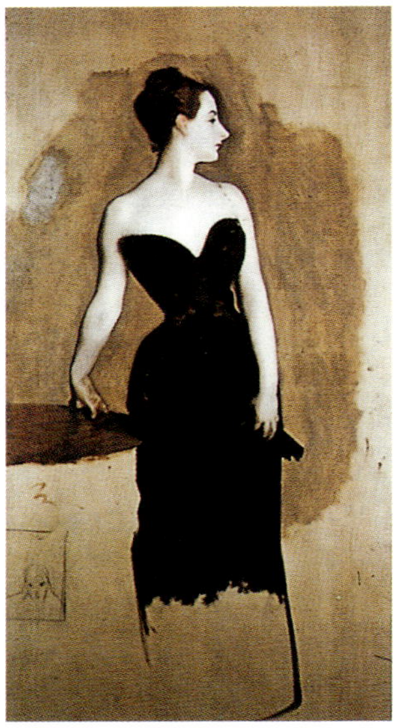

SARGENT
Study of Madame Gautrau
oil on canvas
c.1884. 206.5 × 108 cm
ABOVE Sargent, like Cassatt a celebrated American expatriate, was forced to leave Paris for London after Mme Gautrau denounced the finished portrait that he developed from this study.

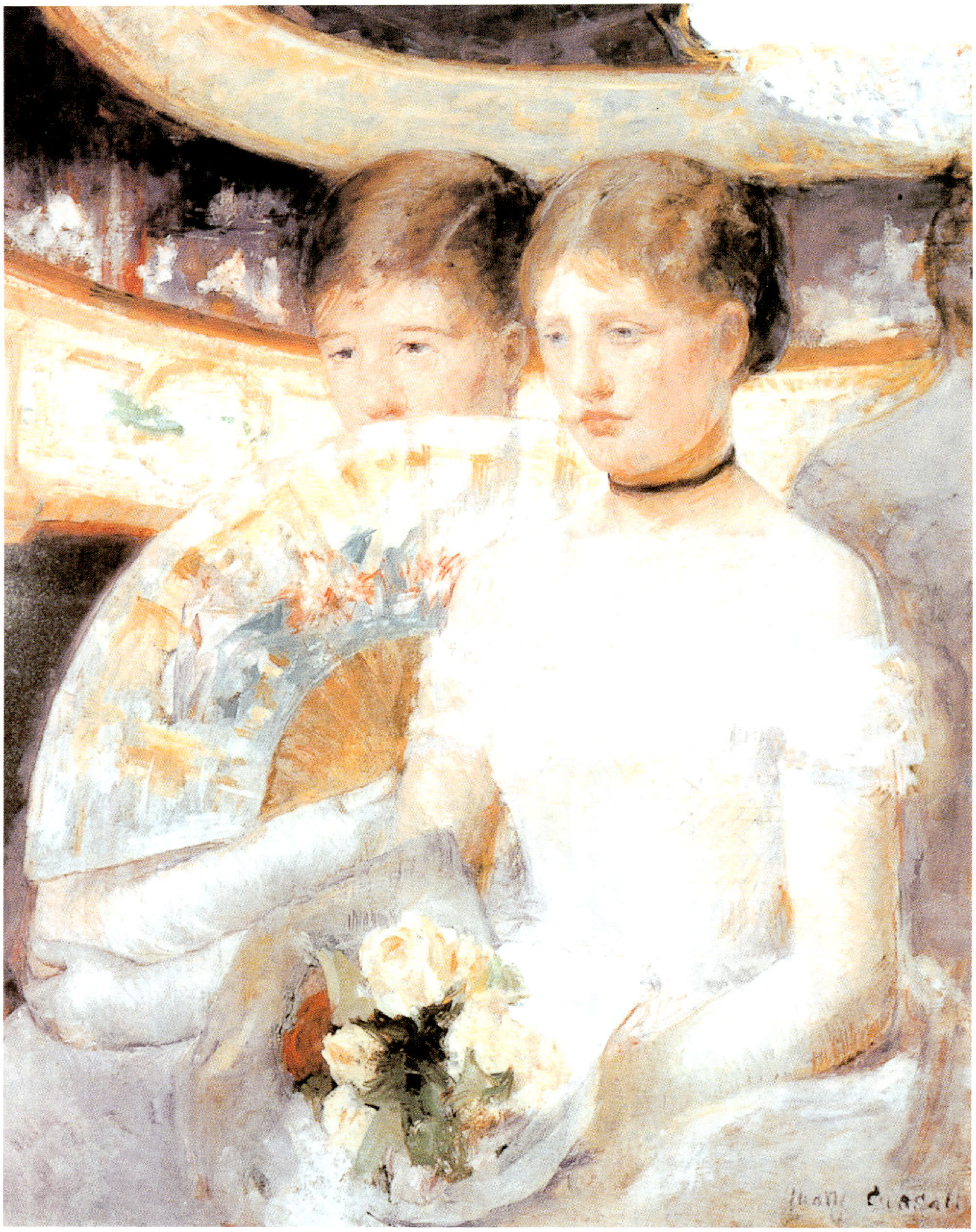

CASSATT
The Loge
oil on canvas
1882. 80 × 64 cm
RIGHT In this composition, another work on the theme of the theatre box which was treated by Renoir, Degas, and Gonzales among others, Cassatt depicts two very dispassionate girls who seem to be waiting for a break in the pose.

On a commercial level, Cassatt was instrumental in introducing Impressionist art into America through her brother, Alexander, and by advising the important collectors Louisine and Henry Osborne Havemeyer. Mary Cassatt was a childhood friend of the suffragette Louisine and it is in no small way thanks to her that from the 1880s onwards substantial amounts of money were available to back the Impressionists in France and endow the United States with a formidable collection of French Impressionist art, in the form of the Havemeyer Collection in the New York Metropolitan Museum.

In 1892, the year she bought her country mansion, Château Beaufresne, Cassatt was commissioned by the Chicagoan Mrs Berthe Honoré Palmer to produce a mural on the theme of "The Modern Woman" for the Women's Building of the World Columbian Exhibition in Chicago. Cassatt's influence in America – although she only returned there twice, in 1898 and 1908 – was now becoming considerable via important patrons such as the Havemeyers and her contacts with the increasing numbers of young American artists coming to study in Paris. Unfortunately the design for "The Modern Woman" has been lost, but photographs show it to be a major work, edging towards a new assertion of the dignity of women's labour and Cassatt's own important status in the world of art.

Although she was effectively a French citizen for the remainder of her life – she was awarded the *Légion d'Honneur* in 1904 – Cassatt maintained that she was "first and last an American". In her last years, suffering from the onset of blindness, increasingly out of touch with the world and bereft of her friends the Impressionists, she became what one visitor to Beaufresne, Forbes Watson, described as, "lonely, unreasonable, and vituperative, still a burning force and a dominant personality, capable of a violent burst of profanity in one breath and, with the next, of launching into a plea to save the coming generation of American art students from turning into café loafers in Paris." She died on 14th June 1926, the same year as Monet, bitter and alone.

CASSATT
Mrs Cassatt Reading
oil on canvas
c.1883. 101.5 × 81.5 cm
Cassatt expresses well the unaffected atmosphere of the home, and the nuances are rendered with great sensitivity.

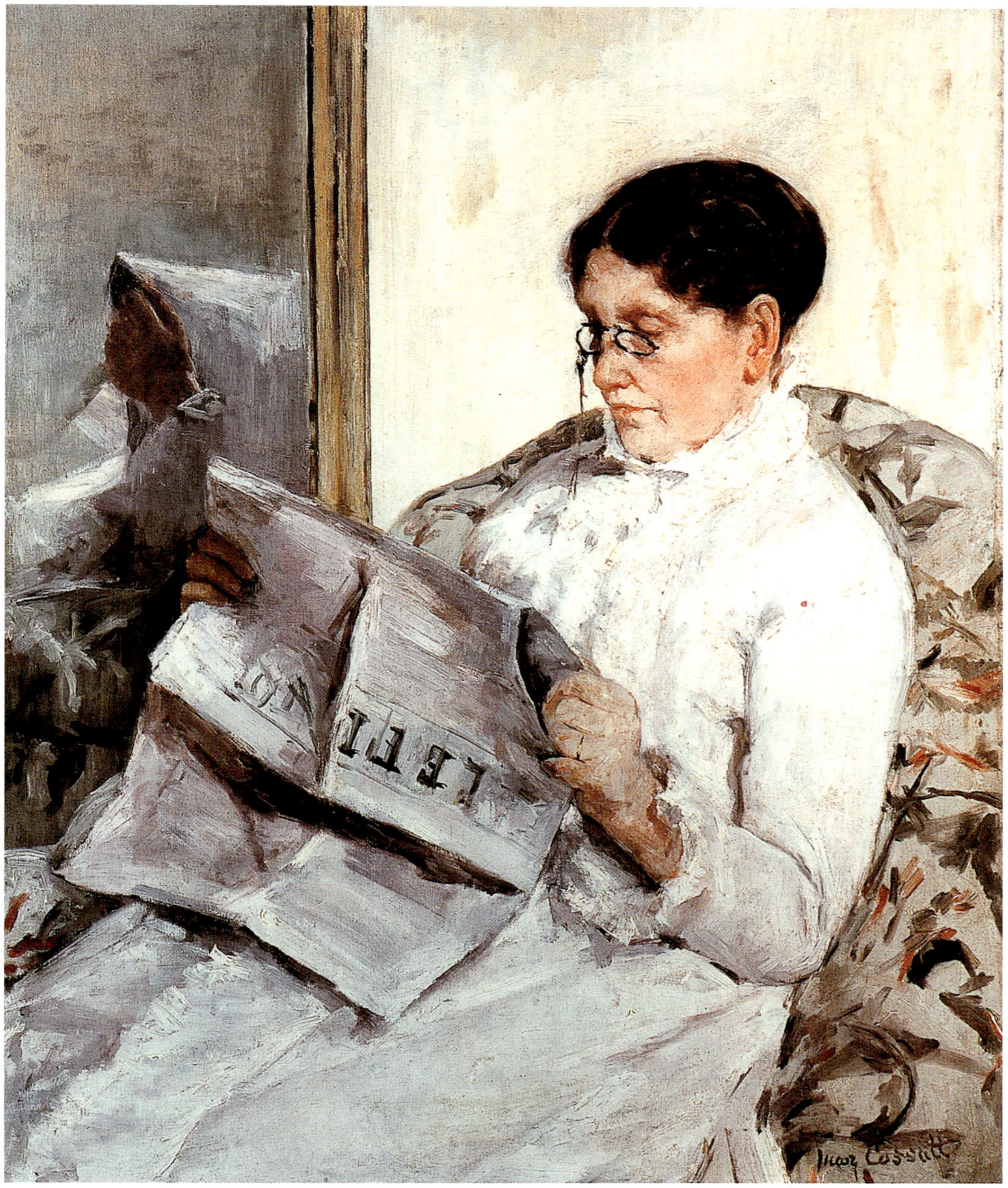

SECTION THREE

THE LEGACY OF IMPRESSIONISM

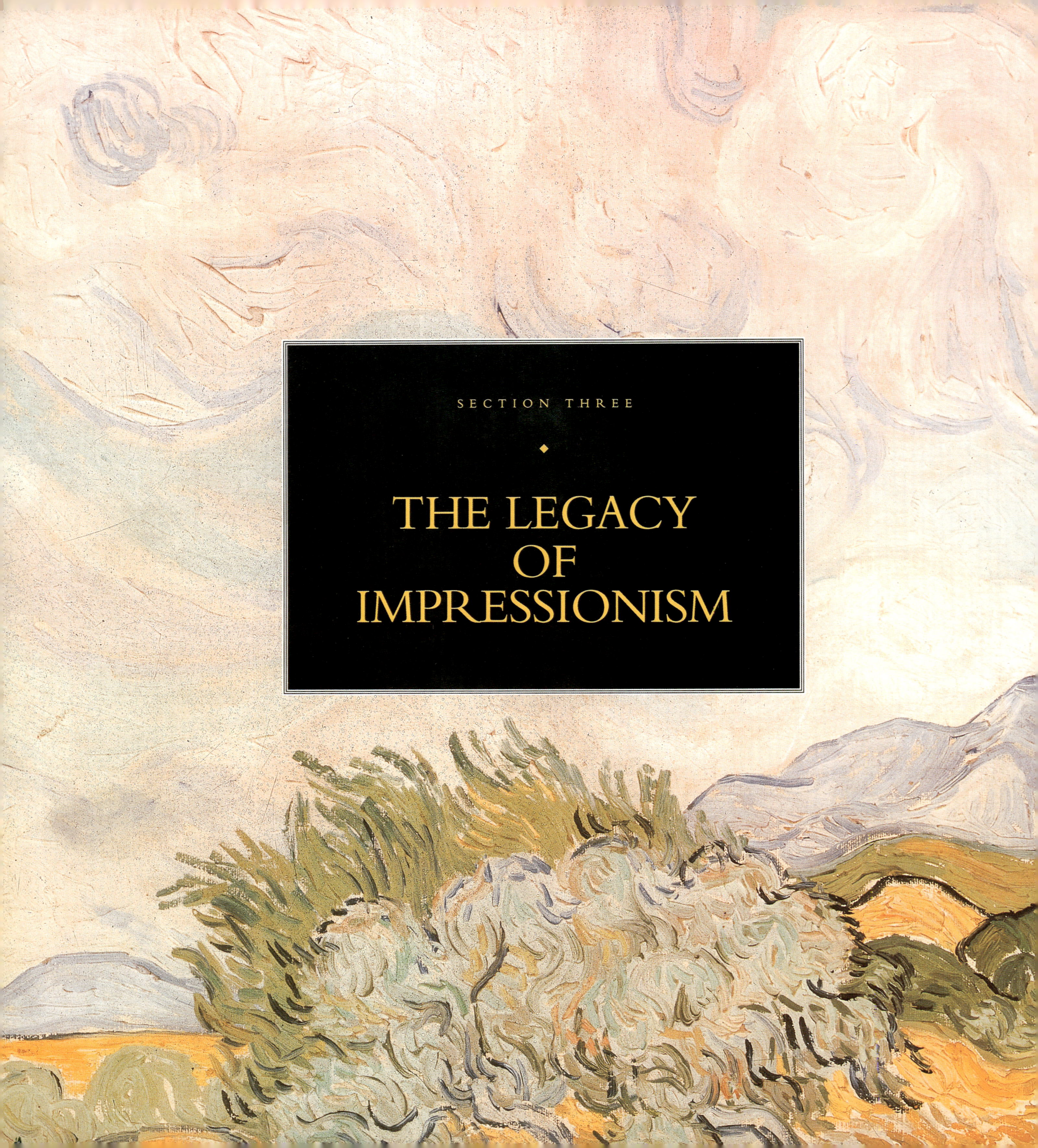

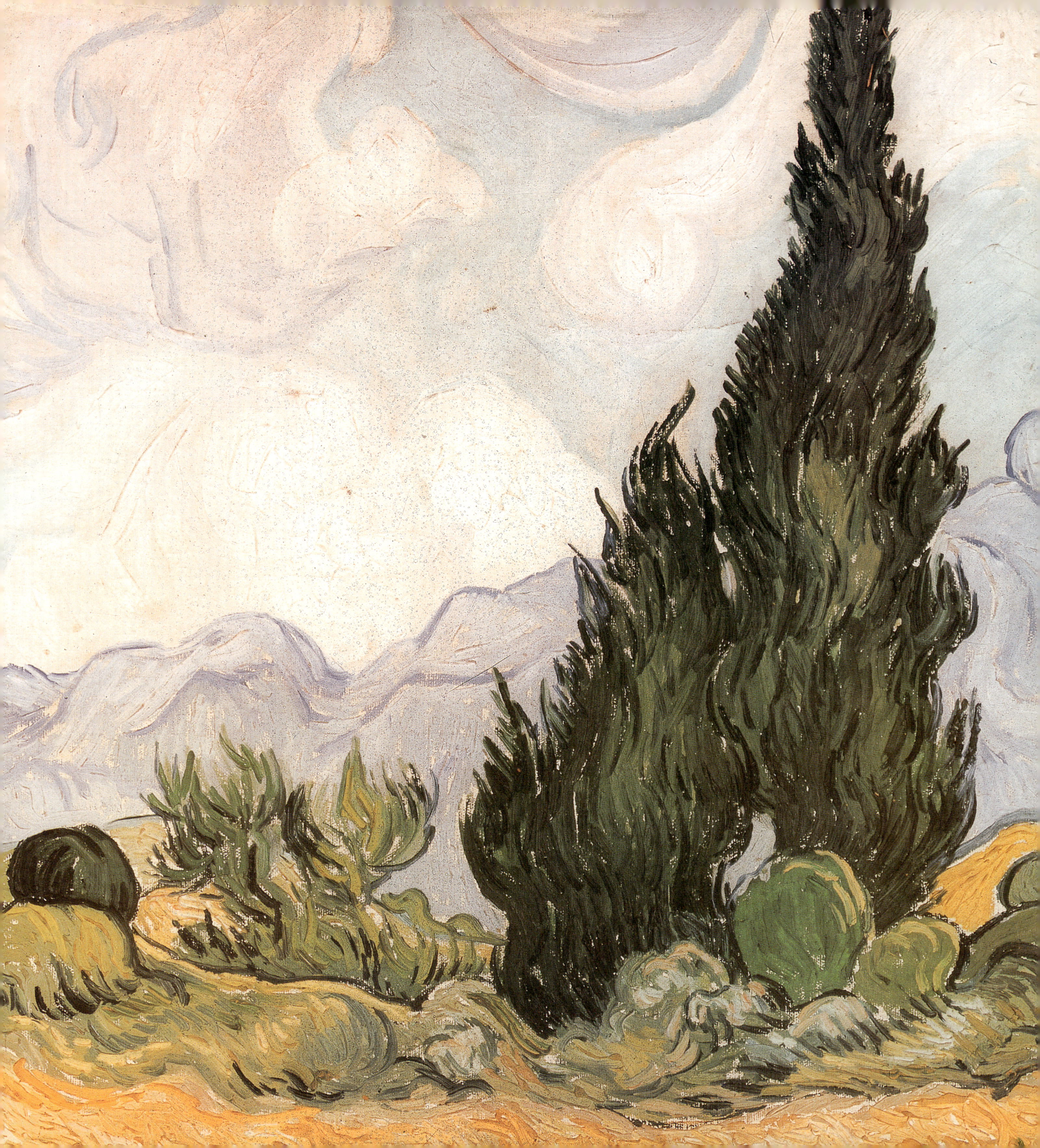

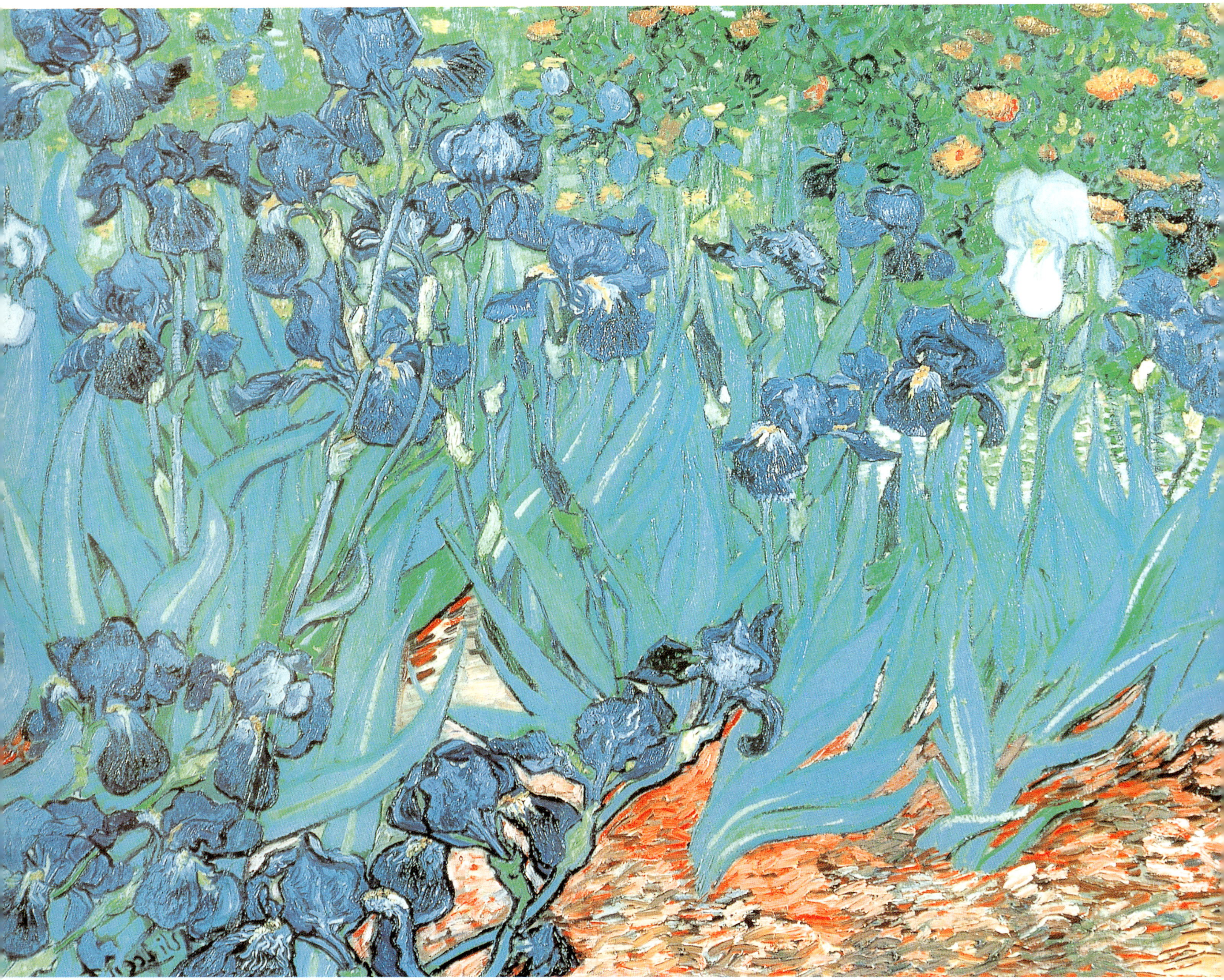

AFTER THE IMPRESSIONISTS

THE GROUP OF ARTISTS which had staged its first exhibition in 1874 had begun to fall apart by the end of that decade. Their differing artistic aims and the desperate need of some of them – Sisley, Renoir, and Monet in particular – to make a better living, could not be supported by the Impressionist exhibitions. So they had sought their fortunes at the Salons and in one-man shows and fared much better outside the group than in it. While all semblance of cohesion amongst the Impressionists was effectively over by the time of the penultimate group show in 1882, their work had filtered into the mainstream of French art and had become the starting point for new tendencies, the first of which was the Neo-Impressionism of Seurat and Signac. Even as this new movement, with its strictly defined aesthetic, was being born, the whole nature of figurative art, of perspective, line, volume – elements which Impressionism had gone some way in questioning – was being challenged in more fundamental ways by artists such as Gauguin, Cézanne, and van Gogh, leading at the turn of the century to the Fauves, dominated by Matisse, and ultimately to the abstraction of Cubism.

Impressionism was assured a future for the time being in Britain, Europe and the United States, but by the start of the 1890s it had arrived at an impasse which it could not negotiate without losing its character. Paris was now the boiling centre with several complementary as well as conflicting new movements vying for and drawing on the legacy of Impressionism.

VAN GOGH
Irises
oil on canvas
1889. 71 × 93 cm
Opposite

VAN GOGH
Cornfield with Cypress Trees
oil on canvas
1889. 72 × 91 cm
Previous page

After the Impressionists

Was it for this I fought? Was it for this bright painting, these patches of colour, these reflections, this decomposition of light? Was I mad?

Emile Zola reviewing the Salon of 1896

The high summer of Impressionism was brief and intense but its after-effects lingered long after many of its first exponents had developed in other directions. In the 1880s Pissarro had fallen under the spell of the Neo-Impressionists Seurat and Signac; Renoir had retreated from the vibrant depiction of scenes from everyday life and was consolidating a classical approach to the problem of the human figure, colour, and line; Cézanne's vision had bypassed Impressionism many years before; only Monet carried on inexorably with his project to realize the *enveloppe*, working on his series paintings and the monumental *Water Lilies* decorations.

Impressionism never had a manifesto and although Degas clearly thought at the very outset of the group's endeavours that it should be a "Salon of Realists", this was not a project to inspire the likes of Monet, Renoir, or Sisley. If it were possible to reduce the brilliant brushwork and tantalizing colouristic

RENOIR
Madame Gallimard
oil on canvas
1892. 80 × 64 cm
Below Renoir's late output did not bring any startling revelations.

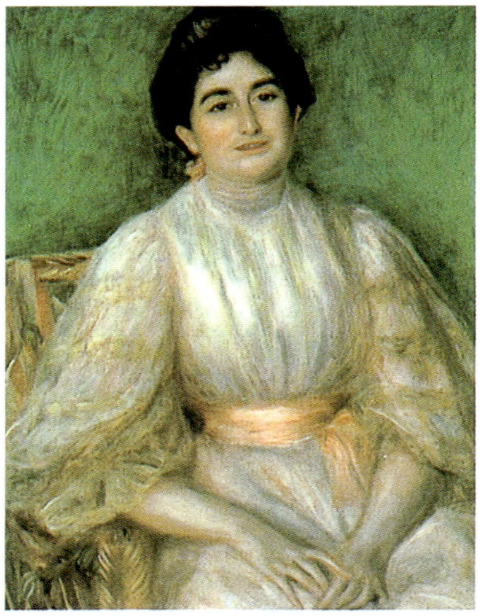

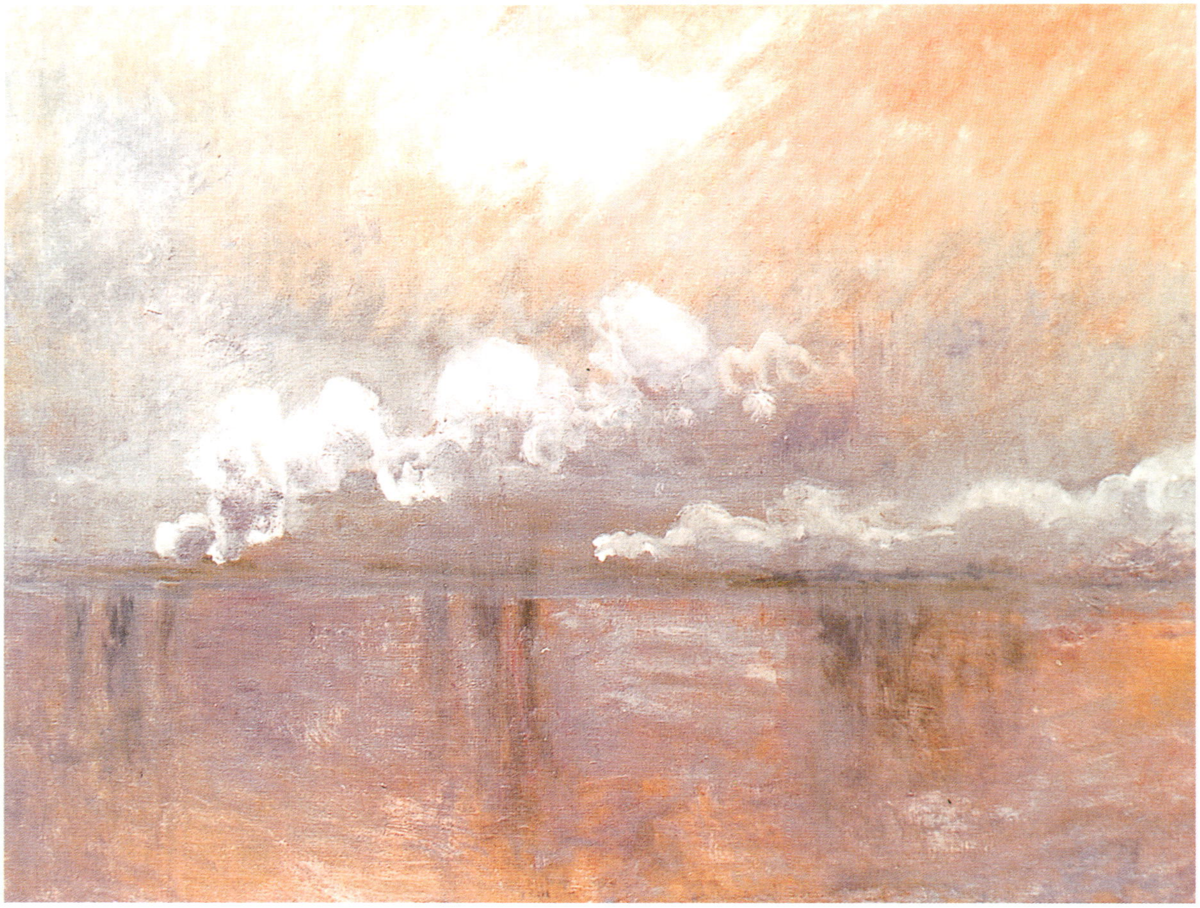

MONET
Charing Cross Bridge
oil on canvas
1902. 71 × 92 cm
Right Monet travelled less, but went to London each winter for several years. In all he painted over a hundred views of the Thames.

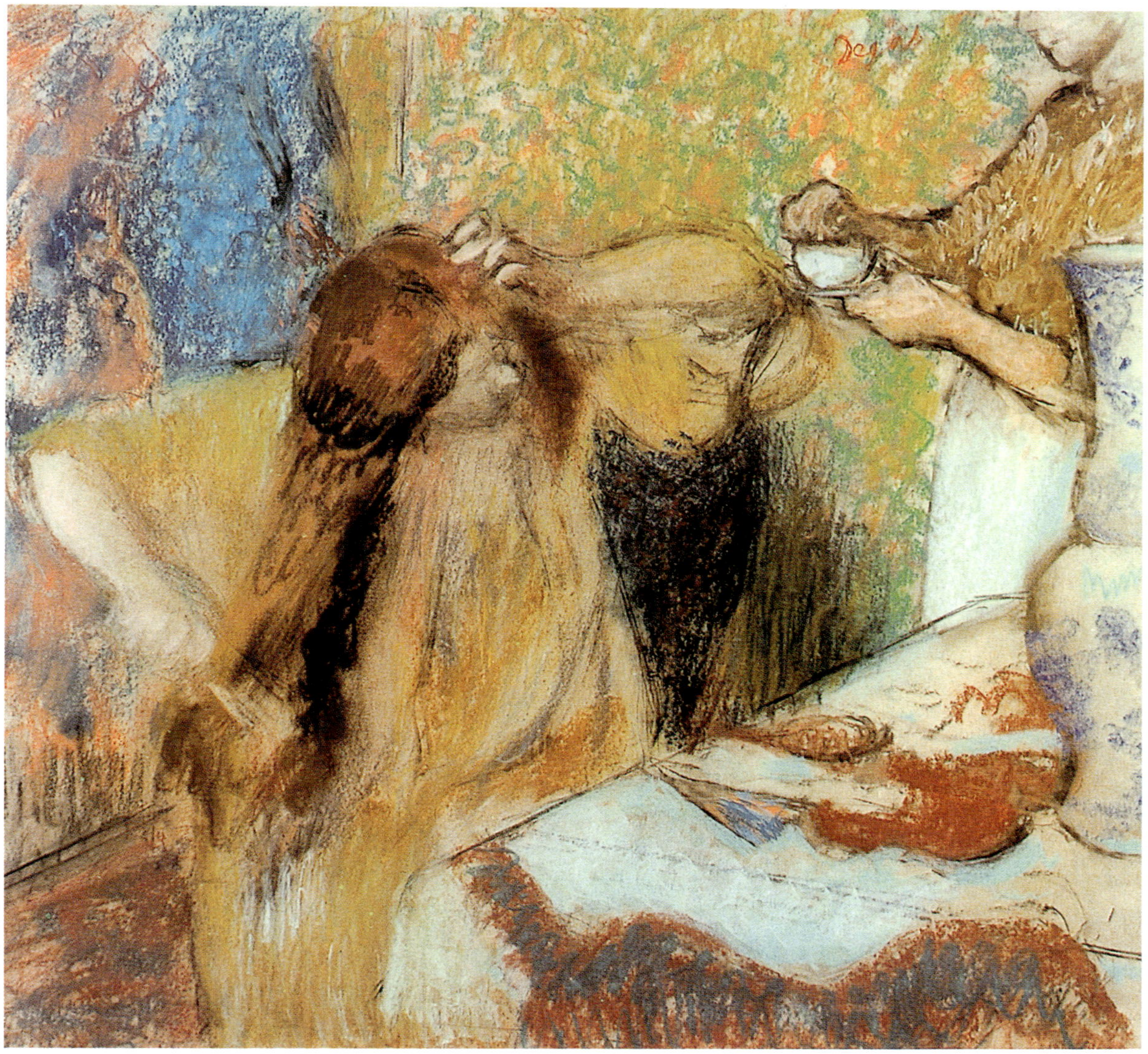

DEGAS
Woman at Her Toilette
pastel on paper
1894. 95.6 × 110 cm
LEFT Degas, whose eyesight was failing, evolved a freer style. He produced a large number of pictures of women at their toilette during these years, a subject which had always been a favourite of his.

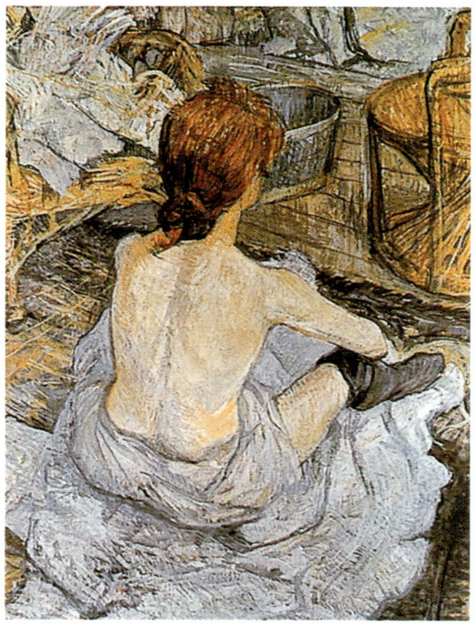

TOULOUSE-LAUTREC
Woman at Her Toilette
oil on canvas
1896. 67 × 54 cm
ABOVE Toulouse-Lautrec was not an Impressionist and did not belong to any particular school. The crippled son of one of the oldest aristocratic families of France, he came from the south and was at an early age an accomplished draughtsman. He was the heir to Degas and some of his subjects are very similar: brothels, women washing, prostitutes, working girls or entertainers. His mood, however, is more cynical and his style accordingly sharper.

effects of Manet's later works to a system, such a system would only succeed in describing Manet's technique, not Monet's or Renoir's or Pissarro's. Yet, after the American expatriate John Singer Sargent had painted by Claude Monet's side in Giverny, it would have been easy to say that his style bore a close resemblance to that of Monet's. Unlike the Divisionism of the Neo-Impressionists Seurat and Signac, which seemed like an inevitable development of Impressionism after the event (it was of course taken up by Pissarro), the internal contradictions of the original nucleus of the Impressionists could never be resolved. The permanence of the archetypal Impressionist painting is to be found paradoxically in the triumph of technique and experience over the impermanence of its subject.

The world had changed since the Impressionists were young men and women carrying out their easels for a day by a bend in the Seine, or an evening sortie to a café concert armed with sketchbook and pen. In the end even Monet had to content himself with creating his own natural world in his garden

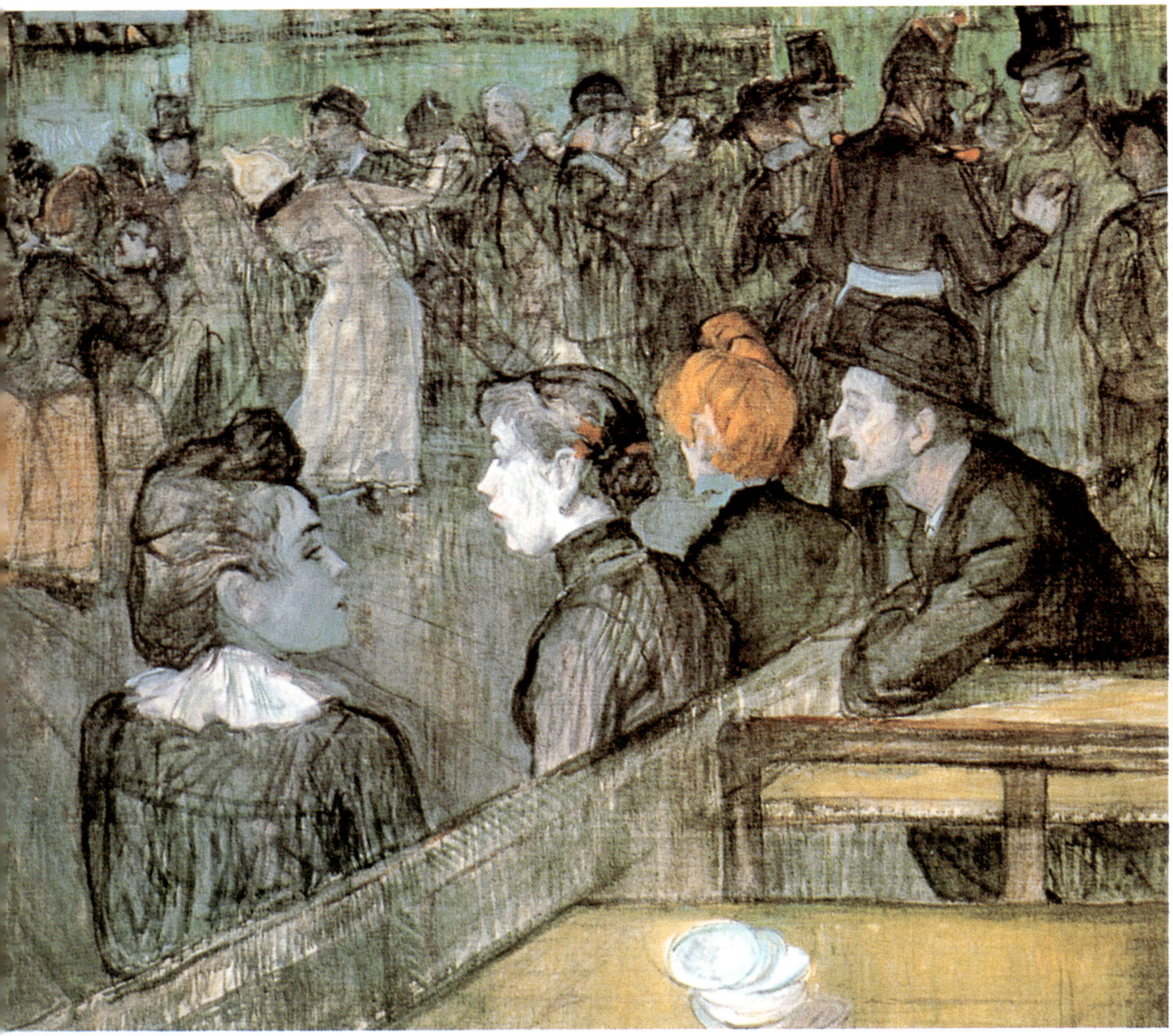

TOULOUSE-LAUTREC
The Moulin de la Galette
oil on canvas
1889. 89 × 99 cm
Toulouse-Lautrec was prone to see life with a cynical eye and to emphasize the character of his figures to the point of making them look grotesque or ugly.

and lily pond. All the talk that drifted up with the smoke to the ceilings of the Café Guerbois and the Nouvelle-Athènes in the 1860s and 1870s was as transient as a glimmer on the water at La Grenouillère, yet out of it had come an association of artists which had flourished briefly, then fragmented, but in the meantime changed the way we see world. In 1892 the critic Georges Lecomte realized that the Impressionists were withdrawing from the naturalistic depiction of reality to make compositions far from nature "so as to realize a total harmony". To paraphrase W.H. Auden, the Impressionists became their admirers. In the 1880s and 1890s young Americans thronged to Giverny to paint *en plein air* in the presence of a self-taught artist whose pictures had once been laughed at by art dealers in London with the words "These are by Monet, the Impressionist, isn't he absurd?"

Nor had French society stood still. Paris had continued to expand and many of the picturesque hamlets around it, where the Impressionists had once worked, had been swallowed up by urbanization. A recent arrival to Paris in 1886, Vincent van Gogh, went out and painted a picture, the desolate *Outskirts of Paris*. As T.J. Clark describes it "there is no town in van Gogh's picture, and no country . . . " This was the aftermath of Baron Haussmann's grandiose plan to rebuild the city: the sweeping vistas of the *grands boulevards* were a world away. *La ville lumière*, the Paris of the Painters of Light with its summery, intimate moments had been abandoned and left to a younger generation of artists more concerned with the inner meaning of things than their outward appearance.

In the political arena the Third Republic had attempted and generally succeeded in consolidating itself throughout the 1880s with a series of laws enshrining republican values. But in the early 1890s when the Dreyfus Affair convulsed France, all the old ghosts began to reappear armed to the teeth. France was a country bitterly divided between Catholic monarchists and secular republicans, Protestants and Jews, and the framing, secret trial and conviction of the Jewish army officer Captain Alfred Dreyfus for espionage he did not commit created a crisis which reverberated in the French body politic for years. Eventually Dreyfus was exonerated, but not

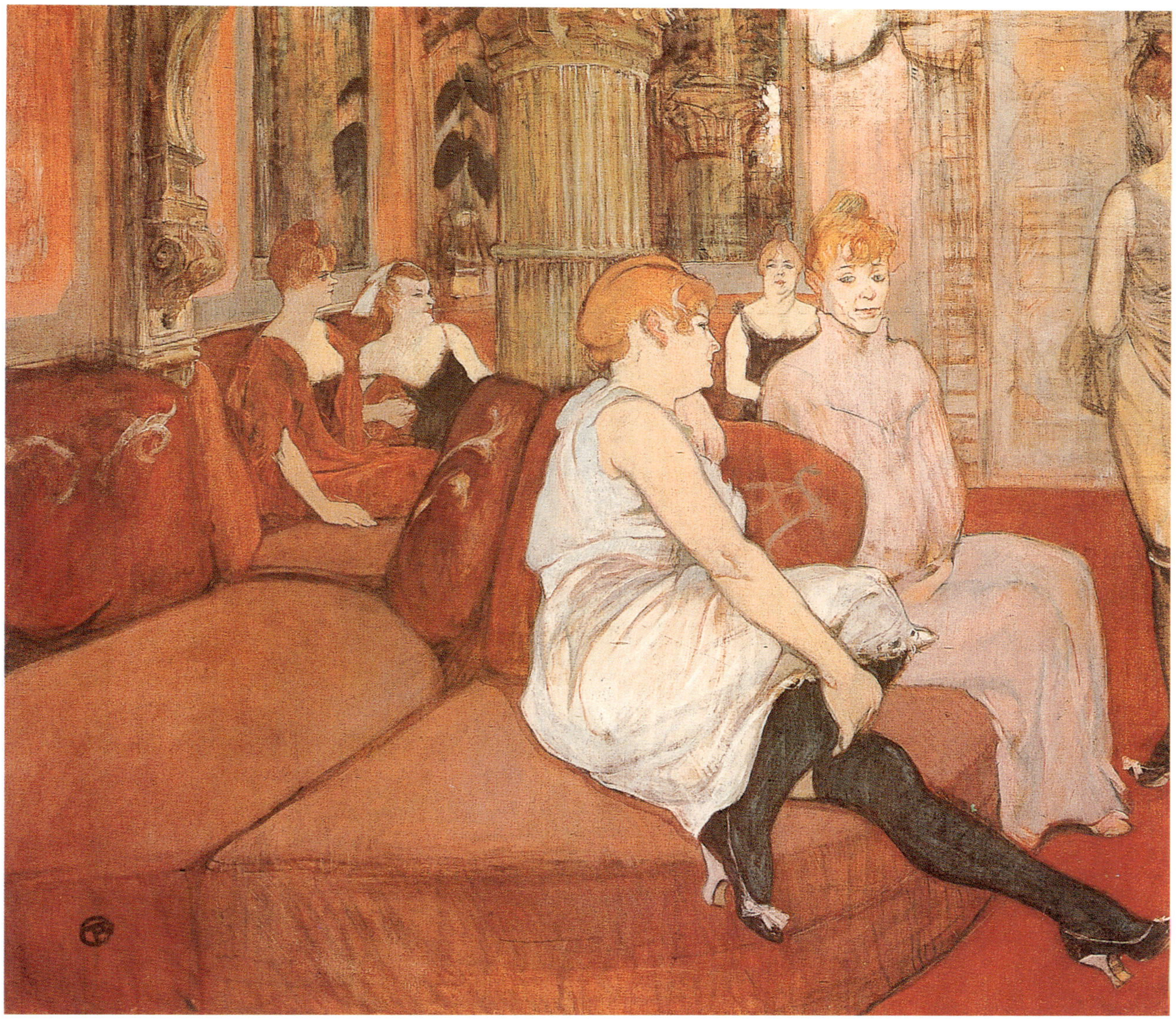

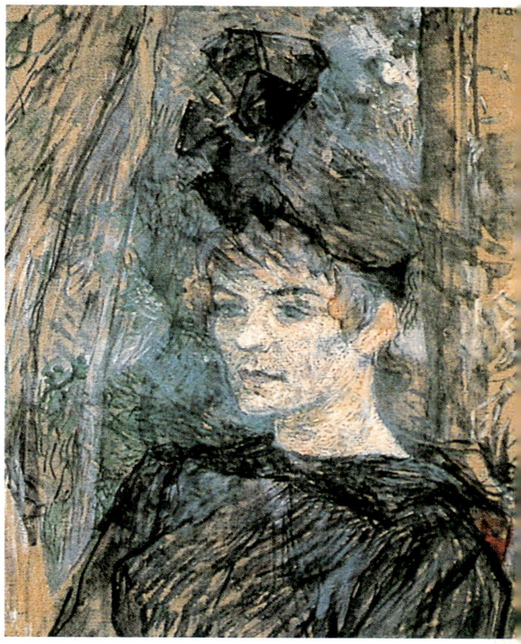

TOULOUSE-LAUTREC
Suzanne Valadon
oil on canvas
1885. 55 × 45 cm
ABOVE Toulouse-Lautrec saw the reality of women who had to face a hard life in a merciless society.

TOULOUSE-LAUTREC
Lovers in Bed
oil on board
1892. 54 × 70.5 cm
LEFT With his nervous brushstroke, thinly applied and often leaving some of the background bare, his pictures are lively and never moralistic.

before friends and families were at each other's throats. Zola was one of the first in the art world to stand up for Dreyfus and he was supported by Pissarro, but Renoir and Degas proved to be virulent anti-Dreyfusards. In 1898 Berthe Morisot's daughter, Julie Manet, was visiting Renoir's studio where the affair was being discussed. In her diary Julie recorded Renoir's opinion: "There are a lot of them [Jews] in the army, because the Jew likes to walk about wearing a uniform . . . " In fact Dreyfus was one of the very few Jews in the French army. Renoir had continued: "They are asking that the Dreyfus Affair be made public, but there are some things which simply can't be said. People don't wish to understand that sort of thing." Julie Manet added, "Monsieur Renoir also let fly on the subject of Pissarro, 'a Jew', whose sons are natives of no country and who do their military service nowhere. 'It's tenacious, this Jewish race. Pissarro's wife isn't one, yet all the children are, even more so than their father.' "

SEURAT AND NEO-IMPRESSIONISM

In 1884 the Groupe des Indépendants was founded to allow unknown and avant-garde artists to exhibit freely. There was nothing new in this idea; the Impressionists' own *Société anonyme* of a decade before had been founded on the same ideals, and like the later Impressionists' group exhibitions the Indépendants' show had no jury and was self-financing. Unlike the Impressionists' shows it was literally a free for all; there was fighting in the exhibition hall, an empty barracks in the Jardin des Tuileries.

In June the same year the organization was reformed and became the Société des Artistes Indépendants. Despite its inauspicious beginnings, it soon became the major outlet for avant-garde artists such as Gauguin, van Gogh and Odilon Redon, as well as more established names like Guillaumin and Cézanne. Amongst the early contributors to the Salon des Indépendants were Georges Seurat and Paul Signac. Seurat was showing the first important work of what was soon to become known as Divisionism, Pointillism, or Neo-Impressionism, his *Bathers at Asnières*.

"The purity of the elements of the spectrum is the cornerstone of technique," Seurat wrote in 1890. "Ever since I first held a brush I had been looking for a formula of optical painting . . . " It is highly unlikely that Seurat had really envisaged a Neo-Impressionist technique at the age of seventeen, but on 15th May 1886, at the age of twenty-seven, he showed his masterpiece, *A Summer Sunday on the Île de la Grande Jatte* (*Un Dimanche d'été à l'Île de la Grande Jatte*), a canvas measuring six

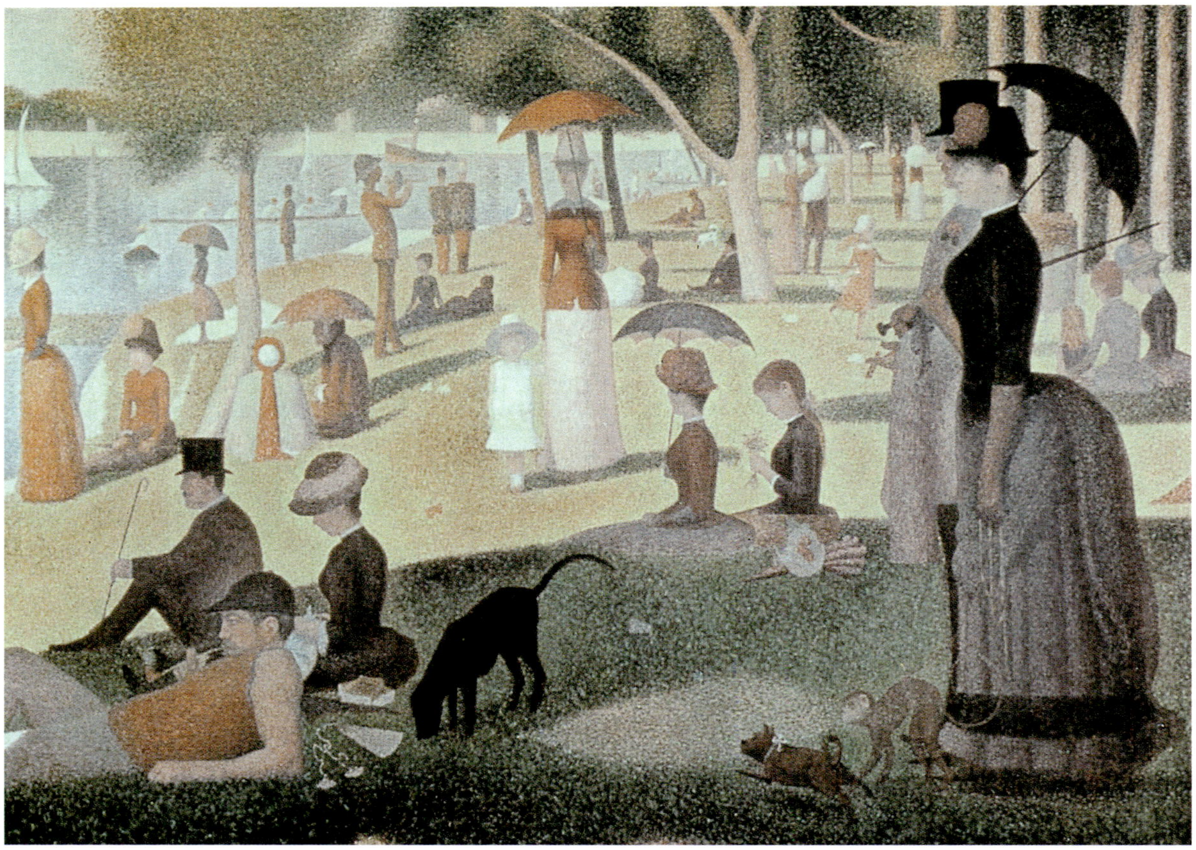

SEURAT
A Summer Sunday on the Île de la Grande Jatte
oil on canvas
1884–86. 206 × 306 cm
This is the culmination of Seurat's achievements, an enormous work in which dots of colour are meant to capture the density of the atmosphere and the precise effect of the light on every surface. Unfortunately, this technique is difficult to match with spontaneity and in this impressive painting, everything is static and lifeless. It already illustrates one of the characteristics of modern art, where the artist's main intention is to illustrate a theory rather than submitting their theory to their subject.

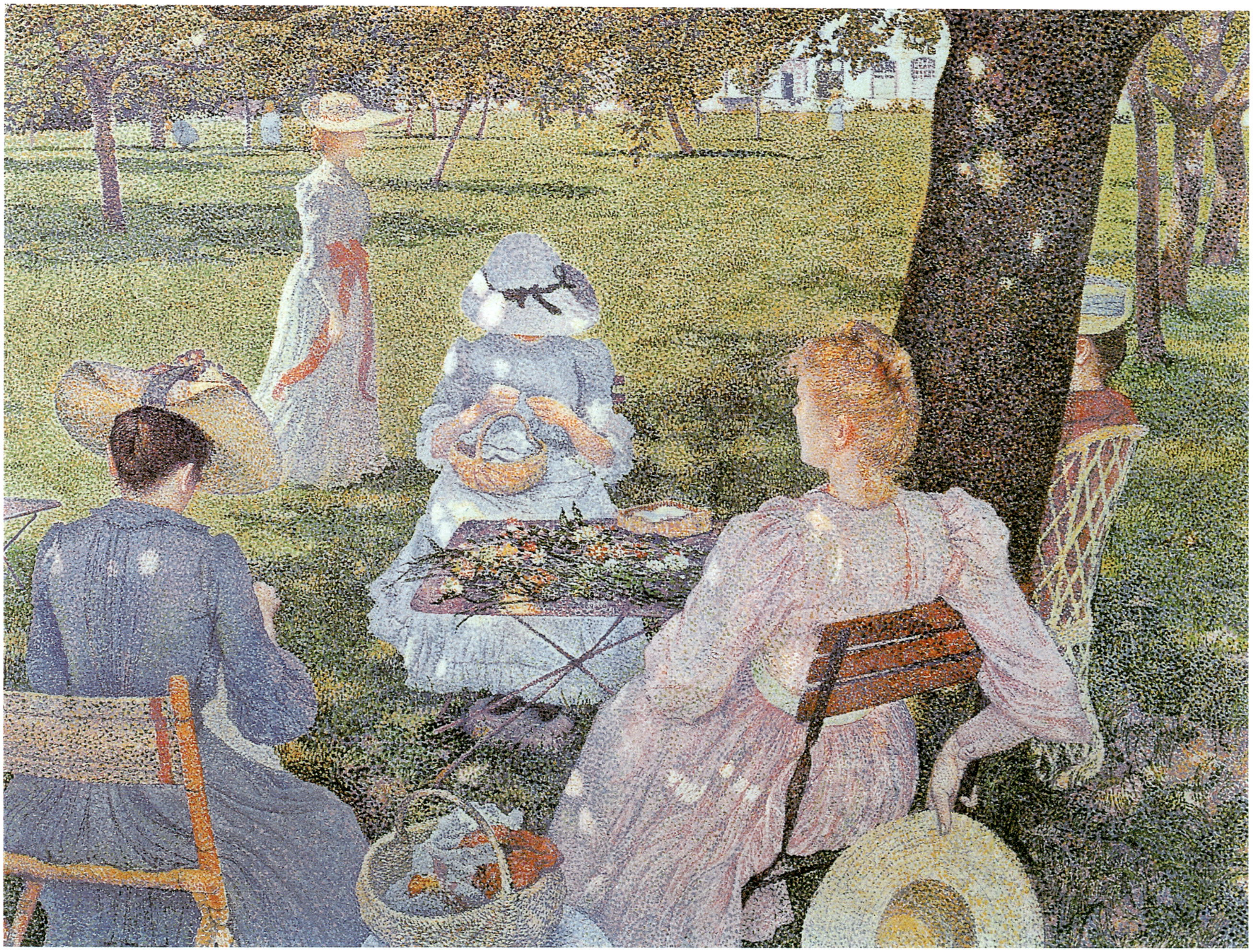

VAN RYSSELBERGHE
Family in an Orchard
oil on canvas
1890. 115.5 × 163.5 cm
This painting, in which Rysselberghe used subtle harmonies of green and purplish colours, was the opposite of the red and green or blue and orange tones used by Seurat. Although his technique imposed a graphic approach, Rysselberghe has produced an atmospheric work which is, from the choice of subject, light in tone and closer to the spirit of the Impressionists than that of the Pointillists.

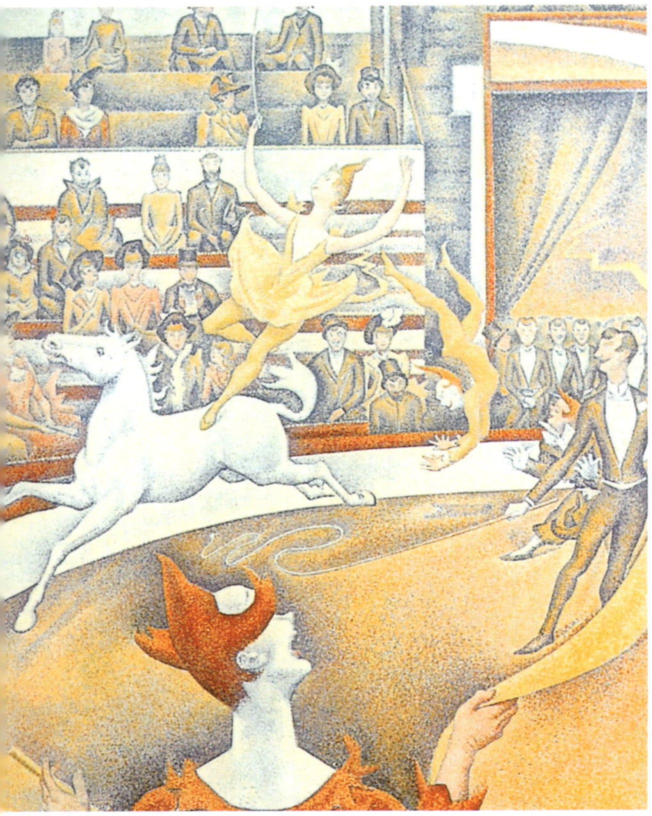

SEURAT
The Circus
oil on canvas
1891. 185.5 × 152.5 cm
ABOVE The picture is inevitably stylized and graphic, lacking in the sensuality of Seurat's predecessors' works, but it has an imaginative and effective composition.

and three-quarters by ten feet. The technique of the painting, which was coined "*neo-impressionnisme*" by the contemporary critic and supporter of Seurat, Félix Fénéon, was a radical development of the small patches and strokes of complementary colour employed by Monet, Renoir, and Pissarro. Seurat had studied amongst others the colour theories of Chevreul and those of the American Ogden N. Rood in his work "Modern Chromatics" which had been translated into French in 1881. The principles of Neo-Impressionism, or Divisionism as its exponents preferred to call it, were described by Paul Signac in his

CROSS
Les Iles d'Or
oil on canvas
1891–92. 60 × 55 cm
RIGHT Cross came from the north of France to Paris in 1881, and received a traditional training, rapidly evolving under the influence of Manet and other Impressionists before he adopted the Pointillist technique in about 1891. He developed it in a very independent and individual manner towards a less dogmatic approach, especially after he moved permanently to the south of France in 1891.

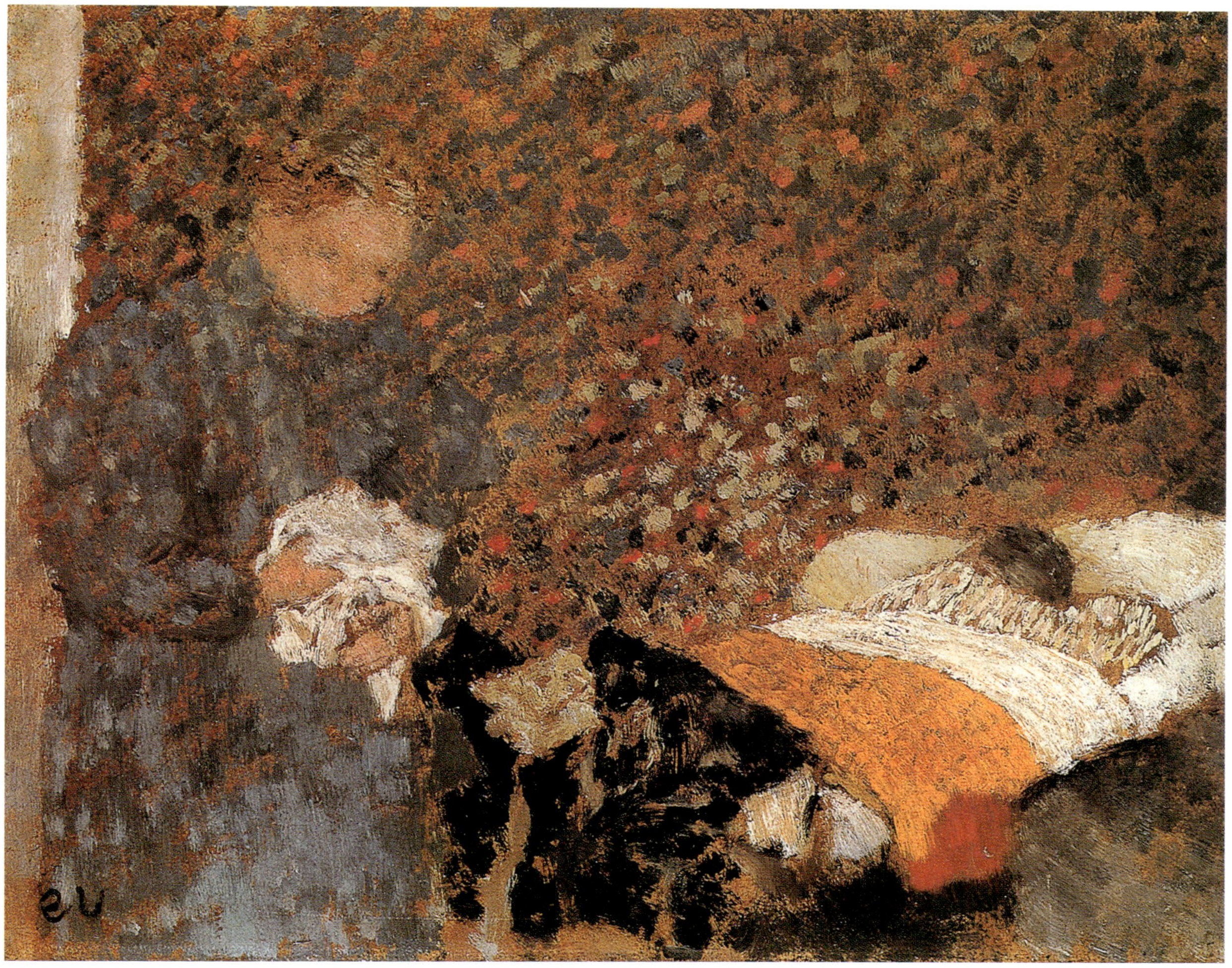

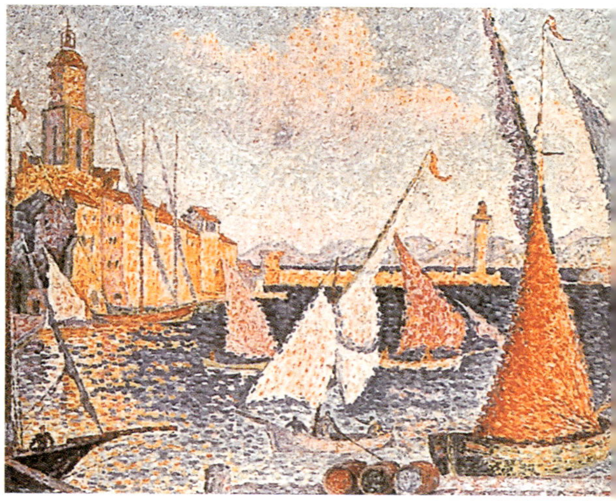

SIGNAC
The Port of St Tropez
oil on canvas
1899. 65 × 81 cm
ABOVE Signac, one of the first Pointillists (he claimed he was the very first), remained one of the artists most faithful to this technique, which he also adapted to his own sensitivity.

VUILLARD
Young woman in Her Sickbed
oil on canvas
c.1892. 20.5 × 26.5 cm
LEFT Here we see the very late influence of Neo-Impressionism on the twenty-four year old painter.

1899 book, *From Eugène Delacroix to Neo-Impressionism*:

> Divisionism is a method of securing the utmost luminosity, colour, and harmony by (a) the use of all the colours of the spectrum and all degrees of these colours without any mixing, (b) the separation of local colours from the colour of the light, reflections, etc., (c) the balance of these factors and the establishment of these relations in accordance with laws of contrast and tone and radiation, and (d) the use of a technique of dots of a size determined by the size of the picture.

This, in essence, is what Neo-Impressionism was all about: a rigorous pseudo-scientific system based on a range of theories and ideas which encompassed colour theory, Delacroix and the work of the Impressionists. But by filtering colour and form through a carefully planned system the whole *raison d'être* of Impressionism – the impression of an immediate representation of a subject – was superseded.

In order to paint *La Grande Jatte* Seurat had to make scaled down but nevertheless substantial sketches in oil indicating the disposition of the basic pigments. Even before this, an exhaustive series of sketches of the site and the characters who would populate it was undertaken before each of the carefully

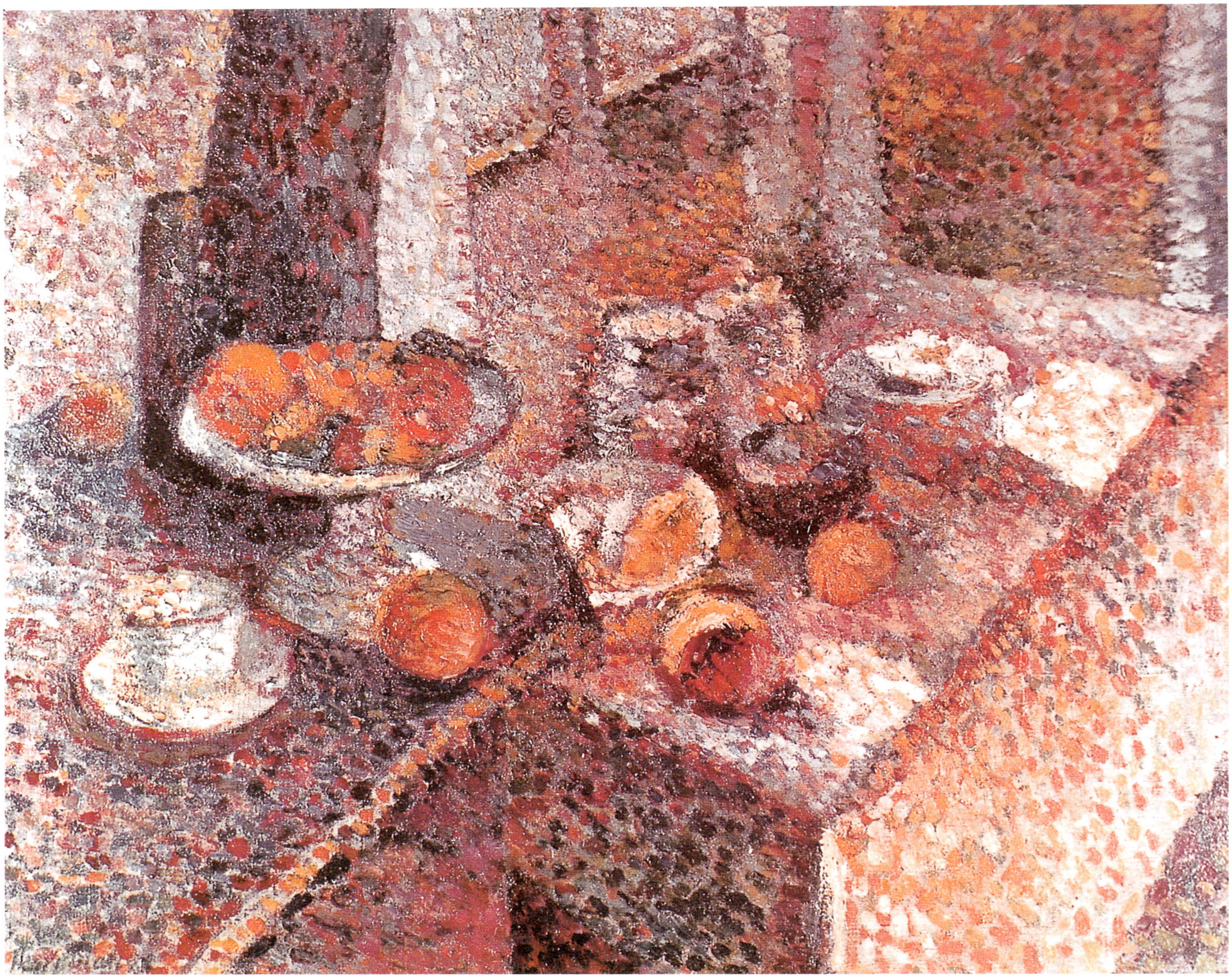

MATISSE
Sideboard and Table
oil on canvas
1899. 67.5 × 82.5 cm
In this still life, Matisse used Pointillism freely on a plain base of colour. This technique, which he probably tried under the influence of Signac, was soon to be abandoned or rather, dramatically altered.

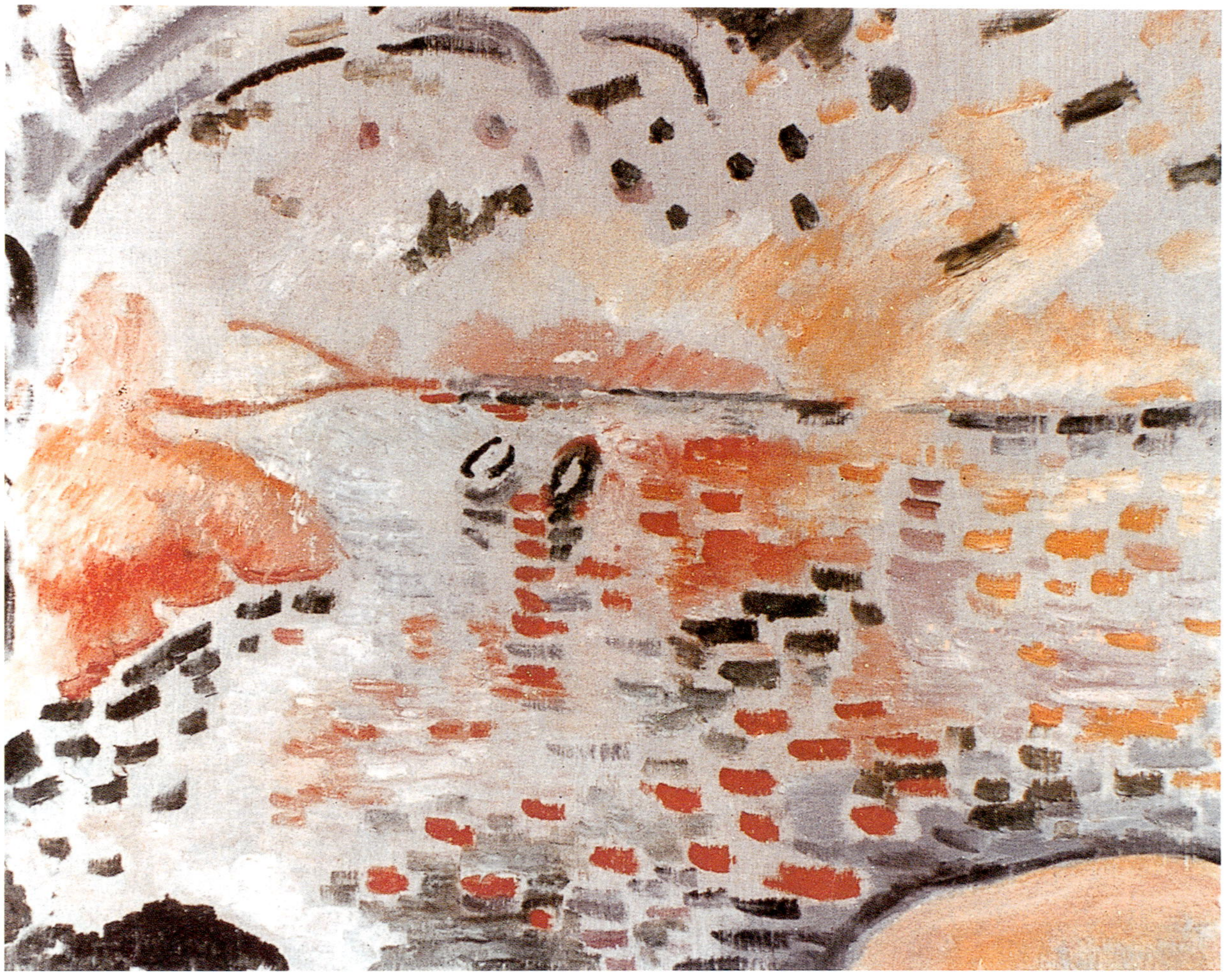

BRAQUE
Small Bay at La Ciotat
oil on canvas
1907. 36 × 48 cm
In this light work, the influence of the Neo-Impressionists is still present, but here the touches of colour are mere indications, and there is also a touch of Cézanne's brushwork in the rendering of the sky. Braque, who travelled regularly to the south of France between 1906 and 1912, often worked at l'Estaque, where Cézanne lived and where he died in 1906. Braque fell more and more under the influence of Cézanne's work.

chosen figures, representing all shades of society, could take their place in the scene.

Pissarro, who was responsible for getting *Le Grande Jatte* shown at the last Impressionist exhibition, had seen the possibilities of the rigid new technique, but he was alone among his contemporaries in making a significant attempt to apply pure Divisionism to his work. Besides, Divisionism was a young man's art. At the age of sixty the rigours of carefully painting in thousands of dots soon took its toll on Pissarro and after a couple of years, during which time he adapted the method to his own technique to great effect, he reverted to a more fluid Impressionist style, saying, "one must yield to one's painterly instinct . . . reason and science run the risk of blunting our feelings."

The artistic expression of emotional and symbolic meaning as seen through line and colour was never an overt part of the Impressionists' work during the 1870s, although it could occasionally surface in emotionally neutral motifs like landscape in the subtlest of ways. This occurred mainly through the careful use of colour. For example when viewing some of Sisley's snowscapes they appear to be intensely melancholic, while the late works of Monet transcend the use of naturalistic colour and come intensely close to an emotional expression of the subject in terms of colour.

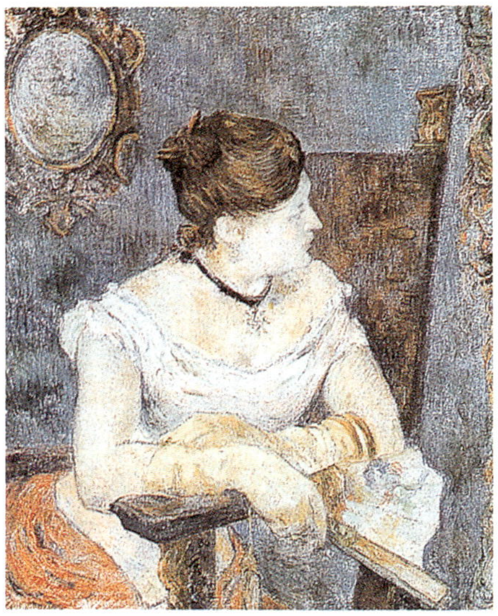

GAUGUIN
Madame Mette Gauguin
oil on canvas
1884. 65 × 54 cm
ABOVE Also a latecomer to painting, Gauguin, like van Gogh, was subject to a variety of influences and evolved rapidly.

VAN GOGH AND IMPRESSIONISM

One artist whose work was radically altered by the consequences of Impressionism was Vincent van Gogh. The short and turbulent life of this painter is legendary. His is the archetypal story of the mad and misunderstood artist struggling to create his own tormented vision of the world. Suffering from an illness, now thought to be epilepsy, which drove him to periodic bouts of extreme depression and mental instability, van Gogh is most often remembered as the artist who cut off his ear as the result of a quarrel with Gauguin and shot himself fatally in the chest at the age of thirty-seven. The potency of the van Gogh myth is compounded by the fact that though he sold few paintings in his lifetime and lived in abject poverty, his paintings are now the most expensive in the world: *Irises*, painted a year before his death in 1890, recently fetched a world record of $49 million (£27.45 million).

Van Gogh was born in northern Brabant in 1853, the son of a Protestant pastor whose family were involved in the art business. From 1869 to 1875 van Gogh worked in art galleries in The Hague, London, and Paris before renouncing the art business and attempting to become a priest in Holland, where he spent three years as an evangelical lay preacher in the Belgian mining region of the Borinage. There he saved no souls, lived in a hovel and gave away his worldly goods before his fanaticism forced the evangelical authorities to remove him from his post. Eventually van Gogh's religious fervour abated and he began to devote himself to art, learning from manuals, studying with his cousin Anton Mauve, and spending some

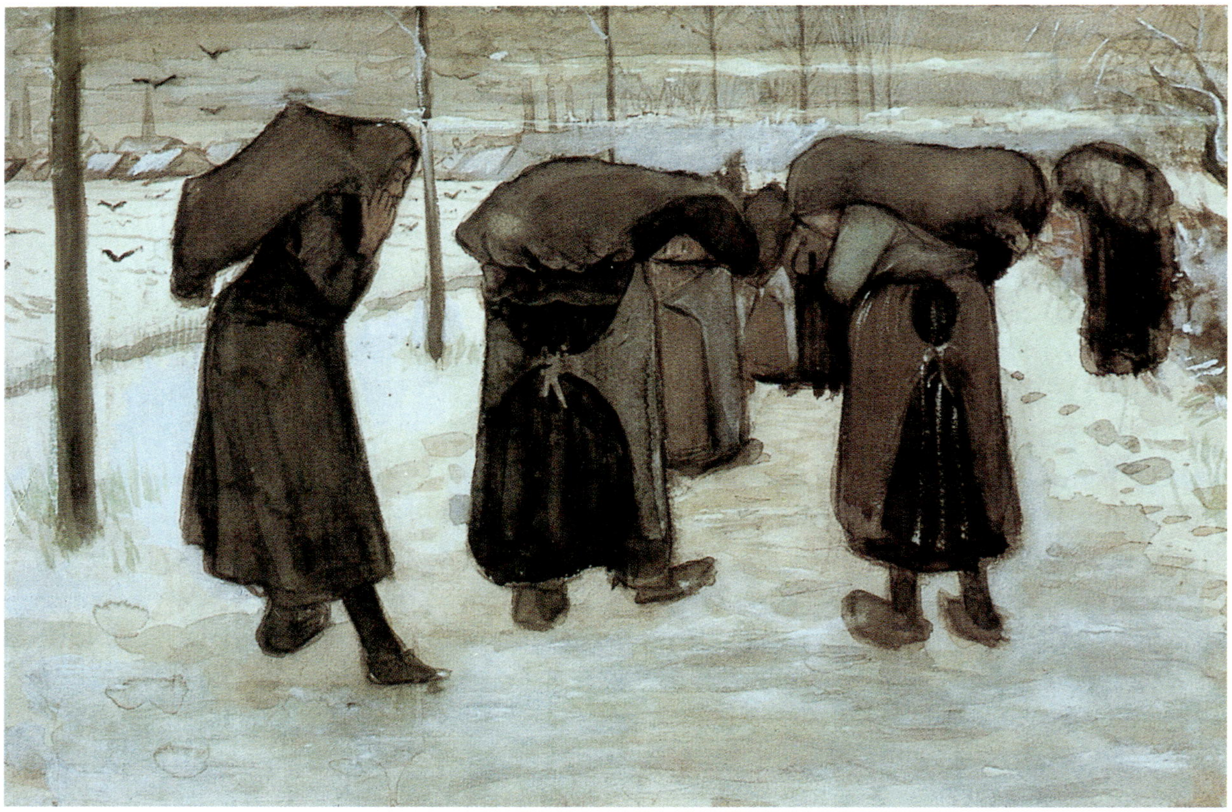

VAN GOGH
Women Carrying Sacks
watercolour on canvas
1882. 32 × 51 cm
RIGHT With van Gogh we leave the tranquillity of the French bourgeoisie and move into the bleak poverty of The Netherlands, where he was trying to find himself. This is rather typical of the dark, unhappy tones of his first works.

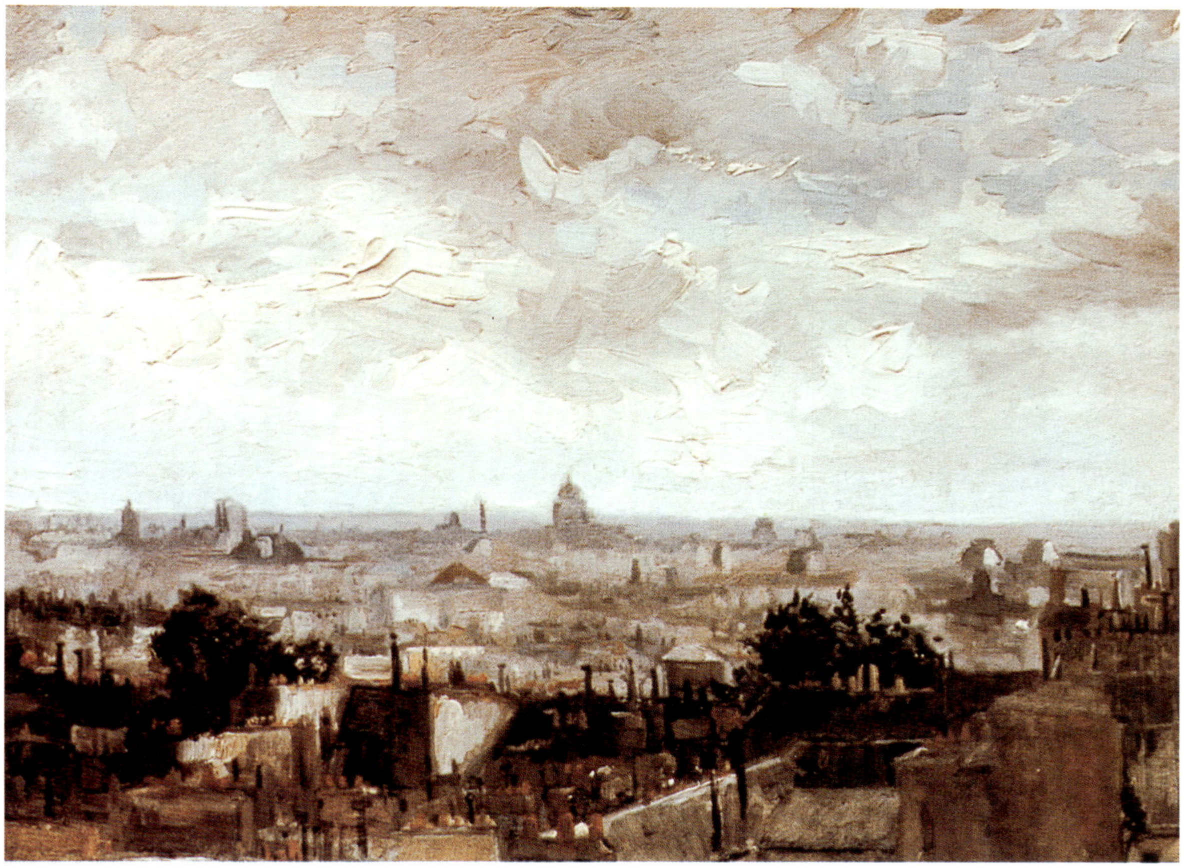

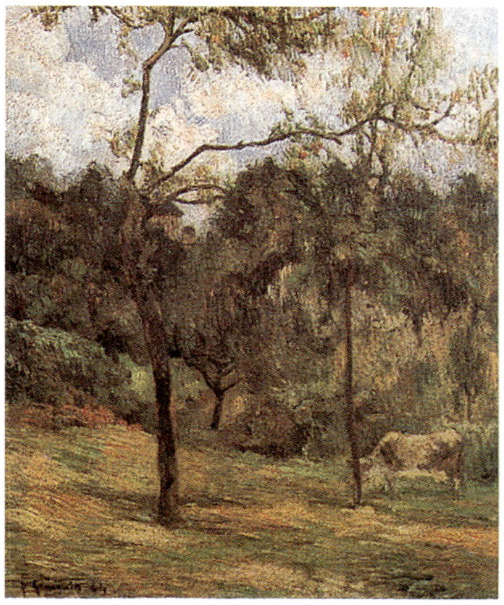

GAUGUIN
Landscape in Normandy
oil on canvas
1884. 56.5 × 46.5 cm
ABOVE Gauguin had often painted with Pissarro in the years since 1879, and with Cézanne since 1881. This is a transitional work, evolving from a multitude of influences, and showing that the artist was still seeking his own mature style.

VAN GOGH
Paris from Theo's House
oil on canvas
1886. 54 × 72 cm
ABOVE LEFT This was painted from his brother Theo's house shortly after van Gogh arrived in Paris. Theo worked for the Boussod and Valadon gallery, and had many connections in the Paris art community. He was able to introduce Vincent to many of the Impressionists and their associates, and particularly close relationships were quickly formed with Pissarro and Gauguin. Contacts with Impressionism at this stage were to have a marked effect on van Gogh's later artistic development.

time at the Antwerp Academy in Belgium. His close contact with the poor and the working class now began to be forcefully expressed in pictures such as *The Potato Eaters*. He wrote that the aim of this picture was "to instil . . . the idea that the people it depicts at their meal have dug the earth with the hands they are dipping into the dish . . . "

Van Gogh became entangled in a succession of disastrous romances that began, unrequitedly, with his landlady's daughter in London, then with his cousin Kee Vos, followed by a part-time prostitute called Clasina (or Sien) Hoornik who modelled for him, and finally a friend of van Gogh's family, Margot Begemann who tried to commit suicide. Van Gogh's relationships were characterized by an intensity that is eloquently and movingly expressed in the many letters he wrote to his brother Theo, an art dealer in Paris.

The monochromatic pictures of working life, so reminiscent of Millet, which van Gogh produced in the dour atmosphere of Holland and Belgium were superseded by an explosion of colour that characterized his work in Paris and the south of France. In France, van Gogh developed his distinctive style of brushwork to express interiors, still lifes, landscapes, and portraits.

Towards the end of the 1880s Paris was swarming with emerging artists eager to make a mark. Friendships were being made and broken as Neo-Impressionism and the new Symbolism vied with established Impressionism. Into this melée came the thirty-three year old Vincent van Gogh, a month before Seurat's *La Grande Jatte* went on show. He had arrived to study at the comparatively

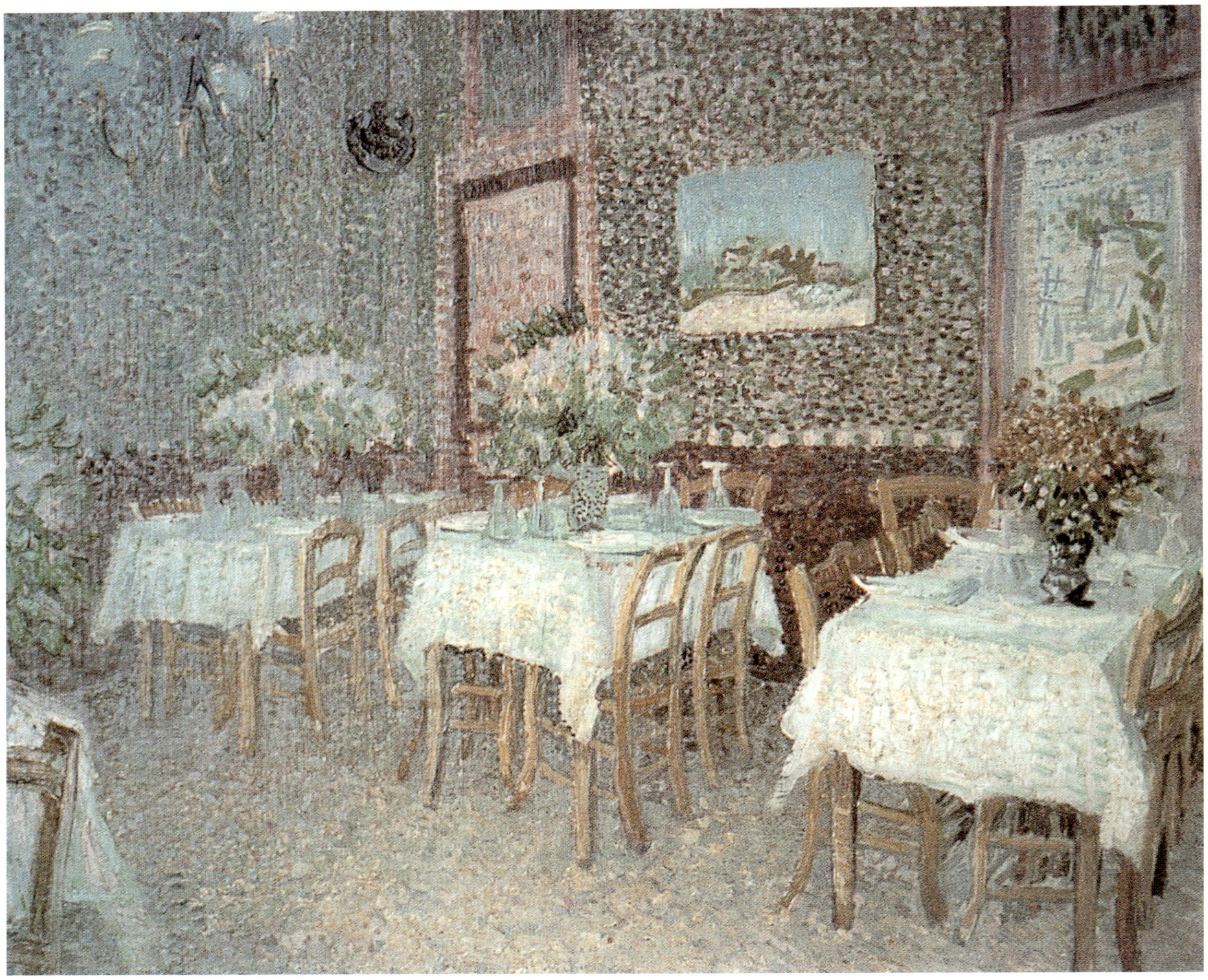

VAN GOGH
Interior of a Restaurant
oil on canvas
1887. 46 × 57 cm
A very unusual work by van Gogh, who met many artists through his brother Theo, who worked in an art gallery. Meeting Pissarro, then experimenting with Seurat's Pointillism, van Gogh produced this very competent and sensitive picture. The tones, northern and subdued, were dramatically abandoned when he arrived in the south of France two years later.

liberal atelier of Félix Cormon where he joined the company of Henri de Toulouse-Lautrec, Emile Bernard, and Louis Anquetin, who had been studying there since 1884. Van Gogh had been in Paris before, in the 1870s, when he had worked for the art dealers Goupil et Cie whose Dutch branch in the Hague he had joined after leaving school – the company had bought van Gogh's uncle's art business in the late 1850s.

Van Gogh's brother Theo worked in Paris for the Boussod and Valadon gallery which had bought Goupils. Theo was a supporter of the Impressionists and the emerging Neo-Impressionists including the newly-converted Pointillist, Pissarro, and his son Lucien. Theo thus knew Monet and Degas and was able to introduce Vincent to them, but it was the Pissarros who had the closest contact with him. Camille Pissarro later introduced Vincent to his friend and patron Dr Gachet. By the end of 1887 van Gogh was also closely linked with Gauguin, who played a crucial role in his brief career.

Van Gogh's encounter with the consequences of Impressionism in Paris had a profound effect. The emancipation of colour which had been achieved by the Impressionists and its subsequent application by the Neo-Impressionists was taken to heart by van

Gogh and expanded far beyond its previous limits. There were other influences too: the Japanese ukiyo-e prints (literally pictures of the floating world), which had influenced Monet and Degas twenty years before, now became important to van Gogh's late but rapid development. In fact, in the last three years of his life van Gogh became aware of and developed elements of everything that was happening in Paris – Impressionism, Neo-Impressionism, the Cloisonnism (flat, bright colour in distinct outlines developed by Toulouse-Lautrec and Emile Bernard), as well as the Symbolism of Gauguin – to reach a new pitch of expression.

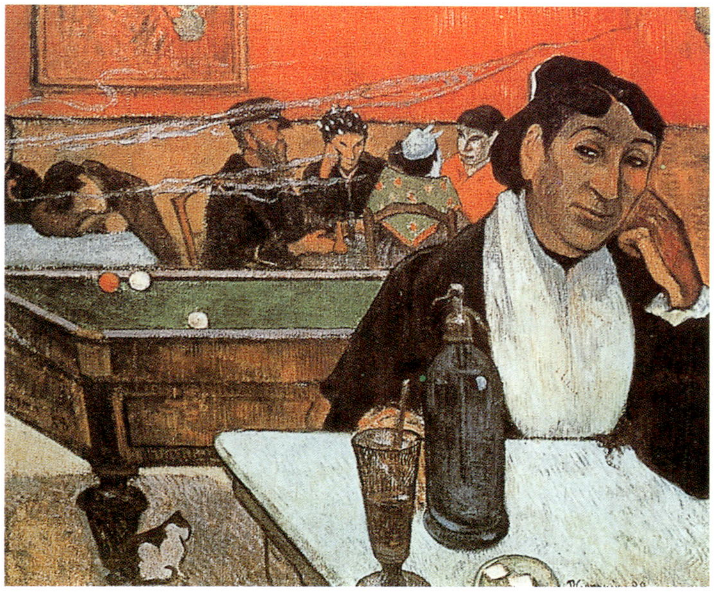

GAUGUIN
Night Café, Arles
oil on canvas
1888. 72 × 92 cm
LEFT Gauguin uses figures more prominently than van Gogh, and has crushed the perspective so that the figures in the background are very small and provide an animated backdrop behind the billiard table.

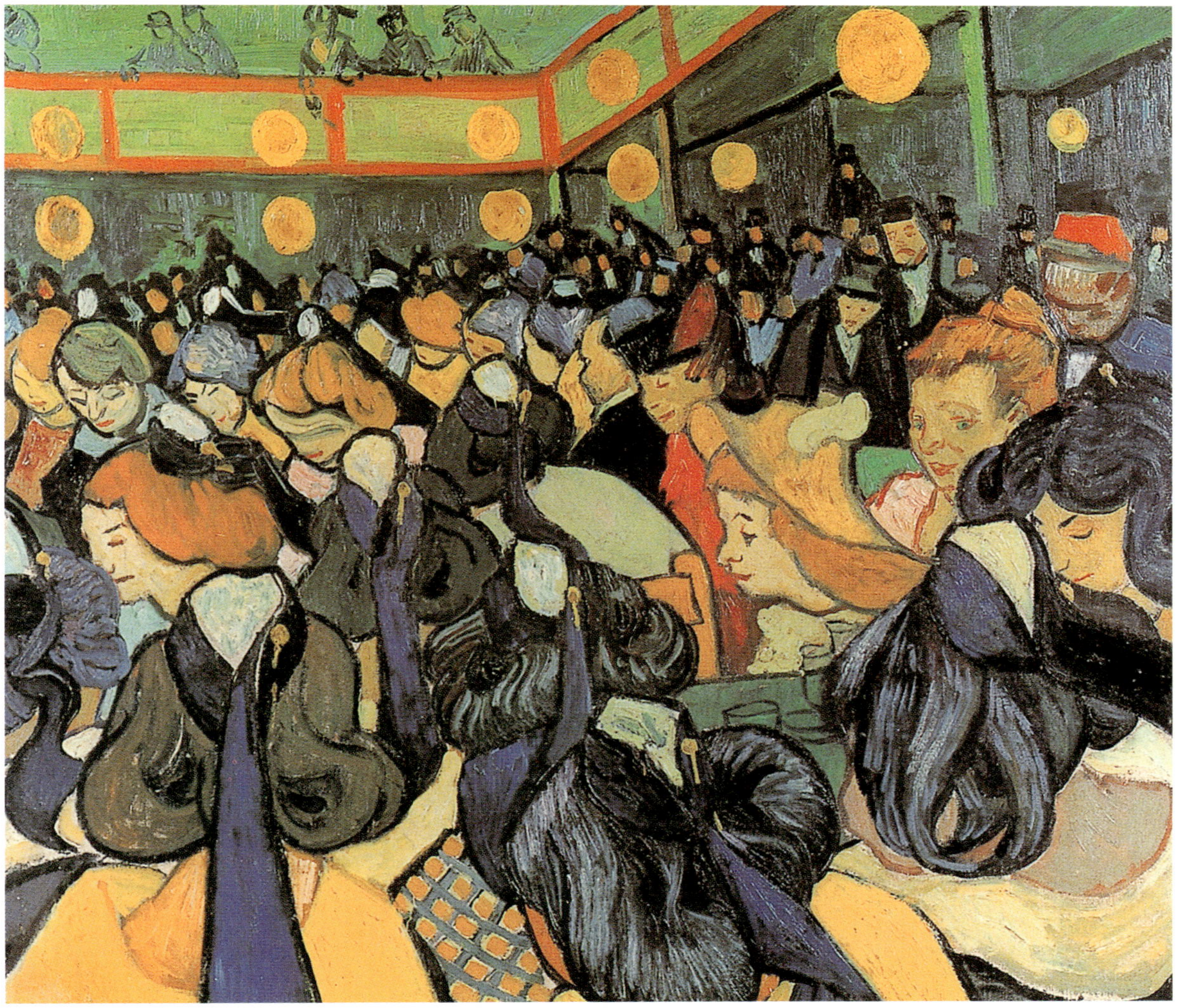

VAN GOGH
The Dancing Hall, Arles
oil on canvas
1888. 65 × 81 cm
LEFT In the south, van Gogh had developed a style unique to him, and under the influence of the luminous climate, began to use extremely bright colours in accordance with his excessive temperament. His bold, rather candid technique, reflects the violence this tormented artist inflicted upon himself.

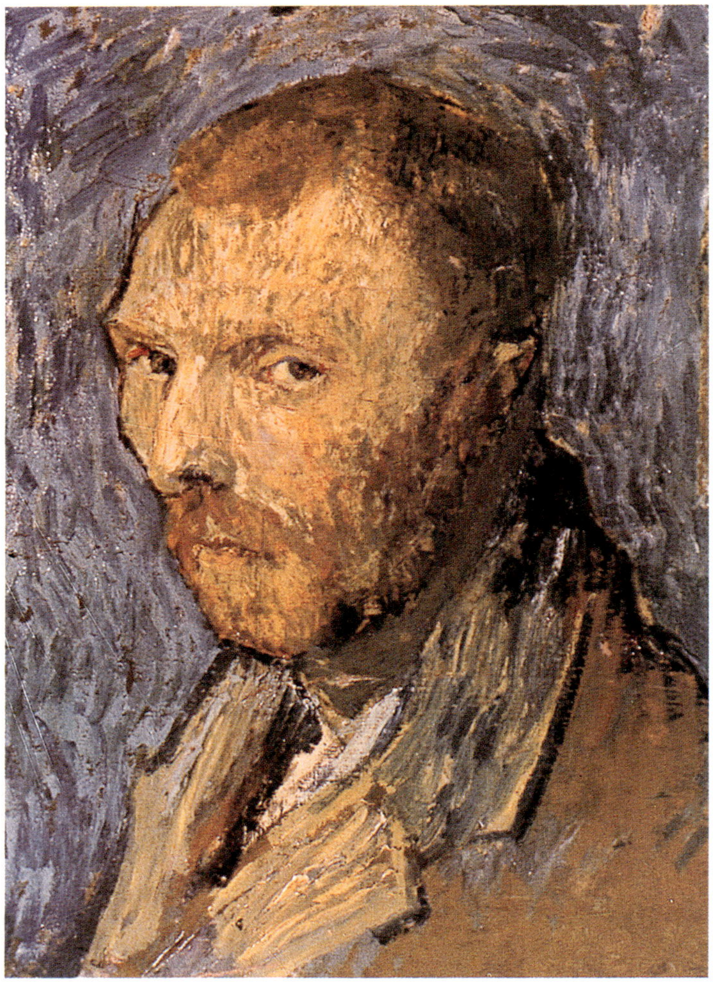

VAN GOGH
Self-portrait
oil on canvas
1889. 51 × 45 cm
Van Gogh spent a year in the hospital of St Rémy where he was treated for mental illness. In this picture, perhaps the most tragic of all his many self-portraits, we see a man suffering from acute depression, hopeless and desperate. The twirls in the background are typical, and he chose to hide the side of his face with the ear he had mutilated after a bitter argument with Gauguin in Arles.

It is reported that Pissarro said after van Gogh's suicide, "this man would either go mad or outpace us all. That he would do both I did not foresee." Whether or not he was mad, van Gogh when writing about his painting *The Night Café* of 1888 described his mission to express himself as follows:

> I have tried to express with red and green the terrible passions of human nature. Look! Through the contrasts between the delicate pink, the blood-red, the colour of vine leaves, the soft Louis XV green, the malachite opposite the yellow-green, the hard blue-green, and all this in the saltpetre-like blackness of the infernal, overheated atmosphere – through all this I try to give expression to the power of darkness that is in the café.

This aptly conveys the personal departure which van Gogh achieved, a departure impossible without the heightened response to colour and form which in their own time had been achieved by the Impressionists.

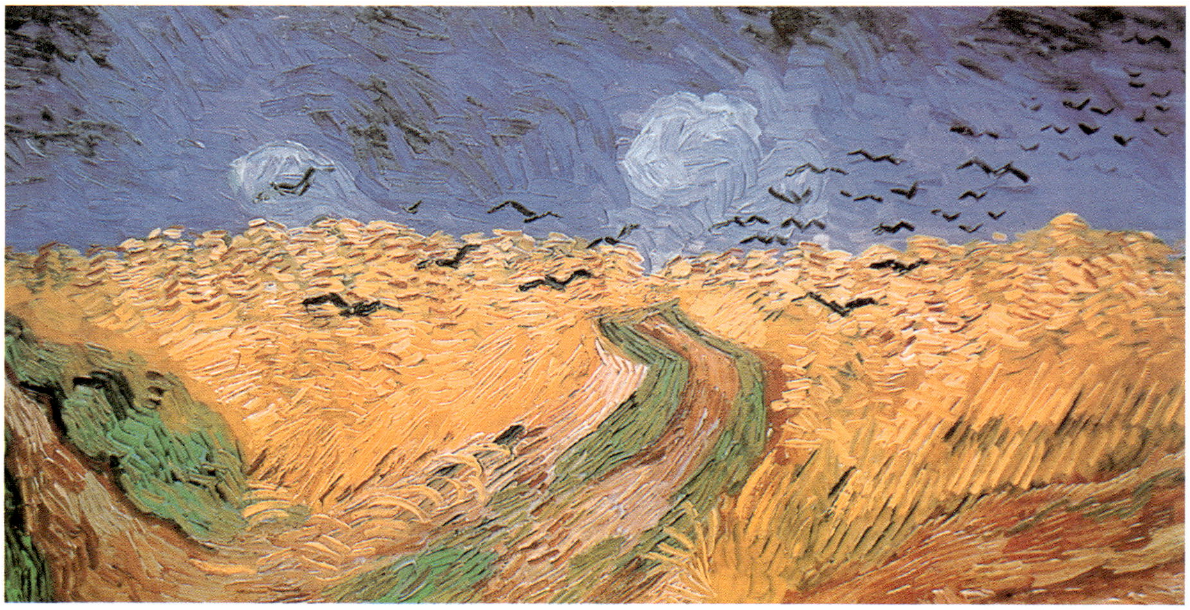

VAN GOGH
Crows above a Wheatfield
oil on canvas
1890. 50.5 × 100.5 cm
This landscape, the last van Gogh painted before his deliberate or accidental death by shotgun, was made in Auvers, where he went to seek the medical assistance of Dr Gachet after leaving the hospital of St Rémy. Van Gogh took with him the intense colours of the south, which we can hardly expect to find north of Paris, and van Gogh manages to render the barest impression of a sun.

PAUL CÉZANNE

Paul Cézanne was born on 19th January 1839 in Aix-en-Provence, the son of a hat-maker who had become a wealthy and prominent local banker. Growing up in a city richly endowed with museums and culture, Cézanne's early life was similar in many respects to that of Manet and Degas, although his relationship with his father was considerably more turbulent. Under pressure from his father to attend law school, Paul briefly attempted it before persuading Auguste Cézanne to allow him to study painting instead. The most important influence on the young Cézanne was his schoolfriend, Emile Zola, whose father was a Parisian engineer working on a project in Aix. Zola and Cézanne had formed a close and formative relationship at the Collège Bourbon, sharing an interest in Baudelaire, Hugo, and the Romantic painters. Zola's ambition was to be a writer, but Cézanne wavered between poetry and painting and was ultimately prompted towards a career as an artist by Zola, whose criticism was later to be of great importance to the Impressionists.

When Zola left Aix for Paris in 1858, Cézanne was desolate and begged his father to let him travel north to what he saw as his destiny in the capital of France. Eventually his father conceded and in 1861 Cézanne joined Zola in Paris, but only stayed six months, studying at the Académie Suisse where he met Pissarro and Guillaumin. He failed the entrance examination to the Ecole des Beaux-Arts, and was forced to return to Aix to work in his father's bank.

In 1859 Auguste Cézanne had bought a magnificent property near Aix called Jas de Bouffan, and here Cézanne set up a studio having left the bank and secured an allowance from his father of 150 francs a month. However, he was soon back in Paris, being introduced by Zola to Manet and Courbet, and meeting students of Gleyre's atelier – Monet, Sisley, Bazille, and Renoir. Throughout the 1860s he swung back and forth between Aix and Paris, unsure of his talents or the direction they were taking and slowly becoming estranged from Zola who was equally unsure of Cézanne's ability. His early work is a violent and erotic strain of Romanticism. Paintings such as *The Abduction* (*L'Enlèvement*), *The Murder* (*Le Meurtre*), *Autopsy* (*L'Autopsie*), and *Skull, Candlestick, and Book* (*Nature mortre au crâne*), all produced in the mid- to late 1860s, show distinctly both a variety of influences from Delacroix to Courbet and a tortured view of the world.

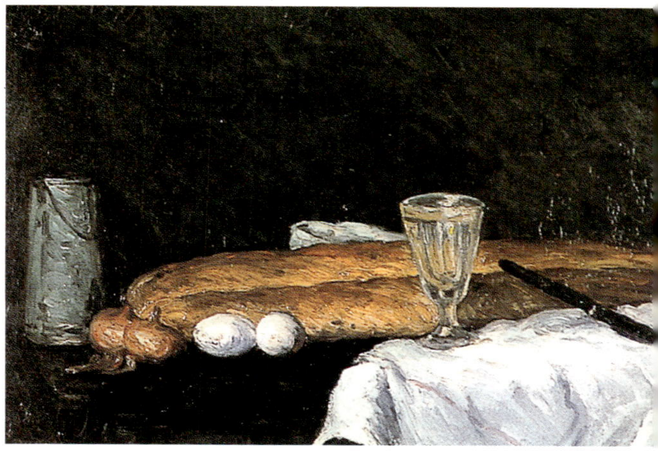

CÉZANNE
Still Life with Knife and Bread
oil on canvas
1865. 55 × 72 cm
ABOVE In this still life, rendered in thick impasto when he was twenty-four, there is none of the ease with which the young Monet executed a rather similar and traditional subject.

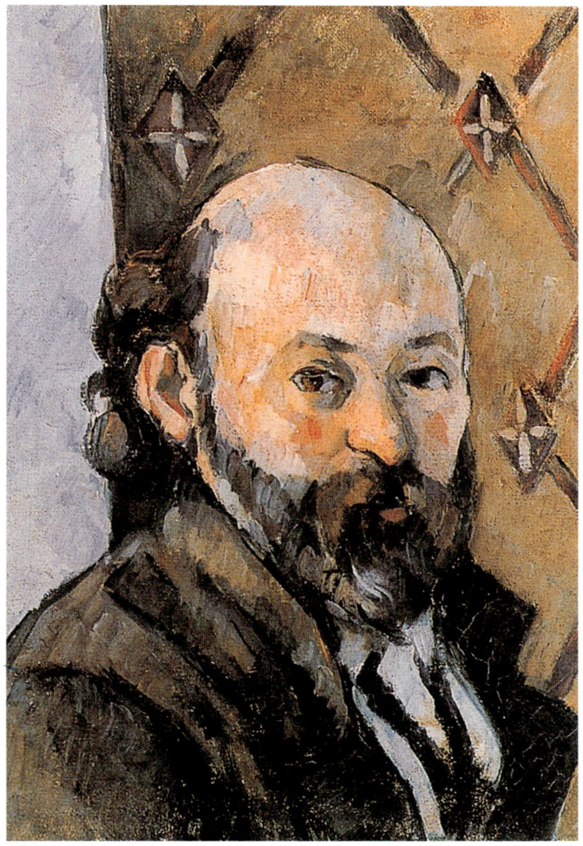

CÉZANNE
Self-portrait
oil on canvas
c.1880. 33.5 × 26 cm
LEFT Cézanne painted a number of self portraits.

A change came in his approach to his work after the French declaration of war on Prussia when he and his mistress, Hortense Fiquet, fled to L'Estaque near Aix. A new vision of nature suddenly takes over in *The Cutting* and *Snow Thaw in L'Estaque* (*Forte des neiges à L'Estaque*), which see Cézanne abandoning the angst-ridden expression of figures writhing in dark landscapes and concentrating on the landscape as a motif in itself. An intensely formative period began in 1872 when Hortense had a baby and all three moved to

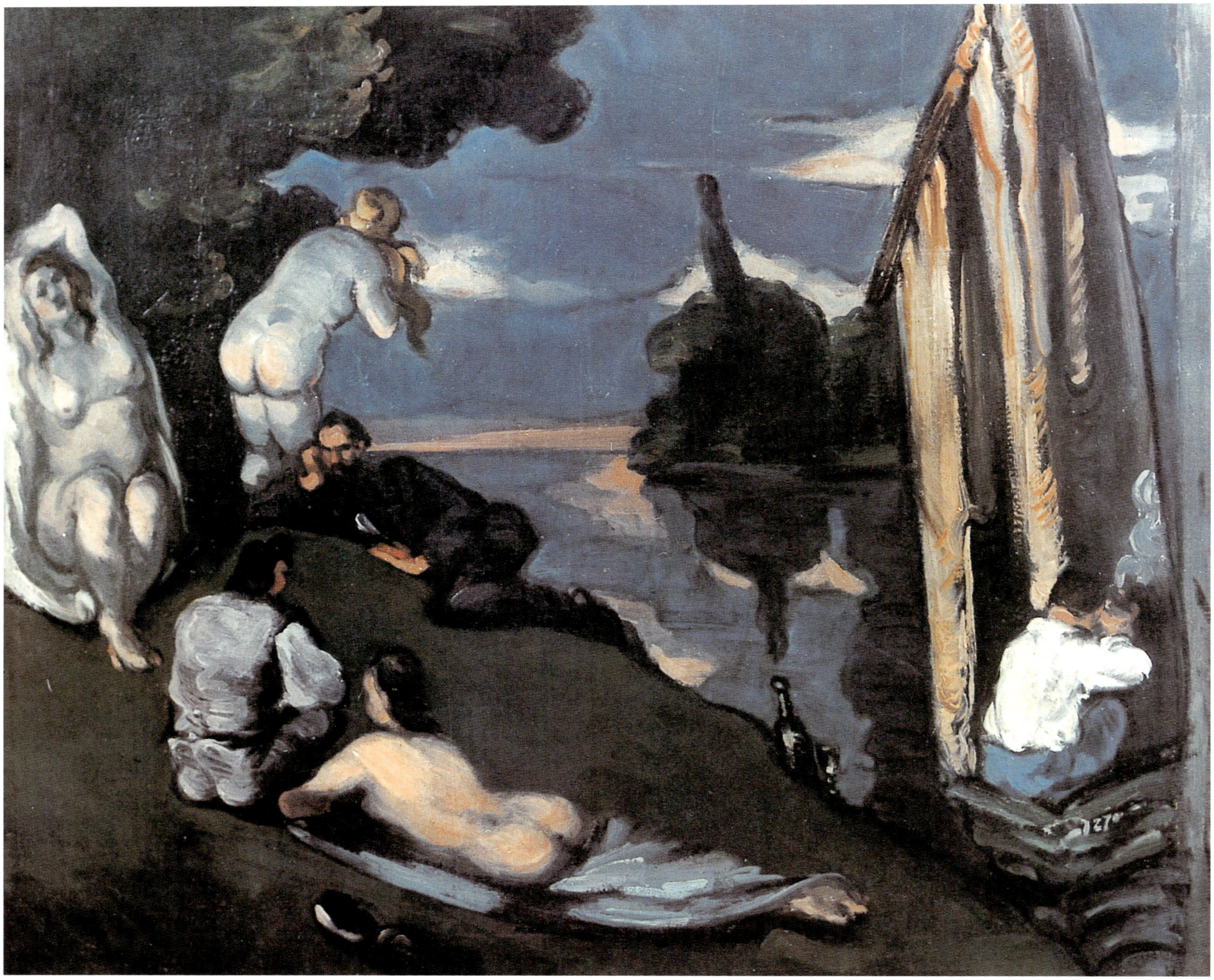

Saint-Ouen-l'Aumône on the Oise near Pontoise where Camille Pissarro was living. The influence of Pissarro now began to manifest itself and it was at this time that Cézanne came the closest to Impressionism he was likely to reach. *The House of the Hanged Man at Auvers* shows Pissarro's influence to particular effect. As Pissarro said many years afterwards " . . . the resemblance of some of his Auvers and Pontoise landscapes to mine is striking. Of course it is true that we were always together, but it is certain that each of us had his own response, which is what really matters." In 1873 Cézanne and his family had moved from Saint-Ouen to nearby Auvers-sur-Oise where a certain Dr Paul Gachet lived. Gachet was a Socialist and a great friend and admirer of many of the Impressionists, especially his neighbour Pissarro. Cézanne, an outcast in his own mind and rejected by many of his contemporaries for being something of a brute because of his seemingly uncultivated manner, was well received at Dr Gachet's house. He was not the last troubled artist to be welcomed there; Vincent van Gogh was often found at Dr Gachet's in the very last days of his short life.

Thanks to his close liaison with Pissarro, Cézanne was one of the contributors to the first Impressionist exhibition in 1874 when he showed *The House of the Hanged Man at Auvers* and *A Modern Olympia*. The critics

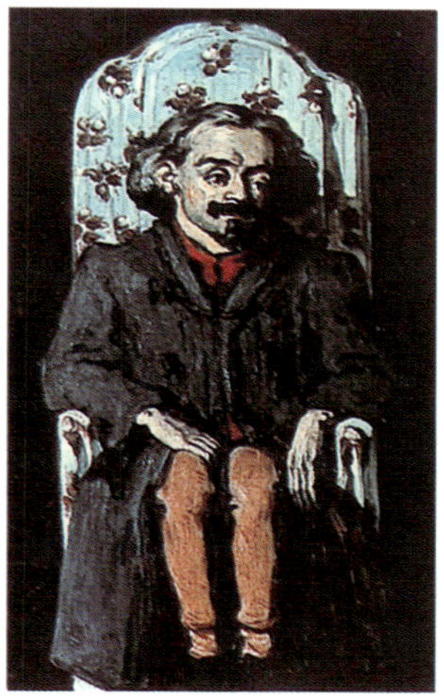

CÉZANNE
Achille Emperaire
oil on canvas
1868. 200 × 120 cm
ABOVE Cézanne used a thick impasto of dark hues worked with a knife. The result is strong but unsophisticated.

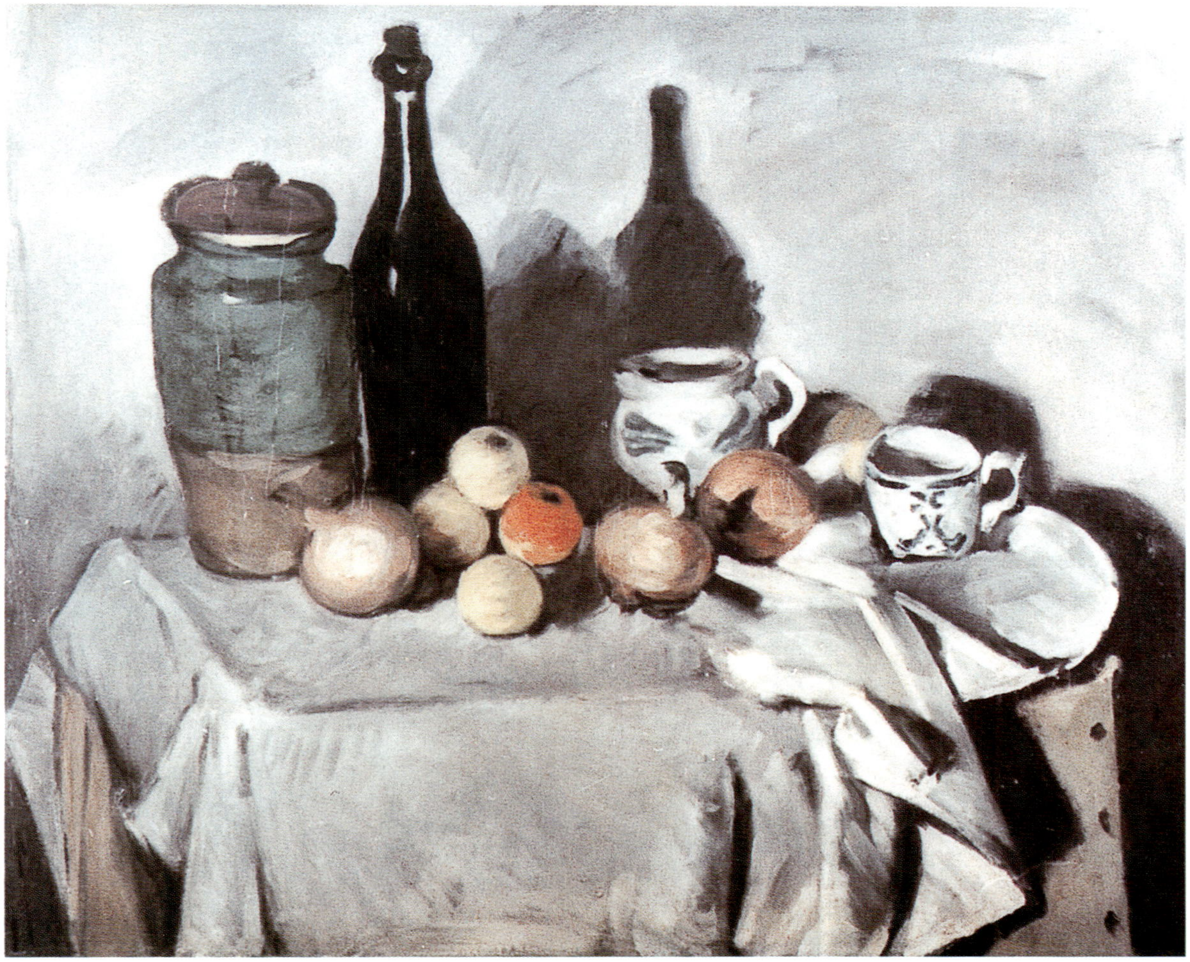

CÉZANNE
Still Life
oil on canvas
1871–72. 63 × 80 cm
LEFT We can now see that he is approaching an individual mode of expression with the strong light projecting shadows on the wall and the various elements of the still life taking shape.

CÉZANNE
Idyll
oil on canvas
1870. 65 × 81 cm
OPPOSITE Drawing on old masters' compositions, Cézanne painted this scene, one of his first series of bathers, a theme he returned to throughout his career.

were beside themselves with outrage. In his infamous satire in *Charivari* Leroy described *A Modern Olympia*, as "A woman folded in two from whom a Negro girl is removing the last veil in order to offer her in all her ugliness to the charmed gaze of a brown puppet. Do you remember the *Olympia* of M. Manet? Well that was a masterpiece of drawing, accuracy, and finish, compared to the one by M. Cézanne." Manet himself was to say of Cézanne's work, "How can you abide such foul painting?"

After the third Impressionist exhibition in 1877, Cézanne no longer participated in the group's shows. Although he remained close to Pissarro and was a vital influence on Renoir in the 1880s, he had eschewed the attempt of Impressionism to depict the effects of light, colour, and atmosphere as exemplified by the whole of Monet's endeavour or Renoir's work of the 1870s. Cézanne sought, as he said, "to make Impressionism more solid and enduring, like the art of the old masters" and to "redo Poussin after nature". This profound concern to reconcile the subject – be it landscape or still life – with a formal, practically geometrical structure developed from deep within Cézanne's perception can be seen in its early stages in the *Bathers* and the *Seine at Bercy* of the mid-1870s. Traditional spatial notions of foreground, background, and depth are eliminated almost at a stroke; his

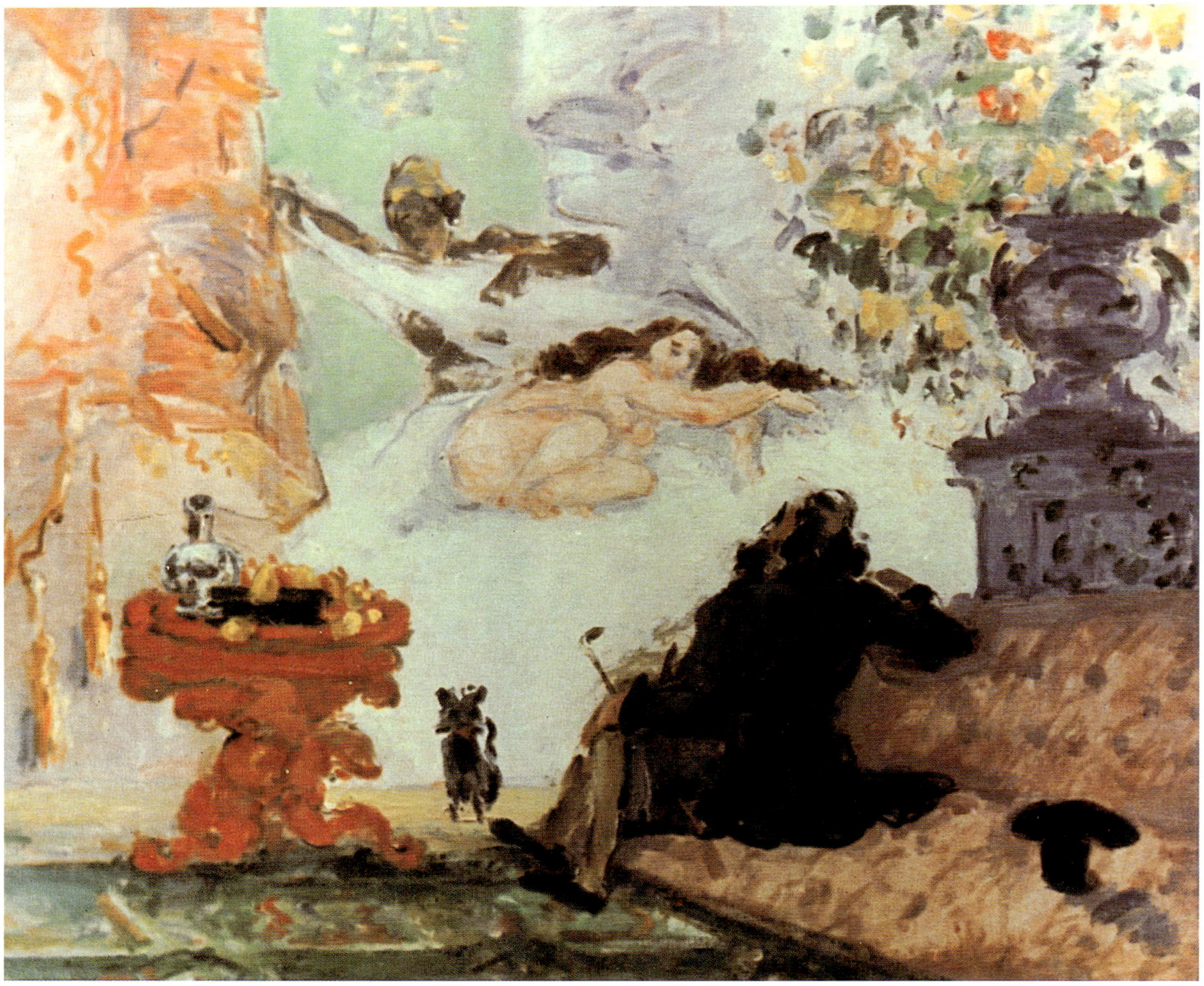

CÉZANNE
A Modern Olympia
oil on canvas
1873–74. 46 × 55.5 cm
RIGHT This is a variation of Manet's famous Olympia *of 1863, but Cézanne himself is in a brothel, turned towards an odalisque whose body is revealed by her maid lifting the sheet covering her crouched body.*

CÉZANNE
Victor Chocquet
oil on canvas
1877. 46 × 38 cm
OPPOSITE Cézanne's portrait of his friend the collector Chocquet is reminiscent of his earlier works in which he used a palette knife.

intention was literally to reconstruct nature from the repertoire of techniques available to him. This fundamental reordering of experience, seen at its height in Cézanne's still lifes, landscapes, and motivic pictures of card-players and nudes in a landscape, is essentially the starting point for Modern art (in fact, Matisse hailed Cézanne a "father to us all"). A letter to the Post-Impressionist painter and critic Emile Bernard written by Cézanne in 1904, two years before his death, reads like the beginnings of a Cubist manifesto: " . . . treat nature by the cylinder, the sphere, the cone, everything in proper perspective so that each side of an object or a plane is directed towards a central point . . . "

In view of his radical rethinking of art it is hardly surprising that Cézanne found little encouragement amongst his fellow artists (apart from Pissarro and Renoir). He was plagued by the same financial insecurity as some of his contemporaries until 1886 when he inherited a quarter of his father's 1.6 million franc fortune. Consistent rejections by the Salon until 1882 further alienated him from the mainstream art market, and the few paintings he did sell were those he displayed in Paris at the shop of the colour merchant Père Tanguy, where other outré painters, notably van Gogh, also held informal exhibitions. It was Pissarro who had introduced him to Père Tanguy and it was also Pissarro who persuaded his patron Victor Chocquet to view Cézanne's works at the colour merchant's. Chocquet was impressed and became

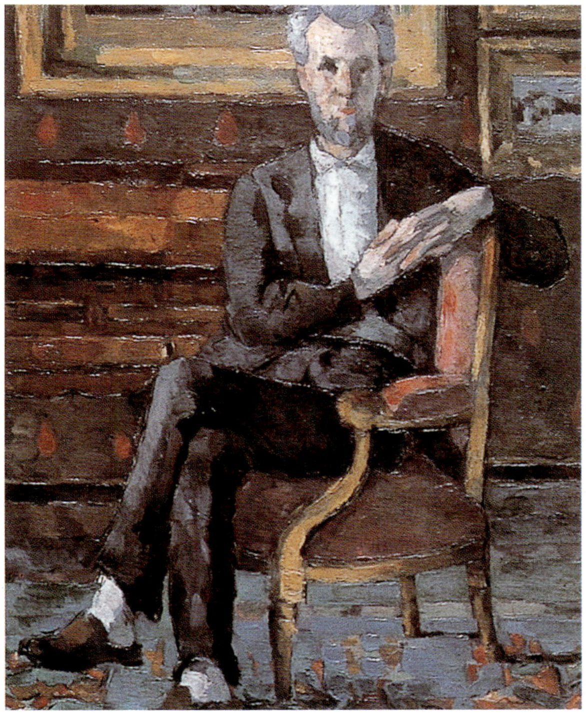

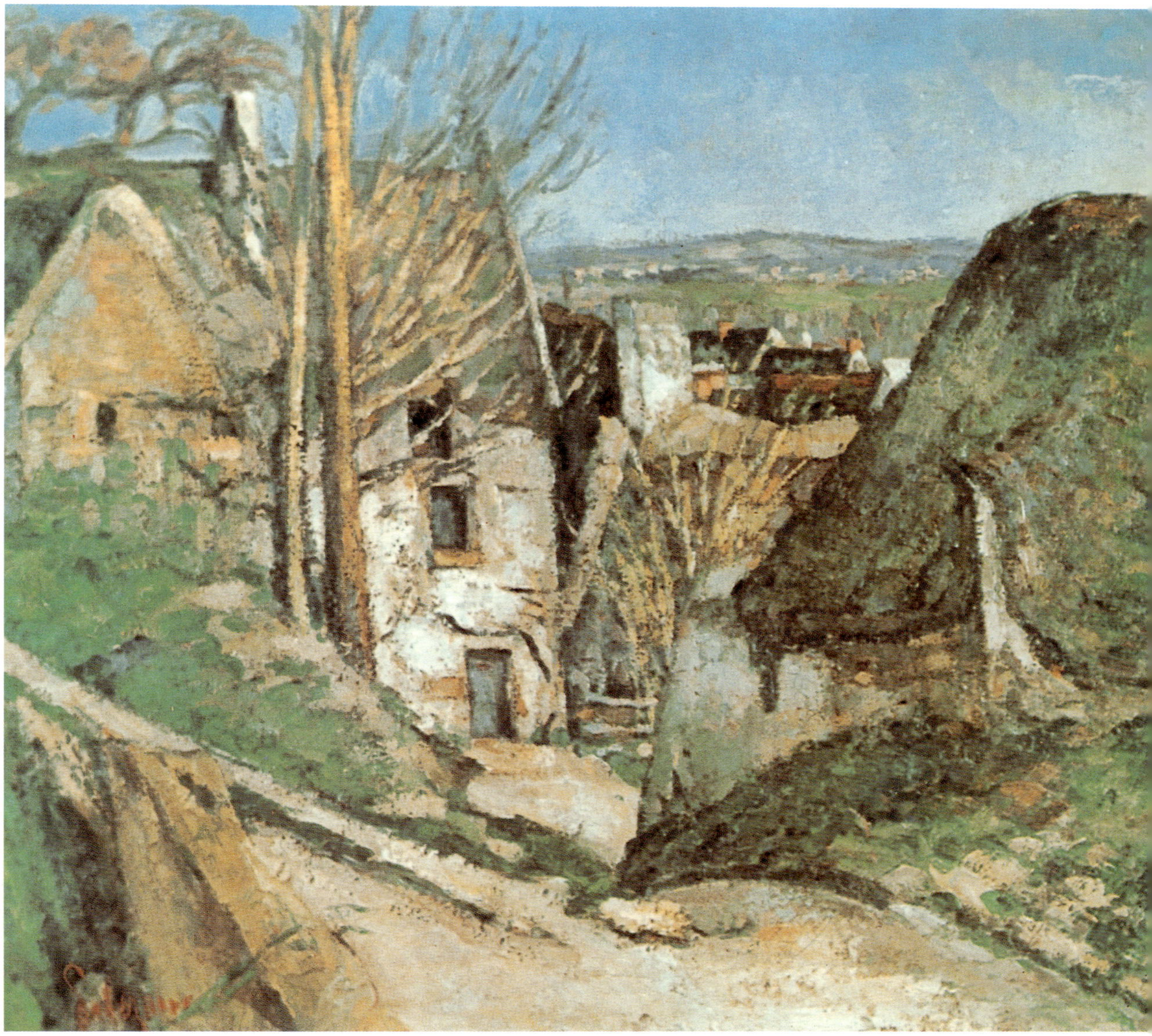

CÉZANNE
The House of the Hanged
Man at Auvers
oil on canvas
1873. 55 × 66 cm
Above The freedom of expression which he was to achieve was, as usual, more the outcome of intensive labour than of instant inspiration.

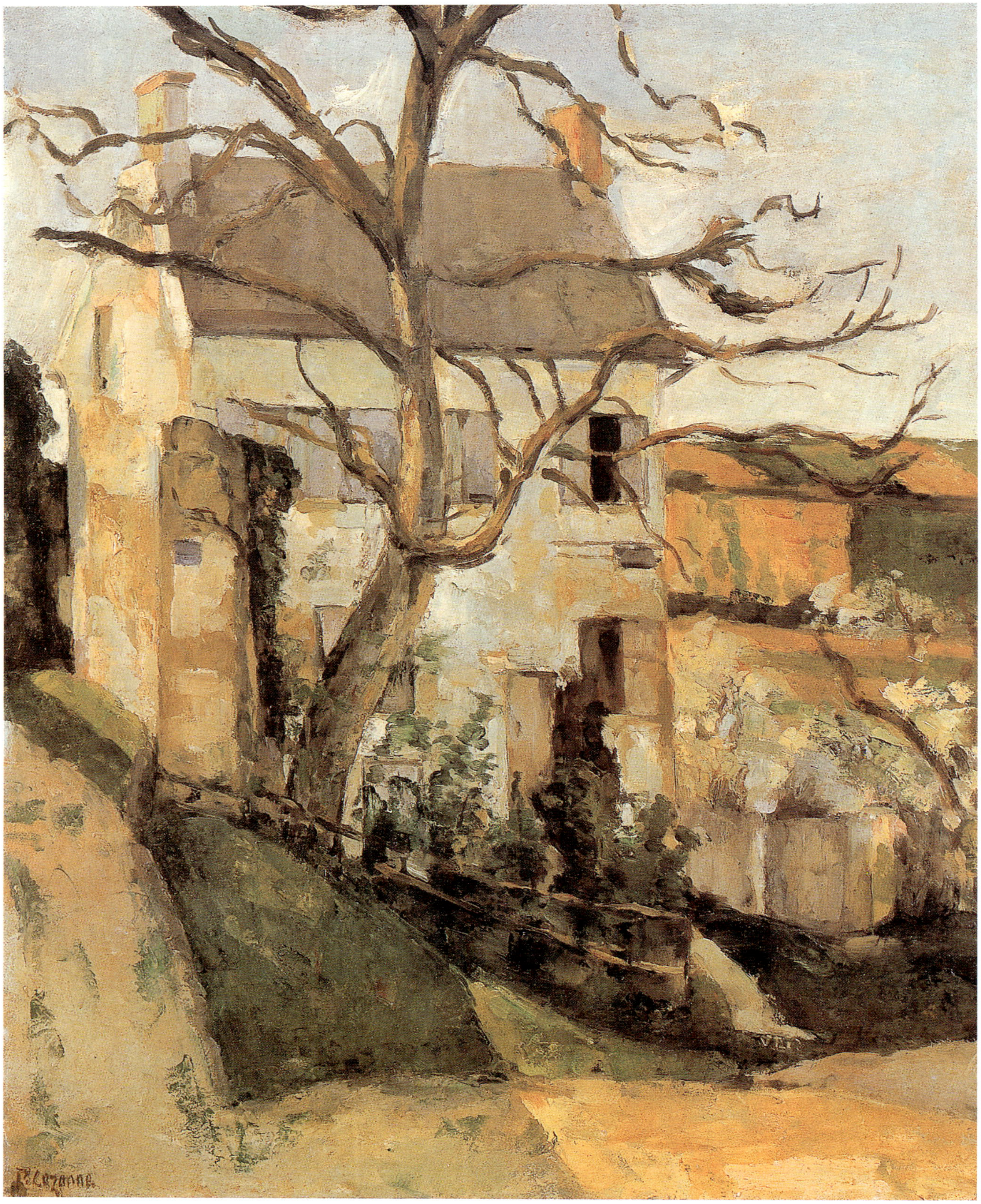

CÉZANNE
House and Tree
oil on canvas
c.1873–75. 66 × 55.5 cm
LEFT Cézanne often worked with Pissarro during these crucial years and learnt from his tolerant and patient elder how to replace his thick, shapeless, and ill-applied impasto with lighter coats of paint. He learnt to structure his pictures and gained in solidity.

CÉZANNE
Panorama of Auvers
oil on canvas
1873–75. 65 × 81 cm
RIGHT Cézanne lived for a while at Dr Gachet's house, which is the tall white building to the left. Here we see the neat touches of the roofs and walls of the houses, the geometry of the landscape as only Cézanne saw it. The painting is perhaps unfinished and Cézanne has deliberately omitted the river Oise and the church which van Gogh was later to make famous. At this point Cézanne was following the example of Pissarro, who said, "replace tonal modelling by the study of colours." Pissarro, willing as always to help a friend, encouraged him to take part in the first Impressionist exhibition, and his participation was one of the reasons Manet gave for refusing to exhibit with the group.

an important collector of Cézanne's works as well as a close friend. He was also instrumental in the showing of *The House of the Hanged Man at Auvers* at the 1889 Exposition Universelle. Two years before, Cézanne had shown along with Gaugin and van Gogh at the exhibition of an avant-garde Belgian group called Les Vingt (The Twenty, because there were originally twenty members), where he again exhibited in 1890.

Cézanne fell out permanently with his childhood friend Emile Zola when the latter

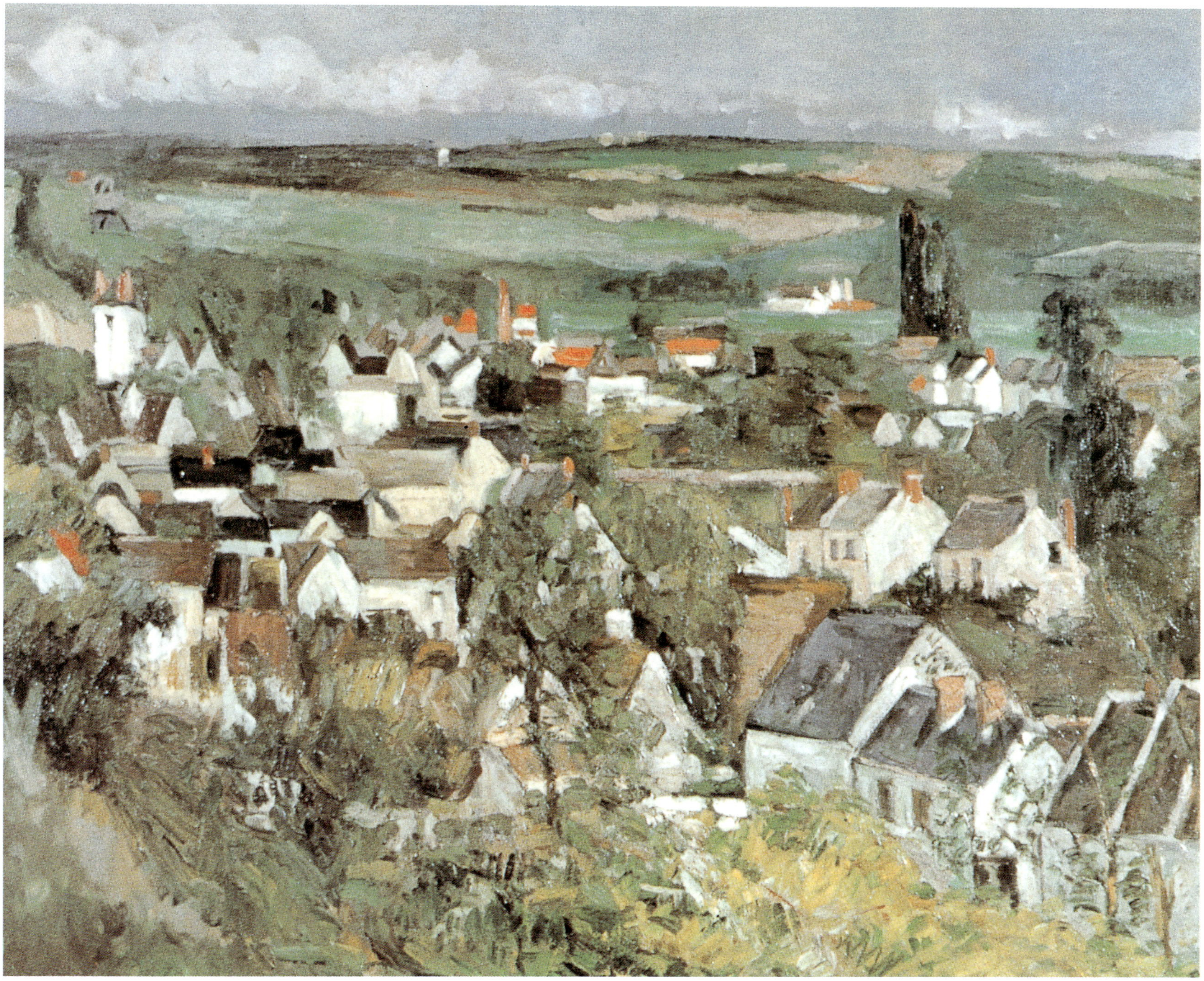

CÉZANNE
Hortense Fiquet
oil on canvas
1877. 72 × 56 cm
BELOW Cézanne's companion Hortense posed for several portraits.

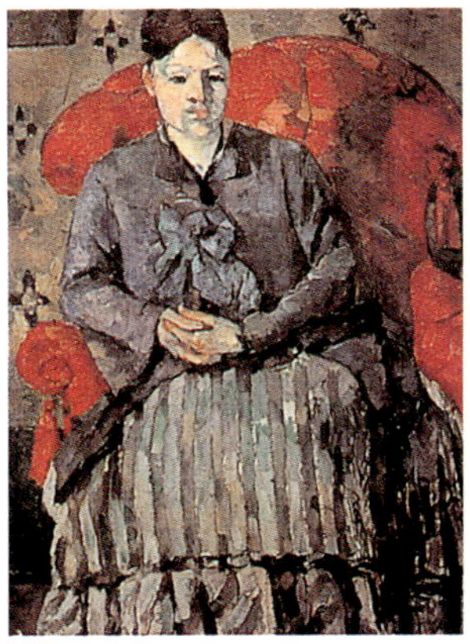

CÉZANNE
Five Bathers
oil on canvas
1877–78. 46 × 55.5 cm
RIGHT Bathers were one of the central subjects in Cézanne's repertoire for nearly half a century. Here they are placed in his own version of an Arcadian landscape, with resonances more obviously classical than contemporary.

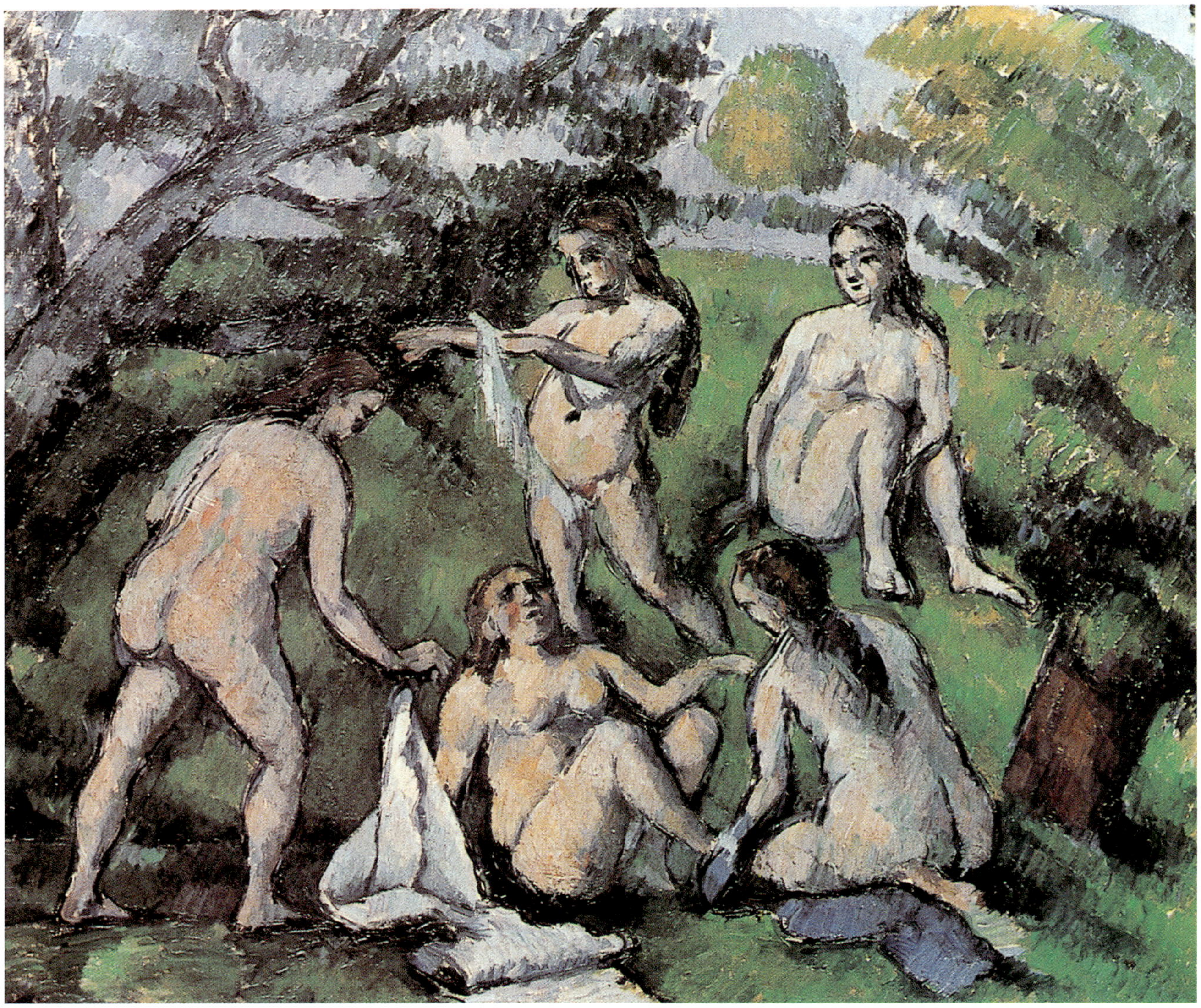

published his controversial novel *L'Oeuvre* (*The Work*) in 1886. Zola had portrayed Cézanne as the character Claude Lantier, a failed painter who commits suicide. Cézanne never forgave him; in any case Zola's support for his early friend had been positively lukewarm throughout the most difficult period of Cézanne's career. In the end there was little love to be lost between the two of them – in 1896 Zola was still describing Cézanne as a "genuis who never matured."

However, Signac had bought a Cézanne landscape from Père Tanguy in 1884 and by the late 1880s a younger generation of artists and critics had begun to value Cézanne's work. By the mid-1890s he was enjoying what was for him a considerable success with his first one-man show at Ambroise Vollard's gallery. A young painter, Maurice Denis, had alerted Vollard to the fifty-six-year-old Cézanne's work and Denis, who had never met Cézanne, later produced an extraordinary apotheosis of the artist. His *Homage to Cézanne* shows the master surrounded by members of the Nabis group, including Bonnard, Vuillard, and Roussel. The perceptive

Denis had the measure of Cézanne. His work, he said, was "the final outcome of the classical tradition and the product of the great crisis of liberty and light which has rejuvenated modern art."

Paul Cézanne died on 22nd October 1906 after he had collapsed on a landscape outing near his home in Aix. He was perhaps the archetypal misunderstood artist, but his fearsome appearance and apparently uncultivated manner belied a mysterious, reclusive, modest nature obsessed with rendering his unique vision of the world: "I paint what I see and how I feel," said the Father of Modernism, "My feelings are very powerful."

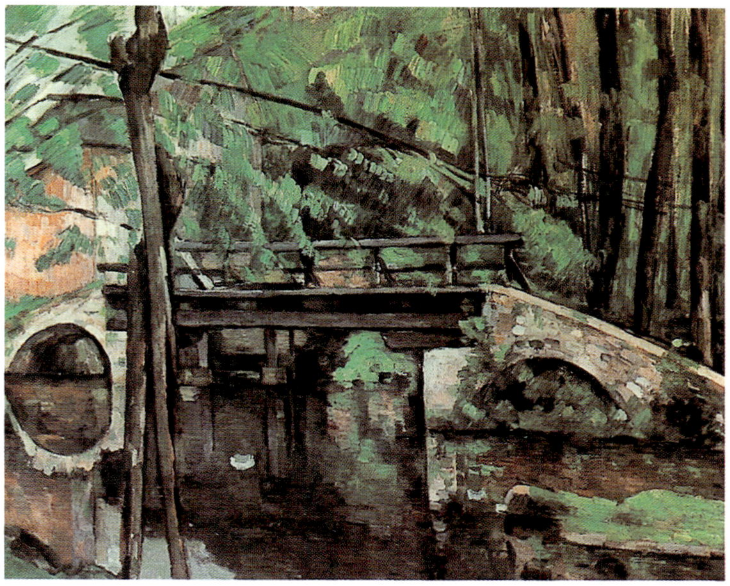

CÉZANNE
The Bridge at Maincy
oil on canvas
1879–80. 58.5 × 72.5 cm
Left Here Cézanne shows his growing interest in the structural elements of landscape. With short brushstrokes he renders a completely unsentimental view.

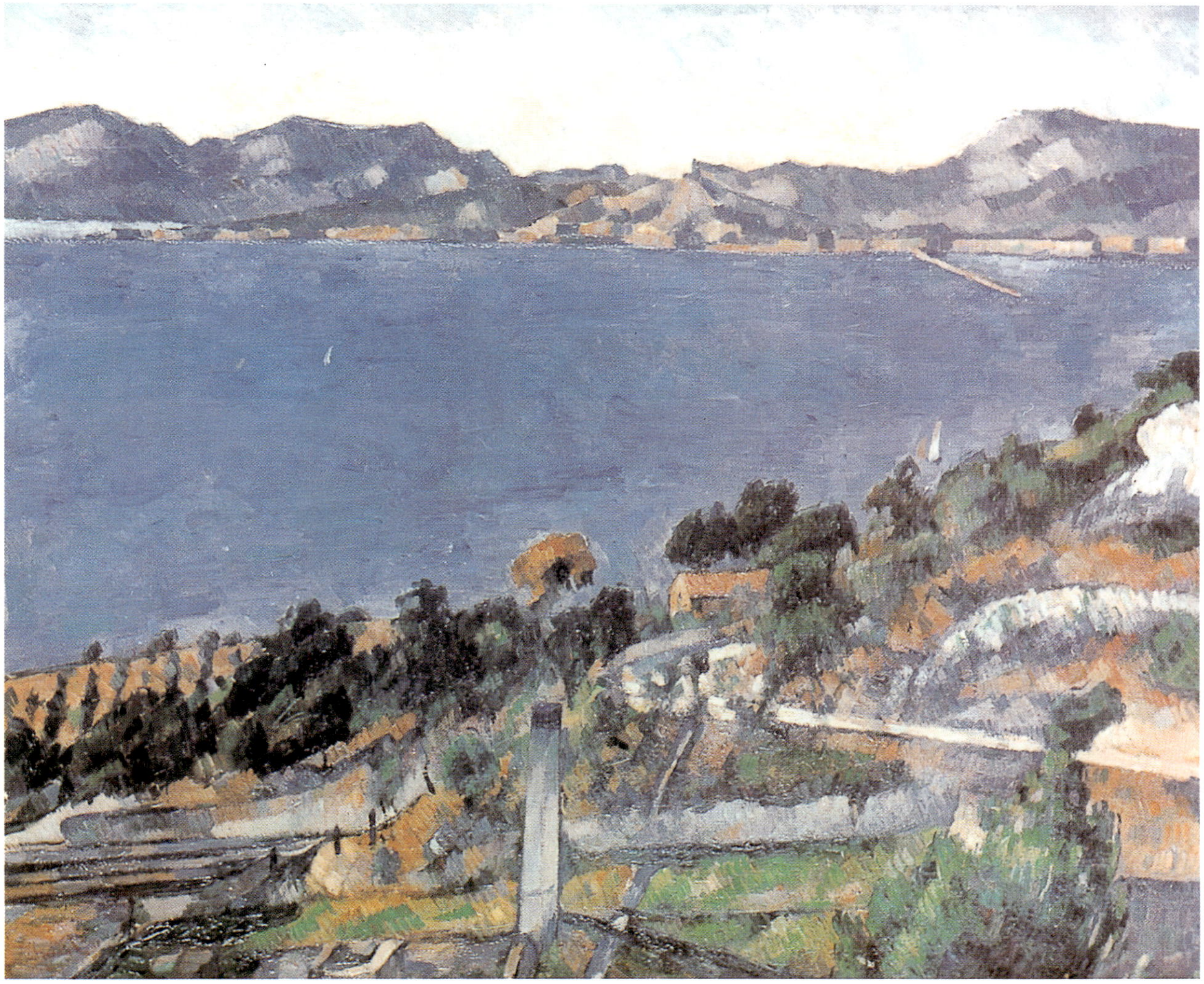

CÉZANNE
L'Estaque, near Marseilles
oil on canvas
1878–79. 59.5 × 73 cm
This work was painted during one of the most difficult periods of Cézanne's artistic career, shortly after the first Impressionist collective exhibition, at which his submissions had been roundly condemned (even by some of the other exhibitors), and just as he was wrestling with the development of a new attitude to colour which was to radically alter his palette.

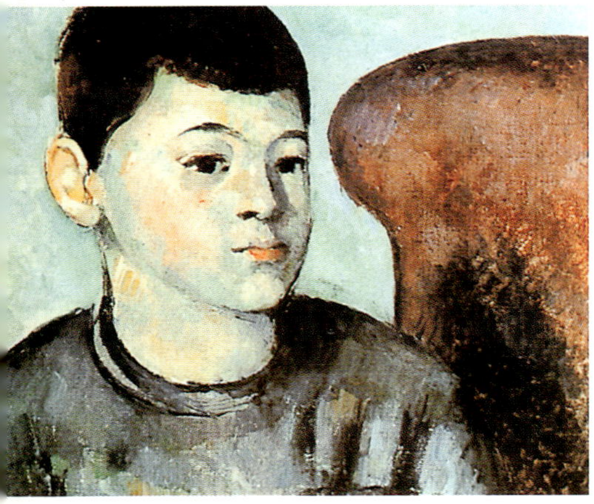

CÉZANNE
Paul Cézanne
oil on canvas
1880. 35 × 38 cm
ABOVE Cézanne loved his son, Paul, and had a good relationship with him. In this small portrait the superfluous details are weeded out and the boy's features are very sensitively depicted.

By the late 1880s Impressionism and Neo-Impressionism were just one of the stylistic options open to the younger artists who had come to Paris to seek fame and fortune. Many of them, including Vincent van Gogh, Henri de Toulouse-Lautrec, Pierre Bonnard, and Edouard Vuillard were thought of at one time or another as Impressionists, though the term had come to signify any artistic position away from what was considered mainstream, naturalistic Salon art. Cézanne and Gauguin who had both been nurtured by the Impressionists (by Pissarro in particular), had developed their own personal modes of artistic expression and had attracted their own followers. Cézanne had moved far away from Impressionism towards a depiction of the world in terms of geometrical structures, and his work was to strongly influence the twentieth-century Cubists, Pablo Picasso and Georges Braque. Paul Gauguin, who had exhibited in the Impressionist exhibitions of 1880, 1881, 1882, and 1886, was passing through what he described as a "Synthesist-Symbolic" period which was to influence Bonnard and Vuillard. And as late as mid-1899, the thirty-year-old Henry Matisse was emerging from the distinct influence of Impressionism into experiments with Divisionism and the ideas of Gauguin. In America and Britain the legacy of the Impressionists lingered well into the twentieth century.

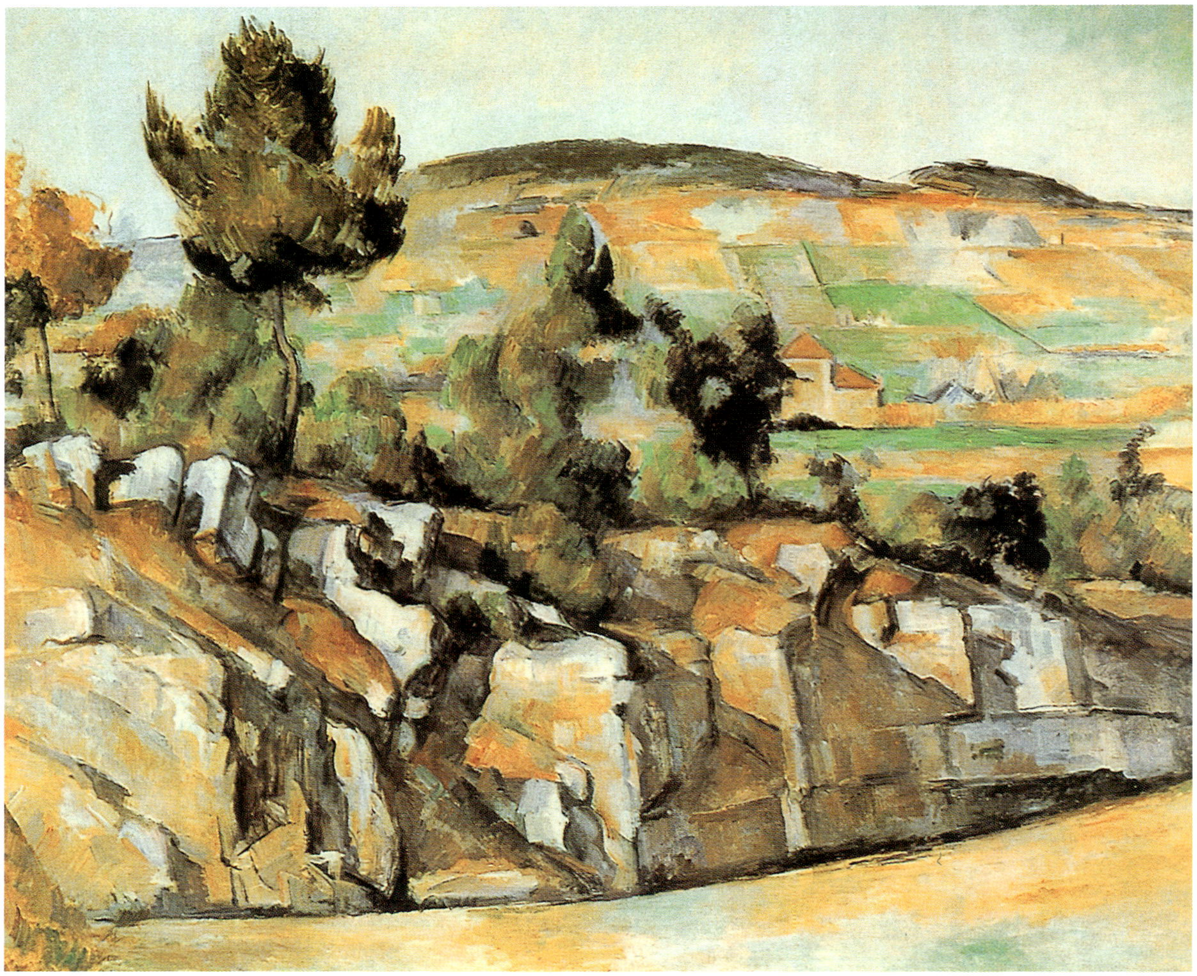

CÉZANNE
Mountain in Provence
oil on canvas
c.1886–90. 63.5 × 79.5 cm
RIGHT Having come to terms with his reworked theory of colour, Cézanne's painting was now beginning to attract the renewed attention and respect of his peers. Both Signac and Gauguin not only came under Cézanne's influence at this time, but also personally purchased some of his paintings.

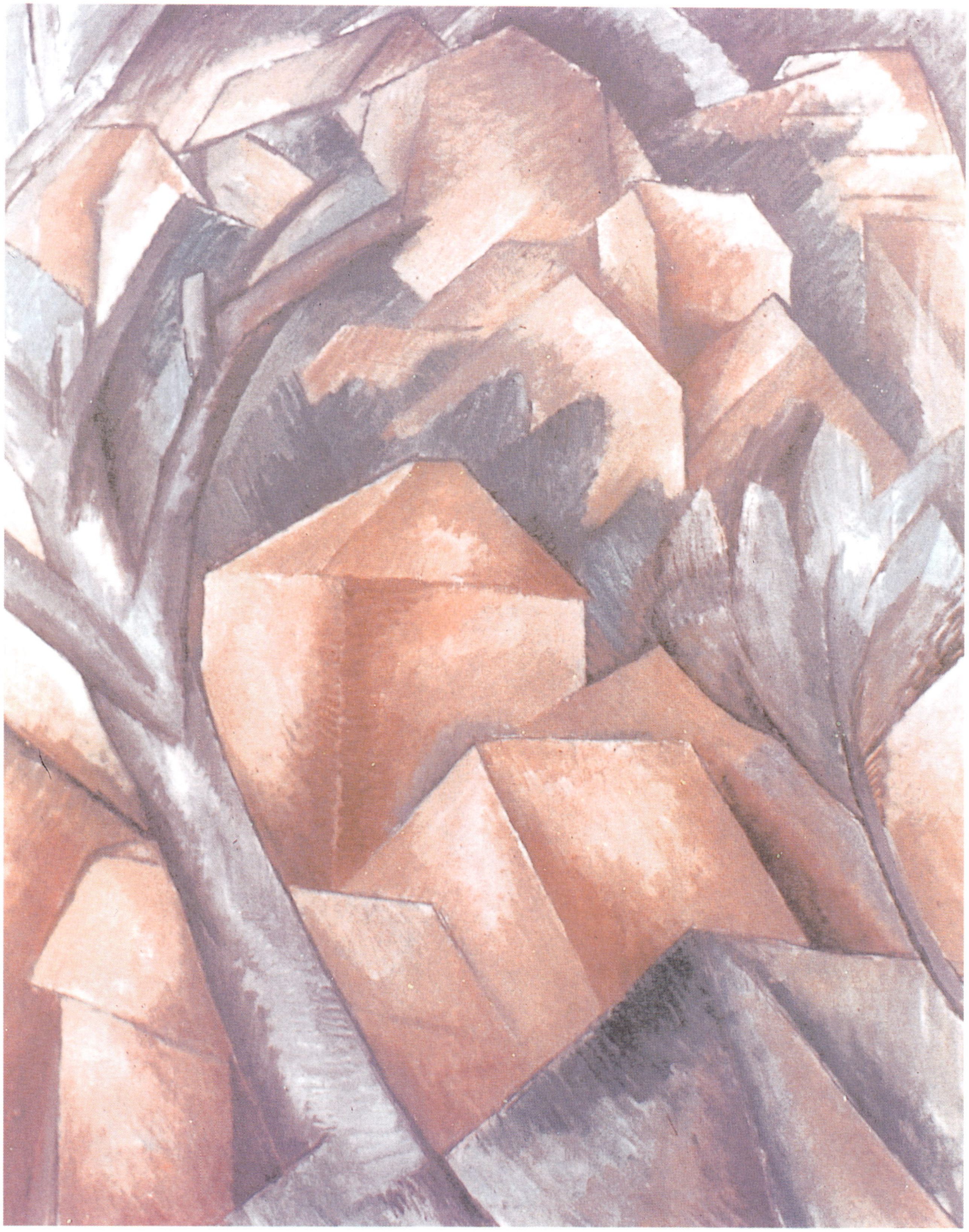

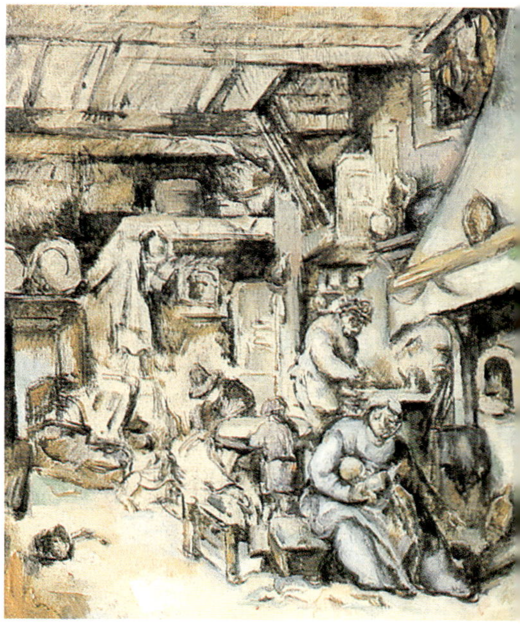

CÉZANNE
The Family
oil on canvas
undated. 45 × 37 cm
ABOVE For sheer pleasure, Cézanne copied, late in life, a small etching by Adriaen van Ostade, dated 1647: he interpreted it in his own style, adding light and harmonious touches of colour. In so doing he transformed a cluttered and dark seventeenth-century Dutch interior into an airy scene, leaving much of the background uncovered.

BRAQUE
House at L'Estaque
oil on canvas
1908. 73 × 60 cm
LEFT In 1907 Braque attended the Cézanne Memorial Exhibition, and the work he saw there completely changed his artistic perspective. Previously on the fringes of the Fauvist school, the work he produced in the period after 1907, together with his introduction to Picasso, saw the preliminary steps towards the foundation of full-blown Cubism.

IMPRESSIONISM IN ENGLAND

In October 1863, reviewing the Salon des Refusés, the English art critic Philip Hamerton wrote in *The Fine Arts Quarterly*:

> Now some wretched Frenchman has translated this [Giorgione's *Fête champêtre* – the source for Manet's *Luncheon on the Grass* (*Déjeuner sur l'herbe*)] into modern French realism, on a much larger scale, and with the horrible modern French costume instead of the graceful Venetian one . . . There are other pictures of the same class, which lead to the inference that the nude, whenever painted by vulgar men, is inevitably indecent.

On 5th June 1900, thirty-seven years after the Salon des Refusés, the art critic of *The Times* reviewed the paintings exhibited in the Exposition Universelle (the occasion when the painter Jean-Léon Gerôme warned the Président of France, Emile Loubet, not to cast his eyes upon "*le déshonneur de la France*") and offered this comment:

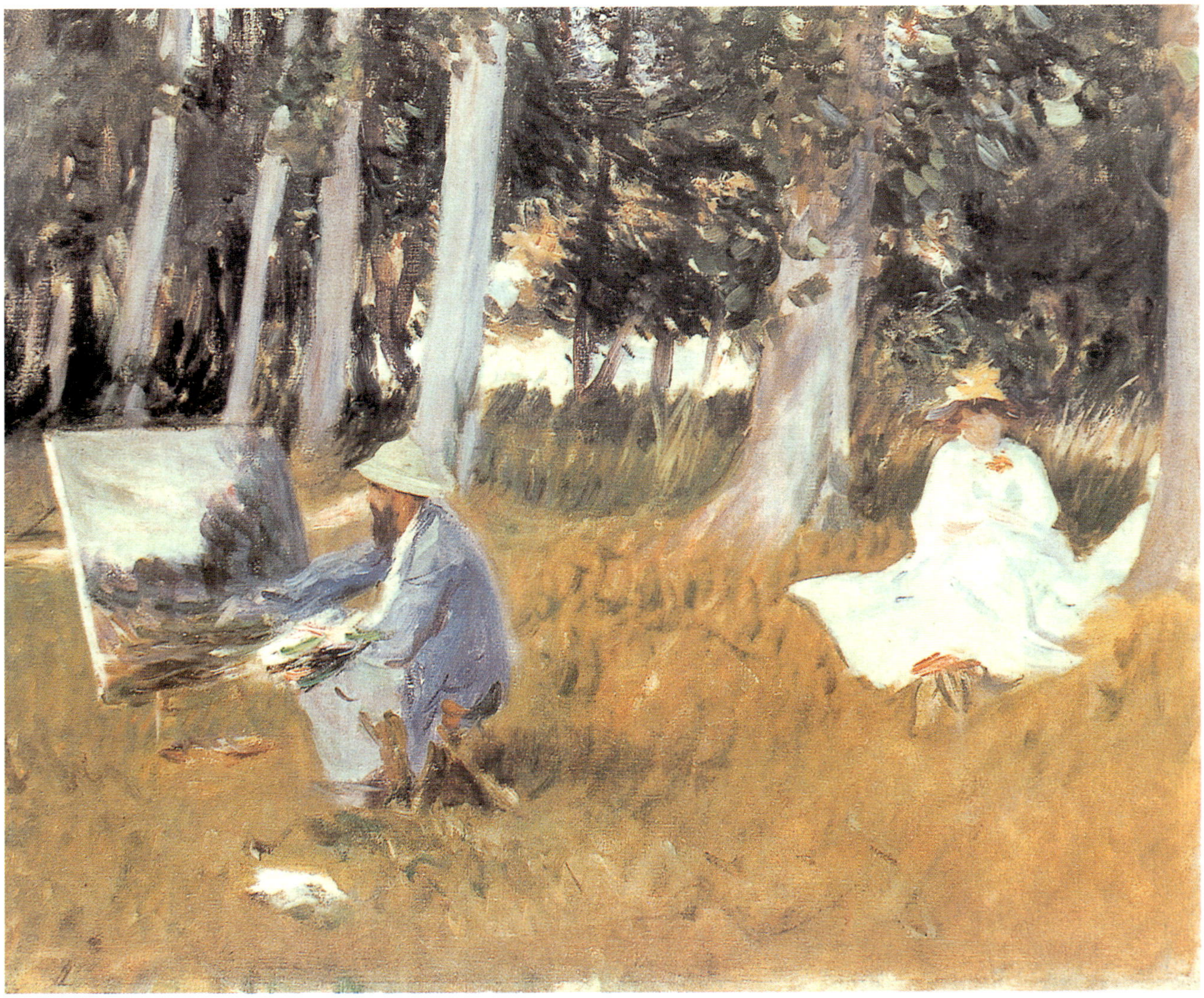

SARGENT
Monet Painting at the Edge of a Wood
oil on canvas
c.1887. 54 × 65 cm
This painting shows Monet at work outdoors and is overtly Impressionistic as befits its subject.

> We ourselves are inclined to think that the craze for the Impressionists' landscapes will not last, but that people will continue to admire Degas for his unique gift of rendering certain movements and certain textures, and Manet for the extraordinary vitality of some of his portraits . . . But that the world, even the cultivated world, will ever see beauty in *Le Déjeuner sur l'herbe* [*Luncheon on the Grass*] . . . is not to be believed.

The most hostile form of the English reaction in the nineteenth century to French Impressionism was characterized by a latent xenophobia and mistrust of the French, which had persisted since the time of the French Revolution in 1789 and the subsequent battles with Napoleon Bonaparte. If Bonaparte thought the English were a nation of "shopkeepers", English critical opinion held that the French were a nation of dangerous and decadent revolutionaries and the Impressionists only helped to convince them of this. It took until the first decade of the twentieth century before the English art establishment could reconcile itself to Impressionism. By the time English Impressionism was a growing force, many artists and critics had dimly begun to recall the exile of Monet, Pissarro, and Sisley in London during the Franco-Prussian War of 1870–71 and their encounter with the work of Turner, Constable, and Crome. This led to an extraordinary revision of art history which was expressed in 1904 by Wynford Dewhurst in his largely sympathetic book *Impressionist Painting: Its Genesis and Development*. In an absurd attempt to claim Impressionism as an English phenomenon he

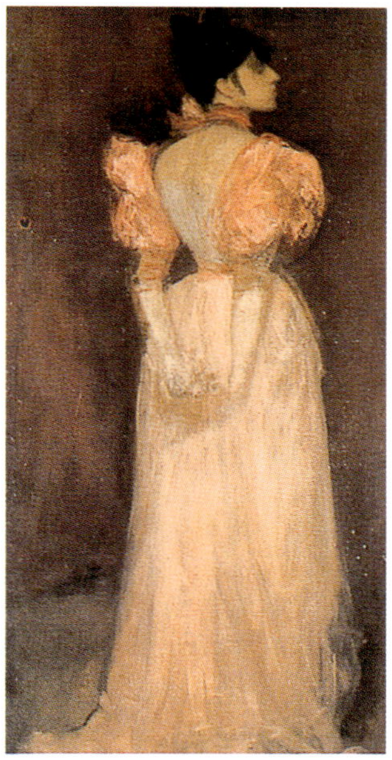

WHISTLER
The Pink Tulip
oil on canvas
c.1870. 190.5 × 89 cm
ABOVE A great admirer of Velazquez, Whistler has used in this portrait a background as dark as those used by the seventeenth-century Spanish master.

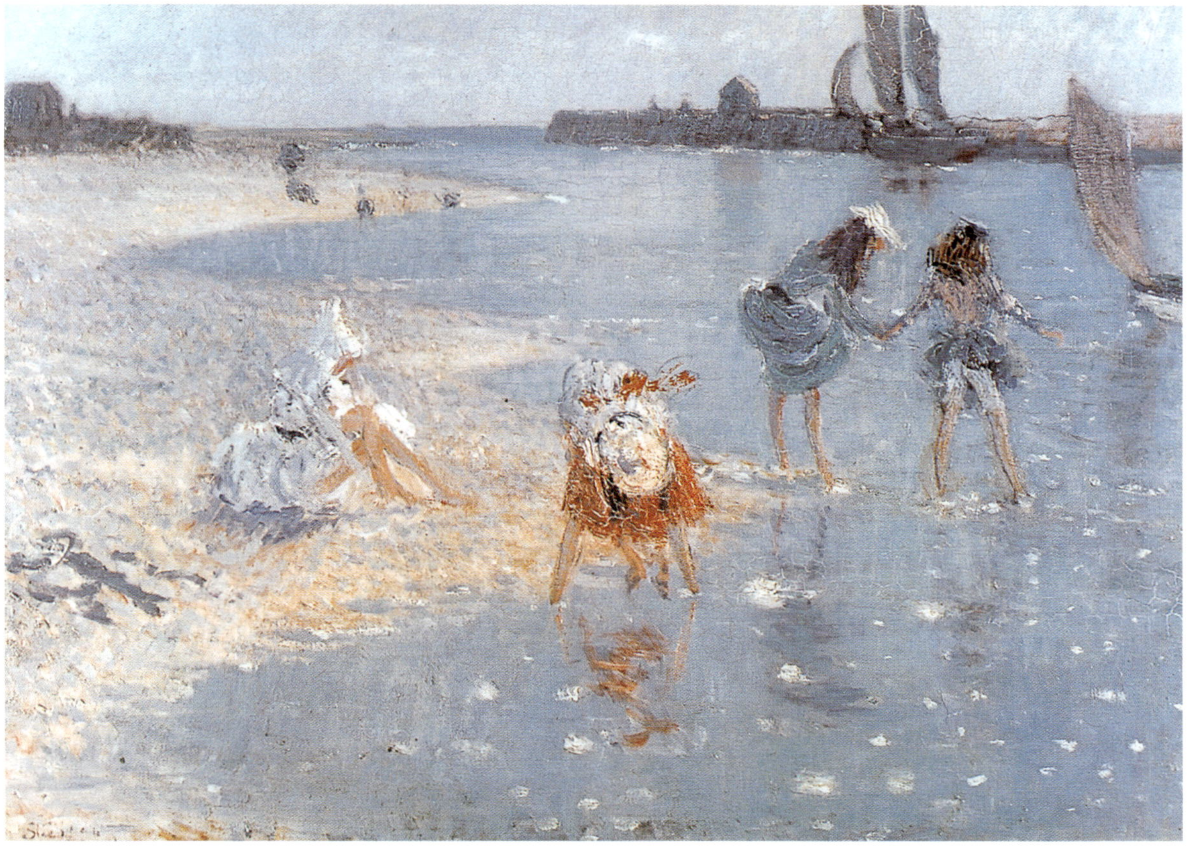

STEER
At the Seaside
oil on canvas
1894. 64 × 92.4 cm
LEFT Steer's paintings show the pleasant scenes found in most Impressionist works, and he treats them with light, elegant layers of brushstrokes reminiscent of Morisot.

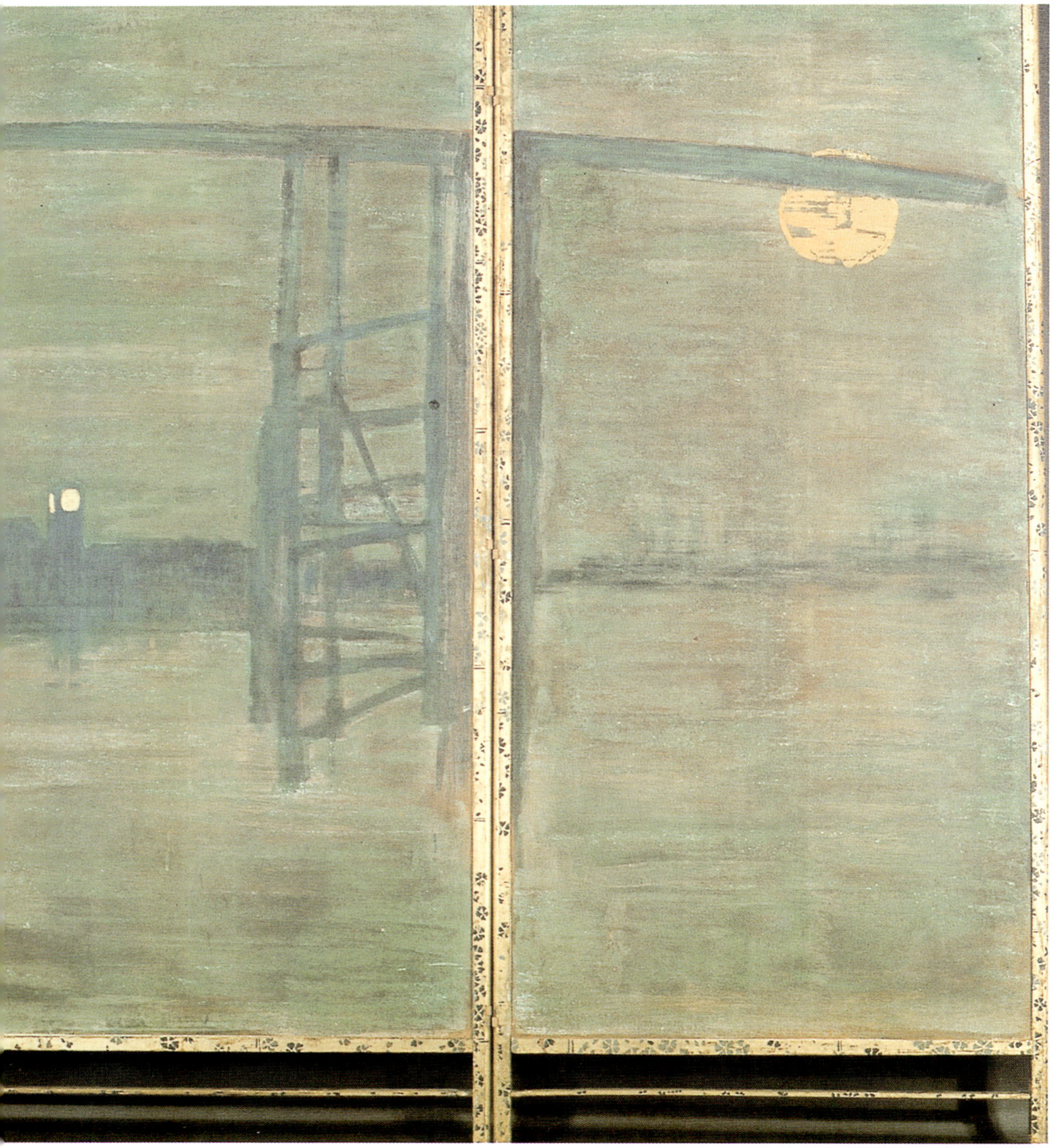

WHISTLER
Blue and Silver: Screen with the Old Battersea Bridge
oil on canvas
1872. 172 × 84 cm
Whistler blended Impressionism and Japanese composition. Degas said of this picture that Whistler "has really found a personal note in this well-balanced expression, a mysterious blending of land and water."

crowed: "Those Englishmen who are taunted with following the methods of the French Impressionists, sneered at for imitating a foreign style, are in reality but practising their own, for the French artists simply developed a style which was English in its conception." While it is true that Turner and Constable may have had a profound influence on Delacroix and the Barbizon school, the cultural and historical distance between them and Monet, Pissarro, Sisley, and Renoir, let alone Manet and Degas, was so great that only the most blinkered of British bulldogs could claim otherwise.

Durand-Ruel's London gallery in New Bond Street was the major conduit of French Impressionism onto the English art market in the 1870s and 1880s. His exhibitions of Impressionist stock from Paris, which he presented as the Society of French Artists, caused much controversy but sold painfully few paintings. The National Gallery and the Tate both resisted offers of Impressionist works. However one enlightened collector, Sir Hugh Percy Lane, offered an important collection of Impressionist works, including Renoir's *Umbrellas* and Manet's *Music in the Tuileries Gardens*, on loan to the National Gallery where they were accepted but then put in storage until 1917.

This philistinism aside, by the late 1880s there was a significant body of English artists who were more appreciative of the important developments in France; an appreciation enshrined in the New English Art Club founded in 1886. Among its members were Walter Sickert, Philip Wilson Steer, George Clausen, Henry Herbert La Thangue, and William Rothenstein, all of whom subtly practised English variants of Impressionism. However, two important figures to influence English

Impressionism were the American expatriates James Abbott McNeill Whistler and John Singer Sargent, a founder member of the Club. Whistler, born in 1834 and thus a contemporary of Pissarro, Manet, and Degas, had left America in 1855 and studied at Gleyre's academy. He soon caused uproar at the 1863 Salon des Refusés with *The White Girl* and was influential in the development of Manet and Degas. Although his flirtation with the beginnings of Impressionism in the 1860s was brief, he was a supporter of Monet, introducing his work to Britain, and the teacher of Sickert. He was involved in a notorious libel action in 1877 against the doyen of English art theorists John Ruskin, who had savagely attacked his picture *Nocturne in Black and Gold: The Falling Rocket.* Although he won symbolic damages of one farthing against Ruskin, the costs of the case were enormous and Whistler was ruined.

John Singer Sargent was born in Boston in 1856 and studied art in Florence and Paris before moving to London and settling in Chelsea in 1884. Throughout the late 1880s he was in frequent contact with Claude Monet, visiting him at Giverny and producing in 1887 his own *plein-air* homage to the master, *Claude Monet Painting at the Edge of a Wood.* Though he made his name with portraiture, Sargent's Impressionist pictures, tangibly influenced by his close contact with Monet, were held in high esteem by his English contemporaries.

The English application of French Impressionism was of necessity always an ambivalent matter, conscious, as most of the Impressionistic English painters were, of their debt to their French neighbours. Nevertheless English art eventually took Impressionism in a watered-down form as its mainstream mode of expression and it held sway in the art academies and clubs until well into the 1920s. The absence of striking images in the English versions of Impressionism is perhaps a symptom of the conservative nature of the society at the turn of the century. Artists like Laura Knight who produced bright and popular beach scenes tinged by Impressionism exemplify the strange and unconvincing awkwardness of expressing English subjects in a French light. Fortunately the impressionable but largely unoriginal English art world was shaken to its roots on 8th November 1910 when Roger Fry organized the first Post-Impressionist exhibition in London with works by van Gogh, Gauguin, Cézanne, Denis, Redon, Matisse, and Picasso. The term "Post-Impressionist" was first coined at the exhibition which stimulated a new generation of artists on to more radical things.

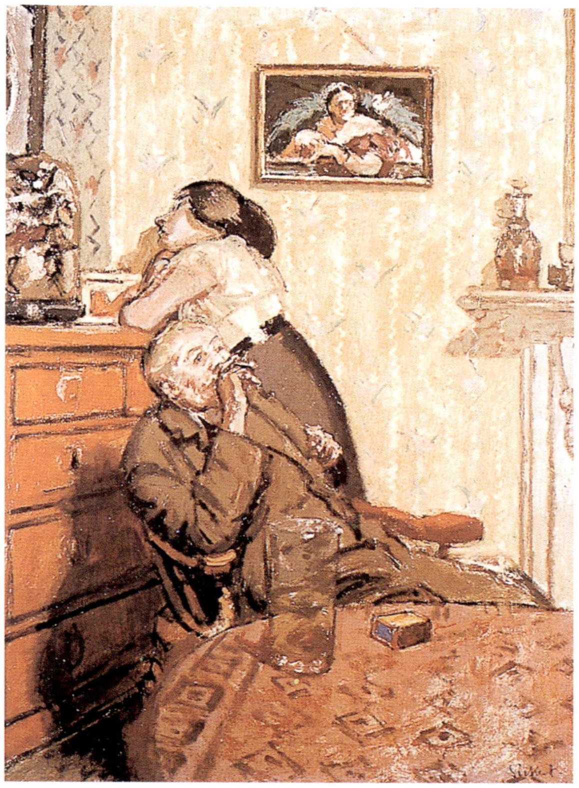

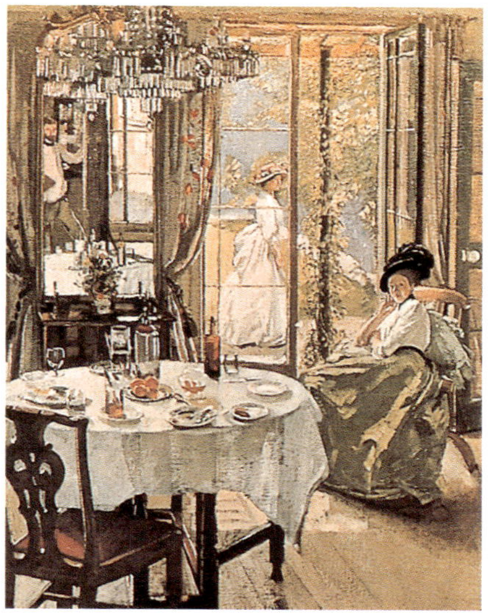

CONNARD
Interior at Chelsea
oil on canvas
c.1914.
ABOVE The artist, who was born in 1875, was one of the founder members of the New English Art Club, partly set up in support of the Impressionists' style and works. In this very late picture, Connard shows how well he has assimilated the lessons of the works Monet was producing at the time of Connard's birth: the light coming from the garden is shed on a relaxed, middle-class interior.

SICKERT
Ennui
oil on canvas
c.1914. 76 × 56 cm
LEFT Sickert's style mainly shows the influence of Degas, and he was attracted by scenes with a social content. This relatively late work is indeed very close to Degas in style and composition.

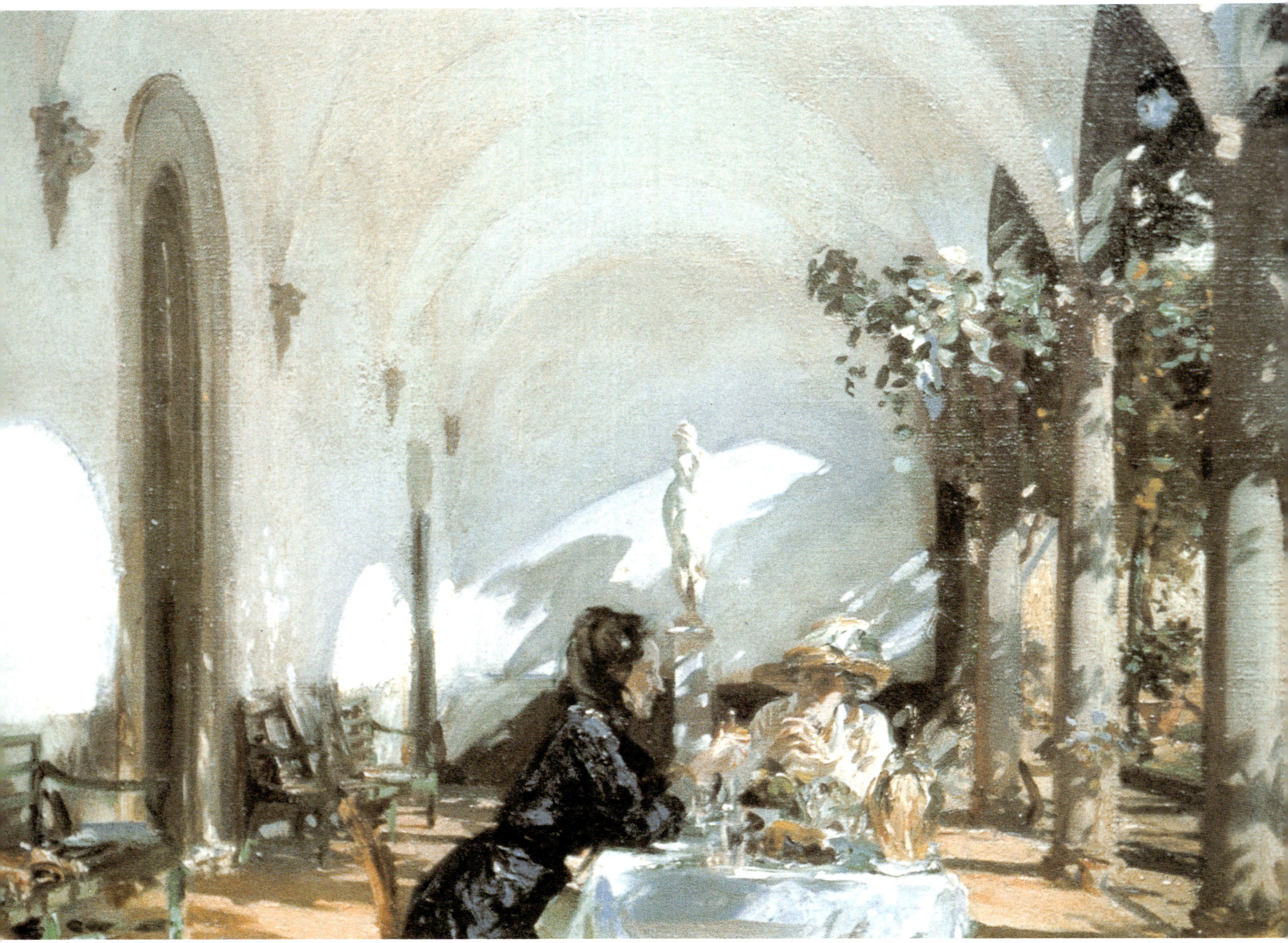

AMERICAN IMPRESSIONISM

WITHIN A DECADE of the first Impressionist exhibition of 1874 the influence of the work of Manet, Monet, Renoir, Pissarro, Morisot and the others was evident to varying degrees all over Britain and Europe – in Belgium, Holland, Germany, Spain, Italy, Romania, and Russia. It also spread to Australia and of course North America.

As we shall see, French Impressionism was received in the United States with much less resistance than in England. It was also inevitable that artists such as Mary Cassatt, so close to the centre of French Impressionism, Theodore Robinson and Lilla Cabot Perry who had worked at Giverny with Monet, would promote Impressionism in the artistic vacuum that existed back home. Two American expatriates in England, Sargent and Whistler, also played an important part in familiarizing their fellow countrymen with Impressionism. Scores of young Americans crossed the Atlantic to study in the ateliers of Paris and elsewhere in Europe in the last two decades of the nineteenth century. They returned to set up their own schools and groups strongly influenced by Impressionism and its aftermath. The result was a brief but late flourishing of the Impressionist idiom in the United States, giving rise to a handful of American Impressionist masterpieces.

SARGENT
Breakfast in the Loggia
oil on canvas
1910. 51.5 × 71 cm
(DETAIL)

American Impressionism

Whether for good or bad, for long or for short, [Impressionism] is the active influence in the art of today . . . it has resulted in an added brilliance of light and color that is refreshing . . .

Modern Art reviewing the Columbian Exposition in Chicago, 1893

The emergence of Impressionism as a dominant force in the hitherto brief history of American art was a development which was inevitable and evolutionary, given the intimate contact between American and French artists in the latter part of the nineteenth century. Americans had in fact been studying art in Paris since the 1840s and returning to set up ateliers to communicate their formal training to their contemporaries, steadily increasing the small number of academically trained artists in the population. The subjects these artists generally chose to paint were portraits, genre works and of course the vast landscape. Several discrete schools of landscape painting had grown up in America by the 1850s centred on specific areas of the country, including the well-known Hudson River School whose notional founder was Thomas Cole (1801–1848). His work, and that of the landscapists who followed him, notably Frederick Church (1826–1900), were spectacular

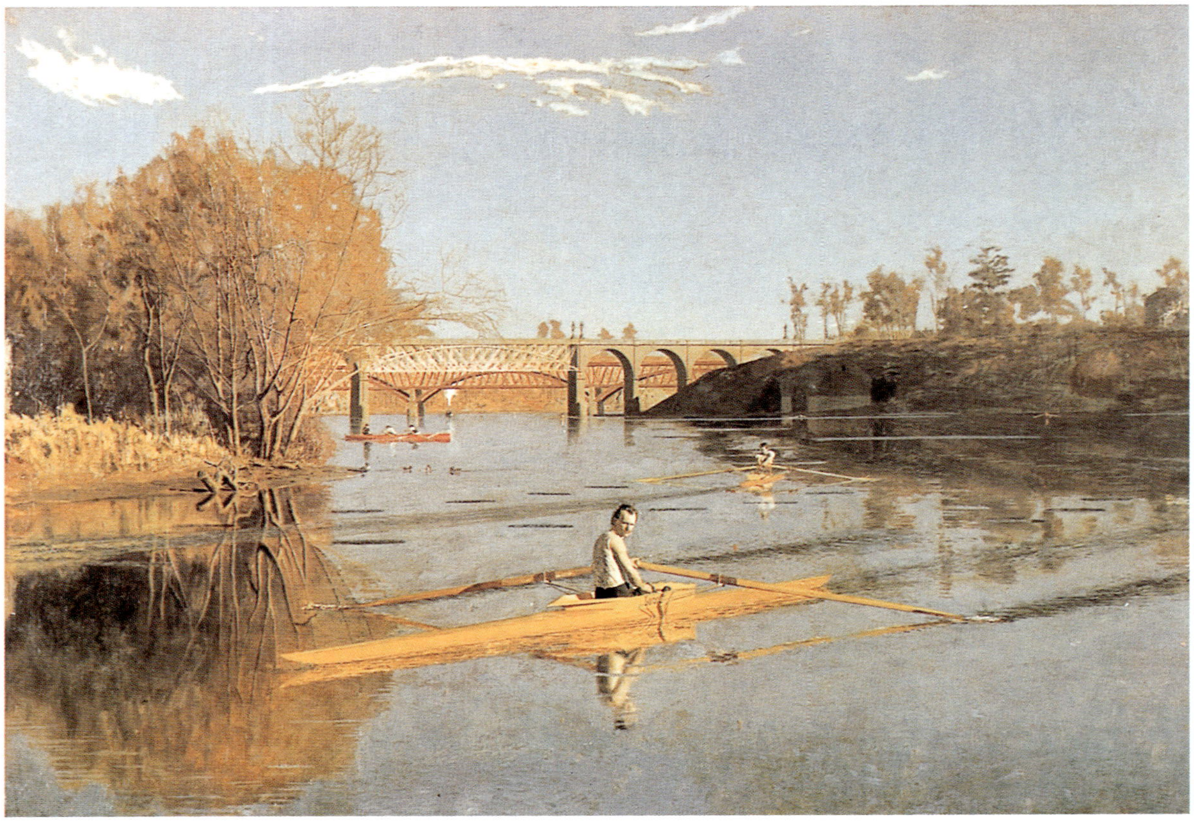

EAKINS
Max Schmitt in a Single Scull
oil on canvas
1871. 82 × 117.5 cm
This picture fails to be Impressionist because Eakins depicted what he knew was there instead of what he really saw, but the subject matter, one of his favourites, and the composition, are very contemporary.

attempts to come to terms with the American landscape using naturalistic and symbolic devices adapted from mainstream European landscape painting. Church's work is an epic attempt to depict the wild forests, the purple-headed mountains and the blood-red skies to the glory of God.

In the absence of Western civilization in great tracts of America, the devout pioneering artists placed their trust in the wonders of God's creation, but individualistic landscapists, such as Fitz Hugh Lane (1804–1865) and John F. Kensett (1818–1872), soon began to concern themselves with the more transitory effects of light and became associated with an important movement known appropriately enough as the Luminists.

By the 1880s, when Impressionism had begun to appear as the modern mode of painting to American artists, the history of post-colonial America itself was barely more than a century old. Nevertheless, the rapid growth of the American bourgeoisie coincided with the influx of French and European Impressionist art, resulting in new ways of depicting modern life. There was, however, no sense in which the American Impressionist would attempt to fulfill Baudelaire's criteria for a "Painting of Modern Life", which Manet and Degas had done some decades before in

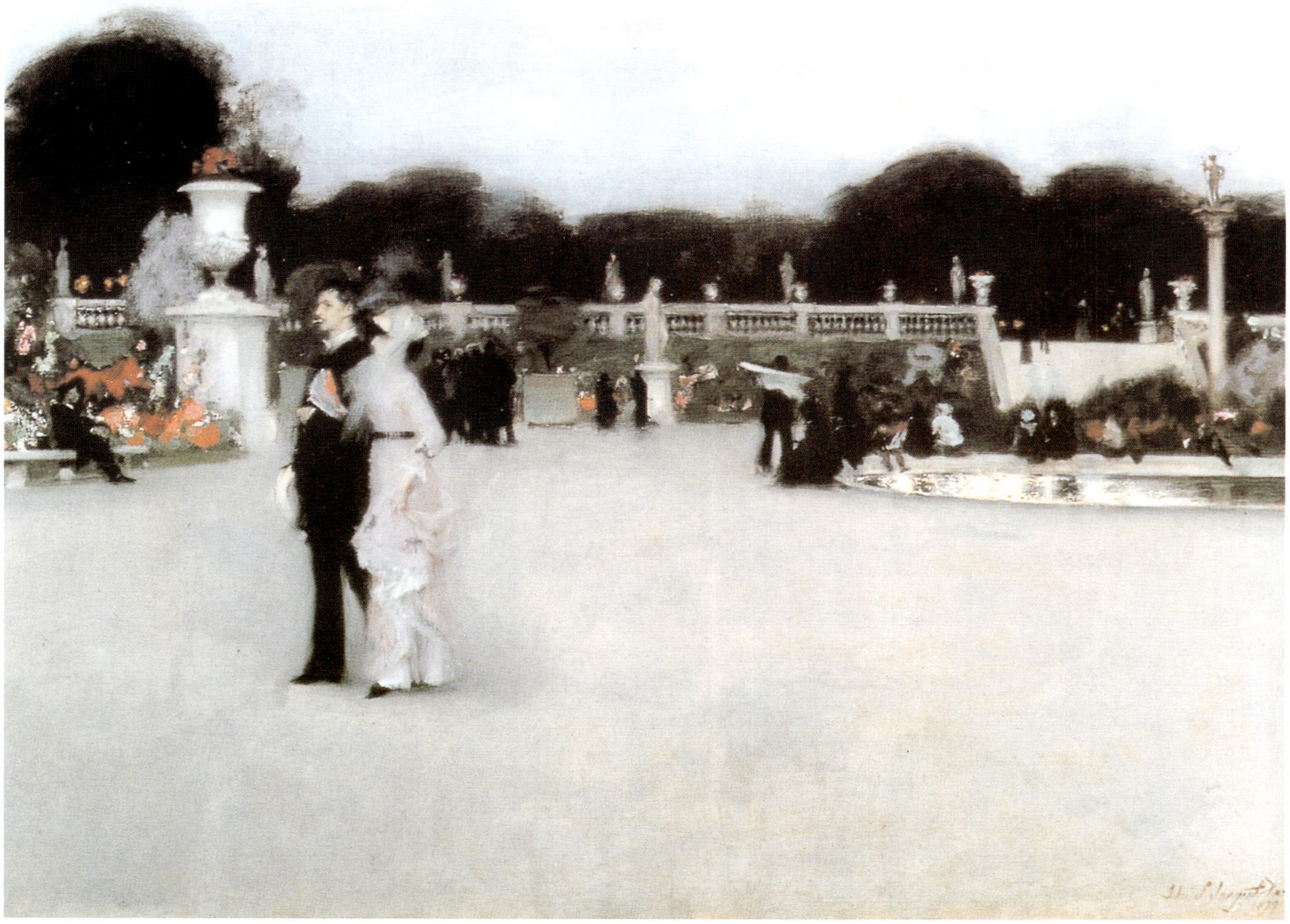

SARGENT
In the Luxembourg Gardens
oil on canvas
1879. 65 × 91 cm
Sargent, along with Whistler and Cassatt, is another American expatriate. Twelve years younger than Cassatt, he had trained in Germany before enrolling in the Beaux-Arts of Paris in 1874. His visit to the Impressionists' show of 1876 was a revelation for a painter who was already fascinated by the changing effects of light. However, his training with the well-known portrait painter Carolus-Duran taught him skills which were to bring him fame and fortune but distract him from purely impressionistic works. We can see in this picture that he has not yet put into practise the stylistic brushwork of his new friends, such as Monet, whom he admired.

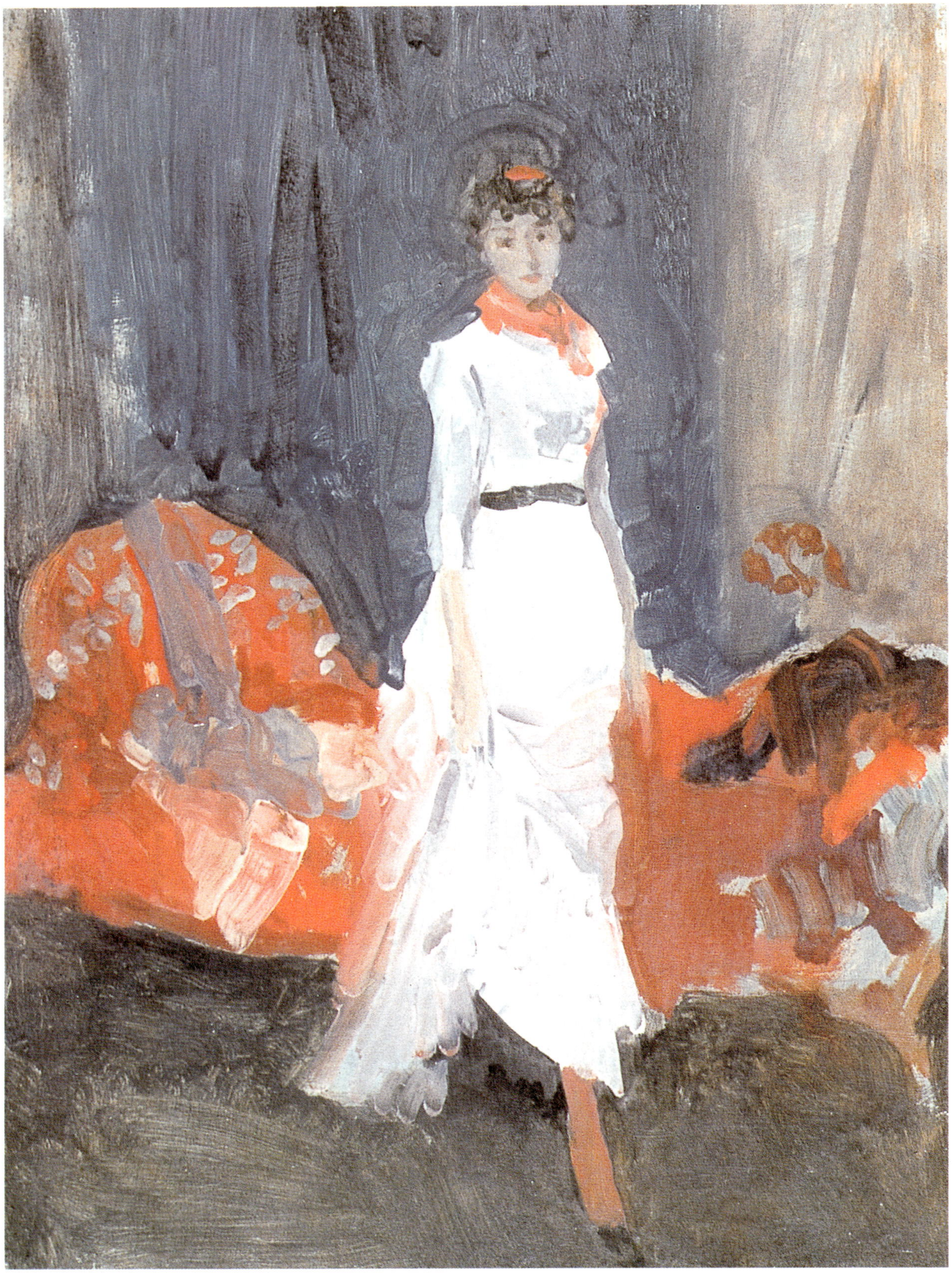

WHISTLER
Arrangement in Pink and Purple
oil on wood
1881–85. 30.5 × 23 cm
LEFT Whistler was at Gleyre's atelier in 1855, a few years before the other young Impressionists. He was closely associated with the movement in the 1860s, and influenced Manet and Degas in particular, both of whom copied pieces by him. By the time he painted this piece he had gone through a period heavily inspired by the new influx of Japanese artefacts into Europe and the United States, and moved on into a phase in which he became allied to the Aesthetic movement. This group was typified by Oscar Wilde in England, who shocked American audiences during his precociously affected reading tour of the United States in 1882.

SARGENT
Mrs Henry White
oil on canvas
1883. 220 × 139 cm
RIGHT Sargent made his fortune with society portraits like this. Not surprisingly, he had studied in Paris with a celebrated portrait painter, Carolus Duran. The influence of Velazquez and Manet is evident in Singer's virtuosic brushwork and detached observation of his subject. Like Manet, Sargent was accused by critics of being cold and impersonal in his vision, although the wealthy queued up to have their portraits painted by the most fashionable portraitist of his day.

Paris. Likewise, as William Gerdts notes, "The Impressionist painters rarely ventured out into raw, unexplored or uncultivated nature, and the concern with wilderness and unbounded space was minimal." It was almost as though the relatively small-scale nature of the landscape of northern France, where Impressionism had been born, had found a corollary in New England and other eastern States where the landscape was similarly bounded, civilized, and manageable.

It is not surprising that probably the first painting by a French Impressionist to be publicly shown in the United States was Degas' *A Ballet*, exhibited at the American Water Color Society in 1878. The picture was lent by Mr J. Elder and had been bought by a close friend of Mary Cassatt, Louisine Elder, later to become Mrs H.O. Havemeyer. Degas had been in New Orleans in 1872, when he began painting one of his first masterpieces, the *Cotton Market*, and his association with the expatriate Mary Cassatt had furthered the links between the New World and the new French painting. A year later Manet's *Execution of the Emperor Maximilian*, previously banned in Paris during the Second Empire because it was perceived as a criticism of Napoleon III's foreign policy in Mexico, was shown in New York. It had been brought over by a Mrs Emilie Ambré of Colonel Mapleson's Italian Opera Company in an attempt to cash in on the painting's notoriety and was put on show at the Clarendon Hotel in New York and then at the Studio Building Gallery in Boston. The poster for the show read: "Come in! Come in and see the famous picture by the famous painter Ed Manet!"

Although Manet and Degas were considered to be the leaders of the Impressionists at the time, the two pictures first shown in

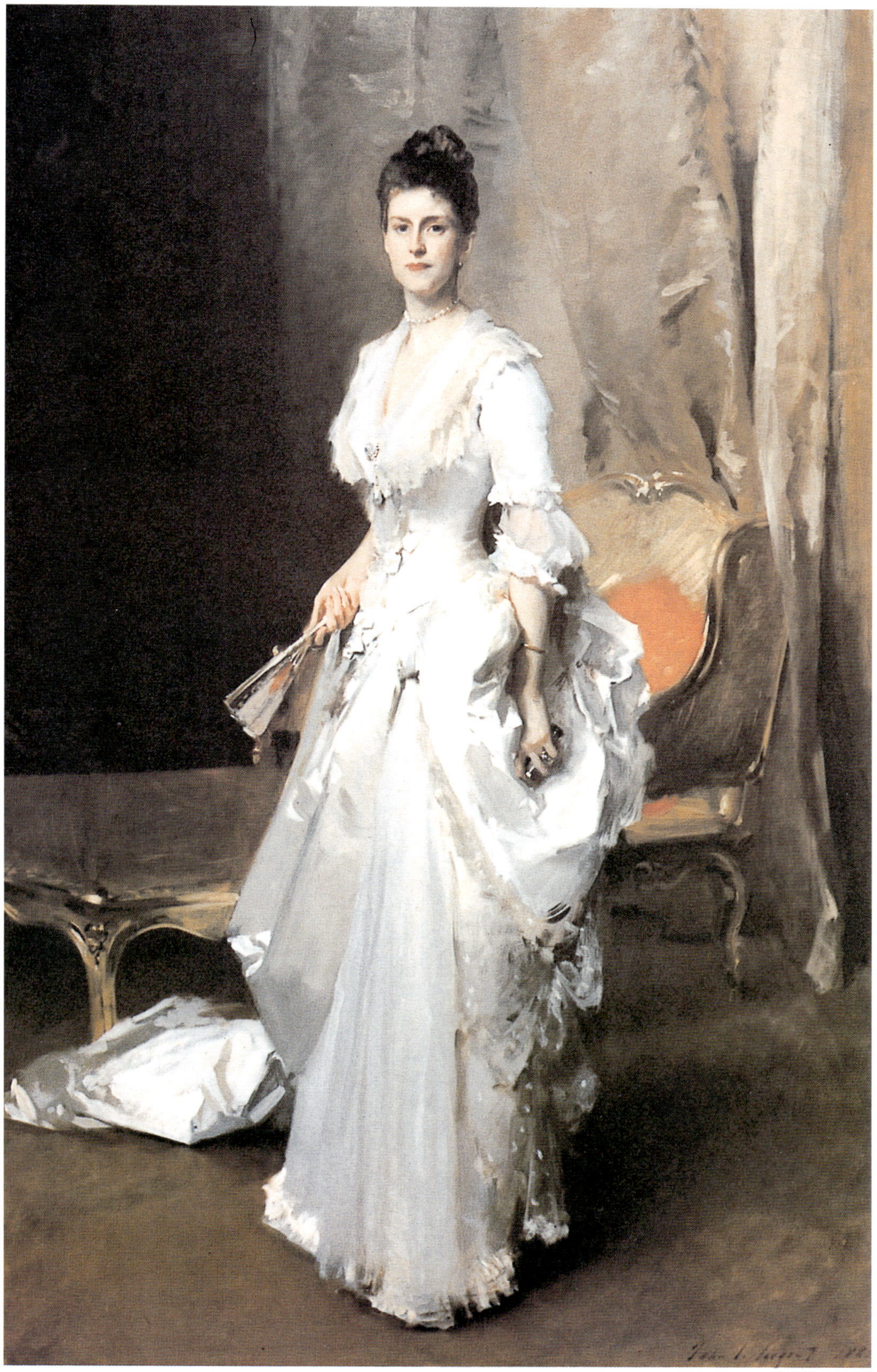

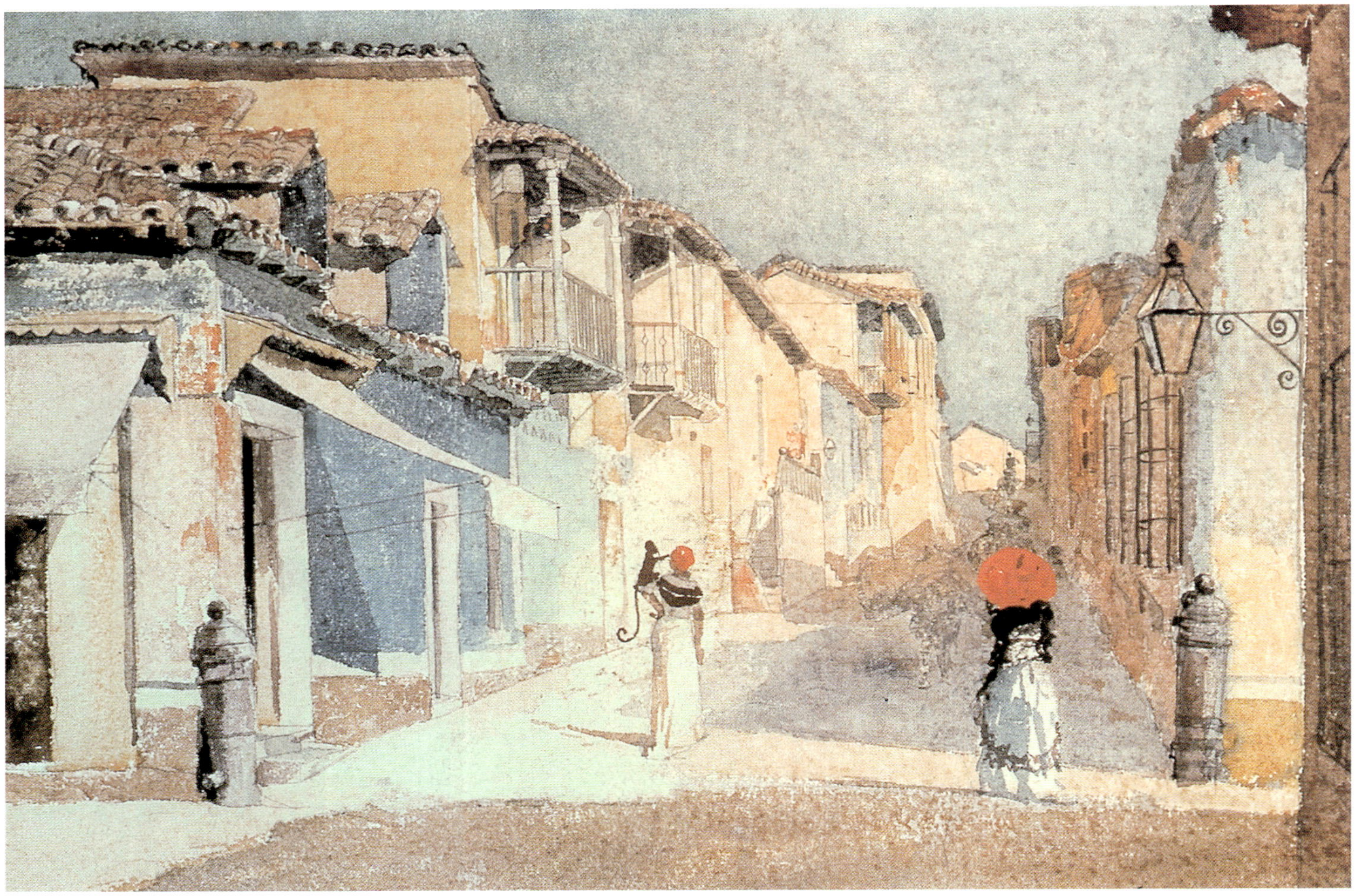

HOMER
Street Scene, Havana
watercolour on canvas
1885. 39 × 44 cm
Homer trained himself from magazines illustrations, but went to Paris in 1867, where he was impressed by Manet's strongly contrasted use of colours. He went on developing his own style, in which light plays a major part. "I paint the subject exactly as it appears," he said, and this could apply to any realist, good or bad, because what matters is the quality of their vision.

America were hardly representative of the main thrust of Impressionism, in the work of Monet, Pissarro, Renoir, or Morisot for example. Thus it was not until 1883 when the major Impressionist dealer Paul Durand-Ruel supplied works for the 1883 International Exhibition for Art and Industry in Boston, sponsored by the French government, that the American public and critics got their first real glimpse of the new painting. The same year William Merritt Chase and Carroll Beck organized the Pedestal Exhibition to raise funds for the base of Bartholdi's Statue of Liberty (Liberty herself had been donated by France), showing several Barbizon and Impressionist works.

The first major Impressionist show in the United States took place in April 1886 when the American Art Association mounted an exhibition under the title "Works in Oil and Pastel by the Impressionists of Paris". The show was masterminded by James F. Sutton and Thomas Kirby and featured Durand-Ruel's stable of artists including Manet, Degas, Monet, Pissarro, Renoir, Seurat, Cassatt, Caillebotte, and Sisley. At the time Durand-Ruel was in serious financial trouble and selling few works in Paris. The New York exhibition was so popular that it enjoyed a second run in the National Academy of Design, where it was augmented by twenty-one Impressionist works from private American

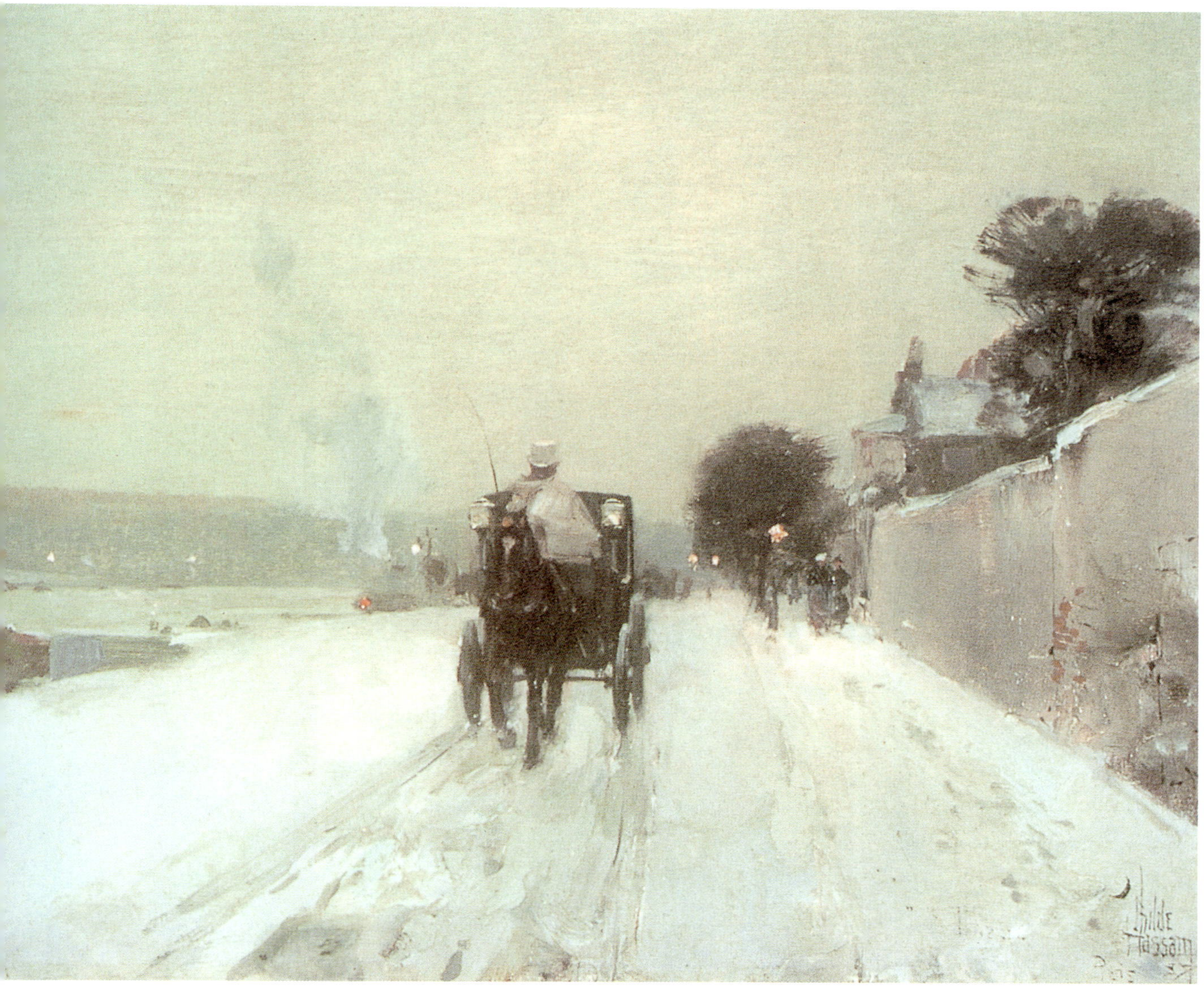

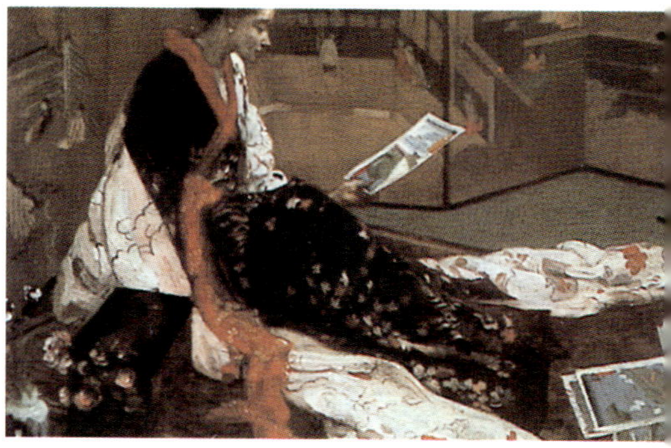

WHISTLER
Harmony in Purple and Gold: the Golden Screen
1864.
ABOVE Whistler was among the very first artists of his time to be fascinated by Japanese art.

HASSAM
Along the Seine, winter
oil on canvas
1887. 20 × 28 cm
LEFT Hassam studied at the Académie Julian in Paris in the late 1880s and produced some overtly impressionistic pictures which are a development of his Boston paintings of 1885–86 and show a concern for perspective strikingly similar to that of Gustave Caillebotte.

collections. In the end Durand-Ruel made $18,000 which saved his desperately ailing business and helped his artists considerably. Sutton had convinced the customs authorities to allow Durand-Ruel to import the pictures tax free under the guise of educational tools for aspiring American artists to study, although a high tariff had to be paid on works that were actually sold in the country.

Compared to the contempt shown to the Impressionists in London, American critics were positively encouraging in their reviews of the 1886 show. One critic by the name of Luther Hamilton writing in *Cosmopolitan* magazine was fulsome with praise; the show was "a glorious protest against the everlasting commonplace, which is another way of saying that its pictures are that rarest thing, a record of the artists' own impressions, not, as usual, their reminiscences of other pictures." Although the American art critics were still to a great extent learning their trade and producing some remarkably naïve opinions, on the whole their attitude, and that of the American

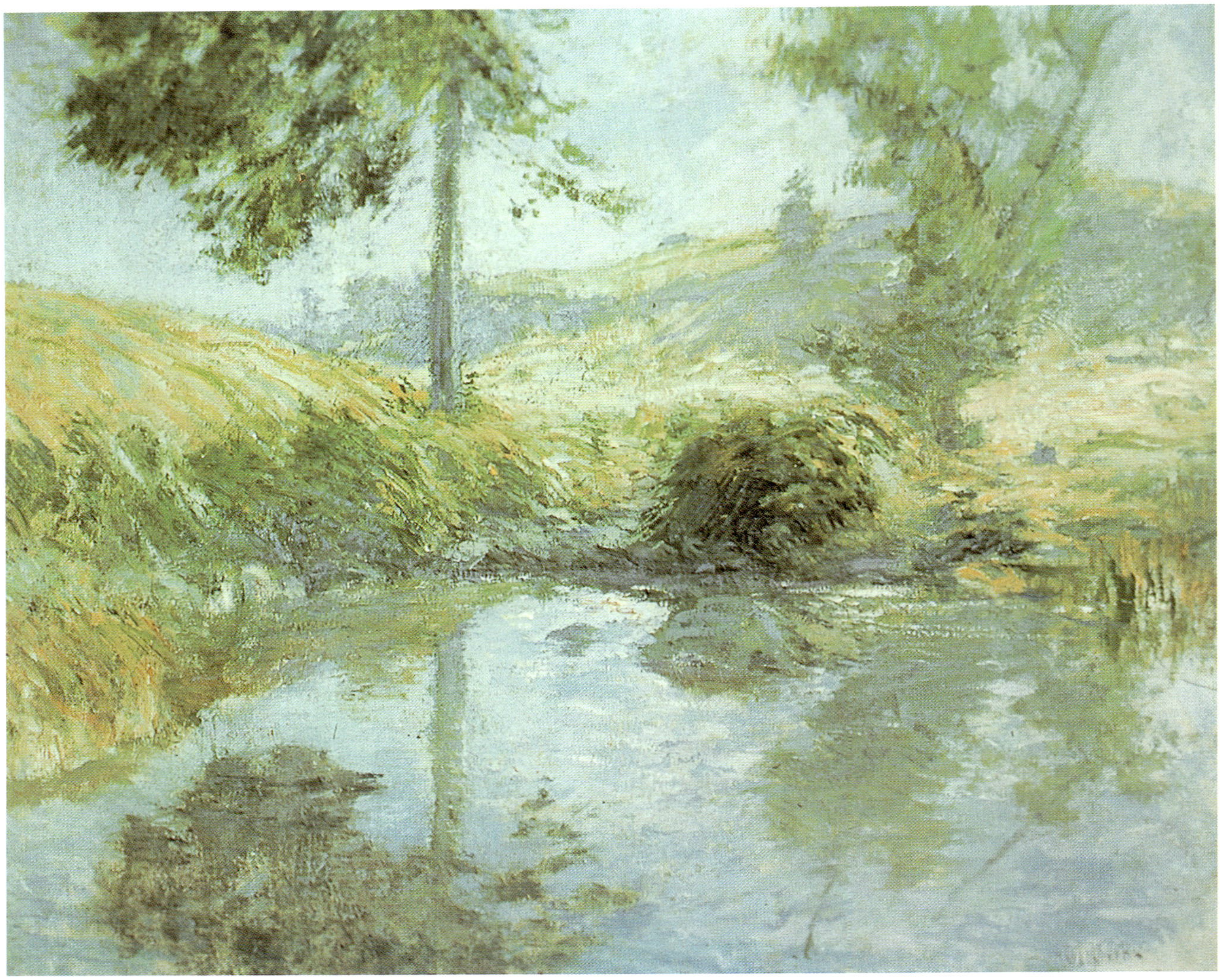

TWACHTMAN
The Pool
oil on canvas
c.1890. 26 × 31 cm
Born in 1853, Twachtman travelled to Europe in 1875, studying in Munich and Venice; where he was accompanied by William Meritt Chase and Whistler, who had some influence over his style. Back in the United States, he settled in New York and married, which provided him with the pretext for another extended trip to Europe, painting with the American Weir in Holland. His visit to Paris was a turning point in his career. He joined a studio in 1883, where he met Hassam, Metcalf and other American students catching up with the last of the Impressionist movement. Of this style, he only kept some elements, short brushstrokes and the effects of light and shade, as in this painting, executed four years after his return home.

public, was refreshingly free of the crusty views shown by many European critics. However, some American artists and critics were less than entranced by Impressionism. The most famous American landscapist of the day, George Innes, whose work was heavily indebted to the Barbizon School, had pronounced somewhat cryptically in 1884 in a letter to the art critic Ripley Hitchcock that: " . . . Impressionism is the sloth enrapt in its own eternal dullness . . . " Despite the deep reservations of Innes and several other critics who were perplexed, especially by the violet and purple tonality, the use of pure rainbow pigments, the lack of chiaroscuro and the dissolution of form in Monet, Morisot and the other Impressionists, the receptive conditions in America by and large favoured the new art and by the end of the 1890s it was firmly entrenched as a valid manifestation. Certainly by 1893 and the Columbian Exposition in Chicago, Impressionism was irreversibly established. As the new Indianapolis periodical *Modern Art* observed in reviewing the Exposition:

> Although the great Impressionists are but meagerly represented, there is no lack of

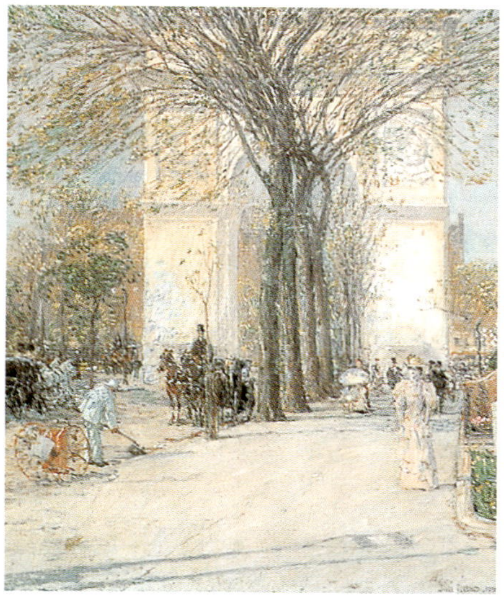

HASSAM
Washington Arch, Spring
oil on canvas
1890. 69 × 57 cm
ABOVE In choosing to paint a frontal view of the monumental arch, Hassam then broke down the overwhelming architecture by placing a row of trees in front of it. In so doing, he avoided to make a purely topographical picture.

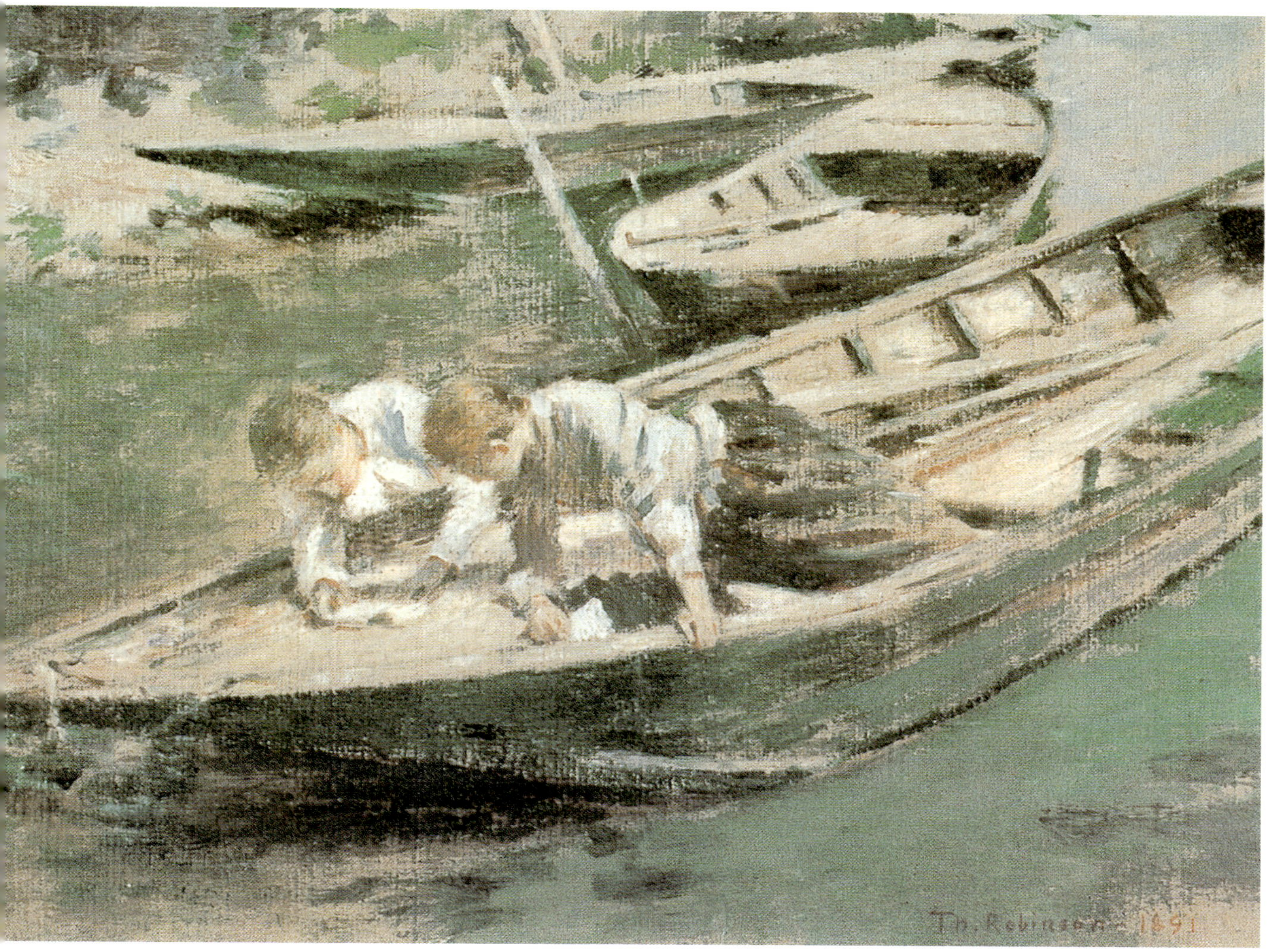

ROBINSON
Two in a Boat
oil on board
1891. 23 × 35 cm
LEFT Had he not died prematurely, Theordore Robinson would probably have been a member of The Ten. Despite the fact that he only took to Impressionism towards the end of the 1880s, he was a vital influence in its popularization in the United States, having spent eight years in and around Paris and a frequent visitor to Giverny. This painting was made after a photograph and displays some of the affinity Robinson also had with the American Realists Eakins and Winslow Homer.

> Impressionism. In fact, one sees it on every hand in the French, American, and Scandinavian collections. Among these nations one feels it on every side. It is in the air, and the great bulk of the pictures show its influence in varying degree. Whether for good or bad, for long or for short, it is the active influence in the art of today. So far, it has resulted in an added brilliance of light and color that is refreshing, and makes a gallery a pleasant contrast to the murkiness of a few years ago, which may even still be seen in some of the art palace exhibitions.

As the historian of American Impressionism William Gerdts notes in his study of the beginnings of the movement, "some of the artists at the Columbian Exposition were dismayed by the Impressionist work and influences. The elderly sporting and animal painter, Arthur Fitzwilliam Tait, complained that the pictures '. . . ain't got no houtlines [sic].' And when the daughter of the Hudson River School landscape painter James Hart was asked if she was an Impressionist, she answered, 'No, I'd like to be, but papa won't allow me!' "

The role of wealthy private collectors was also vital to the encouragement and spread of Impressionism in America. The influence of

Mary Cassatt with the collectors Louisine and Henry Osborne Havemeyer resulted in a major influx of French art, including many important Impressionist works, into the United States. (The Havemeyer collection has been maintained to this day and can be found in the Metropolitan Museum of Art in New York.) By the late 1880s several other collectors, notably Albert Spencer, Desmond Fitzgerald, James S. Inglis, and William H. Fuller, had also begun to invest privately in the Impressionists, and an extensive American market of their work had begun to flourish.

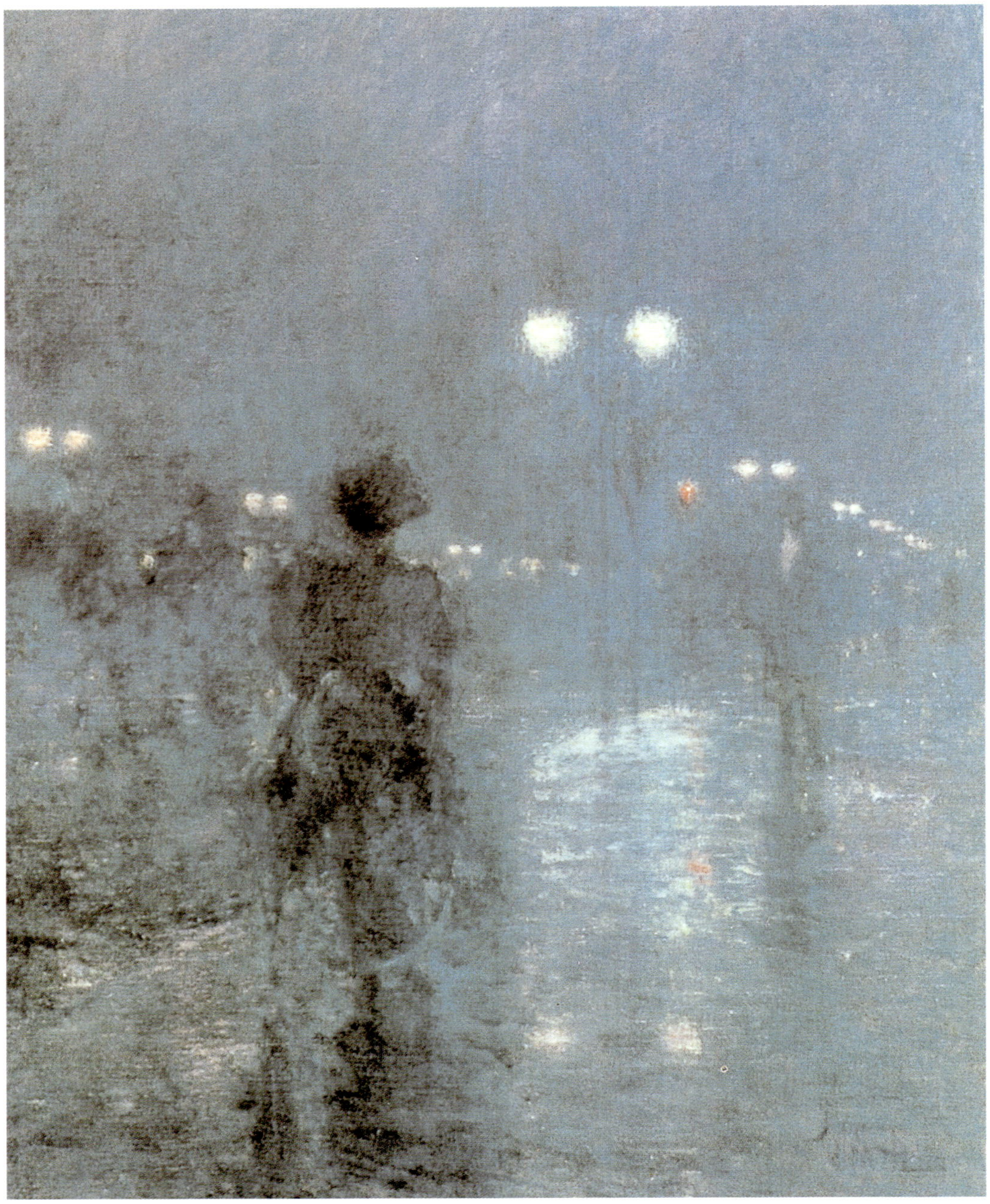

In addition to the expatriates Sargent and Whistler, the American artist Theodore Robinson, born in 1852, was another important link in the growing contact between the Impressionists and the United States. He had studied at the National Academy of Design in New York and arrived in France in 1887. He soon became friends with Monet and spent countless hours painting with him at Giverny and recording his impressions of the great artist in an important diary. Noting the extent of American involvement at the heart of French Impressionism, the *Art Amateur* carried the following report on Boston artists in October 1887: "Quite an American colony had gathered . . . at Giverny, seventy miles from Paris on the Seine, the home of Claude Monet, including our Louis Ritter, W.L. Metcalf, Theodore Wendel, John Breck, and Theodore Robinson of New York. A few pictures just received from these men show that they have got the blue-green color of Monet's impressionism and 'got it bad'." When Robinson returned to the United States in 1892 he became a tireless proponent of Impressionism, encouraging American artists to apply it to their own work.

In 1888, partly to avoid onerous import duties and partly because a substantial market was appearing, Durand-Ruel set up a New York branch which soon became an important outlet for both French and a growing number of American Impressionists. It was here in March 1898 that a group of ten American artists from Boston and New York, many of whom had studied in Paris,

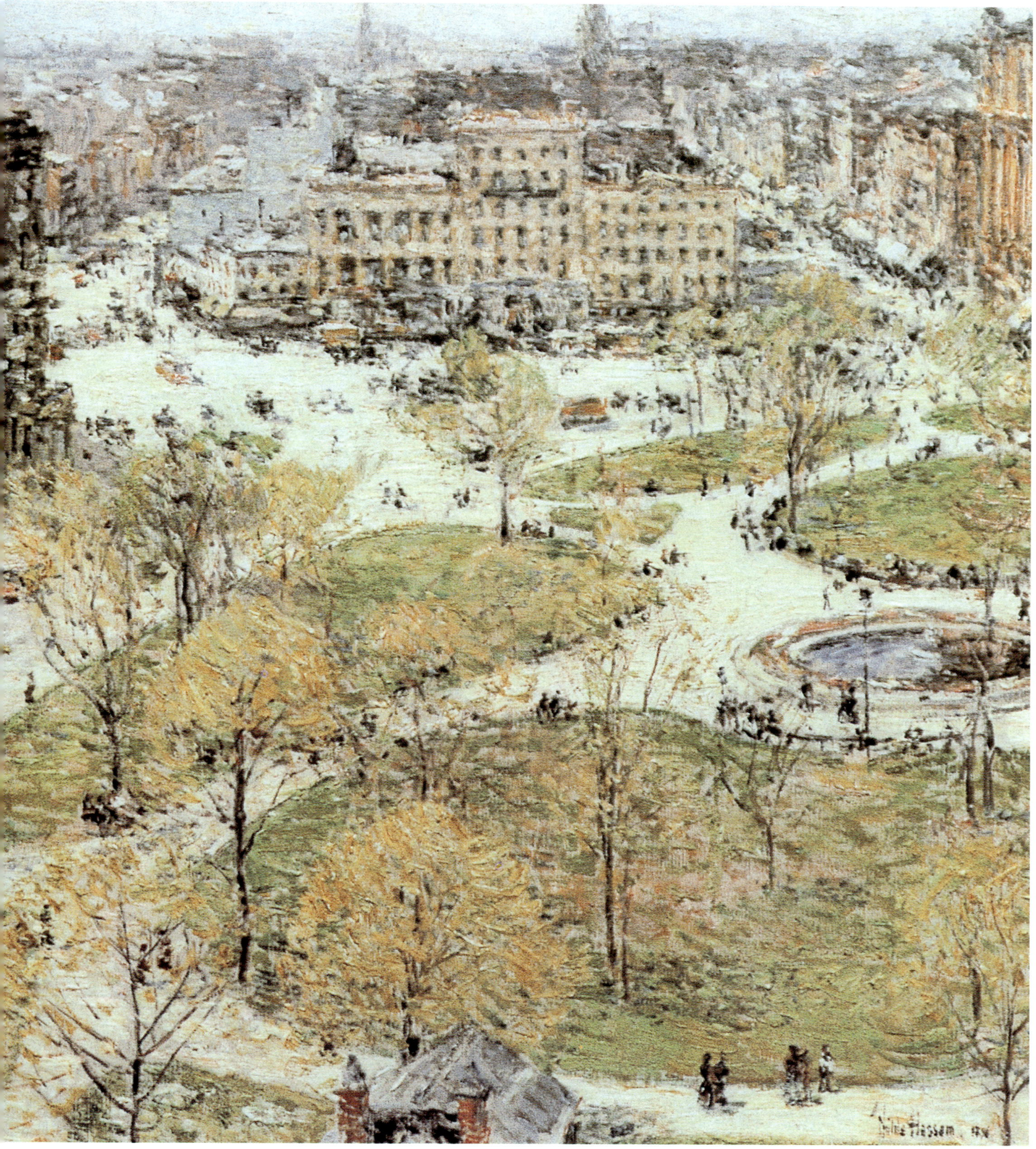

HASSAM
Union Square in Springtime
oil on canvas
1896. 55 × 53 cm
LEFT In contrast to the Impressionists, Hassam did not leave the city, but we can see from this picture that his claim to belong to the Impressionist movement is not without foundation. He had started with urban pictures in the early impressionistic style, and by 1896 he seemed to be mainly influenced by the style of Pissarro's late work.

HASSAM
5th Avenue, Nocturne
oil on canvas
c.1895. 61 × 51 cm
OPPOSITE This Whistlerian scene of New York shows Hassam's much freer style applied to American subjects after his return from Paris in 1889. Hassam lived on 5th Avenue and 17th Street and from this base he devoted himself to depicting the city in a range of moods and weather conditions.

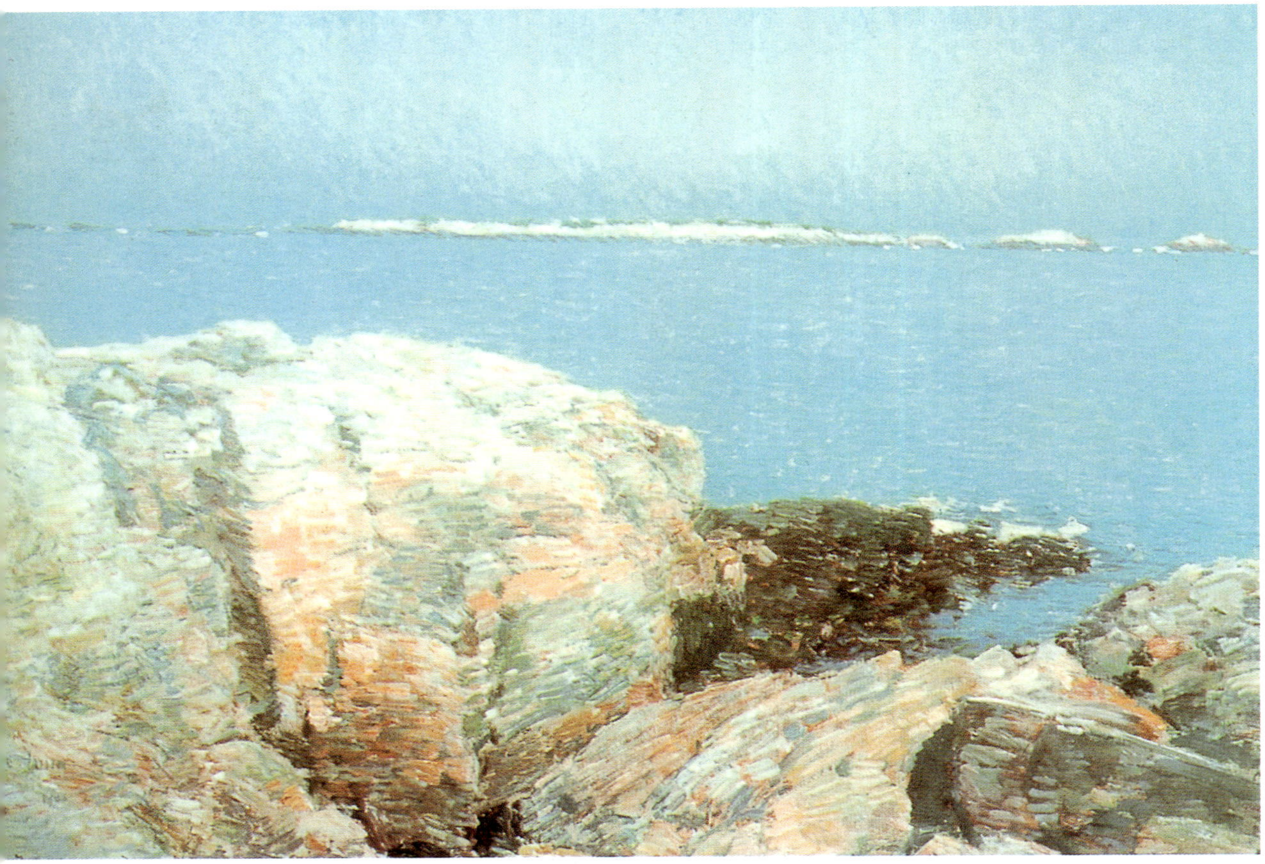

HASSAM
Duck Island
oil on canvas
1906. 49 × 73 cm
Above This luminous picture was painted at the height of American Impressionism, over twenty-five years after the French movement had first exhibited in Paris. The brushstrokes of Hassam are less daring than most of the French artists of the 1880s, but this work has many of the characteristics defining this movement. Meanwhile, Braque and Picasso were already about to start the Cubist movement.

mounted an independent show. They were: Frederick Childe Hassam (1859–1935), Julian Alden Weir (1852–1919), John Henry Twachtman (1853–1902) replaced on death by William Merritt Chase (1849–1916), Willard Metcalf (1858–1925), Edmund Tarbell (1862–1938), Frank Benson (1862–1951), Joseph R. De Camp (1858–1923), Thomas Dewing (1851–1938), Edward E. Simmons (1852–1931) and Robert Reid (1862–1929).

The genesis of "The Ten American Painters" – shortened to "The Ten", as the group came to be known – bears some similarities to the beginnings of the original Impressionists' *Société anonyme* almost a quarter of a century before. "The Ten American Painters" were named by the press, not the artists themselves, who had simply left the Society of American Artists in order to show their work under their own terms. The Society of American Artists had itself been an important forum for new art, breaking away from the National Academy of Design, but its exhibitions had grown too large and generally mediocre for the individualistic talents of The Ten. Although their work was by no means homogenous they showed together until 1918 and thus created the backbone of the American Impressionist movement. Three other names were associated with The Ten at its inception; that of Theodore Robinson, who had died two years before, but would almost certainly have been attracted to the group; Abbott Thayer, who did join (what would have been The Eleven) but ultimately withdrew to stay with the Society of American Artists; and Winslow Homer, who was sympathetic to the group's show but declined its invitation to join.

The Ten did not of course represent all the Impressionists at work in America; figures such as Frederick Frieseke, Robert W. Vonnoh, Allen Tucker, and Edward Henry Potthast were all important Impressionists at work outside The Ten. Nor indeed were The Ten all classical Impressionists. In the late 1890s Impressionism was under attack from several new movements, including Neo-Impressionism, and the beginnings of Post-Impressionism.

Thomas Wilmer Dewing, for example, is regarded as an exponent of Tonalism, a short-lived development of Barbizon landscape painting related to Impressionism, which emphasized a single overall tonality or colour in a subdued, highly atmospheric style avoiding a prismatic palette, and pure pigments applied in swift strokes. Dewing was almost exclusively concerned with the female figure, in some ways a Tonalist Degas. With the

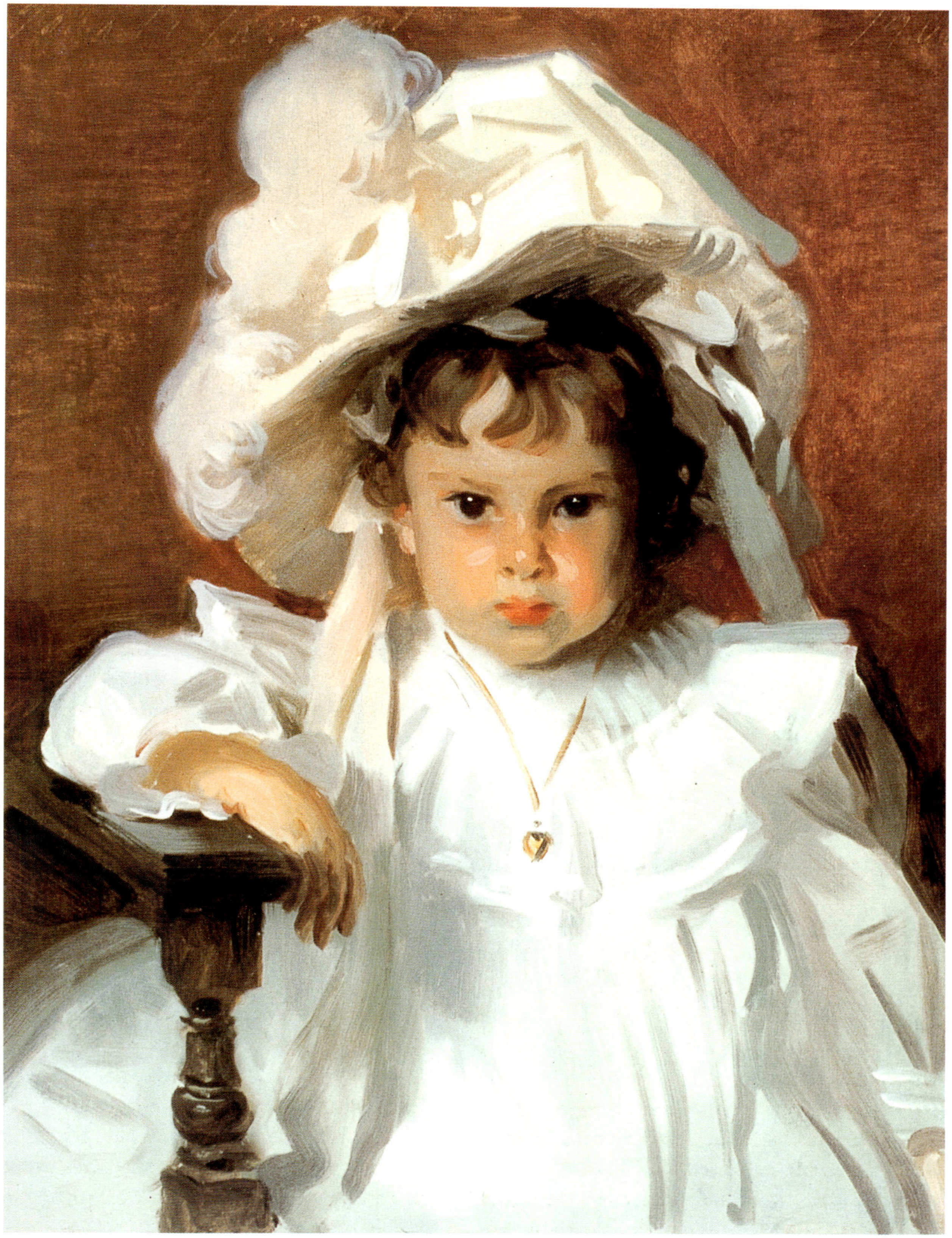

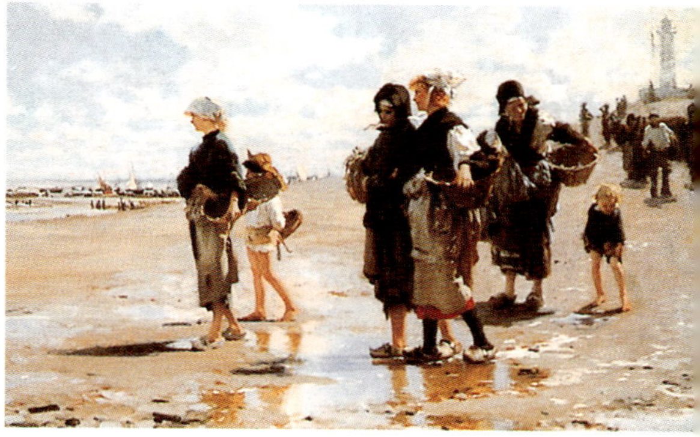

SARGENT
Oyster Gatherers at Cancale, Brittany
oil on canvas
1878. 79 × 123 cm
Above This was the first painting by Sargent accepted at the Salon.

SARGENT
Dorothy
oil on canvas
1900. 60.5 × 50.5 cm
Left Compared with Mary Cassatt's pictures of children, Sargent's portrait is formal and stiffly posed, reflecting the image his clients wanted to see of their offspring in an age when children were to be seen and not heard.

collaboration of his wife Maria Oakey Dewing, who would sometimes paint the natural elements into the pictures, Dewing produced some of the most stunningly ethereal evocations of late nineteenth-century women captured in moments of "deafening silence" and immobility. The land- and city-scapists Metcalf, Twachtman, Weir, and Hassam represent the mainstream of Impressionism in The Ten, although their very individual styles do not fit easily into any textbook definition of Impressionism.

There was nothing radical about the American strain of Impressionism in its choice of urban subject matter either: Impressionists and the members of The Ten stayed away from controversy, depicting cityscapes and figures in a resolutely unchallenged bourgeois environment. But this is not to say that there were no original thinkers amongst the American Impressionists. Even the most heavily influenced of them, Childe Hassam for example, attempted to apply the styles of Monet, Degas, and Renoir to his depiction of America; Hassam's *Union Square in Springtime*, of 1896, vibrates with the memory of Monet's *Garden of the Princess*, but remains true to its American subject.

Amongst his Impressionist contemporaries, the work of John Henry Twachtman

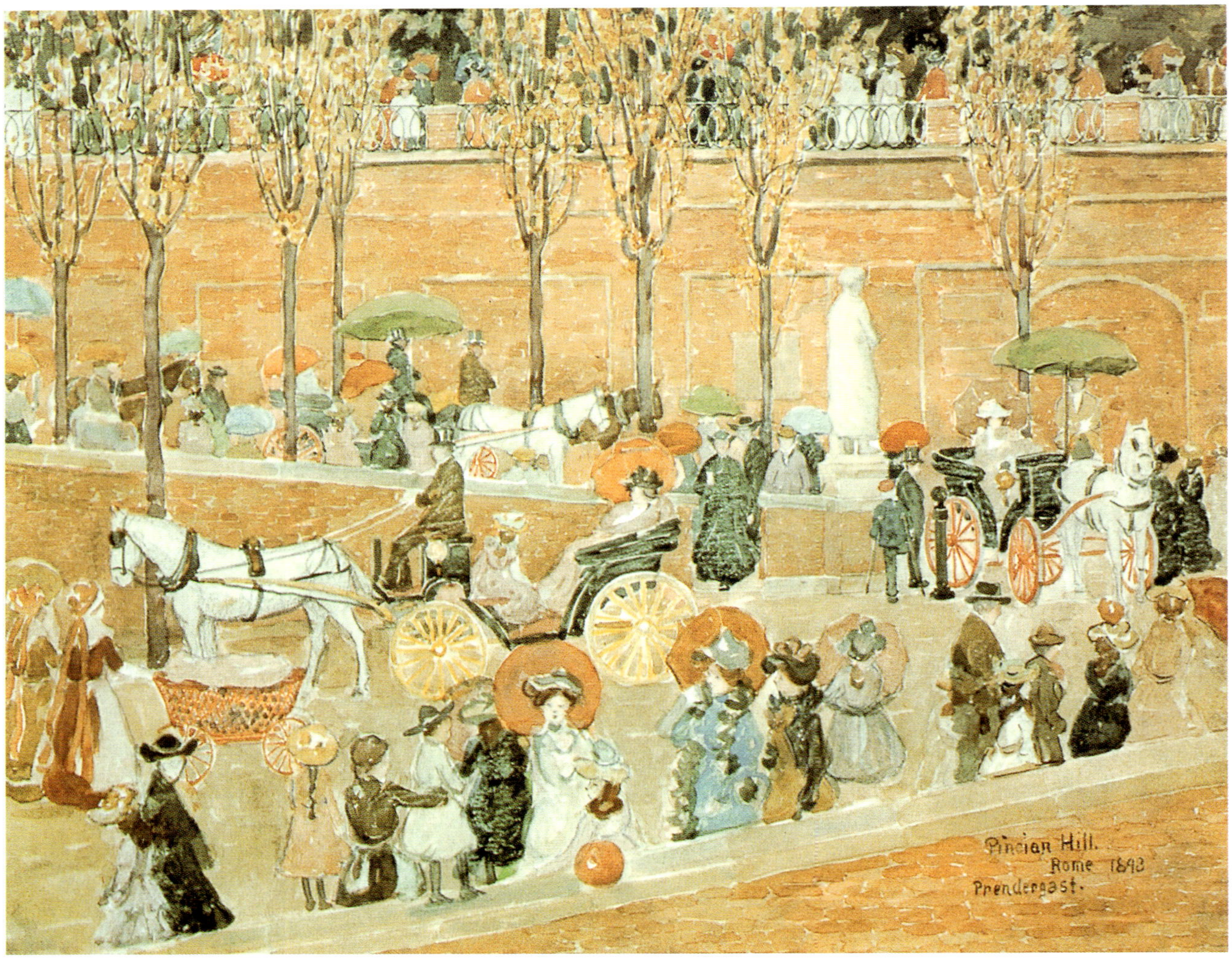

PRENDERGAST
Pincian Hill, Rome
watercolour on canvas
1898. 51 × 67 cm
RIGHT Prendergast came to study in Paris in 1881, where he had a large choice of paintings to look at: the Impressionists had since been succeeded by the Neo-Impressionists, but his preferences were Manet and Whistler.

CASSATT
Sleepy Baby
pastel on canvas
1910. 61 × 49 cm
OPPOSITE Pictures of mother and child were one of the unmarried and childless Cassatt's favourite themes, here rendered in pastel. She had returned to the United States for two years in 1898–99 after twenty years spent in Europe, chiefly in Paris.

shows perhaps the most remarkable sensitivity to the problems of technique and form inherent in what was a movement in a perpetual state of flux. Taking in the innovations of the Post-Impressionists with his treatment of the picture surface as a plane, eschewing naturalistic perspective, he yet manages to convey atmosphere and light in a way that is more consistent with Sisley than Cézanne or Gauguin.

Like their French predecessors, The Ten and the other American Impressionists were widely divergent in their approaches, from Twachtman's melancholy snowscapes, and Dewing's extraordinarily worked figures in interiors to the convergence of a more traditional Impressionism with frank Neo-Impressionism in the work of Frieseke and Weir. Moving away from Impressionism and under the influence of Cézanne and Gauguin, Maurice Brazil Prendergast (1859–1924) had begun in the early 1900s to develop a Post-Impressionist style. He became a member of The Eight (also known as the Ashcan School) which superseded The Ten and other American Impressionists and inaugurated an era of gritty social realism which itself harked back to the maverick realism of Eakins.

In the end Impressionism in America, as in France, England, and Europe, became stale and irrelevant. Whilst it had served a vital role in the late 1880s and into the 1890s, expanding to form schools in New Hope, Pennsylvania; Old Lyme, Connecticut; Woodstock, New York; and in the Midwest, by the time that Robert Henri, W.J. Glackens, George Bellows and the other members of The Eight formed their group in 1907 Impressionism was becoming institutionalized, and thus losing its appeal to a new generation of American artists.

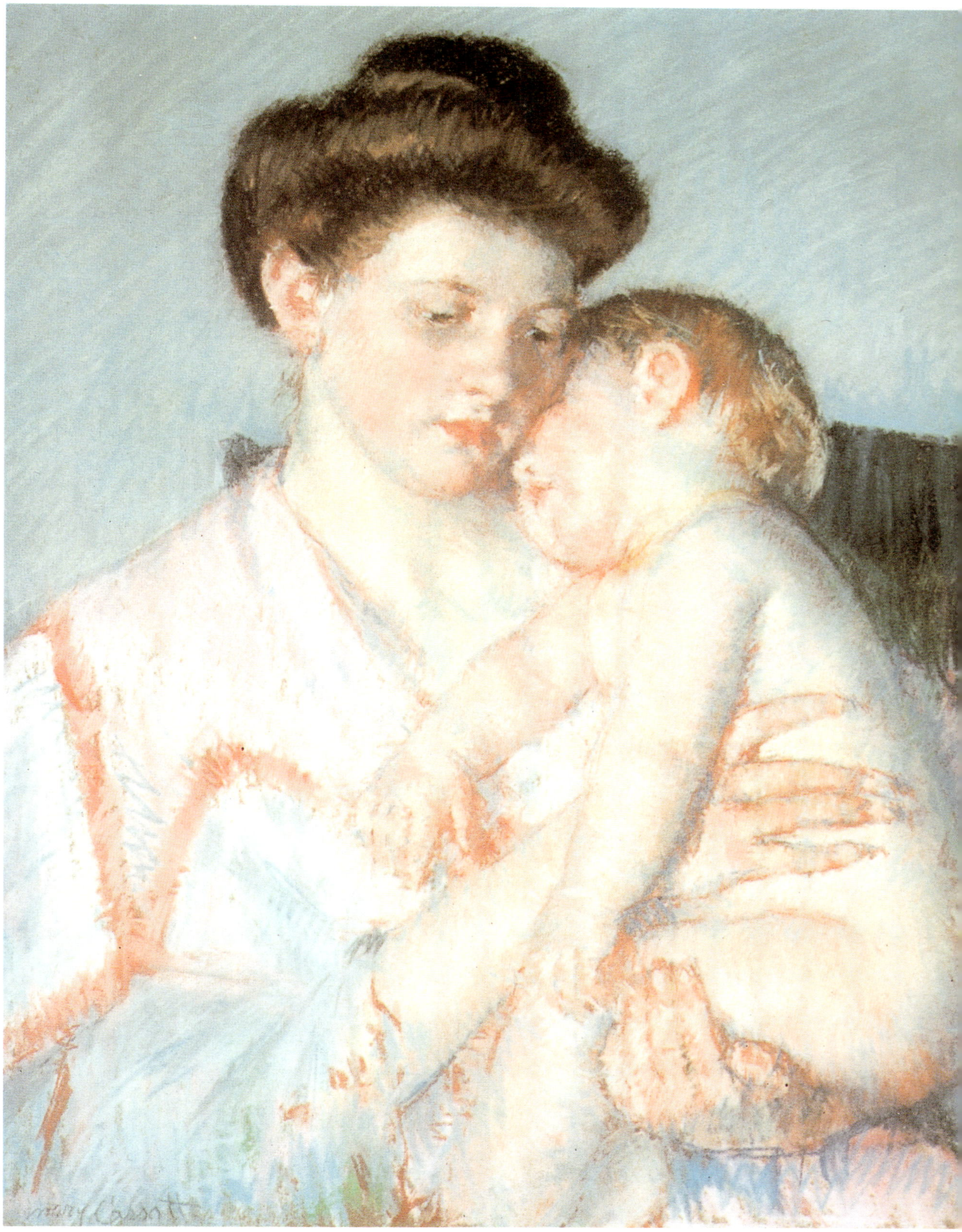

CHRONOLOGY

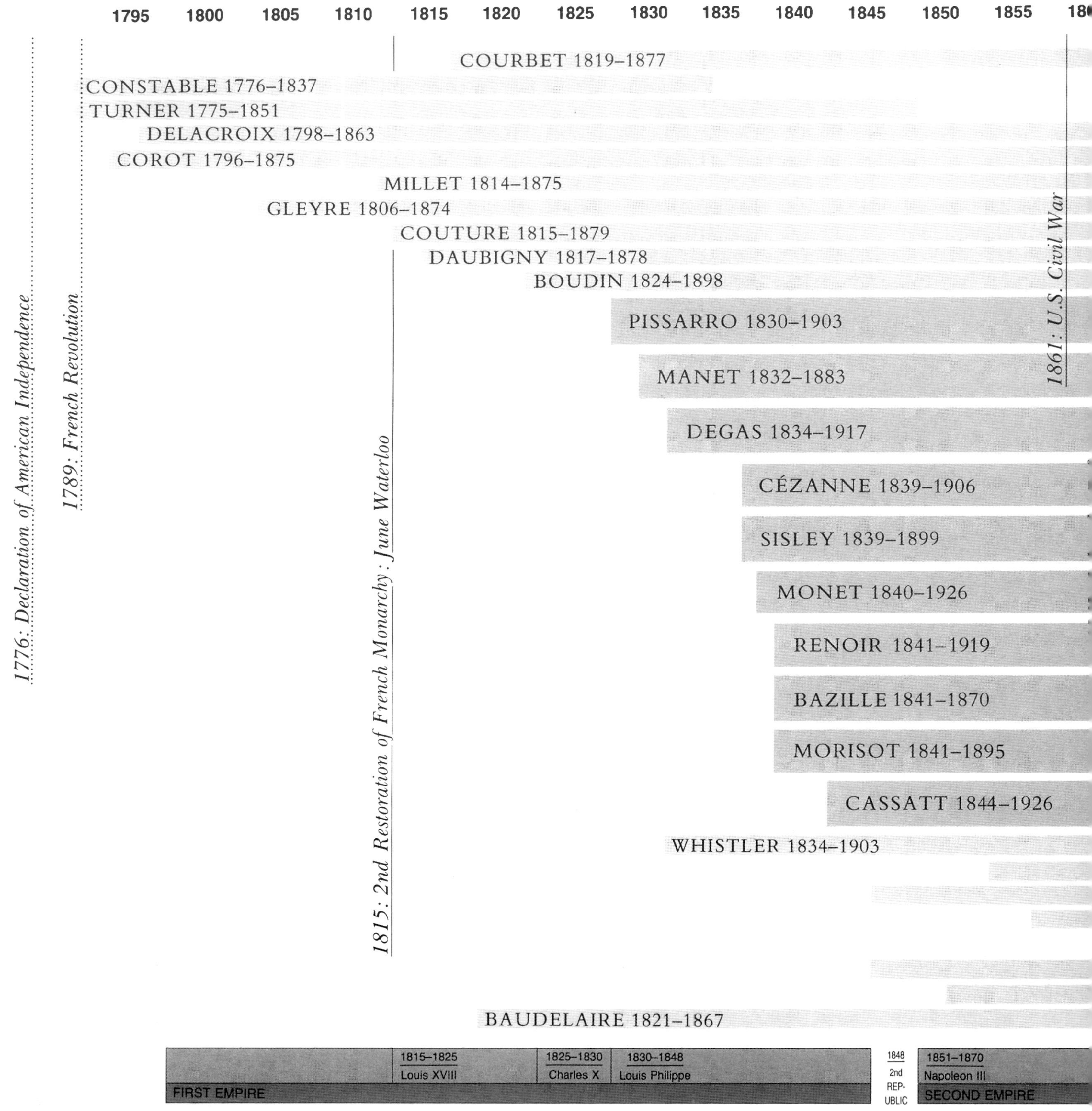
1795
1800
1805
1810
1815
1820
1825
1830
1835
1840
1845
1850
1855
1776: Declaration of American Independence
1789: French Revolution
1815: 2nd Restoration of French Monarchy: June Waterloo
1861: U.S. Civil War
COURBET 1819–1877
CONSTABLE 1776–1837
TURNER 1775–1851
DELACROIX 1798–1863
COROT 1796–1875
MILLET 1814–1875
GLEYRE 1806–1874
COUTURE 1815–1879
DAUBIGNY 1817–1878
BOUDIN 1824–1898
PISSARRO 1830–1903
MANET 1832–1883
DEGAS 1834–1917
CÉZANNE 1839–1906
SISLEY 1839–1899
MONET 1840–1926
RENOIR 1841–1919
BAZILLE 1841–1870
MORISOT 1841–1895
CASSATT 1844–1926
WHISTLER 1834–1903
BAUDELAIRE 1821–1867
1815–1825
Louis XVIII
1825–1830
Charles X
1830–1848
Louis Philippe
FIRST EMPIRE
1848
2nd
REP-
UBLIC
1851–1870
Napoleon III
SECOND EMPIRE

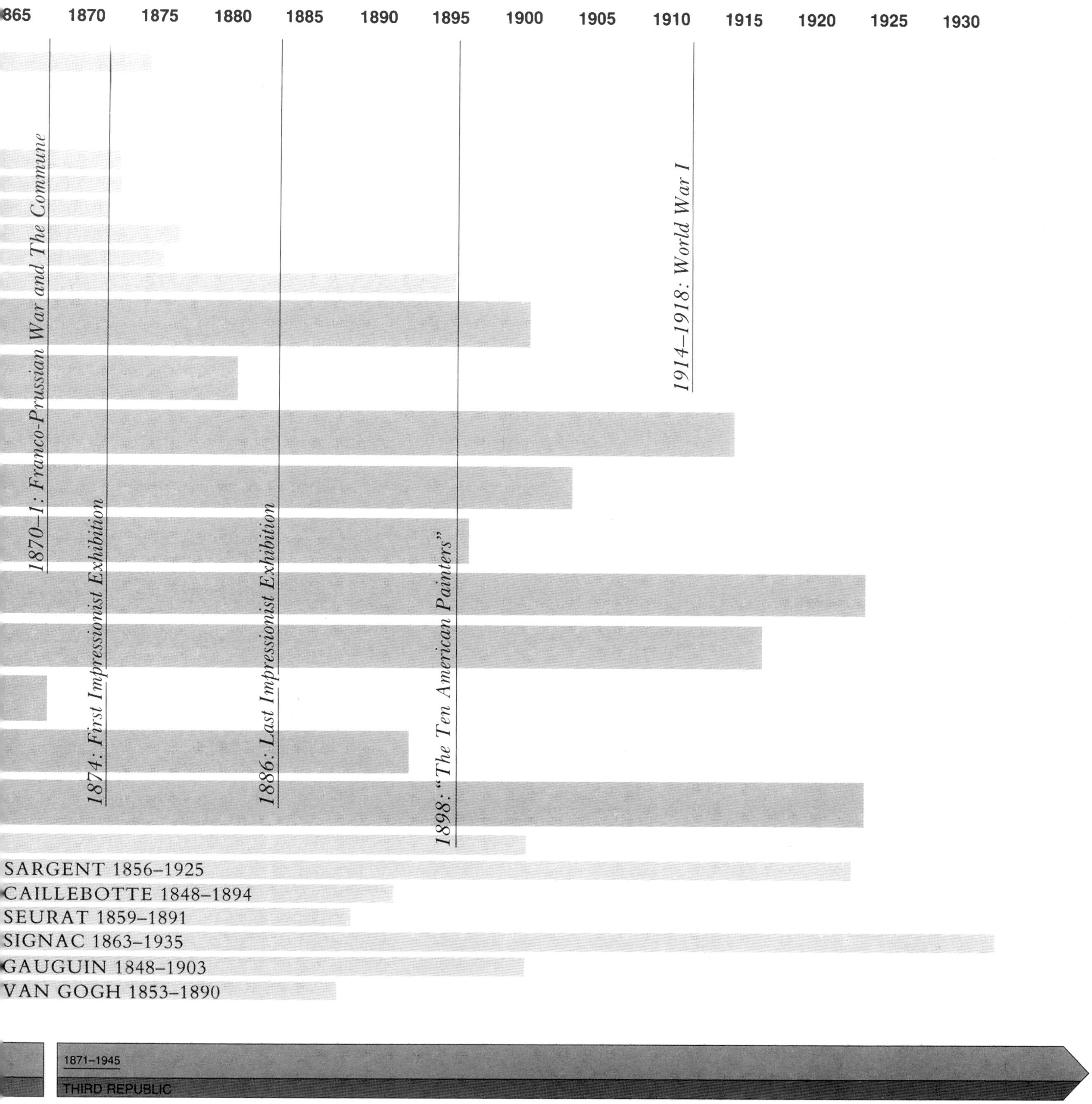

865 1870 1875 1880 1885 1890 1895 1900 1905 1910 1915 1920 1925 1930
1870–1: Franco-Prussian War and The Commune
1874: First Impressionist Exhibition
1886: Last Impressionist Exhibition
1898: "The Ten American Painters"
1914–1918: World War I
SARGENT 1856–1925
CAILLEBOTTE 1848–1894
SEURAT 1859–1891
SIGNAC 1863–1935
GAUGUIN 1848–1903
VAN GOGH 1853–1890
1871–1945
THIRD REPUBLIC

GLOSSARY

Fr. = French; It. = Italian

Academic style Traditional or classical style, the term refers both to the skilful draughtsmanship applied to the paintings, as well as to the biblical, historical, or mythological subjects that were recreated for the scenes.

Académie(Fr.) A study made by art students in the academic style to demonstrate their understanding of technique.

Académie Suisse A lenient académie that Cézanne, Pissarro, and Monet had attended. It supplied no teaching but an abundance of models.

Atelier(Fr.) The studio or school of an artist.

Banlieu(Fr.) A suburb.

Barbizon School The loose group of *plein-airistes* who worked in and around the village of Barbizon in the Fontainebleau Forest during the first half of the nineteenth century. It was highly influential on the young Impressionists.

Cafés-concert The Parisian phenomenon that began in the 1830s. One of the most popular cafés was Folies-Bergère which Manet painted towards the end of his life. The café life was depicted most often by Degas and Toulouse-Lautrec who frequented them.

Chiaroscuro(It.) The effect of an imperceptible change between dark and light in painting.

Cloisonnism A term used to describe a style of painting in flat areas of colour bordered by distinct outlines as in the work of Toulouse-Lautrec, Bernard, and Gauguin.

Cubism Deriving from the work of Cézanne, Cubism was a movement of the early twentieth century whose chief exponents were Picasso and Braque. In its simplest form it expresses the artist's vision in "three-dimensional" geometric shapes and forms on a two-dimensional canvas.

Daguerreotype The early photographic process, devised by Louis Daguerre in the 1840s, of fixing an image on one silver or silver-covered copper plate. It was superceded by William Henry Fox Talbot's method which allowed for the production of paper copies.

Distemper Similar to *gouache*, but using glue as a binding agent. Although impermanent it was occasionally used by Renaissance artists.

Divisionism The term preferred by the Neo-Impressionists to describe their methods of applying small contrasting areas of colour to the canvas. Also known as *Pointillism*.

Ebauche(Fr.) A preliminary study.

Ecole des Beaux-Arts Founded in 1684 as part of the system of the state-controlled patronage of the arts. The school had always emphasized drawing for its younger students and it proved an unshakeable foundation for such graduates as Degas.

Esquisse(Fr.) A sketch.

Facture(Fr.) The way in which each individual artist handles his or her medium. Monet's *facture*, for example, is immediately recognizable.

Fauvism After the French for "wild beasts", *fauves* was a term coined by a critic in 1905 to describe a group of young artists which included Matisse and Derain.

Flochetage The use of flakes (*floches*), or large spots of colour, to break up and give dynamism to matter, colour and form. Used by Rubens, Watteau and especially Delacroix. Pushed to its extreme by the Neo-Impressionists.

Gouache(Fr.) A watercolour paint based on gum as opposed to oils. It has the similar effect of oils but lightens in colour as it dries and tends to crack if used thickly.

La Grenouillère (The Froggery) A popular resort area near Chatou were bourgeois Parisians travelled for long weekends. Both Monet and Renoir painted several views of it.

Grisaille(Fr.) Greyish or monochromatic painting classically used as an underpainting.

Halation An effect produced by early daguerreotypes which, for example, recorded the gently moving leaves of trees as a blurred halo round the edge of the foliage.

Impasto(It.) A frequently used term for the application of paint with a heavily loaded brush.

Japonisme(Fr.) The all-pervading presence of Japanese art in the latter part of the nineteenth century which influenced many Impressionists and Post-Impressionists.

Modelling The depiction of a three-dimensional object on a canvas. Manet was thought by his contemporaries to be a great exponent of "modelling" in oil paint.

Monotype A method of printing using oil paint applied directly to a sheet of glass upon which paper is pressed to obtain a reverse print.

Nabis From the Hebrew word for "prophets", this is the name given to a group of French artists influenced by Gauguin.

Neo-Impressionism Primarily the Divisionist or Pointillist art of Seurat, Signac and their followers.

Odalisque(Fr.) Deriving from the Turkish *odiliq*, it refers to a female slave in a harem. This subject was frequently depicted by Ingres, Delacroix, and later Matisse.

Oeuvre(Fr.) The complete body of work of an artist.

Plein-airisme(Fr.) Open-air painting.

Realism In terms of Impressionism, Realism stood for the representing of ordinary scenes as opposed to the historical paintings of the Romantics. The style was first exemplified by Courbet who brought political connotations to it. Zola adhered to the movement as well and promoted it in his novel *L'Oeuvre*.

Salon Named after the Salon d'Apollon in the Louvre where the first official exhibition of French art was held in 1667. In 1885 the Salon moved to the huge Palais de l'Industrie which was built for the Exposition Universelle of that year.

Salon des Refusés Established in 1863 on the orders of Napoleon III, it included over two thousand paintings which had been rejected by the official Salon of that year. Another Salon des Refusés was held in 1868.

Société anonyme(Fr.) Literally a joint-stock company, and the letters S.A. will appear after the title of a French company. The *Société anonyme des artistes, peintres, sculpteurs, graveurs, etc.* mounted the first Impressionist exhibition in 1874.

Synthetism A movement based around Gauguin and the group of painters at Pont-Aven in the late 1880s that was in direct opposition to Impressionism because it demanded that one paint from memory rather than from nature or life.

Tonal Values The difference between the light and dark areas of a painting.

BIBLIOGRAPHY

ADLER, K. Camille Pissarro: A Biography. *New York: St. Martin's, 1977.*

ADLER, K. Unknown Impressionists. *London: Guild, 1988.*

ADLER, K. and GARB, T. Berthe Morisot. *Oxford: Phaidon, 1987.*

BATAILLE, G. Manet. *Geneva: Editions Skira; London: Macmillan, 1983.*

BOIME, A. The Academy and French Painting in the Nineteenth Century. *New Haven, Conn.: Yale, 1986.*

BOMFORD, D., et al. Art in the Making: Impressionism. *London: National Gallery, 1990.*

BRETTEL, R., et al. A Day in the Country: Impressionism and the French Landscape (Exhibition catalogue). *New York: Knopf, 1984.*

CALLEN, A. Renoir. *London: Oresko, 1978.*

CHAMPA, K.S. Studies in Early Impressionism. *New Haven, Conn.: Yale, 1973.*

CLARK, T.J. The Painting of Modern Life. *London: Thames and Hudson, 1985.*

COBBAN, A. A History of Modern France. 3 vols. *London: Penguin, 1965.*

COGNIAT, R. Sisley. *Paris: Flammarion, 1978.*

DAULTE, F. Alfred Sisley. *London: Cassell, 1988.*

DENVIR, B. Encyclopedia of Impressionism. *London: Thames and Hudson, 1990.*

DENVIR, B. The Impressionists at First Hand. *London: Thames and Hudson, 1987.*

DUNLOP, I. Degas. *London: Thames and Hudson, 1979.*

GORDON, R., and FORGE, A. Degas. *London: Thames and Hudson, 1988.*

GORDON, R., and FORGE, A. Monet. *London: Thames and Hudson, 1989.*

HAMILTON, G. Manet and His Critics. *New Haven, Conn.: Yale, 1954.*

HANSON, A.C. Manet and the Modern Tradition. *New Haven, Conn.: Yale, 1977.*

HERBERT, R.L. Impressionism, Art, Leisure and Parisian Society. *New Haven, Conn.: Yale, 1988.*

HOMER, W.I. Seurat and the Science of Painting. *Cambridge, Mass.: M.I.T., 1964.*

HORN, A. The Terrible Year: The Paris Commune 1871. *London: Macmillan, 1971.*

HOUSE, J. Monet: Nature into Art. *New Haven, Conn.: Yale, 1982.*

ISAACSON, J. Claude Monet: Observation and Reflection. *Oxford: Phaidon, 1978.*

JAWORSKA, W. Gauguin and the Pont-Aven School. Trans. by Patrick Evans. *London: Thames and Hudson, 1972.*

MANET, J. Growing Up with Impressionists: The Diary of Julie Manet. *London: Sotheby's, 1987.*

McCONKEY, K. British Impressionism. *Oxford: Phaidon, 1989.*

McQUILLAN, M. Van Gogh. *London: Thames and Hudson, 1989.*

MILNER, J. The Studios of Paris: The Capital of Art in the Late Nineteenth Century. *New Haven, Conn.: Yale, 1988.*

ORLANDI, E. (ed.) The Life and Times of Delacroix. *London: Hamlyn, 1968.*

POLLOCK, G. Vision and Difference: Femininity, Feminism and the Histories of Art. *London: Routledge, 1988.*

REFF, T. Degas: The Artist's Mind. *New York: Metropolitan Museum of Art, 1976.*

REFF, T. The Notebooks of Edgar Degas. 2 vols. *Oxford: Clarendon, 1979.*

REWALD, J. The History of Impressionism. *London: Secker and Warburg, 1980.*

REWALD, J. Studies in Impressionism. *London: Thames and Hudson, 1985.*

REWALD, J. Studies in Post-Impressionism. *London: Thames and Hudson, 1986.*

ROSKILL, M. Van Gogh, Gauguin and the Impressionist Circle. *Greenwich, Conn.: New York Graphic Society, 1970.*

SCHARF, A. Art and Photography. *London: Penguin, 1968.*

SEITZ, W.C. Claude Monet. *New York: Abrams, 1960.*

SWEET, F.A. Miss Mary Cassatt: Impressionist from Pennsylvania. *Norman, Okla.: University of Oklahoma, 1966.*

INDEX

ACKNOWLEDGEMENTS

Albi, musée Toulouse-Lautrec: p. 303/Giraudon. Amsterdam, Rijksmuseum: p. 20. Amsterdam, van Gogh Museum: pp. 311 left, 314 bottom. Baltimore, Walters Art Gallery: pp. 38 top, 70, 178 right. Berlin, National Gallery: pp. 178 left, 317 left. Boston, Museum of Fine Arts: pp. 56 top, 119 bottom, 165, 186 left, 188, 224 right, 292, 322 left. Cambridge, Fitzwilliam Museum: pp. 236 right, 327 left. Cambridge, Mass., Fogg Museum of Art: pp. 215 right, 236 left. Cardiff, National Museum of Wales: p. 174 top. Chicago Art Institute: pp. 21, 27, 42 top, 51 top, 55 bottom, 64 bottom, 65, 89, 100 left, 110 right, 120 left, 128 right, 140, 155, 159, 171 bottom, 198, 222 bottom, 223 bottom, 255, 267, 270, 285 right, 302, 304, 321. Cincinnati Museum of Art: pp. 34 bottom, 269, 315 top, 334. Cleveland Museum of Art: pp. 25, 74, 247, 340. Cologne, Wallraf-Richartz Museum: p. 256 top. Columbus Museum of Art: p. 319 left. Copenhagen, Ny Carlsberg Glyptotek: p. 161. Dallas, Museum of Fine Art: pp. 275, 337 left, 342, 343 left. Detroit Institute of Art: p. 338. Dijon, musée des Beaux-Arts: p. 160 left. Edinburgh, National Gallery of Scotland: p. 152. Egham, Royal Holloway College: p. 35/Bridgeman Art Library. Essen, Folkwang Museum: p. 233 left/Bridgeman Art Library. Florence, Uffizi: p. 80/Visual Arts Library. Fort Worth, Kimbell Museum of Art: pp. 120 right, 179 top right. Genova, Palazzo Rosso: p. 78 right/Visual Arts Library. Glasgow, Burrell Collection: pp. 123, 195 top. Glasgow, Hunterian Gallery: pp. 327 right, 328. Hamburg, Kunsthalle: p. 175 right/Bridgeman Art Library. Hartford, Wadsworth Atheneum: p. 217 top. Kansas City, Nelson-Atkins Museum of Art: p. 113 bottom. Leningrad, Hermitage: pp. 118 right/Edimedia, 156 right. Lisbon, Gulbenkian Foundation: p. 23. London, Christie's: pp. 47, 56 bottom, 66, 67 top, 129 bottom, 139, 209, 210, 249 right, 251 top, 262, 285 left, 311 right. London, Courtauld Institute Gallery: pp. 181 top, 235. London, courtesy of the Noortman Gallery: pp. 18, 208, 325 right. London, National Gallery: pp. 32, 34 top, 39 right, 46, 97, 106 top, 108 right, 110 left, 137, 141, 149, 157, 164 bottom, 177 left, 185, 197 left, 216 bottom, 217 bottom, 220, 239 right, 240, 242 right, 259 bottom, 278 left, 280 left, 282 bottom, 315 bottom. London, Tate Gallery: pp. 107 right, 196, 221 bottom, 226 left, 260 bottom, 283 top, 294 left, 301 left, 326. London, Victoria & Albert Museum: pp. 31 bottom, 79, 163 bottom. Los Angeles County Museum of Art: pp. 76, 215 left, 279 right. Lugano, Thyssen-Bornemisza Collection: p. 199 left. Lyon, musée des Beaux-Arts: p. 193 right. Madrid, Prado: p. 87 bottom/Visual Arts Library. Mannheim Kunsthalle: p. 87 top/Giraudon. Minneapolis Museum of Art: p. 242 left. Montargis, musée Girodet: p. 50/Giraudon. Montpellier, musée Fabre: pp. 266/Giraudon, 270/Giraudon, 271/Giraudon, 282 top. Moscow, Pushkin Museum: pp. 82/Edimedia, 239 left, 313 top. Munich, Neuepinakothek: p. 131 bottom. Nancy, musée des Beaux-Arts: p. 180 top. New York, Frick Collection: pp. 38 bottom, 168 top. New York, Metropolitan Museum of Art: pp. 24, 53 top, 58, 60, 84 left/Edimedia, 94 bottom, 106 bottom, 173, 174 bottom, 214, 241, 289, 332. New York, Museum of Modern Art: p. 131 top. Northampton, Smith College Art Gallery: p. 341. Oberlin Museum of Art: p. 88 left. Omaha, Joslyn Museum of Art: p. 153. Oslo, Nationalmuseum: pp. 88 right, 310 top, 314 top. Otterlo, Kröller-Müller Museum: pp. 305/Giraudon, 310 bottom, 312. Oxford, Ashmolean Museum: pp. 33, 329 left. Paris, Bibliothèque Nationale: pp. 50/Visual Arts Library, 69 right/Visual Arts Library, 73/Visual Arts Library, 86 left/Visual Arts Library. Paris, Louvre: pp. 31 top, 37/Giraudon/Bridgeman Art Library, 51 bottom/Edimedia, 54 right, 59/Edimedia, 67 bottom/Edimedia, 71 right, 77 top, 77 bottom, 121 right, 151/Giraudon, 293 right. Paris, musée Carnavalet: p. 100/Visual Arts Library. Paris, musée d'Art Moderne de la Ville: p. 48/Edimedia. Paris, musée d'Orsay: pp. 9, 22, 44/Giraudon, 45, 49/Giraudon, 52, 53 bottom, 54 left/Edimedia, 61, 68, 69 left/Giraudon, 71 left, 72, 75 top, 75 bottom, 81, 83, 91, 92 right, 96, 101, 109/Edimedia, 112 right/Giraudon, 114 bottom, 117 top, 117 bottom, 118 left, 121 left/Visual Arts Library, 122, 124 top, 124 bottom, 135, 138, 142, 143, 146 right, 146 left, 147, 148 top, 148 bottom, 150 left, 154, 160 right, 166 bottom, 167, 169/Giraudon, 170 bottom, 176 bottom, 179 top left, 183, 189, 191 left/Giraudon, 192, 193 left, 194 right, 199 right, 202, 207, 212 left, 212 right, 213, 216 top, 218 top, 218 bottom, 224 left, 232, 237, 238, 244, 249 left, 250 right, 251 bottom, 252 left, 253, 256 bottom, 257, 259 top, 260 top, 261 top, 263 right, 264 top, 268, 272/Giraudon, 273/Edimedia, 274/Giraudon, 281 left/Giraudon, 290, 301 right, 306 left, 306 right, 313 bottom, 316, 317 right, 318, 319 right, 322 right, 323 top, 323 bottom, 324 left. Paris, musée Marmottan: pp. 102, 114 top, 119 top, 219 top, 219 bottom, 224 centre, 286, 300 right. Paris, musée national d'Art Moderne: p. 309. Paris, musée Picasso: pp. 194 left, 250 left. Paris, Petit-Palais: pp. 42 bottom, 128 left, 222 top, 248, 264 bottom. Passadena, Norton Simon Foundation: pp. 90 left, 200. Pau, musée des Beaux-Arts: p. 190/Giraudon. Philadelphia Museum of Art: pp. 43, 108 left, 113 top, 164 top, 170 top, 191 right, 201, 246 left, 278 right, 293 left, 333, 336. Private collections: pp. 8, 10, 28, 36, 40, 41 top, bottom, right, 57/Bridgeman Art Library, 63, 64, top, 85, 86 right, 90 right, 92 left, 95, 98, 103 top, 104, 115, 116, 126, 127/Giraudon, 129 top, 130, 134, 144, 145, 150 right, 158, 166 top, 175 left, 179 bottom, 180 bottom, 181 bottom, 182, 186 right, 187, 195 bottom, 197 right, 203, 204, 206, 211 top, 211 bottom, 223 top, 225 left, 226 right, 227, 228, 229 left, 229 right, 230, 233 right, 252 right, 254, 258 top, 261 bottom, 263 left, 265, 276/Giraudon, 281 right, 283 bottom/Giraudon, 284 bottom, 287, 291, 295, 300 left, 307 left, 320. Providence, Rhode Island School of Design Art Gallery: pp. 99, 280 right/Giraudon. Santa Barbara Museum of Art: p. 279 left. St Tropez, musée de l'Annonciade: p. 307 right. Stockholm, Nationalmuseum: pp. 94 top, 205. Strasbourg, musée d'Art Moderne: p. 246 right. The Hague, Gemeentemuseum: p. 84 right. Toledo Museum of Art: pp. 112 left, 156 left, 258 bottom, 284 top. Tournai, musée des Beaux-Arts: pp. 107 left, 125/Edimedia. Washington, Corcoran Gallery of Art: pp. 343 right, 335. Washington, Dumbarton Oaks Library: p. 308. Washington, Freer Gallery: p. 330. Washington, National Gallery of Art: pp. 55 top, 93, 103 bottom, 111, 163 top, 168 bottom, 176 top, 222 top, 289/Edimedia, 294 right, 337 right. Washington, Phillips Collection: pp. 162 bottom, 184, 243, 339 right, 339 left, 344. Williamstown, Clark Institute of Art: pp. 23, 225 right, 231, 245. Winterthur, Oscar Reinhart Foundation: p. 234. Yale University Art Gallery: p. 162 top.